Grave Markers

in

Burke County
Georgia

with 39 cemeteries in four adjoining counties

By:
Lilliam Lewis Powell
Dorothy Collins Odom
and
Albert M. Hillhouse

I0082704

Southern Historical Press, Inc.
Greenville, South Carolina

Please direct all correspondence and book orders to:
SOUTHERN HISTORICAL PRESS, Inc.
PO Box 1267
Greenville, SC   29602-1267

Originally printed: Waynesboro, GA. 1974
Copyright 1974 by: Albert M. Hillhouse
Copyright Transferred 1985 to:
      Silas Emmett Lucas, Jr.
ISBN #978-1-63914-136-4
Printed in the United States of America

TABLE OF CONTENTS

INTRODUCTION

Burke County in 1977 will officially be 200 years old. It was one of the first eight counties created by the Constitution of 1777 after Georgia broke from British control and became an independent State. It retained the boundaries of St. George's Parish, the predecessor administrative unit under the Royal Provincial Government. During a portion of the short period, 1733-1752, when Georgia was a Trustee Colony, and even later, a part of this geographical area was known as "Halifax District".

The first U. S. Census (1790) showed that Burke County with 7064 whites contained approximately 13.3 per cent of all the white population in Georgia, which numbered 52,886. When slaves were included, Burke stood fourth in total population among the then eleven counties.

In 1793 a portion of the original Burke was cut off to help create Screven County, and again in 1796 another portion to form Jefferson County. Not until 1905 did Burke again lose territory, this time toward the creation of Jenkins County. Despite the loss of some of its original area, Burke remains today the second largest county in the State. Its eastern boundary is the Savannah River (across from South Carolina), and its southwest boundary, the Ogeechee River. Neighboring counties are Richmond to the north, Jefferson to the west, and three to the south: Emanuel, Jenkins and Screven.

Burke lies wholly in the coastal plain, just below the fall line which marks the end of Georgia's piedmont area. Its soil is very productive, and well watered by tributaries of the Ogeechee and Savannah rivers, especially by Brier Creek, with its many branches and smaller creeks, which flows diagonally across the county from the northwest corner to the southeast boundary, emptying into the Savannah within Screven County.

The City of Waynesboro is the county seat. Midville and Sardis, both smaller cities, are next in size. Other incorporated, or unincorporated, communities include: Alexander, Blythe (partly in Richmond), Girard, Gough, Keysville, Rosier, Shaw Town, Shell Bluff, St. Clair and Vidette.

A Historic County

Burke is rich in history. A few white settlers began to move into this area as early as the 1740's, and during the 1750's, even before the 1763 Cession by the Indians of more territory to the Crown. This cession treaty also clarified the right to white settlement in all of St. George's Parish.

Burke's history is, in part, reflected in many sites, old extant churches, old homes and church buildings, and ancient graves, such as: an excavation of Indian relics; the fossil oyster shell formations at Shell Bluff which attracted natural scientists as early as 1765 and 1775; the burial site of Dr. Lyman Hall, signer of the Declaration of Independence, and that of his son; two other sites connected with the Revolutionary War; a marker at the site where George Washington spent the night in Waynesborough, May 17, 1791; the probable location of one of Eli Whitney's cotton gins; old boat landings on the Savannah River; the birthplace of the distinguished Methodist missionary to China, the Rev. Young J. Allen; several historical markers which tell of the three-forked march through Burke County by massive Union troops under General Sherman and his subordinate generals, and also of sites where clashes occurred between Union and Confederate units; site of the first school for Freedmen in Burke County during the Reconstruction Period; the Confederate Monument, erected in 1877, in the Waynesboro Confederate Memorial Cemetery, in memory of all the many Confederate dead interred in Burke; five old churches established before 1800, including the second and third oldest Baptist churches in Georgia; four plantation homes, each more than 150 years old; old church cemeteries and a few walled plantation cemeteries, and many soldiers' graves from the Revolutionary War to the present.

A long chronology of documented historic events would have to include such early dates as:

1759 Some Salzburgers moved up from Ebenezer into St. George's Parish and established New Goettingen, now a dead town.

1763 The first courthouse in St. George's was erected.

1765 John Bartram, a British scientist, with his son, visited Shell Bluff to study the fascinating large oyster shell formations, which come to be known as "Ostrea georgiana".

1766 A Presbyterian church on Brier Creek petitioned the Synod of New York and Philadelphia for assistance with supply ministers.

Much of the documentation for such a chronology from the days of Oglethorpe to the present is now in process.

Burke County and Migration

Following the Revolutionary War, and for several decades, the eastern counties of Burke, Richmond, Columbia and Wilkes, were in the path of a substantial

migration flow from such states as Maryland, Virginia,
North Carolina and South Carolina. Augusta was a
natural gateway for settlers seeking virgin Georgia
land made available by successive acquisitions of
territory from Indian tribes. Many new settlers took
up land in Burke, lived out their time and were buried
in the county. But the next generation often moved on,
southwestward and westward, where fresh lands and new
opportunities were more attractive, and later north-
ward in Georgia when Cherokee lands became available.

Cemeteries in Four Adjoining Counties

Included in this book, but located in Jefferson,
Jenkins, Richmond and Screven counties are thirty-nine
cemeteries. In the main they are not far from the
Burke County line. Many include families which have
relatives interred in Burke. Grouped by counties, the
cemeteries not in Burke, but included in this book,
are:

Jefferson

Louisville Revolutionary War	Ways Baptist
Lowry-Alexander	Allen

Jenkins

Big Buckhead Baptist	Jones (Birdsville)
Fairhaven Methodist	Little Buckhead Baptist
Green Fork Baptist	Magnolia Baptist
Habersham Methodist	Murphey
James-Jeffers (on line)	Wallace

Richmond

Atkins-Winter	Cosnahan	Piney Grove Baptist
Bath Presbyterian	Crockett	Rhodes-Allen
Berlin Methodist	Fulcher-2	Tarver-2
Blythe Baptist	Hephzibah	Tinley
Blythe Methodist	Lambeth	Broome
Brothersville	Murphey	Malone

Screven

Brick (Bethel) Methodist	Lovett-2
Hurst Baptist	Odom

Neither Jefferson nor Jenkins have surveyed their
cemeteries; so this book is the sole source. The only
survey of Richmond County cemeteries is a four-volume,
typed study, now available in the Richmond County Library, Augusta. Most of the Richmond cemeteries included in our volume, however, do not appear in the
Richmond survey. The D.A.R. chapter in Sylvania,
Screven's county seat, has completed an independent
survey of Screven cemeteries. This study has not been
published, but can be studied in the Screven County
Library.

Use of the Index

To search for a name in the entire book, begin with the Index. Opposite each name is a cemetery number. The cemetery numbers are given at pages xiii-xvi together with the page number where each cemetery begins. Since within each cemetery the names of the interred are arranged alphabetically, the researcher can quickly pinpoint the name sought.

Omitted from the Index are children who died at age six, or younger. Their names will be found in the same cemetery with their parents. Any research for such children begins with their parents' names.

Relationships between the person found and another, or others, in the same cemetery are indicated by abbreviations, such as wife of, son of, etc. See list of abbreviations.

Abbreviations

Opposite the name of each interred person are two columns. The left-hand one gives the birth date, or age at time of death from which the birth date can be calculated. The right-hand column supplies the death date.

Some of the following abbreviations appear in the name column; others in the birth and death columns; still others in the notes, annotations or other text.

Relationships		Military Service*	
br/o	brother of	Rev War	Revolutionary War
d/o	daughter of	1812 W	War of 1812
f/o	father of	Mex W	Mexican War
h/o	husband of	CSA	Confederate soldier
inf/o	infant of	Sp-Am W	Spanish-American War
m/o	mother of	WW-I	World War I
s/o	son of	WW-II	World War II
sis/o	sister of	Kor W	Korean War
w/o	wife of	Viet W	Vietnam War
		USA	US Army
		USAF	US Air Force
		US Mar	US Marines
		USN	US Navy

*Other military abbreviations, such as rank, unit to which attached, theater of operation, military awards, etc. have been reproduced as found on the markers.

Other

approx.	approximate or approximately
b	born

bkn	marker broken
c.	circa (about)
Co	county or company
d	died
d	day, when age is given
(ed)	editorial
F&AM	Mason
hwy	highway
illeg or ileg	illegible on marker
Jne	June
L	still living, but name on marker
Lic N	licensed nurse
m	month, when age is given
m or md	married
MD	medical doctor
nd	no date given on marker
only date	used most often when only death date is given
Rev	Reverend
rd	road
same date	used when birth & death date are the same
WOW	Woodmen of the World
WOW Cir	Women's Circle of WOW
y	year, when age is given
(?)	in doubt

Annotations

In order to make the book more useful to profession-al genealogists, and others working on family histories, we have researched Bible records, family papers, old will books, obituary notices and other sources, and have used the results to annotate some of the cemeteries.

A special attempt has been made to add the wife's maiden (family) name in order to remedy an omission on the marker which often becomes a stumbling block in tracing her line.

In a few instances we have gone one step further and supplied a "probable lead". For example, the father of Nathaniel Thomas of Burke County could not be ascertained from available sources. Research, how-ever, turned up a biographical sketch of J. Pinckney Thomas, a representative in the Georgia Assembly from Burke County. The date of the latter's marriage was consistent with the birth date of the former; so the annotation suggests only that the latter might be Nathaniel's father.

Annotations are not always identified by the abbre-viation "(ed)", for editorial; but is used frequently enough to alert the reader that not all information under an interred's name appears on the tombstone.

Whenever a marker indicates membership in a

fraternal order, participation in a war, military rank or unit, or church membership, these have been reproduced. Only rarely have these been added by annotations.

The reader will understand, we trust, why it was not practical to provide annotations for all the cemeteries. The main thrust of the book has been to provide the genealogical data on all markers in all Burke cemeteries, plus the same for cemeteries on the periphery of Burke.

Genealogical Materials

For years the professional genealogists left untouched this old county, largely because the county courthouse had twice burned, once in 1825 and again in 1856, destroying valuable public records. During the last decade and a half, however, much has transpired to repair some of the damage and to make Burke an excellent field for genealogical research. We list the new developments:

(1) the discovery in an attic of the County Clerk's receipt book prior to 1825, and a second discovery that the Burke Superior Court minutes for the 1830's and subsequent years survived intact the fire of 1856.

(2) publication by the Heritage Papers of Mary Boudurant Warren's, Marriages and Deaths, 1763-1820 and a sequel for the 1820-1830 decade. Many entries, reproduced from Georgia newspapers, supply material on early Burke families.

(3) a demonstration by Wm. H. Dumont, editor of the National Genealogical Society Quarterly, in his long, 52-page article, "Burke County, Georgia" in the March 1966 edition, that heretofore untouched sources prior to 1800 were available elsewhere than in the Burke courthouse.

(4) the energetic work of the State Department of Archives and History, Atlanta, in photocopying papers from family collections in Burke.

(5) the beginnings of a genealogical collection in the Burke County Library at Waynesboro.

(6) a heightened interest in Burke history and genealogy shown by the weekly newspaper, The True Citizen, under the present ownership and management.

(7) the intensive research by a Burke Countian, Grattan W. Rowland, now living in Atlanta, upon a leading Burke County family, and its interconnections with other families.

(8) the production locally of a 200-page mimeographed history of Burke County for use in the county's high schools, which is now out of print, but is in process of revision and enlargement in scope.

(9) recognition by the Georgia State Historical Commission that Burke is a historic county, as evidenced by establishment in Waynesboro of a State Museum.

(10) publication of the present volume, Grave Markers in Burke County, Georgia. This book provides

a comprehensive treatment of one type of genealogical material. In addition, through its annotations, useful portions of some of the above break-throughs have been systematically pulled together and presented.

Directions to Cemeteries

In order to maximize the inclusion of cemeteries in this book, the directions to each cemetery have been omitted. The rationale is that those who would want to visit one or more cemeteries are but a very small minority of the book's users. For those, however, who wish to visit, a volume of directions has been typed and xeroxed. One copy each has been deposited in the Burke County Library (4th Street), the State Museum (Liberty Street), and the Ordinary Court Office on the first floor of the Burke County Courthouse (Sixth Street), all located in Waynesboro.

For one interested in sight-seeing, we recommend a journey to the Ways Baptist Church (founded 1817) cemetery, near Stellaville in Jefferson County. For charm and beauty this cemetery has no rival among all those included in this book. Especially picturesque are four old, high, rock-walled sections, and two others about eighteen inches high. One high-walled section has lost its name and all its markers. Perhaps on the darkest nights in bleak December and January, the wind and leaves add their sympathetic notes to the moanings of this ancient widowed and childless one.

The best kept is the Sardis Cemetery, situated in the country on a site where once stood a very old church, the predecessor of the present Sardis Baptist Church, which has its house of worship in Sardis. This old cemetery, likewise, has a beautiful setting and is well worth a visit.

The Confederate Monument, erected 1877 in memory of Burke Countians who died in the 1861-65 "Lost Cause", stands tall in the Waynesboro Confederate Memorial Cemetery. This large monument with its inscriptions and the many iron CSA markers, scattered through out the cemetery, are impressive and interesting to many visitors.

Acknowledgments

Our indebtedness extends to many persons who have assisted the authors. Without their help the task would have been much more burdensome and much less successful. Unfortunately, because of space considerations only a few can be singled out for mention here. However, we are in no way less appreciative of the others who have been thanked in person.

For initial advice about methods of approach to such a research project, we are indebted to Mary Bondurant Warren, Danielsville, Ga., the Rev. Silas

E. Lucas, Jr., Easley, S. C. and Elizabeth Pritchard
Newsom, Sandersville, Ga.

For assistance in locating out-of-the-way cemeteries, and in penetrating some overgrown and almost
inaccessible ones, Julian Odom, Joel Crenshaw, Roger
W. Corley, and Alex Gray, each deserve special thanks.

For the loan of useful research material, we are
grateful to Grattan Whitehead Rowland, Atlanta;
Catherine Stewart Jones, Macon; Hugh L. Vallotton,
Valdosta, Ga.; and May Humphrey Edsall, Alexandria,
Va. The last named generously gave us access to
some earlier research on Burke families by her late
mother, Annie MacKenzie Humphrey.

For able advice and assistance in the production
of the book itself, we owe much to Jackie B. Hooks
and Jeanette H. Weathersby, both of Millen, Ga., who
typed the manuscript, and to Wilkes B. Williams of the
Chalker Publishing Co., who counseled us at several
stages on the "musts", as we pressed toward the final
product.

                              Lillian Lewis Powell
                              Dorothy Collins Odom
                              Albert M. Hillhouse

June 30, 1974

LIST OF ALL CEMETERIES WITH NUMBERS
AND
BEGINNING PAGE NUMBERS

ALEXANDER METHODIST
Alexander, Ga.

Name	Birth	Death
Blanchard, Mrs. I.M. w/o Thomas S.	Jan 8 1849	May 18 1922
Blanchard, Thomas S. F&AM Founded Alexander Lodge	Oct 3 1845	Jne 14 1905
Brickett, Mrs. P. R.	Feb 1 1823	Feb 28 1864
Burton, Hattie S.	Dec 27 1861	Jul 17 1865
Carpenter, Tom W. WW-II Ga Tec5 USA	Jan 3 1912	Apr 15 1966
Dixon, Mary E. w/o J.D.	Dec 8 1874	Aug 1 1909
Mauldin, Mary E. d/o Rev. J.D. & M.L.	May 24 1867	Sep 15 1881

McElmurray, Annie Eliza
  w/o John F., Sr. /Shewmake
  d/o Caroline & Joseph A.
	Jne 14 1843	Jan 25 1881

McElmurray, Emmie J. d/o A.E.S. & John F.	Mar 5 1870	Jul 9 1881
McElmurray, Francis Lorraine s/o A.E.S. & John F., Sr.	Nov 23 1874	Jul 4 1932
McElmurray, George Leslie s/o A.E.S. & John F., Sr.	Jul 13 1868	Oct 18 1943

McElmurray, John F., Sr. CSA
  s/o Minis H. & Emily J.
  Capt Co K 32nd Ga
	Nov 15 1842	Dec 18 1911

McElmurray, John F., Jr. s/o A.E.S. & John F. F&AM	May 22 1877	Dec 23 1945
McElmurray, Josie s/o A.E.S. & John F., Sr.	Sep 27 1871	Aug 14 1872
McElmurray, Kate W. w/o Francis L.	Dec 27 1883	Mar 17 1965
McElmurray, Louise Hopkins w/o George L.	Jul 18 1872	Jul 2 1919
McElmurray, Sallie Joe d/o A.E.S. & John F., Sr.	Apr 4 1880	Oct 31 1895
McElmurray, Thomas J. s/o A.E.S. & John F., Sr.	May 9 1876	Jul 6 1905
McElmurray, Virgil S. s/o A.E.S. & John F., Sr.	age 2m 11d	Apr 6 1867
Messex, Augusta	Oct 6 1925	Feb 8 1938
Messex, Cora K. w/o Willie	1884	1968
Messex, Maggie Faye	Jne 4 1943	Oct 8 1943
Messex, Richard H.	May 23 1958	same date
Messex, Willie	1874	1947
Reeves, Annie Farmer	Jul 8 1878	Mar 19 1941
Reeves, John Robert	Sep 13 1883	Feb 6 1954
Reynolds, Mary Annie d/o Mary Lou Shewmake & John W.	May 20 1874	May 21 1874

Rutledge, John
  b Charleston, S.C.
  d Burke Co.
	Oct 14 1793	Aug 25 1864

Shewmake, Caroline L.   Mar 1 1822 Oct 16 1895
    b in So. Car.   /Hankinson
    w/o Joseph A. m/o Sarah, w/o Thomas J. Burton; Mary
    Lou, w/o John Wm. Reynolds; Annie E., w/o John F.
    McElmurray; and Dr. Virgil P. Shewmake (ed).
Shewmake, Joseph A.   Nov 25 1816 Nov 5 1889
    s/o Anna Lassiter (1793-1865) and Joseph (1779-1838),
    both buried in Augusta. br/o Joanna, Anna, Mary,
    Andrew G., Oscar L., John Troup, and Augustus D. (ed).
Shewmake, Virgil P. MD   Apr 10 1841 Jul 20 1862
    only s/o C.L. & Jos. A. Lt Burke Guards CSA; died in
    Richmond, Va., from wound at Battle of Malvern Hill
Thorn, Temperance A.   Oct 31 1877 Sep 26 1906
    w/o G.J.
Vickery, Evelyn Fay   Apr 9 1921 Dec 26 1958
Ward, Leila H.   Nov 25 1885 Mar 29 1946
Wimberly, Mc. W.   Dec 9 1838 Dec 28 1868
Wimberly, W. B. (infant)   nd   nd
Winter, Margie I.   Oct 16 1882 Sep 3 1885
    d/o J.J. & V.T.
Winter, Vollusia T.   Apr 10 1876 Oct 7 1882
    d/o J.J. & V.T.

Notes: This old cemetery also contains two unidentified
brick vaults, one next to the John Rutledge grave; six
unmarked flat slabs, adult size, and one unidentified
grave with well-preserved brick coping.
    The editorial additions to Joseph A. and Caroline
Shewmake were supplied by Mrs. Adele Johnston Bussey,
of Atlanta, a descendant of John Troup Shewmake, who
was a Waynesboro and Augusta attorney and a Georgia
Representative in the Confederate Congress.

2.   ALLEN

Allen, Anna Margaret Evans   Feb 15 1828 Feb 9 1858
    w/o Francis Marion, Sr. CSA
    Co D 48th Reg Ga Inf; Killed at Gettysburg
Allen, Anthoney Marion   1962   1962
    s/o John H. & Delores
Allen, Edna Daisy   Apr 28 1875 Mar 4 1927
    w/o Elisha A.
Allen, Elisha A.   Mar 29 1864 Feb 14 1923
Allen, Fannie Greiner   Jne 22 1856 Aug 20 1900
    w/o William W.
Allen, Francis Marion   Nov 5 1880 Jne 10 1972
    s/o Robert Anderson
Allen, Henry E.   Feb 16 1852 Feb 21 1852
    s/o Francis & Anna M.
Allen, Jefferson B.   Jne 17 1878 Mar 3 1920
Allen, Mabel A.   Jan 29 1884 Feb 13 1961
    w/o Jefferson
Allen, Patricia A.   Aug 23 1958 Sep 21 1969
    d/o John H. & Delores

```
Allen, Robert A.  WW-II          Mar 16 1926   Aug 31 1969
   s/o Daphne A. & Francis M.
   Ga PFC USA
Allen, William Wirt              Aug 30 1850   Feb  4 1908
   s/o Anna M. & Francis M.
Daniel, Louis J.                         nd          1871
Rheney, Pauline Allen                  1854          1882
   d/o Anna M. & Francis M.
```

3.   <u>ALLEN</u>

```
Allen, Priscilla M. Ward         age 28 y     May 13 1835
   w/o Robt. A.                  5 m 8 d
   md Jan 13 1829 (information from Augusta, Richmond Co.
   records)
```

4.   <u>ANDERSON</u>

```
Anderson, Georgia Ringgold       Apr 15 1847   Jul 24 1848
Anderson, James, Sr.             Dec 15 1793   Mar 24 1854
   f/o James, Jr., John M., Augustus H., Elizabeth M.,
   Rosa V., & Ella E.  Will Bk A 144-151
Anderson, John Miller            Sep 23 1832   Feb 28 1854
   d Tampa, Fla.
Anderson, Lawrence Ludlow        Apr 14 1817   Mar 15 1818
Anderson, Malvina P.             age 56y  7m   Mar  4 1865
   2nd w/o James, Sr.  Will Bk A 250-251
Anderson, Mary Ann               Nov 22 1827   Jne 17 1851
Anderson, Mrs. Sarah             Dec 14 1793   Jul 18 1843
   1st w/o James, Sr.
Anderson, Susan Augusta Polk     age 5m  26d   Aug  4 1851
Anderson, William                Sep 22 1822   Mar 15 1834
   s/o James & Sarah
Bradley, Jonas                   age 57y       Dec 11 1815
```

5.   <u>APPLEWHITE</u>

```
Applewhite, Caroline Fullford    Jul 15 1810   Oct 22 1859
   b Jefferson Co., Ga.
   w/o John, Sr. md Feb 15 1828
Applewhite, John, Sr.            Feb  7 1802   Oct 15 1855
   b Wayne Co., N.C.
   first of family to settle in Burke (ed)
Note:  Children of John, Sr. and Caroline:
   Counsel (son)                 Oct 11 1829   Aug 14 1834
   Henry Lawson                  Aug 29 1835   Aug 23 1836
   John N.                       Sep 14 1837   Jul 16 1893
   Louis Jasper MD               Sep 14 1837   Mar  3 1861
      md Isabella L. Phillips
      Aug 16 1860, Augusta, Ga.
   Thomas                        Jne 26 1839   May 12 1840
   Joseph Polhill CSA            Mar 29 1841   Mar 24 1862
      d  Elizabeth City, Va
   Ivanna (dau.)                 Mar 29 1841   Oct 15 1841
      from family Bible  (ed).
```

```
Atkins, Infants (four)                    nd              nd
  each marked "Our Baby"
Atkins, James N.                       1851            1921
Atkins, Langdon M.          Apr 25 1874  Aug 31 1956
Atkins, Lizzie C.                      1860            1929
Atkins, Mary E. Winter      Dec 25 1879  Apr  8 1929
  w/o L. M.
Atkins, Sophia              Apr  4 1838  Apr  3 1922
  w/o Thos.
Atkins, Thomas              Oct 29 1822  May 12 1902
Atkins, Thomas E.                      1877            1964
Barney, Dr. Job S.          Feb 10 1773  Oct 15 1838
  b Richmond, Chesire Co., N.H.
  resident of Richmond Co.,Ga. for 40 yrs.
Bebee, Annie Willie Atkins  Dec  8 1902  Apr 14 1925
  w/o J.M.
Bebee, Jackson McLain, Jr.  Aug 21 1922  Oct 16 1926
Boon, Augusta M.                       1897            1969
Duggan, Helen C. Atkins     May 30 1912  Jne 11 1938
  w/o E.J.
Farris, Margaret D. Atkins  Mar 10 1868  Oct  6 1942
  w/o Wm. E.
Farris, William Edward      Jul  5 1867  May 20 1939
Greiner, Frederick B.       d in 32nd y  Aug 31 1839
  of Philadelphia
Greiner, Mary Anna          May 11 1811  Apr 22 1834
  w/o John P.
  d/o Dr. & Mrs. J.S. Barney
Martin, John W.                        1888            1955
Matthews, Lula M.                      1873            1965
Richardson, James D.        Feb 25 1916  Jul  5 1917
  s/o D.D. & J.E.
Richardson, Jessie Edith    Oct 29 1884  Jne 11 1917
  w/o Dave D.
Winter, Denver G. (Buddy)              1900            1953
Winter, Gordon              Sep 20 1874  Apr 23 1923
  WOW
Winter, Leila A.                       1877            1945
  w/o Gordon
Winter, Robert Herman       Dec 23 1907  Feb 23 1931
```

7.   ATTAWAY

```
Attaway, David              age 69 y    Mar 24 1853
  h/o Eliza Taylor
  s/o Joseph & Edie N.
  f/o Caleb, John, Ellington, Ezekiel, James, and Martha
  Will Bk A 151-152
Attaway, Elijah             May 11 1795  Mar 14 1848
  h/o (1st) Martha; (2nd) Sarah H.
  f/o Abigail, w/o Thomas H. Blount; Martha, w/o Edward
  H. Blount, and Elizabeth, w/o Alexander MacKenzie
  br/o David and Elizabeth, w/o Patrick Cotter
  Will Bk A 31-33
```

```
Attaway, Harlow A.                Jan 12 1888   Oct 25 1898
Attaway, Henry I.                 Sep 13 1890   Nov 21 1905
Attaway, Jesse                    Mar 28 1836   Nov  5 1909
Attaway, Jessie H., Jr.           Dec 26 1880   Sep 15 1914
Attaway, John David               Sep  3 1855   Sep 25 1855
  s/o John & Mary V.
Attaway, Joseph H.                Jan  3 1873   Oct 22 1903
  s/o Jesse  Will Bk A 489-91
Attaway, Rebecca                  Nov  5 1851   Feb 18 1903
  w/o Jesse
Attaway, Thomas                   Jul 23 1823   Sep  1 1915
Attaway, Vernon E.   USA          only   date   Jul  1 1933
  s/o Jesse Will Bk A 489-91
  Ga Pvt ICL 118 Field Arty 31 Div
Kendrick, S. E.                   Nov 19 1864   Jul 27 1917
Vaughn, Jerry M.                          nd            nd
Vaughn, Lizzie                            nd            nd
  w/o J.M.
```

Note: The parents and wives of David and Elijah and the
dates on Joseph H. are information from the earlier
research of Mrs. Anne MacKenzie Humphrey (ed).

8.   BARGERON-BONNELL

```
Bargeron, R. S.                   Jan 18 1862   Jne  7 1862
Bargeron, Robert    CSA           Apr 16 1839   Oct 11 1882
Bargeron, William                 May  4 1835   Jan 31 1864
Bargeron, William Nicodemus       age 5y 11m    May 22 1863
                                  2d
Bonnell, Chas. E.                 Oct  9 1835   Sep  5 1880
```

Note: "E. B." on one foot marker; headstone apparently
removed. One broken marker illegible (ed).

9.   BARK CAMP BAPTIST

```
Archer, Artemus L.                Feb  4 1825   Jne  7 1900
Archer, Georgia V.                Sep 30 1873   Sep 29 1922
  w/o W.E.
Archer, Harry Hughes              Nov 12 1896   Aug  9 1897
  s/o W.E. & G.V.
Archer, Martha Flanders           Jan 28 1824   Mar 19 1910
  w/o Artemus L.
Archer, Robert Lee                Jul  5 1863   Jan  2 1898
Blount, Daisy Netherland                 1898           1936
  1st w/o A.H. Blount, Jr.
  d/o Nora & J.E.
Branan, Hattie Inman              Mar 24 1865   Feb 10 1938
  w/o F.C.
  d/o Jeremiah S. & M.W.
Branan, Ora                       Jul 13 1899   Feb  2 1901
  d/o F.C. & H.I.
Brown, Benjamin                   Aug  8        Nov 13 bkn
                                  age 62y
```

```
Bunn, Hannah Gordy                     Apr 26 1868   Jan 13 1960
  w/o Matthew D.
Bunn, Jake Paul  WW-II                 Dec 12 1907   Jne 11 1957
  Ga Pvt USA
Bunn, Matthew D.                       Apr  6 1867   Mar  5 1956
Bunn, William  WW-I&II                 Apr 16 1893   Jne 20 1949
  Ga Sgt Field Arty
Bunn, William Hiram                    Mar 28 1890   Oct  1 1970
Burton, Charles A.  CSA                Aug 18 1847   Sep  2 1864
  s/o Charles A. & Susan J.  Died from exhaustion in the
  retreat from Atlanta, near McDonough, Ga.
Burton, Charles Malone                 Jne 25 1876   Jul 10 1876
Burton, Charlotte Pepper               age 34 y      Sep  5 1886
Burton, Fannie Malone                  Jan 18 1855   Feb  1 1877
Burton, Hannah E.                      Jne 25 1842   Nov 15 1880
Burton, James G.  CSA                  age 24 y      Jul  2 1863
  Fell at Gettysburg, Pa.
Burton, Musgrove                       Mar 28 1874   Aug 11 1912
  s/o Robt. H.
Burton, Robert H.                      Dec 22 1844   Aug 25 1909
Burton, Robert Pepper                  Aug 31 1886   Dec  8 1886
Burton, Sarah V.                       Oct 10 1837   Oct 31 1896
Burton, Susan J.                       Sep 17 1808   Jan 12 1879
Cole, Private J.                       only  date          1856
  Marker to Cole and Lieut. G.S.J. Price "by their
  comrades in arms, 1856."
Coleman, Jonathan  Rev W                     1750          1825
  Burke Co Ga Mil
  Charter member of Bark Camp Church;  constituted April,
  1788
Cooper, Barbara Anne                         1952          1952
Cooper, R.E.                           only  date          1951
Davis, John L.                               1862          1943
Dixon, Jean H.                         Apr 13 1885   Dec  9 1969
Farrow, Alfred A.                      Dec 15 1836   Aug 15 1903
Farrow, Annie Mae                      Nov  6 1883   Dec 27 1948
Farrow, Delilah                              1831    Jan 30 1896
Farrow, Elizabeth                            1842    Mar 22 1868
Farrow, James H.                       Mar  3 1899   Nov 29 1948
Farrow, Mary A.                        May 28 1847   Mar 19 1914
Farrow, Obed W.                        Jul  4 1897   Apr 10 1950
Farrow, Rachel Murphry                 Feb  5 1865   Mar 27 1952
Farrow, Samuel G. (or C?)              Mar  1 1865   Jne 25 1927
Farrow, Verner E.                      Sep  3 1893   Aug 31 1953
Farrow, Willie Young                   Aug 18 1859   May 11 1938
Fuller, Moses                          Aug 29 1812   May  6 1857
  h/o Laura
Gerald, Elizabeth M.                   Nov 23 1853   Aug  2 1914
Gerald, George T.  CSA                         nd            nd
  Co G 1 Ga Inf
Godbee, C.L.                           May  1 1846   Nov  3 1886
Godbee, Eula E.                        Jne 20 1883   Oct  3 1885
  d/o C.L. & H.I.
Godbee, Infant                                 nd            nd
```

```
Godbee, M.M.                        Feb 29 1844  Feb 25 1883
Godbee, Sammie (infant)             only   date  Mar  8 1882
  s/o C.L. & H.E.
Gordy, Alton L.                     Sep  3 1904  Dec 25 1933
Gordy, Emma O.                              nd           nd
Gordy, Francis                      Dec 25 1842  Jne 14 1923
Gordy, George W.                            nd           nd
Gordy, Lizzie V.                    Sep 11 1881  Mar 24 1930
Gordy, Mattie J.                            nd   Feb    1917
Gordy, N.M.                         Feb  6 1829  Jan  4 1901
Gordy, Nathan N.  CSA                       nd           nd
  Co E 2 Ga State Troops
Gordy, Robert Lowe                  Dec    1911  Jne    1914
Gordy, William Webster              Jan 20 1873  Mar 24 1957
Hammond, Infant                             nd           nd
  s/o Mr. & Mrs. J.T.
Hickson, Annie Louise               Aug 26 1876  Jul 15 1901
  w/o W.H.
Hickson, F.H.                       Mar 31 1848  Nov 24 1913
Hickson, John J.                    Nov  1 1860  Aug  4 1907
Hickson, Lester H.                  Nov  2 1887  Dec 21 1912
Hickson, Sabra A. Kennedy           Mar  7 1852  Sep 10 1925
  w/o F.H.
Hodges, Maud Estelle                Oct 24 1874  May  3 1967
  d/o Sophronia & Troup B.
Hodges, Leslie Inman                Jan  3 1877  Mar  7 1902
  d/o Sophronia & Inman B.
Hodges, Rosa D.                     Apr 30 1864  Oct  9 1889
  d/o Sophronia & Troup B.
Hodges, Sophronia S. Inman          Oct 25 1851  Sep  7 1898
  w/o Troup B.  (buried at Midville)
  d/o Jeremiah S. & M.W.
Hurst, Dennis                              1900         1972
Hurst, Emma L.                             1877         1953
  w/o Steve
Hurst, Steve S.                            1866         1950
Inman, Daniel M.                    Oct 26 1859  Mar  6 1907
  s/o J.S. & M.W.   br/o  J. Frank, James A., Mary,
  Sudie, & Hattie I. Branan from monument  (ed).
Inman, J. Frank                     Jul 12 1862  Apr  4 1907
  s/o J.S. & M.W.
Inman, James A.                     Jul 22 1868  Oct 22 1889
  s/o J.S. & M.W.
Inman, Jeremiah S.                  Jul 26 1828  Oct 22 1889
Inman, Mary F.                      May 19 1855          nd
  d/o J.S. & M.W.  sis/o Daniel, J. Frank, James A.,
  Sudie, and Hattie.  Sophronia S. Inman is listed
  separately on monument from other sisters and
  brothers  (ed).
Inman, Moning W.                    Nov 17 1835  Oct 23 1889
  w/o Jeremiah S.
  m/o three sons and four daughters
Inman, Sudie E.                     Sep 25 1857  Feb 24 1926
  d/o J.S. & M.W.
Jackson, Charles Archer             Jan  9 1879  Feb 11 1949
```

7

Jackson, (infant) d/o Mr. & Mrs. C.A.	only date	1916
Jackson, J.E.	1852	1904
Jackson, Mary Cochran w/o Charles A.	Jan 16 1882	Mar 16 1958
Knight, Louie W.	1900	1943
Knight, Mary Jenkins w/o Robert	Sep 22 1912	May 31 1967
Knight, Robert	Sep 3 1906	Apr 23 1956
Lambert, George A.	May 18 1845	Oct 17 1908
Lambert, Mary E. w/o Geo. A.	Mar 27 1848	Jul 21 1915
Lambert, Virgil s/o G.A. & M.E.	Feb 19 1876	Oct 6 1893
Leaptrot, Jesse A.	age 70 y	May 1 1881
Lee, Maggie	age 26 y	Aug 10 1906
Lee, Mary	age 75 y	Jne 19 1900
Mulling, Deborah 2nd w/o W.J.	Oct 26 1882	Jul 30 1913
Mulling, Mr. E.H.W.	Jan 21 1852	Oct 30 1863
Mulling, Mrs. F.P.	May 22 1834	Jan 19 1887
Mulling, Hattie Cooper 3rd w/o W.J.	Apr 23 1894	Sep 15 1972
Mulling, James A.	Nov 19 1855	Mar 24 1897
Mulling, Jasper s/o W.J. & Susie	Oct 19 1896	Jul 19 1897
Mulling, Mamie Lou eldest d/o J.A. & Mayo	Jul 10 1888	Aug 29 1897
Mulling, Mary Clyde d/o W.J. & Deborah	Sep 15 1907	Oct 1 1909
Mulling, Susie Carswell 1st w/o W.J.	Jne 5 1861	Jul 23 1900
Mulling, W.A.	Aug 26 1829	Dec 10 1889
Mulling, W.J. WOW	May 4 1869	Mar 23 1936
Murphey, Robert A. CSA Co F Cobb's Cav	nd	nd
Murphree, Mrs. Elizabeth	Aug 28 1827	Aug 22 1907
Murphy, Wright CSA Co I 9 Ga Inf	nd	nd
Musgrove, Eliza J. w/o Dr. Wm. C.	May 21 1831	Oct 6 1881
Musgrove, Dr. Wm. C.	Dec 10 1818	Sep 21 1876
Nasworthy, Permelia w/o Wiley	nd	nd
Nasworthy, Wiley F&AM	May 12 1820	Dec 7 1899
Nasworthy, William liberal donor to Bark Camp Church	Jan 1 1800	Dec 10 1857
Netherland, Addie E. w/o Willie P.	1887	1967
Netherland, Ellie Esme	Feb 16 1884	Sep 26 1898
Netherland, Emily d/o W.P. & A.	Jan 2 1917	Mar 8 1918
Netherland, (two infants) of J.E. & N.E.	nd	nd

Name	Birth	Death
Netherland, J. B.	Feb 15 1878	Oct 7 1886
Netherland, James Edward	1868	1930
Netherland, Mary J. Robinson w/o W.P.	Jne 17 1846	Aug 11 1920
Netherland, Nora Culbreath w/o James Edward	1866	1932
Netherland, Robinson	Feb 13 1886	Oct 17 1890
Netherland, W.P.	Sep 21 1843	Jne 29 1901
Netherland, Willie P.	1890	1968
Oliver, Clarence J.	1892	1968
Poston, Thea F.	Aug 1 1894	Apr 5 1972
Poston, Thomas L.	Sep 14 1900	Jne 21 1951
Powell, Emily S.F.	1866	1928
Price, Lieut. G.S.J. See Cole, Private J.	only date	1856
Pritchard, Samuel MacQuin	Jan 26 1858	Dec 24 1908
Robinson, James	Mar 4 1809	Jul 16 1887
Robinson, James M.	Feb 19 1888	Feb 22 1888
Robinson, John R.	Dec 16 1848	Jul 10 1910
Robinson, Kate H. d/o J.R. & S.V.	Oct 27 1898	Mar 23 1916
Robinson, Katherine w/o James	Apr 3 1806	Jne 10 1898
Robinson, Mary Lou d/o J.R. & S.V.	Mar 6 1891	Sep 19 1893
Robinson, Sara Virginia Jones w/o John R.	Mar 2 1864	Dec 21 1938
Robinson, W. J.	Sep 28 1873	Dec 4 1886
Sammons, Clara Lee d/o A.L. & N.J.	age 1y 7m 10d	Sep 23 1863
Sconyers, Mrs. S.N.	Aug 21 1810	Apr 21 1886
Smith, Martha E.	Nov 21 1836	Jan 28 1910
Smith, Wm. E.	Aug 25 1846	Nov 17 1900
Stephens, Ida J. w/o J.Q.	Apr 28 1856	May 22 1881
Stephens, Mattie Clyde d/o J.Q. & I.J.	age 9m 20d	Jul 19 1881
Thomas, Elizabeth	Dec 9 1834	Jne 19 1904
Toole, Charlie E.	Sep 16 1889	Apr 2 1949
Toole, Cora K. w/o W.W.	Oct 26 1902	Jul 5 1959
Toole, E. B.	Aug 30 1857	Jan 3 1927
Toole, Effie Mulling	May 22 1916	Apr 26 1963
Toole, Emma Gordy w/o E.B.	Jan 14 1861	May 9 1945
Toole, James Martin WW-I Ga Pvt 603 SVC BN Engr Corps	Aug 12 1891	Oct 27 1955
Toole, Maggie Woodward w/o James Martin	Jan 29 1906	L
Toole, Robert L.	Jul 16 1896	Sep 10 1938
Turner, Mary J.	Apr 13 1872	Oct 9 1956
Weddon, Jack Edward s/o Warren & Ida	May 22 1911	Jul 2 1944
Wells, Leornia	Feb 6 1872	same date
Wells, Wm. F.	Oct 12 1877	Jul 25 1878

```
Woodward, Alice                      Mar 28 1869    Nov 11 1941
Woodward, Barnes W.                  Feb 11 1871    Jne  3 1941
Woodward, Barney E.                         1900           1936
Woodward, Jessie J.                         1911           1929
Woodward, Mattie Mae                 Jul 11 1893    Jan 30 1908
  d/o E.J. & Alice
Woodward, Paul R.                    Jul 24 1907    Jan 10 1924
Woodward, Pinkie A.                  Oct  2 1871    May  5 1958
  w/o Barnes W.
```

10.   **BATH PRESBYTERIAN**
                 Bath, Ga., Richmond Co.

```
Belt, Richard B.  MD                 age 30y 8m     Nov 27 1852
Burdell, Annie Green                        1859           1951
  w/o Ferdinand V.
  d/o V.A.T. & John G.
Burdell, Ferdinand  CSA              Nov 27 1840    Apr 10 1925
  Co D 2 Regt Ga Inf
Byrnes, James O.                     May 17 1852    Dec 28 1927
Cliett, Fannie Trowbridge                   1891           1971
  w/o Otis J.  d/o Ethel Mc. & J.F.
Cliett, Otis J.                             1897              L
Dent, Ellen                          Aug 22 1860    Mar 13 1861
Dent, Janet Blair                    Dec 19 1865    Jul 17 1887
Dent, John Marshall                  Apr  6 1879    May 31 1879
Dent, Mary Ann                       Mar  8 1859    Apr 26 1859
Dowse, Elizabeth Martha              Apr 11 1794    Mar 27 1854
  w/o Samuel      /Walker
  m/o Susan Clinton & Laura Philoclea.  See sketches of
  Dr. Juriah Harriss and Laura P. Dowse in Myers, The
  Children of Pride.
Dowse, Gideon                        age 3 y        Sep 16 1852
  s/o Sarah Morrison & Gideon
  See sketch of his father in Myers, supra.
Dowse, Samuel                        Oct 10 1786    Nov 16 1856
  md five times:  Harriette Mann, 1807;  Mary Whitehead,
  1812;  Eliza Anciaux Berrien, 1823;  Abigail Eliza
  Sturges, 1827; and Elizabeth M. Walker.  See sketches
  of G. Dowse, L.P. Dowse, J. Harriss, H.H. Jones, and
  Wm. P. White in Myers, supra.
Dwight, Angela                       age 29 y       Oct 12 1836
  w/o Rev. T.M.
Ettelee, Frank                              nd             nd
Eve, Addie W. Trowbridge                    1877           1935
  w/o Benj.
Girardot, Elizabeth H.               Jne  8 1903              L
  w/o Martin E.
Girardot, Infant                            nd             nd
  d/o J.E. & L.E.
Girardot, Janie Elizabeth                   1869           1912
  w/o Louis Edward
Girardot, Louis Edward                      1850           1946
Girardot, Martin E.                  Nov 18 1894    Apr  5 1973
```

```
Goddard, John Wythe                          Aug  6 1851    Sep 10 1925
Goddard, John Wythe                          May 21 1878    Dec 25 1948
Goddard, Mary Amanda Trowbridge              Feb 12 1847    May  4 1913
   w/o John W.
Goddard, Sarah Trowbridge                    Jul 31 1886    Dec 30 1957
   w/o John Wythe
Green, Henry T.                                     1860           1900
Green, James Augustus                        age 1y 3m      Oct 11 1865
   3rd s/o V.A.T. & J.G.
Green, John Gaybard  CSA                      Oct  6 1826    Jul 30 1907
   s/o Gershom & Eliza
   b Burke Co. d Bath, Ga.   Co K 63 Regt Ga Inf
Green, Rosa E.                                      1870           1942
   d/o V.A.T. & John G.
Green, Virginia A. Thompson                  Sep 26 1830    Jan 12 1897
   w/o John G.
   b Richmond, Va.
Harman, William H.                           Apr  6 1841    Jne 17 1916
   Co I 133 Inf Regt Penn Vol
Harris, Jeptha V.                            Oct 10 1838    Oct 29 1838
   s/o Geo. H. & Mary W.
Higgins, Norma L. Churton                    Feb  3 1950    Apr 28 1970
   w/o Michael V.
   m/o Scott E.
Holley, Clifford                             Aug 27 1891    Mar 17 1973
Holley, Clifford Devere, Jr.                 Oct  4 1919    Sep 30 1966
Holley, Gertrude T.                          May 23 1896    May 17 1968
   w/o Clifford
Holley, Infant                               only   date    Oct 15 1954
   d/o S.P. & C.D.
Holley, Sara M. Prescott                     Mar 21 1920              L
   w/o Clifford D.
Holmes, Docia D.                                   1903              L
   w/o Willie R. md Dec 23 1917
Holmes, Willie R.                                  1897           1968
McNatt, Adam                                       1817           1872
   s/o William & Mary
   (unmarked grave) See his sketch in Myers, supra.
McNatt, Infant                                             nd              nd
   of E.T. & Adam
McNatt, Mary Anna                            Apr 23 1840    Sep 23 1848
   d/o Emeline Teresa & Adam
McNatt, Willie                               Jan  1 1855    Nov  9 1855
   s/o E.T. & Adam
Morris, John P.                              Jan 31 1838    Oct 12 1839
   s/o Susan A.W. & Wm. S.C.
Morris, Susan Walker                               1810           1873
   w/o Capt. W.S.C.
   b Burke Co d Brunswick, Ga.
   d/o Bethiah W. & Isaac
Morris, Capt. Wm. St. Clair  CSA                   1812           1871
   b Savannah d Waynesboro  See his sketch in Myers, supra.
Salter, Caroline                             Apr  6 1898    Dec  5 1949
Salter, Zedie  WW-I                          Aug 20 1895    Jan 20 1958
   Ga Pvt USA
```

11

Self, James Thomas	Oct 27 1951	May 21 1966
Skrine, Quintillian	Jul 24 1809	Sep 6 1886
see Walter A. Clark, <u>A Lost Arcadia</u>, 1909.		
Thompson, Sarah B.	1834	1896
Thompson, Susan R.	1828	1906
(in Green Section)		
Thompson, William V.	nd	nd
Trowbridge, Emeline McNair	Aug 15 1858	Mar 28 1953
w/o John Francis		
Trowbridge, Frank Valiton	Oct 26 1857	Mar 5 1925
Trowbridge, Fredric Leonard	Sep 29 1900	Aug 14 1924
Trowbridge, Ida G.	1856	1931
w/o J.W.		
Trowbridge, Infant	Mar 7 1914	same date
d/o J.W. & L.P.		
Trowbridge, J.W.	1853	1931
Trowbridge, James Walter	Dec 23 1889	Jne 13 1941
Trowbridge, John CSA	May 3 1817	Feb 16 1894
Co G9 Regt Ga State Trps		
Trowbridge, John Evans	Jul 2 1898	Oct 7 1899
s/o J.F. & E.M.		
Trowbridge, John Francis	Sep 20 1853	Feb 12 1928
Trowbridge, R.A.	Sep 25 1855	Jne 7 1917
Trowbridge, Raymond	1888	1973
Trowbridge, Sara Louise	Dec 18 1845	Dec 17 1913
d/o John & Sarah M.		
Trowbridge, Sarah M.	Jne 7 1824	Jan 20 1889
w/o John		
Trowbridge, Wm. Alvin	nd	May 7 1931
Ga Pvt Base Hospital 126		
Trowbridge, W. Cecil	Nov 30 1876	May 22 1879
s/o J.W. & I.E.		
Trowbridge, Wm. H.	May 28 1878	Aug 19 1878
s/o J.W. & I.E.		
Walker, Bethiah Whitehead	Nov 13 1771	Sep 4 1851
w/o Maj. Isaac		
Walker, Hester Ann	Sep 13 1796	Sep 3 1818
Walker, Maj. Isaac	nd	Sep 20 1814
West, Eliza Alice Whitehead	1819	1896
(unmarked grave) See sketch of her husband in Myers,		
<u>supra</u>. w/o Dr. Chas. Wm.		
d/o Abigail L. Sturges & John		
West, Eva C.	nd	nd
d/o Eliza A. & Charles W.		
West, Henry Cummings	1859	1904
s/o Eliza A. & Charles W.		
West, Mary Elizabeth	age 14m 8d	Sep 1 1846
d/o Eliza A. & Charles W.		
West, Sarah W. Whitehead	1864	1936
w/o Henry C.		
Whitehead, Bessie	nd	nd
d/o Julia C. & Charles E.		
Whitehead, Burnet Dowse	Oct 27 1842	Apr 18 1844
s/o Julia C. Burnett & Charles E.		

```
Whitehead, Caroline Harlow          age 9m 11d                    nd
   d/o John & Julia M.
Whitehead, Catherine M.             Jan 20 1824   Dec 11 1897
   w/o John B.           /Harper
Whitehead, Charles Julien           Nov  7 1845   Jne 10 1858
Whitehead, Charles Lowndes   CSA    Jne 29 1835   Sep 25 1866
   h/o Sarah A. Whaley
   s/o Julia M.B. & John
   see his sketch in Myers, supra
Whitehead, Curren                   Jan 29 1851   Jul 25 1852
   s/o M.A. & J.P.C., Sr.
Whitehead, George Crawford          age 13d       Jan 24 1843
   s/o M.A. & John P.C., Sr.
Whitehead, Infant                   Nov 27 1852   Jul 15 1854
Whitehead, John                     Dec 14 1783   May 31 1857
   h/o 1st Abigail Lewis Sturges
   2nd Julia Maria Berrien
   see his sketch in Myers, supra
Whitehead, John Berrien             Feb 24 1820   Jul 13 1879
   s/o Ruth L. Berrien & Dr.James
Whitehead, John Philpot Curren,     Jne  6 1813   Dec 21 1883
   h/o (1st) Mary Ann        /Sr.
   Wallace Dent, 1840 (2nd) Margaret Ireland Harper, 1855
Whitehead, John P.C., Jr.           Sep  7 1859   Sep 26 1880
   s/o Margaret Harper & J.P.C.,
                        /Sr.
Whitehead, Julia Maria Berrien      Jne 29 1801   Jan  8 1857
   w/o John
   d/o Major John Berrien (1759-1815) & Williamina S. Eliza
   Moore
Whitehead, Margaret                 age 9m 11d    May  1 1852
   d/o Catherine H. & John B.
Whitehead, Margaret I. Harper       Sep 13 1828   Jan  8 1897
   w/o John P.C., Sr.
Whitehead, Marian Wallace           Jul 17 1848   Nov 16 1849
   2nd d/o John P.C.,Sr.
Whitehead, Mary Ann                 Nov 13 1847   Jan 13 1863
   d/o Catherine H. & John B.
Whitehead, Mary Ann Wallace         Sep  5 1821   Jan 25 1852
   w/o John P.C., Sr.
   d/o John Dent, MD
Whitehead, Mary Dowse               age 22y       Mar 10 1844
   d/o Abigail L. Sturges & John
Whitehead, Robert Connelly          Dec 10 1854   Jul  9 1855
   s/o Sarah E. Connelly & John Randolph
   see sketch of his father in Myers, supra.
Whitehead, Susan Dowse              Dec 28 1843   Aug 27 1846
   d/o Elizabeth McK. & Amos G.
Whitehead, William Dent             Jan 23 1845   May  1 1848
   s/o M.A. & John P.C., Sr.
```

Note: From the intensive research completed by Grattan
Whitehead Rowland, Sr., of Atlanta, the editor has been
able to supply valuable additional genealogical data not
found on the Dowse, West, and Whitehead markers.

The full citation to Myers supra is Robert M. Myers, The Children of Pride, Yale Univ. Press, New Haven, Conn., 1972. 1845 pp. (ed).

11.   BERLIN METHODIST
                         Richmond Co.

Allen, Lillian	1903	1973
Atkins, Annie C.	1863	1937
w/o Pierce R.		
Atkins, H. Samuel	Dec 25 1886	Mar 4 1926
Atkins, Helen L.	1911	1936
w/o L.L.		
Atkins, John G.	Aug 7 1905	Nov 25 1941
Atkins, Lourie L.	1888	1957
Atkins, Pierce R.	1853	1937
Atkins, Virginia Lee	only date	Oct 13 1936
d/o L.L. & H.L.		
Avret, Dozier L.	1907	1951
Avret, Ida Marie Allen	1881	1950
w/o Percy R.		
Avrett, Percy R.	Sep 7 1873	Oct 24 1940
wife's marker gives family name as Avret (ed).		
Bradford, Minnie B.	Oct 26 1893	Jul 13 1968
w/o Thomas P.		
Bradford, Thomas P.	Aug 15 1893	Oct 28 1968
Collins, Benjamin F.	Feb 11 1851	Nov 14 1923
Collins, Hattie B.	Nov 2 1866	Oct 20 1941
w/o James R.		
Collins, James R.	Sep 4 1855	Sep 3 1925
Collins, Jane Averet	Apr 8 1847	Nov 22 1931
w/o Z.W.		
Collins, Marion R.	1886	1955
Collins, Pamelia A.	1890	19--
w/o M.R.		
Collins, Robert Milton	Jne 8 1894	Nov 19 1962
Collins, Walter Derry	Apr 15 1887	Mar 30 1921
s/o Z.W. & Jane E.		
Collins, Zachariah W. CSA	Oct 26 1847	Mar 21 1934
1861-65		
Cosnahan, Alice Elizabeth	Feb 6 1932	Oct 23 1936
d/o John & Mary Skinner		
Cosnahan, John	Aug 17 1897	Jan 19 1939
Cosnahan, Louis Beverly	Dec 31 1925	Oct 24 1927
Cosnahan, Robert Vernon	Feb 22 1936	Feb 25 1936
Hemrick, George Frank	Feb 6 1906	Apr 12 1968
Hemrick, Mattie Lee Shaw	Nov 23 1908	nd
w/o G.F.		
Humphries, Eula Ware	May 31 1882	Oct 29 1967
Lambert, Joseph J. WW-I	Aug 29 1898	Apr 11 1970
Ga PFC Co M 13 Inf		
Miller, Elizabeth C.	Jne 24 1876	Jul 30 1969
Miller, Evelyn	Sep 30 1902	Sep 2 1940
d/o Elizabeth C.		
Neely, Earnest	1905	1961

Name	Birth	Death
Neely, Otis WW-II Ga Cpl Army Air Forces	Dec 11 1909	Apr 8 1960
Neely, William Baxley WW-II Ga 605 AAA Gun Bn CAC	Oct 7 1921	Jan 11 1957
Osbon, Wilma V. w/o Geddings D.	Dec 12 1904	Jne 22 1925
Poole, Mary Skinner Cosnahan w/o O.R.	Apr 4 1901	Jne 9 1950
Prescott, Frankie C. w/o Robt. N.	1892	1923
Prescott, Robert N.	1889	1944
Preston, Larney	May 16 1914	Oct 29 1971
Rountree, Allen Lon Kor W Ga Pfc 1 Marines 1 Mar Div	Feb 4 1930	Apr 24 1951
Rountree, Lewis R. WW-I Ga Cpl 326 Inf 82 Div	Oct 15 1888	Nov 17 1951
Shaw, Charlie B.	Nov 22 1885	Aug 24 1964
Shaw, Hollie Preston, Sr.	Jne 20 1884	Mar 5 1956
Shaw, Larney Preston	Jne 18 1937	Aug 6 1941
Shaw, Rosa Lee Tinley w/o H.P.,Sr.	Jan 20 1884	Oct 25 1938
Shaw, William A.	Jan 5 1891	Oct 24 1963
Skinner, Alice Carten w/o Wm.T.	May 23 1873	Jne 22 1934
Skinner, Audrey Paul (infant)	only date	Feb 19 1941
Skinner, Paul F.	Aug 30 1908	May 1 1962
Skinner, William Jasper	Sep 5 1895	Jan 20 1919
Skinner, William T.	Aug 24 1860	Apr 29 1931
Thompson, Chester E.	Mar 17 1912	Jne 24 1957
Ware, Emma H. w/o E.L.	Mar 2 1907	nd
Ware, Ewing L. WW-II So Car HMI USN	Aug 14 1904	Aug 27 1963
Ware, Zach Garrett	Jul 12 1909	Apr 27 1972
Wingate, Dorothy Collins	1896	1928

12.   BETHANY METHODIST
                         Girard, Ga.

Name	Birth	Death
Armstrong, Emma w/o J.W.	Feb 1 1844	Jan 13 1911
Bailey, Archie B.	May 1862	Oct 1898
Bailey, Georgia Chandler w/o Archie	Oct 16 1857	Dec 21 1923
Bargeron, Ben Frank	1848	1929
Bargeron, C.R.	Mar 21 1885	Apr 2 1907
Bargeron, Edwin	1886	1957
Bargeron, Emma Wimberly w/o B.F.	1851	1930
Bargeron, Frances w/o G.W.	Sep 29 1842	Mar 5 1900
Bargeron, Robert Lewis	1889	1928
Bargeron, Sadie E. w/o Edwin	1894	1961
Barron, Henry Samuel s/o Sarah Moore & Wm. f/o Henry S. & Lizzie	Dec 23 1838	Jan 12 1912

15

Name	Birth	Death
Barron, Henry Samuel	1884	1885
s/o H.S. & Jane		
Barron, Lizzie	1871	1885
d/o H.S. & Jane		
Barron, Mary Jane Dixon	Jul 13 1845	Oct 1926
w/o H.S., Sr.		
d/o Thos. & Elizabeth		
m/o Henry S. & Lizzie		
Barron, Thomas Dixon	Mar 6 1882	Jul 22 1943
Bates, Bathsheba	age 69y 4m	Oct 2 1873
Bates, J.W.	Dec 17 1879	Sep 2 1880
s/o J.F. & E.		
Bates, Leland	Sep 20 1888	Nov 27 1895
s/o John F. & Eugenia		
Bates, Wm. C.	age 84y 4m	Jul 10 1874
Bates, Willie	Apr 15 1885	Jne 7 1885
s/o J.F. & E.		
Blocker, Amanda E.	age 37y 2m	nd
w/o B.M.	15d	
Blocker, Barkley M.	Oct 20 1820	Mar 11 1883
Blocker, Elizabeth A.	Dec 6 1859	Sep 24 1860
d/o B.M. & Amanda E.		
Blocker, Ella F.	Jul 17 1865	May 13 1911
w/o P.B.		
Blocker, Hugh L.	age 10y 11m	nd
s/o B.M. & S.M.	10d	
Blocker, Julia Reed	age 15y 6m	nd
d/o B.M. & A.E.	10d	
Blocker, Pierce Butler	May 27 1863	Feb 22 1941
Blocker, Sarah M. Heath	Sep 1840	Nov 16 1911
w/o B.M.		
Brigham, Ada M. Lewis	Aug 23 1872	May 10 1896
w/o Charlie		
Brigham, Ada Ruth	Dec 14 1892	Nov 15 1972
Brigham, Alma	Jul 15 1889	Sep 1 1889
d/o Chas. & Tulia		
Brigham, Arthur J.	May 19 1879	Apr 3 1962
Brigham, Arthur Julian, Jr.	Aug 3 1912	Jan 2 1925
s/o A.J. & Marie		
Brigham, C.M.T.	Oct 3 1827	Feb 24 1883
w/o Wm.		
Brigham, Caroline	Jne 3 1865	May 20 1875
d/o W. & C.M.T.		
Brigham, Charles C.	1905	1954
Brigham, Charlie	Oct 3 1860	Feb 24 1915
F&AM		
Brigham, Erasmus H.	Apr 17 1854	May 14 1864
s/o W. & C.M.T.		
Brigham, Evans	Sep 13 1884	Mar 1 1887
s/o C.R. & G.V.		
Brigham, Infant	Sep 12 1882	Oct 8 1882
s/o C.R. & G.V.		
Brigham, Infant	Sep 17 1927	Sep 18 1927
s/o T. Powell & Mary D.		

Brigham, Infant s/o W. & C.M.T.	Sep 4 1858	Nov 2 1858
Brigham, J.C. s/o J. & J.C.	Aug 5 1877	Jne 22 1885
Brigham, Joannah Louise 1st w/o Arthur J.	Jan 9 1883	Jul 21 1905
Brigham, John C. MD	Jne 16 1846	Jan 29 1908
Brigham, Julia w/o Dr. J.C.	1853	1950
Brigham, Louise G. w/o Chas. C.	1908	L
Brigham, Marie Reddick 2nd w/o Arthur J.	Feb 28 1883	Dec 9 1968
Brigham, Mary B. w/o Thadieus	1864	1934
Brigham, Mary DeLaigle w/o T. Powell	Jan 19 1898	L
Brigham, Minnie L. w/o Charlie	Jul 5 1878	Mar 12 1953
Brigham, Sarah Caroline d/o Chas. & Ada M.	Nov 20 1895	Jan 20 1903
Brigham, Thadieus R.	1849	1898
Brigham, Thadyes Powell WW-I Ga Pvt 52 Inf	Jan 11 1895	Mar 29 1959
Brigham, Tulia w/o Charles	Nov 28 1866	Jan 25 1890
Brigham, Walter W. F&AM	May 27 1913	Feb 11 1950
Brigham, William	Jan 23 1819	Jne 2 1893
Buxton, Agnes (twin) d/o G.O. & W.L.	Apr 10 1896	Sep 18 1896
Buxton, Allie E., Jr.	Jan 27 1912	May 25 1912
Buxton, Alma White w/o Charles W.	May 11 1910	L
Buxton, Bernard s/o C.W. & D.B.	Nov 23 1901	May 24 1906
Buxton, C.W. F&AM	Jan 21 1873	Jan 1 1915
Buxton, Charles W. s/o C.W. & Daisy	Aug 8 1907	Aug 23 1963
Buxton, Daisy B. Hillis w/o C.W.	Jul 18 1873	Nov 8 1957
Buxton, Doris L.	Apr 26 1914	Jul 25 1914
Buxton, Florence Haeseler w/o Wm. R.	Aug 4 1870	Nov 26 1955
Buxton, Gary	Sep 17 1883	Oct 1883
Buxton, Glover Bass	Mar 3 1870	Apr 19 1921
Buxton, I. Hillis	Aug 14 1899	Nov 19 1964
Buxton, Infant s/o F.L. & M.H.	only date	Jne 16 1924
Buxton, Infant d/o S.H. & Josephine	Mar 27 1885	Jul 14 1885
Buxton, Infant d/o W.R. & F.H.	Dec 21 1890	Dec 23 1890

Buxton, Infant (twin)	Feb 4 1891	Jne 30 1891
d/o G.O. & W.L.		
Buxton, Joseph Haeseler	May 15 1893	Mar 23 1894
s/o W.R. & F.H.		
Buxton, Josephine Dixon	Oct 21 1842	Mar 8 1924
w/o Samuel H.		
Buxton, Josephine McLain	May 9 1853	Dec 31 1913
w/o W.H.		
Buxton, Judah Benjamin	Jne 12 1881	Feb 23 1972
Buxton, Louise Odom	Aug 18 1886	Apr 13 1951
w/o J.B.		
Buxton, Mary Wimberly	Jne 22 1814	Apr 28 1892
Buxton, Mildred B.	Mar 10 1913	Jne 16 1913
Buxton, Natalie (twin)	Feb 4 1891	Oct 20 1898
d/o G.O. & W.L.		
Buxton, Needham A.	Mar 13 1835	Apr 22 1915
Buxton, Oliver	Oct 22 1876	May 8 1914
Buxton, Paul Allen	Oct 9 1907	Apr 28 1909
s/o W.R. & F.H.		
Buxton, Pearl (twin)	Apr 10 1896	Jne 30 1896
d/o G.O. & W.L.		
Buxton, Rosaline Dixon	Nov 7 1858	Jan 31 1938
Buxton, Rosanah	Sep 11 1866	Feb 13 1867
Buxton, Sadie V. Perkins	Sep 4 1876	Jan 16 1959
w/o 1st Bass Buxton		
2nd Harman Perkins		
Buxton, Samuel H.	Mar 1 1813	Dec 29 1896
Buxton, W.A.	Oct 27 1867	Sep 2 1870
Buxton, W.H.	Dec 20 1844	Dec 19 1884
Buxton, Washington G.	age 26y 5m 6d	Aug 26 1853
Buxton, William	May 1 1791	Apr 5 1843
Buxton, William Robert	Sep 10 1864	Oct 5 1938
Chandler, Floyd S.	Feb 9 1899	Oct 24 1954
Chandler, Franklin L.	Aug 18 1942	Dec 27 1967
Ga SP4 USA		
Chandler, Ida Long	Jne 16 1874	Dec 4 1951
w/o W.B.		
Chandler, James B.	Mar 31 1907	May 11 1959
s/o W.B. & I.L.		
Chandler, Louise O.	Apr 16 1911	L
w/o F.S.		
Chandler, Robert W.	1855	1918
Chandler, Willie B.	Nov 11 1863	Nov 30 1934
Chavus, Mrs. Nancy	age 75 y	Oct 10 1839
Claxton, Basheba	1856	1939
w/o James		
Claxton, James	1848	1923
Claxton, Jennie W.	1881	1966
Claxton, Mamie	1884	1955
Claxton, Mell Gertrude	1893	1973
Claxton, Sallie M.	1853	1935
Claxton, Sara E.	1890	1966
Cochran, Arthur Latimer	Dec 26 1900	May 23 1966

```
Cochran, Benjamin R.  WW-I        Oct 26 1895    Mar 31 1970
  Ga Pvt USA
Cochran, Caroline C.              Feb 22 1837    May 24 1887
  w/o G.L.
Cochran, Carrie F.               Jan 27 1871    Jul 10 1898
  w/o E.J.
Cochran, Charlie B.              Jne 21 1861    Jne 29 1928
Cochran, E. Julius               Mar  9 1864    Dec 25 1908
Cochran, Edgar Willie            Oct  4 1862    Oct  4 1866
  s/o G.L. & C.C.
Cochran, Ella L.                 Jan 27 1864    Jan  3 1951
  w/o C.B.
Cochran, George L.               Mar  6 1836    Dec 16 1879
Cochran, George Leslie           Jne  7 1895    Oct  9 1895
  s/o E.J. & C.F.
Cochran, George Lewis            Jul 23 1869    May 14 1955
Cochran, George Metz             Jul 13 1880    Jul 19 1964
Cochran, India H.                Dec 26 1869    Jul 16 1888
  w/o E. Julius
Cochran, India Heath             Jul 15 1888    Nov 11 1888
  d/o E.J. & I.H.
Cochran, Infant                  Jul  9 1898    same   date
  s/o E.J. & Carrie F.
Cochran, Infant                  Jne  1 1900    Jne  3 1900
  d/o G.M. & M.E.
Cochran, Mary E.                 Oct  6 1878    Jne  1 1900
  w/o G.M.
Cochran, Mary Jane Barron        Apr  8 1877    Jne 30 1936
  w/o George Lewis
Cochran, Molly Godbee            Aug 17 1878    Sep  3 1955
  w/o George M.
Cochran, Thomas Lawrence         Apr  9 1867    Oct 15 1905
Cochran, Wm. N.                        1893          1968
Cochran, Woodrow                 May 21 1920    Oct  5 1920
Cox, Louise                                nd   May 25 1864
  w/o W.M.
Cox, Sarah Louise                May 25 1864    Jan 31 1932
  d/o Louise & W.M.
DeLaigle, Janice Elaine          Sep  9 1957    Apr  2 1964
  d/o T.D. & L.S.
DeLaigle, Lucille S.             Dec 11 1905               L
  w/o Theus D.
DeLaigle, Theus D.               Sep  8 1899    Jne  2 1972
DeLaigle, Theus Everette         May 22 1947    Feb 27 1968
  Viet W PH Ga Cpl 621 TC Det 269 Avn Co
Dixon, Bonnie Morgan             Jan 26 1889               L
Dixon, Edd                       Feb 27 1890    Jne 18 1972
Dixon, Elizabeth                 Jul 16 1819    Sep 25 1850
Dixon, Eva Armstrong             Apr 22 1886    Sep 21 1957
  w/o B.M.
Dixon, Frances A.                Aug  3 1838    Jul 15 1883
Dixon, Frank Bartow              Dec 19 1861    Dec 13 1924
Dixon, Infants (three)                     nd             nd
  of W.R. & F.A.
Dixon, Joseph Dennis             Mar  5 1872    Sep  8 1937
```

Dixon, Joyce Malabar	May 31 1873	Dec 26 1944
w/o F.B.		
Dixon, R.J.	Jul 13 1805	bkn 1865
Dixon, Richard Lee	1864	1933
Dixon, Sarah A.	Apr 9 1848	Aug 16 1899
w/o Thos. J.		
Dixon, Thomas	Aug 31 1807	Oct 30 1862
Dixon, Thomas	Aug 5 1866	Dec 1 1866
Dixon, Thomas J.	Apr 12 1840	Dec 29 1911
Ellison, Benjamin Robert	Aug 25 1851	Sep 21 1921
Ellison, Jane E.	May 14 1826	Aug 29 1900
w/o Sam J., Sr.		
Ellison, Jane E.	Apr 16 1868	Feb 14 1897
d/o L.L. & M.A.		
Ellison, John B.	Jan 22 1888	Jne 9 1960
Ellison, L.L.	Oct 18 1848	Sep 2 1899
Ellison, Louisiana Long	Jne 18 1866	Mar 4 1956
w/o Benj. R.		
Ellison, Minnie Lou	Jne 17 1903	Sep 18 1917
Ellison, Samuel J.	Aug 24 1821	Mar 30 1896
Flake, Alice A.	Nov 13 1830	Apr 6 1902
Flake, J.L.	Jul 29 1852	Jan 29 1913
Flake, Marion	May 7 1898	Oct 28 1898
Flake, William	Nov 15 1814	Sep 27 1891
Flake, William V.	1895	1946
Flakes, Wilson	nd	nd
Folds, Junnie WW-II	Jan 31 1908	Jul 31 1952
Ga Pvt 55 Inf Training Bn		
Frazier, Stacy Erwin	Jan 31 1969	Mar 24 1969
Glisson, Alice Houston	Jan 12 1850	Aug 12 1916
w/o Jos. W.		
Glisson, Arthur B.	Apr 6 1881	Nov 5 1908
Glisson, Bessie G.	1876	1937
w/o Henry L.		
Glisson, Duncan G.	1884	1942
Glisson, Henry L.	1874	1935
Glisson, Infant	1926	1926
of D.G. & L.M.		
Glisson, Joseph Lewis	1903	1948
Glisson, Joseph Warren	Oct 13 1843	Apr 19 1916
Godbee, C.G. CSA	nd	nd
Co C 32 Ga Inf		
Godbee, Charlie	1861	1939
Godbee, F.F.	May 11 1854	Apr 10 1881
Godbee, Georgia Thomas	Aug 30 1869	Jne 21 1892
Godbee, James A.	Feb 22 1894	nd
Godbee, Jane M.	Jul 29 1823	Mar 17 1905
w/o Stephen		
Godbee, Joseph Russell WW-I	Apr 8 1895	Jne 25 1972
Ga Pvt USA		
Godbee, Leslie L.	Dec 23 1888	Oct 14 1938
WOW		
Godbee, Lindsey E.	1890	1939
Godbee, Mary	Apr 6 1802	Nov 28 1899
w/o Murchison		

Godbee, Mary Jane	1866	1949
w/o Charlie		
Godbee, Murchison	Mar 18 1814	Dec 3 1876
Godbee, Stephen	Feb 23 1814	Oct 18 1886
Godbee, Willie L.	Feb 19 1888	Mar 10 1960
w/o James A.		
Griffin, Ethel Buxton	Sep 16 1884	Jul 28 1972
w/o J.W.		
Griffin, James W.	Sep 4 1880	Jan 23 1950
Griffin, Joicy M.	Sep 16 1822	Aug 7 1906
w/o Washington		
Griffin, L.E.	Jul 3 1850	Jne 6 1920
Griffin, Martha C.E.	Jul 16 1857	Mar 11 1904
w/o L.E.		
Griffin, Washington	Aug 14 1820	Jul 21 1883
Hall, Bessie B.	Sep 30 1886	May 2 1969
w/o Thomas D.		
Hall, M.B.	Jan 1 1832	Jul 27 1876
Hall, Thomas D.	Aug 3 1873	Feb 19 1951
Hannah, Janie Heath	1881	1967
w/o Robt.		
Hannah, Robert Lee	1882	1948
Hayman, Edna Holland	Apr 25 1892	Jul 26 1964
w/o E.L.		
Hayman, Ernest Leonard	Mar 17 1888	nd
Hayman, James Elbert	Aug 6 1876	Jan 13 1919
Hayman, James E., Jr.	Sep 22 1909	Nov 27 1964
Hayman, Louise Sommer	Nov 21 1912	L
w/o 1st J.E. Hayman, Jr.		
w/o 2nd Duke Dixon		
Hayman, Mattie (Patsy) Griffin	Apr 11 1879	Aug 30 1961
w/o James E.		
Heath, Mrs. Adalaide Chandler	Jul 2 1861	Oct 22 1922
Heath, Alex Alfestus	1871	1936
Heath, Andrew J.	Aug 22 1846	Jul 3 1864
Heath, B.C.	Aug 1 1852	Jul 11 1885
Heath, Benjamin H.	Feb 29 1848	Feb 18 1859
s/o Jordan & Sarah		
Heath, C.C.	Apr 14 1851	Nov 30 1932
Heath, Caroline C.	May 9 1843	Mar 11 1858
d/o Jordan & Sarah		
Heath, Effie	May 10 1910	same date
Heath, Eula L. Odom	Oct 27 1883	Jne 12 1952
w/o Alex. A.		
Heath, Garland C.	Aug 8 1885	Sep 10 1921
Heath, George W.	Aug 24 1853	Jan 27 1881
Heath, Georgia Rosa	Apr 26 1858	Oct 1 1858
d/o R.A. & J.O.		
Heath, H. Walker	Nov 29 1856	Jan 20 1942
Heath, Harney Anderson	Apr 22 1848	Jul 16 1909
Heath, Harriet	Mar 18 1818	Mar 11 1902
Heath, Howard Tatnall	Apr 11 1875	Dec 13 1875
s/o J.B. & M.R.		

Heath, Isabelle M.   Nov 9 1849   Oct 27 1876
  w/o Alex. T. md Jan 23 1876
  d/o Saml. & Eliz. Buxton
Heath, James King   Jne 7 1885   Jul 5 1906
Heath, Jasper E.   Sep 16 1838   Sep 4 1861
Heath, Joseph J.   Nov 30 1877   Jul 12 1912
Heath, Joseph L.   CSA   Jne 13 1842   Apr 12 1862
  d Portsmouth, Va.
  3rd Regt Ga Vol
Heath, Julia Frazier   Jne 2 1846   Aug 26 1908
  w/o Harney A.
Heath, Julius Virgil   Sep 4 1844   Apr 28 1904
Heath, Justin B.   Sep 16 1846   Jan 23 1902
Heath, Kenneth Candler   Feb 14 1906   Aug 1 1906
  s/o H.B. & Lillie
Heath, Leila L.   1890   1968
  w/o Garland C.
Heath, Lessie B.   Jul 7 1879   Mar 1 1902
  w/o O.W.
Heath, Marina   Sep 11 1859   Aug 6 1895
  w/o C.C.
Heath, Martha Leonora   May 1 1847   Feb 22 1908
  w/o S.I.
Heath, Mary Eva   Jne 9 1884   Oct 11 1884
  d/o J.B. & M.R.
Heath, Mary Dorothy   Jan 22 1916   Jne 6 1921
Heath, Mary Rouse   Oct 23 1848   Jul 19 1932
  w/o Justin B.
Heath, Melvina O.   Sep 18 1850   Jne 23 1939
  w/o J. Virgil
Heath, Moses   nd   Mar 3 1874
Heath, Nancey   May 6 1844   Oct 13 1856
  d/o Moses & Harriet
Heath, Oliver Walker   Mar 28 1878   May 20 1933
Heath, O'Neal Buxton   age 87 y   Jan 6 1973
Heath, Rebecca M.   Mar 8 1855   Oct 8 1872
  w/o C.C.
  d/o J.W.H. & E. Godbee
Heath, Richard B.   Apr 15 1870   Oct 28 1950
Heath, Richard Wheeler   Sep 27 1904   Oct 30 1904
  s/o A.A. & Eula Lee
Heath, S.I.   Aug 2 1837   Dec 31 1903
Heath, Thomas Isaac   Jul 6 1868   Oct 5 1875
  s/o J.B. & M.R.
Heath, Wilbur Carson   Aug 23 1918   Sep 12 1918
Herrington, Maria E.   Jan 12 1825   Sep 2 1849
Hicks, Christianna   Mar 18 1815   Apr 20 1902
Hickman, Ada B.   1875   1961
  w/o W. Lee
Hickman, Andrew J.   nd   nd
Hickman, Cleva E. Oliver   Feb 5 1893   Oct 4 1955
  w/o John C., Sr.
Hickman, Florence P.   1875   1901
  w/o James L.
Hickman, Henry W.   1866   1944

```
Hickman, Irene B.                      Aug 19 1901   Jan 15 1969
Hickman, James L.                             1876          1941
Hickman, John Chandler, Sr.           Jan 27 1896   Apr 23 1965
Hickman, Joseph                       Oct 16 1866   Aug  7 1971
Hickman, Maybelle                             1899          1902
  d/o (& Wm. L. below s/o) Florence P. & Jas. L.
Hickman, Melvina C.                           1867          1934
  w/o Henry W.
Hickman, Nona                         May     1898   Jul     1901
Hickman, Sarah R.                             nd            nd
  w/o Andrew J.
Hickman, W. Lee                               1885          1937
Hickman, Walter Augustus              Feb  1 1900   Oct 13 1957
Hickman, William L.                           1901          1901
Hillis, Anna Reddick                  Nov 26 1890   Dec 22 1956
  w/o T.S.
Hillis, Mattie                        Nov 22 1839   Feb 13 1925
Hillis, Robert W.                     Oct 23 1847   Sep 28 1919
Hillis, Thomas Stanley                May 14 1890   Sep  4 1944
Holland, C.Q.  CSA                            nd            nd
  Co C 32 Ga Inf
Holland, Joicy                        Mar  6 1799   Feb 23 1891
  w/o Wm.
Holland, J.M.                         Dec 18 1833   Jan 19 1874
Holland, Joseph Marvin                        nd    Jne 26 1972
Houston, Arthur B.                    Oct 30 1882   Oct  3 1906
Houston, Fanney Bell                  Jul 15 1881   Aug 10 1884
  d/o J. & S.
Houston, Jane Griffin                 Oct  6 1825   Oct  6 1901
  w/o Lewis
Houston, Joseph W.                    Aug 18 1854   Jul 12 1927
Houston, Lewis                        Dec 24 1808   Jan 29 1877
Houston, Mattie Bell                  Jan  1 1871   Oct 16 1879
Houston, Savannah Heath               Feb 18 1853   Jne 26 1911
  w/o Jos. W.
Jackson, A.R.                                 nd    May  8 1882
  w/o H.
Johnson, Ella                         Dec  2 1852   Dec 18 1852
  d/o John & Eliz.
Johnson, Georgia Brown                Nov  1 1861   Aug  4 1862
  d/o John & Eliz.
Jordan, Edwin B.                      Aug 21 1893   Feb 11 1906
  s/o Byron & Carrie E.
Lambert, Infant twins                         nd            nd
  of J.E. & L.
Lambert, S.J.M.                       Sep 30 1866   Oct 12 1868
  d/o J.E. & L.
Lovett, Infant                                nd            nd
  s/o J.D. & Marietta
Lovett, J.R.                          Nov 15 1852   May 16 1920
Lovett, John Dell                     Apr 16 1890   Jne 30 1971
Lovett, Marietta                      Jan 14 1891   Nov  6 1928
  w/o J.D.
Lovett, Virginia Burton               Feb  5 1855   Jan  9 1939
  w/o J.R.
```

```
Mallard, A. Grady                    Sep 27 1888   Dec 29 1949
Mallard, Charles Eugene              Apr 13 1891   Nov 30 1959
Mallard, Dean                        Feb 16 1930   Jne 29 1945
Mallard, Emma Hickman                Mar 29 1873   Aug 22 1968
Mallard, Henrietta Royal             Oct 19 1856   Aug 21 1939
  w/o Leonidas W.
Mallard, Henry Mack                  May 14 1874   Jan 28 1956
Mallard, Jesse Allen                 Apr 10 1905   May 22 1945
Mallard, Joseph Pierce               Sep 11 1890   Nov 22 1951
Mallard, Leonidas Walker             Feb 12 1852   Apr 14 1933
Mallard, Lillie Mae Campbell         Nov 28 1906             L
  w/o Thomas J.
Mallard, Mana Buxton                 Dec 31 1882   Jne 12 1948
  w/o Henry Mack
Mallard, Nannie O.                           1882           1960
  w/o Nease
Mallard, Nease N.                            1890           1969
Mallard, Nina Mae                    Mar 20 1896   May 21 1969
Mallard, Thomas Jefferson            Aug  7 1900   Aug 17 1972
Mallard, Winnie R.                           1892           1972
McMichael, Dewey O.                  Jan 11 1936   Jan 15 1936
  s/o G.D. & J.O.
McNeely, Mary Heath                          1871           1943
McNorrill, Gertrude Elizabeth  Jan 31 1923   Feb 28 1923
  d/o H.W. & M.J.
McNorrill, Hagood Winslow            Jan 30 1926   Jan 31 1926
  s/o H.W. & M.J.
Mobley, Alexander                    Sep 26 1884   Nov  7 1885
  s/o M.M. & F.L.
Mobley, Alma Odom                    May 31 1894   Oct 18 1934
  w/o Grady
Mobley, Benj. H.                     Mar  1 1848   Oct 13 1908
Mobley, Carolyn Rose                 Apr 29 1931   Sep 15 1951
  d/o Nellie & Earnest C.
Mobley, Dell                                 1936           1936
Mobley, Ernest C.                    Feb 14 1885   Apr 30 1953
Mobley, Frances L.                   Apr 27 1859   Aug 29 1920
  w/o M.M.
Mobley, George Washington            Feb 25 1880   Jan 24 1911
Mobley, Grady H.                             1887           1939
Mobley, Ida Alverto                  Jan  2 1872   Oct 17 1878
  d/o B.H. & Melvina
Mobley, Ida Lou                      Jul  3 1898   Nov 29 1899
  d/o M.M. & F.L.
Mobley, Ira A.                       Jul 25 1880   Oct  5 1905
  s/o B.H.
Mobley, John Hervy                           1933           1935
Mobley, Lola                         Oct 27 1875   Jne  5 1907
  w/o G.W.
Mobley, Malcom M.                    Feb  3 1856   Dec  3 1919
Mobley, Martha Frances               Feb 27 1930   Mar 11 1930
Mobley, Nellie W.                    Feb 22 1901   Jan 18 1936
  w/o E.C.
Mobley, Wm. C.                       May 17 1878   Aug  2 1943
```

Moody, A.A.	Apr 20 1871	Aug 13 1872
s/o W.T. & A.		
Murphey, Pearl	Feb 20 1879	Oct 31 1879
d/o L.A. & E.		
O'Banion, C.A.	Sep 12 1856	Aug 3 1916
O'Banion, Hettie E.	Mar 5 1858	Jan 28 1904
w/o C.A.		
Odom, Beverly R.	Jne 24 1855	Oct 29 1929
Odom, Beverly Randall,Sr.	Nov 30 1818	Jne 13 1900
Odom, Elizabeth	Jan 26 1798	Oct 5 1861
w/o Laban		
Odom, Emma Lee Chandler	Nov 25 1895	L
w/o H.B.		
Odom, Evins	1896	1896
s/o James & Lillie		
Odom, Guidella Mears	Apr 27 1875	Oct 10 1941
w/o Jordan		
Odom, Harvey B.	Feb 4 1889	Mar 3 1969
Odom, Houston	May 28 1900	Aug 14 1902
s/o J.R. & N.J.		
Odom, India L.	Feb 21 1890	Jan 30 1941
w/o J. Frank		
Odom, Infant	Aug 27 1919	Sep 7 1919
of H.B. & E.L.		
Odom, Infant	only date	Jne 23 1904
s/o J.B. & G.M.		
Odom, Infant	only date	1896
s/o J.F. & L.J.		
Odom, J. Frank	Jne 17 1883	Aug 15 1956
Odom, Jacob	age 5y 25d	Sep 21 1851
s/o B.R. & Nancy		
Odom, James F.	Dec 5 1862	Aug 9 1928
F&AM		
Odom, James Garnet WW-1	Sep 8 1890	Aug 26 1960
s/o J.R. & N.J.		
Ga Sgt USA		
Odom, James Richard	Feb 2 1862	May 17 1953
h/o Nora Jane Houston		
Odom, James Richard	Jne 29 1902	Nov 11 1902
s/o J.R. & Nora		
Odom, James Thomas	Oct 21 1878	Oct 21 1928
Odom, Joe Wheeler	Jan 27 1899	Feb 3 1900
s/o J.R. & N.J.		
Odom, Jordan Bartow	1864	1947
Odom, Julian P.	Nov 26 1890	Jne 4 1891
s/o S.J. & M.B.		
Odom, Julius Virgil	Sep 4 1844	Apr 28 1904
Odom, Laban	Jan 22 1790	Jne 1 1860
s/o Isaac & Celia		
Odom, Laban, Jr.	1866	1947
Odom, Laban, Sr.	Sep 14 1828	Mar 20 1897
Odom, Lanier L.	Nov 11 1893	Dec 20 1955
Odom, Lillian Dixon	Mar 21 1905	Feb 29 1968
w/o 1st Lanier L.		
2nd Harry Smith		

```
Odom, Lillie                              Nov 18 1872   May 16 1888
    d/o S.H.
Odom, Lillie J.                           Jan 31 1874   Oct  7 1896
    1st w/o Jas. F.
Odom, Louisiana Jane                      Oct 17 1857   Apr 30 1864
Odom, Mamie G.                            Nov  8 1875   Dec  8 1903
    2nd w/o Jas. F.
Odom, Mary B.                             Jne 10 1857   Apr  8 1935
    w/o Sam. J.
Odom, Mary E.                             Sep 27 1864   May 27 1937
Odom, Nancy                               Jan  6 1826   Jne 27 1897
    w/o B.R., Sr.
Odom, Nancy V.                            Jne 30 1854   Sep 10 1880
    w/o S.H.
Odom, Nora Jane Houston                   Oct 25 1864   Dec 17 1931
    w/o James R. md Mar 16 1882
Odom, Samuel J.                           Feb  8 1856   Dec 12 1935
Odom, Sarah E.                            Jul  1 1845   Oct  5 1852
Odom, Sarah Rebecca                       Dec  8 1834   Feb 25 1917
    w/o Laban, Sr.
Odom, Sylester Herrington                 Sep 14 1851   Jul  6 1920
    F&AM
Odom, Thomas Evins                        age 9y        Sep    1876
    s/o B.R. & Nancy
Odom, William Ralph                       Aug  8 1919   Aug  7 1934
    s/o J.F. & Pearl Oglesbee
Odom, Willie L.                                  1869          1948
Oglesbee, Emma Caroline                   Oct 31 1861   Sep 25 1933
    w/o J.N.
Oglesbee, Jasper Newton                   Aug 13 1856   Dec 19 1932
Oglesbee, Mattie O'Banion                 Jan 22 1884   Aug  1 1971
    w/o Wm. L.
Oglesbee, William L.                      Nov 18 1882   Dec 26 1972
Oglesby, Evans L.                                1896          1932
Oglesby, Mattie C.                               1894          L
    w/o Evans L.
Perkins, Sadie V. Odom Buxton   Sep  4 1876   Jan 16 1959
    1st w/o Bass Buxton
    2nd Harman Perkins
    buried next to her first husband (ed).
Powell, Amarinthia                        Jan 14 1836   Jne 10 1905
    w/o Seaborn
Powell, Fairbell Quick                    Dec  1 1837   Jul 11 1966
    w/o Lawton
Powell, Henry Cater                              1854          1929
    s/o A. & Seaborn
Powell, Inez                              Jne  5 1902   Aug 24 1906
    d/o J.E. & Nannie
Powell, J. Evans                          Aug  5 1881   Jul 18 1940
Powell, James B.                          Feb 17 1861   Apr 25 1889
    s/o S. & A.
Powell, Johnnie   WW-II                   Oct 13 1919   May 24 1962
    s/o F.Q. & Lawton
    Ga S Sgt USA
```

```
Powell, Julia Griffin                          1860              1886
   1st w/o Henry C.
   d/o Joicy M. & Washington
Powell, Lawton                                  nd                nd
   s/o A. & Seaborn
Powell, Melker H.                   Sep 22 1904     Jan 18 1937
Powell, Moselle Griffin                    1865              1937
   2nd w/o Henry C.
   d/o Joicy M. & Washington
Powell, Roy                         Sep 15 1907     Jne 20 1909
Powell, Seaborn                     Sep  4 1828     Jul  4 1911
Prescott, Samuel                    Oct 29 1785     Aug  5 1858
Prior, Texie Frazier                Jan  8 1881     Oct 21 1952
Quick, Cameron J.                          1910              1933
Quick, Mrs. Eva                     age 83y         Aug     1960
Quick, George W.                           1864              1930
Quick, Joseph Frazier               Feb  6 1942     Nov 21 1944
Quick, Lewis Grady                  Aug 15 1884     May 13 1951
Quick, Mary W.                             1866              1926
   w/o Geo. W.
Quick, Minor Godbee                 Mar 10 1866     Feb 23 1934
   w/o Richard H.
Quick, Richard Henry                Mar 20 1862     Feb  5 1936
Quick, Richard Henry                       1939              1943
Quick, Robert                              1877              1942
Quick, Virginia                            1885              1964
   w/o Robt.
Rogers, Josephine Rebecca           Nov 14 1840     Apr 16 1863
                        /Buxton
Rouse, Emmie B.                     Jan 15 1855     Feb 24 1913
   w/o J.B.
Rouse, John B.                      Mar 18 1854     May 13 1917
Rowland, Ada                        Mar  8 1876     Dec 15 1962
   d/o Jas. M. & Savannah
Rowland, Benjamin B.                Nov 11 1873     Nov 21 1923
Rowland, Benjamin Franklin          Jan 14 1913     Aug 21 1921
   s/o Eva P. & Jas. M.
Rowland, Eva Powell                 Feb  3 1878     Aug 11 1959
   w/o J.M.
Rowland, James M.                   Aug 26 1821     Apr 19 1897
Rowland, James Monroe               Oct 26 1871     Jul 14 1953
Rowland, Roy A.                     Jul 21 1906     Apr 24 1960
   s/o Eva P. & Jas. M.
Rowland, Savannah                   May 22 1848     Jne 10 1900
   w/o Jas. M.
Rowland, Savannah                   May 18 1902     Aug 17 1902
   d/o J.M. & Eva
Rowland, Victoria                   Sep 27 1842     Oct  5 1864
   w/o James P.
   d/o Sam. H. & Eliz. Buxton
Royal, Atticus Roscoe                      1876              1946
Royal, Claudine O'Banion                   1881              1964
   w/o A.R.
Royal, Emmie                        Sep 23 1883     Sep 26 1904
   w/o A.R.
```

Royal, Infant	Sep 8 1904	same date
d/o A.R. & Emmie		
Sharp, Clifford A.	Mar 18 1920	Oct 6 1971
Ga Pvt USA		
Sharpe, Charlie C.	1868	1940
Sharpe, Grace Quick	1901	nd
w/o Julian Camby		
Sharpe, Julian Camby	1902	1963
Sharpe, M.C., Sr.	Sep 16 1908	Jan 12 1970
Sharpe, Mary F.	1871	1940
w/o Chas. C.		
Sharpe, Mary Virginia	Oct 12 1942	Apr 23 1943
Skinner, Floyd T.	Jne 22 1856	Aug 10 1858
s/o Edmund D. & Mary		
Smith, Emma	nd	nd
d/o Rev. A.B. & Frances		
Smith, Frances R.	Dec 6 1820	Sep 17 1861
w/o Rev. A.B.		
Stephens, Elmer Eugene	Jul 24 1914	Jne 22 1972
s/o Nettie O. & W.V.		
Stephens, William V.	Apr 6 1885	Sep 8 1925
Sturdivant, Alex S.	Jan 2 1884	Apr 18 1968
Sturdivant, Ruth M.	Aug 25 1886	Feb 18 1967
w/o Alex S.		
Tessier, Kitty C.	Jul 23 1858	Sep 13 1863
d/o Dr. M.M. & L.B.		
Tessier, Dr. L.P.	Jne 15 1809	Aug 2 1860
Tessier, Louisiana B.	May 6 1838	Nov 12 1861
w/o Dr. M.M.		
Tessier, Louisiana T.	Mar 1 1860	Sep 22 1863
d/o M.M. & L.B.		
Thomas, Mary	Jul 5 1844	Sep 13 19bk
Utley, Carson	Oct 20 1911	Jan 17 1936
s/o Hattie & William		
Utley, Hattie L. Heath	Oct 10 1882	Nov 3 1961
w/o William M.		
Utley, Wilber	May 27 1923	Aug 4 1941
s/o Hattie & William		
Utley, William Martin	Sep 6 1867	Apr 24 1939
Ward, Ada H.	Jul 22 1876	Dec 17 1966
Ward, Alice Holland	Jul 6 1881	Jne 27 1963
w/o Wm. L.		
Ward, Mary Alice	Feb 20 1909	Apr 5 1910
d/o W.L. & J.A.		
Ward, Seabie Kathleen	Aug 23 1915	Jne 28 1916
Ward, William Fulcher	Apr 27 1902	Apr 3 1955
s/o A.H. & Wm. L.		
Ward, William L.	Nov 27 1866	Oct 16 1953
Ward, William Thomas	Mar 7 1898	Sep 6 1898
s/o W.L. & J.A.		
Wimberly, Henry	Sep 17 1850	May 13 1936
Wimberly, Mary S.	Dec 6 1906	Sep 1 1972
Wimberly, Melvina Spears	Oct 22 1870	Feb 24 1966

BETHEL BAPTIST
Alexander, Ga.

Barefield, Alma Gladys	1907	1920
d/o Mr. & Mrs. J.W.		
Barefield, Annie Margaret	Jne 12 1916	Jne 21 1916
Barefield, Balzora Chance	Sep 29 1859	Aug 16 1940
w/o J.W.		
Barefield, Rev. C.E.	Jne 13 1826	Aug 27 1889
Barefield, Chance C.	Oct 29 1884	Nov 17 1949
Barefield, Corbette	Oct 13 1892	Oct 4 1895
s/o J.W. & C.E.B.		
Barefield, Dewey Hobson	Jul 11 1898	May 30 1959
Barefield, Effie Idell	Sep 21 1889	Jul 13 1964
Barefield, Infant	only date	Oct 17 1918
s/o Mr. & Mrs. J.W.		
Barefield, Infant	only date	1898
d/o J.W. & C.E.B.		
Barefield, Infant	Oct 5 1921	same date
s/o Mr. & Mrs. T.A.		
Barefield, James D.	Aug 4 1907	Jan 2 1954
Barefield, James W.	1882	1945
Barefield, James Washington	Aug 18 1857	Nov 3 1917
Barefield, Jewel	Jne 9 1913	Sep 26 1913
Barefield, Mary Belle Thorne	Jul 8 1901	Jul 22 1932
w/o D.H.		
Barefield, Mattie S.	1882	1960
w/o James W.		
Barefield, Owen R.	Nov 13 1910	Oct 21 1957
Barefield, Sallie Oglesby	Dec 4 1888	Aug 14 1943
w/o C.C.		
Barefield, Tannie A.	Dec 10 1886	Aug 2 1921
Barefield, Thompson	Jan 4 1926	Jne 19 1966
Baxley, Minnie H.	Apr 29 1893	Nov 2 1964
w/o Sidney P.		
Baxley, Sidney P.	Nov 4 1929	Mar 20 1950
Blanchard, Ada Frances Hillis	Oct 28 1878	Sep 8 1958
Blanchard, Alicia Ann	Feb 19 1946	same date
Blanchard, Donna Jean	Dec 3 1944	May 30 1945
Blanchard, Edith Glover	1899	1917
Blanchard, G.P.	Nov 17 1876	Nov 11 1922
F&AM		
marker erected by daughter, Fannie Bell		
Blanchard, John Francis	Dec 24 1912	Jul 16 1962
Blanchard, Julia S.	Aug 12 1867	Aug 22 1909
w/o G.P.		
Blanchard, Sarah Etta	Dec 10 1897	Feb 26 1898
d/o G.P. & J.S.		
Blanchard, Thomas S.	Feb 17 1891	May 5 1893
s/o G.P. & J.S.		
Brawley, William E.	1896	1960
Chance, Ola S.	1879	1960
Claxton, Leslie (infant)	nd	nd
Claxton, Lessie (infant)	nd	nd

Claxton, Lizzie Mae	Feb 15 1892	Oct 10 1912
Claxton, Mary Lou	nd	nd
Claxton, Robert Lee	Feb 2 1869	Dec 23 1921
Coursey, William P.	1929	1929
s/o Mr. & Mrs. H.C.		
Crenshaw, Catherine Jenkins	Dec 23 1890	Jan 27 1969
Elliott, Alford P.	1865	1940
Elliott, John J.	Aug 19 1851	Jul 6 1936
Elliott, Ollie B.	1873	1943
Elliott, Sara Ann	1830	1911
Elliott, Sarrah V.	Mar 29 1886	Feb 3 1909
Elliott, Shultz M.	Feb 14 1868	Jul 21 1948
Ellison, Otis Manor	age 74y	Oct 1 1972
Flakes, Clydell	1935	1945
Flakes, Mary K. Williamson	1895	1940
Godbee, Ada R.	1877	1945
w/o Walker		
Godbee, George W.	1910	1911
s/o Ada & Walker		
Godbee, Infant	nd	nd
s/o Theodow & Frances		
Godbee, Janie	1914	1916
d/o Ada & Walker		
Godbee, Lucile	1912	1914
d/o Ada & Walker		
Godbee, Maggie B.	1905	1906
d/o Ada & Walker		
Godbee, Walker	1870	1958
Hatcher, George William	age 61y	May 6 1969
Hillis, Annie L.	Jul 15 1888	Aug 14 1913
Hunter, Frankie Laurie	1927	1927
Hunter, Hugh David	1944	1970
Hunter, John Henry	Oct 1917	Jul 20 1961
Hunter, Louie Dean Barefield	1904	1951
Hunter, Paul	age 27y	1969
Hunter, Thomas J.	1893	1965
Jackson, ------	nd	nd
four unmarked slabs cover Jackson graves (ed).		
Jenkins, Mallory Lloyd (Nig)	age 62y	Aug 27 1973
Kilpatrick, Laura E.	Mar 10 1858	Jan 5 1932
w/o Wm.		
Kilpatrick, William	Nov 2 1848	Apr 8 1916
Kilpatrick, William P.	Apr 23 1939	Jul 16 1939
Kirby, Roy Leon	1956	1956
McClain, Annie S.	Oct 16 1897	nd
w/o B.B.		
McClain, Britton B.	Oct 11 1896	Dec 23 1965
McMellon, Ada B.	nd	nd
d/o H.A. & Marion		
McMillian, Archie B.	1934	1934
McMillian, Henry A.	1880	1957
McMillian, Marion G.	1908	1934
Miller, Clyde S.	Aug 21 1916	Mar 1 1970
Oglesby, Alford Quinney	Jan 5 1893	Jul 17 1968

Name	Birth	Death
Oglesby, Fannie Baxley w/o A.Q.	Oct 26 1896	nd
Oglesby, Florence R. w/o James J.	Mar 16 1892	Dec 6 1963
Oglesby, James D.	Jul 7 1855	Jan 29 1929
Oglesby, James J.	1885	1943
Oglesby, Maria	nd	nd
Oglesby, Nancy w/o Dawson	Jan 7 1860	Aug 8 1924
Oglesby, Ossie A.	Jul 23 1881	May 3 1890
Oglesby, Shultz C. s/o J.J. & Florence	May 29 1912	Dec. 7 1919
Quick, Mazie Kilpatrick 1st w/o Robert	Dec 16 1933	Apr 14 1961
Sapp, Dennis D. Ga Pvt USA	only date	Aug 28 1938
Sapp, Jesse James	1891	1933
Sapp, William C.	age 51y	Jan 17 1972
Sapp, Willie Langley	1888	1969
Sapps, William C.	Sep 23 1843	Apr 28 1902
Sikes, Adge	nd	nd
Sikes, Birdie C.	1909	1928
Sikes, Doug (infant)	only date	1935
Sikes, Earnest E.	1919	1933
Sikes, Ella Josephine	Nov 7 1878	Apr 21 1965
Sikes, Ella O. w/o Thos. J.	1860	1935
Sikes, Floyd L.	1883	1896
Sikes, G. Leslie	1894	1903
Sikes, Henry Zone	Jul 19 1887	May 17 1965
Sikes, Ida May	Jul 4 1928	Nov 1928
Sikes, Jane C.	nd	nd
Sikes, John T.	1884	1944
Sikes, Lottie Saxon	1897	1969
Sikes, Mary E. w/o John T.	1883	1921
Sikes, Rosa May	1906	1943
Sikes, Thomas J.	1853	1930
Sikes, William A.	Apr 6 1887	Nov 22 1960
Sikes, William H. CSA Co K 32 Ga Inf	nd	nd
Skinner, Caroline w/o Geo. W.	1854	1946
Skinner, Carroll C. WW-II Ga BM 2 USNR Korea	Mar 24 1903	Aug 21 1970
Skinner, E. N. CSA Co C 5 Ga Cav	nd	nd
Skinner, Ezra W.	Jul 19 1906	Dec 17 1949
Skinner, George W.	1850	1923
Skinner, George W.	1890	1935
Skinner, Irene	Jul 17 1905	Nov 4 1918
Skinner, Jennie Lee	Jan 3 1912	Oct 8 1912
Skinner, Lavonia	1867	1940
Skinner, Mamie G.	Feb 21 1892	Sep 12 1904

Skinner, Mattie Lee w/o Sim B.	Sep 14 1893	nd
Skinner, Nellie K.	1901	1935
Skinner, Sallie E.	1878	1921
Skinner, Sim B.	Feb 6 1889	Jne 10 1963
Skinner, Simeon W.	1872	1951
Spires, Chrystbell C. w/o Henry U.	1903	nd
Spires, Henry U.	1897	1959
Spires, Lee G., Jr.	1941	1968
Stephens, Eva Barefield	May 31 1878	Oct 9 1935
Stephens, Jane	Nov 4 1840	1928
Stephens, W. Jack	Mar 15 1868	Feb 25 1926
Thorne, George Jackson	1871	1957
Trader, Bob	1865	1932
Trader, Willie w/o Bob	1869	1937
Watkins, Florence S. w/o J.H.	1897	1969

Watkins, George R.   WW-II   Nov 1 1921   Jne 1 1944·
PH OLC Ga PFC Co G 135 Inf 34th Div   Killed in action
in Italy.

Watkins, James Herschel   age 82y 8m   Oct 14 1968
                                     8d

14.   BETHLEHEM BAPTIST
                          Girard, Ga.

Daniel, Byron MD	Mar 3 1875	Nov 15 1945
Daniel, Charlie s/o W. & E.	Sep 25 1877	Jul 28 1878
Daniel, Elizabeth	Aug 6 1850	Mar 21 1925
Daniel, Elmer Herbert	Sep 15 1897	Sep 13 1898
Daniel, George W.	Jul 13 1870	Nov 8 1901
Daniel, Hattie B. Heath w/o George W.	Oct 11 1872	May 7 1913
Daniel, Infant of Hattie B. & Geo. W.	Apr 23 1896	Jul 17 1896
Daniel, Infant of Hattie B. & Geo. W.	Sep 27 1901	Oct 1 1901
Daniel, Infant of W. & E.	Mar 8 1873	Mar 20 1873
Daniel, Infant of W. & E.	Oct 4 1888	Nov 4 1888
Daniel, Mary Lizzie d/o Geo. W. & Hattie B.	Sep 2 1892	Jan 10 1910
Daniel, Washington	Jul 25 1840	Dec 23 1904
Daniel, Zack	Feb 13 1887	Jan 4 1906
Dixon, Georgia Long	Feb 17 1862	Jul 2 1953
Dixon, Mathew	1889	1932
Dixon, Oran Daniel	May 28 1942	Nov 3 1962
Dixon, Shelly Emory	Feb 14 1907	Sep 11 1973
Dixon, Thomas L.	Oct 21 1859	Feb 25 1920
Dixon, Thomas M.	Aug 23 1947	Aug 24 1947
Dixon, Thomas Quinney	age 85 y	Aug 10 1973
Flake, James Dewey	Oct 8 1907	Jne 18 1949
Flake, James Lanier	Sep 23 1916	Dec 6 1919

Name	Birth	Death
Flake, Marvin B.	1883	Oct 28 1965
Flake, Mary Johnson	Apr 20 1885	Dec 7 1970
Flake, Roger Lester	Jan 26 1882	Aug 17 1922
Frazier, Josie D.	nd	L
w/o Louie H.		
Frazier, Louie H.	1911	1965
Glisson, Anna E.	1877	1957
w/o Robt. W.		
Glisson, Anna Eliza Rhodes	Feb 17 1873	Jul 31 1907
w/o W.J.		
Glisson, Annie M.	1910	1970
w/o Joseph E.		
Glisson, Doris J. (twin)	Jan 18 1947	Jan 20 1947
Glisson, Gerald K. (twin)	Jan 18 1947	Jan 24 1947
Glisson, Joseph E.	1912	1955
Glisson, Lillie Belle Oliver	Mar 30 1889	Oct 28 1930
w/o Wm. J.		
Glisson, Robert W.	1872	1939
Glisson, William Jacob	Nov 25 1868	Aug 1 1921
Glisson, Willie Eva	Oct 23 1914	May 12 1916
d/o W.J. & Lillie		
Godbee, Cleveland D.	Mar 20 1886	Sep 8 1943
Godbee, Della H.	1853	1934
w/o V.W.		
Godbee, Effie (infant)	nd	nd
d/o O.O. & B.A.		
Godbee, Horace Kemp	Aug 13 1916	May 16 1917
s/o Mr. & Mrs. A.K.		
Godbee, Infant	nd	nd
of R.J.		
Godbee, J. L.	Mar 17 1834	Aug 14 1905
Godbee, Lena L.	Jan 7 1902	Jne 16 1902
Godbee, Nettie H.	Jul 31 1894	Sep 27 1970
w/o Cleveland D.		
Godbee, Ritter	age 73y	only date
Godbee, Verdree W.	1851	1932
Godbee, Willie S.	1877	1942
Hayman, Alice C. Prescott	Nov 13 1848	Feb 13 1926
Hayman, Evans G.	1879	1942
Hayman, Infant	nd	nd
Hayman, Lola D.	1886	1965
w/o Evans G.		
Helmly, John W.	Jul 1 1853	Oct 15 1909
Helmly, Martha A.	Jul 3 1848	Sep 23 1921
w/o John W.		
Helmly, Robert L.	Mar 7 1881	Jul 19 1920
Hilles, George	Nov 17 1833	Apr 25 1862
Hilles, Georgia	Dec 4 1860	Jul 2 1862
d/o G. & P.		
Hillis, Amanda Dixon	May 14 1831	Aug 10 1903
w/o William		
Hillis, Catherine	Jul 27 1900	Feb 15 1901
d/o J.S. & S.A.		
Hillis, Cealy Josephine	Jan 29 1851	Sep 22 1865
d/o J.M. & Elizabeth		
Hillis, Charlie Lee	1927	1966

Hillis, Daniel Webster s/o J.M. & Elizabeth	Jan 24 1856	Oct 29 1862
Hillis, Elizabeth Aurelia d/o J.M. & Elizabeth	Sep 22 1858	Oct 9 1862
Hillis, Ellie Godbee	age 66 y	Jan 10 1961
Hillis, Emely B.E. d/o J.M.	May 11 1857	Jul 1 1857
Hillis, Fannie Whitehead w/o H.C., Sr.	Mar 31 1859	May 17 1933
Hillis, Francis Daniel 2nd w/o Jacob	Mar 13 1843	Mar 25 1938
Hillis, George Gordon s/o H.C. & A.F.	Nov 1 1887	Jne 22 1890
Hillis, George Thomas s/o J.M. & Elizabeth	Jne 12 1852	bkn
Hillis, Henry Clayton, Jr.	Feb 24 1886	Jan 10 1919
Hillis, Henry Clayton, Sr.	Oct 10 1854	Dec 1 1926
Hillis, Infant of J.C.	Feb 10 1884	Feb 18 1884
Hillis, Infant d/o J.S. & S.A.	only date	Jan 21 1906
Hillis, Infant s/o T.J. & K.A.	Feb 13 1901	Feb 22 1901
Hillis, Jacob	Oct 1 1819	Dec 7 1881
Hillis, James S.	Sep 23 1860	Jne 5 1923
Hillis, John H. b in Ireland	1784	1864
Hillis, John Meddleton s/o J.M. & Elizabeth	Sep 21 1862	Sep 28 1863
Hillis, John W. s/o J.S. & S.A.	Dec 26 1884	Feb 21 1902
Hillis, Junious S. s/o J.S. & S.A.	Nov 4 1886	Aug 15 1897
Hillis, Kate Houston w/o Thos. J.	Feb 20 1868	May 29 1940
Hillis, Katie W. d/o T.J. & K.A.	Dec 8 1896	May 8 1897
Hillis, Lizzie d/o J.S. & S.A.	Apr 12 1891	Mar 28 1906
Hillis, Mariah McM. w/o John M.	1799	1879
Hillis, Mrs. Martha 1st w/o Jacob	Aug 16 1825	Sep 23 1863
Hillis, Minnie Lee d/o Jacob & Francis	Mar 6 1875	Sep 12 1893
Hillis, Sarah	Sep 20 1822	Oct 11 1880
Hillis, Savannah	Jan 25 1846	Jul 3 1929
Hillis, Susie A.	1866	1943
Hillis, Thomas J.	May 29 1858	Aug 23 1911
Hillis, William	Oct 17 1819	Oct 4 1904
Hillis, Winfield s/o J.S. & S.A.	Jul 17 1889	Aug 7 1890
Hillis, Winnie B. d/o T.J. & K.A.	Oct 14 1888	May 20 1891
Lamb, Willie Lee	Feb 10 1914	Feb 16 1936
Lambert, Hugh	Aug 27 1918	Feb 16 1926

```
Lambert,  Hugh M.                               1897                1952
Lambert,  Wilbert Dukes                           nd    Feb 22 1956
Long,  Ella Virginia             Jan   3 1855    Oct 26 1917
  w/o J.P.
Long,  Infant                    Jul   7 1969    only    date
  d/o Mr. & Mrs. Jimmy
Long,  J.P.                      Mar 28 1845    Dec 14 1921
  F&AM
Long,  James Matthew                            1878                1954
Long,  Minnie Zeigler                           1881                1953
  w/o Jas. M.
Mobley,  Eula                    Oct 18 1884    Jne 28 1889
Mobley,  J.F.                    Sep 20 1861    Jan 13 1917
Mobley,  Oliver                  Mar   7 1884    Jul 31 1884
  s/o Frank & Emilie
Mobley,  Susan E.                Jne 26 1842    Oct 17 1932
  w/o Wm. L.
Mobley,  William L.              May 30 1857    Sep 23 1937
Mock,  Arthur Lee, Jr.           Oct 27 1942    Jul   2 1962
Morris,  Eugenia Virginia                       1858                1926
Muns,  Lucy                      Jne 14 1872    Jul   8 1900
  w/o C.H.
Murry,  P.A.                     Jan 31 1838    Jan 31 1896
  w/o D.
Odom,  Hilda J.                  Apr   5 1916    May 26 1918
  d/o Samuel W. & Bertha T.
Odom,  Sarah                     Jne 30 1859    Sep 17 1898
  w/o B.F.
Oglesbee,  Mary Elizabeth        Jan 15 1830    Jul   4 1893
Oglesby,  Charlie L.             Jne 13 1945    Sep 25 1967
Oglesby,  Ethel Bell             Dec 18 1884    Apr 18 1944
  w/o T.J.
Oglesby,  Henry R.                              1909                1955
Oglesby,  Pauline Anna           Sep 20 1910    Oct 20 1927
Oglesby,  Thomas WW-II           Feb 18 1914    Jne 26 1969
  Ga Tec 5 USA
Oglesby,  Thomas Joseph          Jne 24 1876                 nd
Oglesby,  Willie L.  WW-II       May   7 1916    Sep   5 1970
  Ga Pvt USA
Oliver,  Caroline Bentley        Sep 20 1868    Jul 23 1938
  w/o Lafayette
Oliver,  Emily Ophelia                          1875                1957
Oliver,  Lafayette               Jan   6 1865    Aug 15 1926
Oliver,  Mary A.                 Sep   8 1846    Apr   5 1881
  w/o James H.
Peterson,  Effie Daniel          Feb 24 1884    Mar 17 1962
Proctor,  Margaret P.            Dec 29 1823    Dec 15 1909
  w/o W.P.
Proctor,  Martha A.              Jul   8 1865    Jan 17 1868
  d/o W.P. & M.P.
Proctor,  W.P.                   Jul   5 1829    Mar 25 1911
Sentell,  Mabelle                               1889                1927
  d/o W.T. Wilkins
Sowell,  Georgia E. Freeman      May 17 1869    Jul   7 1902
  w/o Rev. D.L.
```

```
Sowell, Infant                    Jul  4 1902  Jul 28 1902
   s/o Rev. D.L. & G.E.
Watson, Wm.P.                           1916         1971
Wilkins, Mary Arelya                    1860         1946
Wilkins, Savannah                 Nov  5 1850  Nov 18 1902
   w/o W.F.
Wilkins, W.F.                     Apr 19 1845  Nov 10 1923
   F&AM
Zeigler, G. Estell                Apr  3 1901  Oct 22 1901
   d/o W.B. & L.
```

15.   BIG BUCKHEAD BAPTIST
                           Jenkins Co.

```
Hines, Dr. Henry C.               Oct 15 1828  Jan 15 1856
   h/o Caroline Elizabeth  Will Bk A 7-8
Jackson, Ann Everline             age 87y  7m  Aug 22 1889
   w/o George  Joined Baptist Church at this place
   Sep 6 1834
Jones, Batt                       Sep 11 1825  Dec 18 1862
Jones, Caroline E.                age 42y      Jne 28 1869
   d/o Wm. & Sarah Sapp
Sapp, Mary T.                     Jne  4 1797  May 17 1856
   m/o Dr. Henry C. Hines  Will Bk A 7-8
   "She sleeps beside her only son"
Shultz (Schultz), Christian               nd  Aug     1847
   b in Prussia;  lived in Ga 33 y
Thorn, Middleton                  Mar 14 1798  Dec 15 1858
```

Note: The word "Big" was added when Buckhead Baptist
became the mother church of a new church, "Little
Buckhead Baptist" (ed).

16.   BLOUNT

```
Blount, Axalina Clark             Jul 15 1799  Apr  2 1856
   w/o 1st, Ethelred Thomas;  children:  Jethro, William,
   Celia, & Richard;  2nd, James Robinson, Sep 1 1827;
   issue:  Eliza Elizabeth;  3rd, Stephen W. Blount,
   1837;  children:  Robert Broadnax and Edwin Fitz-
   gerald.  Became a member of Brushy Creek Baptist
   Church, 1828.
Blount, Louisa A. Dillard         Aug 10 1843  Aug 14 1882
   w/o Robert Broadnax,  md Dec 22 1859;  children:  Asa
   Holt, William T., Frank A., Maude, and Robt. B., Jr.
Blount, Stephen William           Jan 21 1785  Dec 16 1858
   s/o Stephen Blount of S Car & Savannah (Rev soldier,
   d Sep 16 1804)
   md 1st, Elizabeth Wynn (Winn);  children:  Thomas
   Hamilton, Edward Howard, Henry Jackson, Stephen W.,
   and Jane.
   md 2nd, Axalina Clark (Thomas) (Robinson);  children:
   Robert Broadnax and Edwin Fitzgerald.
```

Penrow, Asa H.	1827	1875
Penrow, Martha A.	1806	187?
Penrow, Martha R.	1816	1879
w/o Asa H.		

Note: For listings above of issue, the editor has drawn upon the earlier research on the Blount and Thomas families by Mrs. Anne MacKenzie Humphrey.

17.
BLYTHE BAPTIST
Blythe, Ga.

Agner, Annie DeLoris	Jne 12 1947	Oct 4 1960
w/o Troy		
Agner, Troy	Jul 28 1948	Jan 26 1966
Auldridge, R. Sisson	Dec 11 1869	Oct 26 1935
Barksdale, John S.	Oct 16 1843	Sep 11 1903
Beall, Evagean Carswell	Oct 27 1886	nd
w/o Wm. W.		
Beall, Monroe (twin)	Nov 20 1924	Nov 23 1924
Beall, Morris (twin)	Nov 20 1924	Jul 25 1929
Beall, William Walter	May 8 1886	Aug 10 1963
Beckum, Doyle (Daddy) J., Sr.	Nov 5 1892	Dec 9 1953
Beckum, John Hyden WW-II	Mar 20 1926	Dec 6 1953
Ga Sgt 630 QM GRREG Co.		
Beckum, Julia Eloise	May 17 1920	May 25 1934
Beckum, Mary Lou Roberson	Jan 9 1898	Jul 1 1970
w/o D.J., Sr.		
Beckum, Willie Mae	1895	1969
Boyd, Susan Weatherford	Mar 24 1878	Jul 16 1941
w/o Newton B.		
Broome, Vernon W.	Jul 3 1903	Dec 17 1955
Burns, Infant	only date	Feb 18 1945
s/o Mr. & Mrs. G. Truett		
Byne, Ida Vallotton	Jul 11 1865	Jul 19 1944
w/o John P. He married (2nd) Corinne Lewis and is		
buried at Sandersville, Ga.		
Cadle, Delilah M.	1844	1920
Carswell, Donalita	Mar 18 1923	Sep 28 1942
Carswell, E. Morris	Dec 5 1877	Aug 17 1913
Carswell, Ida Morris	1856	1946
w/o Jasper E.		
Carswell, Infant	only date	Apr 18 1908
s/o L.A. & E.M.		
Carswell, Jasper E.	1849	1896
Carswell, Linnea Anderson	Oct 27 1887	Apr 22 1908
w/o E.M.		
Carswell, Nannie H.	Dec 8 1883	Mar 13 1916
Carswell, Paul Derry	Aug 21 1890	Sep 19 1925
Cawley, Audley Hill	Mar 5 1905	Jul 15 1942
Clark, Constance	Jne 29 1911	May 22 1913
Clark, Matthias	Dec 2 1869	Apr 20 1951

Name	Birth	Death
Clark, Theodosia Harley w/o Matthias	Apr 30 1874	Apr 1 1937
Cloer, Arlon Brown	Jne 14 1908	Aug 29 1970
Clcer, Beryl Tinley	Oct 25 1941	Mar 10 1970
Cook, Eva Morris	1861	1944
Cook, Fred W.	Apr 7 1890	Sep 6 1953
Cook, Raymond	Feb 9 1920	Jul 22 1922
Council, Andrew Schley s/o R.J. & Lula	only date	Jul 17 1943
Council, Barbara Ann	Oct 13 1946	Jne 14 1970
Dinkins, Bertha	Sep 26 1917	Sep 21 1922
Dinkins, Bertha E. Turner w/o Oliver G.	May 13 1889	Jul 24 1967
Dinkins, Oliver Gary	Jan 29 1884	Mar 1 1920
Dye, Aseneth Walton w/o B.F.	Mar 4 1829	Nov 14 1910
Dye, Benjamin Franklin	Mar 28 1836	Jan 30 1913
Dye, Decima Foss w/o Lewis	Sep 1 1875	Mar 14 1960
Dye, F. Wayne, Sr.	1910	1969
Dye, Lewis Wayne	Mar 23 1875	Jne 26 1940
Dye, Russell F.	1861	1933
Elliott, ------	nd	nd
Fransham, Beth d/o P.D. & D.A.	Aug 10 1964	Dec 29 1967
Fransham, Hilda May Delf w/o Robert R.	Jul 15 1893	Dec 19 1959
Fransham, Robert Reginald	Oct 13 1891	Mar 11 1960
Halford, Alford F. WW-II Ga Pfc 746 AAA Gun Bn CAC	Dec 7 1908	Apr 11 1964
Hammett, Mrs. Martha M.	Nov 12 1845	Jul 31 1919
Hancock, Hazel	1924	1926
Hancock, James T.	1871	1935
Hancock, Mattie M. w/o James T.	1874	1957
Hardy, J.W.	Sep 12 1885	May 26 1916
Haynie, May Trowbridge w/o N.R.	Dec 5 1875	Sep 7 1909
Hendrix, Faythe (infant) d/o Mr. & Mrs. B.S.	only date	Aug 30 1939
Howard, Gordon F.	Aug 6 1924	May 17 1926
Ivey, Benjamine T.	Aug 9 1863	Jne 20 1947
Ivey, Louella P. w/o Benj. T.	Aug 15 1878	Nov 20 1965
James, Dorris Carolyn d/o H.A. & R.E.	1940	1941
James, H. W.	1877	1945
James, Hammond L.	Aug 2 1919	Dec 29 1971
James, Horace A.	Feb 15 1906	Apr 10 1963
James, Louisa Anderson w/o H.W.	1883	1954
Jordan, Carrie L.	Feb 3 1869	Jul 4 1929
Jordan, Henry S.	Aug 30 1833	Apr 8 1904
Jordan, Nannie Morris w/o H.S.	Aug 30 1840	Jne 12 1918

Name	Birth	Death
King, J.B.	Mar 25 1860	Oct 17 1940
King, Modie Templeton Tudor	Jul 16 1868	Oct 31 1957
Lyons, Éliza A.	Jne 25 1848	Aug 21 1909
Mahoney, Mattie Taylor	1880	1930
Martin, Anna Powell w/o George B.	Apr 12 1870	Mar 19 1947
Martin, Floyd A.	Jan 11 1917	same date
Martin, George Berry	Dec 15 1871	Jul 27 1945
Martin, George F.	1892	1973
Martin, Salina Sills	Dec 3 1847	Sep 24 1928
McNair, Addie Jones w/o John W., Sr.	1872	1937
McNair, John W., Sr.	1867	1946
McNair, Juanita	1921	1927
McNair, M. Jones	1894	1960
McNair, Mary	1924	1933
McNair, Sarah w/o M. Jones	1899	1971
Morris, Caroline Hardy w/o Edmond	May 30 1820	Nov 10 1907
Morris, Cathrine d/o G. Walter & Cora E.	1901	1945
Morris, Cora E. w/o G. Walter	1863	1935
Morris, Rev. Edmond	Aug 11 1818	Jul 20 1893
Morris, G. Walter	Oct 14 1858	Dec 10 1918
Morris, Rosa J.	Jne 9 1856	Nov 5 1906
Mundy, Julia w/o R.M.	1891	1949
Mundy, R.M.	1881	1936
Mundy, Roy	1902	1945
Murrow, Hattie Rhodes w/o V.J.	Jan 31 1842	Dec 2 1927
Murrow, Virgil J.	nd	Oct 18 1907
Newman, Franklin H.	1936	1956
Orander, James Boaz	Jne 16 1903	Mar 31 1970
Orander, Marie W. w/o J.B.	Jul 14 1906	Sep 7 1965
Pearce, Dollie Turner w/o H.L., Jr.	Jul 18 1903	Mar 7 1968
Pearce, Henry Lester, Jr.	Mar 31 1905	Mar 19 1954
Phillips, Carrie Whitaker w/o Julian	May 6 1889	Dec 20 1965
Phillips, Julian G.	Oct 18 1883	Jne 28 1966
Radford, Kate A. w/o Wm.	Sep 13 1849	Aug 5 1907
Rentz, Mattie Turner	Oct 30 1889	Oct 16 1926
Reville, Cora Wren w/o Wm. H.	Nov 20 1886	Aug 26 1953
Reville, William H.	May 6 1873	Sep 28 1946
Ricker, Elizabeth P.	Jan 30 1882	Sep 26 1958
Ricker, Ethel	Jan 21 1891	Aug 13 1911
Ricker, Forrest L.	Jul 2 1904	May 7 1967
Ricker, Infant s/o Mada & Paul	only date	1920

Name	Birth	Death
Ricker, James L.	Sep 10 1877	Feb 15 1948
Ricker, Leacy Phillips	1856	1942
w/o Wm. Jas.		
Ricker, Mada Griffin	nd	. L
w/o P.H.		
Ricker, Paul Hayne	1885	1957
Ricker, William James	1850	1915
Saxon, Annie Eliza	Apr 28 1874	Feb 25 1926
Shurling, Clara B. Barwick	1888	1964
Smith, Alice Templeton	Oct 12 1879	Jan 24 1936
w/o Wm. H.		
Smith, Berry H. MD	May 4 1882	Sep 27 1936
Smith, Jannette Carswell	Jne 7 1881	Mar 16 1959
Smith, John Hervey	1911	1971
Smith, Macy B.	May 6 1904	Nov 23 1971
w/o Berry H.		
Smith, Walter S.	Jan 28 1876	May 18 1952
Smith, William Henry	Apr 7 1869	Jan 23 1940
Stapleton, Annie Adams	Sep 25 1875	Jul 12 1933
w/o Wm. A.		
Stapleton, John T.	1907	1926
s/o W.A. & Annie		
Stapleton, Pauline Tarver	Jul 29 1918	nd
w/o Wm. A., Jr.		
Stapleton, Wm. A.	Oct 22 1865	Jul 17 1945
Stapleton, William A., Jr.	Nov 25 1914	May 9 1965
Taylor, Edward C.	May 16 1874	Jul 7 1931
Taylor, Julia D.	Mar 30 1866	Nov 10 1935
w/o Edw. C.		
Tebow, Elnora C.	1871	1950
Tebow, John R.	1854	1927
Temples, Mattie McGee	nd	Jne 15 1954
w/o Jas. Henry		
Tinley, Amelia M.	May 26 1846	Dec 17 1914
w/o J.R.		
Tinley, E.K.	May 19 1874	Jne 25 1906
Tinley, M.M.	Sep 10 1876	Jul 14 1906
Trowbridge, Hattie A.	Mar 7 1854	Aug 6 1918
w/o W.R.		
Trowbridge, Inez B.	Sep 28 1883	Mar 7 1887
Trowbridge, Jones Rufus WW-I	Oct 29 1887	Oct 8 1955
s/o Haseltine Amelia Morris & Wm. Rufus		
1st Lieut Air Corps; Consul US Foreign Service;		
retired 1950		
Trowbridge, W. R.	Nov 29 1852	Aug 13 1911
Tudor, Annie Ethel	Feb 14 1893	Nov 2 1893
d/o Mr. & Mrs. J.M.		
Tudor, Curtis O., Sr.	1889	1961
Tudor, Infant	only date	Nov 15 1891
d/o Mr. & Mrs. J.M.		
Tudor, Infant	only date	Dec 7 1894
d/o Mr. & Mrs. J.M.		
Tudor, J.H.	Aug 29 1858	Jul 6 1895
Tudor, Lena E.	1896	1950
Tudor, Nannie L.	1920	1922

```
Tudor, Sarah M.                       May 10 1915    Jne  6 1916
   d/o C.O. & L.E.
Tudor, Thomas                         age 90y        Aug 12 1911
Tudor, Thomas D.                            1930             1940
Turner, Allen                               1919             1923
Turner, Dave L.                       Apr 13 1894              L
Turner, Fred L.                       Dec 23 1898    Aug 24 1936
Turner, James F.                            1858             1941
Turner, James Willie                  Nov 26 1882    Oct  8 1957
Turner, Samuel Lee                    Apr 15 1900    Feb  3 1927
Turner, Susan J.                            1860             1917
   w/o Jas. F.
Turner, Tiny L.                       Mar 28 1896    Jul 23 1969
   w/o Dave
Walton, Ephily Everette               Feb 26 1826    Aug 28 1903
Weatherford, Clarence E.              Oct 11 1917    Dec 24 1934
Weatherford, Millidge A.              Oct  9 1886    Aug  9 1932
Weatherford, Millidge Robert          Jul 20 1909    Dec 19 1940
Weatherford, Roberta P.               Feb  1 1886    May 21 1949
   w/o Millidge A.
Weatherford, William Harvey           Nov 10 1913    Sep 20 1971
Whitaker, Dixie P.w/o Marvin R.           nd               nd
Whitaker, Marvin R.                         1911             1967
Williams, ------                      only    date          1920
   Unidentified but next to Hoyt C.
Williams, Hoyt C.                           1910             1963
Wood, Alice L. Morris                 Jan 24 1859    Apr 16 1939
   w/o Horatio
Wood, Edmond (infant)                       nd               nd
Wood, Ellen M.                        Nov  2 1891    Jne 23 1892
Wood, H. Bradford                     Oct 19 1892    Feb 27 1938
Wood, Horatio G.                      Nov  9 1829    Feb  8 1912
Wood, Infant                                nd               nd
Wood, Joseph (infant)                       nd               nd
```

18.   BLYTHE METHODIST
                   Blythe, Ga., Richmond Co.

```
Adkins, Mrs. N. M.                    Jne 29 1883    Jan  6 1919
Agerton, Amrintha Lucinda             Apr 29 1834    Jne  1 1912
Agerton, Charley E.                   Dec 26 1866    Jan 26 1896
   s/o E.A. & A.L.
Agerton, Eldred Avery                 Feb 17 1834    Jul 24 1912
Agerton, Mary Lillie                  Mar 25 1862    Aug 14 1921
Agerton, Thomas J.  CSA                     nd               nd
   -Cav Bn Cobb's Ga Legion
Atkins, Thomas Irven                  Nov 27 1879    Apr 25 1921
Atkinson, Emily C.                    Nov 28 1845    Nov  8 1912
   w/o Robt. T.
Atkinson, Robert T.                   Oct 24 1845    May 12 1923
Beckum, Edward Oliver                 Feb 19 1854    Aug 11 1924
Beckum, Grady N.                      Jan  1 1930    Oct 21 1934
   s/o Thelma & Joe H.
Beckum, Jefferson                           1861             1938
Beckum, Joe H.                        Nov 28 1901    Aug 24 1971
```

```
Beckum, Lena May                     Dec 27 1904   Jul 24 1905
Beckum, Martha E.                    Sep 22 1863   Mar 27 1942
Beckum, Nettie V.                    May 16 1893   Jan 11 1907
Beckum, S.B.                         Apr 21 1852   Jne 18 1924
Beckum, Sarah Buck                          1868          1945
  w/o Jefferson
Beckum, Thelma N.                    Dec 12 1900            nd
  w/o Joe H.
Beckum, Wm. H.H.H.                   Oct  1 1897   Jul 17 1899
  s/o J.D. & S.E.
Bell, Clarence L.                           1900          1948
Butler, Sallie Vallotton             Oct 17 1852   Jul 26 1928
  w/o J.J.          /Palmer
Byrd, John L.                        May 27 1873   Dec  7 1944
Byrne, Martin A.  Sp-Am W            May  7 1878   Aug  6 1954
  Qm Sgt Co F 1 Fla Inf
Byrne, Mintie Templeton              Nov  6 1874   Dec 21 1960
  w/o M.A.
Cason, Adam Hillary                  Oct 31 1867   Nov  8 1930
Cason, Mary Cason Williamson         Oct 23 1883   Apr  4 1961
  w/o A.H.
Choate, Kate Saxon                   Sep  5 1890   Nov 15 1969
Cooper, Rosabella Vallotton          Mar  9 1852   Jne 11 1909
Davidson, Caroline                          1851          1927
  w/o Edwin
Davidson, Edwin                             1856          1946
Dinkins, S.K.                        May 25 1845   Nov 19 1914
Dozier, Cleo E.                             nd             L
  w/o J. Louis
Dozier, J. Louis                            1906          1971
Dozier, Louis Oliver                 Aug 31 1877   Jul  4 1953
Dozier, Mary B.                      Oct 25 1915            nd
  w/o R.E., Sr.
Dozier, Mary Irene                   Apr 26 1881   Jul 30 1925
  w/o Louis O.
Dozier, Oliver L.                           1917          1959
Dozier, Robert E., Sr.               May 22 1910   Oct 28 1966
Eubanks, J. Tilla                           1863          1936
Eubanks, Willie T.                          1884          1963
  w/o J. T.
Fletcher, Floyd T.                          1868          1929
Fletcher, Ida Wren                   Jne 14 1874   Oct 21 1963
Fletcher, Lizzie E. Templeton        Jan 11 1860   Jan 29 1923
  w/o F.T.
Fletcher, M.A.                       Nov  1 1834   Dec 17 1917
  w/o G.W.
Goolsby, Eulie Thurston  WW-I               1899          1918
  s/o Wm. F. & H.W.
  6th Regt US Marines; d in action; buried in Argonne,
  France
Goolsby, Harriet Ellen               Jan 21 1860   Mar  2 1931
  w/o Wm. F.      /Whitaker
Goolsby, William Fulton              Apr 23 1860   Jan 13 1942
Graham, Vera Templeton               Jan 24 1894   Aug  3 1953
Graham, Wistar L.                    Nov 15 1890   Apr  6 1951
```

Name	Birth	Death
Greiner, Dove V. WW-I	Dec 31 1893	Apr 10 1952
Ga Pvt 66 Depot SVC Co ASC		
Hardy, Eliza James	May 12 1855	Sep 5 1929
Hardy, Jerry M.	Jan 17 1855	Jan 7 1919
Hardy, Samuel B.	1882	1934
Holley, Willard	Apr 28 1890	Sep 5 1967
Hood, Ad WW-I	only date	Jan 1 1928
Ga Pvt 4 Field Art		
Hood, General Lee	nd	Sep 15 1922
Jenkins, Elizabeth	Mar 24 1848	Aug 14 1918
Lemon, Charles V.	1858	1939
Lemon, Mary J.	1861	1946
Lyons, Clifford J.	1886	1939
Lyons, Irene	1897	19--
w/o Clifford J.		
McNair, Cinnie Rheney	1861	1936
w/o J.K.		
McNair, J.K.	1853	1931
Moore, Julia L.	Apr 23 1856	Sep 1 1901
Newman, B.F.	Dec 28 1870	Jul 25 1932
Nickles, Lula I.	1893	nd
w/o W.R.		
Nickles, Walter R.	1893	1954
Padgett, Jackson L., Sr.	1907	1970
Palmer, Infant	nd	nd
d/o O.H. & L.M.		
Palmer, Infant	nd	nd
s/o S.E. & A.K.		
Palmer, Levin E.	Jul 3 1876	Nov 3 1940
Shriner		
Palmer, Lillie Smith	1891	1954
Palmer, Lucie Mae Reese	Aug 27 1886	Aug 4 1909
w/o O.H.		
Palmer, Mary E. Tinley	Jan 31 1843	Aug 2 1926
w/o Samuel A.		
Palmer, Olin H., Jr.	Aug 19 1920	Jan 12 1944
b Blythe d Cape Gloucester, New Britian		
Palmer, Olin Hagood	Nov 17 1878	Jul 8 1959
Palmer, Samuel Anthony	Feb 1 1841	Jne 28 1926
Palmer, Samuel E.	Sep 6 1864	Jul 3 1906
s/o S.A. & M.E.		
Palmer, Truman N.	Jan 15 1881	Nov 12 1907
Pennington, Fred Cook	May 8 1890	Feb 27 1970
Pennington, Julia Dean	Sep 25 1908	nd
/Heisler		
Pennington, Mary Elizabeth	Oct 2 1905	Aug 26 1944
/Pearre		
Phillips, Joe C. WW-II	Dec 12 1923	Nov 11 1944
Ga Pfc 379 Inf 95 Inf Div		
Phillips, Joseph C.	Jan 17 1880	Mar 29 1930
Phillips, William H.	Oct 30 1926	Aug 18 1934
Phillips, William O.H.	Jan 23 1882	Sep 13 1901
Powell, Inez H.	1875	1944
w/o Jos. C.		
Powell, Joseph C.	1877	1955

Prescott, Allene Aldred	1905	1962
Reese, Laura Mae Wilson w/o P.B.	Nov 25 1863	Jul 7 1930
Reese, Pryor Brooks	Sep 18 1857	Jul 7 1935
Rhodes, Betty	May 24 1918	Jne 14 1964
Rhodes, DeSausure C. WW-I Ga Sgt USA	Feb 8 1897	Apr 20 1970
Rhodes, DeSausure S.	1873	1970
Roberts, Cora Rowland	Nov 23 1873	Aug 5 1949
Roberts, Green W.	Jne 9 1856	Jan 24 1935
Roberts, James R. WW-II So Car Pvt USA	Nov 22 1898	Aug 7 1968
Roberts, Thomas N.	Dec 17 1911	Apr 24 1913
Rowland, Henry B.	Aug 23 1878	Sep 5 1904
Rowland, J. Charley	Oct 2 1885	Jan 12 1954
Rowland, James R.	Jul 31 1845	Jne 18 1898
Rowland, Rosa Lee	1890	1973
Rowland, Sarah B. w/o Jas. R.	May 31 1852	Aug 10 1930
Saxon, Alice Rouse w/o Sam'l A.	Oct 27 1858	Feb 15 1924
Saxon, Benjamin F. WOW	1874	1939
Saxon, Betty Agerton w/o Benj. F.	1870	19
Saxon, Cora Layton w/o Jas. H.	Jne 29 1872	May 10 1951
Saxon, James Henry	Apr 29 1867	Apr 23 1942
Saxon, M.F. m/o I.M. Saxon Young	Apr 29 1835	Feb 28 1918
Saxon, S.A., Jr. (infant)	nd	nd
Saxon, Samuel A.	Oct 4 1850	Feb 29 1924
Shuman, Paul Anderson MD	Nov 30 1885	Jan 24 1956
Shuman, Warren Gilbert MD	Apr 13 1923	Jne 4 1966
Stephens, Ruby Palmer w/o R.H.	Mar 15 1870	Mar 8 1905
Taylor, Jerry Allen	1877	1942
Taylor, Mamie Hardy w/o Jerry A.	1883	1959
Taylor, William Allen WW-II Ga M/Sgt SQB 466 Base Unit AF	Nov 11 1908	Sep 4 1965
Templeton, Andrew	nd	nd
Templeton, Anna D.	Oct 7 1887	Jne 5 1972
Templeton, Annie S.	1881	1958
Templeton, Augustus W.	Jul 8 1860	Dec 14 1929
Templeton, Carrie Rowland w/o A.W.	Feb 25 1876	Jne 22 1965
Templeton, Charles E.	Nov 14 1830	Jul 6 1910
Templeton, Charles E.	Jan 3 1906	Oct 25 1918
Templeton, Charles Ousley	Dec 7 1873	Jne 4 1918
Templeton, Dealphia Walton w/o Charles E.	Oct 28 1839	Aug 20 1905
Templeton, E. Addie S.	Sep 25 1870	May 28 1950
Templeton, Edward Walton	Apr 10 1906	Jne 1 1906

```
Templeton, Emma L.                       Apr  6 1871   May 23 1956
   d/o C.E. & Dealphia
Templeton, Emma R.                       Aug  8 1898   Jne 22 1971
Templeton, Farris Palmer                 Aug 15 1873   Oct  5 1961
   w/o C. Ousley
Templeton, Infant                        Nov  8 1893   Feb 10 1894
Templeton, John E.                       Aug 24 1862   Jne 22 1929
Templeton, Joseph Saxon                       1911          1962
Templeton, Mamie May                     Aug  3 1886   Feb 25 1892
Templeton, Mary Gay                            nd            nd
Templeton, William G.                         1881          1961
Wren, Samuel F.                          Dec  7 1883   Feb  5 1942
Young, I.M. Saxon                        Nov    1861   Mar    1895
   d/o Mrs. M.F.
```

19.   <u>BOTSFORD BAPTIST</u>

```
Bateman, Joseph Hayward                        nd   Mar 24 1960
Bateman, Ruth                                  nd            L
   w/o Joseph H.
Boyd, Allen                              Nov 14 1811   Jan  6 1886
Boyd, Infant                                  1873          1873
   of Mr. & Mrs. J.J.
Boyd, Jefferson J.                       Jan 12 1833   Oct 16 1894
Boyd, Mary Gould                         May  5 1838   May  5 1898
   w/o J.J.
Buford, Ida Lou                          Jan  5 1907   Nov  4 1961
   w/o Jennings
Buford, Jennings B.                      Sep 16 1896            L
Chance, Iola W. Boyd Palmer              Feb  8 1871   Oct 12 1923
   w/o 1st John T. Palmer
   w/o 2nd James Walker
   d/o J.J. & M.G. Boyd
Chance, James Walker                     Nov 28 1869   Jan 20 1960
Chance, Jefferson B.                     Sep  8 1901   Oct 26 1902
   s/o Iola Boyd & J.W.
Daniel, Alice B.                              1881          1964
   w/o Eddie
Daniel, Eddie L.                              1876          1945
Daniel, R. Warren                        May  7 1852   Oct 15 1918
Daniel, William Dunbar                   Aug  9 1881   Nov 21 1915
DeLaigle, Annie Godbee                        1863          1931
   w/o Nicholas
DeLaigle, C. Gaston                      Feb 19 1886   Apr 20 1946
   s/o Annie & N.L.
DeLaigle, H. Milledge                    Mar 16 1888   Jan  3 1907
   s/o Annie & N.L.
DeLaigle, Herbert                        Dec 17 1900   Oct 18 1922
   s/o Annie & N.L.
DeLaigle, Nicholas L.                    Jne 18 1846   Jul 26 1909
DeLaigle, Robert Steadman                     1883          1956
   s/o Annie & N.L.
DeLaigle, Rossie                         Oct 14 1881   Nov 15 1882
   s/o Annie & N.L.
```

```
DeLaigle, Thomas W.                      Jul 30 1893   May 10 1908
    s/o Annie & N.L.
Elliott, John F.                         Apr 14 1827   May 12 1879
Fulcher, Cora Lou                        Mar 26 1898   Oct 18 1911
    d/o W.D. & M.E.
Fulcher, M. Adella Gordon                Oct  1 1875   Sep 30 1922
    2nd w/o Wm. D.
Fulcher, Mell E.                         Oct 20 1859   Dec 28 1900
    1st w/o W.D.
Fulcher, William D.                      Jne 11 1862   Jne  2 1917
Godbee, Emory A.                                  nd              L
Godbee, Emory A., Jr.   Viet W   Dec 10 1949   Nov 13 1971
    s/o Mary C. & E.A.
    Ga Sgt Co A 1 ACFT Maint Bn
Godbee, Mary C.                                   nd              L
    w/o Emory A.
Gordon, Evie A.                          age 21y 6m   Jan  7 1866
    w/o Robert
Gordon, John B.                          Feb 14 1877   Feb 26 1936
Gordon, Mackie                           Jan 25 1866   Nov  8 1868
    s/o Robert & Evie A.
Gordon, Mary J.                          Mar  8 1846   Nov 27 1910
    w/o Robt.
Gordon, Robert                           Dec 11 1828   Jan 21 1886
Hatcher, Annie Powell                         1844              1896
    w/o Dr. Leonidas B.
Hatcher, Arrah N.                        age 48y      Sep 12 1894
    w/o J. Newton
Hatcher, Geraldine A.                    age 56y      Aug  3 1901
Hatcher, J. Newton                       Feb  9 1845   Nov  3 1917
Hatcher, Johnnie Robert                  Jan  9 1871   Oct 15 1872
Hatcher, Dr. Leonidas Benjamin                1834              1897
Hatcher, Robert Claudius                      1865              1920
Hatcher, Theodore L.                     May 17 1869   Nov 10 1966
Hatcher, William J.                      Apr 17 1840   Feb 10 1905
Hatcher, William J.                      Oct 19 1872   Mar  2 1911
Hickman, Henry Lee                       Jan 15 1914   Feb 21 1972
    s/o Howard & Mosie
Hickman, Howard W.                       Jne 24 1890   Jne 17 1950
Hickman, Infant                                   nd              nd
    "Baby" (in Howard W. section)
Hickman, Mosie Tomlin                    Aug  9 1891   Nov 13 1916
    w/o Howard W.
Hickman, Roy (infant)                             nd              nd
    (in Howard W. section)
Hickman, Welbar M.                       Jan 19 1912   Sep 19 1949
Hickman, William Robert                  Apr 16 1880   Apr  3 1920
    WOW
Hill, Alice W.                                1895              1969
    w/o Marion L.
Hill, Caroline Elizabeth                 Nov 14 1833   Sep 21 1863
    w/o Benj. D.
Hill, Eliza Ann w/o Benj. D.     Dec 30 1828   Jan 27 1868
Hill, Henry Ashley                       Aug 18 1868   Dec 19 1936
```

46

Hill, Kate McNorrill w/o Henry A.	Nov 13 1871	Jan 30 1966
Hill, Maria Ben Alice d/o B.D. & C.E.	Mar 6 1859	Sep 5 1868
Hill, Marion L. WW-I Ga Pvt 157 Depot Brigade	Jne 8 1894	Jne 9 1950
Holland, Joseph Ira	Jne 27 1911	Apr 2 1950
Johnson, B.A.	Dec 23 1903	Apr 9 1927
Johnson, Claudia D.	Nov 24 1876	Mar 11 1947
Jones, Addie J. Barefield w/o Wm. P.	Aug 2 1880	Jan 26 1932
Jones, Bernice Sanders w/o James M.	Apr 21 1896	nd
Jones, Fannie A. d/o Emma & Wm. P.	Sep 10 1894	May 18 1896
Jones, Infant of Emma & Wm. P.	Mar 22 1893	Jne 26 1893
Jones, Infant s/o J.M. & R.L.	May 12 1875	only date
Jones, James Morgan	Jul 23 1901	Nov 8 1963
Jones, John Morgan	Jne 24 1846	Dec 15 1893
Jones, Roger R.	Jul 21 1895	Aug 7 1971
Jones, Sarah Emma Rogers w/o Wm. P.	Jne 30 1872	Jul 29 1896
Jones, William Pinkney	Sep 9 1866	Jul 5 1907
Kendall, Mary Clifford Lively d/o M.J. Elliott & Green B.	Nov 22 1877	Aug 10 1957
Lively, Annie Jane d/o Claranella & G.P.	age 28y	nd
Lively, Ashton A.	1907	1962
Lively, Beatrice Hill w/o Matthew Warren	May 3 1903	Sep 22 1964
Lively, Benjamin Fred s/o Claranella & Geo. P.	Sep 10 1870	nd
Lively, Brooks B. (twin) s/o Daisey A. & J.T.	Dec 10 1909	Dec 13 1909

Lively, Claranella
    w/o G.P.
    d/o Rev. L.F. Powell & Sarah Ann
	Sep 9 1850	Dec 30 1916

Lively, Daisey A. 1st w/o James Thaxter	Aug 15 1879	Nov 12 1913
Lively, Edgar s/o Claranella & G.P.	age 2y	nd
Lively, Edgar F.	Jan 9 1897	Feb 5 1924
Lively, Emmie Colson w/o Benjamin F.	Jul 10 1873	Feb 25 1942
Lively, Eugene G.	nd	nd
Lively, Eula B.	1879	1897
Lively, Eulis Gordon (twin) s/o V.H. & Green P.	Nov 6 1907	Nov 26 1967

Lively, George Pierce   CSA
    s/o Jane Boyd & Mark
    Co C 5th Ga Cav
	Jne 30 1844	Aug 20 1927

Lively, George Powell (twin) s/o V.H. & G.P.	Nov 6 1907	Nov 13 1911

```
Lively, Green B.  CSA              Jan 13 1838   Oct 27 1922
  s/o Jane Boyd & Mark
  Co E Cobb's Leg Inf
Lively, Hugh Miller                        1923          1955
Lively, James Thaxter              Mar 28 1879   Nov 11 1952
  s/o Geo. Pierce & Claranella
Lively, Lillie Bly                 age 6m                  nd
  d/o Claranella & G.P.
Lively, Lynn L.                    Mar 22 1883   Mar 12 1955
Lively, Mary Jane Elliott          Feb 23 1844   May 22 1927
  w/o Green B.
Lively, Matthew Warren             Nov 30 1894             L
Lively, Samuel (twin)              Dec 10 1909   Dec 29 1909
Lively, Sarah E.                   Dec 24 1841   Apr  5 1918
Lively, Stella S.                          1913           L
  w/o Ashton A.
Lively, Thomas C.                  age 29y       only   date
Lively, Velma Hill Craft                   1886   Nov 30 1907
  1st w/o Green P.
  m/o Geo. Powell & Eulis G.
Lively, Willie A.                  Sep 24 1911   Aug  8 1912
  s/o Daisey & J.T.
Lockhart, Rhoda (bkn marker)               nd             nd
Lockhart, Mrs. Rhoda               May  2 1800   Dec 10 1868
Lynch, Mary E.                     Feb 15 1896   Apr 27 1959
Martin, Alexander                  Aug 30 1854   Jan 17 1936
Martin, Mary A.                    Jne 17 1858   Oct 21 1935
  w/o Alexander
McElmurray, Mattie J. Lively       Oct 14 1867   Jan 18 1958
  w/o Minus
  d/o M.J. Elliott & Green B.
McNorrill, Alfred Burke            May 30 1912   Jul 29 1969
McNorrill, Beatrice C.                     1915           L
  w/o R.J.
McNorrill, Charlie D.              Aug 13 1864   Feb  4 1893
  b Burke Co.
McNorrill, Charlie Durward         Mar 17 1903   Jne  4 1904
  s/o Norman L. & Eula T.
McNorrill, Effie M.                Oct 12 1884   Aug  2 1968
  w/o N.W.
McNorrill, Eliza A. Godbee         Oct 14 1879   Oct 20 1943
  w/o H.H.
McNorrill, Eula T.                 May 12 1871   Apr 27 1947
  w/o Norman L.
McNorrill, Howell Henry (Bud)      Jan 18 1874   Feb  6 1960
McNorrill, Ida Lou                 Mar 11 1867   Aug 24 1888
  w/o Norman L.
McNorrill, Infant                  Jan 23 1909   Jan 26 1909
  s/o H.H. & Eliza
McNorrill, James T.                Sep 26 1821   Feb 11 1877
McNorrill, James T.                Mar 18 1886   Apr 15 1925
McNorrill, Janey B.                Mar 31 1872   Oct 20 1932
  w/o Dr. W.H.
McNorrill, Jeff                    Jne 10 1877   Sep  2 1881
  s/o W.L. & M.A.
```

Name	Birth	Death
McNorrill, John C.	Nov 4 1872	Nov 24 1918
McNorrill, Joseph W. WW-II	Jan 24 1923	Jne 19 1945
Ga Pfc 184 Inf 7th Div		
McNorrill, Laura	Oct 10 1888	Mar 4 1972
w/o James T.		
McNorrill, Madeline Louisa	May 6 1862	Oct 5 1868
d/o Rev Wm. H.L. & S.E.		
McNorrill, Margaret C.	Nov 17 1915	May 20 1973
McNorrill, Marie	Mar 13 1896	Apr 28 1897
McNorrill, Martha Ann	May 28 1852	Apr 14 1930
w/o Walter L.		
McNorrill, Norman L.	Mar 24 1860	Sep 24 1923
McNorrill, Norman W.	Apr 3 1891	Feb 13 1964
McNorrill, R. Joseph, Jr.	Jul 21 1928	Aug 14 1936
s/o Ethel Reese & R.J.		
McNorrill, Rufus	Aug 13 1864	Feb 4 1893
McNorrill, Rufus C.	Mar 11 1858	Mar 30 1918
McNorrill, Russell J.	1906	1969
McNorrill, Sallie	1829	1879
w/o Rev. Wm. H.L.		
McNorrill, Sarah E.	1803	Mar 10 1886
b Burke Co Member Botsford Church over 50 yrs		
w/o James T.		
McNorrill, Thomas F.	Sep 20 1888	Jan 9 1971
McNorrill, Dr. W.H.	Apr 11 1853	Mar 16 1923
McNorrill, Walter L.	May 10 1851	Feb 1 1919
McNorrill, Willet Howell	Dec 22 1897	Jul 27 1930
McNorrill, Rev. Wm. H.	Mar 31 1826	Aug 27 1875
/LaFayette		
Mead, Sharon Acacia	Jul 21 1953	Mar 17 1971
Miller, Elizabeth	1887	1957
w/o James F., Sr.		
Miller, James F., Sr.	1880	1942
Minor, Allen E.	age 63y	May 14 1967
Minor, Burmah T.	1879	1950
w/o J.E.		
Minor, Infant	1909	1909
s/o J.E. & B.T.		
Minor, John E.	1879	1934
Mobley, A.J.S.	Aug 1818	Apr 1896
Mobley, Clinton	Aug 25 1877	Dec 23 1901
Mobley, Elizabeth Barrow	Aug 1825	Oct 1896
w/o A.J.S.		
Mobley, Hettie Scruggs	1858	1931
w/o James M.		
Mobley, James M. CSA	nd	nd
Sgt Co E Cobbs Ga Legion		
Mobley, Jeff Davis	Jul 18 1860	Feb 27 1907
s/o A.J.S. & Elizabeth		
Mobley, Sue	Jan 24 1844	Oct 27 1901
d/o A.J.S. & Elizabeth		
Mobley, William B.	Oct 6 1872	Aug 22 1909
Palmer, Earnest	Feb 12 1895	Oct 2 1906
s/o Iola Boyd & J.T.		
Palmer, John T.	Apr 10 1867	Nov 12 1895

Palmer, Madeline	Jan 15 1896	Feb 15 1896
d/o Iola Boyd & J.T.		
Powell, Ada Adela	Oct 2 1862	Aug 18 1864
d/o Rev. L.F. & S.A.		
Powell, Rev. L.F.	May 21 1826	Oct 31 1865
Prescott, A.A.	nd	Dec 9 1886
Prescott, Ada B.	Jan 14 1877	Sep 8 1879
Prescott, Ada L.B.	Jan 14 1877	Sep 8 1878
d/o J.F. & L.L. A new and old marker for same person		
Prescott, Arthur O.	Jne 25 1892	Oct 24 1907
Prescott, Jeff F. CSA	May 8 1846	Jan 16 1894
Co D 48 Ga Inf		
Prescott, Jefferson F.	Jan 28 1880	Oct 20 1914
Prescott, Laura L.	Jan 6 1859	Jan 26 1946
w/o Jeff F.		
Prescott, William P.	Oct 7 1888	Jul 22 1955
Redd, Caroline	only date	1886
Redd, William	only date	1873
Reece, John Q.A. CSA	nd	nd
Ga Sgt Co E Cobb's Legion		
Reese, Eliza A.	Nov 11 1833	Jan 8 1881
w/o J.A.		
Reese, Florence	age 6m	1910
Reese, G. Fannie	1844	1922
Thomas, A.J.	age 31y	Jne 7 1876
Thomas, George Sapp	Sep 7 1863	Sep 9 1867
s/o Sarah L. & J.R.		
Thomas, John Robert	Dec 10 1842	Sep 11 1892
Thomas, Mortimore Mack	Mar 5 1862	Nov 3 1910
s/o Sarah L. & J.R.		
Thomas, Sarah Louise	Aug 24 1843	Sep 2 1909
w/o J.R.		
Thompson, Ella	Jul 10 1865	Jne 15 1867
Thompson, John	age 72y	May 5 1882
Thompson, John Lee	Dec 31 1863	Nov 6 1864
Thompson, Sallie	Dec 4 1861	Sep 1864
Thompson, Sarah Jane Wall	age 41y	Jne 15 1873
w/o John		
Tomlin, Annie Mobley	May 9 1881	Dec 10 1967
Tomlin, Benjamin Allen	Mar 7 1902	May 1 1969
Tomlin, Charles E. WW-II	May 6 1912	Jne 18 1971
Ga AIC USAF Korea		
Tomlin, Edwin A.	Sep 29 1832	Mar 24 1892
Tomlin, Evans	age 18y	Jul 24 1904
Tomlin, Hamp O.	1879	1930
Tomlin, Laura Caroline	Mar 2 1834	Feb 18 1884
Tomlin, M. M.	age 68y	Jne 14 1916
Tomlin, Mack W.	Apr 27 1892	May 23 1953
Tomlin, Mary Elizabeth T.	1876	1915
w/o Hamp O.		
Tomlin, Robert A.	Jne 7 1862	Jul 17 1919
Ward, Minnie	Feb 2 1912	Dec 2 1898
d/o C.L. & M.L.		
Weeks, Aaron W. WW-I	only date	Oct 6 1918
Ga Pvt USA		

Weeks, Cathran Ann   Feb 13 1902   Sep 8 1914
  d/o J.E. & E.A.
Weeks, William Henry   Jne 1 1897   Feb 29 1904
  s/o J.E. & E.A.

20.   BOYD-MCBRIDE

Boyd, Robert   Jul 20 1800   Dec 7 1855
Boyd, Ruth W.   Dec 8 1815   Feb 1 1903
Cain, Fannie   Oct 6 1883   Aug 4 1912
  member of Old Bethel Pres. Church
Cain, Mrs. Jane   Jne 16 1859   Nov 12 1915
  w/o E.M.
Cotter, Mrs. Eliza C.   Sep 6 1826   Dec 21 1900
Cotter, James H.   Dec   1826   Nov 10 1894
Davis, W.T.   Aug 4 1849   Nov 23 1898
Heath, Zaida May   Oct 4 1906   Oct 4 1907
Howel, Eola   Mar 31 1860   Dec 23 1862
Ivey, G.H.L. CSA   nd   nd
  Co A 7th Ga Cav
Johnson, B. Jaqueline Rollins Apr 13 1837 Apr 13 1911
  w/o Dr. L.D.
Johnson, Dr. L.D.   Apr 21 1836   Jne 26 1896
  F&AM
Johnson, Marion   Mar 26 1877   Aug 11 1898
  d/o Dr. & Mrs. L.D.
Johnson, Mary Park Fannin   Jne 5 1824   Mar 29 1904
  w/o William B.
Johnson, William B.   Jne 11 1809   Sep 30 1888
McBride, Bertie R.   Feb 24 1889   Aug 16 1928
McBride, Carrie Boyd   Jul 12 1849   Dec 16 1920
  w/o Thomas A.
McBride, Mrs. Clifford A.   Feb 18 1887   Mar 18 1911
  w/o R. Claude
McBride, E. Reginald   Jul 25 1907   May 14 1942
McBride, Fannie H.   1867   1946
  w/o William L.
McBride, Francis C.   May 23 1916   Nov 6 1916
McBride, Helen Sophronia   Jne 9 1884   Dec 19 1944
McBride, R. Claude   Jul 16 1878   Jan 28 1931
McBride, Ruth P.   Feb 9 1876   Aug 10 1962
McBride, T.A.   Sep 11 1851   Aug 15 1909
McBride, William L.   1856   1922
McLendon, Harry WW-I   Jul 5 1877   Dec 2 1962
  S. Car SFC USA
Mountain, Mrs. S.A.   Jne 28 1821   May 18 1896
Murphree, Lillian McBride   Dec 2 1873   Sep 9 1939
Murphree, William James   Nov 13 1900   Apr 26 1956
Murphree, William Jordan   Aug 19 1853   Oct 5 1932
Oates, A.B.   Sep 21 1830   Nov 14 1901
Oates, Amanda C.   Oct 2 1855   Oct 8 1866
Oates, Charlie B.   Aug 10 1866   Mar 26 1868
Oates, Fannie   Oct 17 1853   Mar 22 1896
Oates, Hubert Peel   Jne 8 1893   Dec 9 1893

51

Oates, Infant s/o S.J. & A.B.	only date	1870
Oates, Mary Alice Peel w/o William A.	Feb 25 1868	Apr 7 1899

Oates, Minnie Peel
  w/o Thomas F.
  d/o J.P. & Mary Peel
	Jul 8 1866	Sep 9 1887

Oates, Ralph Leslie	Jul 4 1886	Sep 21 1887
Oates, S.J. Cole w/o A.B.	May 8 1824	nd
Oates, Thomas F.	Mar 4 1858	Oct 29 1888
Oates, William A.	Apr 16 1860	Oct 10 1928
Oates, William Andrew	Jne 21 1898	Aug 20 1898
Rollins, Eliza C. w/o John R.	1872	1937
Rollins, James P. s/o Mary A. & John	Aug 7 1842	Dec 27 1843
Rollins, John	May 5 1809	Jne 1 1876
Rollins, John R. CSA 2 Ga State Troops	1847	1911
Rollins, Mrs. Mary Ann w/o John Rollins	Oct 19 1803	Jan 20 1848
Rollins, Sarah H. w/o John Rollins	Aug 26 1817	Sep 28 1872
Rollins, Thomas McBride	Aug 7 1842	Mar 16 1855
Rollins, William P.	Oct 4 1838	Feb 13 1860
Thompson, Dr. J.M.	Apr 20 1844	Sep 11 1895
Thompson, Jessie John	May 28 1835	Jan 12 1902
Thompson, Lela E. w/o S.A.	Oct 30 1870	Feb 7 1908
Thompson, Norman H. s/o J.J. & M.J. Mays	Oct 3 1902	Sep 11 1904

Note: Amanda C., Charlie B., Fannie, Thomas F., and William A. are all children of A.B. & S.J. Cole Oates, as shown by memorial monument. Individual markers for some are missing; in fact, Amanda C. and Charlie B. are buried in the Lowry cemetery, but their names and dates appear on this monument (ed).

21.   BRICK (BETHEL) METHODIST
                Screven Co.

Andrews, Annie B. d/o Mr. & Mrs. W.D.	Oct 24 1897	Jul 1 1898
Andrews, Dewey H. s/o Mr. & Mrs. W.D.	Jul 15 1899	Mar 31 1900
Andrews, Eliza C. w/o William D.	May 9 1869	Nov 1 1948
Andrews, Infant s/o Mr. & Mrs. W.D.	only date	Sep 24 1888
Andrews, Irma W. w/o Thomas	Feb 9 1903	Oct 19 1970
Andrews, Jannie Flake w/o Walter W.	Apr 13 1890	Dec 27 1948

```
Andrews, John W.                          Jul 23 1893    Jan  8 1898
   s/o Mr. & Mrs. W.D.
Andrews, Lewis Doss  WW-II                Jan 16 1920    Jul 13 1955
   Ga PFC 444 AAA AW Bn
Andrews, Nancy E.                         Jne 26 1872    Dec 28 1876
   d/o W.H. & Sarah C.
Andrews, Ola B.                           Nov  1 1891    Aug 24 1897
   d/o Mr. & Mrs. W.D.
Andrews, Sarah C.                         Jan  8 1845    Jan 18 1914
   w/o W.H.
Andrews, Thomas                           Sep  7 1895    Aug  1 1962
Andrews, Ulysses                          Dec 28 1877    Oct 18 1881
   s/o W.H. & Sarah C.
Andrews, W.H.                             Aug  3 1845    Oct 16 1916
Andrews, Walter William                   Sep  3 1889    May 13 1940
Andrews, William D.                       Nov 22 1861    Apr 28 1928
Atterberry, J.D.                          Sep 24 1814    Jul 10 1871
Atterberry-Mears, Eliza Cogil             Nov  6 1823       c. 1906
   w/o J.D. Atterberry
Bewan (illegible), Emilia                         nd           1871
Bland, Bertha Beatrice                          1924           1964
Bragg, Mattie Williams                    Sep 19 1890    Jan 31 1952
Brown, Ethel St. Clair                    Oct  6 1884    Oct  8 1938
Brown, Eullia                                     nd           1871
Brown, John J.                            Nov  8 1810    Feb 14 1875
   b  Buckingham Co Va
Brown, Mary M.                                  1863    Mar 10 1905
   w/o Sam
Brown, Willie C.  WW-I                    Apr 17 1896    Oct 13 1918
   killed in war    Co B 327th Inf
Brown, Wilton G.                          Oct 20 1893    Jul 20 1914
Brunson, John Wilson                            1863           1929
Brunson, Susie Wells                            1880           1955
   w/o John Wilson
Bullock, William T.  WW-I                 Nov 11 1897    Nov  6 1961
   Ga Wagoner 155 Depot Brig
Buxton, Madeline Mallard                  Oct 19 1879    Feb 24 1970
   2nd w/o Preston B.
Buxton, Mary Eliza                        Oct  5 1884    Jne 14 1962
   1st w/o Preston B.
Buxton, Preston B.                        Jul 23 1875    Jan 20 1963
Cain, Edward Clinton                      Jne  2 1881    Aug 19 1964
Cain, Estelle                             age 3 y              nd
   d/o Mack & Mattie
Cain, Florence                            age 3 y         only  date
   d/o Mack & Mattie
Cain, Lula T. (infant)                            nd           nd
   d/o Mack & Mattie
Cain, Mack R.                             age 38 y             1894
Cain, Mattie E.                           age 38 y             1897
   w/o Mack R.
```

Cain, Sarah w/o J.W.	May 9 1858	Jan 19 1894
Campbell, Mary Elizabeth	1847	1924
Clifton, Linda A. (infant)	only date	Jan 24 1951
Crawford, Anna Mears	1864	1937
Davis, John	May 25 1905	Jan 10 1909
Davis, John Henry s/o J.B. & Mary	Dec 28 1895	May 26 1896
Duggan, Lena Smith	Oct 4 1897	Jan 10 1957
Dunbar, James Vince s/o Geo. R. & Olivia S.	Oct 3 1873	May 5 1942

Dunbar, Nannie Lines
  w/o James V.
  d/o Sam. S. & Nannie B.
	Jan 10 1879	Sep 3 1972

Dunbar, Vince Jr. s/o James & Nannie	Apr 30 1910	Apr 19 1912
Foster, Walter Nesbit	Oct 27 1868	Dec 30 1954
Garvin, Ralbet Lee d/o C.H. & Alice	Jan 21 1874	Jan 7 1886
Gibson, Henrietta Mears	1861	1949
Gibson, Mrs. Nettie B.	age 87y	Feb 9 1949
Gibson, Walter Fleetwood	1872	Oct 5 1935
Harrison, Linton Stiles s/o William K. & Martha M.	Mar 31 1911	Apr 12 1965
Harrison, Martha M. Lines w/o William K.	Nov 18 1868	Aug 31 1949
Harrison, William Kollock	Sep 17 1853	Jul 23 1919
Harrison, William Kollock s/o Kollock & Mattie	Dec 27 1908	Mar 11 1912
Herrington, William J.	Dec 7 1845	Jan 23 1910
Hillis, Jessie Pauline w/o Jinks A.	Aug 6 1886	Jul 9 1965
Hillis, Jinks A.	Jan 29 1871	Jul 18 1955
Hillis, Jinks T. WW-II Ga Pvt USA	Oct 2 1908	Mar 31 1967
Hillis, Johnson H.	nd	nd
Hillis, T.J. WOW	Nov 14 1901	Jul 24 1927
Lines, Caroline S. w/o Samuel J.	Aug 25 1805	Jan 20 1885
Lines, Cecil Raiford	only date	May 14 1917
Lines, Edgar Hudson	Oct 8 1876	Jul 9 1943
Lines, Eugenia S. w/o Stiles B.	Nov 23 1881	Aug 28 1967
Lines, J. Lawrence s/o Samuel S. & Nannie B.	Dec 24 1885	Jne 27 1899
Lines, Julian s/o Samuel S. & Nannie B.	Aug 20 1872	Jan 20 1874
Lines, Lurene F.	Oct 8 1883	Oct 1 1959

Lines, Nannie Bentley Brown
  b Richmond Va
  w/o Samuel S.
	Jne 11 1847	Mar 27 1934

```
Lines, Samuel Sheppard              Nov 20 1827   Feb 23 1916
  b Liberty Co Ga;  d Screven Co Ga
Lines, Stiles B.                    May 19 1874   May 20 1946
Lines, William Bentley  WW-II       Jul  9 1915   Dec 25 1958
  Ga Sgt 563 Base Unit AAF
Maner, John Ogilvie                 Dec 25 1874   Jul 20 1960
Maner, Sallie Mims                  Aug 28 1873   Dec 25 1964
  w/o John O.  md Dec 25 1900
Martin, Maria Dorsey Davidce        Sep 22 1881   Sep 20 1913
  w/o Peyton Wade/or (Davidge)
Martin, Peyton Wade                      1880          1950
Martin, Peyton Wade, Jr.            Sep 21 1912   Jan 29 1957
Martin, Robert Hayne                Dec 12 1847   Jul  2 1928
Martin, Rosalie Elizabeth           age 7m  19d             nd
  d/o Robt. H. & Rosalie W.
Martin, Rosalie Wade                Jan 12 1847   Jan  8 1885
  w/o Robt. H.
Martin, W.E.                        Jan 16 1879   Oct 10 1880
Maxson, Aline Prescott              Jne 29 1909   Dec 29 1959
McCullough, Lorenzo D.              Jul 31 1828   Jan 30 1896
Meads, Ada B.                       Jne 20 1881   Jan  9 1932
Meads, Charlie A.                   Mar 12 1883   Aug 18 1962
Meads, Gerthie T.                   Sep  6 1897   Dec 14 1963
Meads, Sadie Amanda                 Jne  2 1903   Sep 20 1964
Meads, Wade                         Sep  1 1911   Mar 14 1937
Mears, Alice                        Mar  4 1870   Jne 24 1910
Mears, Annie M.                     Mar  8 1875   Jan 16 1914
  w/o J.W.
Mears, Barsheba Lewis               c.   1805               nd
  grandmother of Robert Mears Wade
Mears, C. Raymond                        1893          1918
Mears, Infant                            1902          1902
  of J.W. & Annie M.
Mears, Joab Wilson                  age 65y       Sep  7 1917
Mears, John B.                      Apr 30 1836   Mar 13 1911
Mears, John Wilson                       1871          1933
Mears, Lucy Buford                       1832          1919
Mears, William H.   CSA                  1840          1917
  Co D 47 Ga Inf
Mears, William Melton               Jan 25 1866   Aug  9 1900
Mims, Alice                         Jul 12 1853   May  3 1886
  d/o Dr. B.R. & M.A.
Mims, Allen Lines                   Apr  6 1858   Jne 28 1928
Mims, Bessie Hardeman               May  5 1854   Dec 28 1919
  w/o Allen Lines
Mims, Britton (Mr. B)               Aug 20 1856   May 14 1946
Mims, Dr. Britton Robert            Feb 14 1831   Jan 30 1873
Mims, Emma                               1880          1886
Mims, Emma H.                       Jul 17 1850   Dec 31 1880
Mims, Hattie                        Jan 13 1879   Jul 13 1901
  w/o Frank
Mims, Dr. James A.                  Dec 28 1843   Jan 23 1917
Mims, Judith Scott                  Mar 31 1838   Mar 12 1879
  w/o Thos. S.
  d/o John J. & Martha N. Brown
  b Buckingham Co Va;  d Screven Co
```

Mims, Leslie Brown	Feb 23 1875	Sep 20 1875
s/o Thos. S. & Judith S.		
Mims, Mary Kathleen	Sep 4 1888	Jul 30 1916
Mims, Mary Lessie	Sep 28 1866	Oct 31 1874
d/o Thos. S. & Judith S.		
Mims, Sue Eve	Sep 1 1869	Mar 1 1873
d/o Thos. S. & Judith S.		
Mims, Susie P.	1884	1885
Mims, Thomas S. MD	Jul 31 1820	Dec 17 1906
F&AM		
Mims, Thomas S., Jr.	Apr 20 1847	Nov 7 1895
Newberry, Scott Porter	Feb 5 1953	Mar 13 1959
Odom, Josephene R.	Mar 5 1856	Apr 7 1860
Oliver, Donnie Lee	Feb 7 1948	Jul 15 1966
Prescott, Annie B.	Mar 4 1890	Dec 12 1913
Prescott, Corine	Nov 27 1911	Dec 10 1913
Prescott, Henry Howard	Jul 4 1882	Jan 10 1961
Prescott, Nancy Wimberley	Jan 13 1900	L
w/o Henry H.		
Redding, Cora Ervin	Aug 8 1884	Jan 14 1919
w/o W.P.		
Rider, Elbert	1886	1956
Royal, Joyce Fay	Jan 10 1938	Sep 2 1940
Royal, Lawton B.	Oct 1 1898	Dec 25 1952
Royal, Ruth Andrews	Jul 23 1901	Mar 4 1948
w/o Lawton B.		
Sanders, John Brigham	Dec 12 1902	May 10 1967
Sanders, Katherine	Nov 15 1883	Dec 30 1957
/McClenahan		
w/o Wm. Pinckney		
Sanders, William Pinckney	Feb 14 1877	Aug 3 1951
Simpson, Jesse P.	Aug 28 1877	Aug 16 1906
Simpson, Mollie Mears	Feb 2 1878	Aug 11 1943
Stubbs, Alexander Thomas	Aug 23 1872	Sep 4 1913
WOW		
Stubbs, Amanda C.	1872	1935
Stubbs, Mrs. Mary Moreland	Oct 7 1848	Mar 13 1924
Stubbs, Olan Wytch	Oct 12 1900	Mar 22 1969
Stubbs, Susan Anne	only date	Jul 9 1955
d/o Jo Anne D. & O. Wytch, Jr		
Stubbs, Victoria	1855	1921
Stubbs, Wilton Douglas	Feb 24 1905	May 5 1958
Sullivan, Mellie Anderson	Aug 9 1879	Oct 17 1918
/Wade		
Thompson, Lena Florie	Jan 8 1907	Apr 25 1909
d/o J.W. & Lucy		
Videtto, Frances I. Wade	Dec 27 1807	Oct 2 1853
w/o Henry R.		
Videtto, Henry R.	Dec 13 1811	Feb 27 1889
Wade, Archibald P.	age 19m 21d	May 19 1855
Wade, Arthur Bartow	May 24 1861	Jne 20 1890
Wade, Edward C. CSA	age 22y	1865
wounded at Battle of Sailors Creek; died in Federal		
prison		

```
Wade, Elizabeth Jones              Jul  2 1865   Mar  6 1952
   w/o Capt Jesse
   d/o Seaborn Augustus Jones of Millhaven
Wade, Elizabeth Robert             Nov  7 1817   Oct  4 1883
   w/o Rev. Peyton L.
Wade, Capt Jesse Turpin            Aug 24 1851   Aug 30 1918
Wade, Lieut. Peyton  CSA           age 21y       Nov 16 1861
Wade, Rev. Peyton Lisbey                  1797   Dec 21 1866
   md 1st Sarah Maner Crawford, widow of Rev. John
   Crawford, 1823;
   2nd Elizabeth Robert
Wade, Robert Maner                 Mar  5 1840   Dec  7 1904
   buried Athens,Ga
Wade, Robert Mears                 Nov 15 1875   Apr  2 1899
Wade, Samuel Asbury                Jan  3 1856   Nov  2 1905
Wade, Ulysses P.                   Mar  9 1845   Nov 15 1897
Wade, Walter Barnwell              Jul 12 1858   Oct 20 1882
Wade, Willie Dearing               Nov  2 1898   Feb 12 1900
Williams, Ellis Elton  WW-II       Aug  2 1916   Feb  8 1944
   Staff Sgt Co G 132 Inf
   Lost his life at Bougainville, SW Pac Area
Williams, Infant                   Feb 14 1917   Dec 24 1921
   s/o T.&I.
Williams, Infant                   Aug  1 1918   Jan  9 1919
   s/o S.M.P.V. & M.
Williams, Jessie                          1910          1943
Williams, Leurean                         1913             L
   w/o Jessie
Wood, Joseph                              1860          1907
Wood, William Pinckney             Apr  3 1906   Feb 17 1910
   s/o Chas. & Susie
   parents used an "s" on Woods (ed).
Woods, Charlie A.                         1878          1956
Woods, Mrs. Susie                  age 67 y      Jan 12 1950
```

22.   BROTHERSVILLE
                        Richmond Co.

```
Allen, James                       Apr  5 1859   Sep 14 1913
Allen, Milburn Alexander           Jul 27 1852   Mar 27 1877
   s/o Rev. Jas. W. & Ebbie
Baxley, Mrs. C. Edwina             May  7 1850   May 23 1910
Baxley, Rebecca E. Ward            Apr  5 1838   Dec 17 1892
   w/o Dr. Wm. H., Sr.
   d/o James & Elizabeth
Baxley, Dr. William Henry          Apr  9 1833   Sep 27 1900
Broxton, Alice S.                         1893          1921
Broxton, Fonnie                    Dec 22 1856   May 27 1906
   w/o J.A.
Broxton, Walter A.                 Apr  7 1894   Dec 25 1958
Broxton, Walter M. (Pug)           Sep 18 1935   Sep  4 1951
   s/o W.A. & O.B.
Cadle, Edward E.                   Sep  8 1856   Aug 26 1932
```

Cadle, John E.	Aug 6 1877	May 21 1899
Cadle, Mary A. Broxton	Sep 28 1880	Dec 11 1947
w/o E.E.		
Cadle, Mary E.	Jul 18 1858	Dec 27 1897
Cadle, Maude Bugg	Oct 13 1896	Nov 26 1918
w/o Wm. B.		
Cadle, Moselle	Jne 3 1860	Nov 30 1884
Cadle, Sarah	Jne 27 1884	Aug 27 1884
d/o E.E. & M.E.		
Cadle, Sullivan B.	1827	1883
Cadle, Virginia Netherland	Feb 21 1869	Feb 27 1915
w/o W.E.		
Cadle, W.E.	Jne 27 1870	Apr 11 1922
Cadle, William B.	Apr 29 1888	Sep 18 1967
Clark, C. Edward	Oct 31 1838	Jne 29 1883
Clark, Charles E.	Nov 7 1805	Dec 12 1854
s/o Eleanor & Charles, III		
Clark, Ella G.	Sep 2 1855	Jan 4 1931
d/o S.B. & M.W.		
Clark, Evie L.	Jul 15 1854	Jul 15 1897
w/o Samuel R.		
Clark, H. Leonhardt	Aug 18 1887	Nov 17 1887
Clark, Harold L.	Sep 15 1893	Sep 18 1908
Clark, M. Anna	Jan 21 1848	Sep 4 1864
Clark, Martha R.	Mar 31 1821	Apr 4 1897
w/o Dr. Samuel B.		
Clark, Dr. Samuel B.	Feb 26 1812	Feb 1 1865
s/o Eleanor & Charles, III		
Clark, Samuel R.	Feb 15 1844	Dec 9 1920
Clark, Dr. W. H.	May 14 1840	Mar 29 1867
s/o Evalina & Samuel R.		
Colvin, Edna Cadle	Nov 14 1910	Dec 5 1933
Cushman, Vincey	Apr 25 1830	Feb 23 1894
Dickinson, Anna V. Walker	Sep 23 1847	Aug 15 1922
w/o Capt. W.H.		
Dickinson, Reuben H.	Feb 1 1873	Sep 27 1891
Dickinson, Willard E.	May 3 1886	Aug 28 1915
Dickinson, Capt. Wm. Henry	Oct 5 1839	Oct 1 1897
CSA 2nd Ga Regt		
Ellis, William J.	nd	1920
Francis, Malicia M.	nd	Aug 20 1919
Francis, Tilmon P.	nd	Jan 11 1913
Godbee, Clifford M.	1928	1973
Godbee, Elizabeth M.	1929	L
w/o Clifford		
Godbee, Marion	1948	L
Harris, Franklin	Aug 5 1833	Jul 3 1875
Harris, Thomas J.	Mar 7 1884	Aug 7 1887
Hughes, Charles T. CSA	nd	nd
Corp Co A 20 Ga Inf		
Hughes, Fred	Jul 3 1890	Dec 29 1890
s/o Mary C. & Fred S.		
Hughes, Frederick Strobel	Jul 3 1861	Oct 19 1910
Hughes, George W.	Jul 20 1843	Sep 14 1872
Hughes, Mrs. M. Eugenia	Feb 9 1846	Mar 12 1913

Name	Birth	Death
Hughes, Mary Ella	Jne 5 1870	May 9 1954
d/o Geo. W. & M. Eugenia		
Hughes, Mary George Butler	Nov 8 1870	Aug 29 1893
w/o Fred S.		
d/o Mary Eleanor & Capt. Geo. Butler		
Jinkins, Williams	Nov 3 1803	Oct 21 1876
Jones, Lila Reynolds	1854	1921
Mann, Gertrude Leoline Clark	Jan 14 1890	Mar 16 1971
w/o Rev. David Gilbert		
d/o Evelina A. & S.R.		
McDaniel, G.N.	Mar 5 1869	Jul 15 1912
McNair, Sara B.	1921	1962
Moss, Rev. William B.	Oct 3 1815	Apr 1 1853
Napier, Absolum Roland	Feb 23 1842	Apr 21 1925
Napier, Albert Robin	Mar 28 1903	Apr 25 1968
s/o Edwin & Clara		
Napier, Clara B.	1877	1972
w/o Edwin M.		
Napier, Edwin M.	1870	1933
Napier, Infant	1911	1911
d/o Edwin & Clara		
Napier, Jack Phillips	Mar 4 1914	Feb 10 1958
s/o E.M. & C.B.		
Napier, James Farris	Aug 6 1875	Oct 1 1882
Napier, Julien LeRoy	age 6m 11d	nd
Napier, Mary E.	Nov 16 1842	Dec 25 1913
w/o Absolum R.		
Netherland, Sarah J.	Jul 18 1849	May 18 1881
Prescott, Lina V. Napier	Jul 14 1882	Sep 3 1916
w/o N.H.		
Reynolds, Frank Bartow	Jul 21 1861	Jan 2 1864
s/o J. Jones & Rosa		
Reynolds, Marie Walker	1868	1944
Skinner, T. Baldwin	1866	1931
Smith, Rosa	Sep 5 1859	Jne 20 1929
Stanucha (?illeg.), C.E.	age c. 81y	May 4 1891
Sulvan, Georgia	Apr 25 1858	Feb 2 1897
Timm, Ethel H.	Oct 19 1891	Mar 31 1950
w/o W.F.		
Timm, Infant	Apr 25 1915	May 6 1915
s/o W.F. & E.H.		
Timm, Walter F.	May 29 1891	Apr 13 1939
F&AM		
Tinley, William	1789	Jne 22 1861
b Richmond Co		
Walker, Curran E.	Mar 5 1864	Jne 8 1914
Walker, Howell C.	Jan 19 1847	May 29 1905
Walker, Mrs. M.J.	1790	Aug 6 1872
Walker, S. Eleanora Evans	Apr 15 1843	Jne 1 1925
w/o Wm. E.		
Walker, William E.	Jul 1 1841	Jul 25 1897
Wood, Hermon W.	Nov 1 1881	Jan 22 1947
Wood, Lillian Clark	Aug 19 1881	Oct 31 1952
w/o H.W.		
d/o Evelina Allen & S.R.		

23.   <u>BROWN</u>

Brown, Isabella   age 56 y   Sep 29 1831
   w/o James B.
Brown, J. Singleton   Nov 2 1804   Apr 26 1886
Brown, James B.   Apr 1 1772   Feb 29 1863
Brown, John S.   Aug 5 1839   Sep 20 1864
Brown, Mrs. Martha P.   Oct 13 1818   Mar 2 1852
   w/o J.S.
Brown, Nancy E.   Feb 6 1815   Sep 30 1875

24.   <u>BRUSHY CREEK BAPTIST</u>

Bailey, Harry Roberts   Oct 2 1914   Aug 25 1915
   s/o O.M. & Ethel Roberts
Bailey, Joseph Walter   1885   1940
   1st h/o Susie Roberts
   s/o A.B. (Jack) & Georgia Chandler
Mays, Annie   Aug 27 1872   Oct 16 1898
   d/o M.M. & L.V.
Roberts, Bessie Hill   1860   1936
   w/o Walter Augustus
   d/o Burgess Dozier & Dr. J.C.

Note: Mrs Susie Roberts Sturdivant states that the
following children of her parents, Bessie Hill and
Walter Augustus Roberts, are buried in this cemetery:
Jesse, 12 y; John, an infant; Wm. Prescott, 17 y,
and James Hill, 21 y. No dates are available nor were
the markers found (ed). See <u>ADDENDA</u> p. 312.

25.   <u>BURKE MEMORIAL GARDENS</u>
                    Waynesboro, Ga.

Agerton, Mary Naomi Voss   Nov 3 1900   Nov 24 1972
   w/o Wm. Harry
Anderson, James (Jim)   Sep 21 1952   Apr 6 1963
Arrington, Danny E.   Nov 22 1949   Oct 7 1965
Babb, Carol Dean, Jr.   1972   1972
Bailey, Mamie Lee Wood   Nov 12 1922   Nov 23 1968
   1st w/o W.D., Jr.
Bailey, Marie Glisson   1901   L
   w/o Wm. D., Sr.
   d/o Bessie & Henry
Bailey, William D., Sr.   1894   1953
   s/o Georgia C. & Jack
Barefield, Charlie B.   Feb 24 1920   Sep 19 1972
Barefield, Evelyn Lively   1913   1966
   w/o Roger E.
   d/o Daisey H. & J.T.
Barefield, Roger E.   1911   L
   s/o Mattie S. & J.W.
Barnett, Maude Murray   Jul 29 1919   Apr 15 1971

Barrett, Danita Dale	May 19 1955	Nov 9 1962
d/o Clarice & Aubrey		
Barton, Alvin Edwood	1893	1962
Barton, Sallie Johnson	1895	Jne 2 1971
w/o Alvin E.		
Birge, Stéve Allen	Apr 23 1956	Jne 6 1961
Blackburn, Dorothy W.	nd	L
w/o L. Dean		
Blackburn, Inez Rushton	Mar 30 1919	Sep 11 1967
Blackburn, J.M. WW-II	Aug 8 1921	Jan 28 1970
Ga S/Sgt USA		
Blackburn, L. Dean	1908	1968
Bolton, Rev. W.L.	1910	1971
Bradham, George Herbert	Sep 27 1946	Aug 15 1969
(Sonny)		
Bradham, Ira	Jan 24 1913	Nov 23 1973
h/o Corine Frazier		
Bragg, Ronald	Aug 17 1930	Jan 12 1965
Brigham, Horace D.	Apr 22 1919	Apr 5 1963
Ga Sgt USA WW-II SS		
Brigham, John L.	Aug 13 1903	Jul 26 1957
s/o Joanna & A.J.		
Brooks, Anna Mae	1897	1971
w/o B.H.		
Brooks, Bebee H.	1887	L
Brooks, Infant	only date	Jne 9 1939
d/o Martha J. Lord & Ben H.		
Broome, Jeanette Giles	Jne 7 1922	Oct 5 1971
1st w/o John W.		
d/o Alma M. & Carlyle A.		
Brown, Eddie T.	1910	1965
Brown, Shirley B.	1914	L
w/o Eddie T.		
Brunson, Helen Vogt	1896	1972
w/o Spencer D.		
Brunson, John H.	Oct 2 1905	Jne 12 1964
Brunson, Spencer D.	1895	L
Burns, Jimmy	Mar 11 1954	Jne 29 1961
Canady, Moses Robert (Bug)	Mar 8 1950	Oct 1 1967
Carswell, Francis H.	1918	1919
Carswell, Jack W., Jr.	Apr 21 1948	Apr 16 1969
s/o Loraine & Jack		
Carswell, Milton B., Jr.	Nov 2 1913	Sep 12 1931
Carswell, Moses E.	1915	1916
Cates, Amanda S.	1913	1962
w/o H.B.		
Cates, Hosea B.	1896	L
Chance, Ashley Howard	Sep 20 1927	May 22 1970
h/o Jean Larisey		
s/o Effie & Ashley		
Chance, Boyd M.	Apr 19 1907	Feb 12 1969
Chance, Dama B.	Jne 1 1913	Nov 23 1960
Chance, Guy W.	1894	1965
Chance, Julia B.	1902	L
w/o Guy		

```
Cheeks, Maude Gay                     Sep 20 1919   May   7 1973
Cibulski, Maj. Frederick C.                  1907   Nov   8 1972
  WW-II  Arty US Reg Army
Cibulski, Mina Powell                        1914           . L
  w/o Fred C.
  d/o Fairbelle & Lawton
Claxton, Gladys Brigham               Mar 23 1896   Jne   7 1966
  w/o Thomas B.
  d/o Molly P. & Thadieus
Claxton, Thomas B.                    Jul 31 1897   Nov   1 1971
  s/o Sallie M. & James
Cohen, Mary Nell Porter               May 22 1907   Oct  21 1970
  w/o H.R., Jr.
  d/o Annie & L.J.
Collins, Gladys Broome                        nd            L
  w/o Jesse Otto
  d/o Bertice & John C.
Collins, Jesse Otto                          1895           1966
Cook, Carrie C.                       Oct 18 1907   Oct   3 1959
Coursey, Beth T.                              nd            L
  w/o Harry G.
Coursey, Harry G.                            1912           1966
Cowart, Bennie E., Jr.                Nov 24 1933   Oct  26 1939
Cowart, Bennie E., Sr.                Sep 26 1910   Mar  20 1970
Cox, Frances Rowland                         1910           L
  w/o Miles L.
  d/o Eva P. & J.M.
Cox, Miles L.                                1905           1968
Cullen, Charles W.                           1879           1951
Cullen, Herbert P.                           1903           1966
Cullen, Infant                        only   date           1917
Cullen, Mary Alday                           1858           1936
Cullen, William B.                           1857           1943
Daniel, Albert B.                     Dec 25 1899   Jne  19 1962
Deason, Cindy Marie                   Jul 13 1965   Aug  13 1966
DeLoach, Joseph Allen                        1917   Jan  20 1973
DeLoach, Nell N.                              nd            L
  w/o J. Allen
Dickey, Emerson R. WW-II              Dec 21 1917   Aug  14 1971
  Ga Sgt USA
Dixon, B. Frank                              1896           1971
  s/o Joyce M. & Frank B.
Dixon, Emma Glisson                          1908           L
  w/o Frank
  d/o Bessie & Henry
Dixon, Louise Mobley                  Aug 30 1906   Mar  14 1973
  w/o T.J.
  d/o Nettie R. & Tilden
Dixon, Thomas J.                      Dec 26 1900   Feb  16 1970
  s/o Shellie & Rena D.
Dunn, Craig M.                               1972           1972
Dunn, Mark E.                                1970           1970
Edenfield, Charles G., Jr.            Oct 24 1944   Nov   9 1970
Edenfield, Lloyd B.   WW-I            Oct 25 1899   Sep  25 1959
  1st Lt Ga Inf Res
```

Edenfield, Marceline O.	Jne 15 1928	Feb 16 1972
Ellison, Calvin Otis WW-II	Sep 5 1912	Dec 20 1971
Ga PFC USA		
Faires, Hunter Harry WW-I	Aug 14 1893	Oct 26 1971
Va CMM USN		
Favors, James A. WW-II	Sep 8 1927	Jan 7 1968
Ga Pvt USA		
Felker, Lizzie Tucker	Jan 18 1881	Oct 24 1968
Foster, Patrick J.	Sep 30 1905	Feb 6 1962
Glenn, John Gibson	Feb 4 1882	Oct 28 1960
Glisson, Albert Burney	1911	1970
s/o Bessie & Henry		
Glisson, Allean Knight	1917	nd
w/o Albert B.		
Glisson, Claudia R.	1904	L
w/o Lawson L.		
Glisson, George Lewis, Jr.	Dec 1 1955	Sep 6 1967
(Sonny)		
Glisson, Lawson L. F&AM	1898	1961
s/o Bessie & Henry		
Godbee, Agnes D.	Apr 23 1890	Jan 8 1964
w/o W. King		
Godbee, Oscar J.	Feb 12 1908	Jan 21 1969
Godbee, Owen Monroe	Aug 3 1946	Jne 28 1969
Godbee, Owen O.	1881	1956
Greene, Andrew Judson	Jne 7 1880	May 17 1965
Shriner		
Greiner, John D.	1888	1963
1st h/o Claudia C.		
s/o Ella & John D.		
Greiner, John P.	1897	1968
Greiner, Mary S.	1903	L
w/o John P.		
Griner, Orrie H.	1886	1972
w/o S.L.		
Griner, Seaborn L.	1884	1964
Griner, William P.	Apr 25 1942	Mar 19 1967
s/o Naomi Hillis & T.P.		
Hannah, Clelia R.	1903	1967
w/o James L.		
Hannah, James L.	1903	1961
Harvey, Sheila Kay	Jne 24 1959	same date
Haymans, John Gary	Jul 26 1952	Apr 20 1973
Heath, Glenn W.	Jul 21 1905	Jne 1 1968
Hendrix, James Hubert, Jr.	Jul 2 1951	Aug 15 1970
(Jimmy)		
Herrington, Melody Ann	Apr 5 1963	Jul 23 1966
Hickman, Alva Hillis	nd	L
w/o Sidney A.		
d/o Daisy G. & G.W.		
Hickman, Sidney A.	1903	1969
s/o Annie M. & Washington		
Hillis, Mims Bentley	Apr 29 1923	Oct 16 1973
h/o Henrietta Sturdivant		
s/o Daisy G. & Geo. W.		

Holland, Ellie Mae M.	1895	L
w/o J. Marvin		
Holland, Joseph Marvin, Sr.	1888	1972
Horton, Braudice F.	1915	1965
Hunter, Mary Carolyn	Aug 31 1955	Apr 24 1962
Ivester, Pink L.	1888	1969
Ivester, Ruth I.	1887	Jne 20 1974
w/o P.L.		
Jenkins, Atticus B., Jr.	Sep 27 1919	Sep 8 1971
WW-II Ga Sgt USA		
Jenkins, Willie M.	Oct 16 1903	Jul 25 1971
Johnson, Charles E.	Jul 23 1900	Jan 27 1965
F&AM		
Johnson, Dorothy Dean	Jul 23 1947	Sep 7 1962
d/o Maxine & Cal /(Dottie)		
Johnson, James S.	1903	1961
Johnson, Jodi R.	only date	1972
Johnson, John H.	Nov 8 1892	Jne 26 1965
Johnson, Naomi A.	1904	nd
w/o James S.		
Johnson, Reba Bullock	Aug 19 1920	Oct 18 1972
Jones, M. Silas	1885	nd
Jones, Martin Luther	Jul 16 1902	Dec 21 1952
Jones, Minnie Redd	1881	1970
Jordan, William L. (Buddy)	Oct 7 1944	Jne 17 1968
Kight, Robert E.	Feb 11 1914	Oct 7 1960
Kirkendohl, Mattie M.	1903	1971
w/o Wm. P.		
Kirkendohl, Wm. P.	1892	1955
Kitchens, Grace C.	Oct 8 1922	Jne 6 1963
w/o Wm. I.		
Kitchens, James T.	Jne 14 1892	Jan 29 1961
F&AM		
Kitchens, Kenneth W. Viet W	Aug 29 1949	Sep 30 1971
Ga L/Cpl US Marine Corps		
Kitchens, Mae Snider	age 80 y	Jne 26 1973
Kitchens, William I. WW-II	Oct 7 1918	May 9 1964
Ga MOMM2 USNR		
Lambert, Annie D.	1900	L
w/o R.J.		
Lambert, Robert J.	1893	1963
Lewis, Chelsie Dawes	Apr 10 1925	L
Lewis, Dorothy Hudson	Jan 2 1922	May 17 1968
w/o C.D.		
Little, Robert Timothy	Mar 17 1891	May 22 1966
h/o Margaret Byrom		
Lively, Claudia Crockett	1906	L
w/o 1st John D. Greiner		
2nd M. Warren Lively		
Long, Estelle H.	1897	L
w/o Thos. R.		
Long, Thomas R.	1891	1965

Long, Willie G. WW-I Ga Pvt USA	Apr 28 1896	Dec 18 1966
Mana , Lawrence S. s/o Louisa & H.H.	1899	1963

Manau, Mae Chandler
  w/o Lawrence
  d/o Ida L. & W.B.
	1904	L

Manley, Lee H.	Dec 14 1879	Oct 18 1948
Manley, Mary N. w/o Clyde	Mar 21 1907	May 13 1965
Martin, Grace C. w/o L.A.	1897	L

Martin, James   WW-I
  h/o Idelle Atkinson
  s/o Kalopia & George
  Ohio Pvt Co A 111 Infantry
	Aug 15 1895	Feb 28 1969

Martin, Lonnie A.	1895	1963
McNorrill, Amy Carolyn d/o Betty & Paul/(inf. twin)	only date	Jul 29 1963
McNorrill, Beatrice M. w/o Lee H.	1905	L
McNorrill, Lee H.	1903	1963
McNorrill, Patricia Ann d/o Betty & Paul/(inf. twin)	only date	Jul 29 1963
Meeker, Gilford F.	1880	1942
Meeker, Lillian G. w/o Gilford	1889	nd
Messex, Carey C.	Oct 28 1898	Feb 26 1966
Mincey, Lillie S.	Apr 8 1894	Dec 12 1967
Minor, Dalton L.	1914	1966
Minor, Gertrude B. w/o Jas. D.	1914	L
Minor, James D.	1912	1961
Minor, Lucile R. w/o Dalton L.	1916	L
Mobley, David (infant)	only date	Apr 8 1964
Mobley, Ernest C., Jr.	Oct 22 1933	Nov 5 1972
Mobley, Jack WW-II Ga Pvt USA	Jan 12 1908	Jne 30 1962
Mobley, Lewis	1900	1967
Mobley, Samuel L.	Sep 25 1922	Mar 12 1958
Mobley, Sarah w/o Lewis	1902	L
Mooneyham, Mary F.	Jne 16 1877	Dec 14 1967
Moore, Debra Gail	Jne 3 1961	Jne 4 1961
Murphy, Ira A.	1904	1972

Murphy, Martha Rowland
  w/o Ira A.
  d/o Eva P. & J.M.
	1903	L

Murray, Ora Lee Dixon
  w/o George
  d/o Joyce & F.B.
	Jan 12 1895	Oct 12 1963

Newman, John E.	Jul 20 1908	Dec 31 1962
North, Wright R. WW-II Ga AMSC USN	Nov 25 1913	Jul 18 1966

Odom, George Dewey	Apr 17 1898	Apr 15 1966
Odom, John Bernard	Dec 5 1927	May 15 1930
s/o Julian & Dorothy		
Odom, Lindner	Nov 10 1913	Jul 5 1960
s/o Bertha & Sam F&AM		
Odom, Marie Lee	Dec 7 1896	Apr 4 1965
Oglesby, Ethel Sue	Feb 6 1959	May 27 1964
O'Quinn, Norman Franklin	Dec 4 1949	Feb 11 1969
s/o Vastee Brown & Leroy		
Quick, Carol D.	1907	1973
Quick, Joe Wheeler	1898	1942
Quick, Josie F.	1905	L
w/o Joe W.		
Quick, Lessie Pearl	1929	1935
d/o Josie & Joe W.		
Quick, Pauline S.	1907	L
w/o Carol D.		
Quick, Pearl Oglesbee	1889	L
w/o 1st J. F. Odom		
2nd Willie F.Q.		
d/o Emma & J. N.		
Quick, Wilkins F.	1910	1972
Quick, Willie F.	1892	1968
Quick, Willie Mae Godbee	Jan 1 1912	Sep 13 1973
w/o Twid		
d/o Bertha & Owen		
Quick, Winnie S.	1916	L
w/o Wilkins F.		
Ramage, Joe Choice, Jr.	age 55 y	Sep 22 1973
Rangeley, Douglas Glen	May 9 1911	Jan 23 1973
h/o Sara Brinson		
Rawlings, Bertha R.	Mar 30 1910	Feb 28 1967
Reddick, Timothy	1967	1967
Reeves, Eva B.	1905	1960
w/o Roy S.		
Reeves, Irvin N., Jr.	Jan 23 1947	Oct 23 1960
s/o Katie D. & Irvin		
Reeves, Katie Deason	Sep 17 1925	Feb 15 1959
1st w/o Irvin		
d/o Sallie McC. & Neal E.		
Reeves, Roy S.	1898	1960
Riggs, James L. WW-II	Mar 12 1923	Mar 1 1973
Ga Sgt USA		
Robinson, Moree Mixon	Aug 22 1933	Oct 1 1961
1st w/o Luther		
Rockwell, Reuben L.	Mar 5 1914	May 24 1963
h/o Susie Tucker		
Rogers, Jerry Leo	Apr 21 1949	Sep 21 1969
s/o Winnie I. & Quinton		
Rowell, James B., Sr.	Aug 20 1893	Oct 13 1968
Rowell, Louise Daniel	Mar 27 1894	Aug 13 1963
w/o J.B., Sr.		
Royal, Cleveland Wayne	Jan 14 1938	Mar 8 1967
Royal, Jesse A.	1907	1964

```
Royal, Maggie C.                                1893              1973
  w/o Willie F.
Royal, Thomas Miller Kor W      May 19 1929   Sep 16 1972
  Ga BT3 USN
Royal, Thomas W.  WW-I          Nov 20 1890   Sep 18 1961
  Ga Pvt 5 Co Coast Arty
Royal, Willie F.                                1895                 L
Royal, Willie F.  WW-II         Nov 10 1923   Apr  7 1965
  Ga Tec4 USA
Russell, Doyle Daniel           Nov 15 1889   Jan 16 1970
Russell, Francis Joy            age 16 y      Aug 16 1972
Rustin, Beulah Mobley           May 18 1890   Aug 12 1962
Sapp, Evans H.                  Dec  9 1924   May  2 1961
Sapp, George C., Sr.            Apr 19 1904   Mar 20 1960
Scott, Clarence F.                              1901              1968
Scott, Edward L.                                1899              1964
Scott, Eunice Chew                              1904                 L
  w/o Clarence F.
Scott, Thelma Chew                              1902                 L
  w/o Edw. L.
Secord, Harriet M.              Mar  8 1901   Aug  5 1965
Sentell, Ben L.                 Sep  5 1912   Mar  3 1966
Siekers, Grace B.                               1907                 L
  w/o Sterling J.
Siekers, Sterling J.                            1908              1972
Sikes, G. Leroy                                 1899                nd
Sikes, Herman H.                Jul 23 1916   Nov 16 1963
Sikes, Myron Sidney (Beep)      Mar 29 1952   Oct 20 1971
Sikes, Theresa H.                               1903              1967
  w/o G.L.
Singley, Hudie L.  WW-I         Feb 16 1893   Mar 10 1967
  Ga Cpl USA
Smith, Kenneth Mac              Oct 13 1938   Apr 28 1963
Smith, Walter Mallard           Dec  8 1955   Mar 15 1969
  s/o Eunice & Thos.
Stapleton, Mary B.                              1911                 L
  w/o Robt. L.
Stapleton, Robert L.                            1910              1965
Stone, David Leroy, Jr.         Jul  4 1919   Nov 17 1960
  s/o Myrtis T. & D.L.
Stone, David Leroy, Sr.         Dec 16 1888   Sep  8 1969
Stone, Myrtis Tinsley           Sep 16 1894   Oct  4 1972
  w/o D.L., Sr.
Stone, Paul Sinclair, Jr.       Aug 31 1951   Jul 10 1972
  s/o Gloria C. & Paul S.
Swanson, Genie G.                               1904                 L
  w/o Paul J.
Swanson, Paul J.                                1891              1967
Thigpen, James Ray              Dec  5 1915   Jan 10 1964
Thomas, Clarence Wm.            Sep 10 1897   Jan 14 1969
  h/o May Belle Moxley
Thomas, Clarence Wm., Jr.       Apr  6 1921   Apr 16 1970
  WW-II  Ga Cpl 6 Base HQ & AB SQ AAF
  s/o May Belle & C.W.
Tobias, Franklin C.             Aug 16 1933   Feb  5 1969
```

```
Todd, David Paul   WW-II          Jul  6 1918   Jan  2 1967
  CCK US Marine Corps Res
Vickrey, Christopher Allen        only   date   Oct 27 1972
  (infant)
Walden, Clara H.                         1896              L
  w/o George O.
Walden, George O.                        1899           1953
Walden, Hattie N.                 Jne 16 1894   Nov 11 1961
Ward, Hilton B.                   Dec  3 1918   Jan 29 1966
  s/o Alice H. & W.L.   Shriner
Ward, Joseph B.                          1910           1973
  s/o Alice H. & W.L.
Ward, Martha Daniel                      1915              L
  w/o Joseph B.
Watkins, Silas A.                        1890           1959
Weathers, Tom                     Dec  1 1921   Mar 31 1971
  h/o Lynn
Weaver, Lettie T.                        1898           1970
  w/o Wm. H.
Weaver, William H.                       1897              L
Wells, Josephine Cochran                 1907             nd
  w/o Roy F.
Wells, Roy Franklin                      1901           1968
Wilder, Ann B.                           1907           1972
  w/o Buford S.
Wilder, Buford S.                        1903           1973
Wills, Francis Edward             Jne 10 1901   May  6 1958
Wilson, Annie Oglesby             age 39 y      Aug 28 1972
Wilson, Blanche W.                       1913              L
  w/o Dan F.
Wilson, Dan F.                           1911           1969
Wilson, Sarah Helen               Apr 25 1947   Jan 30 1948
Wood, Charles Preston             Oct 10 1893   May 19 1969
Wyndham, L. Henry                        1907           1964
  F&AM
Wyndham, Rose W.                         1911              L
  2nd w/o L.H.
  (remarried to J. L. Lively)
```

26.   BUXTON

```
Buxton, Mrs. Rebecca              d in her      Aug 18 1831
  w/o William                    40th y
```

27.   CARPENTER

```
Carpenter, Laura Clifford         age 19m 6d    Oct 25 1858
```

Notes: (1) This cemetery contains some remnants of one rock vault and two brick vaults, all above ground, but with no markers (ed). (2) The Applewhite cemetery is very close to this cemetery and in the same wooded area.

68

The proximity suggests that the above infant was
probably a daughter of Craven and Mary Duke Carpenter. A deed in 1870 and one in 1910 (which shows
that title goes back to this Carpenter family)
mention Duke and Carpenter land as adjoining
Applewhite holdings. Craven (Jan 1 1820 - Jan 14
1878) was a son of Bailey and Amelia. Bailey was
a brother of John and a half-brother of George,
Elbert, and Mary Ann. A daughter of Craven and
Mary married Albert B. Saxon. See Will of John
Carpenter, Will Bk A 260-265 for Bailey connection (ed).

28.   CARSWELL

Smith, Benjamin   age 61 y   Dec 24 1835
    Inscription notes that monument was erected by
    E.R. Carswell, grandson.

29.   CARSWELL

See page #308.

30.   CARTER

Carter, Esther   age 45   Nov 13 1810
    1st w/o Isaiah; md Apr 27 1792; d/o Mary Gerhardt
    Duhart and George Walker; mother of Mary and
    Margaret.

Note: Isaiah and his brother, Alexander, were large
landholders in Burke and leading citizens in Waynesborough when it was incorporated as a town in 1813.
George Walker came to Georgia in 1750, married the
daughter of John Duhart in 1756. Esther and Isaiah
had two children; Mary married William Stone of
Milford, Connecticut. He was first a teacher, then
a Waynesboro merchant, and member of the first town
council. The first meeting was in his house.
Margaret married Welcome Allen, a native of New
Hampshire. They lived in Augusta where he was a
prosperous merchant.
    The plantation where Esther Carter is buried
passed into the hands of Samuel Dowse and ultimately the Whitehead family; long known as the
Waterloo Plantation (ed).

31.   CLARK

Carswell, Mrs. Jane Trimble   age 74 y   Oct 23 1834
    w/o Edward

69

```
Clark, Bashie F.                        Apr 22 1861  Mar 28 1866
   d/o J.W. & E.F.
Clark, Charles, III                     Jan 30 1782  Feb  2 1852
   s/o Charles, II & Anna Y.
   md  1st Eleanor Carswell;  2nd Sarah Murphy
Clark, Charles E.                       May 19 1852  Jan  2 1856
   s/o J.W. & E.F.
Clark, Edmund M.                        Jul 27 1827  Aug 31 1864
   b  Burke Co  d  Milledgeville, Ga.
Clark, Mrs. Eleanor Carswell  Dec 18 1785  Feb 17 1826
   w/o Charles, III
   d/o Jane T. & Edw.
Clark, Elisha                           May  9 1839  Dec 17 1856
   s/o Sarah M. & Chas. III
Clark, Mrs. Emily F. Matthews  Mar 24 1824  Feb 13 1897
   w/o Jas. W.
   Emily F. & Jas. W. were the parents of Louisa C.,
   Charles E., Mary C., Bashie F., and J. William.
Clark, Henry Harrison         May 26 1841  May 10 1864
   s/o Sarah M. & Chas. III
Clark, J. William                       Oct  4 1863  Nov  4 1865
   s/o J.W. & E.F.
Clark, James W.                         May 14 1819  Jan 29 1869
   s/o Chas. III & Eleanor C.
Clark, John W. MD                       Nov 27 1821  Feb  8 1857
   s/o Eleanor C. & Chas. III
Clark, Louisa C.                        Jan 17 1848  Jul  4 1848
   d/o J.W. & E.F.
Clark, Louisa C. Matthews     Dec 25 1832  Aug 31 1921
   w/o Edmond M.;  spelled Edmund on his marker (ed).
Clark, Mary C.                          Jul  2 1855  Oct 14 1864
   d/o J.W. & E.F.
Clark, Mrs. Sarah Murphy      Mar 10 1806  Feb  4 1850
   w/o Charles III
   d/o Edmond Murphy

Note:

Clark, Charles, III                     Jan 30 1782  Feb  2 1852
   s/o Charles, II & Anna Yoemans
   md  1st  Eleanor Carswell, 1804; their children were:
                      Born          Married
   Charles Edward     Nov  7 1805  Ann Averett
   John               May  7 1808  d age 2 y
   June Elizabeth     Dec  4 1809  Thomas P. Brown
   Samuel Benjamin    Feb 26 1812  Martha Walker
   Sarah Ann          May 27 1815  Ebenezer Brown
   Levinah Carswell   Mar 25 1817  d age 4 y
  *James William      May 14 1819  Emily Matthews
  *John Wesley        Nov 27 1821  Josephine Lowry
  *Mary Eleanor       Apr 11 1824  John W. Rheney

   md  2nd  Sarah Murphy, 1826;  their children were:
```

```
*Edmund Murphy        Jul 27 1827    Louise Matthews
 Nancy Maria          Nov  2 1828    Levin Taylor
 Nicholas Tally       Jan 24 1830    d  age 8 y
 Frances Emeline      Sep 26 1831    Thomas Tarver
 Georgia Ann          Jan 30 1833    Lewis Collins
 Elizabeth Walker     Oct 25 1834    John Modisette
 Martha Mozelle       Apr 17 1836    John Rodgers
 Robert Evans         Dec 15 1837    d  young
*Elisha Anderson      May  9 1839    d  age 17 y
 Elijah Walker          (twins)      d  age 26 y
*Henry Harrison       May 26 1841    d  young
 Milton Anthony       Dec 16 1842    Mary Roberts
 Thomas Simmons       Sep 14 1844    Adella Cook
 Celestia Victoria    May  3 1846    Louis Modisette
 Infant (unnamed)     Nov  1 1847    d  day of birth
 Susan Augusta        Oct 29 1848    James Smith
```

*indicates those buried in this cemetery; probably
several of the younger children are buried here in
unmarked graves.
Charles, III established and built Clark's Chapel
Methodist Church near this cemetery where some of
his descendants still worship and many others are
buried. Annual family reunions are held there.
This additional information was furnished by the
courtesy of the Clark Family Association (ed).

32.   CLARK

Clark, Mathew   age 41 y   Mar 13 1804

33.   CLARK'S CHAPEL METHODIST

```
Barwick, James Roy           Aug 11 1891    Aug 11 1968
Barwick, James Thomas        Apr 17 1853    Feb 17 1921
Barwick, LeVicie Cook        Apr  2 1847    Jan 25 1930
  w/o Jas. Thos.
Barwick, Mary Lou                   1887            1972
Barwick, Susie May           May 20 1885    Jne 11 1886
  d/o J.T. & L.A.
Clark, Aquilla Matthews      Feb 19 1856    Sep 14 1941
Clark, Bashie Lou            Aug 28 1889    Oct  8 1890
  d/o A.Q. & H.O.
Clark, Frances Marion        Jul  4 1899              L
  d/o Mary Wise & A.M.
Clark, Carlton R.            Feb 15 1878    Feb 21 1894
Clark, H. Clifford Fulcher   Oct 11 1864    Aug 19 1886
  1st w/o Wm. Edgar
Clark, Harriet Lorena        Oct  4 1894              L
  d/o Mary Wise & A.M.
Clark, Hattie Olivia Farmer  Aug  2 1857    Feb 21 1892
  1st w/o A.M.
Clark, Infant                         nd    Jne 19 1903
  d/o Mary Wise & A.M.
Clark, Lewis Henry           Nov 15 1891    Jan 23 1968
  s/o Hattie F. & Aquilla
```

71

Name	Birth	Death
Clark, Lillian Norris w/o Lewis Henry	Sep 1 1899	L
Clark, Mary Lorene Wise w/o A.M.	Nov 11 1867	Jul 16 1958
Clark, Millard Wise h/o Inez Francis s/o Mary Wise & A.M.	Jne 4 1897	Jne 10 1969
Clark, Thomas Edmund s/o Mary Wise & A.M.	Jan 18 1896	Nov 12 1896
Cook, Fred W.	Oct 13 1852	Oct 27 1909
Cook, John A.	May 2 1849	May 15 1912
Cook, Julia Murphey w/o Fred W.	Aug 24 1852	Jul 12 1886
Cook, Maude Greene d/o F.W. & J.M.	Jul 4 1880	Nov 4 1882
Dinkins, C.N.	Mar 20 1850	Jan 2 1909
Dinkins, Cornelia Tinley	1852	1921
Forth, Benjamin Lewis	1855	1916
Forth, Bessie Lee	Nov 30 1893	Jne 17 1898
Forth, Emma Anna Samuel w/o Benj. L.	1859	1941
Forth, Henry G. WW-I Ga PFC Med Dept	Oct 12 1892	May 30 1954
Forth, John Gordon	Jne 12 1879	Feb 9 1962
Forth, Lewis G. (infant) s/o Emma & B.L.	only date	1895
Forth, Mary N.	age 13 y	nd
Forth, Walter W. WW-I Ga Pvt Gen Off Tng Sch	Jan 12 1897	May 2 1952
Fulcher, Ben T.	1893	1946
Fulcher, E. Grover	Mar 17 1887	Oct 26 1953
Fulcher, Fannie w/o Joseph L.	Oct 14 1865	Feb 19 1927
Fulcher, Infant s/o Fannie & Joseph	only date	Aug 1 1900
Fulcher, Joseph L.	Sep 27 1864	Mar 16 1959
Fulcher, Marchia McManus w/o E.G.	Feb 23 1892	Jul 11 1933
Fulcher, Sarah A.	Jul 8 1834	Mar 2 1891
Greiner, Caroll S.	Aug 19 1927	Apr 13 1928
Greiner, Leland S.	Aug 8 1891	Jne 14 1967
Greiner, Leland & Lila (twins)	only date	Jne 20 1929
Holley, J.H.	age 50 y	May 19 1895
Martin, Charles Edwin WW-I s/o Geo. B. & Anna (Pvt)	Apr 20 1897	Feb 7 1917
Melton, Amy	Nov 30 1831	Jne 15 1907
Melton, Edmund CSA Mexican War	Jul 25 1825	Jul 7 1909
Melton, Edmond Louisa w/o R.E. /Elizabeth Clark	Jne 20 1864	Jul 24 1952
Melton, Robert Edmund	Dec 27 1865	Nov 2 1924
Murphey, Ida A.	Jne 13 1876	Jul 15 1899
Murphey, Henrietta Brey w/o J.F.	nd	1885

```
Murphey, John F.                              1846              1901
Palmer, Anna G.                     Jne  6 1880    Aug 18 1962
   d/o Mary Rheney & Wm. C.
Palmer, Anna Rheney                 Dec 13 1860    Dec 29 1943
   w/o J. Price
   d/o Mary Clark & John Wm.
Palmer, Benjamin S.                 May 25 1878    Sep  9 1935
   s/o Mary Rheney & Wm. C.
Palmer, Georgia V.                  Sep  9 1842    Oct 21 1900
Palmer, J. Paul                     Sep 17 1890    Nov  8 1925
   s/o Anna R. & J. Price
Palmer, J. Price                    Jan 29 1862    Jne 26 1937
Palmer, J.T.                        Jul 16 1836    Dec 25 1901
Palmer, Mary Ellen Rheney           Jan 10 1847    Jul 27 1923
   w/o W.C.
Palmer, William Cureton             Dec 14 1836    Sep 11 1898
Perkins, William Robert             age 58 yrs     Jne 24 1917
Petrullo, Deryl Clark               Jan 27 1905    Sep 20 1972
   w/o Luigi
   d/o Mary Wise & A.M.
   d  Washington, D.C.
Rheney, Frank Branch                Nov 16 1886    Mar  1 1953
   s/o Mary Evans & Dr. S.C.
Rheney, Gordon                      Feb    1876    Jul    1876
Rheney, J. William                         1812           1864
Rheney, John W.                     May 28 1810    Aug  3 1883
   s/o Polly Murphey & Charles
Rheney, Lizzie                      Mar  2 1854    Mar  3 1876
   1st w/o Samuel C.
Rheney, Mary                        age 17 m                 nd
   d/o Lizzie & Dr. Samuel
Rheney, Mary Caroline Evans         Jul 12 1859    Dec  9 1947
   2nd w/o Samuel C.
Rheney, R. Toombs                          1854           1872
   s/o Mary E. & John Wm.
   d at Oxford, Ga.
Rheney, Mary Eleanor Clark          Apr 11 1824    Feb 23 1896
   w/o Jno. Wm.
   d/o Eleanor & Chas., III
Rheney, Dr. Samuel C.               May 24 1849    Oct 19 1894
Samuel, Arthur G.                          1881           1899
Samuel, Avis                        Sep 11 1909    Sep  9 1910
   d/o R.A. & F.B.
Samuel, Fannie Bell                 age 42 y       Jan  9 1921
Samuel, Infants (two)                      nd               nd
   of Laura T. & J.B.
Samuel, J. Benjamin                        1855           1918
Samuel, J.H.                        Oct 25 1861    Jne 25 1918
   F&AM
Samuel, Laura Templeton                    1854           1889
   w/o J. Benj.
Samuel, Robert A.                   Dec  8 1859    Oct 29 1917
Samuels, Robert A., Jr.                    1901           1957
Saxon, Maggie May Fulcher                  1896           1925
   w/o J.W.
```

```
Spencer, Mamie Samuel                    1883              1918
  d/o Laura T. & B.V.
Stevens, Andrew Tarver          Oct 15 1884  Oct 14 1943
Stevens, Mary Palmer            Jne 14 1882  Aug  7 1963
  w/o Andrew T.
  d/o Mary Eleanor & Wm. C.
Templeton, Absalom  CSA         Sep 20 1842  Dec 22 1922
  Co D 12 Ga Lt Arty
Templeton, Ben S.                       1824              1893
Templeton, Eliza Murphey        age 70 y     Jan 11 1913
  w/o Absalom
Templeton, Infant               Nov  8 1893  Feb 10 1894
Templeton, Johnnie H.                   1874              1948
Templeton, Julia F.                     1840              1897
Templeton, Mamie May            Aug  3 1886  Feb 25 1892
Thomas, G.E.                    Jul 10 1856  Oct 28 1882
Thomas, Infant twins            only   date  Aug 18 1882
  of Geo. & Adella
Williams, Hal S.                Dec 13 1876  Sep  3 1936
Williams, Margaret Templeton    Dec 28 1879  Jan  1 1959
  w/o H.S.
Williams, Norma Louise          Feb  7 1902  Jul 18 1903
  d/o Norma & Hal S.
```

34.   <u>COLLINS-AVRET</u>

```
Avret, Charlie William          Aug  7 1878  Apr 29 1917
Avret, Eva May                  May  2 1880  Nov 13 1881
Avret, G.G.P.                   Aug  7 1811  Mar  6 1888
Avret, Jesse                    age 53 y     Sep 29 1835
Avret, Mary E.                  May 30 1847  Jul  6 1932
Avret, Nathaniel T.             Aug  2 1845  Nov 29 1917
Clark, Martha A.                Jan 24 1808  Jan 25 1835
  w/o Charles E.
Clarke, Ann B. Avret            Feb  6 1816  Feb 28 1901
Collins, Celia W.               Mar 19 1852  Jne  9 1913
  w/o B.F.
Collins, Gertrude               Nov 20 1880  Nov 27 1881
Collins, Walter Ewing           Jan 20 1879  Dec  8 1881
Corley, Maude Avret             Sep 19 1883  Jan 27 1918
  w/o Terry E.  He is buried in the Hopeful Baptist
  cemetery (ed).
Ware, Robert E.                 Jul 12 1909  Jul 13 1909
  s/o E.L. & W.D.
Ware, Willie D.                 Aug 18 1863  Dec 11 1917
```

35.   <u>CORINTH CHRISTIAN</u>

```
Anderson, Mrs.                          nd                nd
Bates, Alice V.                 Aug 20 1848  Dec 22 1891
  w/o J.W.
  d/o Josiah & A.E. Pollock
```

Bates, Annie J.   Jne 23 1874   May 31 1903
   w/o Jos. C.
Bates, Edward   nd   nd
Bates, Joseph   nd   nd
Bates, Joseph W.   Dec 30 1832   Jan 13 1905
Bates, Robert   nd   nd
Bates, Dr. W.S.   Dec 24 1871   Mar 15 1917
Bennett, Edna Royal   Dec 29 1873   Jul 16 1967
   w/o Ed
   d/o Jane Odom & Mordecai Royal
Burgany, Alice Bates   nd   nd
Buxton, Joseph J.   Jan 21 1873   Mar 28 1911
   Supt. Corinth Sunday School
Buxton, Julian A.   Jul 25 1878   Jan 15 1945
Buxton, Mamie R.   Aug 12 1874   Jul 30 1921
   w/o Joseph J.
   sis/o Charles E. McGregor
Chance, Henry Thomas   Nov 5 1878   Dec 28 1942
Cockcroft, Malvin E.   Sep 22 1892   Jan 10 1936
Cockcroft, Wade H.   Feb 18 1922   Jan 9 1939
   s/o M.E. & A.M.
Connelly, Ella V.   May 5 1848   Oct 9 1882
Connelly, John G.   Jul 4 1816   Dec 9 1883
Connelly, Mary E.   Mar 4 1816   Aug 29 1902
   w/o John G.
Connelly, Richard M.   Nov 22 1845   Dec 23 1911
Connelly, William C.   Jul 6 1839   Nov 14 1895
Connolly, Mary E.   Dec 10 1854   May 1 1929
   d/o John & M.E. Connelly
   Note difference in spelling (ed).
Crosby, Infant   nd   Oct 21 1972
Ellison, James Watson   Jul 31 1893   Mar 15 1962
Frazier, Joseph E.   1914   1953
Glisson, Carrie Bell   Jan 16 1885   Jan 22 1953
   w/o Folson
Glisson, Folson G.   Jan 3 1886   Oct 6 1955
Glisson, Lillian Hillis   Nov 12 1902   Sep 14 1963
Hankinson, Marion   WW-I   Jne 21 1893   Oct 8 1918
   s/o Batt J.   Lost his life in sinking of the Otranto.
   br/o Mrs Julia Ellison
Hankinson, Wm. Bernard   Oct 21 1888   Jul 1 1954
Heath, Judson   nd   nd
Helmly, Essie Strange   nd   nd
   sis/o W.T. (Willie) Strange
Helmly, Hardy P.   Oct 15 1855   Jan 26 1940
Hiers, Mrs. Ida   Apr 5 1882   Aug 9 1959
Hillis, Amanda Pauline   Apr 2 1892   L
Hillis, Beatrice N.   1923   1931
   d/o J.R. & Bessie
Hillis, Ben Wayne   Aug 25 1925   Jul 1 1926
Hillis, Bennie G.   Dec 30 1875   Sep 19 1902
Hillis, Bernard Q.   1932   1933
   s/o J.R. & Bessie
Hillis, Bessie Widener   Apr 23 1890   Jul 9 1969
   w/o Jacob R.

Hillis, Daisy Lee w/o G.W.	Aug 29 1891	Mar 28 1924
Hillis, David Charles s/o Billie K. & Lewis Roy	Jan 10 1955	Jul 2 1956
Hillis, Deady w/o R.J.	Nov 22 1859	Aug 21 1912
Hillis, Eunice	Jan 4 1893	May 27 1943
Hillis, George W.	1886	1955
Hillis, Infant s/o Chester	only date	Jne 25 1943
Hillis, Jacob R.	1882	1941
Hillis, James Richard s/o Chester	only date	Jne 13 1942
Hillis, Martha E.	Nov 16 1877	Jul 18 1928
Hillis, Minjs Ralph s/o Lillian P. & M.S.	Sep 2 1915	Jan 11 1968
Hillis, R.L. s/o Daisy & G.W.	Aug 5 1913	Feb 8 1929
Hillis, Richard Jacob	Aug 27 1854	Jul 31 1938
Hillis, Thomas Quinnie	Mar 6 1887	Feb 19 1968
Hillis, Wesley	Jul 23 1915	Aug 22 1916
Houston, Florence Octavia d/o G.R. & Lessie	Oct 8 1911	Sep 27 1912
Houston, Lessie Lee Hillis	Dec 12 1879	Dec 24 1951
Johnson, Andrew Cleve	1887	1956
Johnson, Ella Mae w/o Andrew	1897	nd
Johnson, Willie (Zeke)	Sep 25 1918	Apr 13 1970
Lamb, Albert B.	Nov 14 1891	Sep 17 1946
Lamb, James B. s/o Albert B.	Nov 17 1928	May 25 1931
Lovett, Annie d/o Tommie & Franklin	Jan 7 1916	Apr 10 1916
Lovett, Franklin E.	Jul 18 1897	Jul 6 1969
Lovett, Maude A.	Jne 22 1885	Jul 24 1961
Lovett, Tommie Mead w/o Franklin E.	May 10 1895	nd
McCullough, Leonard L.	1866	1943
McCullough, Minnie R. w/o Leonard	1886	1959
McGowan, John Hampton	May 1 1846	Aug 27 1914
McGregor, Charles E.	Jan 17 1878	May 11 1938
McGregor, Georgia A. w/o Capt. M.T.	Sep 29 1850	Mar 3 1910
McGregor, Laura Goodson w/o Chas. E.	Dec 26 1876	Nov 10 1944
McGregor, Capt. M.T.	Jne 25 1841	Dec 13 1881
McGregor, Mitt O.	Feb 22 1859	Mar 15 1937
Mobley, Alice Woods w/o Robert	nd	nd
Mobley, Robert br/o Ernest (Jack)	nd	nd
Mobley, Robert Virgil	Apr 22 1884	Mar 4 1936
Oglesbee, Infant s/o J.C. & S.L.	Feb 8 1914	same date

```
Oglesbee, J. Charlie              Sep  9 1886   Nov 26 1968
Oglesbee, Lottie Hillis           Feb  2 1889   Oct 19 1958
  w/o J. Charlie
Oglesby, Frank Joe                Dec 24 1870   Feb 11 1946
Oglesby, Katie Strange            Jul 11 1871   Sep  8 1933
  w/o Frank Joe
Oliver, Eliza Goodwyn             Apr 24 1828   Mar  6 1895
Oliver, Thomas Wm.                Apr 14 1825   May 15 1908
Oliver, Virgil Brooks             Sep  4 1855   Jne  6 1901
Oliver, W. Douglas                Feb 20 1853   Feb  9 1891
Padgett, Deedy Oglesbee           Aug 23 1908   Feb  4 1972
  w/o Rev. John A.
Padgett, Rev. John Albert         Mar 30 1889   Aug 29 1948
Padgett, Richard Newton           Sep 19 1933   Nov 27 1934
  s/o Deedy & John A.
Paris, Martha L.                  Jul  2 1841   Sep 22 1920
Paris, W. C.                      Oct 27 1838   Mar 27 1908
  F&AM
Perry, Charles Otis               Jul 12 1878   Apr  5 1938
Perry, Charlie Fred               Jan 14 1898   Mar 21 1947
Perry, Debra A.                         1963          1963
  d/o Albert.
Perry, Dennis C.                  age 81 y      Jan  4 1970
Perry, Hattie Glisson             May 19 1878   Jne  2 1963
  w/o Charles O.
Perry, Henry Thomas (Jumbo)       Feb 27 1925   Sep 23 1937
Perry, Infant                           nd            nd
  s/o Albert
Perry, Louise S.                  Sep  6 1903   Sep  8 1963
  w/o Thomas A.
Perry, Marion                     Oct  7 1901   Jan  9 1969
  w/o Charlie F.
Perry, Thomas A. (Buddy)          Sep 11 1901   Dec  9 1957
  s/o Jake
Perry, Zelphia Hiers              age 67 y      Jul 20 1967
Pollock, Mrs. A.E.                May 16 1825   Jan 24 1891
Pollock, Josiah                   Apr 29 1821   Oct 24 1898
Reagan, Emmie Cooper              Mar 28 1899              L
  w/o Norman L.
  d/o Mary Wicker & John C.
Reagan, Norman L.                 Aug 25 1891   Mar  6 1973
Reeder, James R.                  Mar    1904   Jan    1935
Reynolds, Mrs.                          nd            nd
  A woman preacher who was taken ill on boat at Stoney
  Bluff and died.
Royal, Alice Tobias                     nd            nd
  w/o Frank
Royal, Mrs. Annie L. Williams     Oct 10 1874   Jan 10 1956
Royal, Doughty                          nd            nd
  s/o Horace
Royal, Eticus                     Oct 11 1904   Oct 18 1904
Royal, Frank                            nd            nd
  h/o Alice Tobias
  s/o Guildford
Royal, Homer Oshey                Aug 17 1885   Jul 28 1942
```

```
Royal, Horace G.                                    nd              nd
  br/o Dr. Guilford
Royal, James Green                        Jne 21 1871  Mar 21 1939
Royal, James W.                           Feb 14 1836  Nov 24 1910
Royal, Jane Odom                                    nd              nd
  w/o Mordecai
  sis/o Richard Odom
Royal, Mattie R.                                  1890            1971
Royal, Mordecai                                     nd              nd
  br/o Wesley and Guildford
Royal, Percy A.                           Aug  5 1895  Apr 29 1918
Sanders, Forest A.                                1915            1971
Sanders, Maggie Weeks                             1908            1969
  w/o Forest A.
Skinner, Etta Rosetta P.                  Jan 27 1905  Dec 29 1972
  w/o J.W.
Strange, Harry                                      nd              nd
  s/o W.T.
Strange, Hattie                                     nd              nd
  sis/o W.T.  According to one source this grave is
  that of the wife of W.T. Strange, Eva Glisson
  Strange, rather than his sister (ed).
Strange, Mary                                       nd              nd
  sis/o W.T.
Tobias, Gertrude Widener                            nd              nd
  w/o John
Tobias, Manie P.                          Jan  7 1900  Feb  6 1943
Weeks, Carl Wayne                                 1960            1960
Weeks, John Perry                         age 55 y     Aug  2 1966
Wells, Infants (four)                               nd              nd
  of Sally
Wells, Sally                                        nd              nd
West, Frances Bartow                      May 15 1861  Mar  4 1950
West, John Calvin                         Mar 15 1853  Apr  2 1923
Widener, Pvt. James W. WW-I               Sep 19 1892  Oct 17 1918
Widener, Willie Allen                               nd              nd
  s/o Abner  br/o Jim, Walter, Glenn, & Emory
Widner, James Hillis                              1921            1941
Woods, Infant                                     1961            1961
  s/o Watson
Woods, Infant                                     1962            1962
  s/o Watson
Woods, William P.  WW-II                  Mar 16 1913  Jul  5 1962
  Ga PFC USA
Yaughn, Anna                              Nov  9 1866  Oct  5 1923
  w/o Asbury
Yaughn, Asbury                            Feb 24 1871  Nov 18 1929


36.                        COSNAHAN
                         Richmond Co.

Allen, Elisha A.                          Jan 23 1900               L
Allen, Evans A.                           Jan 17 1935  Mar 14 1964
  s/o Elisha & Vonnie
```

```
Allen, Vonnie E. Cosnahan        Jne 12 1902              L
  w/o Elisha A.
Avret, Wirt N., Sr.              Mar 14 1901   Jul 12 1934
Cosnahan, Amelia Ann                    1826              1909
  w/o George
Cosnahan, Augustus F.                   1900              1902
Cosnahan, Ethel Ellison          Apr 19 1922              L
Cosnahan, Franklin A.                   1854              1929
Cosnahan, George                        1826              1877
Cosnahan, George E.                     1910              1931
Cosnahan, Leatha S. Knight              1872              1944
  w/o Franklin A.
Cosnahan, Lucy                   Mar  2 1795   Aug  1 1879
Cosnahan, Olin O., Sr.           Sep 22 1914              L
```

Note: The Cosnahan, Crockett, Fulcher (John W), Lambeth and Tinley cemeteries are all just across McBean Creek which is the boundary line between Richmond and Burke counties (ed).

37.   COX

```
Cox, Augustus, B.L.              Mar  2 1842   Aug  3 1854
  s/o Wm. & Sarah Long
Cox, Infant                      Sep  5 1853   Sep 28 1853
  s/o Wm. & Sarah Long
Cox, Milley Floyd                       1765   Feb  3 1848
  b in N.C.  w/o Wm.
Cox, Sarah Louise Long           Oct 17 1821   Sep 25 1853
  w/o William
```
Note: This William (b 1808) was the son of William and Milley Floyd Cox. He is buried in Mt. Zion Methodist cemetery (ed).
```
Cox, William                              nd            nd
  h/o Milley:  b in N.C., moved to Ga. in 1804 (ed).
```

38.   CROCKETT
                         Richmond Co.

```
Allen, Hiram Nott                Nov 10 1881   Dec 31 1881
  s/o Francis M. & Jane E.
Allen, Infant                    only   date   Mar 27 1883
  d/o Francis M. & Jane E.
Crockett, Claudia E.             Jan  9 1845   Jan  6 1882
  w/o Floyd
Crockett, F.  CSA                         nd            nd
  Co B 63 Ga Inf
Crockett, Floyd                  age 77 y      Mar 23 1853
Crockett, Floyd                  Jne  6 1845   May 25 1888
Crockett, Leila Amelia Greiner   Jul 28 1871   Jne  5 1930
  w/o Robt. Edgar
Crockett, Lockey                 age 68 y      Feb 15 1843
  w/o Floyd
```

```
Crockett, Robert Edgar        Jul  1 1871   Aug 12 1938
Crockett, Robert Edgar        Sep 11 1900   Jan 23 1939
Meyer, Carl Crockett          May 14 1902   Apr 21 1950
Meyer, Florrie Crockett            1875           1961
Nott, Walter S.               Feb 18 1811   Feb  2 1868
```

39.   <u>CROSS</u>

```
Cross, Rufus                  Nov  3 1828   Apr 20 1901
   erected by his daughter, Clemmie Perkins
Cross, Sarah                  age 56 y                nd
```

Note: Four footstones, which are not part of the two marked graves found, indicate that at least four others are buried in this cemetery (ed).

40.   <u>DILLARD</u>

```
Dillard, John                 age 56 y      Apr  3 1841
   h/o Nancy M;  f/o Sarah J. (Fryer), Alice A. (Wiggins)
```
and Mary J. (Schaffner). His wife and daughter Alice are buried in the Hopeful Baptist Cem. and the other two daughters in the Hephzibah City Cemetery (ed).

41.   <u>DRONE (OLD CATES)</u>

```
Clemmons, Mary Cates Wynn     Mar 27 1849   Aug 30 1919
Lotz, Effie E.                Dec 15 1886   Apr  9 1910
   w/o Geo. Lotz   d/o Henry H. & Mary Clemmons
Wynn, John F.                 Feb 18 1873   Jan 10 1897
   s/o Joseph & Mary
Wynn, Joseph W.               Mar 27 1842   Oct 20 1877
Wynn, Joseph W., Jr.          Oct 21 1877   Oct  8 1880
Wynn, T. LaFayette            Apr  3 1871   Mar  3 1890
   s/o Joseph & Mary
```

Note: About one-half mile from this cemetery was a smaller one at the Hosea B. Cates home place, but all markers have been removed. However, three graves could be identified from family records (ed).
```
Cates, Elizabeth              age 2 y       Jan 17 1886
   d/o Margaret MacKenzie & Wm. Joseph Cates
Cates, Hosea Berrien          Dec 13 1823   Sep 28 1868
Cates, Susan Douglas Addison  Dec 29 1829   Feb 21 1877
   w/o Hosea B.  md Nov  6 1845
```

42.   <u>FAIRHAVEN METHODIST</u>
                           <u>Jenkins Co.</u>

```
Black, Thomas Lamar           Oct  5 1903   Aug 17 1972
```

Burney, Mary Slater   nd   nd
   w/o John   d/o Eliz. Jones & John D. Slater
Jones, Catherine M. /   Oct 7 1862   Jan 10 1908
   w/o H.P.   Whitehead md Jne 17 1896
   d/o Catherine M. Harper & John Berrien
Jones, Elizabeth Eve Neely   Oct 14 1872   Jne 16 1900
   w/o J.B.
Jones, Ellen Morgan Griffin   Dec 8 1846   Dec 31 1893
   w/o Joel Hurt
Jones, Henry Philip   Nov 27 1846   Mar 3 1909
   s/o James V. & Mary Hurt
   md 1st Lula Chaires; 2nd Catherine Whitehead
Jones, Henry Walter   Feb 14 1891   Jul 6 1908
   s/o J.B. & M.L. Connally
Jones, Henry Wilkes   Sep 25 1824   Aug 9 1900
   3rd s/o H.P. & Sarah Vickers
Jones, Ida Elizabeth Jones   Dec 11 1855   Oct 14 1912
   w/o Philip Sapp
   d/o Seaborn Augustus & Maria Law
Jones, Infant   only   date   Jul 27 1897
   s/o H.P. & C.W.
Jones, Infant   Sep 25 1889   Oct 13 1889
   d/o H.P. & Lula Chaires
Jones, Infant   nd   nd
   s/o J.B. & M.L. Connally
Jones, James Vickers   Nov 3 1863   Apr 7 1930
   s/o Dr. Wm. B. & Sidney Sapp
Jones, Joel Hurt   Feb 14 1846   Sep 1 1909
   s/o James V. & Mary Hurt
Jones, John Sharpe   Apr 21 1896   Jul 27 1958
   s/o Robt. Forth & Madge Sharpe
Jones, Joseph Bertrand   May 23 1859   Feb 2 1908
   s/o H.W. & Martha Aiken
   md 1st Mary Lee Connally; 2nd Elizabeth Eve Neely
Jones, Martha Aikin   Mar 25 1830   Jne 27 1903
   w/o Henry Wilkes
Jones, Mary Lee Connally   May 7 1866   Nov 7 1897
   w/o J.B.
Jones, Percival Connally WW-I   Jul 17 1894   Oct 21 1918
   s/o J.B. & M.L. Connally
   1st Lieut USA Co B 11th Inf 5th Div Killed in battle,
   buried on farm, Verdon Sector, Argonne Forest, France.
Jones, Robert Chapman   May 14 1895   Jne 10 1966
Jones, Robert F.   1899   1899
   s/o Robt. F. & Madge Sharpe
Jones, Robert Forth   May 10 1861   Apr 24 1910
   s/o Jos. B. & Sarah Lewis
Jones, Rosa Chapman   Jan 1 1861   Feb 2 1940
   w/o Jas. Vickers
Jones, Troup   nd   nd
   s/o James V. & Mary Hurt
   died young about 1845-46
Jones, William Beaman   Oct 19 1889   Aug 18 1918
   s/o James V. & Rosa Chapman

```
Law, Annie Jones                        Sep 23 1877  Jan 17 1951
   d/o Robt. & Clara
Law, Clara E. Jones                     Feb 17 1855  Sep 30 1925
   w/o Robert   d/o Martha Aikin & Henry Wilkes
Law, Henry Benson                       Feb 11 1920  Aug 23 1921
   s/o Madelle Benson & Wilkes A.
Law, Infant                             only   date   Nov    1909
   s/o Jos. & Carrie
Law, Robert                             Aug 15 1852  May 23 1912
Law, Robert, Jr.                        Jne 25 1890  Jul  4 1906
   s/o Robt & Clara
Quick, Effie M.                         Feb  8 1889  Apr 10 1931
   w/o Willie F.
Quick, Lula H.                          Aug 15 1910  Sep 18 1929
Quick, Mattie                           Apr  1 1899  May 15 1927
Rosser, Caroline Jones                  Sep 15 1892  Dec 14 1942
   d/o James V. & Rosa Chapman
Rosser, Clarence C., Sr.                Jan  2 1888  Oct  5 1971
Rosser, Clarence Cocke, Jr.    Dec  8 1923  Sep 15 1944
   s/o Caroline Jones & Clarence, Sr.
   WW-II US Marine Corps;  killed in action Palau
   Islands, Pacific area.
Smith, Alison Jones (infant)   only   date   Dec 19 1968
   d/o Caroline Jones & Wilson Smith
Wadley, Rosalie Chapman Jones  Aug  3 1898  May  4 1944
   w/o Richard Barnard
   d/o Rosa Chapman & James Vickers
Wakelee, Miss Kate C.                   Aug 27 1829  Feb  5 1905
   native of Conn.  Relative of Maria Law Jones, also
   from Conn.
White, Michael F. (Mike)                Jne 12 1950  May  1 1971
   s/o Carlton & Jean J.
White, Raymond P.                            1969         1973
```

Note: One old, above-ground, bricked-up vault no
longer has a marker (ed).

43.   FOSTER

```
Foster, James Andrew                    Mar 29 1857  Jne 10 1934
Foster, Katie Belle                     Sep 24 1873  Jul 27 1944
   w/o Jas. A.
Godbee, Lockie                          Feb  9 1875  Jul 25 1901
   w/o Walker
```


44.   FRIENDSHIP METHODIST

```
Allen, William Jefferson                Sep  9 1911  Oct  1 1958
   s/o Jefferson & Mabel
Goetzman, Beverly Jean                  only   date   Dec 17 1969
   d/o Mr. & Mrs. Earnest G. (infant)
```

FULCHER
Richmond Co.

Atwell, Thos. B.	Jan 24 1870	May 16 1892
Colson, Alice	age 1y 1d	Jne 25 1862
d/o J.W. & Caroline		
Colson, Jas. M.	Jan 13 1824	Jul 10 1833
Colson, William	age 58 y	May 7 1851
Colson, Wm. J.	age 8m 3d	Jul 30 1855
s/o J. W. & Caroline		
Fulcher, A. A.	nd	nd
br/o James A.		
Fulcher, Callie C.	Dec 1 1866	Mar 25 1886
d/o Val & Almeda		
Fulcher, Little Carrie	3y 4m 17d	Dec 19 1861
d/o Val & Melvina		
Fulcher, Charlie J.	Nov 12 1858	Sep 29 1923
Fulcher, Cleveland	Jul 21 1884	Sep 18 1884
s/o Edwin & Osee		
Fulcher, Edward Leon	Dec 4 1905	Dec 23 1922
s/o J. E. & Lillie V.		
Fulcher, Elizabeth Huff	1757	Nov 17 1840
w/o James md 1777		
Fulcher, Gratz	age 11m 17d	Apr 26 1879
s/o Valentine & Almeda		
Fulcher, J. A.	Oct 18 1845	Sep 30 1907
s/o James A. & Kiziah		
Fulcher, James Rev War	1755	Mar 23 1839

Note: Family papers in the possession of his great-great-granddaughter state that he and his wife came to Georgia from Virginia (ed).

Fulcher, James A.	nd	nd
Fulcher, Jay C.	age 7y 4m	May 19 1879
s/o Valentine & Almeda	1d	
Fulcher, John, Sr.	1784	Nov 1 1844
s/o Elizabeth H. & James		
Fulcher, John Colson	Oct 14 1814	Sep 10 1882
s/o Mary C. & John		
Fulcher, Kiziah	nd	nd
w/o James A.		
Fulcher, Lillie V.	Dec 16 1876	Sep 4 1911
w/o J. E.		
Fulcher, Lucy E.	Oct 14 1855	Jne 5 1900
w/o J. A.		
Fulcher, M. A.	nd	nd
w/o A.A. aunt of J.A.		
Fulcher, Mary Colson	1791	Nov 14 1867
w/o John		
Fulcher, Melvina Heath	age 34y 3m	Oct 25 1869
w/o Valentine	15d	
Fulcher, Mollie	age 6y 8m	Sep 1 1868
d/o Val & Melvina		
Fulcher, Susie Louise	Aug 3 1911	Jan 23 1912
d/o Mr. & Mrs. J. E.		

```
Fulcher, Valentine                    Nov  9 1828    Jul  9 1880
    s/o Mary C. & John
Fulcher, Valentine                    Dec 18 1880    Jul 26 1882
    s/o Valentine & Almeda
Fulcher, W. H.                                  nd            nd
    s/o J.A. & K.
Fulcher, William, Sr.                 Apr 30 1811    Jan  7 1848
    s/o Mary C. & John
Fulcher, Whitney                      age 6m 11d     Jul 23 1889
    s/o Edwin & Osee
Fulcher, Wm. A.                            1837     Oct     1841
Jones, Esther                         Dec  7 1867    Dec 11 1867
    only d/o J.M. & Fannie A.E.
Jones, Fannie A. E.                   age 21y        Jan 22 1868
    w/o J.M.
Jones, Seleucus R.                    age 8y 4m      Sep  2 1859
    s/o Robt. & Emily                       26d
Loudermilk, Roy S.                    Dec 26 1896    Oct 31 1947
McElmurray, Mary A.                   Dec 18 1818    Jan 27 1887
McE., S. R.   no further identification or dates
Palmer, E. N.  CSA                              nd            nd
    Co C 5 Ga Cav
Smith, A. Eugenia                          1856            1908
Smith, Ann Eliza                           1821            1883
    w/o Robert F.
Smith, Frank A.                            1859            1917
Smith, J. Wyatt                            1863            1938
Smith, Robert F.                           1830            1891
Smith, Sarah I.                            1861            1919
Winter, Anna R.                       Sep 20 1858    Aug 18 1916
Winter, B. G.                         Nov 17 1822    Nov 15 1898
    b  Richmond Co
Winter, B. G.                         Mar 20 1851    Apr 12 1904
Winter, Berry Baxley                  Sep 30 1875    Dec 26 1891
    s/o B. G. & Annie H.
Winter, Cit Meyer                     Jan  7 1882    Jne 21 1884
Winter, Mrs. Elizabeth                Apr 30 1820    Jne 28 1874
    w/o B. G.
Winter, George G.                     Dec 14 1877    Sep 17 1878
Winter, Robert W.                     Mar  8 1886    Aug 24 1887
```

46.   FULCHER
                        Richmond Co.

```
Fulcher, Annie Bessie                 Feb 11 1880    Jul 23 1882
    4th d/o J. W. & Annie
Fulcher, Annie Syms                   Nov 12 1838    Feb 22 1932
    w/o John W.
Fulcher, Beatrice E.                  Mar 16 1884    Jne  6 1886
Fulcher, Etta N.                      May 12 1870    May  6 1886
Fulcher, John W.                      Jul  9 1835    Feb 10 1906
Fulcher, Zelene Baxley                Aug  8 1876    Mar  3 1879
    3rd d/o J. W. & Annie
```

47.   GODBEE

Godbee, Bertha Frances   Oct 13 1848   Oct 19 1905
  w/o Russell J.
Godbee, Charity   Apr 25 1817   Feb 15 1857
  w/o Simeon
Godbee, Charlotte   Mar 20 1834   Jne 1 1899
  d/o Jas. & Sarah
Godbee, James   Jne 17 1800   Sep 26 1869
Godbee, Lafayette   Feb 15 1841   Mar 3 1869
Godbee, Little Lucy   Feb 19 1878   Oct 8 1880
  d/o Raiford & M.J.
Godbee, Mary Jane   Sep 23 1848   Apr 8 1931
  w/o Raiford
Godbee, Raiford CSA   Sep 20 1843   Jan 13 1884
  Co C 5th Ga Cav
Godbee, Little Richard   Jan 23 1870   Oct 25 1878
  s/o Raiford & M.J.
Godbee, Russell Joseph   Oct 30 1848   Sep 29 1923
Godbee, Sarah   Sep 4 1809   Jan 22 1849
  w/o James
Godbee, Simeon   Dec 29 1801   Jul 4 1867
Godbee, Thomas Raiford   c.   1870   Feb   1935
Jones, Emma L.   Jul 14 1878   Sep 10 1919
Smith, Joseph T.   Jul 1 1871   Aug 29 1875
  s/o Rev. A.B. & M.
Smith, Martha Ann Godbee   Jan 18 1868   Sep 24 1868
  d/o Rev. A.B. & Malissa Smith

48.   GODBEE

Godbee, Infant   only   date   Oct 19 1867
Godbee, J.W.H.   Jan 6 1864   Jne 23 1871
Godbee, Savannah   Sep 16 1853   Sep 21 1856
  d/o James C. & Mary

49.   GODBEE

Frazier, Gus WW-I   only   date   Oct 6 1918
Lynch, Hattie   Jne 1 1869   Jul 4 1919

50.   GODBEE

Godbee, James M.   Mar 26 1830   Jan 28 1895

51.   GOODIER

Goodier, Mrs. Emma G.   Apr 1 1846   May 19 1872
  w/o Rev. J. R.   b Mt. Pleasant, Ohio

Note: Mrs. Goodier and her husband were young mission-aries sent during the Reconstruction Period by the Freedmen's Aid Society of the M.E. Church (Northern) to teach in the school which the Society had established at Waynesboro. Both the mother and baby died at child birth and were buried together. It was Mrs. Goodier's request that they be buried close by the wooden building which then served as both a school and a church (ed).

52.   GOUGH

Dawson, William Cullen   Mar 28 1846 Aug 2 1862
Ervin, Iredell Simons   Jan 25 1817 Nov 18 1879
Gough, Celah Ann   Feb 24 1830 Sep 26 1837
   d/o George & Jane
Gough, Elsie Ervin   Apr 21 1796 Oct 20 1834
   w/o George md Jne 24 1827 m/o Parmelia E.
Gough, George   Jan 25 1792 Jul 22 1868
   b in England
Gough, George Henry   Nov 16 1836 Jul 26 1841
   s/o George & Jane
Gough, Jane Dawson   Jul 30 1800 Nov 30 1872
   w/o George md Feb 11 1835 m/o five children
Gough, Joseph Simeon CSA   Aug 10 1842 Mar 10 1918
   s/o George & Jane
   Co F Cobb's Leg Ga Cav Hamptons Div
Gough, Mary Jane   Dec 21 1839 Jul 21 1841
   d/o George & Jane
Gough, William Britten   Nov 30 1835 Dec 13 1835
   s/o George & Jane
Peel, Mary Julia Dawson   Dec 15 1857 Apr 17 1886
   w/o -----Peel   d/o William & Parmelia E.G. Dawson
   d without children
Wimberly, Parmelia E. Gough   Jne 9 1828 Dec 10 1901
                 /Dawson
   w/o 1st William Dawson md May, 1856; w/o 2nd Zack
   Wimberly, md July, 1867; no children

Note: Monument with names on four sides was erected as a memorial to the George Gough family upon death of his son, Joseph S. Gough. Inscriptions have been supplemented by information from the family Bible. Elsie Ervin is spelled Elsey Erwin in Bible (ed).

53.   GOUGH COMMUNITY
                          Gough, Ga.

Brooks, John A.   1889   1950
   loved your grandson - Jr. Brooks
Brooks, Lottie Mae   1894   1938
Brooks, Sadie Gladis   1924   1926
Brown, Capt. Milton A. CSA   Dec 14 1841 Oct 29 1912
   b Burke Co of Lee's Army

```
Cates, Heman Torbit                   Nov 25 1907   May  3 1908
   s/o Heman H. & Ruth L.
Coursey, William P.                   Oct 24 1860   Jne 28 1920
Duke, R. T.                           Jul  1 1820   Feb 22 1906
Hudson, William B.                    Jan  1 1861   Aug 14 1926
McClellan, Mellie                     Mar 25 1907   Mar 19 1911
McClellan, Susan                              1851          1924
Penrow, C. E.                         Jne 19 1881   Jan 25 1948
Robinson, Elizabeth Ponder            Feb 18 1853   Sep  4 1926
   w/o G.B.
Robinson, G. B.                       Nov  9 1850   Nov 18 1910
Robinson, Mrs. James Alice            Jan 25 1860   Oct 24 1910
Robinson, Thomas Edward               Dec 16 1882   Dec 11 1908
```

54.   GRAY

Gray, Mrs. N. (Nancy) C.   Jne 28 1820 Jne 18 1881
   2nd w/o Minchi; m/o eight children: Emily (md Tabb),
   Anderson C., Josephine C., Mary, Savannah D., Judson
   Leroy, Mary Angelina and Minchi B. She was the
   stepmother of two sons of Minchi, Sr., by his first
   wife, viz, Simeon A. and James Gray. Will Bk A
   220-221.

Note: Only one marker was found in what was once a
family cemetery. This marker was broken but the
several parts produced a legible inscription (ed).

55.   GREEN

```
Green, Angerona Christian        age 38 y     Aug 15 1857
   d/o Gershom & Elizabeth
Green, Gershom                   age 41 y     Nov  8 1828
   h/o Elizabeth
Green, Laura                     Jul 23 1828  Oct  2 1831
   d/o Gershom & Elizabeth
```

56.   GREEN

Green, Mrs. Amelia R.   Jul 27 1804 Nov 13 1854
   w/o Jesse P., Sr. m/o Jesse P., II, Moses P., and
   several others who died young.
   Note: Amelia md 2nd John Gaybard Green (1826-1907)
   who is buried in Bath Presbyterian Cem. by his 2nd
   wife, Virginia A. Thompson (ed).
Green, Clara   Jul 9 1863 Oct 2 1870
   d/o Mary Jane & Jesse P., II
Green, Elijah W.   Jan 9 1829 Mar 9 1844
   s/o Amelia R. & Jesse P., Sr.
Green, George Augustus   age 37 y   Aug 2 1885
   s/o Martha T.A. & Moses P.;   the h/o Kate L.
   d/o Nancy C. & Jethro Thomas

```
Green, Jesse P., Jr.                    Nov 28 1831   Nov  9 1840
   s/o Amelia R. & Jesse P., Sr.
Green, Jesse P., II  CSA        Apr 11 1839   Apr 13 1864
   d  at Lake City, Fla., in defense of the Confederacy
   s/o Amelia R. & Jesse P., Sr.;  md Feb 17 1859
   Mary Jane Gresham (1839-1905)  d/o Edmund B. Gresham
   & Sarah M. Anderson;  f/o Jesse P., III, Walter
   Gresham, Sr., and Clara.
   Note:  After Jesse Green's death, his widow md Dr.
   Green Berry Powell.  Her mother was the d/o Elisha
   Anderson, Jr., and Jane McCullers  (ed).
Green, Jesse P., Sr.            Jan 15 1798   Dec 27 1843
Green, Martha Thompson A.       Jan 15 1829   Jan 24 1904
   w/o Moses P.  md Dec 10 1845  d/o Sarah Jones &
   Augustus Harcourt Anderson, Sr.  m/o Moses Edwin &
   George Augustus
Green, Mattie Thomas            Dec 22 1874   Feb  8 1877
   d/o Kate L. & George A.
Green, Moses P.                 Nov 21 1824   Nov 29 1875
   s/o Amelia R. & Jesse P., Sr.  h/o Martha Thompson
   Anderson
Green, Swepson C.               Feb 27 1834   Sep 12 1836
Green, Swepson D.               Sep 18 1836   Aug 22 1840
Green, William Thomas           age 2y 9m     Sep  2 1880
   s/o Kate L. & George A.
```

Note: Augustus H. Anderson was one of three brothers,
James, Elisha, & Augustus, the sons of Elisha, Sr., and
Mary Holzendorf (Rheney) for whom Brothersville was
named. See Will Bk A 105-10 for will of Augustus H.,
Sr. Walter A. Clark, A Lost Arcadia (1909), Augusta,
Ga., 200 pp. contains information on the Anderson,
Green and a few other families of Richmond and Burke
cemeteries (ed).

57.   GREEN

```
Green, Benjamin F.  MD          Aug 25 1802   Dec 26 1829
Green, Catherine Anna           Nov 29 1828   Aug 26 1831
   d/o Sarah & Benj. F.
Green, Sarah Harlow                  nd              nd
   w/o Dr. Benjamin F.  md Dec 5 1827;  d/o Rebecca
   Walker & Dr. Southworth Harlow.*
   * Warren & White, op. cit. 51.  This grave is now
   unmarked  (ed).
```

58.   GREEN FORK BAPTIST
                   Jenkins Co.

```
Alexander, Norwood M.           Jne  7 1901   Mar 29 1967
Alexander, Thelma C.            Jul 23 1913             L
Allen, Infant                   only  date   May  1 1879
Allen, J. W.                          1919           1968
```

Allen, John	Jne 14 1852	Nov 25 1903
Allen, Sarah Jane	Dec 6 1856	Sep 8 1927
w/o John		
Allen, Watson	Apr 10 1892	Dec 25 1921
Attaway, Thomas Bennett	Oct 22 1866	Feb 26 1870
s/o Amos & Sarah		
Barefield, Carolyn	Oct 20 1855	Aug 13 1924
w/o Homer V.		
Barefield, Daisy	Mar 15 1880	Dec 11 1880
d/o H.V. & C.		
Barefield, Harriet	Sep 29 1832	Oct 27 1895
w/o Rev. C.E.		
Barefield, Homer V.	Sep 3 1845	May 16 1927
Barefield, Julian Angus	Nov 27 1898	Nov 3 1953
Barefield, Leila C.	Jan 7 1916	nd
w/o M.B.		
Barefield, Lillie Drake	Apr 13 1877	Oct 1 1968
w/o V.D.		
Barefield, Murice B.	Jul 25 1908	nd
Barefield, Milton Hinch	Jne 15 1905	Apr 10 1966
Barefield, Ruth E.	May 15 1900	Jan 11 1904
Barefield, Sadie Mons	May 28 1912	Jan 12 1969
Barefield, Valda D.	Oct 24 1872	Feb 23 1948
Barton, Frank A.	Aug 5 1897	Jul 12 1909
Barton, James E.	nd	nd
Barton, Marcia E. Deulon	Jne 19 1868	Oct 31 1933
w/o Rufus A.		
Barton, Rufus A.	Jul 25 1864	nd
Becton, E.E.	age 38y	Dec 5 1855
w/o D.A.		
Bell, Amos W. CSA	Dec 3 1834	Sep 28 1899
Ga Pvt Co K 32 Reg Gn Inf		
Bell, Durwin Rhett	Sep 30 1949	Aug 23 1969
Bell, Tom J.	May 19 1867	Feb 10 1933
Bolton, Anna	Oct 11 1887	Apr 2 1963
Bolton, Georgia M.	1903	1969
Bolton, Jas.	1853	Jne 21 1884
Bolton, Octavia M.	Jne 16 1897	Mar 23 1958
Bolton, Robert	1892	1965
Bolton, Washington WW-I	Jne 2 1889	May 6 1971
Ga Pvt Co L 16 Inf		
Bolton, William M.	1898	1946
Bragg, Annie M.	Nov 25 1891	Jul 27 1892
d/o J.E. & O.		
Bragg, Ben	Apr 12 1883	nd
Bragg, Beneta S.	1887	1956
w/o J.L.		
Bragg, Canara E.	Mar 8 1899	Mar 4 1971
w/o R.E.		
Bragg, Cardell	Oct 24 1898	Jul 31 1900
s/o J.E. & Olive		
Bragg, George O.	Feb 21 1879	Mar 8 1932
Bragg, Infant	only date	Feb 3 1900
d/o J.E. & O.		

Bragg, Infant s/o J.E. & O.	only	date	Jan 9 1902
Bragg, Infants sons/o J.F. & O.	only	date	May 12 1903
Bragg, Infant d/o Rufus		1917	same date
Bragg, J. L.	May 19 1875	Oct 18 1918
Bragg, James, Sr.	Oct 12 1845	Apr 12 1912
Bragg, John E.	Jul 1 1871	Oct 29 1918
Bragg, Julian B. s/o Rufus	1930	1931
Bragg, Laura Mintaria w/o James L.	May 20 1876	Jul 21 1900
Bragg, Lillie B. w/o G.O.	Feb 24 1881	Dec 13 1962
Bragg, Marie d/o Rufus	1924	1934
Bragg, Mary Bell	Jan 18 1905	Mar 18 1919
Bragg, Nancy	Aug 27 1846	Sep 30 1910
Bragg, Olive H.	Oct 12 1877	Dec 17 1927
Bragg, Payne	Aug 24 1912	Feb 2 1919
Bragg, R. E.	Nov 25 1880	Dec 7 1910
Bragg, Rufus E.	Mar 12 1896	Sep 10 1969
Bragg, Willie R. w/o Ben	Jne 7 1890	nd
Brinson, B.E. inf. s/o W.T. & S.E.	Jul 17 1871	Nov 3 1872
Brinson, Charles J.	Aug 1 1875	Aug 31 1940
Brinson, Essie H.	Aug 23 1894	nd
Brinson, John A.	Sep 10 1821	Dec 14 1897
Brinson, Maude Joyner	Aug 28 1913	Dec 21 1966
Brinson, S.B. inf. s/o W.T. & S.E.	Sep 16 1876	Jne 20 1877
Brinson, Sarah	Oct 26 1832	Jan 11 1899
Burke, Allie	Mar 31 1896	Jan 12 1908
Burke, Annie Franklin	Apr 16 1855	Mar 4 1902
Burke, Annie Mae	1903	1926
Burke, Annie W. d/o M.D. & A.	May 21 1884	Oct 15 1890
Burke, Billie	1914	1959
Burke, Emma Peel	1884	nd
Burke, Eula Mae	1904	1930
Burke, Eunice H.	Mar 13 1926	Nov 5 1962
Burke, Eva Gladice d/o J.F. & Lena	Oct 5 1906	Jan 2 1909
Burke, Frances Elizabeth	Jul 11 1919	Dec 30 1953
Burke, Lt. George	age 26y	May 19
Burke, Henrietta w/o Homer	1871	1944
Burke, Homer	1870	1942
Burke, India Norris w/o T.W.	Jan 29 1889	Jul 1 1958
Burke, Infant	only date	1930
Burke, Infant d/o Brantley & Ella	May 12 1932	Apr 25 1935

Burke, Infant	only date	Aug 30 1937
d/o Brantley & Ella		
Burke, Infant	Nov 5 1940	Nov 7 1940
d/o Brantley & Ella		
Burke, Infant	only date	Mar 10 1937
d/o J.M. & Christine		
Burke, Infant	Nov 10 1901	Apr 12 1902
s/o M.D. & Annie		
Burke, Infant	only date	Feb 6 1905
s/o P. Z. & Min.		
Burke, Infant	only date	Jne 21 1915
s/o P. Z. & Min.		
Burke, Infant	only date	Apr 5 1916
s/o P.Z. & Min.		
Burke, Ira Bruno	age 61 y	Apr 18 1954
Burke, James E., Sr.	1873	1942
Burke, Josephine	1911	19__
w/o Leon		
Burke, Julia M.	Aug 24 1886	Jul 18 1890
d/o M.D. & A.		
Burke, Lenna Norris	1880	1960
Burke, Leon	1908	1947
Burke, Louise	1910	1931
Burke, Mabel Peel	Oct 31 1903	L
Burke, Major B.	Dec 10 1889	Feb 4 1896
s/o V.L. & L.A.		
Burke, Major Lee	Oct 27 1893	Oct 18 1896
d/o V.L. & L.A.		
Burke, Mandon J.	Feb 16 1878	Oct 19 1951
Burke, Mary E.	Aug 28 1902	Sep 15 1911
d/o J.E. & Emma		
Burke, Melton D.	Aug 30 1850	May 15 1905
Burke, Millard	Oct 8 1879	Jne 21 1908
Burke, Nancy L.	Feb 23 1855	Jul 6 1903
Burke, Needham Valder WW-I	Feb 6 1893	Nov 11 1940
served in France		
Burke, Ola Norris	Aug 20 1886	May 10 1963
w/o M.J.		
Burke, Ralph	1898	1939
Burke, Mrs. Sallie	age 65 y	Jan 25 1941
Burke, Simeon	Jul 29 1845	Feb 1 1904
Burke, Sophia Frances	Aug 17 1843	Feb 6 1915
Burke, T. L., Sr.	Apr 15 1880	Aug 10 1922
Burke, Thomas Watson	May 30 1892	Jan 1 1938
Burke, W. D.	Jan 9 1847	May 15 1886
Cartin, Infant	only date	1892
of J.B. & A.		
Cartin, J. B.	Nov 2 1862	Oct 31 1891
Cartin, Jimmie C.	Oct 27 1887	Aug 27 1889
Chance, Alice Hill	Dec 17 1911	nd
w/o Byron		
Chance, Alma F.	Feb 11 1900	Feb 29 1972
Chance, Byron Lee (Leo?), Sr.	Jul 12 1911	Jul 19 1950

Name	Birth	Death
Chance, Carroll Edwin s/o E.M. & T.C.	Oct 6 1903	Jne 27 1926
Chance, Edwin B.	Sep 23 1922	Oct 27 1936
Chance, Edwin M.	Sep 26 1872	Apr 24 1948
Chance, Fannie Laurie w/o E.F.	Oct 24 1903	Jne 25 1927
Chance, Floyd C.	Mar 1 1844	Apr 6 1929
Chance, Georgia W. w/o Rufus H.	Oct 28 1868	Apr 9 1941
Chance, Infant s/o E.M. & T.C.	Sep 29 1906	Oct 3 1906
Chance, Infant of B.L. & A.H.	only date	May 4 1934
Chance, Infant	only date	Sep 1964
Chance, Malvin W. s/o E.M. & T.C.	Jne 16 1895	Sep 16 1895
Chance, Mozell w/o Floyd C.	Apr 29 1838	Jul 31 1914
Chance, Rufus H.	Sep 26 1872	Feb 10 1950
Chance, Theodosia Hill w/o Edwin M.	Mar 28 1876	Apr 5 1943
Chew, Benjamin F.	Jne 21 1877	Jul 19 1881
Chew, Elizabeth w/o Hon. John Cottle	May 11 1847	Jul 23 1908
Chew, Hon. John Cottle	Aug 19 1841	Mar 16 1890
Clark, Infant s/o Mr. & Mrs. N.T.	only date	Jne 26 1944
Clark, Infant s/o Mr. & Mrs. N.T.	only date	May 12 1945
Clarke, Blanche B. w/o Eugene	Mar 28 1906	nd
Clarke, Dessie B. w/o N.M.	Mar 12 1894	Dec 16 1964
Clarke, Eugene	Mar 8 1903	May 30 1944
Clarke, Mattie J.	1928	1969
Clarke, Minus J.	Apr 24 1898	Apr 16 1944
Clarke, Nannie H. w/o M.J.	Nov 26 1897	May 15 1952
Clarke, Norman M.	Jul 24 1880	May 25 1966
Clarke, Thelma Louise	Sep 16 1924	Oct 3 1925
Cochran, Mamie	1898	1962
Cochran, Sam L. WW-I	Jne 10 1892	May 26 1951
Cooper, Willie Lee	age 65 y	Sep 5 1961
Dickey, Alabel d/o J. & D.	Jan 22 1879	Aug 27 1879
Dickey, Dillia Ann Elizabeth w/o Joseph	Aug 5 1843	Jan 7 1892
Dickey, George W.	Mar 12 1873	May 8 1918
Dickey, Harlow H. WW-II S/Sgt 663 Field Arty Bn	Nov 30 1911	May 17 1951
Dickey, Herbert H. s/o Zollie & Rosa	Nov 1 1916	Oct 26 1970
Dickey, Infant s/o J. & D.	only date	Jan 18 1869
Dickey, Infant d/o J. & D.	only date	Jul 5 1882

Name	Birth	Death
Dickey, Infant	only date	Apr 28 1906
of G.W. & Leslie		
Dickey, Ira	Mar 20 1915	Jan 13 1922
s/o Mr. & Mrs. Madison		
Dickey, Leslie	Oct 31 1883	Nov 13 1906
w/o G.W.		
Dickey, M. A.	Jul 17 1859	Sep 12 1913
w/o Joseph		
Dickey, Madison	1880	1963
Dickey, Rosa M.	Aug 6 1888	Mar 26 1970
w/o Z.W.		
Dickey, Zollie W.	Apr 27 1884	Jul 18 1937
Dietsch, Artimus J.	1901	1973
Dietsch, Dennis C.	Jne 6 1940	Jan 7 1969
U.S.N.		
Dixon, Barbara J.	1960	1970
Dukes, Hardie L., Sr.	Apr 8 1899	Nov 8 1971
Dulon, Elizabeth	Oct 1830	Dec 1897
w/o Thomas		
Forehand, A. S.	Sep 19 1887	Jul 2 1888
Forehand, S. J.	Dec 4 1857	Jne 4 1888
Franklin, Jesse M., Sr.	Nov 3 1824	Oct 30 ____
Franklin, J. M.	May 27 1862	Jul 15 1900
Franklin, King David	Mar 25 1894	Apr 9 1894
s/o H. & I.D.		
Franklin, Nancy A.	Mar 5 1831	Oct 5 1901
Gerken, Frances H.	Sep 18 1818	Nov 1 1898
w/o Charles H.		
Hall, Charlie Bolton, Sr.	Jan 5 1880	Jan 15 1958
Hall, Martha W.	1906	1940
Hargrove, Addie M.	Apr 16 1892	Aug 16 1898
d/o G.H. & P.		
Hargrove, Alma O.	1901	nd
Hargrove, Carey H.	1888	1970
Hargrove, Debra Ann	Nov 23 1954	Nov 25 1954
Hargrove, Florrie B.	Apr 18 1896	Sep 26 1960
w/o G. W.		
Hargrove, G. H.	May 11 1861	Dec 4 1921
Hargrove, George W.	Dec 8 1897	May 11 1957
Hargrove, Infant	only date	Aug 1902
Hargrove, Infant (twin)	only date	Nov 25 1918
s/o G.W. & F.B.		
Hargrove, Infant (twin)	only date	Jul 6 1919
d/o G.W. & F.B.		
Hargrove, Laura P.	Jul 11 1920	May 31 1921
d/o G.W. & F.B.		
Hargrove, Louie B.	Oct 2 1898	May 19 1899
s/o W.B. & Anna		
Hargrove, Mary Will (twin)	May 12 1905	May 26 1905
Hargrove, Pharabe Wallace	Feb 10 1859	May 30 1935
Hargrove, Quinnie	1894	1967
Hargrove, Robert Alston (twin)	May 12 1905	Aug 2 1905
Hargrove, Robert H.	Oct 15 1896	Aug 28 1898
s/o G.H. & P.		
Hargrove, Mrs. Sallie (Josey?)	age 61 y	Dec 1959

Hargroves, Clyde	Sep 27 1897	Oct 9 1897
s/o W.B. & Anna		
Hargroves, J.H.	Apr 13 1882	Jul 15 1883
Hargroves, S. A.	Feb 19 1837	Mar 6 1915
w/o W.B.		
Hargroves, William B., Sr.	Nov 30 1833	Jne 13 1904

Note: Because of their birth dates, William B. and S.A. are presumably not "W.B. & Anna," listed as the parents of several children (ed).

Herrington, Andrew V.	1855	1934
Herrington, Edwin	1900	1900
Herrington, Ezekiel S. WW-I	Feb 12 1894	Jul 6 1970
Herrington, Leila Thorn	1860	1947
w/o A.V.		
Herrington, Leon	1901	1916
Herrington, Lillie Mae Peel	Mar 24 1904	Nov 8 1927
Herrington, Martin M.	1884	1914
Hickman, Mary Ann	Apr 23 1964	same date
Hurst, Arthur Washington	May 9 1886	Jul 5 1887
s/o Wm. & Drucilla		
Hurst, Candacy	Mar 25 1839	Aug 12 1921
w/o James H.		
Hurst, Eula	1891	1968
Hurst, H. Drucilla Peel	Apr 3 1867	Dec 28 1932
w/o William		
Hurst, James A. CSA	Jan 3 1836	Apr 13 1905
Hurst, Lelia	Jne 20 1880	Sep 8 1885
Hurst, William	Feb 12 1859	Nov 4 1933
Jenkins, Alice	Sep 15 1881	Sep 14 1891
d/o J.M. & N.		
Jenkins, Chas. M.	Sep 2 1900	Mar 18 1901
s/o J.M. & N.		
Jenkins, Infant	only date	Apr 18 1903
of J.M. & N.		
Jenkins, Infant	only date	Apr 18 1903
of J.M. & N.		
Johnson, Infant	only date	1960
Jenkins, James M. WW-II	Jne 6 1924	Apr 12 1968
Ga S/Sgt USAF Kor W		
Johnson, R. W.	Jne 30 1825	Jul 7 1905
Joyner, Carlton E.	Mar 25 1926	Mar 6 1927
s/o Mr. & Mrs. C.J.		
Joyner, Carlton J.	Oct 22 1901	Oct 3 1957
Joyner, Estelle B.	Mar 24 1910	Feb 23 1962
w/o P. E.		
Joyner, Infant	only date	Jan 25 1923
d/o C.J. & J.B.		
Joyner, Infant	nd	nd
s/o P.E. & E.B.		
Joyner, Julia B.	Jne 1 1904	nd
w/o C.J.		
Joyner, Palmer E.	Mar 3 1910	Feb 11 1971
Joyner, Thomas Ward	Dec 28 1865	Jul 5 1901
Joyner, Wm. J. WW-I	Oct 23 1896	Jne 4 1968
Kicklighter, John C.	Jne 23 1913	nd

Kicklighter, Robert Walter s/o H.A. Uhrig	Oct 24 1947	Mar 19 1955
Kicklighter, Richard Arnold s/o Mr. & Mrs. John	May 17 1944	Jul 4 1947
Kicklighter, Sue Hall w/o John C. md Aug 3 1938	only date	Jan 5 1918
Lambert, Annie M.	Apr 4 1902	Jan 17 1969
Lester, Alice Cartin w/o J. B.	Jul 12 1865	Mar 3 1924
Lester, Infant of J.B. & Alice	only date	1892
Lester, J. B.	Nov 2 1862	Oct 31 1891
Lester, Jimmie	Oct 27 1887	Aug 27 1889
Lewis, Dessie M. w/o Lovette	Sep 10 1894	May 20 1959
Lewis, George Grady	Feb 2 1909	Jne 14 1968
Lewis, H. S.	Feb 2 1830	Aug 31 1883
Lewis, Infant s/o J.R. & Minnie L.	only date	1897
Lewis, Infant s/o J.R. & M.L.	only date	1900
Lewis, John Robert	1862	1925
Lewis, Lovette	1889	1904
Lewis, Minnie Lee Darlington w/o John Robert	1871	1939
Lewis, Robert L.	Apr 3 1924	Sep 27 1967
Lewis, Wade Hampton s/o J. R. & Minnie L.	1894	1896
Lightfoot, Archibald	Jne 5 1807	May 23 1871
Lightfoot, Mary	Aug 18 1831	May 2 1906
Lowery, Della Grimes w/o L.E.	Jul 21 1882	May 16 1964
Lowery, Lawrence E.	Jne 4 1882	Feb 8 1968
Lowery, Lawrence E., Jr.	Jul 1 1910	Feb 26 1959
Massey, Carol Reginald s/o C.M.	Mar 15 1921	Dec 18 1921
Mays, Carrie d/o Mr. & Mrs. E.O.	Mar 18 1893	Sep 4 1898
Mays, Infant s/o Mr. & Mrs. C.J.	nd	nd
Mayo, Joel E. WW-II Cpl USA	Jul 11 1910	Dec 24 1971
McCoy, Alexander	Apr 3 1834	Jul 26 1912
McCoy, Augustus C. s/o J.M. & Martha	Sep 20 1859	Feb 9 1897
McCoy, Elizabeth	1835	Apr 18 1911
McCoy, Francis B. s/o J.M. & M.	age 2m 11d	Oct 11 1861
McCoy, Infant inf/o R.L. & Annie	only date	Jul 27 1880
McCoy, Infant d/o R.P. & L.R.	only date	Dec 2 1888
McCoy, Infant of R.P. & L.R.	only date	Jul 5 1898

95

McCoy, John s/o J.M. & M.	age 6y 5m 2d	Oct	2 1860
McCoy, John M.	Aug 20 1824	Apr	9 1894
McCoy, Martha W. Perkins w/o John M.	Mar 21 1824	May 14 1881
McCoy, Samuel h/o Nancy	Apr 2 1838	Apr 16 1904
McCrackle, Beverly Ann d/o John	only date	Mar 20 1955
McGlohorn,_____ WW-I	only date	Nov 26 1925
McGlohorn, Atticus H.	Aug 7 1884	Dec 27 1942
McGlohorn, Fannie B.	1890	1966
McGlohorn, Groover	Jan 12 1919	Feb 23 1943
McGlohorn, Grover WW-I Ga Recruit 31 RCT Co Gen Serv Inf	only date	Oct 13 1918
McGlohorn, Infant of Henry & Hesteran	only date	Jne 30 1900
McGlohorn, John WW-I Ga Pvt 26 Regt CAC	nd	Nov 26 1925
McGlohorn, Madron s/o Henry & Hesteran	Sep 4 1905	Jan 4 1906
McGlohorn, Miriam	May 16 1925	Jne 7 1925
McMillan, Nancy	age 87y	Jne 20 1903
Messex, Ethel Raygood w/o J. A.	Mar 28 1885	Jul 26 1951
Messex, Infant of Mr. & Mrs. Ray	only date	Sep 6 1939
Messex, James Andrew	Oct 25 1889	nd
Mock, Eva L.	1903	1972
Mock, Sol	1901	1940
Moore, Mollie	Feb 24 1849	Dec 29 1919
Moore, Thomas	Dec 10 1839	Aug 27 1913
Murphy, Eddie	Dec 24 1893	Feb 16 1973
Murphy, Sylvetta Sharp	Jan 14 1911	nd
Murrow, Sarah W. Thorn w/o Rev. J.B.	May 29 1831	Nov 10 1898
Norris, J.N.	1846	Oct 7 1922
Norris, Martin Bartow s/o J.N. & S.	Mar 14 1891	Oct 27 1898
Norris, Sabra w/o J.N.	Apr 12 1861	Jul 17 1928
Oglesby, Charles O.	Oct 17 1941	Mar 18 1950
Palmer, Estelle B.	Mar 24 1910	Feb 23 1962
Peel, Bennie F. s/o L.S. & Mary	Oct 5 1871	Mar 16 1874
Peel, Bennie W.	1874	19__
Peel, Dempsey Frank	May 17 1851	Feb 28 1920
Peel, Edgar Preston s/o D.E. & Susan	Jul 31 1880	May 1 1884
Peel, George Mills	Nov 10 1905	Aug 31 1910
Peel, Gussie w/o R. L.	Oct 1 1884	nd
Peel, Harriett w/o Levi S.	Sep 21 1812	Jan 9 1890
Peel, Henry F. s/o L.S. & M.	Dec 4 1888	Mar 20 1893

96

Peel, Infant	only	date	May 20 1887
s/o L.S. & M.			
Peel, Infant	only	date	Sep 30 1903
s/o Mr. & Mrs. Percy			
Peel, Infant	only	date	Dec 10 1877
s/o W.M. & Olive			
Peel, Johnie Otis	Sep 11 1897	Jne 23 1905	
Peel, Levi	Jne 10 1814	Jne 10 1895	
Peel, Levi S.	Dec 11 1846	Dec 31 1920	
Peel, Lula M. Bragg	Dec 7 1886	Feb 25 1967	
w/o L.L.			
Peel, Luther L.	Apr 23 1882	Oct 4 1960	
Peel, Mary	Jne 29 1850	Sep 4 1927	
w/o Levi S.			
Peel, Mary Frances Wallace	Feb 12 1854	Oct 19 1920	
Peel, Mathew W.	1885	1953	
Peel, Olive Dickey	Jne 9 1844	Jul 29 1909	
w/o W.M.			
Peel, Quinton	Jne 1 1882	Feb 12 1900	
Peel, R. E.	Jul 1 1853	Mar 18 1914	
Peel, Robert Lee	Feb 14 1874	Jul 24 1947	
Peel, Rosa Lee	1876	1943	
w/o Bennie W.			
Peel, Sebron Lafayette	age 1y 7m	Aug 21 1873	
s/o W.M. & Olive	9d		
Peel, Susan McCoy	Apr 24 1857	Jne 3 1940	
w/o Dempsey F.			
Peel, W. M.	Nov 29 1840	Mar 14 1923	
Peel, Wade H.	Feb 22 1878	Oct 12 1916	
Perkins, Eliza	age 29 y	May 10 1863	
w/o Marshall			
Prince, Dewey	1904	1963	
Prince, L. W.	Feb 20 1878	Sep 10 1936	
Prince, Lila Norris	1883	1962	
Pye, Walter F. WW-II	Feb 25 1911	Sep 8 1959	
Ga M/Sgt LM USA			
Rabitsch, Augustus F.	Feb 12 1878	Jul 4 1928	
Rabitsch, Infant	only	date	Apr 21 1904
Rabitsch, Infant	only	date	Dec 15 1905
Rabitsch, Infant	only	date	Sep 14 1911
Rabitsch, Infant	Aug 25 1914	Sep 1 1914	
Rabitsch, Infant	same	date	Dec 16 1909
d/o W. R. & Isabella			
Rabitsch, Isabell	1873	1949	
w/o W. R.			
Rabitsch, Virginia E.	May 27 1886	Dec 23 1929	
w/o Augustus F.			
Rabitsch, W. R.	nd	1871	
Redd, Corneilus E.	1872	1939	
Redd, I. H.	Jne 26 1868	Sep 27 1916	
Redd, Isadore H.	Jne 10 1914	Nov 23 1972	
s/o Melba Redd Johnson			
Redd, John E.	Jan 14 1861	Apr 2 1928	

Redd, Nancy A.	Nov 8 1843	Oct 3 1909
w/o Wm. A.		
Redd, W. A.	May 15 1838	Oct 16 1911
Redd, Wanda Sue	Oct 14 1963	Dec 14 1963
d/o Mr. & Mrs. Wilbur		
Reynolds, Bessie Lou Hargroves	Dec 31 1889	nd
w/o Thos. W.		
Reynolds, Cleo	only date	Jul 18 1920
inf d/o Mr. & Mrs. T. W.		
Reynolds, George M.	Dec 19 1900	Jan 18 1973
Reynolds, Infant	nd	nd
Reynolds, Joe Ellis	Jan 16 1907	Oct 20 1970
Reynolds, Joseph W.	Sep 7 1860	Dec 4 1933
Reynolds, Martha	Dec 2 1830	May 14 1905
w/o Wright R.		
Reynolds, Theresa T.	Apr 1 1865	Dec 2 1958
w/o Joseph W.		
Reynolds, Thomas Wright	Oct 6 1889	Nov 5 1969
Rowe, Rosa M.	Mar 10 1900	Mar 26 1900
d/o W. & E.		
Salley, Albert	Nov 21 1944	nd
Salley, Theresa J.	Jan 27 1963	Mar 23 1973
Salley, Wray Jean	Sep 24 1945	Mar 22 1973
Seats, Joe Clarke	Dec 24 1843	Feb 22 1920
Sharpe, Alquin H.	May 4 1912	1969
Sharpe, Katie Bragg	Jne 3 1889	Apr 27 1966
w/o Robert D.		
Sharpe, N. (?)	only date	1966
Sharpe, Robert David	Nov 17 1883	Dec 15 1949
Shonk, Micky Lee	1965	1965
Shonk, Nicky Lee	1965	1965
Smith, James	Jan 1932	Sep 1939
s/o Roy & Ella		
Sowell, J. Alex	1904	1973
Spence, Dyte Olliff	Jul 8 1899	May 24 1932
w/o Emory O.		
Spence, Emory Olliff	Sep 30 1928	Nov 12 1928
Stalnaker, Mary L.	May 2 1834	Apr 10 1911
Stephens, Frances	Sep 10 1920	Jne 22 1923
Stephens, Myra B.	Oct 30 1901	Aug 15 1927
Taylor, Roy W.	Feb 9 1909	Nov 9 1969
Thompson, Brent Allen	Dec 2 1972	Dec 12 1972
Thorn, Abigal	Mar 25 1902	Jne 3 1904
Thorn, Henry Lee	Aug 22 1880	Sep 30 1886
Thorn, Infant	only date	Dec 15 1889
Thorn, Leslie	Feb 29 1888	Apr 11 1902
Thorn, M. B.	Jul 31 1833	Dec 29 1901
Thorn, Mary A.	Jne 12 1838	Feb 2 1907
Thorn, Mattie Moore	Oct 3 1860	May 22 1884
Thorn, Thomas W.	Dec 20 1890	Jne 20 1901
Thorn, W. B.	Apr 1 1877	Mar 4 1941
Thorn, Wadie A.	Feb 10 1882	Jan 28 1883
Thorne, Anna	Mar 3 1869	Dec 25 1929
w/o Edwin L.		
Thorne, Edwin L.	Aug 16 1854	Mar 26 1932

Wallace, Arthur Larie	Jan 17 1883	Jan 30 1951
Wallace, Barney V.	Aug 24 1895	Jan 3 1911
s/o S.V. & W.K.		
Wallace, Beuliah V.	Jan 19 1890	Apr 3 1890
Wallace, Cora Lee	Dec 13 1894	Dec 11 1935
Wallace, Cora Thorne	Apr 1 1866	Nov 10 1960
w/o E.N. md 1st T.W. Joyner		
Wallace, Curtis Waldo	Jan 23 1933	Dec 1 1935
Wallace, D.D.	Oct 4 1827	Oct 20 1873
Wallace, Dora L.	1894	1972
w/o E.N.		
Wallace, Enoch N.	Jul 2 1861	Apr 29 1939
Wallace, Enoch N.	Sep 30 1892	Mar 12 1971
Wallace, Esther J.	Jul 14 1861	Aug 22 1914
w/o E.N.		
Wallace, Frances Hall	Dec 1 1900	May 29 1933
w/o Lafe Pence		
Wallace, Infant	Mar 18 1900	Apr 3 1900
d/o E.N. & E.J.		
Wallace, Infant	only date	Oct 30 1938
d/o Robt. & Pauline		
Wallace, Isaiah Wellington	Feb 25 1852	Sep 20 1853
s/o D.D. & Jincy		
Wallace, Jennie Brinson	Dec 18 1870	Jne 30 1873
Wallace, Jessie Herrington	Sep 15 1895	Apr 17 1970
w/o Matthew		
Wallace, Jincy	Sep 29 1828	Nov 7 1906
Wallace, John Thomas	Jan 16 1924	Jan 17 1970
Wallace, Lafe Pence	Aug 15 1893	Jan 30 1941
Wallace, Lottie Zeigler	Jne 25 1879	Mar 20 1971
w/o Arthur Larie		
Wallace, Matthew	May 13 1891	Jan 9 1967
Wallace, Osceola	Sep 10 1889	Jne 26 1890
inf/o S.V. & W.K.		
Wallace, Pauline H.	Jne 27 1904	nd
w/o Robert		
Wallace, Pauline V. Perkins	May 16 1843	Feb 15 1919
w/o Robert W.		
Wallace, Robert	Jul 21 1891	Jan 14 1968
Wallace, Robert W.	Jne 20 1854	Jan 28 1942
Wallace, Rozzie	1873	1920
w/o Clarence W.		
Wallace, Rubye Faye S.	Feb 22 1926	nd
w/o John T.		
Wallace, S. Victor	Jne 14 1865	Dec 19 1946
Wallace, Styring W.	Feb 9 1888	Oct 30 1889
s/o S.V. & W.K.		
Wallace, Tommie	Jul 31 1902	Feb 23 1904
s/o S.V. & W.K.		
Wallace, Winnie K.	Sep 28 1863	Jne 4 1933
w/o S. Victor		
Weese, Thomas Eugene Viet W	Jne 6 1944	Mar 23 1971
Ga Pvt Ord Dept		
Wiggins, John K. WW-II	Nov 8 1922	Dec 27 1971
Williams, Betsy	May 17 1892	May 4 1906

Williams, Hoke		1910	1944
Williams, Infant	only	date	Mar 11 1890
s/o S.B. & J.D.			
Williams, Infant	only	date	May 10 1898
s/o S. & J.L.			
Williams, Infant	only	date	Jul 14 1899
s/o S. & J.L.			
Williams, Infant	Aug 1 1918	Jan 9 1919	
s/o S.M. P. & M.			
Williams, John E.		1897	1946
Williams, Maggie A.		1873	1958
Wilson, Bertie Waters		1899	nd
w/o David C.			
Wilson, David C.		1884	1950

59. GREINER

Greiner, Robert H. CSA   Aug 7 1845 Nov 3 1920
  b Augusta, Ga.
  Co A 27 Bn Ga Inf

60. GRESHAM

Gresham, Job   Jul 20 1781 Jne 6 1846
  b King & Queen Co., Va. Member Baptist Church
  Note: This Job, the founder of the Gresham family in
  Burke Co., was the son of Job and Mary Byne of King &
  Queen Co., Va. Some time before 1800, however, the
  father Job moved his family to Lincoln Co., Kentucky,
  but this son, when he was not more than 18 or 19 years
  old, struck out on his own and with one companion came
  on horseback from Kentucky to Burke Co. where his
  grandfather, the Rev. Edmund Byne, and a large family
  (including grown sons) had settled in 1785, having
  migrated from Virginia. Initially, Job worked for
  his uncle, Thomas Byne (ed).
Gresham, Mary Jones   Jul 10 1785 Jan 21 1812
  b Burke Co. w/o Job
  Note: Mary, the daughter of John & Margaret Walker
  Jones, married Job about 1800-1801. They had three
  children, a daughter who died in infancy and two sons,
  Edmund Byne and John Jones. She died when her second
  son was born. Her grave marker reads, "This stone
  erected to Mary Jones Gresham by her son for whose
  life she gave her own." Walter A. Clark, A Lost
  Arcadia, 1909, pp. 161-163, treats of the Gresham
  family. See also Testimonials to the Life and
  Character of John Jones Gresham, John Murphy & Co.,
  Printers, Baltimore, 1892, especially pp 61-72, and
  the sketch of John Jones Gresham in Myers, The
  Children of Pride (full citation supra, p. 14 (ed).

HABERSHAM METHODIST
Jenkins Co.

Adams, Bessie Lou Jenkins	Mar 2 1910	Jan 20 1949
w/o T.M. /Arrington		
buried beside her first husband		
Adams, Joel M.	Jul 22 1860	Oct 21 1896
Adams, Sara	Sep 26 1855	Apr 18 1904
w/o Joel M.		
Adams, T.M.	age 37 y	Dec 11 1929
Allen, Daisy Landing	Jan 26 1880	Apr 15 1962
w/o D.B.		
Allen, David Benton	Nov 27 1887	Nov 27 1939
Allen, George Edward	Jul 3 1859	Jul 5 1915
Allen, Mary	Sep 13 1861	Jne 4 1901
w/o Geo. Edw.		
Anderson, James T.	1873	1946
Anderson, Mamie C.	1879	1933
w/o James T.		
Andrews, Ronald Comer	Sep 25 1910	Nov 28 1936
Bargeron, James A. WW-II	Jan 28 1923	Dec 23 1943
Ga PFC Coast Arty Corps	d Fiji Islands	
Bargeron, Kenneth	Apr 8 1935	Feb 1 1936
s/o Sidney & Julia		
Bargeron, Minnie L.	1890	1969
w/o Tannie R.		
Bargeron, Sam	1915	1954
Bargeron, Tannie R.	1880	1946
Baxley, Elias J.	Aug 3 1865	Dec 8 1939
Baxley, Emma Lou	Dec 29 1874	Dec 9 1935
w/o Elias J.		
Baxley, Infant	nd	nd
Baxley, Mary E.	Aug 29 1865	Mar 9 1911
w/o E.J.		
Baxley, Walter	Apr 25 1900	Jan 21 1901
Baxter, Fannie C.	Feb 28 1857	Jul 21 1914
Baxter, George F.	Feb 25 1858	Nov 3 1913
Baxter, Walter F.	Feb 1 1899	Mar 6 1906
Bell, Abbie Jane	Aug 26 1861	Jan 13 1931
w/o Henry G.		
Bell, Alcimus Overn	Dec 2 1903	Aug 25 1967
Ga Pvt Co C 29 Inf		
Bell, Almeade G.	1864	1928
Bell, Amanda J.	1857	1914
Bell, Amarintha	Feb 10 1886	Dec 5 1886
d/o Feddy D. & Fanny F.		
Bell, Berry	age 64 y	Jne 12 1973
Bell, Berry A.	1851	1901
Bell, Dora Allmond	1899	1967
w/o John Wesley		
Bell, Edgar T.	Oct 24 1917	Oct 10 1943
Bell, Edla C.	1899	nd
w/o James H.		
Bell, Elizabeth C. Langley	1835	1918
w/o Isaiah A.		
Bell, Ella Fair	1846	1937

```
Bell, Emma                                    1888      Feb 12 1950
Bell, Fannie                                  1890             1892
  d/o Mr. & Mrs. F.D.
Bell, Fannie Crozier                          1856             1890
  w/o Fred D.
Bell, Feddie Clark               May 15 1888      Jul 28 1915
  w/o Seaborn D.  d/o G.W. & Susan
Bell, Frederick D.               Sep    1858      Apr    1919
Bell, Hallie Henry               Oct 27 1888      Nov 25 1934
Bell, Henry Green                Sep  7 1859      Nov 11 1911
Bell, Hoke S.  WW-II             Dec 13 1905      Apr 10 1943
  Ga 1st Lt 135 Inf 34 Div
Bell, Isaiah A.                               1832             1904
Bell, J. B.                      Jan 23 1887      Mar  9 1897
  s/o H.G. & Abbie J.
Bell, James Horace                            1896             1967
Bell, Joe B.  WW-II              Jul  4 1907      Aug 20 1958
  Ga PVT USA
Bell, Joe, Sr.                                1910             1971
Bell, John Wesley                             1844             1894
Bell, John Wesley  WW-I          Jul  5 1889      Oct  8 1954
  Ga Sgt USA
Bell, Lloyd  WW-II               Feb  3 1903      Aug 18 1966
  Ga PVT USA
Bell, Maggie Chance              Mar 20 1879      Apr  5 1946
  d/o Geo. E.C. & Mittie  sis/o Edw. F.
Bell, Malary A.                  Nov  7 1881      Jul 17 1886
  s/o H. G. & Abbie J.
Bell, Mary Ola Herrington        Feb    1894      Sep    1915
  w/o E.B.
Bell, Ozzie F.                                1876             1930
Bell, Seaborn O.                 Feb 29 1876      Nov  3 1934
Bell, Wm. Kendrick               Jul 12 1929      Feb 12 1934
Bell, Wm. Thomas                 Feb 15 1882      Jne 24 1952
Bell, Willie  WW-II              Jul  8 1906      Oct 14 1965
  Ga PVT USA
Bell, Willie A.                               1872             1917
Bell, Willie M. Chance           Jan 29 1883      Jan  9 1923
  w/o Wm. T.
Black, Arthur                    Jne 30 1886      Aug  8 1958
Brinson, Andrew Jackson          Apr 20 1869      Oct 10 1945
Brinson, Carnie H.  WW-I         Jne  9 1892      May 24 1958
  Ga CPL USA
Brinson, Cyperon A.                           1861             1923
Brinson, DeWitt C.               age 70 y         Jul 23 1966
Brinson, Douglas                 Sep 10 1864      Oct  4 1949
Brinson, Mrs. E. A.              Jne 13 1829      Apr  4 1901
Brinson, Fannie H.                            1857             1926
Brinson, James B.                Oct  3 1885      Dec 28 1962
Brinson, Jasper Douglas          Sep  1 1926      Feb 23 1941
  s/o Carnie & Mildred
Brinson, Jasper E.                            1860             1933
Brinson, L.M.                    Mar 16 1866      Jan  9 1901
Brinson, Lilla B.                Dec 25 1895      Dec 29 1966
  w/o Jas. B.
```

Name	Birth	Death
Brinson, Maggie H.	1864	1955
w/o J.E.		
Brinson, Mattie Lou	Aug 1 1876	Jul 4 1934
w/o Andrew J.		
Brinson, Mildred Jenkins	Nov 3 1896	Oct 26 1928
w/o C.H.		
Brinson, Myra E.	Oct 28 1920	Jul 26 1923
d/o Ranse & Leta C.		
Brookins, Nellie Sapp	Aug 19 1888	Sep 8 1958
Brookins, William Judge	Sep 11 1883	Jan 27 1965
Broxton, Annie E.	Apr 15 1874	Aug 22 1889
Broxton, Infant	only date	Aug 22 1888
d/o Mr. & Mrs. S.L.		
Broxton, Ira	1926	1967
Broxton, Octavia	Oct 20 1851	Oct 23 1944
w/o Seaborn L.		
Broxton, Seaborn L.	Nov 28 1846	May 20 1911
Bryant, Woudia M.	Jul 3 1904	Nov 4 1926
Butler, Farah Bell	1886	1912
Butler, Mary W.	Jan 17 1897	nd
w/o Tate		
Butler, Tate	Nov 30 1884	Dec 19 1958
Carpenter, Infant	May 11 1906	May 19 1906
d/o J.N. & Julia S.		
Carpenter, Joe Brown	Dec 1 1881	Feb 25 1920
Carpenter, John N.	1853	1930
Carpenter, Josephine S.	Aug 26 1869	Oct 8 1901
Carpenter, Julia C.	1881	1923
Carpenter, Julius Malcolm	1883	1956
Carpenter, Maggie Reeves	1888	1966
w/o J.M.		
Carpenter, Nannie M.	Jul 11 1900	Dec 14 1901
Carpenter, Nina Lee Reeves	Oct 23 1886	Mar 3 1920
w/o Joe Brown		
Carpenter, Sam M.	age 83 y	Jan 21 1973
Carpenter, Thomas E.	Oct 3 1887	Dec 20 1928
Chance, Addie Roberson	Jne 12 1874	Jan 17 1942
w/o Willie Darden		
Chance, Alfred	nd	nd
br/o Geo. E.C.		
Chance, Aura Wade	Mar 20 1895	Oct 17 1917
Chance, Daisy Reeves	Jul 28 1878	Jne 6 1925
w/o Edw. F. d/o Geo. W. & Caroline L.		
Chance, Edward Franklin	Feb 16 1874	Mar 24 1952
s/o Geo. E.C. & Mittie		
Chance, Ella R.	1865	1943
w/o James H.		
Chance, Mrs. F.C.	Jan 28 1855	Aug 27 1927
Chance, Frances Reeves	Mar 4 1854	Apr 21 1938
Chance, Francis Neely	nd	nd
s/o James H. & Ella		
Chance, G.A., Sr.	Feb 22 1880	Mar 27 1948
Chance, George E.C.	Mar 14 1846	May 6 1920
Chance, Henry C.	1880	1951

Chance, James Daniel	Jan 30 1890	Jul 2 1913
s/o W.D. & Addie		
Chance, James F.	Feb 14 1825	Jne 22 1892
Chance, James H.	1858	1920
Chance, Louis Duncan	Jul 10 1849	Apr 8 1909
Chance, Mae H.	1889	19__
Chance, Mary V.	Nov 30 1836	Jan 23 1922
w/o James F.		
Chance, Mittie	Feb 20 1850	Aug 30 1926
w/o Geo. E. C.		
Chance, Tommie Gussie	Nov 30 1885	Mar 17 1959
Chance, Willie Darden	Mar 9 1861	Jne 5 1920
Chester, Eugene H.	Feb 24 1901	Sep 15 1959
Chester, M.E.A.	Mar 8 1873	Jne 18 1885
d/o J.J. & M.A.D.		
Chester, Mattie R.	Aug 1 1872	Feb 17 1959
Chester, Willie B.	Feb 28 1870	Feb 3 1945
Clark, Emily	Jan 27 1823	Sep 9 1907
w/o John		
Crozier, Amrintha Davis	1827	1913
w/o Elbert B.		
Crozier, E.B.	Nov 27 1824	Feb 9 1897
Crozier, John T.	Feb 25 1852	Apr 8 1887
s/o Elbert & Amarintha		
Cullen, Mittie M.	Apr 19 1910	Jne 23 1948
Daniel, Mary Lillian	Oct 11 1901	Mar 8 1902
Flakes, Edward L. WW-I	Mar 7 1896	Aug 30 1969
Ga PVT USA		
Flakes, Infant	only date	Jne 17 1958
Godbee, Almanda	Jul 6 1831	Jne 30 1915
w/o J.R.		
Godbee, Fannie M.	Apr 26 1871	May 29 1904
w/o J.L.		
Godbee, Homer E.	May 10 1858	Feb 18 1912
Godbee, James R.	Nov 30 1826	Feb 1 1897
Godbee, Mattie Hargroves	Oct 10 1865	Nov 6 1934
w/o Homer E.		
Godbee, Twiggs R.	Mar 25 1888	Aug 19 1963
Greiner, Palmer Kay (infant)	only date	Dec 19 1960
Gunn, Seabie Reeves	1913	nd
Gunn, Terry	1905	1964
Haeseler, Sarah Reese	Nov 12 1837	Apr 1 1918
Hall, Mary Kilpatrick	Oct 19 1853	Mar 15 1929
w/o Verdery		
Hargrove, H. Melton	1849	1907
Hatcher, John Earnest	Sep 5 1907	Jan 10 1911
s/o W.A. & M.L.		
Hatcher, Julian C.	1904	1934
Hawes, Marion Lee	1884	1964
Hawes, Sadie Chance	1895	nd
w/o Marion Lee		
Heath, Nina C.	Jne 30 1881	Jan 29 1968
Herrington, B. Terrell	Aug 9 1888	Aug 18 1968
Herrington, Berry	Jan 26 1818	Aug 27 1886
s/o Martin & Nancy		

Herrington, Essie B. w/o W. Holmes	Aug 31 1890	Dec 8 1970
Herrington, Frances L. w/o Berry	Mar 25 1832	Nov 17 1895
Herrington, Infant	nd	nd
Herrington, Stephen M. s/o Martin & Nancy	Nov 28 1825	Jul 7 1881
Herrington, W. Holmes	Mar 27 1882	Mar 7 1959
Hillis, Wilbur Cleveland	May 1 1916	Jul 28 1964
Hopper, Claude W.	Nov 26 1862	Nov 8 1904
Hopper, Infant s/o C.W. & Mattie M.	Jne 19 1887	Nov 10 1887
Hopper, Mattie Rogers w/o Claude W.	Jne 28 1867	Mar 4 1944
Horton, Katie K. w/o Leonard H.	1898	nd
Horton, Leonard Hayes	1889	1952
Jackson, J. Clinton	1914	1971
Jenkins, Agnes C. w/o Berry	May 20 1848	Jan 10 1926
Jenkins, Carrie Brinson w/o Wafford B.	1878	1912
Jenkins, Charles J.	Dec 20 1910	Jul 20 1964
Jenkins, Charlie	1880	1935
Jenkins, Cora Chance	1877	1969
Jenkins, Frank	1871	1933
Jenkins, George Pierce	Jne 9 1877	Nov 29 1965
Jenkins, Hattie L.	1878	1947
Jenkins, Inez Reeves w/o Geo. Pierce	Dec 12 1880	Jan 2 1956
Jenkins, Infant s/o Mr. & Mrs. F.H.	nd	nd
Jenkins, Izatus	Aug 30 1876	Aug 8 1962
Jenkins, Jane E. Kilpatrick	Oct 26 1846	Oct 20 1899
Jenkins, L. Berry	Jan 7 1842	Mar 31 1916
Jenkins, Malva Bell w/o Izatus	Jan 18 1882	Mar 31 1939
Jenkins, Minnie Lee Bell w/o Pead H.	Aug 26 1873	Jan 24 1905
Jenkins, Pead Harrison	Nov 10 1862	Sep 24 1933
Jenkins, Rufus Rogers s/o Wilson & Jane	Jan 1 1875	Sep 13 1889
Jenkins, W. Ben	Jan 31 1906	Jul 3 1918
Jenkins, Wafford Bennias	1870	1945
Johnson, Emma Lee Jenkins w/o W.O.	Feb 20 1899	Apr 5 1927
Joiner, Allie B.	Oct 12 1899	May 10 1900
Joiner, Anna w/o Thomas	Dec 11 1861	Aug 7 1943
Joiner, Ellen D. w/o Thomas	Apr 9 1829	Jne 13 1893
Joiner, Emily Skinner w/o Tillman	Mar 28 1851	May 14 1908
Joiner, Ethel	Sep 5 1917	Jul 11 1918
Joiner, Johnnie s/o T.D. & Emily	Aug 19 1889	same date

Joiner, Lula M. w/o Matthew E.	Aug 8 1872	Nov 24 1921
Joiner, Mark T. WW-I Ga PVT USA	Mar 11 1894	Feb 8 1972
Joiner, Matthew E.	Sep 17 1866	Nov 1 1934
Joiner, Minnie L.	Jul 11 1894	Oct 21 1900
Joiner, Thomas	Jan 6 1828	Aug 15 1922
Joiner, Tillman D.	Dec 13 1849	Jne 24 1930
Joiner, Willie Wade s/o T.D. & Emily L.	Dec 1 1886	May 29 1891
Joiner, Winnie E.	Jan 9 1897	Jul 19 1904
Joyner, Albert W., Sr.	1915	1964
Joyner, Bertha H.	1898	1972
Joyner, Jethro Clinton	Apr 24 1907	Sep 30 1928
Joyner, Lillie Stone w/o Wm. Frank	May 26 1867	Sep 20 1928
Joyner, Robert Dewey	Feb 6 1900	Feb 14 1924
Joyner, William Frank	Dec 1 1849	Sep 5 1928
Kilpatrick, Buford Dalstine WW-II Ga T Sgt USAF Korea s/o Ella G. & Freeman G.	Nov 23 1909	Aug 24 1955
Kilpatrick, Ella C. w/o Freeman G.	1868	1916
Kilpatrick, Freeman G.	1858	1918
Kilpatrick, John W. WW-I Ga PVT USA	Feb 3 1892	May 12 1967
Kilpatrick, Louis Dean s/o Ella C. & Freeman G.	Aug 30 1901	Oct 28 1930
Knight, Mrs. Daisy Flakes	age 58 y	Oct 6 1969
Lambert, George W.	1870	1949
Lambert, Hattie L. w/o Geo. W.	1873	1958
Lambert, James A.	Sep 10 1833	Feb 27 1908
Lambert, James W. Viet W Ga PFC USA	May 26 1941	Jul 15 1970
Lambert, L.L.	May 18 1876	Sep 18 1901
Lambert, Walter Lee	Apr 30 1915	Sep 19 1959
Landing, Eliza w/o William G.	Aug 29 1835	Mar 13 1912
Landing, Elvira Bell w/o Ransom	Oct 15 1829	Aug 3 1923
Landing, Katie Lambert	Sep 27 1877	Jan 12 1958
Landing, Ransom	Jan 27 1847	Jan 21 1917
Landing, William G.	Dec 26 1835	Dec 30 1907
Landing, Willie Waldon	Jul 22 1870	Nov 7 1935
Lariscy, Josie R.	1903	1947
Lewis, Audrey C. w/o Willie R.	Mar 24 1897	Jne 20 1968
Lewis, George W.	May 9 1854	Jne 15 1916
Lewis, J. A. h/o Sallie	Jan 1 1855	Dec 22 1910
Lewis, John Wesley	Feb 8 1851	Dec 9 1930
Lewis, Lena d/o Geo. & Lena	1894	1900
Lewis, Lena E. w/o Geo. W.	Apr 9 1871	Jne 19 1895

Lewis, Willie R.	Sep 10 1894	Nov 16 1955
McClure, Mattie Alma	Sep 12 1887	Nov 25 1887
d/o H.E. & Alma		
Messex, Charles W.	Dec 10 1891	Jne 22 1899
Messex, L.J.	Aug 22 1852	Dec 19 1927
Messex, Martha	Jan 20 1865	Jan 29 1941
Oglesby, Hattie Nora	Oct 9 1892	Apr 14 1928
d/o W.R. & E.B.		
Perry, J. D. F&AM	1821	1899
Perry, J. H. F&AM	1850	1876
Prescott, Argyle B.	Sep 20 1900	Jul 31 1960
Prescott, Carl Oscar	Dec 1 1898	Jan 31 1966
Prescott, Eugene W.	Sep 31 1904	Jan 14 1958
Prescott, Georgia Fordham	Nov 14 1903	Feb 1 1965
w/o Carl O.		
Prescott, Joseph Powell	Mar 5 1873	Sep 19 1926
Prescott, Leila Bargeron	Dec 3 1872	Aug 7 1945
w/o Joseph P.		
Prescott, Robert L.	1908	1940
Prescott, Sylvia	Jul 6 1936	Jul 2 1945
d/o Carl O. & Georgia Fordham		
Prescott, Wilbur H.	1902	1934
Prickell, Penny R.	May 8 1961	May 12 1961
Pritchett, John W.	Feb 13 1861	Sep 4 1941
Pritchett, Mary J.	Feb 2 1873	Jne 13 1950
Reese, Joel W.	May 9 1832	Jne 17 1869
Reese, Narcissa	Oct 1 1855	Oct 10 1932
Reeves, Caroline L.	1846	1916
w/o George W.		
Reeves, Comfort	1812	1885
w/o Riley		
Reeves, Cora D.	1861	1930
w/o D. B.		
Reeves, David B.	1858	1928
Reeves, George W. CSA	1844	1914
s/o Riley & Comfort		
Co E 7 Ga Cav		
Reeves, Helen	Oct 7 1896	Dec 29 1896
Reeves, Herman Urquhart	Oct 10 1877	Jne 15 1901
s/o W.S. & M.A.		
Reeves, Lessie Broxton	1890	1971
w/o Victor H.		
Reeves, Lola L.	Mar 19 1883	Mar 2 1965
w/o Riley W.		
Reeves, Marion	Sep 29 1900	May 27 1901
d/o C.O. & M.L.		
Reeves, Marion WW-II	Nov 8 1917	Jan 25 1963
Ga Cpl USA BSM		
Reeves, Mildred M.	Jan 17 1894	Aug 8 1895
Reeves, Mittie Reese	1865	1902
w/o Riley W.		
Reeves, Riley	1818	1883
Reeves, Riley W.	Aug 24 1864	Jan 14 1940
Reeves, Rosa Wilcox	Nov 20 1863	Jne 16 1936
w/o Simeon Lee		

Reeves, Sim A.	Mar	8 1897	Sep	11 1971
Reeves, Simeon Lee	Aug	28 1862	May	23 1940
Reeves, Thomas Warren	Apr	8 1876	Jan	23 1906
Reeves, Velpeau		1910		1924
Reeves, Victor H.		1885		1970
Roberson, A.J.		1807	Feb	6 1872
Roberson, Turner	Apr	1805	Apr	26 1879
Robinson, John T.	Jan	7 1852	Nov	11 1928
Rogers, Alliean Lucile	Oct	12 1877	Sep	24 1906
w/o L.P.				
Rogers, Infant		nd		nd
d/o L.P. & A.L.				
Rogers, Infant		nd		nd
s/o L.P. & A.L.				
Rogers, J. Rufus	Mar	15 1828	Mar	1 1908
Rogers, Nancy B.	Mar	29 1843	Nov	9 1899
w/o J. Rufus				
Royal, Benjamin F. CSA		nd		nd
Co E Cobb's Ga Legion				
Sheppard, Sara G.	Nov	5 1896	Sep	3 1955
buried in Godbee section				
Sikes, Fannie L.	Sep	23 1885	Apr	25 1968
w/o Thomas R.				
Sikes, Thomas R.	Oct	15 1883	Apr	18 1929
Skinner, Alice Maud Bentley	Nov	3 1877	Dec	3 1959
w/o Robt. L.				
Skinner, Benjamin Franklin	Nov	15 1860	Jne	10 1938
Skinner, Mrs. F.E.	Jul	10 1829	Mar	21 1888
Skinner, J. H.	Sep	24 1826	Nov	10 1906
Skinner, Jonas Hardy	Mar	9 1903	Nov	9 1971
Skinner, Mattie Trueza Chance	Feb	21 1870	Jan	10 1930
w/o Benj.				
Skinner, Robert Lee	May	7 1865	Feb	27 1946
Spencer, Alvin H. WW-II	Jne	23 1911	May	14 1963
Ga PVT USA				
Ward, Mrs. A.E.	Dec	22 1858	Feb	7 1902
Whitfield, Bryant W. F&AM	Apr	1 1836	Mar	18 1893
Whitfield, Nancy		nd	Aug	23 1889
w/o Bryant W.				
Williams, Lou Hall	Feb	9 1877	Aug	14 1925
w/o M.F.				
Williamson, Bertie C.	Jne	26 1924	Aug	9 1924
Williamson, Harman H. WW-I	Sep	11 1889	Jne	1 1951
Ga Pvt 309 Repair Unit MTC				
Williamson, Lillie E.	Dec	23 1888	Jan	4 1969
w/o Harman H.				

62.   HALL

Hall, John, Esqr.   age 27 y   Jan 20 1792
  s/o Mary & Lyman and their only child
  Notes: (1) His mother was the d/o Samuel and Hannah
Osborne of Fairfield, Conn. and his father an MD, the
s/o Mary Street & John Hall of Wallingford, Conn.

(2) Dr. Hall, a leading citizen, first of St. John's
Parish, played a distinguished role in the American
Revolution; later served as Governor of Georgia.
Death came on Oct. 19, 1790 after he had moved to
"Montville", his Burke plantation. His son was interred beside him in the plantation cemetery and the
two graves enclosed by an iron fence. Many years
later, upon erection of a memorial to Georgia's three
signers of the Declaration of Independence--George
Walton, Lyman Hall, and Button Gwinnett-- Hall's
remains were removed and placed under an imposing
monument on Greene Street, Augusta. William D'Antig-
nac, who then owned the plantation, shipped the
marble slab from the brick vault to Hall's Connecticut home town. The original Burke grave site was
memorialized in 1936 by the National Society of the
DAR as follows: "Site of Lyman Hall's original
grave marked by the Georgia Society and Edmund
Burke Chapter."
    The widowed mother of John died on the plan-
tation, Nov 18, 1793. Thus, within a three-year
period, this line of the Hall family ended (ed).

63.   HARRELL

Harrell, Bessie Celia	Jne 16 1888	Sep 28 1890
Harrell, Beulah V.	Mar 15 1897	Feb 16 1898
Harrell, Leslie F.	Aug 4 1892	Aug 30 1893
Harrell, Mary E.	Oct 19 1852	Mar 23 1906
w/o T.A.		
Harrell, Mary L.	Aug 13 1887	Sep 20 1909
Harrell, Monson Perry	Mar 14 1891	Aug 8 1894
Harrell, Porter T.	Feb 6 1887	Jan 27 1910
Harrell, Pressley	Sep 3 1906	Dec 3 1906
s/o Mr. & Mrs. C.S.		
Harrell, Thomas A.	Sep 28 1849	Feb 11 1910
Thomas, James M.	Oct 20 1825	Nov 18 1904

64.   HATCHER

Hatcher, Mrs. Christian C.   Aug 25 1806 Apr 18 1837
  w/o Edward
Note: No will of an Edward Hatcher was re-recorded
after the Burke courthouse fire of 1856. Fragmentary
data in the earlier research notes of Mrs. Anne Mac-
Kenzie Humphrey indicate that an Edward Hatcher died
about 1847 leaving a widow, Savannah, nee Palmer,
who subsequently married Floyd Crockett; also that
Green B. Powell married Ann Charlotte, a daughter of
this Edward. It is not clear from the notes, however,
whether or not Ann was the daughter of Savannah. The
1972-74 cemetery project shows that an Edward Hatcher
married "Mrs. Alice" (d. 1822) and an Edward married

"Mrs. Christian C." (d. 1837). If these three re-
ferences to Edward Hatcher are all to one person,
Alice, Christian C. and Savannah were then his three
wives in that order (ed).

65.   HATCHER

Dixon, Mamie Lee   age 12y 28d   Oct 8 1900
Hatcher, Augusta Virginia   May 27 1848   Mar 16 1918
Hatcher, Virginia Rosa L.   Jne 3 1891   Mar 24 1906
  d/o R.L. & Willie G.

66.   HATCHER-REYNOLDS

Hatcher, Mrs. Alice   age 22y 6m   Aug 10 1822
  w/o Edward   22d
Reynolds, Mrs. Jane   age 18 y   Sep 9 1820
  w/o John W. Note: On Mar 13 1827 he married Sarah
Ann Sturges, d/o Samuel Sturges (ed). *
*Warren & White, op. cit., p. 106.
Reynolds, Jane Abdelle Marion age 6m 12d   Nov 2 1820
  only child of Jane & J.W.

67.   HEATH
                  Girard, Ga.

Barefield, Annie Bell   Jne 13 1873   Sep 1 1914
Bergeron, John   Dec 27 1813   Feb 3 1884
Heath, Frances   Nov 25 1830   Oct 15 1857
  w/o Samuel
Heath, George W.   1833   1912
Heath, Henry   Jne 15 1798   Dec 4 1857
Heath, Isaac I.   Apr 3 1802   Nov 6 1866
  s/o Jordan
Heath, Samuel   Apr 12 1825   May 20 1895
Heath, Sarah M.   1849   1910
  w/o G.W.
Spears, Carrie Belle   Nov 11 1892   Aug 9 1897
  d/o H.M. & Linnie B.

68.   HEPHZIBAH
                  Richmond Co.

Acton, Alma Tharpe   Aug 26 1913   Feb 5 1924
  d/o Jas. C. & Mattie May
Acton, James Crockett   Apr 4 1880   Feb 25 1962
Acton, Mary   nd   Jan 14 1939
  d/o Wm. D. & Mary T.
Acton, Mary Torrance   nd   Nov 18 1917
  w/o Wm. D.
Acton, Wm. Dandridge CSA   Dec 10 1837   Feb 19 1891
  b Frankfort, Ky. d Hephzibah

```
Adkins, Cephier H.                      Jne  6 1891                L
  w/o Henry G., Sr.
Adkins, Henry G,, Sr.   WW-I            Feb  5 1890    Mar  3 1971
  Ga PVT USA
Allen, Daniel R.   WW-I                 Nov  5 1895    Nov 11 1951
  So Car Pfc Base Hosp
Allen, William Rhodes                   Jne 19 1849    Jul 23 1909
Alley, Thomas King   WW-I               Oct  5 1889    Feb 24 1969
Antonopoulos, George Gene               Nov 29 1949    Feb 11 1950
  s/o Martha Rhodes & George
Atkins, Eulie Lovelace                  Oct 12 1885    Oct 19 1931
Atkins, John L.                         Mar  2 1853    Jne 23 1907
Atkins, Savannah Bell                   Nov  8 1858    Oct 25 1919
Baker, Harold Thomas                    Oct 14 1945    Nov 22 1968
  Ga PVT US Marine Corps
Banks, Francis Louise                   Sep 23 1909    Feb 12 1914
Bargeron, Alexander Lawton              Jan 15 1876    Aug 18 1914
Bargeron, Josie Louise Turner          Aug 10 1874    May 14 1963
  w/o A.L.
Baxley, Alice Bush                      Oct 10 1873    Oct  9 1925
  w/o Dr. Wm. H., Jr.
Baxley, James Ward                      May 12 1862    Aug 27 1917
  s/o Rebecca Ward & Dr. W.H., Sr.
Baxley, Margaret Pauline Allen         Nov  1 1880    Feb 13 1916
  w/o J.W.
Baxley, William Henry, Jr. MD           Jul 22 1864    Apr 22 1938
  s/o Rebecca E. Ward & Dr. W.H., Sr.  grand s/o Eliza-
  beth & James Ward  Burke Co  Will Bk A 188-189  (ed).
Beall, Dr. J. R. F&AM                   Feb 22 1850    Mar  1 1918
Beall, Mary S. Bowls                    Dec  5 1842    Apr 14 1926
  w/o Dr. J.R.
Berrong, Edna Layton                         1891           1964
  w/o Millard A.
Berrong, Millard A.                          1897           1944
Black, Elizabeth B.                          1888             nd
  w/o Wm. Mack
Black, William Mack   WW-I              Jne 15 1884    Mar 27 1973
  Ga Sgt US Army
Blizzard, Christopher N.  WW-II Nov 24 1921    Aug 10 1968
  Ga Tec 5 US Army
Bostock, John L.                        May  2 1854    Jne 19 1934
Bostock, Julia L.                       Feb 25 1854    Nov 14 1933
  w/o John
Bowen, J. Angus  Kor W                  Mar 11 1931    Nov 30 1950
  Sgt Med Co 31st Inf Regt
Brandon, James R.                       Nov 26 1899    Jul  7 1926
Brandon, Rachel Vallatton              Jan 11 1866    Aug 14 1947
  w/o Wm. H.
Brandon, William H.                     Feb 16 1853    Aug  8 1917
Braswell, Jimmie Cook   WW-II           May  9 1931    May  1 1951
  PFC 805 Army Unit
Brenzikofer, Russell C.                 Apr 26 1889    Feb 22 1925
  F&AM
Broadwater, Josephine Hudson           May 31 1861    Oct  7 1945
  w/o R.E.
```

Broadwater, Robert Edward CSA   Apr 26 1845   Dec 15 1931
Burch, Carlos K.   1944   1944
Burch, Infant   only   date   Aug 1 1943
   d/o G.W. & M.L.
Burch, Macie I.   Jan 3 1912   May 24 1951
Burch, Mary   May 15 1908   Sep 16 1952
   w/o Ollie W.
Burch, Ollie W.   Apr 29 1901   Aug 10 1973
Burch, Tumie D.   Jne 15 1898   Dec 5 1970
Burch, William Henery   Sep 5 1886   Jul 5 1948
Burkhalter, Laura Eva Eubanks   1873   1963
   w/o Riley H. m/o Ollie (md Weldon Rheney)
Burkhalter, Riley H.   1875   1964
Butler, John Denver   May 28 1914   Mar 12 1965
   h/o Allie Rheney
Cadle, Joseph E.   Mar 27 1878   Nov 29 1916
Cantrell, John Fletcher   May 31 1892   Nov 23 1898
   s/o Rev. F.D. & Ginevra
Carpenter, Allie J. WW-I   Sep 8 1892   Sep 1 1959
   So Car Engi US Navy
Carpenter, Dennis Stonewall   Aug 27 1908   Oct 9 1945
Carpenter, Doyle Woodrow   Mar 14 1924   Nov 1 1927
   s/o A.J. & Grace   / (Bubber)
Carpenter, Gertrude I.   1878   1928
Carpenter, Irene W.   Jul 31 1874   Feb 17 1961
Carpenter, Louis Sherfield   Jne 8 1912   Sep 23 1949
Carpenter, Preston B.   Sep 29 1866   Nov 5 1918
Carroll, Mattie Ruth   Aug 14 19__   Sep 12 1933
   d/o Mr. & Mrs. J. D.
Carswell, Mrs. Alice Winburn   Mar 20 1881   Jan 19 1902
Carswell, Arthur Eugene   Mar 10 1879   May 30 1938
   md 1st Helen Murphey,   2nd Edna Kiser (1 child, Betty
   Louise)
Carswell, Charles M. CSA   May 29 1846   Jan 4 1915
Carswell, Charles M.   Jan 15 1896   Oct 7 1972
Carswell, Egenardus Ruthven MD   Oct 22 1822   Feb 27 1891
   s/o Matthew & grandson of John (who was son of
   Alexander & Isabella Brown). md Sarah A. Prior, Nov.
   2, 1847. Ordained Baptist Minister, 1853 f/o three
   sons and three daughters (ed).
Carswell, Eunice   Oct 21 1910   Aug 8 1915
   d/o W.D. & L.E.
Carswell, Fannie Janes   Nov 14 1848   May 18 1921
   w/o Rev. J.H.
Carswell, Frances   Mar 19 1899   Jul 16 1900
   d/o F.W. & M.L.
Carswell, Franklin W.   Aug 6 1860   May 26 1926
Carswell, H. Eliza   Jne 16 1825   Apr 12 1892
   w/o Matthew J. d/o Harriet E. Jones & Rev. J.H.T.
   Kilpatrick (ed).
Carswell, Miss Hattie E.   Nov 13 1854   Feb 20 1909
Carswell, Helen Murphey   Jan 5 1892   Mar 7 1928
   b & d Hephzibah w/o A. Eugene d/o Lee Murphey
Carswell, Ida Satcher   Mar 10 1891   Dec 13 1959
   w/o Jas. A.

Carswell, Infant   nd   nd
  of F.W. & M.L.
Carswell, Infants   nd   nd
  of F.W. & M.L.
Carswell, J. Frank   Apr 15 1882   Dec 6 1952
  b Hephzibah d   Brunswick, Ga. h/o Jane Pearce
Carswell, Rev. J.H.   Jan 21 1849   Apr 7 1918
Carswell, James A. CSA   Sep 24 1844   Dec 5 1915
  F&AM   s/o John Franklin & Mary Jones Kilpatrick
Carswell, James A. WW-I   Mar 10 1894   Dec 28 1957
  Ga Cpl Cen MG Off Tng Sch
Carswell, Jane Pearce   Jne 30 1887   Sep 6 1939
  b Olena, Ill. d Augusta, Ga. w/o J. Frank;
  no children
Carswell, John Franklin   Dec 25 1817   Oct 31 1882
Carswell, John Miller   May 6 1879   Mar 30 1892
  s/o James A. & Lavinia
Carswell, Lavinia Miller   Nov 20 1852   Nov 18 1922
  w/o James A.; d/o Cornelia Polhill & Dr. B.B.;
  m/o Cornelia Ellet (Walker), Mary Orlean (md Wm. R.
  Walton), John M., John Frank, James Joseph, Louis
  McHenry, & Louise (md Gus York) (ed).
Carswell, Leila Bullard   1858   1926
  w/o Charles M.
Carswell, Linnie Estelle   Apr 25 1876   Oct 10 1924
  w/o Wm. Davis /Netherland
Carswell, Lizzie M.   Aug 8 1906   Apr 4 1962
Carswell, Louis McHenry (infant)   nd   nd
Carswell, Miss Mary E.   Aug 20 1857   Oct 27 1909
Carswell, Mary Jones Kilpatrick Dec 24 1823   Jul 5 1882
  w/o John Franklin d/o Harriet E. Jones & Rev. J.H.T.
Carswell, Matthew J. CSA   Jan 18 1822   Apr 12 1887
Carswell, Minnie I.   Jan 13 1868   Mar 2 1936
  w/o Franklin W.; member WOW Circle
Carswell, Dr. Thomas Janes   Apr 6 1877   Feb 10 1913
  s/o J.H. & M. Fannie Janes
  L. I., PH GMD
Carswell, Velma Winston   Jne 29 1908   May 18 1909
  d/o F.W. & M.L.
Carswell, W. LaFayette   1901   1928
Carswell, Walton Norris   1914   1936
Carswell, William Davis   Apr 23 1880   Apr 5 1950
  F&AM
Clark, Edward Percival   Dec 2 1869   Mar 12 1952
  s/o M.A. & Chas. E.
Clark, Essie May   Mar 31 1880   Feb 19 1961
  d/o M.A. & Chas. E.
Clark, Eva Edwina   Apr 16 1876   May 22 1896
Clark, Martha Allen   Jul 15 1848   May 13 1911
  w/o Chas. Edw.
Clark, Sarah Elizabeth Rheney Feb 28 1856   1935
  w/o Walter A. md Oct 24 1880.
Clark, Walter Augustus CSA   Mar 5 1842   1914
  s/o Martha Rebecca Walker & Dr. Samuel B.; grandson
  of Charles Clark who established Clark's Chapel.
  Author of A Lost Arcadia. See his book, pp. 153-59 for

information on the Clark family (ed).

Clonan, Joseph   Dec 15 1895   Jne 6 1966
Cook, Laura Jane   Mar 28 1856   Sep 12 1847
Cooper, Peyton S.   age 25 y   Nov 13 1840
Courtney, Altaman S. CSA   nd   nd
  Co H 2 S. Car. Arty
Crockett, Virginia Davis   Feb 22 1879   Feb 24 1904
Cromartie, Henry Richard   Sep 21 1875   Sep 11 1939
  b Bladen Co., N.C.   d Augusta, Ga.
Cromartie, Lena Murphey   Sep 17 1885   Nov 26 1967
  b Hephzibah   d Augusta, Ga.   w/o Henry R.
  d/o Lee Murphey
Crowford, Lois Carswell   Oct 15 1883   May 29 1920
Curtis, Alice Fryer   1854   1918
  w/o Dr. Lebbeus
Curtis, Lebbeus MD   1847   1909
Curtis, Lucile   1892   1914
Davis, James J.   Aug 17 1832   Nov 12 1896
Davis, Louisa Edith   Jan 17 1803   Jne 8 1874
  w/o Rev. Jas.
Davis, Sarah Anne Kilpatrick   1831   1895
  w/o Rev. Wm. H.   d/o Harriet E. Jones & Rev. J.H.T.
  Kilpatrick. Clark, op. cit., 171 (ed).
Davis, Sarah Atkins   Nov 20 1883   Oct 28 1906
Davis, Virginia L.   Nov 5 1838   Feb 23 1915
  w/o James J. m/o Inman Davis
Davis, Rev. William Hudson   Aug 1 1826   Apr 18 1879
Delph, Emma Gertrude   only date   1873
Delph, John Gordon   Feb 18 1880   Jan 31 1925
Delph, Sarah Elizabeth   Nov 18 1842   Feb 17 1918
  w/o Rev. W.I.
Delph, Waring Hudson   Jne 18 1875   Nov 1 1904
Delph, William Ioor CSA   Sep 1 1842   Aug 20 1930
  Sgt Major 1 So. Car. Inf
DeVaughn, Ethel Walker   nd   Mar 26 1950
DeVaughn, Lovick Pierce   Apr 10 1874   May 21 1938
Devereaux, A. W.   1875   1913
Devereaux, Caroline Ethleen   Jul 10 1906   Jul 18 1906
  d/o A.W. & P.E.
Devereaux, David McDowell   Jan 16 1909   Mar 10 1909
  s/o A.W. & P.E.
Dickson, James D.   1887   1945
  F&AM f/o J.D., Jr., Randolph, Warren and Belva
Dinkins, Martha H.   1882   1951
  w/o Oscar
Dinkins, Oscar L.   1878   1926
Dobson, Florine Carpenter   Jan 12 1900   Jne 24 1971
Duffie, Alice Shaw   1872   1943
  w/o J.N.
Duffie, John Noah   1871   1951
Ellis, Sarah M.   Mar 4 1882   Aug 24 1955
  w/o Wm. H.
Ellis, William H.   May 12 1872   Jan 26 1948
Ellis, William Tyler   Sep 7 1921   May 11 1942
  s/o W.H. & Sarah

```
Englett, Sudie                      Feb 27 1873   Jan 28 1948
  w/o Thos.
Englett, Thomas                     Jan 11 1870   Dec  7 1957
Eubanks, Arthur Brooks                      1875          1957
Eubanks, Roberta Burkhalter                 1879          1970
  w/o A.B.
Eubanks, Roy L.                             1901          1945
  h/o Margaret Dennis
Evans, Mary Sophronia               Apr 16 1836   Dec 24 1925
Farmer, Ann Knight                  Mar 18 1825   Apr 12 1900
  w/o Berry
Farmer, John W.                     Apr  7 1848   May  1 1892
Farmer, Ruhamah McCook              Sep  2 1850   Jne 24 1899
  w/o John W.
Farmer, Willie Belle                Feb 22 1887   Dec  1 1888
Foss, Dr. C.J.                              1828          1896
Foss, Charlie                               1852          1920
Foss, Eliza A.                              1839          1900
Foss, Emma H.                               1873          1952
Foss, Emmie Kilpatrick              Sep 12 1875   Apr 21 1914
  d/o Emma H. & Rev. W.L. Kilpatrick
Foss, James V.                              1869          1951
Foss, Julian                                1903          1905
Foss, Laura                         Nov    1860   Jul    1927
Foss, Lillian K.                            1875          1915
Foss, R.H.                                  1862          1944
Frost, Florence                     Apr 13 1885   Aug 13 1886
  d/o Lula M. & U.B., Sr.
Frost, Louise Guion                 Mar 12 1905   Sep 25 1946
  d/o Lula M. & U.B., Sr.
Frost, Lula Miller                  Feb  4 1864   Nov 21 1942
  w/o U.B., Sr. d/o Cornelia Polhill & Dr. B.B. Miller;
  m/o Florence, Ruth (md Adrian C. Ford), U.B., Jr.,
  Robert Cecil, Thomas Harry, & Louise Guion (ed).
Frost, Ulysses Barney, Sr.          Apr  8 1846   Jan 17 1931
Fryer, Benjamin E.  CSA             age 55 y      Jan 17 1879
Fryer, John Benjamin                Feb 19 1860   Mar 25 1911
  s/o Sarah Dillard & Benj. E.
Fryer, Marian Cain                  Nov  1 1861   Dec 11 1945
  w/o John Benj.; d/o Jane Marian Cain & James Granberry
  Cain (a cousin) (ed).
Fryer, Sarah I.                     age 56 y      Jne  9 1888
  w/o Benj. E.  d/o Nancy & John Dillard. d  Augusta
Fulcher, Frances Saxon              Feb  6 1892   Mar 30 1948
  w/o Percy C.
Fulcher, Joe  WW-II                 Apr  1 1917   Jul  3 1964
  s/o Frances Saxon & Percy   Ga CSC US Navy
Fulcher, Kinnard S.  WW-II          Jne 20 1920   Apr 15 1963
  s/o Frances & Percy C.   Washington Pvt USA
Fulcher, Larry Grady                Feb  1 1936   Apr 20 1942
Fulghum, Mrs. Mary                  age 67 y      May    1915
Ganus, Frances Turner               Oct 28 1920   Jul 18 1958
  d/o Mr. & Mrs. Henry
Ganus, Leonard A., Sr.                      1900          1935
  F&AM  h/o Rosalie
```

```
Ganus, Leonard Allen              Aug 23 1921   Jan 19 1963
Ganus, Levin A.                           1858          1924
   F&AM
Ganus, Susie Wimberly                     1874          1943
Garrett, Dr. Henry C.   CSA      Sep 22 1836   Aug 25 1892
   b Edgefield, S.C.    d Hephzibah
Godbee, John Raiford   WW-I      Mar 25 1893   Mar 17 1951
   md 1st Susie Hardin, 1 child, J.R., Jr; 2nd  Mary W.
   Marchman, no issue;  s/o Minnie A. & Thomas Raiford;
   Ga 2d Lt 121 Inf 31 Div
Godbee, Minnie Armstrong         Apr 13 1872   Aug 18 1956
   w/o Thos. R.    d/o Emma Dixon & John Walker Armstrong
Goodin, C. Lee                   Jul 20 1911   May  9 1948
Goodin, Clinton Loree            Dec 20 1938   Jan 29 1946
Goodin, Curtis Nathan            Sep  9 1924   Aug 28 1926
Goodin, Fannie Mae               Feb 27 1918   Mar  4 1918
Goodin, J. D. W.                 Apr  8 1863   Sep 18 1927
Goodin, John Barnum              Nov 20 1907   May 27 1964
Goodin, Mollie Blackston         Sep 23 1885            nd
   w/o J.D.W.
Hall, D. Emmett                           1906          1937
Hall, Ida Davis                  Sep 24 1859   Jne 25 1894
   w/o Joseph A.
Hall, Infant                              1935          1935
Hardin, Claude F.                Sep 19 1899   Jul 14 1969
Hardin, Doris W.                 Mar 19 1929   Feb  1 1969
   (in Weathersbee section)
Hardin, Hazel M.                 Oct 17 1906            nd
   w/o C.F.
Hardy, Ruby Loree                Feb  6 1920   Jne 11 1965
Harter, Alexander                         1904          1950
Harter, Carrie G.                         1909          19__
   w/o Alexander
Helmly, Mary E.                  Nov 23 1920            nd
   w/o W.R., Sr.
Helmly, Willie R., Sr.           Feb 21 1918   Apr 26 1969
Henderson, Benjamin                       1881          1963
   br/o Claude C.
Henderson, Claude C.             Nov 16 1884   Jul 30 1948
Henderson, J. Thurmond           Dec  2 1894   Dec 28 1933
   br/o Claude C.
Henderson, James Lewis           Sep  4 1852   Nov  4 1918
Henderson, John C.  WW-I         Mar 13 1891   Jne 24 1970
   h/o Louise Ellington  br/o Claude C.
   Ga Pvt USA
Henderson, Lottie C.             Dec 13 1886   Dec 26 1926
Henderson, Martha Adelaide       Jan 24 1853            nd
   w/o Jas. Lewis   /Beall
Henderson, Ruth K. Lansdell      Jne 19 1909   May 14 1958
   w/o Claude C.  d/o R.A. & Ruth K.
Hill, Elizabeth                           1851          1926
Hill, Green                               1849          1923
Hill, Hasseltine                          1838          1923
Hogarth, Kathryn L. (infant)     only  date  May 17 1945
   d/o H.E. & V.R.
```

Hogarth, Virginia Rooks   Jul 28 1912   L
  w/o H.E. d/o Lillian Lansdell & Asa H. Rooks
Holcomb, J. Polhill   Apr 2 1881 Sep 8 1881
  s/o Louisa Polhill & Flavius Josephus (both buried in
  Midville City Cemetery).
Holmes, David S. CSA   Mar 17 1846 Apr 23 1912
  b Wilkes Co. d Augusta, Ga.
Holmes, Emma Kilpatrick   Oct 22 1849 Mar 18 1923
  w/o David S.   /Carswell   md Dec 7 1876, Hephzibah
Holmes, Furman K.   Feb 9 1884 Mar 18 1921
Hudson, Cyrus CSA   Feb 23 1814 Dec 28 1886
Hudson, David J.   Mar 5 1888 Dec 23 1912
Hudson, Emily   Jan 13 1823 Apr 1 1898
  w/o Cyrus
Hudson, Florence A. Fryer   Sep 17 1849 Apr 22 1904
  w/o J.G.
Hudson, Hamilton Stephens   Jan 29 1854 Oct 13 1886
  s/o Cyrus & Emily
Hudson, Robert Emmette   May 31 1855 Aug 28 1891
  s/o Cyrus & Emily
Hudson, William Preston   Jne 14 1849 Aug 5 1915
Hudson, Willie   1852   1921
Hurst, William Lansing, Jr.   Nov 6 1930 Dec 12 1930
  s/o W.L. & V.A.
Hutchinson, Edwin Colon   Apr 23 1875 May 13 1935
Hutchinson, Estelle Carswell   Mar 31 1896 May 8 1936
  2nd w/o Edwin C.
Jenkins, Ella B. Johnson   Aug 6 1882 Jul 13 1932
Jenkins, John J.   Jul 22 1908 May 28 1909
Jenkins, Martha Lindsey   Jan 1 1881 Oct 15 1959
Jenkins, William J.   Jne 2 1878 Apr 30 1948
Jennings, Estelle Glisson   Dec 13 1909   nd
  w/o Geo. H.
Jennings, George Henry   Mar 25 1907 May 18 1967
Johnikin, John Wesley   Jan 10 1865 Dec 5 1935
Johnikin, Minnie Mira Lee   Apr 2 1885 Jul 3 1934
  w/o John W.
Jones, Anna Willie Hughes   Dec 3 1868 Aug 4 1904
  w/o Henry S.
Jones, Lieut. Batt Rev War   nd   nd
  6 Co Ga Batt'n
Jones, Henry S.   May 1 1864 May 8 1926
  F&AM WOW
Jones, Kathleen Lacy Moss   Oct 3 1882 Mar 3 1963
  w/o Henry S. m/o Carlton, Margaret (md Schuyler
  Clark), & Randolph
Jones, Mary Estelle   Nov 4 1871 Jne 12 1895
Jones, Mary Jane Jenkins   Jan 5 1876 Jan 2 1950
Jones, Rosalyn Randall   Oct 30 1841 Feb 23 1916
  w/o Thos. H.
Jones, Thomas   Mar 18 1830 Aug 16 1875
Jones, Thomas Hill   Mar 4 1867 May 25 1886
Jordan, Carl Andrew WW-II   May 1 1919 Oct 19 1968
  Ga T Sgt US Army
Kelley, James Madison   Mar 20 1866 Mar 2 1911
  WOW

Kelley, Julia O.   1866   1930
Kelley, Thomas Leon   WW-I   Dec 24 1895 Jan 12 1973
  s/o Essie Cumming & Dr. Geo. W., Jr.   Ga Mech USA
Kilpatrick, Emma J. Hudson   Mar 17 1843 Aug 13 1926
  2nd w/o Rev. W. I. m/o Andrew J. (MD), Ruth (md Lansdell), Emma (md Foss), & Derrelle D. See Clark, op.
  cit., 172 (ed).
Kilpatrick, James Hall   Feb 8 1864 Sep 12 1865
  s/o Rev. W.L. & S.E.
Kilpatrick, Lella (infant)   nd   nd
  d/o Emma H. & Rev. W.L.
Kilpatrick, Sarah E. Schick   Feb 7 1832 Jne 27 1872
  1st w/o Rev. Washington L. b Savannah m/o George P.
  & Henry H., both of Burke; Lizzie (Hunter), Sarah
  (md Winslow Hamilton), and Eliza (Gaffney). See
  Clark, op. cit., 172 (ed).
Kilpatrick, Rev. Washington L.   Oct 18 1829 Aug 3 1896
  s/o Harriet E. Jones & Rev. J.H.T. Note: Other side
  of tombstone gives 1828 as year of birth (ed).
Kilpatrick, Willie (infant)   only date Nov 9 1880
  s/o Emma H. & Rev. Washington L.
Kilpatrick, Wycliffe (infant)   nd   nd
  s/o Emma H. & Washington L.
Kimbrough, Mary Ella Crockett   Jan 1 1866 Nov 12 1949
King, Robert B., II Viet W   Nov 19 1943 Aug 21 1971
  Ga A3C US Air Force
Kiser, Ethel O'Dell   Aug 4 1888 Mar 31 1956
  w/o R.H.
Kiser, Romey H.   Jul 26 1881 Jul 3 1961
Landreth, Bennett E.   1880   1944
Landreth, Mae Ridlehoover   1895   1970
  w/o B.E.
Langley, Robert E.   Jul 11 1945 Aug 29 1945
Lansdell, Anna Cody   Nov 27 1845 Dec 29 1925
  w/o Edwin Erwin   d/o Elizabeth A. Lewis & B.F.
Lansdell, Dare Singleton   Feb 19 1880 Dec 25 1923
  s/o Anna C. & Edwin E. 1st h/o Jennie Godbee
Lansdell, Edwin Erwin CSA   Dec 17 1845 Jne 20 1901
  s/o Luke & Emeline f/o Robt. Cody, R. Addison, Sr.,
  N. Eugenia Murphey, Lillian Rooks, and Dare S.
Lansdell-Clonan, Jennie Godbee May 28 1895 May 1 1968
  w/o Dare S.   md 2nd Joseph Clonan; d/o Minnie Arm-
  strong & Thomas Raiford Godbee; m/o Myrtle (md Wm. H.
  Saul), and Virginia (md Julian F. Lewis) (ed).
Lansdell, Joseph Truett   Mar 27 1920 Sep 3 1951
  s/o R.A. & R.K.
Lansdell, Rinaldo Addison   1875   1937
  s/o Anna C. & Edwin E.
Lansdell, Ruth Kilpatrick   1878   1960
  w/o R.A. d/o Rev. W.I. & Emma Hudson; m/o Anna
  (Walker), Cyrus Hudson (md Sarah Cook), Ruth (md Claude
  Henderson), Lillian (md B.S. McElmurray), Emily, a
  missionary to China (md Dr. J.D. Weatherspoon), R.
  Addison, Jr. (md Ida Padgett), and Joseph T.
Layton, John L. CSA   Oct 20 1841 Oct 29 1908

Layton, Minta Cook   Jan 17 1855   Jne 2 1929
   w/o John L.
Ligon, Mrs. Mernemia J.   age 72 y   Apr 15 1876
   w/o Thomas Marshall, md 1821; d/o John Rhodes; sis/o
   Matilda Rhodes who married Thomas Hatcher in 1820, and
   Lewis B. Rhodes. Clark, op. cit., 45 (ed).
Lindsey, Alva Dixon   Dec 22 1885   Aug 18 1969
   2nd w/o J. Robert
Lindsey, Bessie Guye   Sep 22 1915   Nov 8 1939
   1st w/o J. Robert
Lindsey, J. Robert   Aug 4 1910   nd
Marks, Annie B. Atkinson   Oct 3 1878   Nov 31 1962
   w/o W.T.
Marks, W.T.   1884   1949
Mayne, Anna Carswell   Oct 10 1868   Jul 17 1903
Mays, Leonard W.   Sep 17 1858   Sep 2 1935
   s/o Lou V. Franklin & M.M. Mays
Mays, Marvin W.   Sep 11 1898   Jul 3 1925
   s/o Mary Jane & L.W. No children
Mays, Mary Jane   Oct 28 1867   Apr 15 1913
   w/o L.W. d/o Mr. & Mrs. Wilkins of Columbia Co., Ga.
   m/o Marvin W., Hubert, and Gertrude
McGee, Thomas Ellis   Nov 12 1903   Oct 31 1959
McLelland, Beulah Vernon   Jan 4 1890   Feb 4 1964
   w/o Jos. E.   / Johnson
McLelland, Cornelia H.   1854   1939
McLelland, Joseph E.   Jul 26 1875   Feb 11 1959
Meigs, Eliza A.   Jul 25 1825   Feb 21 1906
Meigs, James   nd   Dec 27 1925
Meigs, Mary Bowman   nd   Aug 15 1943
   w/o James
Michaels, Terry I.   1955   1955
Michaels, Wayne Bruce   only   date   1956
Miller, Cornelia E. Polhill   Jan 30 1834   Jne 6 1922
   w/o Dr. Baldwin B. d/o Julia Guion & Rev Joseph;
   m/o Lavinia C., Joseph B., John P., Ruth McHenry,
   Louisa (Lula) Maria, Benj. F., & Robert Lee, MD (ed).
Miller, Evans Smith   Jan 31 1883   Oct 9 1957
Miller, Sidney Lucile Turner   Sep 11 1886   Jul 16 1971
   w/o Evans S.
Mims, Brian R.   Aug 22 1935   Oct 26 1963
   s/o Louise Rhodes & G.B., Sr.
Mims, Fred Henry   Feb 7 1888   nd
Mims, Guy Baxley, Sr.   Apr 1 1894   nd
Mims, Harry A.   Apr 14 1911   Aug 25 1970
Mims, Ida Dixon   Oct 24 1894   Oct 8 1970
   w/o L.M.
Mims, Jack V.   Sep 29 1914   May 1 1950
Mims, Louise Rhodes   Jne 1 1899   Dec 20 1971
   w/o Guy, Sr., d/o Pauline & Walter F. Rhodes
Mims, Lucile Malcolm   Nov 9 1883   nd
Mims, Nellie E. Ray   Apr 4 1896   Oct 2 1969
   w/o Fred

```
Mims, Nellie Sue                    May  8 1929   Sep 22 1930
   d/o Mr. & Mrs. Fred H.
Mims, R. Leslie                          1886             1919
Mims, Susie Baxley                       1857             1937
Mims, T.K.                          Jan 18 1892   Nov  6 1963
Minor, Annie May Jones                   1903             1950
Murphey, Harriet Carswell           Feb  3 1861   Jne 29 1930
   w/o Henry Lee  m/o Helen (md Eugene Carswell), Mildred
   (md Geo. W. Vance), Lena (md H.R. Cromartie), & Jim
   (ed).  b  Whitfield Co., Ga.  d Hephzibah
Murphey, Henry Lee                  Jan 26 1862   Nov 21 1942
   b  Burke Co  d Hephzibah
Murphey, John M.C.                  Jan 23 1868   Aug  8 1925
   f/o Edwin, Marie (Moore), & Emmie (Powell)
Murphey, N. Eugenia Lansdell        Apr 25 1870   Oct  2 1940
   w/o John M.C.  d/o Anna C. & Edwin E.
Murphey, Sarah Jones                Jul 24 1837   Jul 17 1923
   b  Burke Co  d Hephzibah  w/o Wm. R.
Newman, Cora R.                          1899             1957
Newman, Dock J.  WW-II              May 20 1921   Sep 10 1954
   Ga Pvt 1083 Guard SQ AAF
Newman, Jim W.                      Mar 22 1898   Jne  5 1966
Newsome, Gertrude R.                Oct  5 1888             nd
   w/o Homer
Newsome, Homer C.                   Sep 19 1892   May 13 1968
Norris, Gussie S.                        1874             1955
Norris, Lucia A.                         1906             1948
Norris, Walton Alonzo                    1865             1946
Olenik, Charles, Jr.  WW-II         May  5 1917   Oct 16 1948
   PH  N.Y. PFC 168 Engr Combt Bn4 Inf Div
Oxyner, Bessie Watson                    1874             1932
Oxyner, James Luther                     1861             1941
Patterson, Rosa Carswell            Oct 10 1914   Nov 21 1961
   b Rosier, Ga  d Columbus, Ohio
Pearre, Emma Cody                   Dec  4 1847   Nov 12 1915
   d/o Elizabeth Ann Lewis & Benj. F.
Perkins, Effie                      Dec 25 1859   Sep  6 1897
   w/o G.W.
Pickett, Cora O.                    Oct 21 1893   Nov 19 1966
Porter, Francis H.                  Jul  9 1939             nd
Porter, Gloria W.                   Apr  6 1943   Apr  2 1972
   w/o F.H.
Powell, Emily B.                    Jne 28 1883   May  7 1968
Raborn, Addie Lee                   Jne 16 1909   Apr 19 1925
   d/o S.P. & E.M.
Raborn, Alice Mae                   Dec 26 1915   Mar  5 1928
Raborn, Alvin H.                         1899             1958
Raborn, Alvin H., Jr.                    1934             1946
Raborn, Effie May Goodin            Apr 24 1892   Apr 21 1925
   w/o S.P.
Raborn, James T.                    Aug  4 1884   Mar 27 1938
Raborn, M.M. (Doc)                       1875             1971
Raborn, Rhodia H.                        1878             1934
Raborn, Sarah E. Burch              Dec  5 1885   Nov 10 1953
   w/o Jas. T.
```

Raborn, Sim P. 1888 1949
Reynolds, Amelia Virginia Nov 13 1867 Feb 6 1935
 w/o Foster P. /Dickinson m/o Foster, Jr., Henry
 D., Elizabeth and Rosa.
Reynolds, Foster Pierce F&AM May 22 1865 Apr 25 1935
Rheney, Charlie R., Jr. Apr 12 1898 Aug 19 1927
Rheney, Clarence A. Oct 15 1892 Nov 1 1939
 h/o Mabry Carswell
Rheney, Earl F. WW-II Aug 25 1908 Nov 16 1972
 Ga Sgt USA br/o Weldon, Clarence & George. Earl
 never married.
Rheney, Emma B. Aug 23 1873 Dec 2 1943
Rheney, George King Jul 30 1901 Nov 22 1961
 h/o Inez Dinkins
Rheney, Infant nd nd
 s/o Clarence & Mabry
Rheney, LeRoy H. May 24 1894 Aug 2 1970
Rheney, Mabry Carswell nd L
 w/o Clarence A. m/o Leila Rheney Spearing
Rheney, Weldon Eve 1896 1955
 h/o Ollie Burkhalter
Rhodes, A. Sterling Jul 31 1875 May 3 1927
 Note: Records in Richmond Co. on the Rhodes family
 go back to Absalom, Sr., Aaron, and their sister
 Nancy. According to Clark, op. cit., 47 these three
 Rhodes, and probably a cousin John (father of Lewis
 B.), came from North Carolina to Richmond Co., probably in 1783 or 84. Nancy's grave marker still
 stands in the Edmund Murphey cemetery and there is
 good evidence that Absalom, Sr., and Aaron are also
 interred there. See Note at end of that cemetery
 listing. Lewis B. and his wife, Mary White Rhodes,
 his sister, Mrs. M.J. Ligon, his eldest son, Absalom
 W., this son's wife, Susan C., are the oldest of the
 family buried in the Hephzibah cemetery (ed).
Rhodes, Absalom CSA Feb 15 1844 May 13 1915
Rhodes, Absalom W. Mar 27 1811 Apr 21 1893
 s/o Mary White & Lewis B.
Rhodes, Andrew Miller Jul 24 1841 May 26 1844
 s/o Absalom W. & Susan C.
Rhodes, Augusta Holliday age 63 y May 15 1904
 w/o R.L.
Rhodes, Charles J. CSA nd nd
 s/o Absalom W. & Susan C.
Rhodes, Chesley M. Nov 15 1879 Jan 21 1943
Rhodes, Chesley Marvin, Jr. Nov 7 1905 Nov 7 1971
Rhodes, Clarence A. Jan 11 1871 Sep 27 1921
Rhodes, Clarence Alvin Jne 17 1920 Jne 18 1920
Rhodes, Clifford E. Jne 13 1882 Aug 8 1945
 s/o Fannie Cogle & Absalom
Rhodes, Crystal Elaine Oct 8 1956 May 31 1966
 d/o Wayne & Hazel
Rhodes, Cynthia Brown Nov 7 1959 May 31 1966
 d/o Wayne & Hazel

Rhodes, Elizabeth Loraine   Jul 3 1914 Jul 1 1929
    d/o W.E. & P.S.
Rhodes, Eugene Cartwright   Jul 2 1895 Jne 18 1973
    s/o Pauline & Walter E.
Rhodes, Fannie H. Cogle   Feb 15 1847 Jne 15 1929
    w/o Absalom They were the parents of W.T., Sr.,
    Foster, Clifford, A. Sterling (md Kate Adkins), Wesley
    (md Lillie Adkins), and Hattie (md Geo. F. Sullivan)
    (ed).
Rhodes, Foster G.   Dec 22 1886 Mar 29 1965
    s/o Fannie Cogle & Absalom
Rhodes, George Byron   Aug 30 1900 Jan 7 1902
    s/o Sterling & Kate
Rhodes, Gussie Mims   Dec 19 1889 Mar 9 1920
    1st w/o Willie T. m/o W.T., Jr., & Fannie Sue Rivers
Rhodes, Hattie   age 6m   1878
    d/o R.L. & A.A.
Rhodes, Infants (two)   nd   nd
    of C.M. & L.A.
Rhodes, Kate Atkins   Oct 5 1879 Jan 3 1932
    w/o A. Sterling
Rhodes, Laura H. Layton   Mar 26 1895 Feb 4 1963
    w/o Eugene
Rhodes, Lewis B.   age 48 y   Feb 4 1836
    Note: Born in 1788. In Clark, op. cit., a misprint
    shows his birth as Mar 10 1778 (ed).
Rhodes, Maggie May   nd   Sep 23 1903
    d/o A.W. & S.C.
Rhodes, Mary White   Sep 7 1788   Oct 9 1875
    w/o Lewis B. md Feb 5 1810; their children were:
    John R. (md Araminty Haynie); Absalom W. (md Susan C.
    White); Thomas R. (md 1st Marie Watson, 2nd Sarah A.
    Pardue); Val W. (md 1st Mary G. Fox, 2nd Margaret M.
    Jones); Mary B. (md W.W. Walker); Tilman (md Sarah
    R. Wolfe); James William, Lewis Allen, Lewis Bobo,
    William Peyton, & Hiram Jones. For other descen-
    dants of Lewis B. & Mary White, see Clark, op. cit.
    45-46 (ed).
Rhodes, Mary Elizabeth   Nov 7 1881 Nov 19 1966
    w/o Chesley M.   /Atkins
Rhodes, Mollie   nd   Nov 5 1907
    d/o A.W. & S.C.
Rhodes, Pauline E. Simon   Feb 11 1872 Feb 20 1930
    w/o Walter E.
Rhodes, R. L.   age 68 y   Apr 7 1906
    s/o A.W. & Susan C.
Rhodes, Susan C. White   Jne 30 1812 Aug 4 1895
    w/o Absalom W. (who was the son of Lewis B.)
Rhodes, T.S.W.   age 38y 7m   Dec 1 1855
Rhodes, W.E., Jr.   1917   1940
Rhodes, W. T.   Mar 3 1919 Dec 31 1968
Rhodes, Walter E.   Jul 28 1868 Jul 12 1930
Rhodes, Walter Warren   1876   1897
    s/o R.L. & A.H.

```
Rhodes, Warren White               age 15 m       Jan  3 1851
   s/o A.W. & S.C.
Rhodes, Wm. Peyton                 Jan 30 1827     Apr 14 1874
   s/o Mary White & Lewis B.
Rhodes, Willie T., Sr.                  1884            1950
   s/o Fannie Cogle & Absalom   md 1st Gussie Mims,
   children: W.T., Jr. & Fannie Sue (Rivers)  2nd Marie
   Reborn,  children: Wayne & Ronnie  (ed).
Ridlehoover, Jack B.  Kor War  Apr  2 1932     Aug  1 1970
   Ga Sp 4 USA
Roberts, Alexander H.                   1892            1945
Roberts, Desse A.                  May 14 1894     Nov  7 1965
Roberts, James Henry                    1884            1902
Roberts, John Eben                      1883            1903
Roberts, John Henry                Jan 30 1841     Sep 11 1914
Roberts, Louisa Amelia Simon       Oct  4 1856     Dec  6 1933
   w/o John Henry
Roberts, Maizie E.                      1889            1952
Roberts, Mary Louise                    1886            1886
Roberts, Titus Alganon                  1887            1902
Roberts, William Eugene                 1882            1885
Robsky, Louise Bargeron            Jul  2 1905     Jan 22 1966
   d/o Josie Turner & A.L.
Rooks, Asa H.                      Aug 21 1860     Jne  3 1921
Rooks, Lillian Lansdell            Feb 27 1876     Oct 30 1947
   w/o Asa H.   d/o Anna C. & Edwin E.
Royal, Loretta Ethel Turner        Sep 23 1883            nd
   w/o Dr. Louis B.
Royal, Loretta Helen               Jne 30 1916     Jul  3 1916
   d/o Ethel T. & Dr. L.B.
Royal, Dr. Louis Bartow  MD        Jul 11 1876     May 11 1952
   F&AM
Rupert, Mrs. Lula                        nd             nd
   d/o R.L. & A.A. Rhodes
Schaffner, Fred L.                 Nov 30 1861     Feb  9 1926
   s/o Mary D. & John F.
Schaffner, Dr. John Frederick      Feb 21 1831     May 10 1881
   CSA   b Charleston, S. C.
Schaffner, Julien D.                    1876            1892
   s/o Mary D. & John F.
Schaffner, Mary Dillard            Sep 14 1840     May 25 1922
   w/o Dr. John F.   d/o Nancy & John Dillard
Sewell, Anna Fryer                 Sep 24 1881     Jan 27 1973
   w/o H. Warner   d/o Marian Cain & John Benj.
   m/o Marian F. & John F. Sewell  (ed).
Sewell, H. Warner                  May 25 1879     Sep 26 1940
Schick, Elizabeth S. Cline         Mar  9 1809     Aug 11 1881
   w/o Peter
Sills, Archie John  WW-II          Mar 24 1913     Apr 21 1956
   Illinois PFC 810 Base Unit AAF
Simon, Camille                          1857            1920
Simon, Infant  J.A.                     1931            1932
Simon, John A.                          1868            1937
Skillman, Ervin E.                       nd             1971
Skinner, Cathorine W.                   1872            1959
```

```
Skinner, G. Millard                           1903         1949
Skinner, Harvey T.                            1898         1936
Smith, Charles O.                  Jul 15 1870  Nov 17 1902
Smith, Charles Otto                Feb 24 1907  Sep 18 1964
Smith, Mary Eliza Carswell         Mar 27 1874  Aug 29 1962
  w/o Dr. Bryant J.
Smith, Sarah H. Carroll            Oct 15 1870  Apr 18 1921
  w/o Thos. E.
Smith, Thomas E.                   Mar 30 1868  Dec 27 1925
Steed, Gertrude Hudson             Jul  9 1848  Jan 29 1932
Stewart, James Robert              Feb  8 1926  Mar 24 1928
Stewart, Julia Burch               Oct  3 1893            nd
  w/o Wm. A.
Stewart, William A.                Sep 20 1880  Sep 21 1949
Story, Adeline Burmah              same   date  Jul 15 1895
Story, Agnes                       Jan  5 1876  Feb 10 1877
  d/o S. G., Sr. & Burmah
Story, Anderson Gresham                     nd           nd
  inf. s/o S.G., Jr. & Ida Gresham
Story, Charles                              1878        1942
  s/o S.G., Sr. & Burmah
Story, Chester E.                           1880        1956
  s/o S.G., Sr. & Burmah
Story, Emily Burmah Steed          Sep 15 1841  Apr 20 1896
  w/o S. Gaines, Sr.   m/o (in addition to those buried
  in Heph. Cem.)  S.G., Jr. (Waynesboro), Frank, Ida
  (md  McDaniel), Jessie (md McFarJane) & Suzie  (md
  Savage).
Story, Infant                               nd           nd
  of S.G., Jr. & Ida Gresham
Story, Paul                        Apr 21 1872  May 25 1873
  s/o S.G., Sr. & Burmah
Story, Ruth Winter                 May  9 1880  Feb 24 1964
  w/o Charles   d/o Artemecia Meigs Thomas & Lewis
  Vinton Winter   m/o Dorothy, Ruth, Charles, Steed
  & Lewis.
Story, Samuel Gaines, Sr.          Apr 23 1825  Jul 28 1892
Story, William Steed               Nov  3 1868  Mar  7 1905
  s/o S.G., Sr. & Burmah. Never married.
Sullivan, George F. Franklin                1851        1917
Sullivan, Hattie Rhodes                     1877        1941
  w/o Geo. F.   d/o Fannie Cogle & Absalom
Thompson, Algie Lewis              Dec 28 1888  Jne  5 1957
Thompson, Cordelia Henderson       Oct  3 1892  May  7 1959
  w/o A.L.
Timmerman, Dr. John P.                      1874        1944
Timmerman, Mayme E.                         1879        1968
  w/o Dr. John P.   m/o Francis, J.P., Jr. William,
  Elizabeth & Wayne.
Timmerman, Sarah Inez              Sep  4 1911  May 27 1912
  d/o John P. & M.E.
Traylor, A.A.  CSA                 Feb 10 1837  Jul 17 1908
Traylor, Alpha L.                  Sep 27 1875  Feb 14 1957
Traylor, Emmie Winter              Aug  6 1875  May 30 1972
  w/o Alpha L.   d/o Artemecia Meigs Thomas & Lewis
  Vinton Winter
```

124

```
Traylor, Mary                          Aug 17 1851   Oct 25 1911
  w/o A.A.
Turner, Claude A.                            1925           1928
Turner, Claude Amelia                  Aug 12 1889   Mar 10 1972
Turner, Della W.                       Apr  3 1890   Apr  3 1950
Turner, Fred E.  WW-I                  Mar  3 1893   May 27 1918
  Co E 28th Inf  First Div A.E.F.  killed in action
  Battle of Cantigny, France.
Turner, Harriet M. Carswell                  1887           1943
  w/o Joe E.
Turner, Henry B.                       Jul 11 1871   Sep 12 1932
Turner, Joseph S.                      Oct 13 1849   Mar  6 1933
Turner, Julia B. Britton                     1885           1957
  w/o Joe E.
Turner, Kathryn J.                           1921           1925
Turner, Loretta Rowe                   Nov  3 1851   Jul 28 1931
  w/o Jos. S.
Turner, Riley M.  CSA                  age 83 y      Nov  8 1897
Turner, W. Clayton, Jr.                      1913           1972
Turner, Wilbur C.                            1880           1938
Tyler, Infant                          only  date    Apr 21 1920
  s/o Dr. & Mrs. L.V.
Tyler, Infant                          only  date    Jan  7 1922
  d/o Dr. & Mrs. L.V.
Ulm, Beulah R.                               1889           1970
Ulm, John Clinton  WW-I                Mar 29 1889   May 23 1947
  Ga F 2C US Navy
Usher, Auvergne  WW-II                 May 10 1881   Apr  1 1962
  Ga PFC USA
Vance, Clifford                        Aug 11 1894   Jan  8 1914
  s/o W.F. & S.E.
Vance, Effie                                 1903           1935
  d/o W.F. & S.E.  Note: Effie, Ethel & Eva A. were
  triplets (ed).
Vance, Ethel                                 1903           1936
  d/o W.F. & S.E.
Vance, Eva A.                                1903           1939
  d/o W.F. & S.E.
Vance, George Washington               Oct  9 1896             L
  s/o W.F. & S.E.
Vance, Horace L.                             1901           1932
  s/o W.F. & S.E.
Vance, Matilda                               1911           1934
  d/o W.F. & S.E.
Vance, Mildred Murphey                 May 22 1895   Feb 21 1959
  w/o George Washington  d/o Lee Murphey
Vance, Reba Layton                     Nov 27 1892   Jne 13 1934
  w/o Fred, Jr.
Vance, Robert E.                             1914           1956
  s/o W.F. & S.E.
Vance, Sallie H.                       Sep 21 1871   Nov  7 1948
  w/o W.F.
Vance, William Fred, Jr.  WOW          Oct  4 1892   Feb 11 1972
  s/o W.F. & S.E.
```

```
Vance, Willie F.                         Jul 31 1867    Jan 26 1917
Walker, C. Ellet Carswell               Mar 20 1873    Nov 16 1894
  w/o Lyttleton Harwell   d/o Lavinia M. & James A.
  m/o Ellet
Walker, Foster Clark                     Sep  1 1904    Nov 20 1905
Walker, Foster Pierce Clark             Sep 14 1884    Sep  7 1904
  w/o Benj. H.
Walker, Kate B. Wicker                   May  9 1875    Jul  9 1900
  w/o L.F.
Walker, Lena Allen                              1879           1914
  w/o Curran Evans
Walker, Margaret Jones                   Aug 10 1854    Feb 15 1918
Warner, Infant                           only    date   Aug 14 1915
  s/o Geo. & Edna
Weathersbee, Annie Kate                  age 5 y                 nd
Weathersbee, John H.                     Oct 27 1903    May 18 1969
Weathersbee, John Hampton, Jr.          Jne  9 1931    Sep 19 1931
  s/o J.H. & Ruth
Weathersbee, John P.                              nd    Dec 12 1919
Weathersbee, John P., Jr.               Sep 13 1889    Dec  1 1946
Weathersbee, Julia H.                             nd    Dec 26 1897
Weathersbee, Ruth N.                     Jan 28 1912             nd
  w/o John H.
Weatherspoon, Emily Lansdell                    1913           1973
  w/o Rev. Dr. Jesse D.   d/o Ruth K. & R.A.   She was a
  missionary to China   (ed).
Whitaker, Almeda                         Apr 25 1888    Oct 23 1890
  d/o L.F. & R.H.
Williams, Annie B.                       Jul 28 1884    Jul 17 1969
Williams, Geo. E., Jr.                   only    date   Sep 19 1954
Williams, Infant                         only    date   Dec 14 1937
  s/o J.L. & L.V.
Williams, J. LeRoy                       May 12 1885    Jne 30 1937
Williams, J. LeRoy, Jr.                 Sep 14 1922    Jne 14 1923
Williams, Lena Vance                     Jul 28 1903    Sep  8 1970
  w/o J.L.   d/o W.F. & S.E.
Williams, Mary Sanders                   Aug  5 1876    Jan 10 1954
  w/o Willie C.
Willis, Laviece Ann Jenkins              Apr  1 1852    Apr  1 1929
Willis, Lewis A.                         Jan  8 1891    May 19 1927
Willis, William W.                       Oct 10 1861    Sep  1 1940
Wilmer, Harriet Davis                    May  5 1856    Jne 22 1928
Woodward, Ada Cook                       Mar 28 1860    Jan 24 1939
  w/o Robt. H.
Woodward, Celestia C.                    May 12 1890    May 20 1967
  d/o Ada C. & Robt. H.
Woodward, Maggie Vance                   Nov  3 1900    Sep 28 1957
  w/o Robt. E.   d/o W.F. & Sallie H.
Woodward, Margaret Lucile                Apr  7 1895    Apr 14 1948
  WOW Circle   d/o Ada C. & Robt. H.
Woodward, Robert E. WOW                          1881           1946
Woodward, Robert H.                      Nov 23 1855    May  4 1923
Woodward, Roy Wideman                    Jne  5 1900    Oct  2 1952
Woodward, Samuel C.                      Oct  9 1883    Jne 16 1963
```

Woodward, Wyman P.   1890   1951
  h/o Marie Oxyner (Whisnant)
Zimmerman, Belva Dickson   1918   1959
  w/o William   d/o James D. Dickson, Sr.

69.   HERRINGTON

Herrington, Andrew J.   age 5y 1m   Apr 26 1833
                                    18 d
Herrington, Archibald M.   age 37 y   Nov 16 1853
                                    10 m
Herrington, Julius P.   Sep 9 1859   Aug 11 1860
Herrington, Martin   age 64y 5m   Aug 1 1850
                                     5d
Herrington, Nancy   Jan 10 1792   Aug 25 1860
  w/o Martin Note: Two children of Martin and Nancy
  are buried in the Habersham Methodist cemetery (ed).
Sapp, Abbie   Feb 14 1861   Oct 16 1882
  w/o W.C.

70.   HICKMAN

Hickman, Annie B.   Apr 1 1878   Aug 1 1913
  1st w/o N.A., Sr.
Hickman, Infant   Sep 26 1905   same   date
  d/o N.A. & A.B.
Hickman, Infant   Jul 24 1906   Jul 27 1906
  s/o N.A. & A.B.
Hickman, Infant   Aug 8 1907   same   date
  s/o N.A. & A.B.
Hickman, Jesse and wife   nd   nd
  (unmarked graves) grandparents of James Warren
  Hickman (ed).
Hickman, John Wesley   Apr 7 1915   Sep 1 1917
Hickman, Joseph W.   Mar 8 1851   Jne 18 1911
Hickman, Mariah   Dec 26 1852   Oct 4 1922
  w/o Joseph W.
Hickman, Martha Hickman   c. 1873   Jul 8 1930
  w/o Jim
Hickman, Mary J. Andrews   Feb 6 1888   nd
  2nd w/o Noah A., Sr. Her birthdate appears on the
  double marker with N.A., but she, and her son, N.A.,II,
  are buried in the Old Sardis cemetery (ed).
Hickman, Noah A.   Sep 18 1880 Jne 11 1945
  md 1st Annie B.   2nd Mary J.A.
Sturdivant, Lillie R.   Sep 6 1886 Dec 21 1912
  w/o W.E.

Note: In this vicinity there remains one marked grave,
Solomon Godbee, no dates, with the inscription, "Respect
other graves nearby." (ed).

```
Arrington, Sallie Amanda        Jne 10 1861   Aug  7 1888
Beckum, Mary Jane               Oct 11 1816   May  3 1893
Blackstone, Annie Inglett              1906             L
  w/o Wm. M.
Blackstone, William McKinley    age 72 y      Nov 16 1972
Brown, Infant                           nd             nd
  s/o J.S. & Sarah D.
Brown, Sarah D.                 Oct      1825  Apr 20 1875
  w/o J.S.
Brown, Walter H.                age 4y 1 m              1858
  s/o J.S. & Sarah D.
Broxton, Burke S.                      1902            1924
Broxton, Chas. W.               May 13 1855   Sep  2 1931
  h/o Sarah
Broxton, Charlie R.             Mar 11 1887             nd
Broxton, Ethel S.               Mar 16 1892   Mar 16 1951
  w/o Charlie R.
Broxton, Nannie J.              Apr  8 1894   May 23 1960
Broxton, Sarah                  Jne 27 1862   Jan 25 1935
  w/o Chas. W.
Byne, John R.                   age 34y 7m    Jan 17 1875
  s/o Caroline Tarver & Oliver H. Perry 3d
  f/o John Perry Byne who is buried at Sandersville,
  Ga.  (ed).
Byne, Oliver H. Perry           Aug 25 1815   Sep  3 1868
  md  Caroline Tarver of Richmond Co., 1838;  parents
  of John R. and Sarah Alice, who md Henry Rudolph
  Williams  (ed).
Carswell, Enoch H.              Oct 28 1814   Feb 17 1863
  s/o Mary Palmer & Alexander, II
Carswell, Nancy Janette         Sep 26 1820   Sep 14 1867
  w/o Enoch H.  d/o Mary Miller (1786-1863) & Samuel
  McNair (1770-1841) of Greene Co., Ga.  (ed).
Carswell, William Felix         Oct  9 1883   Nov  1 1884
  s/o Mary Fannie Janes & Rev. J. Hamilton
Cason, Adam T.                  Sep  5 1827   Nov 14 1902
Cason, John R.                  Oct 14 1871   Nov  2 1903
Cohn, Allen K.                         1955             L
  s/o V.B. & K.L.
Cohn, Janet M.                         1949             L
  d/o V.B. & K.L.
Cohn, Kenneth L.                       1922             nd
Cohn, Michael J.                       1960             L
  s/o V.B. & K.L.
Cohn, Nathan O.                        1947             L
  s/o V.B. & K.L.
Cohn, Vivian B. Graig                  1926            1961
  w/o Kenneth L.
Cook, Ella                      Dec 13 1853   Mar  2 1863
Corley, Allie Templeton         Nov 18 1869   Dec  5 1944
  w/o William E.  m/o Roger W.
Corley, Georgia Loren           Mar 11 1904   Aug 17 1970
  w/o Samuel Templeton
```

Corley, Infant   age 1d   Jan   1928
  d/o Sam & Georgia
Corley, Mary Atkins   1852   1919
  w/o Bird (who is buried in Saluda Co., S.C.);
  m/o William E.
Corley, Terry E.   1874   1939
  h/o Maud Avret, who is buried in the Collins-Avret
  cemetery; br/o Wm. E. f/o James (ed).
Corley, William E.   Jul 1 1872   Jne 15 1939
Daniel, Bryan   Jne 2 1799   Jul 10 1864
Daniel, Bryan McDuffie   Jan 27 1834   1883
Daniel, Emeline Miller   Jul 3 1842   Jne 13 1921
  w/o Theodore F. d/o Emeline McKinney (d. 1844)
  & Thomas Miller (d. 1851) of King & Queen Co. Va. (ed)
Daniel, Harriett   Sep 26 1806   Nov 4 1880
  w/o Bryan
Daniel, Isabella H.A.   Nov 26 1831   May 23 1912
  d/o Harriett & Bryan
Daniel, Jasper G.   May 15 1837   1871
Daniel, Louisa J.   nd   Aug   1877
  w/o B.M.
Daniel, Robert Toombs   1847   1865
Daniel, Theodore F.   May 24 1840   Feb 14 1920
Daniel, Thomas B.   Dec 6 1866   Aug 22 1901
Daniel, William Baldwin   CSA   May 24 1843   Apr 29 1862
  died with disease contracted in the service of his
  country (ed).
Dillard, Anna Jones   age 28y 5m   Sep 3 1869
Dillard, Mrs. Nancy M.   Oct 12 1807   Feb 18 1868
  w/o John m/o Sarah Fryer, Mary Schaffner, and Alice
  Wiggins. See Dillard & Hephzibah City cemeteries (ed)
Fulcher, Carlton L.   Jne 29 1859   Nov 1 1864
  s/o J.L. & E.F.
Fulcher, Cora Smith   Oct 29 1891   Aug 7 1957
  w/o Thomas H.
Fulcher, Emily F.   May 2 1829   Sep 19 1863
  w/o John LaFayette
Fulcher, J. LaFayette   1825   1909
Fulcher, James C.   Nov 4 1868   Jne 22 1949
  s/o John LaFayette
Fulcher, John Berry   1851   1933
  s/o John LaFayette
Fulcher, Mrs. Mamie E.   May 13 1874   Nov 28 1906
Fulcher, Moselle Melton   1857   1932
  w/o John Berry d/o Mr. & Mrs. Templeton
Fulcher, Sarah A.   Dec 23 1839   May 13 1879
Fulcher, Thomas H.   Oct 11 1889   Oct 25 1967
  s/o Moselle Melton & John Berry
Gaines, Mrs. Louisa   nd   Sep 30 1880
Henderson, J. Lewis   May 13 1896   Sep 9 1897
Hillis, Charlie Rasmus   Mar 30 1880   Apr 21 1944
Hillis, Mattie Broxton   May 24 1900   nd
  w/o Chas. Rasmus
Ivey, Infant   age 5 d   only   date
  s/o J.M. & E.E.

Ivey, Infant   age 5 d   only   date
  s/o J.M. & E.E.
Johnson, Clarence Lucious   Sep 2 1886   Jul 21 1952
Johnson, Eva B. Fulcher   Aug 12 1896   L
  w/o 1st Clarence L. 2nd Grover E. Fulcher
  d/o Charles Broxton, Sr.
Johnson, Gracie A.   Apr 20 1921   Feb 26 1925
Johnson, Mrs. Nancy   Jne 27 1786   Aug 28 1855
  w/o Moses   d/o Mary Cureton & George Palmer
  m/o Herschel V. Johnson, Georgia Governor, U.S.
  Senator, candidate for U. S. Vice-President on ticket
  with Stephen A. Douglas, Confed. Senator, distinguished lawyer and judge. See Johnson & Palmer
  cemeteries (ed).
Joiner, Infant   nd   nd
Key, Rev. Joshua   Feb 9 1786   Nov 11 1862
  b Edgefield Dist., S.C.   md 1st Elizabeth Tarker-
  sley, 1806; 2nd Martha Barksdale of Edgefield Dist.,
  1811; 3rd Elizabeth Marshall Scott; 4th Mrs. Mary
  McNatt. f/o Rev. Thomas D. & Capt. Joshua S., by
  second marriage.
  Note: Some data above are from the earlier research
  of Mrs. Anne MacKenzie Humphrey (ed).
Key, Joshua Scott   Sep 2 1817   Dec 12 1876
  s/o Rev. Joshua
Key, Mrs. Mary McNatt   1790   1871
  w/o Rev. Joshua   md Jne 22 1823. By first marriage
  she was the mother of Adam McNatt. Will Bk A 342-44.
  See Bath cemetery for her son and his family (ed).
Kilpatrick, Harriet Eliza   Nov 4 1791   Mar 16 1863
  2nd w/o Rev. J.H.T.   md Jan 23 1822 d/o Mary and
  Batt Jones. m/o Rev. Washington L., Rev. James
  Hines, and three daughters: Mary (md Carswell)
  Harriet Eliza (md Carswell), and Sarah Ann (md Rev.
  W. H. Davis), Clark op. cit., 171. She was also
  the grandmother of Dr. Wm. Heard Kilpatrick, educa-
  tional philosopher and professor, Columbia University,
  N.Y. City. Fothergill, op. cit., 126 (ed).
Kilpatrick, Rev. James H.T.   Jul 24 1788   Jan 9 1869
  b Iredell Co., N. Car. Migrated to Louisiana.
  Soldier War of 1812. Married in La. Miss Tanner;
  one son, Robert T., MD. Clark op. cit., 171. Moved
  to Georgia; pastor of Big Buckhead Church, 1828-56;
  outstanding minister and leader in the Hephzibah
  Baptist Association (ed).
Loren, Harvey L., Sr.   1906   1965
Loren, Pearlie S.   1920   nd
  w/o H.L., Sr.
McKinley, Robert L.   Nov 30 1922   May 6 1973
Morris, Eugenia Carswell   Dec 8 1851   Jne 3 1927
  w/o Whitfield Lee   d/o Janette & Enoch Carswell
  m/o Enoch (buried Dublin, Ga.), Jasper H., Ethel (md
  R. W. Corley), Harriet Eugenia (md Jordan) & Kath-
  erine J. (md Vallotton) (ed).
Morris, Jasper H. WW-I   1895   1918
  Lost at sea. See Note 1 (ed).

```
Morris, Whitfield Lee              Dec  9 1860  Aug 31 1925
  s/o Joe Morris & ------ Delaughter
Palmer, Miss Elefare Josephine              1832          1903
Palmer, Isabella Tarver            Feb 13 1793  May 20 1863
  w/o Benjamin   d/o Etheldred (b  1770 in N. Car.) &
  Mary Robinson Tarver   m/o six children  (ed).
Palmer, Mary Matilda Brown                 1808          1881
  w/o William   md 1827
Palmer, Miss Mary Sabine                   1831          1903
Palmer, Miss Michigan Adelaide             1842          1871
Palmer, Robert C.                  Aug      1852  Aug     1884
  h/o Sallie   f/o Olin Palmer
Ricker, James Luther                         nd  Jan  5 1897
Ricker, Mary L.                    Jne 23 1852  Mar 24 1867
  d/o Jas. L. & Melvina
Ricker, Melvina Gaines                     1828  Mar  3 1907
  w/o Jas. L.
Roberts, L. P.                     Sep  8 1845  Mar 30 1881
Tarver, Adline Youngblood          Apr 28 1835  May  6 1914
  w/o Dred Clayton    m/o Wm. Gardener, Abbie Palmer
  (never married), Smith Clayton (buried at Gaffney,
  S.C.), & Samuel Etheldred  (ed).
Tarver, Benjamin Ruffin            Dec 17 1854  Mar 11 1863
  s/o Noah S. & Narcissa
Tarver, Dred Clayton               Jul  7 1827  Mar 10 1910
  also listed in family records as Etheldred, Jr.  (ed).
Tarver, Fleming Eliphlet MD        Feb  4 1851  Oct 29 1907
  s/o Robinson & Anley   Vurdic;  practiced medicine
  in Burke Co  (ed).
Tarver, James Elhannon             Jan  7 1857  Mar 22 1918
  s/o Noah S. & Narcissa
Tarver, Jaqueline E. Farmer                 1860          1938
  w/o James E.   no children   b Jefferson Co.
Tarver, Julia Smith                May  5 1858  Jul 19 1868
  d/o Noah S. & Narcissa
Tarver, Mark                       age 64 y      May  6 1849
Tarver, Mary (Molly) L.            May  3 1859  Sep 13 1933
  w/o Wm. G.       / Vallotton   d/o Nancy Wise &
  John R. Vallotton m/o Effie Tarver Stone (Mrs. J.H.),
  John R., Lillie Kate, Ruffin Nolan & Thomas Frederick
  (ed).
Tarver, Narcissa Youngblood        Nov 14 1833  Apr 18 1914
  w/o Noah Smith   m/o Lula (md  T.W. Pilcher of
  Augusta, no children)  (ed).
Tarver, Noah Smith                 May 12 1824  Apr 28 1892
Tarver, Sarah                              1792  Sep 29 1869
  w/o Mark
Tarver, William Gardener           Jul 17 1860  Jne  4 1940
  s/o Dred C. & Adline Youngblood
Thomas, E. S.                      age 70 y      Jan 27 1905
Thomas, Mrs. Joanna E. Palmer              1828          1902
  w/o William   md 1851
Traylor, Artemecia Elizabeth       Dec 13 1901  Jne 21 1902
  d/o Alpha L. & E.W.
```

Vallotton, Elizabeth A. Erwin   . . . . nd - Jul 3 1885
   b Richmond Co.   w/o 1st ------Tinley 2nd   Robert R.
   Vallotton   d/o Nancy Daniel & Richard Erwin (or Ervin)
   m/o Mary & James Tinley (ed).
Vallotton, Robert R.   Jne 1 1824 Oct 13 1887
   s/o Sarah Tarver & Francis Stephen   br/o John R.
   His parents, brother & wife's half-sister are buried
   in the Vallotton cemetery   (ed).
Walton, C.R.   age 17 y   Apr 12 1883
   only s/o Efali & Mary V.   d while attending M.G.
   Military & Agriculture College at Milledgeville, Ga.
Walton, Nancy   age 84 y   May 9 1877
Ward, Johnson L.   age 83 y   Jne 10 1897
Weatherford, Emmitt Daniel   Mar 20 1920 May 2 1970
   WW-II Ga S Sgt USA
White James Daniel   1865   1926
White, Thomas Clyde WW-I   Jul 27 1895 Nov 17 1941
   Ga PFC USA
Wicker, E. A.   1837   1919
Wiggins, Alice Dillard   1835   1924
   w/o Amos W.   d/o John & Nancy M. Dillard
Wiggins, Amos B. (Buck)   1856   1941
   s/o Amos W. & Alice D.
Wiggins, Amos W.   1816   1883
   s/o Amos   See Wiggins cemetery (ed).
Wiggins, Clarence R.   Sep 27 1901 Feb 1 1930
   s/o A.B. & M.G.
Wiggins, Maud I. Greiner   1865 Jne 24 1954
   w/o Amos B. m/o Alice (md Marion Hill)
Wiggins, Nancy Virginia   age 20 y   Jne 25 1859
   Note: A governess from Mississippi who came to teach
   the Carswell children; not kin to the other Wiggins
   (ed).
Winter, Artemecia Meigs   Apr 22 1852 Nov 3 1939
   w/o Lewis V.   /Thomas   md Dec 14 1871
   m/o Davis, Emmie (md Traylor), Ruth (md Story) &
   Bertha (md Carswell) (ed).
Winter, Lewis Vinton CSA   Jan 22 1847 Mar 26 1925
Wise, Nancy Daniel   1799   1862
   w/o 1st Richard Erwin (or Ervin) 2nd Frederick Wise
   m/o Elizabeth A. Erwin, Nancy F. Wise (Vallotton) &
   Thomas Wise, CSA (buried in Richmond Co. above Blythe)
   (ed).

Notes: (1) A monument stands in this cemetery "In
memory of Alexander Carswell (1727-1803), John Carswell (1760-1817), George Palmer (1750-1820), Patriots
of the American Revolution; also to Jasper H. Morris
(1895-1918) Soldier World War I, Lost at Sea." See
the Carswell and Palmer cemeteries where the first
three mentioned are buried (ed).
      (2) Rev. Edmund Byne, long the pastor of Rocky
Creek Baptist Church, was the moving spirit in esta-
blishing Hopeful Baptist, although the latter was
not actually organized until 1815, about a year after
his death. According to church records, he was

132

buried February, 1814, not far from the planned location of the new church, but today no one can identify
the grave site. He had served as a Rev. War soldier
in Virginia; became the founder of the Byne family
in Burke Co., having moved from King and Queen County,
Va. in 1785 and settled with his family on the north
side of Brier Creek. Family records place the number of children at twelve, but we list here only the
eight who could, at least, be partially documented:
Mary Byne md Job Gresham (this couple settled in
Lincoln Co., Ky.); Sarah md Philip Lumpkin,
General William ** (1758-1824), a brigade commander
in the Ga. Militia and a senator for 13 years in
the Ga. Legislature; Anne (1776-1851) md Augustine
Harris; Frances md Moses Walker of Brunswick Co.,
Va.; Thomas an outstanding Burke Baptist layman,
about 1810; Lewis* md Martha* (d 1817), mother of
twelve, and Edward*, who married Milly* (1753-
1806). See **Warren & White, op. cit., 19 and
*Warren, op. cit., 16 (ed).
    (3) The 1820 U.S. Census for Burke Co.
lists nine Bynes as heads of families: Elijah,
Enoch, George, Henry, John, Lewis, Richard, Thomas,
and William. Some of these are sons of the first
generation in Burke (ed).

72.   HUDSON

Hudson, R.V. (Mrs. Jenny)   Nov 16 1835 Sep 24 1914

73.   HUGHES

Hughes, Dr. Edward   age 30 y   Jul 8 1833
Hughes, Mrs. Julia   age 42 y   Feb 26 1852
  w/o W.W.
74.   HURST

Hurst, John   age 64 y   Sep 30 1831
Sanders, Benjamin I.   Nov 20 1877 Jan 9 1881
Sanders, Elizabeth C.   May 31 1880 Jne 14 1881

75.   HURST BAPTIST
                       Screven Co.

Andrews, Ernest Samuel   Mar 18 1908 Jan 15 1945
  s/o Josephine
Andrews, Josephine   Jul 10 1867 Sep 4 1938
Andrews, Mary Emma   Jan 17 1878 Aug 13 1946
Archibald, C.T.   Apr 10 1854 Apr 12 1922
Bargeron, Ora D.   Mar 29 1901 Jan 19 1970
Beasley, Eva Agnes G.   Aug 18 1909 Sep 4 1964
  w/o W.T., Jr.
Beasley, Marvin D.   Oct 1 1941 Dec 21 1959
  s/o W.T., Jr. & Eva A.

```
Beasley, Wm. T., Jr.  WW-II        Sep 17 1914    Oct  4 1968
   Ga S/Sgt 35 TK Bn 4 Armd Div SS PH
Biggs, Joseph A.                    Oct 21 1880    Jul 29 1895
   s/o J.A. & N.A.
Blackburn, Georgia N.               Sep 11 1861    Jan  3 1927
   w/o James R.
Blackburn, James R.                 Aug  6 1849    Aug 13 1906
Bonnell, Mrs. Clara R.              age 84 y       Feb 18 1950
Bonnell, J. Crawford                     1896            1971
Boyed, Infant                       Apr  3 1824    same   date
   d/o J.G. & Sarah
Boyed, Laura L.                     Oct 18 1861    Feb  4 1897
   w/o J.G. Boyd
Boyd, Carrie Bell H.                Jul 17 1874    Jan 20 1957
Boyd, Crawford Lee                  Apr 10 1890            nd
Boyd, James G.                      Mar 21 1858    Dec 28 1935
Boyd, Mollie F.                          1888            1958
Boyd, Willie L.                     Sep 10 1893    Jan 23 1906
   s/o J.G. & Laura L.
Broxton, Florie B.                       1900            1951
   w/o J.L.
Broxton, James L.                        1894            1969
Bryan, Mollie Hillis Lariscy        Apr  4 1902    May  3 1956
Callison, George R.                      1902            1949
Chance, Beulah Bell                 Jul 10 1924    Jul 27 1925
Chance, Callie Marie                Jne 27 1893    Sep 27 1894
   d/o J.H. & E.M.
Chance, Dicy Davis Smith            Sep 29 1834    Dec 17 1923
   w/o Willoughby
Chance, E.L.                        Aug 11 1874    Apr 29 1890
Chance, Lillie May                  Oct 11 1893    Oct 27 1894
   d/o R.R. & S.A.
Chance, Willoughby                  May 30 1820    Mar  9 1876
Clayton, Inez                       Apr 20 1916    Jne 11 1916
   d/o W.H. & M.E.
Clayton, T.J.                       Mar 16 1914    Sep  8 1914
   s/o W.H. & M.E.
Click, James M.  WW-I               Dec  5 1896    Sep 14 1953
   Cpl 323 SVC Par Unit MTC
Daley, Jenny                        Mar  8 1878    Dec 22 1880
   d/o T.W. & N.A.
Davis, Mrs. Abbie                   Aug 15 1873    Dec  6 1892
   d/o Mr. & Mrs. J.A. Joyner
Davis, Annie Skinner                Nov  3 1866    Apr 23 1941
   w/o C.S.
Davis, C.S.                         Oct  8 1866    Jan  9 1919
Davis, Capers Bob                   Jne 12 1876    Sep 25 1947
Davis, Charley                      Mar 14 1839    Aug 24 1886
Davis, Charlie H.                   Aug 15 1897    Dec  1 1966
Davis, Dessie Mae Brown             May 21 1896    Apr  8 1957
   w/o J.N.
Davis, Julia A.                     Mar 16 1841    Feb 17 1913
Davis, Layuna R.                    Aug 20 1910    Feb  4 1930
   w/o Chas. H.
Davis, Mrs. Liddie                  May 19 1844    Dec  6 1923
```

Davis, Mary L. Skinner	Jan 31 1897	Feb 8 1944
w/o Jesse N.		
Davis, Minnie L.	Apr 25 1883	Sep 30 1889
Davis, Roblin	Feb 7 1839	May 1 1899
Davis, Rolan R.	Oct 3 1901	Oct 24 1901
s/o C.S. & A.L.		
Davis, Rolin R.	May 2 1878	May 18 1899
Davis, Susia I.	Jan 29 1872	Jul 8 1894
Davis, Willie J.	Feb 29 1872	Mar 28 1901
Dennis, Carrie Mae Joyner	Nov 24 1906	Jul 14 1930
Dickey, Angus S.	1872	1941
Dickey, Annie Sarah Broxton	Sep 28 1898	Nov 26 1948
w/o Minis A.		
Dickey, Atys S.	Aug 27 1898	Aug 22 1962
Dickey, Gilbert R.	Jan 5 1908	Aug 15 1933
Dickey, Infant	only date	Jan 11 1932
d/o Mr. & Mrs. Gilbert R.		
Dickey, Lola E.	1878	1955
w/o Angus S.		
Dickey, Minis Albert	Mar 10 1896	Aug 9 1963
Dukes, Infant	only date	Oct 11 1936
of Mrs. Pearl N.		
Dukes, Pearl N.	Feb 5 1905	Oct 11 1936
Elliott, Amanda Andrews	Feb 10 1857	Sep 5 1928
w/o Augustus		
Elliott, Augustus D.	May 22 1853	Oct 3 1922
Elliott, Cora Lee Davis	Jne 21 1893	Jne 18 1937
w/o W.G. sis/o Mary Lee Skinner		
Elliott, Norman	Mar 30 1886	Sep 30 1928
Godbee, Byron C.	1916	1961
Godbee, Capus Mulky	Mar 1 1903	Aug 21 1906
s/o R.S.		
Godbee, Colquitt C.	Dec 7 1877	Sep 7 1952
Godbee, Corene	Jul 8 1911	Sep 2 1925
d/o G.G. & R.A.		
Godbee, Darrol	1960	1961
Godbee, David	1957	1961
Godbee, Eugene WW-II	Dec 13 1907	Sep 12 1961
Ga Sgt 2132 Base Unit AAF		
Godbee, Homer Capus	Mar 21 1904	Feb 18 1907
s/o C.C. & Rozzie		
Godbee, Infant	only date	Jne 25 1924
d/o Lindsey & Luna		
Godbee, Infant	only date	Dec 24 1918
s/o Lindsey & Luna		
Godbee, Jesse W. WW-II	Apr 8 1915	May 10 1945
Ga PFC 305 Inf 77 Div		
Godbee, Joseph Henry	Dec 22 1892	Aug 9 1972
Godbee, Julia	Aug 3 1914	Aug 14 1914
d/o Mr. & Mrs. J.H.		
Godbee, Lena	Oct 18 1921	Dec 11 1923
d/o Mr. & Mrs. J.H.		
Godbee, Lois Inez	Oct 30 1921	May 20 1934
d/o Lindsey & Luna		
Godbee, Luna	nd	illeg

Godbee, Mabel	Mar 13 1897	nd
w/o Joseph Henry md Dec 18 1913		
Godbee, Martha E.	1931	1961
Godbee, Reba	Feb 4 1928	Dec 4 1928
d/o Mr. & Mrs. J.H.		
Godbee, Rozzie T.	Sep 7 1878	Dec 19 1960
w/o Colquitt C.		
Godbee, Wesley T.	1918	1964
Griffin, Cleveland E.	Jan 14 1886	Nov 17 1918
Griffin, Dora Dean	Jan 1 1916	Jne 24 1916
d/o C.E. & E.L.		
Griffin, Eva L.	Jan 29 1900	nd
w/o Hemon T.		
Griffin, Hemon T.	Oct 30 1890	Aug 23 1958
Griffin, Henry T.	Oct 30 1882	Mar 20 1883
s/o Thos. & J.R.		
Griffin, Isabella I.	Feb 18 1874	Aug 22 1882
d/o Thos. & J.R.		
Griffin, Jane E.	Dec 10 1826	Oct 30 1891
w/o Sampson		
Griffin, Jane R.	Dec 25 1847	Feb 18 1922
w/o Thomas E.		
Griffin, Lillian G.	Apr 15 1880	Dec 18 1954
w/o W.L.		
Griffin, Marion Thomas	Aug 8 1900	Jul 27 1936
Griffin, Mattie J.	1911	nd
w/o Vance A.		
Griffin, Mollie A.V.	Jan 11 1884	Sep 6 1886
d/o Thos. & J.R.		
Griffin, Stella	Nov 15 1916	same date
d/o C.E. & E.L.		
Griffin, Thomas E.	Sep 21 1850	May 28 1924
Griffin, Vance A.	1911	1972
Griffin, W.L.	Apr 4 1876	Apr 8 1929
Griffin, Willie E.	Mar 8 1906	Feb 12 1967
Griner, Arrie Oglesbee	1892	1939
Hamilton, John L.	Sep 20 1892	Dec 18 1941
Hann, Ina Mae	Jan 15 1896	Jul 13 1898
Hann, Lillie P.	Oct 29 1895	Jne 14 1897
d/o Homer & Josephine		
Hill, Austin Mathew, Sr.	Jan 4 1892	Nov 25 1964
h/o Susie W.		
Hill, H.C., Jr.	Feb 13 1883	Jne 28 1908
s/o H.C. & L.A.		
Hill, H.M.	Feb 4 1878	Jul 20 1925
Hill, Harvey A.	Sep 2 1886	Oct 17 1950
Hill, Henry Clay	Jul 16 1852	Jan 7 1916
Hill, Kaye Ermene (infant)	same date	Mar 23 1940
Hill, Lucy A.	Aug 13 1856	Mar 29 1940
w/o H.C.		
Hill, O.F.	Dec 30 1875	Mar 5 1878
s/o H.C. & L.A.		
Hill, Susie W.	nd	nd
w/o Austin M.		

Name	Birth	Death
Hillis, Lula M. w/o Walter R.	Apr 10 1878	Jne 6 1942
Hillis, Mattie d/o W.R. & L.M.	Oct 6 1907	Oct 8 1907
Hillis, Walter R.	Jul 18 1868	Oct 10 1930
Hiott, Dewey Perry	Mar 27 1899	Aug 8 1939
Holland, Infant d/o Mr. & Mrs. H.I.	Oct 26 1925	same date
Hotchkiss, Daniel A.	age 57 y	nd
Hotchkiss, Howell R. s/o Mr. & Mrs. Daniel	nd	nd
Hotchkiss, James D.	Jan 16 1860	Mar 7 1887
Jenkins, Berry, Jr.	Sep 23 1869	Aug 15 1936
Jenkins, Cornelia R. w/o Wm. J.	1875	1938
Jenkins, Ellie Gertrude w/o Thos. H.	Jan 25 1900	Oct 25 1920
Jenkins, Ervin V.	Nov 27 1885	Aug 23 1968
Jenkins, Ida Hillis w/o Berry, Jr.	Jne 25 1872	Aug 15 1924
Jenkins, Infant s/o Mr. & Mrs. W.J.	Jul 16 1916	Oct 10 1916
Jenkins, J. D.	Dec 30 1919	Sep 8 1934
Jenkins, J. Hershel	Apr 1 1882	Nov 26 1927
Jenkins, Jennie Joyner w/o Ervin V.	Aug 30 1884	Oct 8 1951
Jenkins, Leo Frank	Oct 25 1909	Oct 4 1963
Jenkins, Paul Hubert	Dec 1 1909	Nov 15 1939
Jenkins, William J.	1872	1937
Johnson, Gussie M. w/o Ransom W.	Nov 25 1905	nd
Johnson, Ransom W.	Dec 1 1898	Aug 23 1947
Joyner, Abbie d/o B.M. & W.E.	Nov 20 1905	Feb 19 1906
Joyner, Adel L. w/o Triggs	Feb 26 1880	May 4 1904
Joyner, Adeline	Jul 28 1850	Mar 18 1914
Joyner, Alice Smith	Apr 7 1877	Jne 17 1959
Joyner, Britt Mims	Jan 1 1885	Dec 6 1929
Joyner, Cathryn J.	May 6 1912	nd
Joyner, Cinthia E. d/o Jas. E. & Lennie	Dec 26 1902	Feb 27 1908
Joyner, Clarence F.	Sep 22 1906	Sep 29 1938
Joyner, Cuthbert	Mar 10 1842	Feb 13 1926
Joyner, Cynthia Elizabeth	Mar 24 1881	Sep 16 1885
Joyner, D. Triggs	Apr 1 1876	Mar 16 1937
Joyner, Emma R. d/o C. & Jane	Jne 22 1875	Sep 25 1915
Joyner, Fed	Jan 3 1879	Sep 25 1953
Joyner, Frank M.	Aug 27 1878	Jul 9 1951
Joyner, J.E.	May 31 1869	Nov 25 1914
Joyner, J. W.	Aug 2 1870	Dec 5 1884
Joyner, Jane w/o Cuthbert	Oct 23 1840	Sep 23 1906

Joyner, Jane E.	Aug 25 1866	May 1 1878
Joyner, Jimpsey	May 14 1847	Nov 13 1918
Joyner, Jimpsey M.	Feb 7 1901	Dec 6 1941
Joyner, Josephine Rowe	Jan 28 1875	May 10 1950
Joyner, Joshua	Apr 5 1846	May 15 1901
Joyner, Lennie B.	Sep 20 1880	Nov 2 1967
Joyner, Leroy G.	Apr 4 1906	Sep 26 1971
Joyner, Lucy	Nov 17 1842	Jul 12 1907
w/o Jimpsey J.		
Joyner, Lucy Ophelia	Jan 11 1904	Mar 18 1904
d/o Britton M. & W.E.		
Joyner, Moses P.	Oct 23 1871	Sep 9 1923
Joyner, Sarah L.	Nov 4 1897	Aug 31 1902
d/o F.M. & Alice		
Joyner, Sidney Franklin	Mar 12 1906	Nov 29 1936
Joyner, T.W.	Oct 21 1910	Mar 28 1971
Joyner, Turlie Sikes	May 19 1869	Jne 13 1956
w/o Fed		
Joyner, Willie Sowell	May 22 1887	May 29 1951
Joyner, Woodrow Wilson	Feb 8 1916	Jul 6 1918
Kirkland, George W.	1872	nd
Kirkland, Mary O.	1879	1944
Lambert, Gladys V.	Aug 1 1909	nd
w/o Willie S.		
Lambert, Willie S.	Aug 2 1906	Jul 15 1972
Lariscy, John Etheredge	Dec 18 1889	Oct 26 1965
Lariscy, Norma Broxton	Dec 28 1901	nd
w/o John E.		
Lee, Minnie Hillis	Oct 27 1897	Aug 1 1962
w/o Walstein		
Lee, Walstein L.	Dec 15 1908	nd
Lovett, James Mark	May 22 1886	Nov 5 1962
Mobley, Mrs. Luna Chance	age 79y 3m	May 24 1966
Mobley, Margaret	1862	1940
sis/o James G. Boyd		
Mobley, Minus WW-II	Jan 10 1899	Jne 17 1949
Pvt 305 MP Escort Gd Co		
Mobley, Winnie B.	Mar 23 1879	Dec 20 1904
Moore, John M.	Mar 1 1878	Jne 26 1939
Moore, Tomsie A.	Jan 2 1880	Aug 30 1961
w/o John M.		
Morris, Adolphus, Sr.	Nov 26 1886	Sep 5 1954
Morris, Daisy S.	Nov 14 1892	May 11 1965
w/o Adolphus, Sr.		
Morris, Infant	nd	nd
s/o Mr. & Mrs. W.A.		
Morris, Infant	nd	nd
s/o Mr. & Mrs. W.A.		
Morris, James Lovick	Oct 19 1909	May 23 1927
s/o Mr. & Mrs. W.A.		
Morris, John H. WOW	Jan 21 1894	Sep 13 1918
Murray, Crawford S.	May 16 1883	Jan 21 1969
Murray, Lula T.	Oct 2 1889	Jan 10 1952
w/o C.S.		
Oglesbee, -------	nd	nd

Name	Birth	Death
Oglesbee, Elenor	Apr 17 1905	Sep 27 1905
d/o Jas. & J.E.		
Oglesby, Ada Andrews	Oct 12 1893	Jul 14 1946
w/o Thos. W.		
Oglesby, Albert s/o James	1906	1936
Oglesby, Georgia A.	Sep 8 1843	Sep 19 1883
w/o Henry		
Oglesby, Henry	Nov 17 1835	Nov 17 1898
Oglesby, Ivy	Oct 6 1914	Sep 9 1919
s/o T.W. & Ada A.		
Oglesby, James	1880	1945
Oglesby, Thomas Watson	Jne 1 1892	nd
Oglesby, Willie	Apr 27 1877	Sep 19 1880
Oliver, Lula Estelle	Mar 19 1909	Jul 5 1918
d/o W.R. & N.V.		
Oliver, Nina T.	Nov 27 1880	Sep 24 1957
Oliver, William R.	Nov 13 1874	Mar 13 1942
Pye, Charlie Edward	May 5 1911	Aug 9 1933
Rackley, Fanny	Feb 18 1872	Dec 10 1902
Rackley, John A.	Apr 1 1829	Feb 25 1908
Rackley, Zilpha E.	Feb 4 1832	May 4 1897
w/o J.A.		
Radcliff, Floy S.	May 13 1912	May 8 1963
Reddick, John I.	Apr 3 1821	Jan 13 1897
Reddick, Sarah	Apr 26 1831	Nov 13 1882
w/o John I.		
Roberts, Clarence H.	Mar 21 1879	Oct 25 1883
s/o S.H. & E.G.		
Roberts, Jane E.	Nov 30 1859	Dec 6 1903
w/o M.H.		
Roberts, Jessie M.	Feb 8 1892	Nov 13 1904
d/o M.H. & J.E.		
Roberts, M.H.	Mar 8 1861	Nov 12 1904
Rowe, Albert W.	Jul 29 1899	Feb 2 1943
Rowe, Charles D.	Feb 7 1910	Jan 9 1939
Rowe, Ella Chance	May 1 1874	Dec 4 1957
Rowe, Roe Ann	1858	1907
Rowe, William M.	Dec 15 1872	Feb 24 1942
Sing, Maude Hillis	Jan 9 1900	Oct 24 1953
Skinner, Alfred C.	Jan 3 1894	Oct 12 1894
s/o W.E. & A.T.		
Skinner, Eliza	1903	1961
Skinner, Lovett C.	Feb 22 1897	May 9 1956
Skinner, Nillie	May 28 1872	Jul 5 1937
w/o W.E.		
Skinner, Roye M.	Feb 28 1900	May 26 1901
s/o W.E. & Nillie		
Skinner, Sadie Gertrude	Feb 1 1928	Jne 18 1928
d/o L.C. & E.S.		
Skinner, Susan M. Joyner	Mar 2 1868	Feb 11 1957
Skinner, Tilman G.	Feb 2 1895	Sep 12 1895
s/o W.E. & A.T.		
Skinner, W.E.	Jul 20 1870	Feb 15 1949
Skinner, William Hubert	Jul 20 1935	Jan 22 1936
s/o L.C. & E.S.		

Smith, Clarence L.	May 23 1890	Aug 24 1958
Smith, Grady D.	Oct 25 1891	Aug 1 1968
Smith, Isaac H.	Jne 28 1879	Dec 1 1937
Smith, J.H.	Jne 9 1887	Mar 22 1893
s/o J.H. & S.J.		
Smith, James H., Sr.	Jul 27 1849	Nov 5 1920
Smith, Martha	Feb 24 1881	Jan 29 1955
Smith, Mattie L.	age 90 y	Feb 27 1973
Smith, Ruth Hillis	Oct 26 1894	Mar 1 1960
Smith, Mrs. S.J.	May 27 1856	Jne 20 1915
w/o James H.		
Thompson, A.S.	Aug 3 1867	Nov 20 1885
Thompson, Alexander Horace	Feb 11 1889	May 22 1893
s/o J.W. & M.A.		
Thompson, Amanda	Feb 16 1859	Dec 14 1945
Thompson, Earl	Jan 31 1891	Jul 17 1904
Thompson, Essie Mae K.	1907	1939
w/o Ira J.		
Thompson, Evelyn	1916	1972
Thompson, George W.	Feb 14 1884	Apr 26 1958
Thompson, H.M.	Nov 8 1851	Mar 23 1925
Thompson, Infant	nd	nd
of H.M. & Sarah		
Thompson, Infant	Apr 4 1904	Jul 20 1904
of J.W. & M.A.		
Thompson, Ira Joseph	1907	1926
Thompson, J.R.	Nov 24 1882	Jne 20 1884
Thompson, Jimmie D.	1931	1939
Thompson, John R.	Dec 14 1831	Dec 24 1870
Thompson, Mattie L.	Oct 12 1886	Oct 31 1918
w/o Geo. W.		
Thompson, Miley	Nov 18 1893	Jan 19 1898
Thompson, Myra Kimbrell	Dec 20 1896	Sep 15 1966
Thompson, Nancy	Jan 15 1835	Oct 2 1905
Thompson, Pearl K.	Oct 2 1904	nd
w/o Geo. W.		
Thompson, Susie E.	Mar 4 1888	Jan 20 1890
Thompson, Thomas Allen	Feb 2 1892	May 3 1972
Walker, Anna	Oct 10 1893	Jne 27 1942
w/o James		
Walker, James	Jne 11 1890	Nov 9 1943
Wallace, Henry Harrison	Jne 12 1898	Jne 5 1901
Wiley, Mrs. Pearl	age 65 y	Jne 10 1967

76.   INMAN

Francis, India Walton	Aug 5 1854	Mar 29 1928
w/o Franklin M.		
Inman, Alfred	Mar 14 1795	Jan 6 1851
He joined the Baptist Church at Bark Camp Apr 22 1831		
Inman, Alfred J.	Sep 26 1864	Oct 10 1864
s/o D.A. & Maryann L.		
Inman, Allen	Oct 10 1806	Feb 24 1859

Inman, Mrs. Ava	Jne 10 1813	Jan 11 1870
w/o Allen		
Inman, Daniel Rev War	nd	nd
Ga Mil		
Inman, Daniel A.	Dec 11 1825	broken
Inman, George Washington	May 1 1849	Oct 13 1850
s/o Jeremiah & Mary A.		
Inman, Indianna E.	age 8m 3d	Jul 7 1851
d/o Daniel A. & Maryann L.		
Inman, James Daniel	May 14 1840	Dec 20 1840
s/o Jeremiah & Mary A.		
Inman, James G.A.	Sep 10 1851	Apr 8 1852
s/o Allen & Ava		
Inman, Jeremiah	Mar 26 1809	May 22 1869
a member of the Baptist Church since 1849		
Inman, Jeremiah A.	Dec 7 1857	Oct 9 1863
s/o J. & M.A.		
Inman, Mary E.E.	Oct 15 1849	Feb 22 1850
d/o Allen & Eva		
Inman, Melvina V.	age 4y 4m	Mar 14 1857
d/o D.A. & Mary L.	14d	
Inman, Sophia	age 52y 7m	Mar 28 1854
w/o Alfred		
Inman, William Allen	Feb 6 1851	Sep 24 1852
s/o Jeremiah & Mary A.		
Inman, William D.	Sep 20 1840	Jul 6 1841
s/o Allen & Ava		
Inman, Willie James	Feb 7 1863	Sep 24 1863
d/o J. & M.A.		
Jones, Clarence Malcom	Aug 19 1862	Aug 11 1863
s/o M.D. & V.L.		
Jones, Edward Crosland	1890	1895
Jones, Elizabeth	age 43 y	Sep 12 1846
w/o Mathew Jones		
Jones, Francis M.	Jne 3 1866	Sep 27 1870
s/o Malcom D. & Virginia L.		
Jones, Infant	Mar 11 1857	same date
s/o Francis A. & Mary T.		
Jones, James M.	Jan 22 1823	Jul 6 1849
Jones, Louisa A.	age 15y 10d	Mar 9 1845
eldest d/o Mathew & Elizabeth		
Jones, Malcom Bennett	Mar 1 1858	Aug 1 1863
s/o F.A. & M.T.		
Jones, Malcom D.	nd	Sep 29 1869
Jones, Mathew	age 45 y	May 13 1840
Jones, Thomas	age 2y	Oct 1840
s/o Mathew & Elizabeth		
Jones, William M.	Aug 30 1864	Jul 28 1865
s/o Malcom D. & Virginia L.		
Price, Mrs. Mary Ann	Jan 9 1834	Jan 5 1853
Consort of Dr. J.R. Price		
Wallace, Mrs. Ava M.	Feb 3 1819	Jan 21 1859

Jackson, J.C.	Nov 13 1844	Apr 6 1906
Jackson, Rockanna	May 10 1845	Aug 12 1916
w/o J. C.		
Knight, James CSA	nd	nd
Co D 48 Ga Inf		
Martin, Emmie Collins	1875	1944
w/o Luther E.		
Martin, Luther Evans	1875	1942
Mixon, Annie Gertrude	Jne 26 1884	Sep 6 1917
w/o W.H.		
Mixon, W.C.	Oct 17 1901	May 21 1902
s/o W.H. & A.G.		

78.   JAMES-JEFFERS
                    Burke-Jenkins Line

Allen, Mrs. Parris C.	Jan 10 1878	Jne 27 1907
w/o G.E. Allen		
Blackburn, Marietta W.	nd	nd
Blackburn, Robert L.	nd	nd
Chance, James M.	Dec 5 1875	May 4 1888
s/o J. & S.		
Chance, Susan	Nov 22 1848	Nov 24 1898
w/o J. Chance		
Gibson, Sarah Jessie James	Dec 21 1903	Aug 10 1928
w/o George		
James, Charles F.	May 11 1870	Apr 29 1938
James, Infant	Apr 22 1895	same date
d/o C.F. & O.J.		
James, Infant	only date	Feb 22 1896
s/o C.F. & O.J.		
James, Infant	only date	Sep 12 1897
d/o C.F. & O.J.		
James, Infant	only date	Feb 18 1899
s/o C.F. & O.J.		
James, Jessie	nd	bkn inscrp
James, Ophelia J.	Feb 22 1870	Jan 12 1925
w/o Charles F.		
Jeffers, Alma Pearl	Dec 19 1881	Apr 28 1953
w/o C.T.		
Jeffers, Benjamin	1870	1952
Jeffers, Charles Thomas	Mar 22 1890	Jan 22 1935
Mixon, Ina James	May 27 1906	Dec 15 1954
Scarborough, Emilne	age 55 y	Jne 29 1901
w/o W.L.		
Williams, Charlie	nd	Sep 15 189-

Note: Cemetery contains 15 additional adult graves
but without inscriptions: eleven with concrete slabs,
three with brick copings only, and one with wooden
marker. Two infant graves have concrete slabs (ed).

JENKINS

Jenkins, Alex	May	7 1883	Aug	1 1954
Jenkins, Archibald	Feb	15 1841	Feb	15 1857
Jenkins, Betsie	age	61 y		nd
Jenkins, Caroline	Dec	18 1843	Jul	2 1922
Jenkins, Clarence	Aug	28 1898	Jne	16 1899
s/o L.M. & M.F.				
Jenkins, Dorothy	Oct	25 1923	Jan	6 1941
w/o Wesley				
Jenkins, Dwight	Sep	28 1904	Aug	31 1951
Jenkins, Eliza	Jul	15 1849	Jul	15 1853
Jenkins, Emma B.	Dec	17 1884	May	17 1952
w/o Henry T.				
Jenkins, Hattie A.	Apr	11 1887	Feb	6 1904
d/o L.M. & M.F.				
Jenkins, Henry T.	Aug	12 1881	Jul	25 1947
Jenkins, Littleton M.	Sep	27 1858	Sep	28 1931
Jenkins, Lonnie	Oct	5 1896	Nov	2 1896
s/o L.M. & M.F.				
Jenkins, Loyd	Sep	12 1905	Aug	9 1924
s/o Mr. & Mrs. Alex				
Jenkins, Mary F.	Jul	16 1861	Sep	7 1921
w/o L.M.				
Jenkins, Mary H.	Sep	9 1908	Mar	23 1965
w/o Dwight				
Jenkins, Ola	Dec	10 1883	Aug	22 1961
w/o Alex				
Jenkins, Thomas W.	Nov	16 1922	Jne	20 1924
s/o H.T. & E.B.				
Joyner, Elizabeth	Dec	8 1836	Jan	31 1923
Long, Emma F.	Jne	5 1889	Aug	12 1936
w/o J.C.				
Long, John C.	Oct	6 1884	Sep	22 1921
Long, John Thomas	Aug	2 1911	Aug	19 1911
s/o J.C. & E.F.				
Murray, Mary E.	Feb	7 1838	Sep	13 1887
w/o Enoch				
Parkerson, Daisy J.	Dec	9 1891	Dec	4 1964
Parkerson, Henry I.	Jan	2 1888	Nov	21 1969
Parkerson, Myrtle	Nov	15 1917	Mar	25 1920
Sanders, Frank	Mar	9 1948	Jne	16 1956
Sanders, Robert	Dec	29 1949	Jne	16 1956
Sanders, Wayne	Jul	8 1946	Jne	16 1956
Scott, Joyce	Aug	14 1930	Aug	15 1930
Skinner, Lottie Jenkins		1894		1967
w/o Sim Thomas				
Skinner, Sim Thomas		1898		1956
Skinner, Thomas Watson	Feb	19 1944	Jne	23 1944
s/o L.M.				
Smith, Martha	May	26 1836	Sep	28 1913
Van Norstran, Frank E.	May	15 1887	Aug	9 1932
Van Norstran, Mildred J.	Sep	29 1927	May	15 1928
Ward, Infant	only	date	Dec	18 1929
of Mr. & Mrs. T.E.				

Ward, Infant   only   date   Jan 27 1933
    d/o Mr. & Mrs. T.E.

80.   JOHNSON

Johnson, Moses   nd   Sep 22 1837
    d on 60th birthday See Nancy Johnson in Hopeful
    Baptist (ed).

81.   JONES (BIRDSVILLE PLANTATION)
Jenkins Co.

Falligant, Amanda Burney   nd   nd
    w/o Joseph d/o Mary Slater & John Burney
Franklin, Ben, Sr.   Mar 25 1884 Mar 24 1971
Franklin, Ben, Jr.   Dec 26 1913 Apr 27 1970
Franklin, Mary Edwin Perkins   Jne 11 1918 Dec 4 1964
    w/o Ben Franklin, Jr.
Franklin, Susan Elizabeth (Bessie) Jones
    w/o Ben, Sr.   Dec 25 1890 Apr 8 1969
    d/o M.J. Anderson & Geo. W. grand d/o Dr. Wm. B. &
    Sidney S. She was the 8th mistress of the Birdsville
    plantation home (ed).
Jones, Ada   Jne 3 1852 Jul 29 1853
    d/o W.B. & S.S.
Jones, Anderson Harcourt   Oct 16 1893 Oct 2 1913
    s/o George W. & Mattie
Jones, Emory C. Freeman   Mar 26 1844 Oct 13 1875
    w/o Dr. Wm. B.
Jones, George Washington   Oct 14 1860 Sep 28 1905
    s/o Dr. Wm. B. & Sidney S.
Jones, Henry Philip   Dec 27 1788 Oct 1 1853
    s/o Philip & Elizabeth Huckabee md 1st Sarah Vickers;
    2nd Mary Forth (Wells); 3rd Mary Hampton (Fullwood)
Jones, Infant   Jan 29 1866 Aug 27 1866
    s/o H.W. & Martha Aiken
Jones, Infant   nd   nd
    s/o J.V. & Rosa C.
Jones, Infant   Jul 28 1843 Aug 26 1843
    s/o Jos. B. & Sarah A.
Jones, James Henry   Jul 5 1850 Aug 20 1851
    s/o J.B. & S.A.
Jones, James Vickers   Apr 22 1812   1879
    eldest s/o H.P. & Sarah Vickers; md Mary
    Elizabeth Hurt
Jones, John Forsyth   Oct 10 1839 Mar 29 1844
    s/o Henry P. & Mary Wells
Jones, John Paul   May 8 1856 Dec 4 1883
    s/o J.B. & S.A.
Jones, Joseph Bertram   Oct 10 1817 Dec 29 1896
    s/o Henry P. & Sarah V.
Jones, Joseph Whitfield CSA   Apr 13 1848 Feb 14 1865
    s/o J.B. & S.A. killed in action

Jones, Lyman Hall   Mar 21 1851   Mar 4 1852
    s/o H.W. & M.A.
Jones, Martha (Mattie) Jones   Oct 3 1860   Nov 12 1886
    w/o Geo. W.   /Anderson
Jones, Mary Forth Wells   illeg   Jul 17 1840
    w/o Henry Philip/(nee Forth)
Jones, Philip Rev War   Jul 16 1759   Nov 6 1789
    b N. Car.   h/o Elizabeth Jones of Wilkes Co., his
    cousin; s/o Francis & Elizabeth Huckabee
    Ga Mil Rev War
Jones, Sarah A. Lewis   Nov 15 1822   Jne 1 1871
    w/o J.B.
Jones, Sarah Vickers   Nov 29 1790   Mar 18 1835
    w/o Henry Philip   d/o James & Penelope Murphey
    Vickers   m/o Harriet Almira, James Vickers, Melvina
    Virginia, Joseph Bertram, Sarah Ann, Henry Wilkes,
    William Beaman, and Penelope Elizabeth (ed).
Jones, Sidney Ann Elizabeth   Oct 30 1833   Jne 1 1870
    w/o Dr. William Beaman /Sapp   d/o Everett &
    Frances Allen Sapp Will Bk A, 80-81.
Jones, Sidney Johnson   Nov 15 1864   Jul 10 1865
    d/o J.B. & S.A.
Jones, Stella Susan   May 19 1857   Dec 30 1913
    d/o J.B. & S.A.
Jones, Walter Beaman   Sep 5 1875   Nov 20 1876
    s/o Dr. Wm. B. & Emory F.
Jones, Wesley   Oct 28 1844   Dec 11 1879
    s/o J.B. & S.A.
Jones, Wilkes Aiken   Aug 20 1868   Oct 28 1887
    s/o H.W. & Martha Aiken
Jones, William Beaman MD   Feb 23 1827   Mar 30 1886
    s/o H.P. & Sarah V.   md 1st Sidney Ann Elizabeth
    Sapp; 2nd Emory C. Freeman; 3rd Mamie F. Chaires
Jones, William Wirt   Aug 31 1850   Jul 16 1852
    s/o W.B. & S.S.
Law, Lena Alethia   Jan 23 1881   Jan 23 1885
    d/o Robt. & Clara Jones
McElmurray, ------ .   nd   nd
    dates and parents of this boy unknown
Parsons, Henry Philip   Mar 10 1844   Oct 26 1847
    s/o Thomas & Melvina
Parsons, Julia Virginia   Oct 18 1839   Dec 16 1847
    d/o Thomas & Melvina
Parsons, Melvina Virginia   Mar 27 1814   nd
    w/o Dr. Thomas   d/o Henry Philip & Sarah Vickers
Parsons, William James   Nov 3 1845   Mar 30 1847
    s/o Thomas & Melvina
Note: The Birdsville Jones Family, compiled by Miriam
Jones Brinson and Susan Elizabeth Jones Franklin, 66 pp.
(n.d. typed), is the definitive work on this family.
The limited edition was distributed only to family
members (ed).

Barnes, Eliza J.   age 31 y   Aug 23 1852
   w/o William E.   d/o Margaret & Seaborn H. Jones
   m/o John A. Note: Wm. E. of Augusta, Ga. was a
   Confed. soldier, the s/o John A. & br/o George T.
   See Clark, op. cit., 148 (ed).

Barnes, Infant   nd   1848
   d/o Eliza J. & Wm. E.

Barnes, Infant   nd   1852
   d/o Eliza J. & Wm. E.

Jones, Abraham Henry   Nov 18 1792 Jne 18 1798
   s/o Sarah & James

Jones, Infants (two)   nd   nd
   of Evalina Toombs (niece of Robert Toombs) &
   John James

Jones, James Rev War   May 1 1755 Jan 9 1809
   s/o Martha Jones & Abram (not related; she was of a
   Bristol, Eng. family). James was b in Edgecombe
   (later Halifax) Co., N. Car. Captured by British at
   fall of Charleston. Lawyer and planter. Several
   times member of Georgia Legislature. Acquired the
   Canaan plantation after the Rev War. Fothergill,
   op. cit.,61, 101, 102   (ed).

Jones, James William   Feb 15 1799 Jul 29 1799
   s/o Sarah & James

Jones, Margaret A. Jones   Jul 7 1800 Jan 26 1893
   w/o Seaborn H. b on Burke plantation which in the
   1890's was known as the Moses Walker place, The
   True Citizen, Feb 18, 1893. She was also a Jones
   but not a kinswoman of Seaborn. m/o Mary, Eliza
   Barnes, John James (U.S. Congressman and distinguished lawyer), & Sarah M. See Fothergill, op.
   cit., 108; also Bascom Anthony, Fifty Years in
   the Ministry, Macon Ga., 1937, 144 et seq for a
   fine tribute to this lady (ed).

Jones, Sarah Jones   Dec 4 1761 Oct 13 1817
   w/o James (a cousin). md in Amelia Co., Va. Couple
   moved to St. George's Parish (later Burke Co.) in
   1773.   d/o Keziah & Henry Jones (listed by British
   as "St. George's Parish Rebel Colonel"; he represent-
   ed the parish in the pre-war efforts to unite the
   Colony against the British).   m/o Mary, Jane Ann,
   Seaborn H., & James W. See Fothergill, op. cit.,
   102, 153-4 (ed).

Jones, Sarah Margaret   Dec 28 1786 Sep 4 1789
   d/o Sarah & James

Jones, Sarah Margaret   Sep 11 1789 Oct 10 1810
   d/o Sarah & James

Jones, Seaborn Henry   nd Nov   1859
   s/o Sarah Jones & James b near Waynesboro, Fothergill, op. cit., 108. Note: John J. Jones, Waynesboro,
   owns two very fine portraits of Seaborn and Margaret,
   his paternal great grand parents (ed).

Notes: (1) The two above family cemeteries have been designated by their original plantation names: Birdsville, once in lower Burke but now in Jenkins Co. and Old Canaan, near Waynesboro. The latter family is not known by its plantation name but as the Col. John Jones family (ed).
(2) Mary and Sarah M., both daughters of Margaret and Seaborn H., never married. They are buried in this cemetery, one probably in a brick above-ground vault which, like one or two others, has lost its marker over the years (ed).

83.   KEYSVILLE METHODIST
                    Keysville, Ga.

Adkins, William Clarence	Oct 8 1930	Mar 15 1931
s/o Mr. & Mrs. P.B.		
Amerson, Harry	1939	1959
Amerson, John Willis	Dec 9 1914	1966
Arrington, Daisy	May 21 1910	Feb 22 1937
Arrington, Dora	Dec 26 1871	Feb 16 1929
w/o R.A.		
Arrington, George W.	Sep 16 1863	Feb 6 1914
Arrington, Infant	only date	Jne 14 1925
of Mr. & Mrs. A.C.		
Arrington, Martha Lynn	Feb 23 1962	Jan 4 1963
Arrington, Reece A.	1870	1943
Arrington, Silas A. CSA	nd	nd
Co B 59 Ga Inf Mus		
Austin, Theo Woodward	Jne 16 1890	Oct 13 1918
w/o C.F.		
Banks, Alice T.	Sep 7 1860	Oct 15 1919
Banks, James R.	Mar 10 1861	Jne 16 1924
Banks, John William	May 2 1886	Mar 7 1903
s/o J.R. & D.T.		
Baston, William H.	Nov 20 1856	May 12 1902
b Columbia Co., Ga.		
Blackston, Mamie B.	Mar 24 1891	Oct 11 1968
Blackston, William B.	Jan 22 1881	Mar 21 1959
Bowling, Eula Mildred	Aug 15 1912	Nov 2 1920
Clark, A.N.	Jul 11 1888	Jul 15 1929
Clark, Adela Louise	Nov 14 1853	Oct 2 1893
w/o Thomas S.		
Clark, Catherine Hite	1851	1917
w/o H.W.		
Clark, Eula May	Jne 19 1885	Jul 19 1913
Clark, Henry Washington	1852	1933
Clark, Thomas S.	1844	1906
Cook, Alice Eugenia	1860	1915
w/o Thos. J.		
Cook, George Rufus	Jul 15 1875	May 23 1907
Cook, Harriet Daniel	Apr 3 1883	Aug 24 1967
w/o Jas. W.		
Cook, James W.	Sep 28 1878	Dec 26 1943

Name	Birth	Death
Cook, Mary Lou d/o T.J. & A.E.	Mar 16 1891	Feb 2 1906
Cook, Pauline	Feb 6 1916	Feb 3 1917
Cook, Reece (infant) "Baby Reece" in Cook section	only date	May 8 1960
Cook, Thomas J.	Jan 27 1849	Jul 28 1896
Daniel, B. Gertrude Drummond w/o John W.	Sep 4 1882	Jul 1 1961
Daniel, Fannie J.	Jne 30 1873	Feb 5 1945
Daniel, John W.	Sep 9 1878	Dec 27 1951
Daniel, N.G. s/o N.G. & G.E.	Nov 26 1913	Mar 31 1914
Daniel, R.T., Sr.	Jul 31 1870	Jan 15 1920
Dixon, Annie Delorious	Nov 11 1919	Oct 26 1920
Dixon, Infant of Mr. & Mrs. J.I.	Aug 23 1908	same date
Dixon, Mildred Charline	Oct 29 1929	Sep 22 1934
Dixon, Sadie Martin	1882	1968
Dozier, A.G.	1870	1915
Dozier, Alice	Oct 4 1904	Aug 30 1909
Dozier, Charlie H.	Aug 14 1899	Sep 23 1966
Dozier, Elizabeth Ann w/o Charlie H.	Mar 19 1902	Mar 26 1930
Dozier, Lizzie L. w/o Robt. H.	Mar 12 1867	Dec 13 1909
Dozier, Mrs. R. H.	Oct 2 1877	Sep 22 1950
Dozier, Robert H.	1860	1935
Eason, Charles A.	Dec 4 1929	Jul 2 1931
Eason, Infant d/o Mr. & Mrs. T.C.	only date	Nov 5 1928
Eason, Infant d/o Mr. & Mrs. T.C.	only date	Mar 21 1939
Eason, Robert H.	Apr 23 1918	May 25 1959
Evans, Mamie Skinner w/o Ray W.	Feb 28 1918	nd
Evans, Ray Willard	Jan 15 1916	Aug 18 1971
Evans, Walter Otis s/o Mamie S. & Ray W.	Jne 28 1946	Oct 13 1968
Eve, B.H.	Jne 27 1855	Oct 30 1909
Eve, Robert B.	Nov 12 1891	Oct 2 1958
Gay, Florence Burton	1939	1952
Gay, Lamar Isaac	age 62y 3m	Sep 11 1968
Greenway, Elizabeth Ann w/o Henry H.	Apr 26 1838	Sep 6 1900
Greenway, Henry H.	1841	1911
Griffin, Mary Clark Blount	1883	1962
Gunn, Lewis A.F. WOW	Dec 18 1874	Jan 20 1919
Harris, Johnnie T.	Nov 6 1906	Jul 30 1909
Holley, Andrew J.	Mar 3 1925	May 22 1942
Howard, Lenton H.	Nov 3 1889	Mar 21 1957
Howard, Willard	May 30 1915	Sep 22 1939
Jenkins, Theodore s/o Mr. & Mrs. J.H.	Sep 9 1909	Apr 17 1936
Johnson, Mary Dozier w/o Wm. O.	1893	1972

Name	Birth	Death
Johnson, William Otis	1891	1965
Kendrick, John P. CSA	nd	nd
Co C 20 Ga Cav		
Kendrick, William Robert	age 57 y	Jan 21 1962
Lively, Frank	Aug 21 1883	Dec 31 1902
McNair, James Daniel F&AM	Dec 13 1884	May 10 1940
McNair, Mary Ellen	Aug 22 1887	Oct 25 1912
w/o J.D.		
Moore, Louise Adelia	Oct 13 1887	May 19 1913
Newman, Elizabeth S.	1892	1933
Newman, Leon Alonza	1876	1972
Padgett, Beatrice Sherrer	May 29 1906	nd
w/o H.L., Sr.		
Padgett, Boyd P.	Oct 17 1849	May 24 1935
Padgett, Elbert P.	Aug 9 1873	Jul 30 1965
Padgett, Hubert Lester, Sr.	Nov 13 1906	Apr 14 1949
Padgett, Infant	Nov 19 1902	Feb 15 1903
s/o E.P. & N.H.		
Padgett, Louiza	Dec 8 1841	Dec 8 1906
Padgett, Mary E. Williamson	Jne 5 1876	1955
w/o Boyd P.		
Padgett, Myrtle G.	1921	1960
Padgett, Nannie Hassie	Nov 3 1881	Apr 25 1913
w/o E.P.		
Padgett, Nannie Hassie	Apr 24 1913	May 17 1913
d/o E.P. & N.H.		
Padgett, Ruby A.	Mar 2 1905	Oct 19 1907
b Keysville d Augusta		
Parker, Jimmie	1943	nd
Parker, Thomas A.	1847	1907
Parker, Wilton J. WW-I F&AM	Aug 8 1891	Mar 8 1958
Ga Pvt HQ Co 324 Inf		
Parker, Zebula W.	1857	1903
w/o Thomas A.		
Perkins, Clarence E.	Mar 6 1878	Aug 26 1947
Perkins, Everette N.	Aug 27 1911	Mar 23 1912
Perkins, Harvey E.	May 9 1906	Jne 28 1925
Perkins, Mollie G.	Apr 2 1872	Sep 18 1906
w/o W.M.		
Perkins, Nannie L.	1893	1918
w/o H.G.		
Perkins, Nonie K.	Dec 12 1886	nd
w/o Clarence E.		
Pool, Floid	Feb 5 1906	Feb 24 1906
s/o L.P. & J.A.		
Pool, Samuel Lawrence	Sep 7 1850	Apr 14 1923
Pool, Sarah Jane	May 23 1860	Jan 23 19---
Powell, Charles E.	Oct 14 1878	Jne 23 1925
Powell, Vera M.	Dec 4 1888	nd
w/o Charles E.		
Robinson, John	Jan 4 1945	Feb 7 1945
Simmons, Lillian M.	1905	1971
Skinner, Lany	1878	1959
w/o Oscar T.		

```
Skinner, Oscar T.                            1873              1959
Smith, Annie Mae               Feb 19 1901    Nov  1 1971
  w/o Lon
Smith, Curby Lee                             1890              1949
Smith, Lon                     Oct 10 1899    Dec 22 1951
Smith, Lucia Williamson                      1894              1927
Stephens, Tampa J.                           1899              1973
Strickland, B.P.               Dec  5 1911    Mar 19 1914
  s/o C.S. & B.P.
Strickland, Pearl              Apr 24 1893    Dec  7 1911
Turbeville, B.L., Jr. (infant) only   date    Jne 27 1943
Turbeville, Brite L. WW-II      Jul 28 1919   Mar 31 1947
  Ga 1 Sgt 311 Field Arty Bn B.S.M.
Watts, James WW-II             Jne 20 1912    Oct  2 1965
  Ga Pvt US Marine Corps
Way, B. Leroy                  Jan  7 1878    Aug 30 1942
Way, Evie Cook                 Oct  5 1880    Jan 26 1966
Whitaker, Addie M.                           1900              1954
Whittle, Laveta                Dec 31 1898    Jne 14 1916
  w/o John W.
Williams, Lucy M.                            1888              1973
Williamson, Ida Ethel          Dec 17 1879    Aug 11 1935
Williamson, Julia Malinda      Jne  6 1856    Jan 16 1916
  w/o Thomas P.   /Phillips
Williamson, Thomas P.          Jan 26 1848    Aug 15 1925
Woodward, Ashley P.            Mar 23 1882    Feb  2 1947
Woodward, Catherine Stallings  Aug 19 1854    Jne  2 1932
  w/o J.M.
Woodward, James Monroe         Jne 11 1852    Jul  7 1920
Wren, Annie Cook               Oct  5 1880    Apr 19 1954
  w/o Albert A.
Wright, Bunyon                               1880              1966
Wright, Ida G.                 Apr  8 1881    Jan 21 1956
  w/o Tom W.
Wright, Thomas P.                            1846              1917
  b Mattox Co., Va.
Wright, Tom W.                 Oct 20 1883                     nd
```

84.   KNIGHT

```
Atwell, Mary A.                Feb 23 1850    Jul 12 1913
Knight, Alton P.   WW-II       Oct  6 1904    Feb  7 1948
  Ga PFC 339 Inf
Knight, Ben E.                 Dec 23 1874    Jan  7 1956
Knight, Otis E.                Jul 14 1895    Aug 31 1910
Knight, Sallie C.              Jne  1 1874    Apr 25 1972
  w/o B.E.
Knight, William Baxley                       1898              1943
```

85.   LAMBERT

```
Godbee, Synthia (bkn)          age 74 y       Jne  1 1881
Lambert, Alice L.              Feb 12 1869    Oct 20 1883
  d/o J.E. & L.
```

150

```
Lambert, Infant                              nd              nd
  of J.E. & Louisa
Lambert, James A.                   Apr 25 1883   Oct  8 1885
  s/o J.E. & A.E.
Lambert, Louisa                     Jul 27 1844   May 24 1881
  w/o J.E.
Lambert, S.J.E.                     Sep 10 1873   Oct 12 1878
  s/o J.E. & L.
```

86.   LAMBETH
                    Richmond Co.

```
Lambeth, Amos P.                    Mar 27 1828   Jul 21 1908
Lambeth, Lucy Patterson            Apr 10 1788   Oct 24 1855
  w/o Thos.
```

87.   LITTLE BUCKHEAD BAPTIST
                    Jenkins Co.

```
Atkinson, John                      Apr 20 1806   Apr  6 1874
Atkinson, Susan                     Dec 16 1823   Dec 18 1870
Awtry, Infant                       only   date   Aug 12 1904
  s/o Mr. & Mrs. A.E.
Belcher, Deborah                    Sep 20 1847   Jne 16 1908
  w/o G.W.
Belcher, Donnie D.                           nd              nd
  s/o G.W. & Deborah
Belcher, Eddie                               nd              nd
  s/o G.W. & Deborah
Belcher, G.W.                       Sep  7 1851   Apr 16 1914
Belcher, Infant                     Dec  3 1896   Dec  5 1896
  d/o T.W. & M.L.
Belcher, Infant                              nd              nd
  s/o G.W. & Deborah
Belcher, Isaiah C.                  Aug 16 1843   Jan  7 1876
Belcher, Minna                      Jul 23 1869   Jul  2 1898
  w/o Thomas W.
Belcher, Minna Lucile               Mar 23 1898   Aug 29 1898
Belcher, Roxie E.                   May 22 1843   Jne 28 1895
  w/o Isaiah C.
Bell, Elizabeth S.                  Nov  6 1858   Oct 14 1886
  w/o B.E.
Brinson, Annie E.                   Sep 27 1895   Apr 28 1968
  m/o Carlton Brinson & Ann B. Alexander
Brinson, Bonnie C.                  Mar 10 1873   Nov 13 1878
  s/o R.A. & S.A.
Brinson, Camilla                    Feb 16 1907   Jul  2 1907
  d/o J.C. & Donie
Brinson, (children)                          nd              nd
  of T.J. & Susannah
Brinson, Daisy                      Nov 23 1884   Sep 20 1885
  d/o J.C. & Modhalry
Brinson, Daniel Champion            Apr  8 1852   May 26 1913
Brinson, Daughter                            nd              nd
  next to Dora Alma   (ed).
```

```
Brinson, Donie Attaway              Sep  8 1865   May   9 1934
  w/o J.C.
Brinson, Dora Alma                  Feb  8 1876   Jan 23 1961
Brinson, Harlow A.                  Jul 31 1898   Dec 22 1940
  f/o Carlton & Ann
Brinson, J.P.                              nd            nd
Brinson, John Crawford              Dec 21 1862   Feb  3 1914
Brinson, John Farmer                Apr 19 1893   Dec 22 1941
  Lt Col of Inf USA;  f/o John Farmer, Jr., Philip
  Wren & Mary Lucie
Brinson, Johnnie                    May  4 1889   Oct  8 1890
  s/o J.C. & Modhalry
Brinson, Junette Sasser             Apr 12 1861   Mar 11 1942
  w/o D.C.
Brinson, Lamar                      Mar 25 1897   Aug 20 1897
  s/o J.C. & Donie
Brinson, M.A.                       Feb 17 1828   Jne 13 1885
  w/o Simeon
Brinson, Malene                     Jul 11 1895   Aug  6 1897
  d/o J.C. & Donie
Brinson, Modhalry                   Sep  7 1865   Feb 18 1891
  w/o J.C.
Brinson, Nancy                             nd            nd
  w/o J.P.
Brinson, Ralph H.                   Jne 13 1879   Jne 19 1933
Brinson, Simeon                     Mar 21 1823   Oct  1 1883
Brinson, Son                               nd            nd
  next to Dora Alma   (ed).
Brinson, T.J.                       Oct 31 1849   Sep 14 1904
Burke, Dean Estella                 Sep 14 1885   Apr  6 1896
Burke, Joseph M.                    Sep 12 1893   Aug 23 1895
  s/o J.E. & M.A.
Burke, Julian C.                    Sep 25 1882   Aug 23 1889
Burke, Mary A.                      Oct  1 1864   Aug  2 1896
  w/o J.E.
Burke, Mary Etta Lewis              Mar  4 1857   Sep 16 1928
  w/o W.E.
Burke, Sallie E.                    Oct 25 1863   Aug 29 1903
  w/o W.E.
Burke, William Edward               Mar 20 1856   Dec 29 1925
Calhoun, Mrs. A.M.                  Dec  2 1822   Jul 17 1880
Cogland, Mary J.                    Jan 31 1836   May 14 1906
  Mother
Coughlin, James                            nd            nd
Coughlin, Mary                             nd            nd
Coursey, Daisy                      Dec 20 1876   Mar 17 1906
  w/o W.P.
Coursey, Minnie                     Oct  3 1902   Jul 24 1904
  d/o W.P. & Daisy
Daniel, James                       Feb 17 1878   Dec 18 1944
Daniel, James C.                    Sep  6 1914   Nov 27 1915
Daniel, Lessie Lee                  Sep  7 1887   Nov 26 1931
Edenfield, Allie B. Reynolds        Jan  4 1900   Aug  6 1935
Eidson, Mary H.                     Oct 10 1897   Apr  9 1959
```

Ellison, Charlie S.W.	Feb 11 1860	May 3 1867
only s/o J.H. & N.A.		
Ellison, James H.	Jan 28 1831	Aug 28 1903
Ellison, Nancy Brinson	Dec 4 1841	Feb 18 1900
w/o J.H.		
Ethridge, Winnie Mae	Dec 16 1888	Dec 14 1968
Glisson, Herbert L.	age 3m	nd
s/o H.C. & S.S.		
Glisson, Homer C.	Jul 5 1831	Jne 24 1886
Glisson, Mary F.	Nov 3 1845	Nov 27 1910
Glisson, Susannah S.	Sep 23 1836	Jne 7 1875
w/o H.C.		
Gregory, A.B.	Dec 10 1825	Oct 6 1854
Gregory, Clyde	Dec 25 1910	Jne 4 1912
s/o A.B. & Ruby		
Gregory, John Brinson	Mar 4 1854	Nov 8 1896
member Magnolia Church		
Gregory, Polina	Jne 11 1884	Sep 7 1884
d/o J.B. & Emma		
Griffin, Mary Elizabeth	Aug 17 1885	Jne 30 1906
w/o James E. /Brinson		
Hargrove, Jane E.	Aug 8 1876	Aug 16 1876
d/o J.G. & S.F.		
Hargrove, Sarah F.	Sep 11 1837	Jul 7 1896
w/o J.G.		
Hargroves, John G.	Mar 25 1836	Nov 6 1910
Note: no "s" on his wife's and daughter's markers		
(ed).		
Hayes, Florice	Jul 21 1895	Aug 11 1896
d/o W.A. & Susie		
Hayes, W.A., Jr.	Mar 11 1904	Jul 24 1906
Herrington, Dallie M.	1881	1943
w/o S.M.		
Herrington, Myrtis Lucile	Sep 13 1901	Jul 16 1910
d/o S.M. & D.M.		
Hillis, Alice E.	age 23y 9m 2d	Jan 1 1892
Hillis, Elizabeth	Nov 3 1827	Mar 24 1884
Hillis, Infant	Mar 15 1898	Mar 22 1898
d/o A.E. & S.R.		
Hillis, J.M., Jr.	Feb 12 1854	Sep 1 1886
Hillis, James M.	Jan 28 1819	Mar 6 1883
Hillis, Maud	Oct 6 1894	Jne 13 1896
d/o A.E. & S.R.		
Hillis, Sallie	Jan 3 1876	Jul 23 1901
w/o A.E.		
Hillis, Simeon	Oct 10 1827	Nov 19 1895
Hillis, W.W.	Oct 19 1864	Mar 31 1894
Hurst, Coral D.	Mar 18 1874	Dec 24 1901
w/o S.N.		
Jackson, Rev. George L.	Feb 6 1811	Mar 31 1901
s/o John & Sarah Whitfield . b Screven Co Ga;		
called to ministry 1846		
Jackson, Mamie Gertrude	age 1y 2m 17d	Jne 27 1883
youngest d/o Geo. A. & Lavinia J.		

Jackson, S.Z. F&AM	age 31y 4m'	Jul 19 1878
Lanier, Rev. T.B.	Mar 15 1831	Jne 24 1902
Lester, Henry W.	1921	1973
McCoy, Mary	Jul 1793	Dec 23 1871
McCoy, S. Marshall	Aug 22 1890	Sep 9 1908
s/o R.P. & Lena R.		
McLendon, Green Bell	Nov 7 1892	Mar 22 1944
Ga Seaman 2CL USNRF		
McLendon, Moselle E.	Jne 9 1861	Apr 23 1915
w/o D.W.		
Miller, Josie Brinson	Jne 26 1876	Aug 4 1909
Mock, Bessie Whitfield	Mar 20 1871	Aug 18 1898
w/o Frank P.		
Moxley, Mary B.	Sep 27 1832	Aug 25 1882
w/o N.J.		
Moxley, Nathaniel J.	Apr 20 1829	Nov 15 1899
Murrow, Birdie E.	age 9 m	nd
d/o F.L. & M.S.		
Murrow, Carrie	age 1y 10m	Nov 21 1869
d/o Rev. W.J. & Cynthia	17d	
Murrow, Cynthia	age 55 y	Jul 4 1882
w/o Rev. W.J.		
Murrow, F.L.	Mar 7 1848	Nov 19 1914
Murrow, Mary Stueart	Aug 19 1853	Dec 19 1934
Murrow, Nina	age 3y 1m	Oct 28 1867
d/o Rev. W.J. & Cynthia	2d	
Murrow, Rev. W.J.	Oct 12 1822	Jan 30 1892
Parker, Infant	only date	Jne 1905
s/o R.H. & Allie M.		
Peel, Daniel Leroy	Sep 16 1905	Oct 16 1905
s/o M.L. & N.S.		
Peel, Ethel	Jne 15 1909	Aug 6 1909
d/o M.L. & W.T.		
Peel, Henry	Nov 11 1906	Jan 5 1907
s/o M.L. & N.L.		
Peel, Henry W.	Feb 1 1845	Sep 18 1887
Peel, Infant	Jne 23 1911	Aug 18 1911
d/o M.L. & N.T.		
Peel, John Franklin	Feb 13 1908	Apr 26 1908
s/o M.L. & N.T.		
Peel, John T. CSA	nd	nd
Co A 22 Ga Inf		
Peel, Lottie Avice	Jne 18 1910	Aug 26 1910
d/o M.L. & N.T.		
Peel, Lucy L. Sikes	Aug 8 1848	Oct 31 1922
w/o John T.		
Peel, Mongin LeRoy Sp Am W	Feb 14 1876	Mar 1 1955
Btry F 1 Regt Arty		
Peel, Nina Their	Feb 13 1876	Jne 4 1941
Peel, Susannah Wallace	Mar 12 1841	Jan 28 1910
w/o Henry W.		
Perkins, A.J.	Jan 17 1845	Oct 31 1868
Perkins, Ada M.	Feb 23 1871	Feb 25 1871
d/o G.W. & Mollie C.		
Perkins, Adella	Oct 9 1876	Oct 17 1876

Perkins, B.L.	Apr 9 1806	Sep 11 1854
Perkins, C.E.	Jan 31 1853	Jan 28 1917
Perkins, Carlos A.	Sep 11 1880	Oct 10 1895
s/o S.A. & M.A.		
Perkins, Charlie E., Jr.	age 6y 11m	nd
Perkins, Estella M.	Mar 14 1869	Apr 10 1871
d/o G.W. & Mollie C.		
Perkins, Ethelyn Murrow	Sep 7 1876	Jul 6 1934
Perkins, Eunice A.	Apr 2 1886	Feb 25 1909
Perkins, G.J.	Nov 20 1837	Nov 9 1854
Perkins, Gertrude	Aug 31 1884	Sep 20 1884
Perkins, Henry C.	May 15 1897	Dec 23 1927
Perkins, Infant	nd	Apr 28 1870
s/o N.M. & M.F.		
Perkins, Infant		nd Feb 24 1871
d/o N.M. & M.F.		
Perkins, Lizzie A.	Mar 5 1854	Feb 1 1897
w/o Jno. H.		
Perkins, Mrs. Mary Drucilla	Jul 3 1830	Nov 13 1887
Perkins, Mary Kittrell	Jul 23 1870	Sep 23 1935
Perkins, Mittie A.	Jul 1 1860	Apr 18 1892
w/o S.A.		
Perkins, Mollie C.	Jul 30 1845	Dec 18 1886
w/o G.W.		
Perkins, Mose	Apr 14 1895	Nov 24 1931
Perkins, Newton M.	Jul 7 1824	Feb 29 1872
Perkins, Newton Milton	age 4m 11d	Aug 31 1872
s/o N.M. & M.F.		
Perkins, P.P.	Nov 22 1886	Aug 31 1888
Perkins, Samuel Hillis	Jul 30 1888	May 25 1889
s/o S.A. & M.A.		
Perkins, Sarah	Apr 7 1810	Sep 25 1872
Perkins, Sarah F.	Mar 4 1812	Jan 17 1879
Perkins, Street A.	Jne 17 1858	Jan 1 1924
Perkins, Street A., Jr.	Jne 23 1896	May 5 1908
Perkins, Susan A.	Sep 12 1843	Apr 8 1863
Perkins, Susey	Oct 9 1867	Feb 14 1872
Perryman, A.M.	age 63 y	Nov 19 1890
Reynolds, Arye E.	Jul 29 1885	Nov 5 1970
Reynolds, Children	nd	nd
of S.D. & Mary		
Reynolds, George W.	Feb 12 1848	Sep 1 1919
Reynolds, Henry T.	Nov 24 1856	Nov 8 1870
s/o Ambrose Wright & Martha		
Reynolds, Henry W.	Aug 5 1897	Jan 14 1921
Reynolds, Infant	nd	nd
s/o S.D. & Mary		
Reynolds, Infants (4)	nd	nd
wooden markers; no inscriptions, but located near to		
Lula Parker & W.D. Reynolds (ed).		
Reynolds, Josephine Perkins	Jul 3 1849	May 29 1919
w/o W.M.		
Reynolds, Lula Parker	Jan 2 1869	Jne 8 1890
w/o W.D.		

```
Reynolds, Mamie B.                    Apr   4 1877   Nov   2 1894
   w/o S.D.
Reynolds, Mary McCoy                  Sep  21 1871   Mar  27 1934
   w/o S.D.
Reynolds, Narcissus Peel                    1873            1963
Reynolds, Newton M.                   Mar   6 1881   Jul  18 1937
Reynolds, S.D.                        Apr   8 1873   Jul   5 1928
Reynolds, Susannah                    Mar  20 1839   Apr   5 1868
Reynolds, Susannah Atkinson           Aug  30 1856   Jan  11 1926
   w/o George W.
Reynolds, W.M.                        Jan   1 1842   Aug   2 1906
Reynolds, William D.                  Oct  19 1857   Jul   4 1926
Royal, Delmar Audley                  Oct  24 1912   Jul  12 1915
Sorrier, G. Josephine Brinson         Jan   9 1844   Jul  19 1918
   w/o C.A.
Wallace, A.B.                         Jul   3 1830   Mar  25 1902
Wallace, A.B.                         age 1y 3m      Jul   2 1862
   s/o A.B. & R.C.                        26d
Wallace, Candice E.                   Jan  18 1841   Jne  13 1899
Wallace, Charles LeRoy                age 2y 9m      Jul  19 1854
   s/o A.B. & J.E.
Wallace, E.J.                         Feb   8 1806   Mar  10 1871
Wallace, Emma                         Nov  27 1853   Jul   7 1892
   d/o A.B. & J.E.
Wallace, Emma Perkins .               May  18 1852   Jan  16 1879
Wallace, Fannie H.                    Feb  13 1856   Jne  17 1874
   w/o S.B.A.
Wallace, J.E.                         age 20y 10m    Aug  13 1854
   w/o A.B.
Wallace, Katie                        Jan  15 1880   Oct   4 1880
   d/o F.R. & L.A.
Wallace, Lillie                       Dec   5 1861   Jne  24 1892
   w/o Dr. F.R.
Wallace, Mary                         Jan   5 1788   May  10 1860
   w/o William, Sr.
Wallace, N.S.                         Sep   7 1837   Apr   8 1906
Wallace, Pearle                       Dec  16 1882   Feb  19 1903
   d/o N.S. & Virginia
Wallace, R.C.                         age 46y 11m    Nov  15 1879
   w/o Dr. A.B.                           18d
Wallace, S.B.                         Feb  13 1805   Nov   7 1866
Wallace, S.B.L.B.                     Dec  17 1854   Feb  24 1928
Wallace, Sarah J.                     age 28y 4m     Oct   9 1871
   w/o Wm. B.                             16d
Wallace, Sarah Mozelle                age 4y  4m     Sep  23 1854
   d/o A.B. & J.E.
Wallace, Susie                              nd              nd
   d/o F.R. & L.A.
Wallace, Virginia Brinson             Nov   8 1847   Aug   3 1922
   w/o N.S.
Wallace, William, Sr.                 Apr   4 1789   Mar  10 1856
Ward, Ann L.                          Dec  18 1842   Sep  22 1923
   w/o Thomas A.
Whitfield, B.E.   CSA                       nd              nd
   Asst Surg Co C 32 Ga Inf
```

LIVELY

Lively, Elizabeth Kimbrel   Dec 31 1821 Dec 1 1898
   w/o Alexander
   Note: She was his second wife. Her name and dates,
   as well as those of his first wife, appear on his
   marker in old Sardis cemetery (ed).

89.   LIVELY

Lively, Jane Boyd   Nov   1805 May 12 1881
   w/o Mark
Lively, Rev. Mark   Feb 27 1791 Jan 31 1852
   md in Richmond Co. Feb 4 1836

90.   LIVELY-HOLLAND

Broxton, Ella V.   Mar 16 1858 Oct 14 1884
   w/o S.L.
Godbee, Hamens H.   May 9 1876 Jul 31 1879
   s/o J.R. & Amanda
Holland, Ruth   age 76 y   Nov 8 1901
   w/o John
Lively, Adin   Apr 17 1856 Apr 30 1862
Lively, Jno. T.   Mar 13 1795 Mar 27 1880
Lively, Verlinda   May 24 1836 Aug 7 1861
   1st w/o Alexander; her name and dates also appear
   on his marker in the Sardis cemetery (ed).
O'Banion, Martha   Jan 25 1821 Aug 16 1901
Royal, Henry   age 26 y   Sep 23 1856

91.   LOUISVILLE OLD REVOLUTIONARY WAR
                    Jefferson Co.

Bostwick, Chesley Rev War   nd   nd
Bostwick, Nathan   Rev War   nd   1817
Gamble, John   Rev War   nd   nd
Gamble, Hon. Roger L.   age 60 y   Dec 20 1847
Gunn, James   age 48y 4m   Jul 30 1801
                                    17d
Jones, Joseph Maybank   age 26y 8m   Jan 5 1831
   of Liberty County s/o Joseph
Lawson, Roger Rev War   nd   nd
McDermott, Andrew   Feb 12 1801 Oct 14 1860
McDermott, Andrew   May 9 1843 Mar 14 1873
   s/o Owen & Bd.
McDermott, Bdelia   Mar 11 1811 Sep 15 1881
   w/o Owen
McDermott, Charles   Mar 25 1849 Aug 7 1862
   s/o Owen & Bd.
McDermott, Daniel   Nov   1827 Aug   1829
   s/o Owen & Bd.
McDermott, Eliza   May 9 1837 Nov   1844
   d/o Owen & Bd.

```
McDermott, George                    May 14 1839  Nov      1855
  s/o Owen & Bd.
McDermott, James                     Aug 20 1845  Aug 22 1863
  s/o Owen & Bd.   Listed as 1845 on a tall shaft of all
  the children - 1848 on a separate marker (ed).
McDermott, Joseph                    Aug     1835  Nov      1839
  s/o Owen & Bd.
McDermott, Julia                     Jul     1841  Jan      1844
  d/o Owen & Bd.
McDermott, Louise Martha             Feb 22 1847  Jul 28 1862
  d/o Owen & Bd.
McDermott, Mary Ann                  May     1829  Sep      1832
  d/o Owen & Bd.
McDermott, Michael                   Nov  4 1830  Sep      1834
  s/o Owen & Bd.
McDermott, Owen                      Mar  9 1806  Jan 27 1877
  b  County Sligo, Ireland
McDermott, Susan                     May 10 1831  Sep  3 1839
  d/o Owen & Bd.
McDermott, William                   Aug  4 1833  Sep  4 1839
  s/o Owen & Bd.
Tomlinson, Aaron  Rev War                    1748  Apr 12 1828
Wright, Ambrose  Rev War                      nd            nd
Wright, Ann Fromington               May 10 1854  Jul 24 1854
  d/o M.H. & A.R.
Wright, Carrie Hazelhurst            Aug 11 1858  Mar 23 1859
  d/o Carrie C. & A.R.
Wright, Mary H.                      Dec 28 1825  Jne 23 1854
  w/o Col. A.R.    md Apr 26 1843
  d/o Mary & Dr. Wm. Savage
Wright, Mary Hubbell                 May 10 1854  Aug  2 1854
  d/o M.H. & A.R.


92.                        LOVETT
                        Screven Co.


Griner, Infant                       Oct  3 1893  Oct  7 1893
  s/o Joseph & F.L.
Hankinson, Thyrza Y.                 May 13 1872  Nov 21 1910
  w/o Robt. A.
Hill, Amelia Lovett                  Oct 12 1892  Sep  6 1949
  w/o Fielding M.
Hill, Arthur                         Jan 30 1888  Oct 13 1888
  s/o F.M. & C.C.
Hill, B.D.                           Apr 18 1806  May 24 1877
Hill, Beulah B.                      Jul 29 1913            L
  w/o C.M. Mack
Hill, C.M. Mack                      Aug 11 1909  Feb 11 1972
Hill, Carrie C.                      Oct 24 1867  Dec 25 1905
  w/o Fielding M.
Hill, Fielding M.                    Dec 11 1862  Jne 19 1938
Hill, Infant                                 nd            nd
  d/o Uley & Irene
```

```
Hill, Irene H.                        Jan 30 1878                    nd
  w/o Uley H.
Hill, Uley H.                         Aug 25 1870      Nov 28 1930
Hill, Willie Holmes                   Sep 17 1918      Mar  6 1936
Kemp, Alexander Stephen               Feb  1 1861      Aug 16 1936
Kemp, Eliza J.                        Feb  1 1872      Nov 21 1925
  w/o Alex. S.
Kemp, Louisanna V. Littlefield        Jan 23 1859      Dec 12 1899
  w/o Alex. S.
Kemp, Lovett H.                             1894             1964
Kimbrell, Arnold D.                   Nov  8 1900      Feb 21 1932
Kimbrell, Green B.                    Apr 24 1874      Jan  5 1947
Kimbrell, Mary F.                     May  9 1879      Oct 13 1964
  w/o Green B.
Kimbrell, Robbie E.  WW-II            Mar 12 1921      Dec 11 1944
  Ga Staff SGT 330 Inf 83 Inf Div
Kittles, Jane Elizabeth               age 31 y         Oct 20 1840
  w/o John R.
Littlefield, Annaliza                 Jan 14 1851      Mar 24 1855
Littlefield, Martha C.                Feb 22 1821      Nov 19 1898
Littlefield, Samuel H.                Sep 13 1813      Jan 23 1883
Littlefield, Thomas Harrison          Mar  1 1846      Sep  5 1846
Littlefield, Yulie Crawford           age 2y 6m        Oct 11 1863
                                          25d
Lively, Abel                          age 47 y         Mar 23 1834
Lovett, A.J.                          age 16y 8m       Nov  9 1832
                                          20d
Lovett, Berrien M.   CSA                   nd               nd
  Co B 7 Ga Cav
Lovett, Berrien M.                    Sep 12 1902      Mar  4 1941
Lovett, Elizabeth Bates               Dec 20 1836      Jan  2 1902
  w/o John F.
Lovett, Exie Lewis                    Jan 24 1897      Nov  4 1950
Lovett, Hamilton L.                   Mar  6 1801      Jan 25 1839
Lovett, Hamilton L.                   age 7y 4m        Apr 29 1847
                                          13d
Lovett, John F.                       age 55y 7m       Jan  7 1851
                                          4d
Lovett, John F.                       Apr  3 1823      May 31 1890
Lovett, Marjorie Ercelle              only   date      Mar 17 1920
  d/o W.A. & E.S.
Lovett, Mary V.                       age 15y 10m      Nov 30 1852
                                          1d
Lovett, Mollie E.                     Jul 21 1871      Jan 16 1903
  w/o Wm. H.
Lovett, Rebecca                       age 73y 10m      Jul 30 1848
                                          14d
Lovett, Thos. F., Sen.                age 58 y         Apr  9 1830
  b  in So. Carolina;  for many years a citizen of
  Georgia
Lovett, Thomas F.                     age 59y 4m       Feb 22 1852
                                          22d
Lovett, Thomas F., Jr.                age 20y 2m       Sep 28 1852
Lovett, Warren P.                     Sep 10 1874      Jne 29 1911
Lovett, Wm. Atkinson                  Aug 12 1894      Jul 28 1941
```

```
Lovett, William H.                      Jan 22 1868    Apr  1 1943
Lovett, Wm. H.H.                        Oct 15 1840    Oct 13 1871
Lutes, Infant                           Dec 28 1920    same   date
   s/o Mr. & Mrs. Leroy M.
Lutes, Leroy M.                         Sep 23 1900    Aug 15 1959
Lutes, Marion June                      May 14 1939    Sep 24 1941
Mays, Kathleen Lutes                    Dec  9 1895    Mar 18 1958
McBride, James                          age 38 y       May 31 1837
   b Londonderry, Ireland;  for many years a citizen
   of Georgia
McBride, Sarah Rebecca                  age 7y 2m      Oct 14 1843
   d/o James
Mobley, Agnes E.                              1901           1965
Mobley, Henry Grady  WW-I                      nd             nd
   Ga Pvt 156 Depot Brig
Mobley, Infant                                 nd             nd
   s/o J.H. & M.H.
Mobley, John Thomas                     age 52 y       Jul    1963
Mobley, Julian H.                       Jne 28 1888    Oct 15 1925
Mobley, Julian H.  WW-II                Aug  7 1909    Jne 10 1953
   Ga Pvt Btry B 817 AAA AW Bn CAC
Mobley, Mary Helen                      Aug 31 1888    Sep 11 1931
Mobley, Mary Louneal                    Aug 15 1911    May 15 1930
Mobley, Nettie Reddick                  Feb 26 1885    Apr  1 1954
Mobley, Robert W.                       Jne 20 1874    Jne 21 1877
   s/o J.M. & M.V.
Mobley, Samuel Tilton                   Oct 26 1876    Jan 26 1942
Mobley, Sidney L.  WW-II                Dec 30 1921    Dec 30 1967
   Ga Tec 5 USA
Mobley, Thomas Lovett                   Aug 20 1878    Dec  7 1930
Mobley, Mrs. V.R.                       Jne  5 1855    Mar 20 1919
   w/o J.M.
Murray, Dempsey  CSA                           nd             nd
   Co K 32 Ga Inf
Murray, Mary A.                         May 10 1819    Jan 17 1879
   w/o Dempsey
Murray, Rosa Hurst                      May 14 1855    May 31 1888
   w/o S.W.L.
Odom, Candacy                           Oct  7 1852    Mar 30 1922
   w/o J.C.
Odom, Corrie Kemp                       Nov 30 1885    Apr 25 1943
   w/o Walter, Sr.
Odom, Laura Jane                        Mar 11 1847    Jul  1 1917
   w/o N.
Odom, Lillie L.                         Jne  4 1890    May 12 1950
   w/o Ulysses
Odom, Ulysses                           Mar 14 1872    May  5 1937
Odom, Walter, Sr.                       Oct 27 1879    May 19 1952
Odom, Wilson R.  WW-II                  Mar  7 1918    Jne  6 1957
   Ga Pvt USA
Reives, Martha Eugenia                  age 16y 4m     May 17 1846
   d at Troy Female Seminary           6d
Smith, Emma                             Apr 13 1884    Nov 30 1904
   w/o G.E.
```

LOVETT
Screven Co.

Anderson, Albert Sydney	Apr 21 1879	Jne 7 1950
Anderson, Charles E. WW-II	Oct 17 1908	Jan 28 1942
Ga Lt jg USNR		
Anderson, Etta Lovett	Oct 6 1874	Aug 21 1939
w/o Albert Sydney		
Herrington, Archibald	1869	1907
Herrington, Emily E.	Dec 20 1845	Aug 13 1874
Herrington, Emily Eulalie	Oct 30 1875	Jne 7 1878
Herrington, Florence M.	Apr 6 1872	Jne 6 1873
Herrington, Jennie	1889	1889
d/o Wm. J. & Jennie		
Herrington, Lucy A.	1850	1869
Herrington, Lucy Bell	Jul 24 1877	Aug 28 1886
Herrington, Marion	1887	1887
inf/o Wm. J. & Jennie		
Hiers, Infant	nd	nd
d/o Mr. & Mrs. J. Perry		
Hiers, J.P., Jr.	Aug 16 1904	Aug 24 1904
Hillis, Edna Lovett	Sep 20 1868	Sep 23 1897
Lovett, Caroline Jane Wade	Dec 29 1819	Nov 16 1885
w/o William H.		
Lovett, Cecil Arlington	Aug 10 1878	Oct 9 1916
Lovett, Infant	1869	1869
of Wm. R. & Mary E.		
Lovett, Infant	1871	1871
of Wm. R. & Mary E.		
Lovett, J.C.	Sep 25 1815	Jan 2 1898
Lovett, John Cuyler CSA	Sep 5 1846	May 26 1865
Co D 27 Bn Ga Inf		
Lovett, Lucy	Jan 7 1795	Jan 11 1878
w/o Robert W. d/o James & Emily Williamson Roberts		
Lovett, Lucy Elizabeth	May 27 1854	Dec 5 1868
d/o Robt. W. & Eliz M. Andrew		
Lovett, Marietta Adeline	Jan 11 1835	May 25 1915
w/o Dr. Robt. Watkins		
Lovett, Martha	Feb 3 1844	Nov 16 1864
Lovett, Mary Elizabeth	Jul 17 1846	Oct 20 1886
w/o Wm. R.		
Lovett, Mattie H.	1874	1945
w/o Richard L.		
Lovett, Parmelia H.	Aug 26 1826	Jne 1 1910
Lovett, Preston H.	Aug 2 1860	Sep 2 1884
Lovett, Richard L.	1863	1942
Lovett, Robert Wade	Feb 2 1797	Mar 5 1878
s/o John F. & Eliz. Bonnell		
Lovett, Rev. Robt. Watkins MD	Nov 11 1818	Jul 2 1912
Faithful minister of M.E. Church and a beloved		
physician		
Lovett, Sarah Isabella	May 18 1836	Nov 9 1864
w/o Robert W. d/o Z. & M.C. Brownen Price		
Lovett, William H.	Jul 23 1821	Dec 9 1861
Lovett, William R.	Mar 23 1845	Aug 21 1927

LOWRY—ALEXANDER
Jefferson Co.

Agerton, Edward Thompson	Oct 15 1859	Nov 27 1938
Agerton, Mrs. Elmina	Mar 12 1828	Dec 23 1905
w/o John W.		
Agerton, Infant	only date	1883
d/o E.T. & S.M.		
Agerton, Maggie Lois	Feb 13 1897	Jul 3 1897
d/o E.T. & S.M.		
Agerton, Moffatt Spencer	Jan 27 1900	May 26 1900
Agerton, Sarah Martha	Feb 9 1858	Aug 27 1920
w/o Edward T.		
Agerton, William Edward	Nov 1 1884	Jul 23 1898
s/o E.T. & S.M.		
Alexander, Mrs. A.J.	Apr 6 1815	Jan 25 1874
w/o W.S.		
Alexander, David, Sr.	age 48 y	May 9 1836
Alexander, Elizabeth Ann	Oct 24 1834	Aug 24 1837
Alexander, Fannie	Mar 20 1852	Oct 16 1927
Alexander, Green David	Feb 1827	Jne 2 1848
Alexander, Infant	Aug 19 1849	Feb 4 1850
s/o W.S. & A.J.		
Alexander, J.W.	Sep 11 1810	Dec 2 1872
Alexander, John	Apr 12 1889	Sep 15 1890
Alexander, John David Hugh	Sep 11 1856	Jul 10 1933
Alexander, Lou Ellen Johnson	Feb 11 1856	Oct 19 1933
w/o John D. Hugh		
Alexander, Margaret Louisa	Jul 5 1858	Apr 10 1863
d/o J.W. & M.C.		
Alexander, Marion Colley	Feb 20 1903	Sep 8 1904
Alexander, Martha Ann	Oct 4 1809	Nov 12 1841
Alexander, Mary A.J.	Mar 4 1812	Oct 27 1853
w/o J.W.		
Alexander, Mary Adeline Woodes	May 21 1841	Oct 12 1843
Alexander, Mary Caroline	Dec 2 1816	Jan 27 1887
w/o John Woods /Bothwell		
Alexander, O.J.	Jul 4 1834	Sep 13 1890
Alexander, Mrs. Sarah	age c. 54y	Sep 8 1842
Alexander, Sarah	May 8 1905	Jne 16 1910
Alexander, W.S.	Jan 21 1812	Jul 31 1892
Alexander, Wm. Green	May 9 1837	Nov 9 1840
Bell, Effie Dawson	1880	1929
w/o Robert L., DD		
Brown, Clarence Dawson	Sep 3 1915	Sep 24 1915
s/o T.B. & Eugenia		
Brown, Eugenia Dawson	Oct 6 1876	Jul 23 1927
w/o Thomas B.		
Brown, Mary Alexander	Apr 4 1911	Jul 27 1912
d/o T.B. & Eugenia		
Brown, Thomas B.	1875	1930
Brown, Thomas Burrell, Jr.	Aug 31 1912	Dec 22 1919
Causey, J.W.A.	age 26 y	nd
Causey, John W.A.	Feb 14 1861	Aug 8 1887
Causey, Johnnie	Jne 26 1887	Nov 8 1941

Causey, Susie G.	Jul 8 1860	Sep 19 1931
w/o John W.A.		
Daniel, S.J.	Mar 25 1851	Sep 1 1875
w/o J.R.		
Daniel, Sarah Julia	Aug 14 1875	Nov 2 1875
d/o S.J. & J.R.		
Darley, Tarlton	nd	nd
and daughter		
Dawson, Belle Boyd	1876	19--
w/o Clarence H.		
Dawson, Clarence Henry	1874	1948
Dawson, Eliza	Sep 22 1838	Jul 23 1930
Dawson, Eliza Alexander	Aug 25 1910	Apr 27 1911
d/o C.H. & Belle		
Dawson, Eugenia Patterson	Nov 19 1845	Apr 12 1870
d/o A.L. & Caroline		
Dawson, Fannie Belle	age 16 m	nd
Dawson, J.B.	age 65 y	nd
Hadden, Mrs. Mary	Oct 5 1770	Aug 8 1858
b Burke Co d Louisville, Ga.		
Harden, Asa P.	Apr 16 1889	Jne 3 1895
s/o R.A. & M.E.		
Ivey, Mrs. Sallie	1898	1935
Kicklighter, Fredrick	Nov 12 1842	Jul 13 1897
Kicklighter, John W.A.	Jan 11 1874	Jan 30 1884
s/o Frederic & M.A.		
Lawson, Mrs. Mary	1814	Nov 1837
Lowry, David P.	Sep 3 1824	Aug 31 1868
Lowry, Harriet	nd	nd
w/o W.S.		
Lowry, Mrs. Jane A.	Nov 11 1836	Dec 2 1906
w/o D.P.		
Lowry, Rev. Joseph	age 64 y	Jul 23 1840
b S. Car. Presbyterian. Marker erected		
by congregations he had served.		
Lowry, Mary Pressly	nd	nd
w/o Rev. Joseph. Buried in Ebenezer Church yard		
between Louisville and Wrens.		
Lowry, Mrs. Ruth	Sep 26 1826	Feb 7 1855
w/o D.P.		
McCanless, Wm. R.	nd	nd
McIver, James B. WW-II	Apr 26 1904	Jul 6 1965
Ga PHM3 USNR		
Mosley, Edith Lee	Oct 4 1909	Feb 12 1910
d/o Mr. & Mrs. G.S.		
Murphy, Frances Marie	Sep 24 1897	Feb 10 1899
d/o C.M. & G.D.A.		
Murphy, Sidney P.	Feb 8 1838	Jne 27 1915
Murphy, Willie Pinkney	Oct 26 1903	May 22 1905
s/o C.M. & G.D.A.		
Oates, Amanda C.	Oct 2 1855	Oct 8 1866
Oates, Charley B.	Aug 10 1866	Mar 26 1868

Note: Amanda C. & Charley B., buried here, are the
children of A.B. & S.J. Cole Oates, who with several
other children are buried in the Boyd-McBride cemetery.

The names and dates of these two also are inscribed
on the memorial monument there (ed).

Name	Birth	Death
Patterson, Augustine Little	Feb 1 1815	Jul 24 1897
Patterson, Caroline Strong	1823	Aug 31 1847
w/o A.L.		
Patterson, Mrs. Eleanor L.	age 66y	Aug 6 1845
Patterson, Ellen Edgeworth	Aug 3 1830	Apr 4 1885
w/o A.L.		
Patterson, James E.	age 19y 7m	Nov 19 1830
Patterson, John Rev War	nd	nd
Pvt Ga Mil Bickman's Co		
Patterson, Joseph L.	Mar 2 1845	Jan 1 1846
Patterson, Mary C.	Mar 3 1812	May 18 1817
Patterson, Mittie J.	Nov 19 1859	Jne 15 1887
d/o A.L. & Ellen		
Patterson, Nancy J.	Mar 19 1818	Dec 22 1836
Patterson, William	Jul 4 1776	Sep 21 1862
Patterson, William Augustine	Aug 3 1862	Nov 1865
s/o A.L. & Ellen		
Peel, Rachel Oakman	Apr 27 1851	Oct 15 1852
d/o Richard & Sarah J.		
Peel, Richard Lawson F&AM	Dec 15 1827	Apr 23 1860
Penington, Thos., Jr.	Jul 1 1855	Jan 3 1890
Pennington, Minnie A.	Feb 26 1854	Jan 4 1887
w/o Thos., Jr.		
Pennington, Minnie A.	Jan 4 1887	Aug 9 1887
d/o T. & M.A.		
Ponder, Mrs. C.A.	Aug 7 1832	Jan 22 1863
w/o W.J.		
Ponder, C.A.	age 7m 4d	nd
d/o W.J. & C.A.		
Ponder, Elizabeth S.	age 20 y	Nov 21 1866
w/o Wm. J. d/o A.J. & B. Davis		
Ponder, Percy E.	Mar 10 1881	Dec 9 1898
s/o E.E. & I.B.		
Ponder, W.J.	Jan 10 1825	Feb 24 1886
Smith, Henry McPherson	Jne 25 1865	Apr 15 1938
Smith, Mattie Alexander	Jan 24 1871	Mar 29 1950
w/o Henry M.		
Trimble, J.C.	age 27 y	May 31 1852
Trimble, Joseph L.	age 1 y	nd
Trimble, William Emette	age 12 y	nd

95.   LYNCH

Name	Birth	Death
Lynch, Rebecca A.	1852	1912
w/o Wm. H.		
Lynch, William H.	1850	1926
Lynch, William W.	Jan 7 1880	Oct 29 1910

MAGNOLIA BAPTIST
Perkins, Ga., Jenkins Co.

Bargeron, Clara Perkins	Mar 7 1876	Aug 27 1944
Bargeron, Jessie Perkins	Dec 12 1872	Sep 2 1966
w/o Dr. Thos. F.		
Bargeron, Dr. Thomas Franklin	Apr 22 1865	Nov 22 1947
Bittinger, Sarah L.	May 20 1860	Mar 11 1925
Bittinger, Solomon S.	May 6 1858	Jne 4 1935
Buxton, Ione Perkins	Feb 20 1902	May 29 1957
Chance, Abram Anthony	Nov 5 1864	Sep 2 1909
Chance, Abrom A.	Aug 20 1898	Mar 19 1899
s/o A.A. & S.M.L.		
Chance, Aline O.	Jan 18 1893	Oct 31 1963
w/o Shep R.		
Chance, Jessie Thorne	Sep 29 1899	nd
w/o John T.		
Chance, John Thomas	May 2 1895	Apr 25 1947
Chance, Lila Deasia	Jul 12 1887	Oct 20 1897
d/o A.A. & S.M.L.		
Chance, Ralph, Pvt. WW-II	Sep 13 1923	Dec 6 1943
s/o Shep & Aline d in service		
Chance, Shep R.	Jan 22 1891	May 3 1954
Chance, Simeon Reeves	Apr 8 1882	Mar 6 1937
Chance, Sudie M.L.	Aug 5 1868	Apr 19 1899
w/o A.A.		
Daniel, Frank R.	1911	1973
Daniel, Magna O.	1904	L
Godbee, Edna Perkins	Jan 2 1869	Dec 18 1931
Harrell, Charles S.	age 29 y	Jne 2 1890
Haws, Joseph	Oct 26 1836	Jne 8 1876
Haws, Susan	age 52 y	Aug 18 1888
w/o Joseph		
Haws, William B.	Jan 21 1862	Aug 18 1890
Hickman, Harry	1910	1963
Hopper, Robert L.	Dec 21 1900	Jan 2 1968
Jeffers, Nancy A.	age 83y 11m	Sep 16 1895
w/o Wm.	16d	
Jones, Frederick Sparks	Oct 10 1889	Jul 27 1973
h/o Virginia Perkins		
Jones, Lona Perkins	Sep 22 1913	Jne 28 1955
Knight, Miss Jannie	age 51 y	Nov 1906
Lake, A. Paris D.	Feb 25 1856	Aug 12 1899
w/o M.S.		
Lake, Beulah Miriam	Sep 16 1914	Jul 13 1916
Lake, Eva Thorne	Nov 26 1888	Mar 3 1971
w/o J.S.		
Lake, Julian Shepard	Oct 17 1878	Aug 21 1929
Lake, Mongin Lamar	Jul 6 1894	Jul 31 1900
s/o M.S. & A.P.D.		
Lee, Ida Moss	Apr 27 1907	Apr 28 1952
Lewis, Infant	Jul 12 1929	Jne 25 1930
d/o Mr. & Mrs. J.S.		
Lewis, James H.	Mar 2 1921	Apr 25 1973

```
Lewis, Jonas S.                      Aug 18 1889                  nd
Lewis, Lessie Chance                 Apr  2 1897   Feb 16 1971
  w/o Jonas
Lewis, Nancy A. Perkins              age 76 y      May 16 1893
  w/o John
Oglesbee, Mrs. Alice                 May 11 1885   Jan 31 1927
  w/o Avner A.
Oglesbee, Avner A.                   Aug 16 1883   Oct  9 1939
Oglesbee, Cleveland N.               Jul  6 1916   Aug  7 1923
  s/o Mr. & Mrs. A.A.
Perkins, Ann Barnes                  Sep 15 1889   Nov 25 1947
  w/o J.G.
Perkins, Beatrice                    Sep  4 1879   Mar 15 1908
  w/o J.G.
Perkins, Bessie S.                   Jne  8 1877   Sep 30 1964
Perkins, Capers D.                   Sep  3 1865   Feb 18 1922
Perkins, Crawford                    Jne  4 1856   Apr  3 1904
Perkins, David Mills                 Mar 17 1870   Dec 17 1889
  s/o S. Mills & Tallulah
Perkins, Dr. E.A.  CSA               Mar  8 1849              1893
  s/o Frances A. & Dr. David S.  Served with Pruden's
  Artlry Battery from Milledgeville. F&AM. Sketch in
  Samuel A. Echols, Biographical Sketches, Georgia's
  General Assembly of 1878.  Atlanta, 1878, pp. 103-4
  (ed).
Perkins, Elizabeth Eve                       1944              1944
  d/o Mr. & Mrs. Geo. M.
Perkins, Ethel                       Aug  6 1882   Aug 16 1925
  w/o Harman H.
Perkins, Eudora C.                   Jan 30 1879   Jan 17 1951
  w/o J.B., Sr.
Perkins, Mrs. Frank                          1904              1953
Perkins, Fred W., Sr.                Oct 22 1877   May  4 1938
Perkins, Fulton J.                   Jne 11 1881   Dec  9 1918
Perkins, Fulton Jerome               Mar 21 1900   Dec  7 1900
  s/o F.J. & Mabel S.
Perkins, George C.                   Sep  8 1854   May 14 1893
Perkins, George Mills                Nov 12 1910   Jan 18 1972
  h/o Eva Smith
Perkins, Georgie Adele               Jan  4 1893   Dec  7 1919
Perkins, Harman Hampton              Jan  9 1874   Jul 10 1959
Perkins, Hugh C.                     Dec 23 1879   Sep 27 1916
Perkins, Infant                      only    date             1893
  d/o R.L. & Ida J.
Perkins, Ira E.                      Jne  8 1890   Jul 10 1926
Perkins, Irene                       Jne 11 1904   Apr 10 1970
Perkins, Iris Irene                  May  1 1886   Nov 22 1969
  w/o Jno. H., II
Perkins, J. Byron, Sr.               Nov  9 1875   Sep 24 1952
Perkins, James G.                    Jan 12 1880   Dec 31 1941
Perkins, James G.                    Sep 25 1907   Jne  6 1908
  s/o J.G. & M.B.
Perkins, John H., II                 Dec 20 1879   Jan 15 1929
```

Perkins, Julia E. Jackson   1850   1922
  w/o Dr. E.A.   md Sep 29 1870   d/o Rev. George L.
  Jackson
Perkins, Julian Edwards   May 24 1918   Sep 21 1958
Perkins, Lena May   Apr 17 1894   Nov 8 1899
  d/o Robt. L. & Ida J.
Perkins, Lois R.   Mar 17 1921   Jne 11 1963
Perkins, Louisa   age 7y 7m   Jul 27 1865
  d/o S.E. & S.W.   27d
Perkins, M.D. Lamar   Jul 8 1860   Aug 18 1929
Perkins, Mark Edward   MD   Jne 18 1885   Mar 1 1934
Perkins, Marshall   Nov 7 1834   Feb 22 1903
Perkins, Mary Tallulah   Jul 25 1846   Mar 13 1889
  w/o Simeon Mills
Perkins, Mattie Sapp   Jne 9 1844   Jne 11 1913
Perkins, Mildred P.   Dec 28 1899   Oct 31 1964
Perkins, Minnie Attaway   Feb 16 1862   Mar 15 1917
  w/o M.D.L.
Perkins, Montine Lanier   Jne 30 1881   Jne 18 1956
  d/o E.A. & Julia
Perkins, Myrtis Dasher   Sep 9 1889   Jan 3 1949
  w/o Mark E.
Perkins, Myrtle   Apr 24 1884   Sep 11 1900
  w/o S.W.
Perkins, Nell Alberta   Feb 6 1915   Oct 13 1927
Perkins, Robert Lee   Dec 24 1873   Mar 17 1918
  h/o Ida J. Rodgers
Perkins, Shepard E.   Jan 26 1829   Feb 22 1899
Perkins, Shepard Watson   Feb 27 1872   Jul 11 1935
Perkins, Simeon Mills   Nov 19 1830   Jan 13 1886
Perkins, Susan W. Clark   age 39y 3m   Jul 31 1874
  w/o S.E.   24d
Perkins, Virginia Barefield   Feb 13 1858   Sep 29 1945
  md twice: Geo. Perkins & Wesley Lewis
Perkins, Walter Cleveland   Oct 25 1887   Apr 28 1943
Powledge, Gideon   Dec 10 1886   Dec 21 1966
Rackley, Mrs. Ada Perkins   May 12 1879   Feb 13 1962
Riddle, John A.   age 61 y   Oct 17 1917
Rodgers, ------   nd   nd
  On each side of Nancy J. is an adult grave marked
  by brick coping (ed).
Rodgers, Nancy J. McCullar   Jan 9 1855   Jan 31 1902
  w/o J.A.
Smith, Nathaniel   Mar 7 1821   Feb 10 1908
Thorne, Beulah Perkins   Apr 2 1868   Nov 2 1942
  w/o Thos. J.
Thorne, Brooks M.   F&AM   Sep 30 1894   Dec 14 1924
Thorne, Thomas J.   Jne 5 1862   May 18 1934
Wallace, Clarence C.   Feb 9 1867   Feb 3 1952
Wallace, Ola Anna   1886   1946
Ward, Amos E.   Sep 3 1861   Apr 30 1932
Ward, Madge Evelyn   Apr 28 1903   Jne 26 1904
Weeks, Effie L.   Jne 9 1894   Sep 4 1968
Young, Annette Perkins   Jul 28 1882   Sep 4 1958
  w/o Clyde W.

Young, Clyde William   Jul 21 1888   May 8 1973

97.   MALABAR

Malabar, John   age 63 y   Mar 6 1877
    b in England   first of his family in Burke Co
    md a Miss Godbee   f/o Joe, Morgan, Letha (Smith),
    Annie, Virilla, Joyce (Dixon), (Bethany Methodist
    cem) & Ben F. (Waynesboro Magnolia cem) (ed).

98.   MALLARD

Chance, Carrie Mallard	Dec 30 1894	Feb 10 1969
Click, Lilla A. Mallard	Feb 19 1898	Dec 31 1922
w/o J.M.		
Cochran, Minnie Belle	Sep 28 1875	Apr 25 1893
Godbee, Frank M.	Sep 27 1883	Oct 17 1883
s/o M.F. & M.J.		
Godbee, Linnie L.	Jul 11 1881	Nov 10 1887
d/o M.F. & M.J.		
Heath, Henry W.	Jne 14 1902	Oct 7 1903
s/o R.L. & K.M.		
Heath, Infant	only date	Nov 18 1915
s/o R.L. & K.M.		
Heath, Infant	only date	Apr 24 1917
d/o R.L. & K.M.		
Heath, Infant	only date	Aug 14 1924
s/o R.L. & K.M.		
Heath, Katie Mallard	Feb 10 1881	Jne 25 1964
w/o Richard Lee		
Heath, Richard Lee	Dec 20 1880	Jne 7 1964
Holland, Aaron N.	Jul 29 1851	Oct 29 1918
Holland, Annie Lee	May 2 1901	May 22 1902
d/o J.V. & A.E.P.		
Holland, Annie M.	Apr 1 1801	Apr 15 1857
Holland, Annie P.	1874	1950
w/o J. Virgil		
Holland, Elizabeth	Dec 28 1850	Oct 29 1931
w/o Aaron		
Holland, Ernest L.	Jne 5 1916	Jan 17 1929
s/o J.V. & A.E.P.		
Holland, Frances	1890	1936
w/o Norman		
Holland, Francis Laurie	Sep 31 1914	May 18 1915
Holland, Harold Thomas	May 7 1927	Apr 16 1970
Holland, Hubert A.	Nov 8 1916	Jne 27 1931
Holland, Infant	only date	Apr 3 1913
d/o J.C. & Elizabeth		
Holland, Infant	Apr 30 1907	same date
d/o J.V. & A.E.P.		
Holland, Infant (twin)	only date	Oct 29 1919
s/o Mr. & Mrs. J.C.		
Holland, Infant (twin)	only date	Oct 29 1919
d/o Mr. & Mrs. J.C.		

```
Holland, J. Virgil                          1875              1969
Holland, John                   Jne 13 1830    May   2 1911
Holland, Joseph H.                          1878              1953
Holland, Julius V., Jr.         Jul 18 1899    May   4 1912
   s/o J.V. & A.E.P.
Holland, Katie R.                           1878              1944
   w/o Joseph H.
Holland, Lucille B.             Jul   2 1910    Apr 16 1965
   w/o Harold T.
Holland, Norman                             1876              1941
Holland, Pauline                Dec 15 1911    Jan 18 1812
   d/o J.V. & A.E.P.
Holland, Rhonda Celeste         Jul 27 1961    Sep   2 1961
Holland, Richard Laval          Dec   5 1922    Dec 19 1960
Holland, Wilbur W. s/o J.V.     May   8 1910    Nov 25 1912
Joyner, Charles E.                          1904              1958
Lively, Robert L.               Jan 26 1867    Dec 18 1896
Mallard, Arnold A.              Dec 11 1827    Jan 26 1905
Mallard, Arnold A.              Dec   6 1905    May   5 1921
   s/o J.L. & Bertha
Mallard, Bertha Rowland         Oct 27 1877    Oct 28 1965
   w/o Jos. L.
Mallard, Beulah Mae                         1895              1898
Mallard, Carol Lawton                       1914              1926
Mallard, Catherine Holland      Feb   7 1833    Apr 20 1912
   w/o Arnold A.
Mallard, Ellafair Godbee        Oct 22 1860    Sep   1 1940
   w/o Wm. H.
Mallard, Eugene B.              May   8 1869    Jul 22 1869
Mallard, Fairy Belle            Jne 12 1887    Aug   6 1899
   d/o W.H. & E.
Mallard, George W.              May   8 1853    Jan 12 1856
Mallard, Infant                             1887              1887
   s/o James & Savannah
Mallard, Infant                 Jan 18 1904    Jne   5 1904
   d/o J.L. & Bertha
Mallard, Infant                 only    date                 1897
Mallard, Infant                 Mar 28 1895    Mar 31 1895
   s/o W.H. & E.
Mallard, James M.               Jul 16 1856    Sep 30 1928
Mallard, James Oscar            Jne 28 1915    Jne   6 1916
   s/o J.L. & Bertha
Mallard, Jerry Lou              Apr   6 1882    Jne 14 1898
   d/o W.H. & E.
Mallard, Jessie Stephens                    1920              1921
Mallard, Johnnie Arnold                     1893              1914
Mallard, Joseph L.              Jne   6 1870    Apr 11 1932
Mallard, Joseph Thomas                      1909              1910
Mallard, Laurie                             1902              1907
Mallard, Leila P.                           1870              1953
   w/o Pleasant G.  Their children included:  Minnie Lou,
   Johnnie Arnold, Beulah Mae, an unnamed baby, Laurie,
   Joseph Thomas, and Jessie Stephens  (ed).
Mallard, Lorenzo W.             May   8 1853    Oct 25 1867
Mallard, Martha R.              Jul 10 1864    Aug 13 1864
```

Mallard, Minnie Lou   1890   1891
Mallard, Pleasant G.   1867   1919
Mallard, Rayford   Aug 5 1935   Aug 22 1935
  s/o Evelyn Campbell & Lonnie B.
Mallard, Savannah Godbee   1863   1887
  w/o Jas. M.
Mallard, William H.   Mar 12 1858   Jne 12 1936
McNorrill, Katherine   Oct 22 1921   Dec 11 1921
  d/o W.H. & Beatrice
Poston, Grady W.   Mar 23 1936   Oct 19 1936
  s/o R.L. & H.M.
Sturdivant, Bob   1878   1950
Sturdivant, Charlie R.   Apr 18 1900   Aug 31 1925
Sturdivant, Infant   Sep 28 1902   Oct 8 1902
  s/o Mr. & Mrs. E.B.
Sturdivant, Rosa   1879   1942
  w/o Bob
Sturdivant, W.E.   1880   1933
Tuten, Lee M.   1900   1930
Vickery, Stafford   F&AM   Jan 26 1895   Mar 8 1936
Willingham, Julia G.   1900   1972

Note: History of The Mallard Family, cited in the
"Introduction", is a useful additional source (ed).

99.   MCBEAN

Beesley, Sarah   Oct 6 1799   Mar 6 1880
Brown, Tarlton H.   Jne 25 1904   Feb 25 1945
Coats, Mrs. Mamie V.   May 3 1869   Sep 7 1887
  w/o Fleming B. d/o Thomas & M.A. Preskitt
Cosnahan, Thomas R. WW-I   Sep 2 1894   May 2 1952
  Ga Pvt 326 Inf 82 Div
Duke, Mrs. Mary   Aug 20 1804   Apr 18 1886
Johnston, Kathleen Miller   1875   1923
Knight, Miss Frances   Nov 15 1847   Nov 6 1886
Knight, Infant   only   date   Apr 17 1886
  s/o R.W. & L.A.
Knight, John W.   Oct 30 1841   Feb 21 1864
Knight, Julia   Dec 18 1814   Jne 4 1904
  w/o R.W.
Knight, Julia H.   Sep 19 1887   Jne 26 1888
  d/o W.W. & Mary J.
Knight, Laura   Feb 6 1859   Oct 16 1912
  w/o Robert W.
Knight, Lillian G.   1883   1969
Knight, Lizzie P.   Nov 8 1885   Sep 5 1888
  d/o W.W. & Mary J.
Knight, Lonnie   Apr 24 1880   Oct 3 1886
  s/o W.W. & Mary J.
Knight, Lucian Edward   Mar 1 1882   Aug 6 1930
Knight, Lucyann V.   Jne 2 1851   May 28 1871
Knight, Mary J. Polatty   Apr 7 1856   Jul 2 1931
  w/o William Walton

Knight, Robert W.	Aug 24 1818	Nov 9 1873
Knight, Robert W.	Jne 16 1855	Apr 20 1927
Knight, William Walton	Sep 5 1849	May 3 1912
Meyer, Rebecca J.	age 44 y	Aug 25 1892
Miller, Mrs. Anna	Aug 10 1859	May 14 1911
w/o Bates		
Miller, Annie S. Wood	Nov 27 1866	Jul 6 1940
w/o Bates d/o Harriet Crawford & John Henry		
Miller, Bates	May 25 1860	Aug 23 1917
Miller, Mrs. Nancy	Dec 27 1840	Oct 19 1906
Miller, Sallie Bates	May 21 1886	Jul 30 1900
d/o Bates & Anna		
Miller, Sarah Hanson	Dec 23 1849	May 19 1921
w/o Stephen		
Miller, Stephen	Nov 26 1855	Sep 12 1908
Miller, Unia	May 6 1890	Jul 2 1890
d/o Bates & Anna		
Miller, Sgt. W. Henry CSA	nd	nd
Co C 2 Ga SS		
Peek, Infant	only date	May 27 1967
s/o M.J. & Cleila		
Peek, Marion John WOW	Jne 3 1897	Mar 24 1966
Pickering, Mrs. S.Z.	Feb 5 1845	Jan 5 1908
Preskitt, Mattie A.	Sep 22 1840	Mar 16 1926
Preskitt, Sarah V.	May 21 1857	Mar 22 1876
w/o Dr. A. Preskitt		
Preskitt, Thomas	Jan 9 1844	Dec 11 1927
Preskitt, Thomas F.	Oct 9 1870	Jne 9 1959
Smith, David J.	Apr 15 1830	Mar 8 1887
Smith, Marion D.	Nov 11 1865	Jan 2 1879
Smith, Verlinder	Sep 9 1838	Nov 22 1908
Vaughn, Jesse A.	Mar 9 1859	Nov 30 1862
Ward, Al Jarona Prescott	1834	1908
w/o Calvin		
Ward, Alonzo W.	Apr 16 1880	Jan 10 1909
s/o Al Jarona & Calvin		
Ward, Calvin (Boss)	1830	1895
Note: First of this family to come to America; settled first in a community in S.C. which became known as Ward; later came to Burke Co (ed).		
Ward, Bessie A.	Jan 28 1893	May 26 1906
d/o Minnie S. & Seaborn H.		
Ward, Clara May	Oct 10 1887	May 14 1906
d/o Al Jarona & Calvin		
Ward, Daniel Knight	Sep 20 1897	Feb 18 1968
s/o Minnie S. & Seaborn H.		
Ward, Mrs. Emma J.	May 24 1861	Aug 24 1924
in Peek section		
Ward, George W.	Sep 15 1877	Sep 16 1883
s/o Al Jarona & Calvin		
Ward, Lockey L.	May 8 1867	Jan 9 1886
d/o Al Jarona & Calvin		
Ward, Mary Alice	Mar 18 1906	Apr 7 1962
w/o Daniel K.		

Ward, Minnie Spotswood   Mar 13 1859 May 21 1935
    w/o Seaborn H.   d/o Sarah Elizabeth Henley & George
    Walton Knight;   half sis/o Lucian Lamar Knight,
    distinguished Ga. historian. See Evelyn Ward Gay,
    Lucian Lamar Knight, The Story of One Man's Dream,
    Vantage Press, N.Y., pp. 11, 16, 17, 57, & 163 (ed).
Ward, Robert W.   Jan 12 1883 Jul 31 1938
    s/o Minnie S. & Seaborn H.
Ward, Seaborn Harris   Jan 1 1854 May 26 1916
    h/o Minnie S.   s/o Al Jarona & Calvin

100.   MCNATT

McNatt, Wm.   age 50y 6m   Nov 21 1820
                                   21d
    Note: Probably the father of Adam McNatt, prosperous
    Burke planter in the next generation. Part of family
    buried at the Bath Presbyterian Church cemetery (ed).

101.   MCNORRILL-REDD

Powell, Mrs. Sarah Ann   nd   May 18 1861
    w/o Rev. L.F. He is buried at Botsford Baptist Church
    Cemetery next to his second wife and their child (ed).
Thompson, Mrs. Ann Maria   Apr 22 1787 Dec 2 1859

102.   MEAD

Mead, Infant   May 16 1901 May 21 1901
Mead, Lecie   nd   May 18 1901
    w/o Thos.   d/o William Strange
Mead, Thomas   Nov 5 1852 May 18 1924

103.   MIDVILLE CITY

Anderson, Robert L.   Feb 28 1889 Jan 30 1940
Anderson, Robert M. WW-II   Nov 30 1915 May 23 1944
    s/o Robt. L. 1st LT USAAF. Lost his life over Burma
    flying the Hump
Atkinson, Essie Elianor Brack   Nov 8 1888 Jan 16 1919
    w/o Jack   d/o Chappin & Dixie Brack
Attaway, E.C.   Apr 9 1882 Mar 16 1930
Barnes, Goodwin Malcolm   Dec 31 1882 May 31 1943
    h/o Elizabeth Smith   s/o John Monroe & Sarah
    Clements Barnes of Meriwether Co., Ga.
Baxter, May Bell   Jne 9 1883 Mar 9 1913
    w/o W.E.
Baxter, William E.   Dec 12 1883 Dec 8 1932
Baxter, William Ellington, IV   Feb 16 1963 May 21 1966
Bent, Hyland Fairbanks MD   Nov 17 1875 Apr 22 1969
Benton, Roby Hinton WW-II   Oct 2 1905 Aug 12 1964
    Ga PFC USAAF
Bernstein, Katie   1901   nd
    d/o Charlie Coleman

172

Berrstein, Louis 1889 1953
Brack, Anna Dixie Jordan 1865 1961
  w/o Chappin; sis/o Mary P. Jordan Drew; m/o Ernest
  Harcourt, Essie Eleanor (Atkinson), Rooney Jordan
  (buried in Augusta), Annie (Poindexter), Pauline
  Hermann (md Ben Lanier Lane) & Eugene Adolphus.
Brack, Benjamin C., Sr. Jan 18 1865 Jan 1918
  s/o Jane H.M. & Miles Fields
  md 1st Victoria Jones 2nd Mamie Lee Franklin
Brack, Benjamin Calvin Jne 26 1911 Nov 16 1929
  s/o Mamie & Benj.
Brack, Chappin McCullers Oct 29 1858 Oct 19 1926
  s/o Jane H.M. & Miles Fields
Brack, Ernest Harcourt Dec 21 1886 Aug 22 1960
  s/o Chappin & Dixie
Brack, Jane H. McCullers Nov 21 1831 1898
  w/o Miles Fields; d/o Matthew Calvin McCullers
  m/o Ottis LeVert, Chappin McCullers, & Benjamin
  Calvin, Sr. (ed).
Brack, Mamie Franklin Apr 21 1885 Nov 7 1935
  2nd w/o Benj.
Brack, Mattie Rebecca Tudor Dec 28 1891 Mar 24 1948
  w/o 1st Burwell Jordan Drew; 2nd Ernest Harcourt
  Brack; m/o Myrtice Melonae Drew by first marriage.
Brack, Ruth Oct 29 1894 1912
  d/o Victoria & Benj.
Brack, Victoria Jones Feb 12 1873 Mar 16 1904
  1st w/o Benj. C.
Brinson, Fannie King May 6 1884 nd
  w/o John T.
Brinson, John Thomas Apr 22 1884 Mar 2 1964
Brown, Annie E. Zeigler 1868 1933
  w/o S.W.
Brown, Benton B. Mar 30 1929 Jan 14 1967
Brown, Robert Leonard Jne 21 1891 Jan 10 1964
Brown, Roy T. Apr 3 1895 Apr 15 1961
Brown, Shadrach Willard 1862 1922
Bunn, Fred L. Oct 1 1894 Apr 30 1971
Bunn, Sadie Coleman Dec 6 1902 L
  w/o Fred L.
Burch, Infant only date Jul 1 1964
  s/o Mr. & Mrs. Fred P.
Burch, Steve E. Jan 1 1959 Aug 27 1970
Burchfield, Wm. H. May 1927 Aug 1963
Burke, Caroline L. Jne 25 1841 Aug 11 1917
Burke, Henry S. Dec 2 1842 Nov 8 1900
Burke, Willie J. May 15 1874 Dec 6 1893
Burke, Willie Marion Feb 9 1903 May 29 1904
Burton, Isabelle age 70 y Oct 6 1909
  w/o Uriah
Burton, Uriah CSA nd nd
  CSA iron marker next to his wife's grave is believed
  to mark his grave (ed).

Name	Birth	Death
Chandler, Louie Lawson s/o Ida Long & W.B.	Oct 6 1901	Jne 4 1961
Chandler, Martha Ann w/o Louie	Aug 15 1911	L
Coleman, Charles L. WOW	Jan 5 1867	Aug 6 1925
Coleman, Grace Gordy w/o W. Arthur	Dec 2 1916	Dec 31 1972
Coleman, Mollie E. Crawford w/o Charles L.	Feb 1 1876	Apr 2 1958
Coleman, Pearl Elizabeth d/o Laura Drew (Coleman) (McNeely)	Mar 15 1901	Mar 4 1922
Coleman, W. Arthur	Nov 17 1909	L
Coleman, William Matthew	Jan 12 1877	May 25 1954
Courtney, Mae Mulling w/o John d/o Mattie Helen & W. Lawson Mulling	nd	nd
Crawford, Elizabeth m/o T.M. Drew	nd	nd
Crosland, David F.	Apr 9 1874	Apr 13 1967
Crosland, Ruth Drake w/o D.F.	Oct 5 1907	L
Cross, Charlie W. WW-I Ga Pvt Inf	Apr 15 1896	Mar 26 1947
Cross, Doris Bunn w/o Rufus E.	Jne 14 1908	May 20 1969
Cross, Edwin s/o Lannye & Ellie	Jne 12 1926	Sep 4 1939
Cross, Joseph Ellie F&AM	Jne 22 1884	Sep 4 1939
Cross, Lannye Drew w/o J. Ellie d/o Joseph Drew, Sr. & Florence	Jan 13 1893	Oct 7 1962
Cross, Lynwood s/o Lannye & Ellie	Aug 5 1919	Sep 6 1939
Cross, Mary E. Ponder w/o Robert E.	1875	Mar 20 1949
Cross, Robert E.	1873	1952
Cross, Ronald s/o Lannye & Ellie	Sep 21 1931	Sep 4 1939
Cross, Rufus Edward	Feb 29 1900	Jan 17 1966
Curry, Daisy	1920	1968
Curry, Diane	1943	1957
Davis, Joel Adam, Jr. s/o Gladys Baxter & Joel	Aug 24 1932	Sep 23 1956
Davis, Joel Adam, Sr.	May 2 1876	Jne 3 1956
Dell, Elizabeth Brown Smith d/o Robert Leonard Brown	Oct 7 1916	Jne 16 1948
Drew, Bonnie E. d/o Mary P. Jordan & T.M.	Sep 26 1883	Feb 8 1885
Drew, Burwell Jordan s/o Thos. Douglas	Feb 14 1889	Dec 12 1954
Drew, Charley R.	Dec 25 1879	Nov 27 1918
Drew, Edith Edel d/o Thos. D. & Mary P.	Aug 24 1885	Sep 11 1885
Drew, Evelin Letitia d/o T.D. & M.P.	Mar 29 1904	Jne 26 1904

Drew, Florence O.   Jan 25 1872   Dec 27 1957
   w/o Joseph D., Sr.   m/o Joseph D., Jr.,Florence
   (Lane), Thos. A., Theopolus, & Lannye (Cross)
Drew, Frank Armstrong   Aug 27 1923   Nov 27 1958
   s/o Laura & Williby
Drew, George M.   Aug 1 1871   Sep 22 1905
   h/o Virginia Lane   f/o Martha, George, & Mary Belle
Drew, Guy D.   Oct 19 1900   Jan 30 1971
   s/o T. Douglas & M.P. Jordan
Drew, Guy D., Jr.   Jan 14 1940   L
   s/o Pearl New & Guy D., Sr.
Drew, Infant   only   date   Mar 23 1908
   s/o Burwell J. & Mattie R.
Drew, Infants (twins)   only   date   1890
   sons of T.D. & M.P.
Drew, Jeremiah CSA   nd   nd
   CPL Co K 28 Ga Inf Note: A marker but he is not
   buried there (ed).
Drew, Jerry H.   Apr 7 1866   Aug 19 1924
Drew, Jerry Hobson WW-II   Nov 26 1907   Jul 31 1942
   s/o Laura & Williby Ga Fireman ICL USN
Drew, John Jordan   Jne 27 1965   Jne 29 1965
   s/o John & Phyllis
Drew, Joseph D., Jr.   May 6 1904   Mar 29 1953
Drew, Joseph D., Sr.   May 1 1869   Apr 12 1938
Drew, Laura Earnest   Nov 28 1884   May 1 1971
   w/o Williby B.
Drew, Laura Myrtle   May 31 1914   Jan 17 1915
   d/o W.B. & L.E.
Drew, Mamie Helen   Nov 27 1887   Jne 12 1889
   d/o T.D. & M.P.
Drew, Martha   Nov 16 1914   Dec 1 1915
   d/o Mary Inman & Paul
Drew, Martha Ann Bennett   Jan 12 1842   Jan 12 1910
   m/o T. Douglas, Jerry H., Joseph D., Sr., George M.,
   Williby B, Laura McNeely, Charley R., Wilson D., Sr.
   and Paul. b Statesboro, Ga.
Drew, Mary Inman   Jne 6 1889   Sep 14 1967
   w/o Paul
Drew, Mary P. Jordan   1860   1946
   w/o 1st T.M. Drew 2nd T. Douglas Drew
   d/o Mattie E. Allen & James Pinkney Jordan;
   m/o (by 2nd marriage) Burwell J., Myrtice Corrine,
   Thelma Edwin, and Guy Douglas (ed).
Drew, Ora Bell Womack   Oct 10 1884   Nov 1 1971
   w/o Jerry H.
Drew, Paul   Dec 29 1885   Jan 30 1973
Drew, Paul Daniel   Feb 26 1916   Feb 10 1948
   s/o Mary Inman & Paul
Drew, Pearl New   Sep 25 1911   L
   w/o Guy D., Sr.   d/o Lucy Missouri Cowart & John
   Morgan New of Twin City, Ga.
Drew, T. Douglas   1860   1938
Drew, T.M. F&AM   Feb 14 1855   Sep 8 1887
Drew, Williby B.   Feb 14 1874   Sep 13 1958

```
Drew, Wilson D., Sr.              Feb 20 1884   Jan 12 1943
Duffie, Sallie M.                 age 43y 14d   Mar 14 1892
Duffie, W.W.  MD                  Sep 11 1837   Aug 11 1911
Farmer, Tevis Smith               Jul 18 1888   Feb  5 1971
   w/o James Frank   d/o Mary Murphree and Patrick
   Bartow Smith
Felker, William O.                       1880          1960
Franklin, Charlie M.M.            Nov 14 1853   Mar 27 1922
Franklin, Louisa Hart             Nov  6 1858   Apr 18 1928
   w/o C.M.M.
Franklin, Rohema Smith            Dec 17 1878   Aug 27 1954
   w/o S.W.
Franklin, Samuel W.               Feb  1 1877   Nov  7 1934
George, Edith Poindexter          Jul 21 1916   Jan 28 1961
   w/o Harlan   d/o Annie Brack & Amos Wilson
   Poindexter
George, Myrtice H.                Jan  3 1892   Aug 22 1967
   w/o Wm. M., Sr.
George, Wm. Mood, Sr.             Jne  4 1884   Feb  1 1970
Glover, Fred C.                   Sep  8 1894   Sep 22 1962
Gray, Virginia                            nd    Jan 15 1974
   w/o W.A.  He is buried in Swainsboro, Ga.  (ed).
Green, Bertie L. Lamb             Sep 15 1888   Dec  8 1961
   w/o Roger N.
Green, Jim                               1894          1960
Green, Roger N.                   Mar  5 1888   May 25 1961
Green, Walter, Sgt.  WW-II        Apr  1 1922   Feb  1 1945
   s/o Georgia & Jim   killed in action;  buried in
   Epinal Cem. France
Greene, James Elmer  WW-II        Feb 12 1919   Dec 22 1950
   Ga Sgt 28 Field Arty Bn
Ham, Mrs. S.E.                    Feb 27 1847   Aug  8 1909
   w/o O.W.  bkn marker  (ed).
Hamm, Jesse Thomas                Jne 19 1883   Jul 31 1946
Hamm, Mollie S.                   Jul 23 1882   Jul 10 1956
   w/o J.T.
Hancock, William Bruce            Mar 28 1904   Nov  3 1960
Hand, C.M., Jr.                           nd           nd
Hand, Claude Matthew              Aug 10 1880   Nov  5 1940
Hand, Eddie C.                            nd           nd
Harris, ------                            nd           nd
   an unmarked adult grave next to Dr. E.A. Harris
Harris, Edwin Adolphus  MD        Apr 17 1867   Jan 11 1910
   F&AM
Harris, Infant                    only   date   Feb 18 1904
   d/o Dr. & Mrs. E.A.
Harris, Infant                    only   date   Apr  1 1906
   d/o Dr. & Mrs. E.A.
Herndon, George A.                Dec 15 1909            L
Herndon, Katherine Poss           Oct 16 1913   Dec 13 1972
   w/o Geo. A.
Herrington, Crawford Stanley      Sep 11 1891   Oct 24 1949
   (Pat)
Herrington, Mary Lou Nasworthy    Dec 25 1908            L
   w/o C.S.  md 2nd Fred C. Glover
```

176

```
Herrington, Minnie Stone          Feb 28 1876    Nov  7 1965
     /Reaney Boyd
Hickson, Annie Toole              Feb 22 1898               L
  w/o Arthur L.
Hickson, Arthur Lawton            Oct 16 1879    Jan 27 1960
Hickson, Charlie Edward                  1881    Jne 26 1931
Hickson, Edgar Gardner, Sr.       Mar 17 1911    Apr 27 1963
Hickson, Ernest Willie            age 39 y                nd
  s/o Sadie & C.E.
Hickson, Florrie I. Drew          Jul  6 1912               L
  w/o Edgar G.   md 2nd Zane Kofford
Hickson, Sadie Inman                     1887    May  2 1963
  w/o C.E.
Higdon, John H.                          1862               1951
Higdon, John Thomas               Sep 11 1917    May  6 1968
Higdon, John Vurney   WOW         May  1 1893    Sep 19 1956
Higdon, Pheby A.                         1862               1937
  w/o John H.
Hodges, Troup B.                  Jan  6 1851    Oct  3 1902
  h/o Sophronia Inman   See Bark Camp cemetery (ed).
Holcomb, Flavius Josephus         Nov    1849    Apr    1934
Holcomb, Lizzie                   same  date    Oct 12 1886
  d/o F.J. & L.P.
Holcomb, Louisa Polhill           Apr    1845    Dec    1892
  w/o Flavius   d/o Julia Guion & Rev. Joseph Polhill
Houston, E.N.                     Aug 23 1848    Apr 17 1897
Houston, Florence A.              May 22 1848    Apr 10 1885
  w/o E.N.
Houston, Julian                   age 1y 1m                nd
  s/o E.N. & F.A.                      9d
Hudson, Jennie F.                 Aug 18 1901    May 26 1971
  w/o N.J.
Hudson, Noah J.                   Feb  4 1886    Jul 19 1959
Inman, Alfred Gaynor                     1872    Jne  6 1936
Inman, Alice                      Mar 15 1878    Aug 30 1958
Inman, Claude                     Sep 11 1894    Mar  9 1913
  s/o Florrie & Daniel
Inman, Daniel M.                  Oct 26 1859    Mar  6 1907
Inman, Florrie                    Dec  8 1858    Sep 21 1917
  w/o Daniel
Inman, J. Emmett                  Sep 27 1873    Apr  3 1919
Inman, Jerry S.                   Jne 22 1884    Apr  4 1906
Jenkins, Mrs. Adelaide            Nov  2 1844    Mar  2 1907
Jenkins, Avery D.                 Dec 25 1834    Feb 16 1907
Jenkins, John Evans                      1880               1928
Jenkins, Laura N.                        1873               1955
Jenkins, Margaret Brinson         Jne 24 1920               L
  w/o T.C.
Jenkins, Tyrus Cobb               Dec 10 1916               nd
Jenkins, Tyrus Wayne              Apr 21 1942    Nov 22 1969
  Ga EN3 USN
Jeffers, Savannah A.              Dec 17 1876    Nov 10 1959
Johnson, Barney A.                Aug 14 1893    Apr  4 1931
Johnson, Jack                     only  date    Nov 22 1913
  inf s/o Thelma Drew & J.C.
```

Jones, Corinne Dickerson   1876   1947
    w/o Joe
Jones, Elizabeth Inman   Jan 10 1857   Apr 6 1937
    w/o James M.   d/o Mary & Daniel
Jones, Francis A.   Jne 14 1827   Aug 20 1885
    s/o Matthew
Jones, George Law   Jul 5 1880   Nov 4 1969
Jones, Gussie Smith   Oct 19 1889   Jan 25 1971
    w/o Seaborn A.   d/o Mary & Patrick Bartow Smith
    sis/o Mrs. Elizabeth Smith Barnes & Tevis Smith
    Farmer
Jones, Guy M.   age 2y 9m   Jul 21 1884
    s/o J.M. & E.S.   3d
Jones, James F.   age 1y 7d   Jul 24 1877
    s/o J.M. & E.S.
Jones, James Matthew   Jne 24 1852   Jan 19 1921
    s/o Mary F. & F.A.
Jones, Julian M.   age 1y 11m   Sep 21 1881
    s/o J.M. & E.S.   23d
Jones, Mary A.   Dec 9 1846   Feb 11 1886
Jones, Mary B.   age 4y 3m   Mar 12 1878
    d/o J.M. & E.S.   12d
Jones, Mary F.T.   Oct 13 1833   Apr 24 1881
    w/o F.A.
Jones, Paul A. WOW   Dec 6 1877   Jan 1 1917
    s/o Eliz. I. & J.M.
Jones, Pauline Wallace   Jan 22 1888   Nov 23 1970
    w/o Geo. Law
Jones, Philip Sapp, Jr.   Apr 27 1939   Aug 28 1964
Jones, Philip Sapp, Sr.   Jne 30 1909   Jne 10 1966
Jones, Seaborn Augustus   Feb 2 1883   May 11 1948
Jordan, Mattie Elizabeth Allen age 87 y   Oct 2 1927
    w/o James Pinkney (who was s/o John); d/o Patience
    Pierce & William Allen; m/o Mary P. Jordan (Drew),
    Mattie Helen (Mulling), Anna Dixie (Brack), Benjamin,
    Wm. Henderson, John Allen and James.
    Grave is beside Anna Dixie but marker is gone (ed).
Kelley, Roy Orestes   Jul 1 1903   Aug 9 1960
Kennedy, Harry P.   Jul 8 1904   Feb 14 1970
Kennedy, Helen C.   Dec 22 1931   L
    w/o H.P.
King, Eddie Bertha Meads   Apr 18 1889   L
    w/o 1st Claude M. Hand   2nd James S. King
King, James Saffold   Aug 21 1904   Feb 28 1966
Kirkman, John M.   1857   1915
Knight, Charlie WW-I   May 18 1897   Jan 16 1948
    Ga Pvt Inf
Knight, Johnnie WW-II   Mar 25 1904   Feb 2 1971
    Ga Pvt USA
Lane, Florence Drew   Oct 15 1907   Aug 3 1951
    w/o Ben   d/o Joseph D., Sr. & Florence
Lastinger, David A. F&AM   Sep 9 1880   Jan 5 1956
    Methodist Minister

Lowe, Mary E. Veazey   May 22 1886   May 27 1952
  w/o Dr. Wm. R; d/o Martha Willcox & Frank C.;
  m/o Wm. R., Jr., Mary Veazey, & Miriam Elizabeth;
  b Jacksonville, Ga.   d Midville
Lowe, William Robert MD   Apr 13 1885   Nov 13 1950
  s/o Annette & Rev. Charles b Warren Co., Ga.
  d Midville
McClelland, Daniel Edward   Sep 3 1904   Mar 30 1957
McGarr, Irene Toole   Mar 31 1898   Jul 1 1927
  w/o W.J.
McGarr, Margaret Bland   Mar 7 1862   Nov 20 1940
McGarr, Walter J., Sr.   Nov 24 1896   Jne 6 1964
McNeely, John Russell   Jul 3 1879   Nov 18 1934
McNeely, Laura Drew   Apr 26 1876   Aug 16 1934
  w/o 1st ------ Coleman, issue Pearl Elizabeth &
  Milton; w/o 2nd John Russell McNeely, issue Paul.
Moxley, Benjamin Lee   Apr 19 1898   May 5 1968
  h/o Reba Campbell   s/o Katharine Lowery & Wm. Jasper
Moxley, George Jordan   F&AM   Jul 15 1900   Jne 20 1958
Moxley, Gladys Lamb   1922   L
  w/o H. Eugene
Moxley, H. Eugene   1919   1973
  s/o Carrie & George J.
Moxley, Homer Leonard   F&AM   Oct 24 1896   Aug 4 1953
  h/o Sudie
Moxley, Ralph William   F&AM   Aug 19 1918   Apr 19 1956
  s/o Sudie & Homer
Mulling, Annie McGolrick   Apr 29 1860   May 4 1935
Mulling, Charles B.   1876   1941
  s/o Fannie & Wm.
Mulling, Charles B., III   Feb 24 1943   Sep 27 1946
  s/o Louise Snooks & C.B., Jr.
Mulling, Claiborne Sneed   Jne 21 1895   Aug 5 1962
  s/o Annie McG. & Isaac J.
Mulling, Claiborne Sneed, Jr.   only   date   Mar 15 1926
  inf s/o Johnnie & Claiborne
Mulling, Cora G.   Sep 28 1902   Sep 10 1965
  w/o Eggie
Mulling, Henrietta G.   Nov 19 1940   Dec 30 1963
  d/o Cora G. & Eggie
Mulling, Isaac Jefferson   Jne 9 1863   Oct 3 1937
Mulling, Johnnie Bell Lamb   Sep 2 1898   L
  w/o Claiborne Sneed
Mulling, Mrs. Kate I. Shaw   1884   1953
  w/o Charles B.
Mulling, Mattie Helen Jordan   Dec 31 1863   Dec 2 1936
  w/o W. Lawson   m/o Otis, Pipkin, Cora Elizabeth
  (1900-05), Lillie Mae M. Courtney & Julian Lamar (ed).
Mulling, Pipkin H.   nd   nd
  s/o Mattie Helen & W. Lawson
Mulling, Susie Nasworthy   Apr 2 1890   Apr 27 1970
  w/o Wm. C.
Mulling, W. Lawson   nd   nd
  h/o Mattie Helen

Mulling, William C.   1886   1936
  s/o Annie McG. & Isaac J.
Murdock, Susie A.   May 11 1874   Apr 8 1930
  w/o Thomas C.
Murdock, Thomas C.   Jne 15 1878   May 27 1932
Murphree, Augustus William   May 25 1831   Dec 29 1883
  s/o Martha Jane Jones & Wright Murphree
Murphree, Charles Musgrove   Jne 20 1872   Mar 18 1948
  s/o Elizabeth Jordan & Augustus Wm.
Murphree, Charles O.   Jan 31 1903   Jul 1 1962
  s/o Charles Musgrove & May Parker
Murphree, Dora Alice Hurst   May 21 1909   May 1 1967
  w/o 1st Mr. Gordy; /Gordy   issue two children;
  2nd Robert M. Murphree; sis/o Mrs. Toby Chandler
Murphree, Elizabeth T. Jordan   Jne 12 1840   Jul 17 1913
  w/o Augustus W.   d/o Rhoda Gamble & Mr. Jordan
  m/o four sons: Charles Musgrove, Robert Madison,
  John Byne, & Jones Jordan Murphree; and three
  daughters: Mrs. J. W. Sandeford, Mrs. P.B. Smith,
  & Mrs. Susan Murphree Sheppard (ed).
Murphree, Jones Jordan   Mar 19 1862   Dec 8 1897
  s/o Elizabeth T. Jordan & Augustus W.
Murphree, John Byne   Jne 21 1868   Dec 11 1924
  s/o Elizabeth T. Jordan & A.W.
Murphree, Jones Jordan   Sep 15 1908   Mar 27 1971
  s/o Charles Musgrove & May Parker
Murphree, Letitia Inman Hodges Feb 20 1880   Apr 4 1967
  w/o John Byne   d/o Sophronia I. & Troup B.
  m/o Mrs. Donald Thomas (Atlanta), Mrs. Asa Patterson
  (Atlanta), & Mrs. Joseph B. Jones (Midville) (ed).
Murphree, Lou Dudley   Jul 4 1867   Mar 16 1951
  w/o Robert M.   d/o Wm. Crosland of Bennettsville,
  S. Car.
Murphree, May Parker   May 16 1877   Apr 13 1952
  w/o Charles Musgrove d/o Mozelle & Rufus Parker
  of Ogeechee, Screven Co., Ga.
Murphree, Robert Augustus   Oct 20 1899   May 3 1901
  s/o Charles Musgrove & May Parker
Murphree, Robert Madison   Oct 21 1859   Jan 12 1932
  s/o Elizabeth Jordan & Augustus W.
Murphree, Robert M.   1905   1943
  s/o Charles Musgrove & May Parker
Murphy, Elton H.   Apr 12 1921   Oct 28 1959
Murphy, Spike (infant)   only   date   Dec 15 1966
Myers, William Henry   Apr 17 1908   Jul 8 1909
Nasworthy, J.B.   May 4 1878   Sep 16 1911
Nasworthy, Louise Rheney   Sep 19 1897   Jan 13 1970
  w/o N.L.
Nasworthy, W.C.   1902   1959
Norvell, Ruth Stone   May 17 1894   Jul 10 1931
Odom, Fred   Sep 4 1912   Jan 27 1973
Odom, Thetis G.   Sep 8 1914   L
Owens, Joseph Holmes   Oct 29 1876   Feb 5 1933
Owens, Leila Hickson   Oct 3 1882   Dec 6 1918
Owens, Ronald Morgan   Feb 25 1922   Mar 7 1922

```
Peel, Bettie A.                          Feb 22 1855   Sep 20 1926
Perkins, Clemmie Cross                   Apr  8 1857   Feb  9 1938
Phillips, Lula Jones                     Nov  3 1854   Nov  3 1911
  w/o Frank    d/o F. & F.A.
Pippin, Nancy Jewel Brown        Jul 18 1896   Jan 19 1957
  w/o Thos. E.   d/o Lucinda & Wesley C. Brown
  b Twin City, Ga.    d Midville
Pippin, Thomas Edward            Oct 23 1885   Aug 23 1965
  s/o Sara Harrel & Taylor  b Thomas Co., Ga.
  d Midville
Poindexter, Amos Wilson          Aug 24 1886   Jan 10 1968
  h/o Annie Brack
Ponder, William H.                        1847            1886
Poston, Florence                 May  3 1910   Jne  2 1910
Poston, Maggie Lee               Sep  1 1903   Jne  2 1904
Poston, Robert L.   F&AM         Aug 20 1873   Mar 13 1924
Quick, Lucille W.                Sep 10 1902            L
Quick, Norman Lester  WW-I       Mar 20 1897   Oct 25 1971
  Ga PEC USA
Read, Julia V.                            1932            1936
Read, Leola Mae Robinson         Aug 16 1884   May 23 1966
  w/o W.E.
Read, Vivian                              1902            1936
Read, William Embry              Sep 10 1883   May 21 1955
Read, William Embry, Jr.                  1907            1928
Reaney, Robert Miller            Oct 18 1849   Dec  1 1911
Renfroe, Sidney Jones            Apr 12 1879   Jne  1 1959
  w/o John   d/o Ida E. & Philip S. Jones
Rheney, Charles C.   WW-I        Jan 31 1890   Apr 10 1968
  Ga 2d Lieut USA
Rhodes, Carol                    Sep 19 1916   Dec 10 1917
  d/o J.C. & Rebecca
Rhodes, James Carroll            Nov  6 1881   Feb 12 1955
Rhodes, Pauline Carolina         Feb 14 1846   Feb  2 1919
  w/o Jas. Walker
Rhodes, Pauline Carolina         Jne 18 1920   Jul 30 1959
  d/o J.C. & Rebecca T.
Rhodes, Rebecca Tripp            Dec  5 1887   Feb 24 1934
  w/o James C.
Riggs, Bruce                     Oct  8 1903            L
Riggs, Nannie Lou                Nov 12 1905   Dec 11 1971
  w/o Bruce
Roberts, Bessie W.                        1890            L
  w/o Geo. D.
Roberts, George D.                        1889            1958
Robinson, Richard                Sep  5 1923   Feb  2 1966
Robinson, Richard M.             Jul 19 1954   Jne 28 1967
Rountree, Carrie Cross           Oct  9 1880   Oct  6 1951
Rountree, Grace W.               Mar  5 1925            L
  w/o H.J., Jr.
Rountree, Hugh J., Jr.           Jul 25 1919   Mar 20 1971
Sammons, E. Levi                 Dec  2 1875   Apr  2 1908
Sandeford, Beatrice Murphree     Jul 13 1858   Feb  7 1925
  w/o John Wesley   d/o Eliz. T. Jordan & Augustus Wm.
```

```
Sandeford, Evelin Clyde            Feb  3 1880   Jul 29 1883
   d/o J.W. & B.M.
Sandeford, Infants (two)                     nd            nd
   sons/o J.W. & B.M.
Sandeford, Jane                    Sep 23 1929   Mar 19 1936
   d/o Grace Smith & Ralph
Sandeford, John Wesley             Mar  5 1847   Dec 19 1924
Sandeford, Ralph Herman            Nov  3 1890   Jan 31 1956
   h/o Grace Smith   s/o Beatrice Murphree & John Wesley
Sconyers, A.H.                     age 72y 9m    Nov  3 1902
Sconyers, G.D.  CSA                          nd            nd
   CSA iron marker next to his wife's grave is believed
   to mark his grave  (ed).
Sconyers, Mary Ann Ascenath        Oct  4 1840   Feb  9 1885
   w/o A.H.
Sconyers, Nancy                    Nov 13 1849   Sep 16 1889
   w/o G.D.
Scott, Ernest L.                   Nov 22 1890   Aug 21 1964
Seeger, Charles B.                 Jan 21 1922   May 30 1922
   s/o C.B. & C.E.
Seeger, Charlie Brannan            Dec 16 1881   Jan 19 1952
Sheppard, Susan Murphree           Nov 28 1862   Jan 10 1941
   See Smith, Susan Murphree  (ed).
Sherrod, Evelyn Eastmead           Sep  4 1922   Jul 30 1971
Sherrod, Sydney Phyllis            Sep 16 1949   Aug 10 1964
   d/o Evelyn Eastmead
Shinaberger, George Benjamin       Feb 15 1933   Jan 26 1957
Shinaberger, Howard Louis          Aug  4 1902   Feb 27 1972
   Lt. Col 180 Inf 45 Div;  Combat Inf Badge;
WW-II, B.S.M. AR Com.
Sikes, D.P.                        Sep 13 1859   Oct 14 1886
Smith, Alice A.                    Nov 25 1886   Feb 17 1887
   d/o Mary M. & Patrick Bartow
Smith, Eli Sidney  F&AM            Feb 14 1879   Sep  8 1930
Smith, Hattie Ponder               Jul 17 1881   Apr 19 1955
   w/o Eli S.
Smith, Hazel Parish                      1904          1950
Smith, Homer W.                    Mar 31 1858   Mar  9 1885
   s/o Patrick H.
Smith, L.E.                              1870          1944
   s/o Wm. & Martha Jordan
Smith, Mary Ann                    Jul  5 1832   Sep  3 1899
   w/o Patrick H.
Smith, Mrs. Mary E.                Aug 28 1858   Jul 22 1896
   w/o J.A.
Smith, Mary Murphree               Sep 29 1864   Dec 31 1912
   w/o Patrick Bartow   d/o Elizabeth T. Jordan &
   Augustus Wm. Murphree
Smith, Patrick Bartow              Mar  1 1861   Aug 17 1903
Smith, Patrick H.                  May 20 1834   Dec  9 1891
Smith, Robert Homer                May  3 1894   Dec 13 1960
   s/o Mary Murphree & Patrick Bartow
   br/o Mrs. Elizabeth Smith Barnes
```

Smith, Susan Murphree   Nov 28 1862   Jan 10 1941
  w/o 1st Homer W. Smith; 2nd W.G. Freeman 3rd Henry F.
  Sheppard. She is buried beside her first husband's
  grave (ed).   d/o Elizabeth T. Jordan & Augustus
  W. Murphree
Smith, William Devotie   Nov 2 1878   Apr 16 1907
Spence, Henry Baxley   Jan 24 1907   May 11 1966
Spence, Marjorie Coleman   May 31 1908   Nov 27 1968
  w/o Henry B.
Stevens, Carl A.   1886   1964
Stevens, Henrietta Mulling   Jul 26 1893   Jne 18 1947
Stockton, Letitia Jones   Jan 10 1876   Jul 9 1953
  w/o William J.
Stockton, Louise Frances   Mar 1 1905   L
  d/o Letitia Jones & Wm. J.
Stockton, William Joseph   Aug 17 1858   Jul 3 1934
Stockton, William Joseph, Jr.   Oct 24 1908   Dec 28 1972
  s/o Letitia Jones & Wm. J.
Stone, Drucilla Joiner   Apr 9 1854   Sep 14 1934
Stone, James Glenn   Dec 16 1905   Jne 6 1906
  s/o Mr. & Mrs. J.G.
Thigpen, Hubert L.   Apr 28 1918   Sep 20 1920
Thigpen, Leona Watson   Jul 22 1881   Jne 17 1959
Thorne, Virginia G. WW-II   Feb 6 1922   Feb 8 1967
  Ga 1st LT Army Nurse Corps
Thurman, John B., Sr.   Aug 26 1891   Sep 14 1965
Thurman, Para Zona Roughton   Sep 23 1884   Apr 2 1962
  w/o John B.
Thurman, Sidney W.   Apr 16 1919   Jan 24 1966
  s/o Para & John B.
Toole, Caroline Hickson   Dec 20 1874   Nov 26 1967
Toole, Elbridge Hamilton   May 30 1878   Apr 19 1957
Toole, Frank E. F&AM   Dec 29 1916   Jan 8 1968
Walden, Charlie T.   Sep 14 1884   Jan 22 1936
Walea, Lamar Taft   Nov 21 1908   Oct 28 1940
Wall, Charles Henry WW-II   Oct 29 1915   Jul 3 1943
  s/o V.H. & T.H. S/Sgt African Theatre. Missing in
  action
Wall, Mary Lucile   Jul 1 1908   Jne 17 1910
  d/o T.H. & V.H.
Wall, Thomas Hylmon   Jul 25 1881   Sep 8 1945
Wall, Vashti Hughes   Feb 19 1887   Mar 6 1971
  w/o Thos. H.
Wasden, Howard R.   Dec 29 1908   Sep 29 1938
Wasden, Howell Anderson   Mar 6 1872   Jul 25 1956
Wasden, Infant   only   date   Jne 17 1914
  s/o Mr. & Mrs. H.A.
Wasden, Ray S.   Apr 6 1911   Nov 9 1937
Wasden, Sallie L. Franklin   Feb 9 1905   Oct 23 1954
  w/o H.A.
Wasden, Sallie R. Franklin   Jan 19 1879   Jne 26 1944
  w/o H.A.
Wells, Frank Phillips   Nov 18 1906   Jan 9 1972
  s/o Frankie Jones & Inman F.

                          183

```
Wells, Frankie Jones                    Nov 17 1885   Apr  6 1945
    w/o Inman F.
Wells, Infant                           only    date  Jan 18 1911
    s/o J.H. & Annie
Wells, Inman F.                         May  6 1879   Feb  8-1932
    s/o Mollie Inman & George
Wells, Julian Harris, Jr.               Mar  3 1909   Sep 25 1910
Wells, Kathleen Hatcher                 May 13 1910   Feb 11 1956
    d/o Mamie Cox & L.E. w/o Frank P.
Williams, Lula Mae                      age 83 y      May 18 1953
Winburn, Bess Jones                     Feb 20 1888   Jne 25 1963
    w/o R.L.    d/o Eliz. & J.M.
Winburn, Robert Lee                     Jne 14 1884   Jan 22 1965
Wingfield, Bessie Stone                 May  2 1884   Mar  3 1955
Wingfield, Charles Norwood              Mar 10 1873   Sep 18 1941
Wingfield, Charles Norwood, Jr. Sep 28 1918   Oct 23 1955
Womack, Roy A.                                  1918          1951
Woods, Mannie Eugene                    Jan 30 1894   Nov 26 1958
Youngblood, Benjamin Brack              Jan 29 1937   Jul  7 1940
Youngblood, Dorothy Drake               Jan  5 1911   Nov 23 1945
    w/o Robert E.
Youngblood, Joseph Montgomery           Jan 30 1939   Jul 12 1940
Youngblood, Lillie Stone                Feb 28 1876   Feb 15 1958
    w/o Sam
Youngblood, Mary Clyde                  Jne 10 1906   Feb  2 1907
    d/o Mr. & Mrs. I.S.
Youngblood, Robert Evans                Aug 31 1903          nd
Youngblood, Sam                         Aug 28 1875   Nov  9 1948
```

104.   MILLER

```
Miller, Baldwin Buckner  MD      Oct 31 1798  Feb 24 1873
    s/o Frances Mann & Richard Miller, King & Queen Co.,
    Va.  Moved to Georgia in 1823 after studying medicine
    at Univ. of Penn.   md 1st Rosa Anderson (Morrison),
    2nd Cornelia E. Polhill  (ed).
Miller, Benjamin F.              Aug 17 1867  May 18 1875
    s/o Dr. B.B. & Cornelia E.
Miller, Infant         .                  nd          nd
    of B.B. & Rosa A.
Miller, Rosa Anderson Morrison        c. 1799          1851
    w/o 1st John Morrison;  2nd Dr. Baldwin B. Miller.
    She was d/o Mary Holzendorf (Glenn Co.) & Elisha
    Anderson, Sr., and sis/o James Anderson, Sr., Elisha,
    Jr., & Augustus H., Sr.   m/o Sarah A. Morrison
    (Dowse), Robert Morrison, Frances M. Miller (Schley)
    & B.B. Miller, Jr.  (ed).
Miller, Rosina S.                Jne  5 1832  Jul 12 1832
    d/o Dr. B.B. & Rosa A.
Schley, Baldwin Miller                c. 1847          1870
    s/o Frances Miller & Henry J.  b Burke Co., but came
    to manhood in Texas;  d at his grandfather's plan-
    tation in Burke Co  (ed).
Schley, Eliza                    Mar  5 1848  Oct 29 1851
    d/o Frances Miller & Henry J.
```

Schley, Henry   Apr 22 1850   Sep 7 1850
   s/o Frances Miller & Henry J.
Schley, Rosa A.   Sep 7 1854   Aug 13 1855
   d/o Frances Miller & Henry J.

Notes: 1) Parents of the four Schley children are
buried in the Wharton cemetery, Wharton, Texas. Frances
Mann Miller, d/o Dr. B.B. & Rosa Anderson (Morrison),
was born Jul 30 1828, d 1901. Henry Jackson Schley
was the son of Gov. Wm. Schley. See his sketch in
Myers, The Children of Pride, p. 1670 (ed).
        2) B.B. Miller, Jr., b Oct 21 1835, md about
1859 Vannah Chew of Augusta, d in Texas about 1869.
Their two children did not reach adulthood. His widow
married Henry Landrum of Augusta. For additional data
on the Millers, see Hephzibah cemetery, Clark, op. cit.
36, 37, 126, and The Miller, Polhill and Other
Families, op. cit., 1-47 (ed).

105.   MIXON

Mixon, Annie G.   Jan 16 1916   Mar 15 1916
Mixon, Carol Twiggs   Sep 9 1877   May 28 1881
Mixon, Charley J.   1851   1931
Mixon, Clara P.   1859   1940
   w/o C.J.
Mixon, Ellawease   Feb 12 1908   Sep 17 1908
Mixon, Essie Lundy   Mar 19 1887   Aug 29 1966
   w/o Geo. Henry
Mixon, George   Jne 29 1820   Jne 7 1874
Mixon, George Henry   Feb 7 1882   Mar 1C 1959
Mixon, Lila Gertrude   Feb 2 1884   Aug 3 1885
Mixon, Mamie M.   Jne 26 1889   Jne 7 1913
Mixon, Narcisus B.   Mar 28 1824   Apr 26 1890
   w/o George
Peek, Ethel N.   1894   19--
   w/o N.L.
Peek, Noah L.   1888   1946

106.   MOODY

Mallard, Kittie   Nov 3 1869   Nov 27 1905
   w/o L.D.
Mallard, Loula   Mar 21 1900   Jul 24 1900
   d/o D. & K.L.
Moody, Adalaid   Feb 24 1848   Jan 14 1930
   w/o Walter T.
Moody, Gara Ernestine   Aug 12 1886   Apr 29 1910
   d/o W.T. & A.
Moody, Infant   age 2 m   Mar 12 1833
   d/o W.T. & Adalaid
Moody, Sweet Julia   Mar 17 1878   Dec 29 1898
   d/o W.T. & A.
Moody, W.T.T.   Jan 26 1876   Aug 10 1882
   s/o W.T. & A.

Moody, Walter T.   Jul 28 1840   Apr 29 1908

107.   MT. ZION METHODIST

Auldridge, Andrew K.   Jne 22 1848   Mar 25 1921
Auldridge, Jessie   Nov 20 1851   May 23 1919
Bush, Annie L. Cox   Feb 15 1873   Feb 5 1902
  w/o Sterling   d/o Laura & Thos. B.
Chance, Abram   Nov 26 1846   Nov 9 1886
Chance, Annie Eliza   Aug 27 1876   Jul 25 1877
  d/o A. & V.E.
Chance, Elizabeth Estelle   Oct 29 1880   Oct 13 1901
  d/o Abe & E.W.
Chance, Infant   Jan 19 1872   only   date
Chance, Infant   Jan 21 1873   only   date
Chance, Infant   Sep 20 1877   only   date
Chance, Joel F.   Sep 5 1882   Sep 27 1908
Chance, Reuben W.   Jan 15 1884   Jul 22 1885
  inf s/o A. & F.W. Chance
Chance, Virginia E.   Dec 6 1843   Nov 25 1878
  w/o Abram
Cox, Mrs. Ann   Mar 4 1809   Apr 3 1887
Cox, Cicero H. MD   1866   1935
  s/o Aurelia Holcomb & Wm. R.
Cox, George Henry   Feb 7 1867   Jul 22 1867
  s/o Wm. R. & S.O.
Cox, Helen Corine   age 6 y   nd
  d/o Alona & P. Duncan
Cox, Henry Ashton   Jan 7 1897   Dec 14 1897
  s/o H.O. & D.M.
Cox, Henry O.   Feb 12 1871   Mar 15 1907
  s/o Laura R. & Thos. B.
Cox, Infant   age 1 m   nd
  of Alona & P. Duncan
Cox, Infant   only   date   Jan 18 1906
  d/o Mr. & Mrs. J.T. Cox
Cox, Jinks   nd   nd
  h/o Maude Wimberly   s/o Alona & Duncan
Cox, John T.   Jan 14 1865   Nov 24 1906
  s/o Laura R. & Thos. B.
Cox, Laura E. Rogers   Nov 14 1847   May 16 1905
  w/o Thos. B.   d/o Sarah & Thos.
Cox, Marion Wimberly   age 2 y   nd
Cox, Ola   Dec 28 1868   Sep 1 1870
  s/o Laura R. & Thos. B.
Cox, Ophelia   age 21 y   Dec 2 1870
  w/o Wm. R.
Cox, Patterson Duncan CSA   Mar 14 1847   Jne 5 1896
  s/o Sarah Long & Wm. R. Co C 5th Ga Cav Regt See
  sketch in A. St. Clair-Abrams, Manual & Biographical
  Register – State of Georgia for 1871-2, Atlanta,
  1872, p. 45 (ed).
Cox, Sallie M.   Jne 17 1875   Oct 6 1886
  d/o Laura R. & Thos. B.

186

Cox, Theona Alona Fulcher   Feb 12 1842   Feb   7 1905
  w/o P. Duncan   md 1867   d/o Louisa W. & Vincent W.
  Note: Family Bible gives "Theone" as the correct
  spelling. Descendants state that marker is in error
  (ed).
Cox, Thomas B.   Nov 30 1841 Dec 21 1914
  s/o Esther Hust & Jno. Heyward
Cox, William Randolph   1808   1873
  s/o Milley Floyd & Wm   md 1839 Sarah Long (1821-1853);
  issue Wm. B., Augustus B.L., Mary Aurelia, Patterson
  D., Zaccheus L., & an unnamed infant; md 2nd Louisa
  Heath (or Huff) of Girard; issue Sarah Louise;md 3rd
  Aurelia Holcomb; issue: Cicero and Anna (md Lanier).
  See Will Bk A, 364-5. Sarah Long is buried in the
  Cox cemetery and Louise H. in Bethany Methodist (ed).
Cox, William Long   age 14 y 8m   nd
  s/o Alona & Duncan
Eason, Loula May   Sep 20 1876 Dec 18 1903
  w/o E.R.
Fulcher, Julia E. Hughes   1852   Feb   1920
  w/o Simpson R.
Fulcher, Simpson R. CSA   Jan 19 1845   Oct   2 1920
  s/o Louisa W. & Vincent W.
  Co C 5th Ga Regt Anderson's Brigade
Fulcher, Willie Warren   Jul 16 1871 Jne 17 1896
  s/o Julia & Simpson R.
Gordon, George M.   Dec 14 1850 May 31 1878
Hammond, C. D.   age 49y 2m   May 14 1894
  d home at McBean   3d
Hammond, Charles D.   Sep 27 1891 Oct 18 1918
  s/o Elizabeth W. & C.D.
Hammond, Elizabeth Winter   Feb 12 1849   Apr 24 1925
  Erected by her three children: George, Lessie, and
  Clarence
Jones, Aurelia Holcomb Cox   Feb 5 1840 May 3 1912
  w/o 1st Wm. Cox 2nd R.T. Jones   d/o William Holcomb
  who came to Ga. in 1838 from Conn. b Lexington, Ga.
  (ed).
Jones, Florence V. Rogers   Aug 24 1864 Dec 10 1901
  w/o Lindsey
Jones, Infant   Jne 10 1889 only   date
  s/o Florence & Lindsey
Jones, Lindsey E.   Oct 10 1854 Aug 13 1908
Jones, Robert Thomas   May 22 1825 Aug 27 1907
  s/o Sarah E. Thomas & J.M. Jones. md 1st Emily Calsom
  2nd Aurelia Holcomb (Cox). f/o Robt. P. & Thos. D. by
  second marriage. See sketch in Memoirs of Georgia,
  Southern Hist. Ass'n., 1895, Vol II, p. 369 (ed).
McElmurray, J.K. CSA   Apr 18 1829 Apr 14 1862
  d from typhoid fever; battle plains of Virginia
McNorrill, Virginia Fulcher   Jne 19 1843   Feb 8 1869
  w/o Dr. K.P.   d/o Louisa & Vincent W.
Mills, Floyd L.   Jne 24 1884 Aug 18 1896
Mills, Sarah M.   Dec 29 1842 Dec 8 1897

Name	Birth	Death
Prescott, Effie d/o B.G. & M.B.	Dec 30 1905	Dec 23 1906
Prescott, Elizabeth M. w/o Britton	Apr 4 1843	Nov 20 1906
Prescott, Kathryn Blanche d/o B.G. & M.B. / (Missie)	Mar 5 1907	May 30 1909
Preskitt, Ebenezer	Nov 9 1849	Dec 27 1871
Preskitt, H. Russell	Jne 1 1852	Apr 24 1924
Preskitt, Henrietta	Dec 25 1858	Jan 21 1943
Preskitt, Ina Lou (infant) d/o M.H. & A.L.	Jan 19 1905	Apr 1 1911
Preskitt, Infant s/o A. & L.M.	Jan 19 1881	Jan 21 1881
Preskitt, Lobealia	Jan 23 1854	Sep 12 1875
Preskitt, N.H.	Nov 18 1811	Aug 28 1880
Preskitt, William E. s/o H.R. & H.H.	Sep 15 1874	Jan 22 1876
Reese, Ethel Belle only d/o H.C. & C.B.	May 26 1892	Oct 16 1893
Reese, H. Carl	Mar 20 1894	May 13 1909
Reese, Henry Chance	May 11 1860	Nov 28 1910
Reese, Marion	Jne 24 1905	Jne 22 1910
Roberts, George D. CSA Co D 2nd Regt Ga Vol Inf ANV	nd	nd
Rogers, C. Fulwood s/o Sarah & Thos.	Dec 8 1859	Jne 25 1861
Rogers, Florence V. 3rd d/o F. May & T.W.	Nov 18 1898	Aug 29 1899
Rogers, Infant twins ds/o John & Sarah J.	only date	Jan 1 1867
Rogers, James H. s/o Sarah & Thos.	Dec 28 1849	Sep 15 1872
Rogers, John M.	May 23 1845	Mar 7 1892
Rogers, May Godbee	May 5 1875	Jul 25 1941
Rogers, Sarah w/o Thomas	Aug 21 1826	Dec 21 1895
Rogers, Sarah C. d/o Sarah & Thos.	May 28 1858	Mar 17 1869
Rogers, Sarah F. 2nd d/o F. May & Thos. W.	May 4 1897	Aug 15 1897
Rogers, Sarah J. w/o John M.	May 10 1847	Nov 30 1903
Rogers, Thomas	age 59 y	Nov 11 1876
Rogers, Thomas Britton	Aug 31 1852	Nov 21 1905
Rogers, Thomas W.	Aug 7 1875	Aug 1 1953
Syms, Albert J.	Sep 4 1829	Aug 20 1905
Syms, Emily V. Smith w/o Albert J.	Nov 18 1833	Jul 27 1907
Syms, Laura Lavenia d/o E.V. & Albert J.	Aug 28 1855	Sep 29 1861
Syms, Sarah Nathelia d/o A.J. & E.V.	Mar 30 1859	Sep 26 1861
Warner, Amanda	Apr 12 1827	Dec 25 1911
Warner, Mary C.	1866	19--
Warner, Samuel L.	1865	1936

Wedder, Susan Irene   Feb 17 1894   Apr 12 1912
  d/o S.I. & Carrie
Williams, Amelia C.   Sep 27 1846   Jne 27 1881
  w/o John H.
Wimberly, Julia A.   Dec 19 1832   Dec 24 1894
  w/o Wilson J.   md Jan 15 1851
  d/o Nancy & Peter Mathis (ed).
Wimberly, Wilson Joseph CSA   Apr 19 1829   Sep 20 1892
  s/o Mary Cox & Wiley   Note: He was the father of
  William Mathis Wimberly, whose wife was Mrs. Callie
  Chandler Wimberly (ed). 1st Lt,Jones Hussars,
  organized Aug 4 1863.
Winter, John G.   Aug 24 1869   Oct 22 1898

108.   MURPHEY
                        Jenkins Co.

Murphey, Alexander   Apr 8 1801   Dec 24 18---
Murphey, Caroline Eliza   Aug 14 1846   Oct 2 1866
Murphey, Margaret   Jul   1805   Nov 6 1885

109.   MURPHEY
              Hephzibah, Ga., Richmond Co.

Bullard, Mrs. Elizabeth Ann   Oct 26 1826   Jul 29 1851
  w/o Needham d/o Nancy Carswell & Nicholas Murphey
  (son of Edmund by his second marriage). Clark,
  op. cit., 30.
Evans, Robert H.   age 52 y   Jul 20 1856
  d at his residence in Richmond Co. h/o Elizabeth Ann
  Murphey, who was a d/o Nancy Rhodes & Edmund Murphey.
  Clark, op. cit., 30 & 33.
McTyre, Mary   1763 Nov 20 1830
  Note: Clark, op. cit., 40 refers to a Holland McTyre
  who served as a judge of the Richmond Co. Inferior
  Court in the 1820's. Mary may have been a part of
  his family (ed).
Murphey, Edmund Rev War   Nov 24 1745 Dec 10 1827
  md 1st Betsey Ann Gibbs, issue James & Nancy Ann who
  married Aaron Rhodes; md 2nd Nancy, the sister of
  Absalom Sr. & Aaron Rhodes; issue five sons and five
  daughters. For Edmund and his descendants, see Clark,
  op. cit., 26-34 and Woodson, op. cit., 36 & 45 (ed).
Murphey, Nancy   Feb 10 1787 Mar 20 1819
  1st w/o Nicholas md Feb 7 1805   d/o Mr. & Mrs.
  Collins   Clark, op. cit., 30.
Murphey, Nancy Rhodes   May 30 1764 Aug 12 1825
  2nd w/o Edmund md Feb 10 1785   m/o five sons and
  five daughters, Clark, op. cit., 28 & 30.
Rhodes, Absalom, Jr.   Aug 20 1791 Sep 4 1820
  s/o Absalom, Sr. by his first marriage   f/o one child
  Thomas, who migrated to Alabama. See Clark, op. cit.,
  42.
Rhodes, Elizabeth   age c 3 y   nd

Rhodes, Mary Barton   1773   Feb 14 1823
   2nd w/o Absalom, Sr.   md 1796   m/o two sons and
   five daughters. See Clark, op. cit., 42.
Rhodes, Mrs. Nancy Ann   age 47 y   Oct 26 1822
   w/o Aaron   d/o Edmund Murphey by his first marriage
   m/o William J. & Lavinia. Clark, op. cit., 47-49.
   Note that Clark places her death at Oct 6 1833 (ed).

Notes: 1) Our check of this cemetery produced only
seven graves with inscriptions, three less than
existed when Reese, op. cit. made his survey in June,
1936. We have, however, reproduced his information
on Mrs. Bullard, Absalom Rhodes, Jr., and Elizabeth
Rhodes (ed).
       2) Since Absalom Rhodes, Sr.'s second wife,
Aaron's wife, their sister, Nancy Rhodes Murphey, and
Absalom, Jr. are all buried here, it is highly probable
that Absalom, Sr. is also in this cemetery. Aaron
Rhodes (b 1805), however, is not buried there; grave
site unknown according to Clark, op. cit., 48 (ed).
       3) This cemetery contains several graves mark-
ed with stones but without any inscriptions. In
addition, four footstones with initials: JCM, CEM,
EM, and JM, are not matched by headstones with inscriptions (ed).

110.   MURPHREE

Murphree, Abraham W.   Jul 21 1829   Nov 11 1840
Murphree, Emily Virginia   Sep 1 1824   Sep 14 1848
   2nd w/o Wright   d/o D. & Ann M. Corker
Murphree, Hannah E.   May 28 1824   Aug 10 1839
Murphree, Infant   Mar 26 1843   Apr 2 1843
Murphree, James A.   Nov 23 1826   Dec 3 1827
Murphree, James M.   Apr 5 1834   Sep 30 1835
Murphree, Jane M. Jones   Oct 1 1802   Mar 30 1843
   w/o Wright   d/o Hannah Hadley & Thomas (seventh son
   of Abram Jones)   m/o Augustus Wm. & Margaret Jones
   Murphree) Fothergill, op. cit., 148-49 (ed).
Murphree, Malachi   Dec 31 1804   Jan 28 1855
Murphree, Susan J.   Aug 16 1836   Oct 19 1839
Murphree, Wright   Dec 3 1797   Nov 13 1853
   Notes: 1) Wright Murphree was the father of
Augustus Wm. (md Elizabeth T. Jordan of Jefferson Co.)
and Margaret Jones Murphree (md John S. Byne).
Fothergill, op. cit., 148-9. See Midville & Waynes-
boro cemeteries (ed).
       2) An earlier generation than Wright included
John (Rev soldier), Mills, and Elizabeth Brack
Murphree. Dates on the two last-named are available
from Brack family records.
Murphree, Elizabeth Brack   Feb 25 1765   Dec 19 1817
   w/o Mills   sis/o Benjamin Brack (Rev War)
Murphree, Mills Rev War   Apr 21 1756   1825
   The above three are probably buried in this cemetery
   (ed).

Jenkins, Bartow C.	Oct 16 1896	Nov 11 1906
Jenkins, Bob J.	Apr 16 1898	Jul 16 1898
Jenkins, Elbert Norwood	Nov 23 1899	Aug 16 1914
Jenkins, Eula E.	Jul 18 1907	Apr 25 1908
Nasworthy, Sallie E.	Aug 21 1905	May 20 1906

d/o G. (or Q?) C. & Ida

112.   ODOM
                     Screven Co.

Odom, Caroline	Jul 6 1827	Sep 22 1891

w/o Nicholas

Odom, John C. CSA	nd	nd

Co D 47 Ga Inf

Odom, Nicholas	age 74y 1m	Jne 3 1901

113.   OLD CHURCH

Barron, E.T.	age 9 y	nd
Barron, Lavina	age 26 y	Dec 8 1835

w/o Wm. J., Jr.   Note: Memorial shaft to Lavina and
Wm. J., Jr. mentions four children but no names or
dates are given (ed).

Barron, Mary J.	age 3 m	nd
Barron, S., Jr.	age 42 y	Jul 26 1846
Barron, Sarah Brumette	1770	1868
Barron, William J., Jr.	age 52 y	Oct 13 1850
Barron, William, Sr. Rev War	age 84 y	Oct 25 1836

Ga Mil

Barton, Mrs. Sarah	age 49y 8d	Jan 18 1864

w/o Dr. Willoughby   m/o Nancy, Eugenia & Josephine
Barton; also three Bostwick children. See Floyd C.
Bostwick infra (ed).

Bell, Infant	nd	nd
Bell, Robert Lee	Aug 1865	Nov 1885
Bell, S. Jones	Jne 3 1870	Oct 10 1874
Bell, Sarah G.	nd	Aug 1876

w/o Seaborn J.

Bell, Sarah Lewis	1834	1870
Bell, Seaborn J.	1876	1876
Bell, Seaborn J., Sr.	Jan 25 1837	Aug 2 1901

s/o Elizabeth & Simeon   br/o Mary, Martha, Simeon
& John W.   bro-in-law of Elisha Watkins. See Simeon
Bell (d 1869) Will Bk A, 289-90.

Bell, Virgil H.	Jne 6 1860	Sep 16 1908
Bell, William K.	Sep 1866	Apr 1900
Berrien, Eliza Godbee	Aug 24 1842	Sep 9 1917

w/o 1st Homer V. Godbee; 2nd Thomas M. Berrien

Bostwick, Floyd C. CSA	age 24 y	Nov 4 1863

Died from effects of wounds received at Chickamauga
br/o Caroline L. Herrington & Comfort S. Bostwick;
stepson of Dr. Willoughby Barton. Will Bk A, 229.

```
Brumett, John                          age 60 y        Aug 17 1806
Brumett, Susanah                       age 50 y        Mar 11 1810
   w/o John
Carpenter, John W.                     Nov 15 1849     Feb  7 1907
Carpenter, Josephene Rebecca           age 8y 4m       Nov 22 1853
   d/o Cellirnize & Calvin                      23d
Carpenter, Laura                       age 3y 7m       Aug 15 1857
   d/o Cellinnize & Calvin                     12d
Carpenter, Lula V. Hutchins            Dec  2 1855     Apr 28 1902
   w/o John W.
Carpenter, S. Vania                    age 40 y        May 10 1856
Carpenter, Sydnia                      age 30d         May  9 1852
   d/o Cellinnize & Calvin
Carswell, John Devine                  Jul 16 1841     Feb 28 1868
   s/o Sarah Ann & John Wright
Carswell, John Wright            Oct  7 1806   May 21 1885
   s/o Sarah Wright & John (who was the s/o Isabella
   Brown & Alexander) Will Bk A, 493-495.
Carswell, Linda Royall             Oct 30 1844   Mar 22 1896
   w/o John D.  b Burke Co   d/o James Henry Royal
   m/o Porter W. & John D. Carswell (of Savannah)
Carswell, Mrs. Sarah Ann           Sep  9 1811   Nov 21 1869
   w/o John W.      /Devine   md  Jan 28 1835
   m/o Anna Eliza Moselle (md W.A. Wilkins) & John
Crymes, Alice                          Feb 18 1868     Nov 13 1883
   d/o W.O. & S.B.
Crymes, Loula Meda                     Dec 19 1869     Dec 18 1873
   d/o W.O. & S.B.
Crymes, William Oscar                  Apr  7 1840     Sep 23 1887
Godbee, Fannie May                     May  4 1873     Jan 10 1874
   d/o Homer V. & M. Eliza
Godbee, Homer V.  CSA                  Jan 20 1837     Jan 18 1878
   F&AM   1st h/o M. Eliza   bro/o Russell J. Godbee
   Will Bk A, 424.
Godbee, Homer V.                       Oct  7 1876     Oct 16 1897
Jones, Little Jimmie                        nd              nd
   s/o R.F. & P.W.
Lewis, Infant                               nd            1836
Lewis, John Rev War                         nd              nd
   2 NC Mil
Lewis, Ransom                             1807            1883
   h/o Sarah A.  f/o Samuel E., Mary E. Godbee, James T.
   & Wilbur F. Lewis.  Will Bk A, 511.
Lewis, S.                                   nd            1850
Lewis, Sarah Barron                       1810            1886
Lewis, Wilbur F.  CSA                  Jan  9 1845     Nov  3 1922
   Co C 5th Regt Cav  s/o Ransom Lewis
Lewis, William E.                           nd         Apr 19 1833
McElmurray, Edmund Burke               Feb  9 1885     Nov 30 1886
   s/o Mary Chandler & Thos. J.
   Note:  Mary C. was the 2nd wife of Thos. J.
   See Will Bk B, 36-39.
McElmurray, Emma Jane                  Aug 22 1883     Oct 31 1884
   d/o T.J. & M.C.
```

McElmurray, Genevieve   Jul 7 1879   Oct 7 1880
  d/o T.J. & M.C.
McElmurray, Infant   Mar 21 1872   still born
  of T.J. & L.B.
McElmurray, Louisa Barron   Jul 14 1845   Sep 24 1873
  1st w/o Thos. J.   m/o Wm. L., Judson, Mrs. Tommie
  B. Gray & Minis. See Thos. J. McElmurray, Will Bk
  B, 36-39.
Moore, Elizabeth Penelope   Jul 13 1844   Dec 21 1881
  w/o J. Wm. Shultz. d/o Mary & Hill Sandeford
Moore, John William Shultz   Sep 28 1843   Jul 4 1883
  s/o Martha & William   br/o Ella Sarah Warnock, Mary
  Catharine & Prayler Clanton Moore. See William
  Moore, Will Bk A, 132-134.
Moore, Marther Emma   Jan 16 1881   Mar 20 1885
Moore, Mary Catherine   Nov 6 1878   Oct 27 1881
  d/o Elizabeth & Shultz
Moore, William Hugh   Nov 8 1876   Mar 6 1877
  s/o Elizabeth & Shultz
Mulkey, W.A.   age 40y 3m   May 10 1856
  Leaving a wife and two sons   5d
Rogers, Harriet   age 20 y   Sep 22 1856
Royal, Hetty Bell   Jul 5 1813   Apr 21 1836
  1st w/o Jas. H.
Royal, James Henry   Jan 15 1811   May 8 1878
  b Burke Co   d Augusta   f/o Linda R. Carswell &
  Rebecca E. Mollen (Mrs. John T.); uncle of Mary
  E. Mandell. Will Bk A, 431-2.
Royal, Joanna L.   Feb 19 1814   Nov 29 1844
  2nd w/o Jas. H.
Royal, Nancy G.   Sep 28 1801   Jne 21 1873
  3rd w/o Jas. H.
Sandeford, Hill   Aug 21 1806   Sep 4 1880
  f/o Rebecca R. Dean, Eliz. P. Moore, John Wesley
  Sandeford & William Capers Sandeford. Will Bk A,
  446-47.
Sandeford, Mary   Sep 1 1811   Dec 12 1895
  w/o Hill   md Nov 6 1832
Smith, Essie G.   Nov 11 1885   Oct 17 1896
Smith, Frances Bell   1839   1908
  w/o Walden B. of village of Habersham   d/o Abigille
  & James Bell, Sr. sis/o Ella (md Ransom Landing),
  Joseph & James W. See James Bell, Sr., Will Bk A,
  337-339.
Smith, Ida L. (infant)   nd   nd
Smith, John G.   Oct 19 1887   Nov 10 1887
Smith, Seaborn J.   Sep 20 1883   Jne 12 1886
Whitfield, James M.   Apr 20 1824   Jan 25 1874
  consistent member of the M.E. church for 35 yrs.
  s/o Jane & Lewis. br/o Nancy, Mary Whitfield (Burton)
  & Bryant. See Lewis Whitfield, Will Bk A, 142-143.

Notes: 1) S. Vania Carpenter was added from a 1969
listing of Old Church markers by Jesse Stone. Data on

Frances Bell Smith came from a similar survey made by
Mrs. Chandler W. Wimberly (ed).
2) This cemetery is on land which belonged
originally to the Parish Church of St. George's.
Nearby stood the Episcopal established house of worship, but after the Rev. War the congregation had
scattered and the land and building became state
property. There is some evidence that over the
decades more than one denomination used the original building for worship, but in 1830, upon peti-
tion, the State legislature vested title in a
local Methodist Society. The Methodists flourished
there, and in 1853 a new and larger building was
built. In the twentieth century, however, the
congregation lost members to urban churches and
eventually the building was abandoned. Title
passed to the American Legion Post. Unfortunately,
the building was destroyed by fire in the 1930's,
but the cemetery remains under American Legion
care (ed).

114.   PALMER

Palmer, George Rev War   1750   1820
   4th Co Ga Batt'n
Palmer, Mary Cureton   age 81 y   1832
   w/o George
   Note: George and Jonathan Palmer, the forebears of
   the Palmer lineage in Burke, moved in 1792 from
   Rockingham Co., N. Car. to Columbia Co., Ga., together with three other brothers and two sisters. George
   and Jonathan later moved to Burke. Jonathan married
   Margaret White. For descendants of these two brothers, see Pound, op. cit., 313-20 (ed).

115.   PARSONS

Parsons, Sarah M.   age 23y 29d Jan   1835
   w/o John A.

116.   PEMBERTON

Pemberton, Atton   age 65 y   Apr 17 1811
   b in England   Note: Pemberton married the widowed
   mother of James Madison Reynolds. All his property
   was left by will to two step-sons, Wm. Henry R. and
   James Madison R. Will Bk A, 192-194 (ed).

117.   PINEY GROVE BAPTIST
                   McBean, Richmond Co., Ga.

Bass, Arlie M. WOW   Jne 4 1879 Nov 12 1934
Bass, Selma Broome   1888   1922
   w/o Arlie M.

194

Name	Birth	Death
Broome, Edith Brunson w/o Wm. Thomas	1879	1956
Broome, William T. WW-II Ga Pvt 921 Tech Sch SQ AAF	Nov 16 1903	Dec 4 1962
Broome, Wm. Thomas	1870	1938
Collins, Jerushia K. w/o Minus	Aug 19 1881	Aug 30 1971
Collins, Kathleen	Jul 20 1904	Aug 20 1946
Collins, Minus M.	May 20 1870	Oct 19 1922
Crozier, John Henry s/o Peggy Goodson	Oct 5 1959	Oct 7 1959
Cunningham, Mary E.	only date	Apr 1946
Dickey, Claudie Mae	age 12y 1m 8d	Jul 29 1936
Dickey, Otto B. WW-I Ga Pvt USA	Dec 30 1896	Oct 12 1966
Floyd, Raymond L. WW-I S Car Cpl 335 Field RMT SQ QMC	Nov 13 1895	Oct 15 1965
Fulcher, Barney Dunbar	Mar 18 1893	Dec 31 1955
Fulcher, Benjamin Gilbert	Sep 16 1871	Apr 22 1944
Fulcher, Benjamin Gilbert	Oct 10 1889	Oct 26 1942
Fulcher, Florence Collins w/o Willie E.	Sep 20 1902	Feb 6 1958
Fulcher, James Russell	Oct 24 1901	May 2 1963
Fulcher, Jerry Howard	Aug 10 1913	Mar 26 1960
Fulcher, Maryam Meyer w/o B.G.	Oct 12 1872	Jan 30 1947
Fulcher, Willie Dorothy d/o Willie & Florence	Apr 9 1924	May 29 1925
Fulcher, Willie E.	Apr 18 1897	Feb 14 1966
Godbee, Etta Fulcher w/o W.C.	Feb 8 1895	Mar 1 1919
Goodson, Hoyt M.	Sep 14 1885	Jne 21 1951
Goodson, Lillie Lively	Mar 15 1897	Jan 25 1968
Hair, Laura Richardson w/o Winton A.	Oct 1 1880	Nov 28 1936
Hair, Winton Andrew	Sep 9 1973	Aug 20 1951
Hawes, Infant d/o J.B. & D.L.	nd	nd
Howell, Floyd	Aug 11 1912	Feb 22 1965
Howell, Julia Mae w/o Floyd	Jul 31 1916	L
Knight, Enoch Walker	age 84y 2m 29d	Nov 16 1961
Knight, John J.	1878	1951
Knight, Lillie May	Nov 2 1905	Jan 29 1918
McCombs, Charles	Oct 23 1916	Feb 4 1925
McCombs, Ivey	Sep 17 1913	May 31 1963
McCombs, John	May 6 1866	Dec 26 1926
McCombs, John H.	Dec 6 1911	Jne 30 1921
McElmurray, Lizzie	1840	1927
Meyer, Bertie Miller w/o William Wallace	Aug 24 1888	Feb 6 1972
Meyer, Carrie H. w/o William W.	1865	1937

Meyer, Julian Lofton	Jne 12 1887	Dec 28 1943
Meyer, William W.	1862	1932
Meyer, William Wallace	Dec 1 1888	Aug 23 1942
Miller, Annie Louise Fulcher	Mar 26 1891	Aug 3 1973
w/o Marshall A.		
Miller, Benjamin S., Jr.	Jne 8 1936	Jan 12 1963
Miller, Marshall A.	Mar 20 1884	Jan 13 1948
Mixon, C.J. (Buss)	Jne 4 1902	Feb 11 1952
Mixon, Chester	Aug 8 1904	Sep 15 1912
Mixon, Ella R.	Jul 29 1879	Jne 14 1967
w/o Theodore F.		
Mixon, Mary M.	1847	1927
Mixon, Pat M.	1887	1944
Mixon, Theodore F.	Feb 7 1873	Dec 18 1934
Moore, Wyatt L. WOW	Aug 26 1886	Jne 26 1938
Moseley, Joseph H.	Sep 29 1885	Jan 17 1963
Moseley, Mattie A.	Jan 20 1886	Oct 11 1952
w/o Joseph H.		
Muck, Robert C.	Jul 24 1945	May 10 1971
Peek, John Marion	nd	nd
Price, Annie Susie	Jan 9 1923	L
w/o Merritt Carl		
Price, Merritt Carl	Oct 23 1921	L
Price, Wallace T.	Oct 10 1952	Jul 16 1959
s/o Annie S. & M. Carl		
Quattlebaum, Polly Kneece	Mar 31 1899	nd
w/o Wm. James, Sr.		
Quattlebaum, Ralph B.	1928	1937
Quattlebaum, William James,	Mar 4 1883	Mar 7 1964
/Sr.		
Rabun, Raymond R.	1891	1958
h/o Vicie P.		
Reese, Hilda F.	Jne 7 1919	Sep 30 1966
Saxon, Jewell Ann	Dec 6 1937	Dec 27 1957
Saxon, Mae Martin	Nov 12 1911	May 20 1973
w/o Wesley Lane		
Saxon, Roy D.	Jne 13 1931	Aug 8 1931
Saxon, Wesley Lane	Jan 11 1901	Jul 25 1969
Self, Opal L.	Jan 21 1923	Feb 8 1968
Sims, Crettie F. Roark	Dec 28 1890	Apr 2 1961
w/o Sidney Oscar		
Sims, Howard H.	Jne 12 1917	May 2 1943
Sims, Sidney Oscar	Apr 10 1892	Apr 29 1956
Syms, Harry B. WW-II	Jul 25 1918	Jne 18 1970
Ga Cpl USA		
Syms, McDuffie	1924	1957
Syms, Thelma P.	Jan 17 1924	Jne 17 1965
Tinley, Berry S.	1916	1969
Tinley, Kenneth	Oct 13 1959	Apr 12 1969
Tinley, Lamar A.	Oct 12 1909	Jan 14 1965
Tinley, Mary E. Johnson	Jne 24 1883	Sep 20 1966
(Gennie)		
Tinley, Mildred W.	1914	L
w/o Berry S.		

Tinley, Robert L.	Jan 21 1919	Nov 16 1959
Usher, Rebecca Peek	nd	nd
Way, Carolyn Meyer	Jan 6 1918	Jan 23 1951
w/o James C.		
Westbrook, Mrs. D.A.	Aug 3 1861	Jan 19 1934
w/o David A.		
Westbrook, David A.	Apr 16 1853	Jul 2 1936
Westbrook, John S.	1889	1935
Wilcher, Leroy	1919	1969

118.   POLHILL

Polhill, Fannie Williams   Jne 5 1855   May 14 1859
  d/o Mary Williams & Augustus Polhill of Jefferson Co.
Polhill, Rev. Joseph   Apr 2 1798   Dec 2 1858
  s/o Mary Anderson & Thomas Polhill of Chatham &
  Effingham counties   b Effingham Co. Ordained a
  Baptist minister Nov. 1832. Sketch appears in
  History of the Baptist Denomination in Georgia (by the
  Christian Index)1881, pp. 424-26.
Polhill, Julia J.   Feb 19 1799 Jan 23 1863
  w/o Rev. Joseph   md 1819; d/o Jemima Hackett &
  Frederic Guion, New Rochelle, N.Y.; m/o John G.,
  Cornelia Ellet (Miller), Josephine R. (Smith), Augus-
  tus, Julia J. (Cross), & Louisa (Holcomb). For
  additional data on Polhill family, see The Miller,
  Polhill, and Other Families, op. cit., pp 56-77 (ed).

119.   RED HILL

Dixon, Elizabeth	Oct 2 1838	Jul 17 1925
w/o T.J.		
Dixon, G. Shellie	1874	1956
Dixon, Infant	only date	Apr 22 1831
of J.R. & L.T.		
Dixon, Pearl	Oct 28 1832	Sep 26 1835
d/o J.R. & L.T.		
Dixon, Rena Perry	1880	1954
w/o Shellie		
Dixon, Thomas James	age 82 y	Aug 31 1836
Helmly, Matha S.	1827	1912
Perry, Bartow Kor W	nd	Sep 2 1972
Perry, Charles J.	Jne 15 1857	Jne 11 1926
Perry, Cliford	Feb 23 1928	Jne 24 1970
Perry, Frances K.	Aug 22 1894	Feb 4 1954
Perry, Infant	nd	nd
of C.J. & Mattie		
Perry, Infant	nd	nd
of C.J. & Mattie		
Perry, J. Preston	Jan 15 1886	Nov 10 1959
Perry, Mattie Helmly	1858	1944
w/o C.J.		
Roberts, Mary	Dec 13 1858	Jul 10 1880
d/o J. H.		

197

Royal, Alice E.	Sep 7 1891	Sep 27 1891
d/o Guilford & F.G.		
Royal, Frances G.	1852	1929
w/o Guilford		
Royal, Guilford	Apr 14 1838	Jne 6 1911
Royal, Henry	Nov 4 1888	Dec 8 1907
s/o G. & F.G.		
Royal, Howard A.	Apr 30 1897	Jne 11 1912
Royal, Ida E.	Oct 4 1872	Oct 7 1887
d/o Guilford & F.G.		
Smith, Infant	May 28 1885	May 29 1885
d/o R.J. & C.J.		

120.   <u>REYNOLDS</u>

Reynolds, Joseph Smith   age 34 y   Jan 1 1841

121.   <u>RHODES-ALLEN</u>
              Hephzibah, Ga., Richmond Co.

Brack, Eleazer   age 74 y   Oct 11 1801
   See Clark, <u>op. cit.</u>, pp. 18 & 35; also <u>Note</u> at end of
   this cemetery listing   (ed).
Miller, Infant   nd   nd
   of B.B. & R.S.
   <u>Note</u>: A still born infant of Rosa S. Anderson
   (Morrison) and Dr. B.B.   (ed).
Rhodes, Martha   age 19 y   Jne 9 1841
   d/o Wm. J. & Martha
Rhodes, Mrs. Martha Allen   age 44 y   Jne 30 1843
   w/o Wm. J. d/o Elizabeth Anderson & Robert Allen
   (See <u>Note</u> at end of this cemetery listing). See also
   Clark, <u>op. cit.</u>, for Robert Allen and some of his
   descendants (ed).
Rhodes, Mrs. Mary J.   age 21y 2m   May 14 1860
                                           10d
Rhodes, Robert A.   age 25y 10m   Apr 19 1860
                                           11d
Rhodes, William J.   Jan 13 1799   Jan 23 1866
   s/o Nancey Murphey & Aaron. See Clark, <u>op. cit.</u>,
   47-49 & 52 for his life and some of his descendants
   (ed).
Note: This old walled cemetery contains some internal
evidence which suggests that it was early an Anderson-
Allen cemetery. Elisha Anderson, Sr. married first a
sister or daughter of Eleazer Brack, which accounts
for Brack's burial there. Their only child, Elizabeth
Anderson, married Robert Allen of plow fame. Rosa
Anderson, mother of the Miller infant, was also a
daughter of Elisha Anderson, Sr., but a half-sister of
Elizabeth Anderson Allen. Later, one daughter of
Robert Allen, Elizabeth, married Alexander Murphey,
which might account for our finding an "E.M." foot-
stone (which no longer has a headstone), and another

daughter, Martha Allen, married Wm. J. Rhodes, thereby adding another family dimension. Against this background one might speculate that the nine now-unmarked brick graves, all in one part of the cemetery, include Elisha Anderson, Sr. and three of his four wives, Elizabeth Anderson Allen and perhaps an unmarried daughter of hers. Robert Allen, however, moved to Columbia County after his second marriage, and is believed to be buried there. Clark, op. cit., referred to this old cemetery as the Allen cemetery. Reese, op. cit., designated it as the Old Rhodes cemetery (ed).

122.   ROCKY CREEK BAPTIST

Applewhite, Ivanna   Mar 29 1841 Oct 15 1841
  d/o Caroline & John Note: See Applewhite cemetery
  (ed).
Applewhite, John N.   Sep 14 1837 Jul 16 1893
  s/o Caroline & John md 1st Sarah A. Floyd, Apr 27,
  1862; 2nd Sarah Ann Owen, Jan 1, 1864; 3rd Nettie
  Duke, Feb 26, 1873. Note: marriage dates from
  family Bible (ed).
Applewhite, Louis William   Jne 19 1861   nd
  s/o Louis J. & Belle   b in Augusta
Applewhite, Nettie Duke   Sep 7 1828   Nov 5 1912
  3rd w/o John N.
Applewhite, Sallie   Nov 20 1868 Nov 8 1894
Cates, Mary Ann Rebecca   Dec 31 1830   nd
  w/o Robert H.   /Knight   md Sep 8, 1844
Cates, Lieut. Robert H. CSA   May 21 1824 Sep   1891
  f/o F.M. Cates, Sr.
Saxon, Ransom Y.   Jan 19 1833 Feb 14 1908

Notes: 1) This cemetery was badly damaged in the 1920's by state highway construction. Data on Ivanna A., Louis William and the two Cates graves were supplied from family Bibles (ed).
        2) Dr. Louis Jasper Applewhite, MD, a brother of the above John N., is buried in the Magnolia cemetery, Augusta. His dates are: b Sep 14, 1837 d Mar 3, 1861 md Isabella L. Phillips. See Reese, op. cit. (ed).

123.   ROSE DHU
                        Vidette, Ga.

Agerton, Edith Madeline   Mar 8 1924   Apr 23 1927
  d/o Eva M. & W.T., Sr.
Agerton, Francis M.   Feb 25 1916 May 14 1917
Agerton, George   1857   1945
Agerton, John R.   Aug 15 1890 Aug 1 1959
Agerton, John S.   Mar 28 1918 Jul 10 1919
Agerton, Mamie S.   Apr 25 1893 Jul 15 1969
  w/o John R.

Name	Birth	Death
Agerton, Nellie	1869	1941
w/o George		
Agerton, Walter T., Sr.	Apr 27 1901	Aug 4 1969
Alexander, Francis Pressly	Sep 20 1896	Sep 21 1971
Devoted member of Bethel Assoc. Ref. Pres. Church		
Alexander, Hugh Causey	Nov 3 1908	Nov 4 1948
Alexander, Hugh Causey, Jr.	Jne 12 1942	Jne 3 1972
Alexander, Infant	Feb 23 1939	Feb 25 1939
s/o H.C. & Annie E.		
Alexander, James F.	Jan 27 1881	Mar 28 1956
Alexander, Minnie Oates	Jul 15 1889	Oct 3 1960
w/o W.J.		
Alexander, Pearl Oates	Jan 14 1884	Dec 17 1969
w/o James F.		
Alexander, William J.	Sep 20 1891	Sep 11 1959
Babb, Hulen B. WW-I	Aug 14 1896	May 2 1955
Pvt Co B 22 Engineers		
Bailey, Hugh M., Jr.	Jne 20 1919	May 1 1940
Bailey, Hugh McMaster	Sep 12 1896	Dec 3 1960
Banks, Julian WW-I	nd	May 10 1933
Ga Pvt 157 Depot Brig		
Banks, Neva C.	Dec 25 1905	Jul 3 1930
Barber, Nell C. d/o Sam	Jan 5 1926	Aug 18 1973
Barber, Sam M.	Mar 28 1884	Apr 7 1965
Bass, Eligah O.	1881	1939
Bass, Katie Walker	Sep 14 1887	Jne 28 1973
Blount, Wiley Dillard (Mutt)	Jan 3 1892	Mar 6 1967
Burch, Lula Bussey	1860	1940
w/o Dr. J.J. MD		
Burke, Charles A.	Feb 8 1879	Nov 21 1933
Burke, L. (infant)	only date	Jan 7 1940
Burke, T. (infant)	only date	Jan 6 1939
Carpenter, Howard H.	Sep 23 1902	Feb 19 1970
Cates, Heman H.	1883	1920
Cates, James Samuel	Sep 23 1862	Jne 25 1938
Clark, John B.	Aug 20 1861	Mar 28 1921
Clark, Savannah Palmer	Oct 19 1865	Jul 16 1930
w/o John B.		
Davis, Alice Jane	Sep 25 1884	Mar 16 1939
w/o Eugene L.		
Davis, Eugene Levi	Jne 25 1884	Nov 8 1930
Davis, Irene S.	1892	1927
Davis, Robert E.	Aug 31 1908	Aug 7 1954
Diehl, William T.	Sep 15 1875	May 11 1943
Dunn, Eva Lott	Aug 15 1892	Jne 13 1964
w/o James O.		
Dunn, James O.	Jan 30 1887	May 28 1962
Flories, Eujuano Lee WW-II	May 23 1908	Feb 6 1972
Sgt Co E 193 Inf Tng Bn		
Goodwin, Hazel Bass	1916	1955
Heggs, Clem C. WOW	Oct 28 1891	Jan 16 1918
Heggs, Nona Broxton Johnson	Jne 21 1884	Oct 8 1940
w/o Clifford C. WOW Circle		
Hillis, Jake L.	Nov 13 1905	Jne 29 1969
Methodist Minister (1929-1969)		

Horton, Martha S.	May 5 1878	Feb 4 1939
w/o Wm. B.		
Horton, William B.	Nov 6 1870	Mar 21 1940
Hudson, Roff L.	Oct 22 1887	Feb 20 1954
Ivey, Anna Elizabeth Reagan	May 3 1869	Apr 14 1942
w/o Wm. H.		
Ivey, Clara M. Pressley	Apr 4 1911	Apr 21 1937
w/o Ernest W.		
Ivey, William Henry	Jne 24 1861	Apr 13 1939
Johnson, Alice F.	May 12 1863	Sep 11 1935
Johnson, Cora	1912	1943
Mother and Babe		
Johnson, J.B. WOW	Feb 4 1867	Jan 8 1916
Johnson, Jessie E.	May 23 1862	Sep 21 1915
Johnson, Robert E.	Mar 24 1918	Apr 26 1930
Johnson, Susie Mae Sessions	Dec 1 1886	Apr 24 1927
w/o W.S. WOW Circle		
Johnson, William Sidney	Sep 16 1886	Mar 15 1937
Kelly, Charles Benjamin	Sep 19 1882	Feb 14 1944
Kelly, Susan Jenkins	Apr 24 1878	Jne 19 1962
w/o Chas. Benj.		
Kitchen, Alyce Rowland	Jul 7 1898	Oct 25 1938
w/o Claude R., Sr. d/o J.E.		
Kitchen, Claude Ray, Sr.	May 11 1898	Dec 23 1963
Kitchens, Cyrus White	Oct 11 1887	Nov 2 1960
Kitchens, Tressie Gay	Mar 5 1891	Oct 5 1964
w/o C.W.		
Martin, Annie Mae Davis	Aug 19 1885	Mar 1 1960
w/o John H.		
Martin, John Hamilton	Mar 19 1881	Feb 9 1939
Martin, Wiley Richard	Oct 26 1932	Apr 29 1972
Mays, James Allen	Aug 2 1900	Jan 4 1972
Mays, Joseph Jones	1870	1953
Mays, Mary Jessie	1877	1950
w/o J.J.		
Mays, Ruby Murphy	1907	1930
McBride, Frances Shivers	Dec 27 1900	L
w/o Owen C.		
McBride, Letitia S.	Apr 30 1896	Oct 26 1952
w/o T.G.		
McBride, Owen Clinton	Mar 29 1900	Jan 27 1970
McBride, Sarah Agerton	Nov 26 1892	May 1 1961
w/o Wm. B.		
McBride, Thomas G.	Jul 12 1888	Jul 27 1964
McBride, Thomas G. WW-II	Aug 20 1915	Mar 19 1968
CMI US Navy		
McBride, William B.	May 25 1893	Sep 3 1966
McCarver, Commie Gay	Apr 24 1883	Jul 2 1969
w/o Wm. Cullen		
McCarver, William Cullen	Aug 12 1882	Jul 24 1955
McCarver, Wm. Cullen, III	Jne 10 1947	Nov 17 1947
Mosley, Charles Seaborn	Jul 10 1884	Oct 22 1954
Mosley, Clifford	Sep 10 1913	Sep 29 1923
Mosley, Ida Bussey	May 13 1858	Feb 28 1932
w/o S.H.		

Mosley, S.H.	Feb 24 1850	Nov 16 1928
Mosteller, Luther	1858	1930
Mosteller, Sarah J.	1872	1953
Moxley, Cathrine Lowry	1862	1954
w/o William J.		
Moxley, William Jasper	1860	1946
Paradise, Lena Bussey	Jne 29 1862	Apr 23 1942
Peel, Robert J.	Jan 21 1870	Mar 17 1941
Peel, Sarah Whigham	Jul 6 1875	Dec 20 1966
w/o R.J.		
Penrow, John Ralph	Sep 7 1912	Oct 22 1968
Ponder, E. Gordon WW-I	1887	1918
Corp 490th Aero Sqdn		
Ponder, Edw. E.	1859	1928
Ponder, Ida B.	1858	1925
w/o Edw. E.		
Powell, Vera Mosley	Sep 24 1908	Sep 15 1946
Rollins, Henry Ulysses	1878	1951
Rollins, Johnnie Belle Burke	1888	1950
w/o H.U.		
Rollins, Owen Burke	Jan 14 1928	Dec 3 1929
Rowland, Anna Renfroe	Sep 2 1874	Mar 20 1940
w/o Jacob Elmo		
Rowland, Dorothy Pearson	Dec 23 1923	nd
w/o James Elmo		
Rowland, Jacob Elmo	Mar 29 1868	Sep 15 1958
Rowland, James Elmo	Apr 23 1904	Jul 22 1967
Rowland, Mae	Apr 21 1956	Jne 18 1956
d/o Robt. L. & Jane B.		
Rowland, Mae R. Thompson	1894	1936
w/o Thos. R.		
Rowland, Thomas R.	1890	1940
Saxon, Clarence	1903	1968
Saxon, Gertrude	1895	1919
Saxon, James M.	1869	1935
Saxon, Lena H.	1873	1944
Shaffer, C. Allen	1945	1945
Shaffer, Charles H. WW-II	Jan 21 1895	Dec 16 1957
Sanford, Fla. Police		
Shivers, Gilbert H.	Oct 4 1875	Jul 21 1962
Shivers, Ola Agerton	Nov 24 1888	nd
w/o G.H.		
Smith, Eva Weeks	Sep 3 1899	Feb 28 1972
w/o J.R.		
Smith, James Russell	Apr 10 1897	Apr 8 1964
Smith, Mattie A.	Dec 31 1878	Apr 13 1955
w/o Robt. H.		
Smith, Robert H.	May 5 1878	Mar 7 1951
Thomas, Addie Smith	Jne 4 1895	May 18 1971
w/o John Samuel		
Thomas, Alisa Ann	1962	1962
d/o John & Jean		
Thomas, Jody (infant)	only date	Apr 21 1969
s/o Mr. & Mrs. J.B.		

Thomas, John Samuel	Feb 18 1881	Aug 3 1964
Thomas, Teresa Ann	1962	1965
d/o John & Jean		
Thompson, John Lee	Apr 23 1900	Jne 3 1966
h/o Leona Horton		
Thompson, Ruth Newell	Oct 19 1911	Dec 26 1928
d/o S.A.		
Thompson, Ruth Swan	May 30 1876	Mar 30 1961
w/o S.A.		
Thompson, Seaborn A.	Apr 24 1868	Feb 26 1953
Wells, James M. Sp-Am W	May 28 1876	Oct 11 1954
Pvt Co K 2 Regt Ga Inf		
Wells, Julia Wiley	age 84 y	Oct 8 1958
w/o James M.		
Whigham, John J.	1845	1922
Whigham, Mary Cotter	1850	1926
w/o Jno. J.		
Wren, John Andrew	May 2 1935	Sep 15 1969

124.   ROSIER

Little, John Rosier	Sep 3 1875	Dec 8 1875
s/o Rosa V. & William		
Little, Rosa V. Rosier	Oct 26 1854	Jan 5 1876
w/o William d/o Martha A. & John A.		
Rosier, Frances Sophia	Jul 17 1856	Sep 4 1857
d/o Martha A. & John A.		
Rosier, Infant	same date	Jan 8 1850
d/o Jane H. & John A.		
Rosier, Infant	same date	Nov 14 1857
s/o Martha A. & John A.		
Rosier, Jane Hellen	Jan 8 1819	Jan 16 1850
w/o John A.		
Rosier, John A.	Nov 8 1815	Jan 16 1874
md 1st Jane H. 2nd Martha A. children by first wife: John Anderson, Sarah J. Winter, and infant; by second wife: Mary Elizabeth, Rosa V. (Little), Frances Sophia and infant.		
Rosier, John Anderson	1842	1842
s/o Jane H. & John A.		
Rosier, Mary Elizabeth	Aug 1 1852	May 13 1863
d/o Martha A. & John A.		
Rosier, Sarah J. Winter	Apr 28 1843	Oct 9 1868
d/o Jane H. & John A.		

125.   RUSSELL
                   Keysville, Ga.

Howard, Aquilla Lynne	Jan 20 1953	Feb 4 1968
d/o Ruth Russell & Leonard		
Lucky, Seth McCallan	Feb 22 1911	Apr 10 1936
Marshall, Geneva Russell	Sep 5 1913	nd
w/o J.W.		

```
Marshall, Julian Wilson          Jan  9 1914                    nd
Russell, Elvie H.                Jan 18 1894                    nd
   w/o Rev. Q.V.
Russell, Mozell                  Jan 21 1922   Aug 12 1933
   d/o Q.V. & E.H.
Russell, Rev. Q.V.               Oct  6 1889   Jne 26 1959
Russell, Richard H.              Feb 25 1924   Mar 15 1931
   s/o Q.V. & E.H.
```

Note: Next to the Russell family cemetery is an Annex
in which morticians were permitted to bury certain
former patients of the Keysville Nursing Home. This
Home is owned and operated by the Marshall-Harmons who
are a part of the Russell family. Data from the Annex
are listed separately so as not to be confused with
family genealogy (ed).

```
Davis, Alice                                nd  Mar 26 1963
Davis, Robert Lee                Mar      1884  Jan 22 1962
   s/o Sarah & Wm. A.  He was not married   (ed).
Goss, James (Jimmy)              Mar 11 1883  Aug  6 1963
   s/o Zack
Harrison, Floy Smith             Nov 19 1881  Dec  7 1960
   w/o Wm. H.   d/o Brantley Smith
Harrison, William H.             age 83 y     Nov 12 1959
Nolan, Mittie                         1893    Mar 16 1969
Taylor, Nancy                         1875            1959
Whiteside, Roscoe                Jan  5 1900  Nov 12 1959
   s/o Dela Ladbetter & Robort
```

126.   SARDIS
                         Sardis, Ga.

```
Allen, Mrs. F. O.                age 64 y     Oct 24 1911
   w/o Rev. J.H.
Allen, Rev. J.H.                 Oct 29 1832  Jan 25 1896
Bailey, Edward Farrow F&AM       Apr 26 1899  Sep 13 1946
Bailey, Lloyd Kenneth            Oct 13 1928  Oct  3 1972
Baley, Elizabeth Skinner         Mar  2 1830  Mar 21 1923
   w/o David
Barefield, Julia Godbee          Feb 26 1871  Aug 18 1908
   w/o Hugh   d/o Abigail P. Herrington & Ezekiel
Bargeron, Amelia Ann             Feb 27 1875  Apr 17 1896
   d/o Martha Hurst & John T.
Bargeron, Annie Laura            Jne 27 1886  Apr 16 1887
   d/o Martha Hurst & John T.
Bargeron, Benjamin F.            Mar 18 1826  Oct 28 1911
Bargeron, Benjamin Franklin      Mar 16 1881  Aug 19 1964
   s/o Martha Hurst & John T.
Bargeron, Carlton                Apr  5 1903  Oct 29 1969
   s/o Rebecca R. & Jeff D., Sr.
Bargeron, Carrie V. Robinson     Oct 29 1866  Apr  5 1937
   w/o H.H.
Bargeron, Corene Roberts         Oct  3 1896            L
   w/o Floyd L.
```

Bargeron, Ebbie A.   Jul 11 1886   Jul 10 1921
   s/o Thomas W. & Ida B.
Bargeron, Edward James   Sep 7 1859   Feb 11 1931
   s/o Benj. F.
Bargeron, Eliza Ann   Jne 21 1829   Jan 27 1906
   w/o John
Bargeron, Ellen Robinson   Dec 1 1871   Mar 10 1894
   w/o J.D.
Bargeron, Ernest   Dec 17 1908   Apr 14 1909
   s/o W.M. & Mollie
Bargeron, Ethelyn Butler   1915   L
   w/o H. Ralph
Bargeron, Eva T.   1892   L
   w/o Grover C.
Bargeron, Ezekiel N.   Jne 1 1831   Nov 17 1916
   half-br/o Benj. F.
Bargeron, Floyd L.   Jne 10 1888   Dec 7 1968
   s/o Ellen Robinson & Jeff D., Sr.
Bargeron, Franklin D., Jr.   Apr 2 1961   Apr 4 1961
   s/o Mr. & Mrs. F.D.
Bargeron, George W. (Bose)   Oct 19 1870   Dec 12 1939
   s/o John
Bargeron, Grover C.   1884   1968
   s/o Henry H.
Bargeron, H. Ralph   1909   nd
   s/o Eva T. & Grover C.
Bargeron, Hampton W. WW-I   Mar 15 1889   Apr 9 1958
   s/o Thos. W.   Ga CPL 3 Casual Co
Bargeron, Hattie J. Smith   Sep 22 1867   Mar 20 1925
   w/o B.F.   /Herrington
Bargeron, Henry H.   Sep 25 1853   Jan 13 1916
   s/o John
Bargeron, Ida B.   Dec 14 1861   Sep 16 1943
   w/o Thos. W.
Bargeron, Infant   same date   Jul 1 1918
   s/o Mr. & Mrs. F.L.
Bargeron, Infant   only date   Sep 14 1930
   d/o Mr. & Mrs. J.M.
Bargeron, Infant   same date   Aug 29 1911
   s/o Robert & Pearl
Bargeron, Infant   only date   Nov 4 1913
   s/o W.K. & Mamie J.
Bargeron, Infant   1899   1899
   s/o Y.E. & Clyde G.
Bargeron, J. Claud   Oct 3 1863   Apr 10 1927
   s/o John
Bargeron, Jeff D.   1861   1937
   s/o ------- Sapp & Franklin
Bargeron, Jeff D., Jr.   Jan 5 1909   L
   s/o Rebecca R. & Jeff D., Sr.
Bargeron, John CSA   Oct 20 1828   Jul 20 1918
   Alexander Greys,   Co K 32 Reg Ga Vol Inf Army of
   Tenn.

Bargeron, John Jones WW-I   Jul 18 1891   Nov 28 1962
    s/o Hattie Rackley & Edw. J.
    Ga PFC Co A 304 Ammo Train
Bargeron, John Michael   Jne 13 1909   Jul 22 1923
    s/o Lottie Parker & Linton S.
Bargeron, John Tyler   Dec 26 1850   Dec 29 1927
    s/o Benj. F.
Bargeron, Joseph Green   Sep 20 1857   Jan 8 1945
    s/o Ezekiel N.
Bargeron, Katie Bell   Feb 18 1890   Oct 13 1961
    w/o B.F.
Bargeron, Lewis F.   Apr 23 1859   Mar 15 1930
    s/o John
Bargeron, Linton S.   Aug 1 1872   Oct 9 1913
    s/o Ezekiel
Bargeron, Mrs. Lottie Parker   age 89 y   Dec 24 1973
    w/o Linton S.
Bargeron, Lucile H. Hickman   Apr 28 1911   L
    w/o Carlton
Bargeron, Lula Hattie Rackley   May 4 1872   Mar 15 1966
    w/o Edw. J.
Bargeron, Marcus Warland   1873   1938
    s/o John
Bargeron, Martha Hurst   Jne 9 1854   Aug 21 1940
    w/o John T.
Bargeron, Mary   Jan 29 1909   Oct 29 1910
    d/o Mr. & Mrs. W.A.
Bargeron, Mary Odom   Mar 14 1873   Sep 3 1959
    w/o Wm. A.
Bargeron, Mary Rebecca   Aug 24 1838   Oct 30 1926
    w/o Ezekiel N.
Bargeron, Maud   Dec 31 1886   Jan 29 1905
    w/o B.F.
Bargeron, Nancy E.   May 12 1847   Sep 13 1902
    w/o Benj. F.
Bargeron, Ora Ellison   Oct 14 1878   Jan 19 1970
    w/o Geo. W.
Bargeron, Percy H.   Dec 14 1900   Dec 3 1971
    s/o Geo. W. (Bose) & Ora
Bargeron, Rebecca Robinson   1874   1938
    w/o Jeff D.   d/o Joanna Reddick & Ezekiel
Bargeron, Ruth (infant)   only   date   1898
    d/o Y.E. & Clyde G.
Bargeron, S. Mills   Feb 23 1893   Feb 13 1926
Bargeron, Sarah Martha   Oct 5 1850   Jul 27 1885
    w/o H.H.
Bargeron, Theone Robinson   Mar 13 1923   L
    w/o Jeff D., Jr.   d/o Irene Smith & Ivens L.
Bargeron, Thomas W.   Jan 19 1859   Feb 10 1938
    s/o Ezekiel
Bargeron, W.L. Kilpatrick   Aug 28 1896   Sep 8 1896
    s/o Wm. & M.S.
Bargeron, Watson K.   Sep 22 1891   Feb 13 1951
    s/o Henry

```
Bargeron, William A.              Aug 27 1868   Oct   4 1934
  s/o Benj. F.
Bargeron, William Leslie          Jul 23 1875   Jul   1 1942
  s/o George C.
Baughman, Ethel May               Oct 10 1897   May 31 1898
  d/o W.C. & L.
Baughman, Infant                  Aug 24 1899   same    date
  s/o W.C. & L.
Baughman, J.A., Jr.               Oct 22 1862   Dec 31 1928
Baughman, J.A., Sr.  CSA          Feb 24 1832   Mar 14 1904
Baughman, Lester                  Jul 25 1902   Oct 13 1902
  s/o W.C. & L.
Baughman, Lilla                   Mar 12 1878   Nov 15 1902
  w/o W.C.
Baughman, Mrs. Sarah              Mar 24 1836   Aug   2 1923
  w/o J.A.
Baughman, W.S.  F&AM              Aug 22 1873   Oct   4 1916
Bell, Mrs. Addie Kirkland                1903           1973
  w/o Berrien
Bell, Berdie Brinson              Jan 14 1887   Jul   7 1966
  w/o Wm. D., Sr.   d/o Ariann Bland & Mills James
Bell, Elbert Berrien, Jr.         Dec 10 1923   Nov 22 1941
Bell, Elbert Berrien, Sr.                1887   Mar   2 1952
Bell, Eugene                      Nov 22 1903             L
Bell, Hardie J.                          1884           1972
Bell, Lucy Lovett                 Sep 16 1857   Feb 14 1949
  w/o Seaborn Jones, Lt.,CSA
Bell, Preston Wade                Jul 18 1882   Apr   9 1949
Bell, William Daniel, Sr.         Dec 18 1887   Oct 31 1933
  s/o Lenora Davis & Seaborn
Bell, Willie S.                   Feb 26 1902   May 19 1972
Berry, Charlie                           1855           1910
Berry, Eliza                             1861           1905
  w/o Charlie
Blount, E. M.                     Jan 15 1852   May 16 1926
Blount, Mrs. Lou Setta B.         May  7 1867   Jan 16 1946
  w/o E.M.
Bonnell, Albert Judson            Apr  6 1908   Aug 21 1973
  h/o Myrtie Bell Hillis   s/o Mary Oliver & Bryant
Bonnell, Ann                      Aug  3 1875   Aug 26 1925
  w/o L.L.
Bonnell, Charles Otis  F&AM       Jul 25 1873   Apr 12 1929
Bonnell, Clyda                    Apr  9 1898   Sep 15 1917
  d/o A.D. & C.L.
Bonnell, James Everett  WW-II     Jan 25 1913   Mar   1 1942
  s/o Mamie & Jas. R.   Killed in action South of Java
Bonnell, James P.  F&AM           Jul 25 1878   Jan 26 1915
Bonnell, Louisa                   Oct  4 1842   Mar 17 1914
  w/o Chas. E.
Bonnell, Mamie Ellison            Jan 13 1881   Feb 15 1960
  w/o Jas. P.
Bonnell, Mamie Joe                       1880           1949
Bonnell, Myrtie H.                May 19 1909             L
  w/o Albert J.  d/o Annie Laurie Trader & Charlie R.
  Hillis
```

```
Bonnell, Robert S.                        Sep 20 1869   Aug 30 1951
Boyd, Ruth S.                             Sep  1 1897   Jul  3 1928
Brigham, Mary Dennison                    Oct 20 1890   Jne 16 1960
   w/o Wm. L.
Brigham, William Lewis                    Jan 19 1894   Mar 22 1964
Brinson, Annie Beulah                     Oct 30 1875   Feb  6 1900
   w/o Geo.
Brinson, Annie Beulah                     Dec 25 1899   May 17 1900
   d/o G.F. & A.B.
Brinson, Douglas Brigham                  Oct 11 1896   Apr     1897
   s/o G.F. & A.B.
Brinson, George F.                        Dec 16 1873   Apr 13 1909
   s/o Martha E. & Frank L.
Buckley, Sylvia Faye Campbell             Aug 15 1935   Oct  3 1971
   d/o Myrtie Kimball & B.
Burke, Myrtis Smith                              1900          1949
Buxton, Dwight Lafayette                         1882          1883
Buxton, Ellie Edith                              1884          1887
Buxton, Jefferson LaFayette               Jan 31 1838   Dec  5 1906
Buxton, Jefferson Lamar                          1886          1887
Buxton, Moody Bliss                              1878          1882
Buxton, William Eugene                           1866          1869
Cates, Alice V.                           Feb  1 1880   Feb 11 1902
   w/o John
Cates, Elijah B.                          Oct  2 1822   Nov 17 1904
Cates, Florrie                            Mar 23 1900   May 16 1901
   d/o D.J.P. & J.E.
Cates, Henry Judson                       Feb 27 1892   Aug 10 1915
   s/o D.J.P. & Josephine
Cates, James B.                           Jan 22 1849   Nov 27 1862
Cates, Jennie E.                          Aug 16 1874   Jan 16 1882
   d/o G.F. & Mattie
Cates, Mary Sapp                          Nov  6 1826   Feb  8 1906
   w/o Elijah B.
Chance, Infant                            only   date  Dec 30 1922
   d/o Mr. & Mrs. M.P.
Chance, Madison Watt                             1879          1935
Chance, Susie                             May 17 1854   Nov 29 1918
   w/o William
Chance, Susie F.                          Sep 21 1885   Feb  1 1948
   see Griner, Susie F. Chance
Chandler, Charles Coutteau                Oct 22 1912   Jne 10 1918
   s/o J.J. & M.L.
Chandler, Francis Marion                  Nov 26 1914   Jul 28 1930
   s/o Maggie L.B. & John J.
Chandler, George M.  CSA                  Jul  8 1846   Sep  6 1906
   Cpl Co D 27th Ga Batt
Chandler, Infant                          Jan 18 1895   same   date
   d/o J.J. & M.L.
Chandler, Irene Mae                       Feb  6 1890   Jan 15 1916
   w/o Jas. A.   /Herrington  d/o Hazeltine & Tom
Chandler, Jane L. Darlington              Feb  8 1823   Jne 21 1876
   w/o Wm.  d/o Martha Hankinson & John Armstrong
```

```
Chandler, John J.                    Nov 22 1872   Aug 19 1940
    s/o George M.
Chandler, Lillian Scruggs            Sep 17 1887   Aug 16 1966
    w/o Richard D.
Chandler, Maggie Lou Bargeron        Nov 22 1878   Jan  3 1974
    w/o John J.  d/o Martha Hurst & John T.
Chandler, Martha Eugenia             Sep  1 1910   May 10 1912
    d/o J.J. & M.L.
Chandler, Minis J.                           1877          1938
Chandler, Norma Lou                  Apr 14 1890   Feb 27 1915
    d/o Norma W. & Dr. Wm. H.
Chandler, Norma Wimberly             May 11 1855   Feb 21 1931
    w/o Dr. Wm. H.   d/o Julia Ann Mathis & Wilson Joseph
Chandler, Richard Darlington         Sep  5 1882   Feb 20 1962
    s/o Jane D. & William
Chandler, Robert   CSA                       1830          1893
Chandler, Robert Tyler               Jul  7 1908   Sep 22 1909
    s/o J.J. & M.L.
Chandler, Sarah E.                           1842          1919
    w/o Robert
Chandler, Sarah E.(Little)           Aug 14 1884   Aug  2 1885
    d/o Sarah & Robert
Chandler, Thomas J.                  Feb  2 1875   May 20 1913
    s/o Sarah & Robert
Chandler, William   CSA              Jan 22 1822   Mar 15 1909
    s/o Susannah Boyt & George    5th Ga Regt
Chandler, William Hamilton MD        Apr 29 1851   Oct 24 1916
    s/o Jane L. Darlington & Wm.
Chandler, William Wilson             Sep 11 1875   Feb 14 1905
    s/o Norma & Dr. Wm. H.
Chew, John C., Jr.                   Sep  8 1871   Jul 26 1873
Chivers, Carol H.                    Mar 18 1911   Mar  5 1963
Chivers, Sara B.                     Nov 26 1911              L
    w/o Carol H.
Coughlin, Cordile                    Jne 30 1911   Jan 11 1927
Coughlin, Mrs. Georgia E.            Sep 16 1853   Jne  3 1888
Coughlin, Massie Taylor              Aug 15 1883   Sep 30 1953
    w/o Olin H.
Coughlin, Olin Herrington            Jan 28 1885   Jan 30 1956
    grand s/o Mary Hurst & Bill Herrington
Coughlin, William Davis              Dec 25 1921   Jne  9 1930
Cullen, Ida C.                       Aug 15 1903              L
    w/o Wyatt
Cullen, Wyatt A., Sr.                Jne 10 1893   Aug  4 1950
Davis, Bertha R.                     Feb    1909   Jan    1968
    w/o Raymond
Davis, Raymond                       Sep    1902   Sep    1965
Elliott, George Sherman, Sr.         Sep  1 1902   Sep  1 1969
Elliott, Gus  WW-I                   May 20 1895   Nov 14 1969
    Ga Pvt USA
Elliott, Hattie Lovett               Oct  3 1884   Aug 29 1919
    w/o W.G.
Elliott, James Howard                        1902          1944
Elliott, Mattie Lovett               Oct  3 1884   Sep 26 1903
    w/o B.F.
```

Elliott, William Gibson   Sep 12 1882   Feb 29 1948
Ellison, Ada Lavinia   Aug 29 1872   May 22 1915
  w/o J.L.
Ellison, Annie Herrington   Nov 30 1892   L
  w/o Lovick P.   d/o Hattie Smith & Martin Luther
Ellison, Benjamin F.   Jul 19 1854   Jne 17 1883
  s/o Cynthia & Robt. F.
Ellison, Clara V. Ellison   Dec 31 1859   Oct 18 1897
  w/o Jacob L.
Ellison, Cynthia H.   Jan 25 1819   Nov 7 1883
  w/o R.F.
Ellison, Emily T.   Aug 20 1861   Feb 18 1892
  w/o B.F.
Ellison, George Evens   May 1 1884   Sep 10 1884
  s/o R.J. & J.E.
Ellison, Hattie Lou   Apr 11 1905   Mar 30 1915
  d/o Ada Bargeron & Jacob L.
Ellison, Jacob Lawrence   May 31 1849   Jan 18 1929
  s/o Cynthia H. & Robt. F.
Ellison, Linwood   Jan 1 1874   May 30 1883
Ellison, Lovick Pierce   Feb 15 1887   L
  s/o Clara V. & Jacob L.
Ellison, R.F.   Aug 7 1801   May 3 1876
Ellison, Robert J.   Nov 11 1847   Jul 28 1900
Ellison, Robert P. WW-II   Aug 16 1917   Dec 9 1968
  s/o Annie H. & L.P. Ga CPL USA
Ellison, Walter W. WW-I   Jan 13 1887   Jne 16 1968
  Ga Mech USA
Ellison, Warren   May 3 1887   Jne 10 1887
  s/o R.J. & J.E.
Ellison, Warren Marshall   Jan 24 1935   Mar 7 1935
  s/o Annie H. & Lovick P.
Glisson, Infant   Jul 19 1885   same   date
  s/o I.C. & N.A.
Glisson, Irving Clayton   Apr 21 1850   Sep 25 1916
Glisson, Nannie A.   Dec 14 1848   Nov 8 1927
  w/o Irving C.
Godbee, Attie Bailey   Feb 24 1871   Mar 21 1951
  w/o N.L.
Godbee, Clarence   Mar 5 1891   Apr 27 1926
  s/o M. Jeroline & Moses F.
Godbee, Claudie   Sep 3 1893   Aug 26 1898
  s/o M.F. & M.J.
Godbee, Francis Bartow   Apr 4 1862   Sep 25 1929
  Shriner   s/o Martha G. & Jim
Godbee, Hampton S.   1884   1953
  s/o Jeroline & Moses F.
Godbee, Harry Evans   Oct 27 1893   Dec 4 1963
  s/o Sara Cates & Francis Bartow
Godbee, Hattie C.   1884   1939
  w/o Hampton S.
Godbee, James Thomas (Tommy)   1928   1939
  s/o Elizabeth Herrington & Harry E.

Godbee, Martha Jeroline   Aug 29 1863   Sep 13 1936
   w/o M.F.
Godbee, Moses F.   Sep 15 1857   Jul 8 1928
   s/o Martha Godbee & Jim
Godbee, Needham   Jul 24 1888   Apr 28 1959
Godbee, Newton Lawrence   Dec 19 1870   Apr 30 1931
   s/o Martha Godbee & Jim
Godbee, Sara Cates   Mar 28 1861   Feb 29 1948
   w/o F.B.   d/o Mary Sapp & Elijah B.
Godbee, William Hamilton   Jan 21 1914   May 29 1914
Graham, Abner Francis   Aug 19 1823   Jul 16 1877
   A second marker shows birth date as Aug 10 (ed).
Graham, Dr. Almond A.   Mar 16 1854   Mar 21 1895
Graham, George W.   Apr 4 1861   Jul 1 1926
Graham, Lula Mills   May 9 1876   Jul 24 1936
   w/o Geo. W.
Graham, Sarah E. Rackley   Jne 13 1825   Aug 19 1898
   w/o Abner F.
Griner, Susie F. Chance   Sep 21 1885   Feb 1 1948
   w/o 1st Madison W. Chance   2nd _____ Griner
Haeseler, Joe A.   Mar 29 1910   Feb 8 1936
   s/o Edna B. & Julian G.
Hamilton, Florrie Oliver   Jan 25 1901   L
   w/o John L.
Hamilton, John L.   Sep 20 1892   Dec 18 1941
Hamilton, Stella Bargeron   Mar 8 1928   May 7 1959
   w/o J.H., Jr.
Hargroves, Henry   age 74 y   Aug 20 1871
Hargroves, Martha   age 69 y   Jne 17 1877
   w/o Henry
Herrington, Abigail   Jul 20 1834   Aug 18 1906
   w/o Martin M.
Herrington, Mrs. Anna H.   May 6 1855   Sep 4 1924
Herrington, Carrie V.   Jne 20 1873   Jne 18 1932
   w/o Stephen A.
Herrington, David L.   Aug 31 1903   Nov 25 1904
   s/o W.H. & Mittie
Herrington, Emily Lovett   Jul 5 1880   Dec 28 1961
   w/o Geo. W.
Herrington, Ethel   Mar 17 1882   Jne 26 1908
   w/o Seaborn A.
Herrington, Eva A.   Jne 15 1877   Feb 23 1905
Herrington, Eva Lovett   Sep 4 1872   Feb 17 1965
   w/o S.A.
Herrington, F.K.Z.   Jan 31 1863   Oct 18 1889
Herrington, George W.   Nov 29 1901   Aug 12 1902
   s/o W.H. & Mittie
Herrington, George Washington   Jan 2 1876   May 9 1924
   s/o Mary Hurst & Wm.
Herrington, Grover C.   Dec 23 1891   Jul 31 1911
   s/o Hazeltine Bargeron & Thomas Y.
Herrington, Hattie J.   Nov 14 1891   Dec 13 1924
   w/o N.P.

Herrington, Jared I.   Jan 21 1858   Sep 10 1933
  s/o Mary Hurst & Wm.
Herrington, John Fletcher   Feb 9 1858   Sep 17 1918
  s/o Abigail Prescott & Martin
Herrington, Julian R.   1922   1970
  s/o Ethel Haeseler & Seab
Herrington, Kathryn   1927   1964
Herrington, Laura Rackley   Jne 16 1861   Dec 7 1948
  2nd w/o J.F.
Herrington, Martin Luther   Nov 19 1865   Nov 24 1903
  s/o Abigail Prescott & Martin
Herrington, Mary Hurst   Sep 12 1834   May 1 1922
  w/o William
Herrington, Maybelle   Jul 22 1892   Aug 29 1904
  d/o S.A. & Carrie
Herrington, Mittie L.   Dec 1 1865   Feb 23 1948
  w/o Herschel
Herrington, Myra Mae   Jul 12 1922   Mar 19 1924
  d/o Hattie J. & Nathaniel P.
Herrington, Nannie H. Cates   Dec 31 1857   Oct 12 1923
  w/o Seaborn R.
Herrington, Nathaniel Pierce   1891   1947
  s/o Hattie Smith & Martin
Herrington, Ola B.   1880   1952
  d/o Nannie Cates & Seaborn R.
Herrington, Robt. C.   Jul 6 1881   Jne 4 1913
  s/o Nannie Cates & Seaborn R.
Herrington, Seaborn A. WOW   Oct 10 1875   Dec 26 1935
Herrington, Seaborn R.   Nov 4 1848   Jul 16 1915
Herrington, Seaborn Roan   Jul 8 1891   Oct 14 1942
  s/o Nannie Cates & Seaborn R.
Herrington, Stephen A.   Nov 21 1859   Sep 11 1939
Herrington, Thomas Y. F&AM   Apr 5 1850   Jan 9 1898
Herrington, Virginia A.   Aug 11 1861   May 18 1909
  w/o John F.   /Hargrove   d/o Sarah Perkins & John
  Green   md May 14 1882
Herrington, W.H.   Oct 18 1855   Dec 4 1934
Herrington, Wm. M. . CSA   Jne 5 1834   Oct 5 1898
  Pvt Co D 27th Ga Batt
Herrington, Willie B.   Sep 3 1877   Apr 6 1917
  s/o Nannie Cates & Seaborn R.
Herrington, Zack   Apr 5 1891   Apr 13 1892
  s/o J.F. & A.V.
Hickman, Mary A.   Feb 6 1888   Jne 10 1965
  w/o Noah A., Sr.
Hickman, Noah Allen WW-II   Sep 5 1920   Nov 23 1944
  Ga S/Sgt Co K 8 Inf 4th Div BSM-PH 8 OLC
Hillis, Wm. Wycliffe MD   Oct 8 1884   Oct 19 1968
  h/o Mildred Kent   s/o Clayton & Frances Whitehead
Hurst, G.W. CSA   Feb 12 1813   Dec 14 1895
  Burke Sharpshooters
Hurst, Margaret A.   Jne 5 1816   Apr 25 1904
  w/o G.W.
Hurst, Shellie F.   Dec 23 1872   Sep 5 1878
  s/o T.J. & Sallie V.

```
Hurst, Walter Judson                          1892              1954
Jenkins, Barbara Annette       Jan  8 1938                       L
   d/o L.A. & Ruby K.
Jenkins, Charles M.            Oct  2 1894                       L
Jenkins, Edith Joyner          Apr 11 1898                       L
Jenkins, Henry Wesley          age 53 y          Oct  6 1973
Jenkins, J.N.                  Feb 11 1885       Jul 26 1930
Jenkins, J. Carroll            Sep 25 1911       Aug 26 1970
Jenkins, Jasper N.             Oct 26 1915       Nov 24 1969
Jenkins, Lawrence Alvis        Aug 14 1901       Mar 13 1971
Jenkins, Lonnie Albert         Sep  1 1905       Nov  3 1964
Jenkins, Nannie Reddick               1897              1966
   w/o Thos. H.
Jenkins, Lt. Roy M.  WW-II     May 30 1925       Jne 25 1947
   s/o Edith J. & Charles M.  Bombardier, AA Corps;
   killed on night flight, Luzon, P.I.
Jenkins, Ruby Kent             Nov 10 1919                       L
   w/o Lawrence A.
Jenkins, Thomas H.                    1893              1943
Jenkins, Viola J.              Jul 26 1919                       L
   w/o J.C.
Johnson, Deborah Lynn          Oct 25 1956       Oct 30 1956
Johnson, Levy                         1916              1973
Johnson, Rosa A.               Jne 14 1912       Aug 31 1972
Kemp, Charlie Clarke           Aug  3 1892       Nov  2 1918
Kirkland, Alma Rogers          Jan  9 1887       Aug 23 1948
Lambert, Lula                  Jan 15 1882       Aug 22 1885
Lanier, Charles F., Jr.        Mar  1 1922       Mar 10 1923
   s/o Sara Chandler & Chas. F.
Littlefield, Exie E.                  1909              1970
   w/o Irvin C.
Littlefield, Irvin C.                 1903                       L
   s/o Sam
Lively, Alexander  CSA         Feb 25 1832       Oct  1 1912
   4th Cpl Jones Hussars
Lively, E. Alexander (Guy)     Sep  8 1879       Jan 31 1957
   s/o Sara Cates & Matthew
Lively, Mrs. E. Alexander      age 82 y          Jan 27 1968
   w/o E.A.  Note:  Mrs. Lively's name was Nell
   McCrary (ed).
Lively, Elizabeth              Dec 31 1821       Dec  1 1898
   2nd w/o Alex.
Lively, Julian H.              May  1 1878       Sep 15 1938
   s/o Sara Cates & Matthew
Lively, Martha Victoria        Jul 30 1852       Dec 30 1883
   w/o Dr. M.M.
Lively, Matthew                Nov 20 1857       Nov 16 1882
   s/o Alexander & Verlinda
Lively, Verlinda               May 27 1836       Aug  7 1861
   1st w/o Alex.
Long, Alma Wren                       1902                       L
   w/o Frank E.
Long, Frank E.                        1900              1972
Long, John Rayford  F&AM       Apr  8 1920       Nov 13 1970
```

213

Lovett, Agnes E.   1896   1940
Lovett, Alexander James   CSA   1838   1905
  Co E Cobb's Legion 1861 Pris. Rock Island, Ill.
  1863-65
Lovett, Crawford L.   Sep 13 1911 Sep 5 1968
Lovett, Frances F.   1917   1929
  d/o Agnes & J.M.
Lovett, Idarie   1942   1949
Lovett, Infant   only   date Dec 13 1947
  d/o Elwood & Ida
Lovett, James M.   Mar 12 1880 Jul 26 1961
Lovett, Lucy Ann Ellison   1838   1911
  w/o Alex. J.
Lovett, Pamela (infant)   only   date   1962
  d/o Mr. & Mrs. T.M.
Lovett, Thomas Wayne   1950   1950
Lovett, Tracey (infant)   only   date   1938
  s/o Agnes & J.M.
Mallard, Simmie Arnold   Oct 14 1886 Feb 8 1960
McElmurray, Emily J. Leslie   Aug 31 1818 Feb 4 1888
  b S Car   w/o Minis H.   d/o Sarah Hankinson &
  Wm. (?) Leslie
McElmurray, Minis Hunter   Jne 8 1809 Jul 29 1869
  s/o Martha Hankinson & Andrew
McElmurray, William L. CSA   Jan 11 1839 Oct 3 1861
  s/o Emily J.L. & Minis H. Burke Sharpshooters
  2nd Reg Ga Vol d Manassas Junction of typhoid
McMaster, Infant   only   date Aug 1 1897
  s/o Eula C. & Dr. David
McMillian, William D.   1877   1948
Meads, George L.   Aug 29 1907 Mar 7 1961
Meads, J.H.   1880 Jan 14 1959
Meads, Mattie B.   Nov 13 1881 Jan 30 1955
  w/o J.H.
Meads, Moses   CSA   May 21 1846 Nov 29 1924
Meads, Pauline D.   Sep 20 1904 Jan 14 1971
  w/o George L.
Mills, Carlton Joy, Sr.   Aug 13 1885 Mar 8 1941
  s/o Susan Littlefield & John A.
Mills, Elizabeth   Sep 15 1825 Jul 9 1874
  w/o W.H.
Mills, George L.   Mar 13 1882 Sep 21 1928
  s/o Susan Littlefield & John A.
Mills, Ina Herrington   Jan 2 1884 Jan 26 1943
  w/o C.J., Sr.   d/o Adelaide Hargrove & John F.
Mills, John Alexander   1850   1933
Mills, Sarah Kemp   1810   nd
  w/o Stephen B.
Mills, Seabie Bell   May 7 1889 Aug 2 1966
  w/o Geo. L.
Mills, Stephen B.   1805   1853
Mills, Susan Littlefield   1849   1919
  w/o John A.

Mills, Wm. Herbert, Sr.   Oct 14 1909   May 5 1969
  h/o Claudine Tolbert   s/o Ina Herrington & Carlton
  J., Sr.   F&AM
Mobley, Jennie Bonnell   Jul 25 1878   Oct 21 1962
  w/o W.O.
Mobley, Ulysses E.   Sp-Am W   nd   nd
  Co L 2 Ga Inf
Mobley, William O.   Mar 30 1879   Jul 29 1966
  h/o Jennie B.
Murray, Infant   same   date   May 12 1940
Norris, Elizabeth Hearn   May 17 1871   Aug 19 1959
  w/o Wm. H.
Norris, William Henry   Apr 5 1865   Apr 6 1952
Odom, Henrietta   Jul 24 1845   Apr 22 1919
  w/o S.H.
Oliver, Caroline C.   Sep 26 1826   Jan 19 1893
  w/o Wm. H.
Oliver, Eleanor Chance   1882   1938
  w/o Shelley V., Sr.
Oliver, Elizabeth   Nov 6 1850   Dec 30 1880
  w/o C.J.
Oliver, John William   Oct 8 1940   Aug 31 1960
Oliver, Mary Elizabeth   Oct 5 1944   Dec 1 1945
Oliver, Shelley V., Jr.   1900   1957
  s/o Eleanor C. & S.V.
Oliver, Shelley V., Sr. MD   1854   1926
Parker, Jimmy Milton, Jr.   Aug 8 1967   Nov 29 1967
Perry, George D.   F&AM   Jan 25 1882   Apr 21 1947
Porter, Leila A.   1867   1943
  w/o Wm. H.
Porter, William H.   1875   1961
Rackley, Amanda   Feb 2 1842   Oct 24 1924
  w/o Seaborn F., Sr.
Rackley, Cathleen   Sep 13 1904   Nov 5 1904
  d/o C.F. & W.B.
Rackley, Crawford F.   Aug 23 1873   Nov 2 1942
  s/o Amanda & Seaborn F.
Rackley, Crawford Mills   Oct 14 1909   Mar 28 1951
Rackley, Crawford Willie   Mar 15 1900   Jul 19 1900
  s/o C.F. & W.B.
Rackley, Emily Chapman   1895   1968
  w/o R. Gray
Rackley, Freddie Virginia   Jan 14 1870   Oct 2 1964
  d/o Amanda & Seaborn F.
Rackley, Infant   Sep 20 1903   Oct 6 1903
  d/o C.F. & W.B.
Rackley, Infant   May 16 1903   same   date
  of S.F. & E.M.
Rackley, Infant twins   same   date   Aug 13 1902
  of C.F. & W.B.
Rackley, Jas. F.   CSA   Apr 17 1842   Aug 10 1921
  Pvt Alexander Greys, Co K 32 Reg Ga Vol Inf Army of
  Tenn
Rackley, Julia   Apr 25 1845   Jne 20 1915
  w/o Jas. F.

Rackley, Lovett Francis   Sep 13 1875   Apr 20 1893
   s/o S.F. & A.W.
Rackley, Mattie Lee   May 21 1874   Feb 7 1892
   d/o S.F. & A.W.
Rackley, R. Gray   1889   L
   s/o Amanda & Seaborn F.
Rackley, Robert E.   Sep 29 1867   Aug 14 1889
   s/o Amanda & Seaborn
Rackley, Robert Hubert   Apr 4 1904   Aug 20 1961
Rackley, Seaborn F.   CSA   Nov 13 1831   Feb 28 1917
   Alexander Greys, Co K 32 Reg Ga Vol Inf Army of Tenn
Rackley, Seaborn F., Jr.   Nov 14 1881   Oct 17 1914
Rackley, William Fulton   Mar 26 1877   Apr 10 1893
   s/o S.F. & A.W.
Redd, Billy Franklin   WW-II   May 4 1933   Jne 9 1954
   Ga PFC 2 Armored Cav   Death date of June 11 on
   military marker   (ed).
Redd, Billy Joe Falvey   1941   1950
Redd, Edith B.   May 8 1886   Oct 19 1953
Redd, William C.   Mar 9 1900   Jan 24 1959
Reddick, A. Dawson   Mar 9 1859   May 21 1927
Reddick, Andrew D. (Bug)   Oct 5 1928   Jul 31 1973
   F&AM
Reddick, Bessie Long w/o L.H.   Jan 16 1887   Oct 26 1939
Reddick, Frances K.   Aug 5 1933   Mar 7 1945
   d/o G.W. & L.M.
Reddick, George W.   CSA   Sep 16 1841   Dec 28 1907
Reddick, George Washington   May 19 1885   May 14 1957
Reddick, Leslie Heman   Jan 18 1881   Jne 3 1946
Reddick, Louie L.   Aug 19 1893   Apr 24 1909
   s/o G.W. & M.J.
Reddick, Lucy Mae   Aug 28 1907   Feb 23 1971
   w/o Geo. W.
Reddick, Mary J.   Dec 8 1857   Jne 24 1915
   w/o G.W.
Reddick, Thomas   CSA   Oct 4 1844   Oct 16 1906
   Alexander Greys, Co K 32 Reg Ga Vol Inf Army of Tenn
Reeves, Sarah Smith   Sep 23 1904   L
   d/o Bunyan A. & Sallie R.
Reeves, William Grady   Sep 10 1926   Oct 22 1931
   s/o Mr. & Mrs. Sim
Robinson, Cecil Golden   Sep 5 1896   Mar 13 1897
   s/o E.W. & Zula
Robinson, Donna Ferrell   Sep 5 1955   Nov 13 1972
   d/o Grace & Jimmy
Robinson, Dora Bell   Jul 27 1890   Sep 23 1907
   d/o W.H.J. & M.E.
Robinson, Ellaree Zeigler   Sep 5 1907   L
   w/o S.J.
Robinson, Emory W.   Jne 5 1908   Feb 17 1962
   s/o Zula Mills & Ezekiel W.
Robinson, Ezekiel W.   Jul 21 1874   Aug 14 1948
   s/o Susan Mills & Lemuel
Robinson, George W.   Feb 17 1873   Nov 7 1929

Robinson, Grace B.	Nov 6 1931		L
w/o Jimmy R.			
Robinson, Hattie J.	Aug 4 1874	Jne 4 1932	
w/o Geo. W.			
Robinson, Jerome	Sep 20 1956	Nov 13 1972	
s/o Grace & Jimmy			
Robinson, Jimmy R.	Nov 13 1929		L
s/o Loraine Mincey & Loy			
Robinson, Lemuel CSA	Feb 4 1843	Jan 15 1903	
Robinson, Lola	Nov 18 1901	same	date
inf/o G.W. & H.J.			
Robinson, Mary Baughman	1868		1953
w/o Walter H.J.			
Robinson, Mary E.	Jul 21 1874	Sep 29 1887	
w/o Walter R.			
Robinson, Ola	Nov 18 1901	May 20 1902	
inf/o G.W. & H.J.			
Robinson, Ralph Mills	Mar 4 1900	Apr 4 1962	
s/o Zula Mills & Ezekiel W.			
Robinson, Sidney J.	Apr 3 1903		L
s/o Hattie Kemp & Geo. W.			
Robinson, Susan E.	Aug 12 1833	Sep 4 1895	
w/o Lemuel			
Robinson, Walter H.J.	1863		1933
Robinson, Zula Mills	Mar 26 1875	Jne 30 1944	
w/o Ezekiel W.			
Rogers, Dudley	Jan 11 1862	Aug 29 1931	
Rogers, Sallie W.	Mar 17 1860	Jne 3 1940	
w/o Dudley			
Sapp, Fannie S.	May 4 1902		nd
w/o McKinley			
Sapp, Mary A.	1892		1960
Sapp, McKinley	Apr 4 1898		nd
Sapp, Sarah	Apr 19 1799	May 12 1857	
w/o Wm.			
Sasser, Annie Laura	May 19 1888	Sep 12 1965	
w/o Henry L. /Herrington			
Sasser, Elnora Robinson	Jan 28 1869	Oct 14 1942	
w/o Jos. Edgar			
Sasser, Henry Lemuel	Dec 7 1890	Oct 5 1946	
Sasser, Infant	Sep 11 1902	Sep 15 1902	
of J.E. & E.L.			
Sasser, J. Louvert	Jul 3 1900	Sep 25 1935	
Sasser, Joseph Edgar	Jan 13 1866	Dec 18 1944	
Sasser, Ocie	Jul 19 1896	Nov 11 1897	
d/o J.E. & E.L.			
Sasser, Wesley H.	Sep 23 1894	Oct 18 1895	
s/o J.E. & E.L.			
Sasser, Willie Henrietta	Nov 11 1905	May 3 1960	
Skinner, L. Milton	1920		L
Skinner, Mary Dell	1923		L
Skinner, Thomas W.	1944		L
Smith, Bunyan A.	Jan 20 1873	Oct 29 1927	
Smith, Cleo W.	Mar 14 1898	May 4 1944	

```
Smith, James B.  Shriner          Nov 12 1880    Feb  8 1936
Smith, Laura Bell                 Nov 27 1861    Jan 15 1932
Smith, Lyddie                     Nov 14 1816    Apr  7 1898
Smith, Lydia Frances (Fannie)     Jan  2 1879    Dec  8 1962
Smith, Nancy Hargrove             Jan 18 1844    Sep  5 1929
Smith, Philip E.  F&AM            Feb 27 1891    Apr 26 1948
Smith, Sallie Robinson            Jne 16 1872    Dec  7 1947
    w/o Bunyan
Smith, Thomas J.                  Nov 19 1882    Sep 19 1905
Stephens, Agnes Ethel             Feb  3 1881    Jne  3 1885
    d/o J.F. & J.E.
Stephens, Clara Lula              Jan 28 1879    May 21 1881
    d/o J.F. & J.E.
Stephens, Joanna E.               Feb 20 1856    Feb 26 1929
    w/o John F.
Stephens, John F.                 Apr 15 1850    Sep 26 1904
Stowe, James Ferguson             Aug 25 1972    Aug 26 1972
    s/o Mr. & Mrs. Noel R.
Varnadoe, Henry M.                Jul  5 1883    Aug 31 1942
Varnadoe, Rosaline G.             Feb 18 1902              nd
Videtto, Henry A.   CSA           Jne 15 1840    Feb 27 1880
    1st Lt.  Alexander Greys, Co K 32 Reg Ga Vol Inf
    Army of Tenn
Videtto, Mary L. Graham           Feb 25 1847    May 18 1882
    w/o Henry A.
Walker, Arthur Jerome             Sep 11 1947    Apr 16 1965
Walker, Arthur N.                 May  7 1925    Aug  8 1969
Walker, Robert C.                 Mar  4 1891    Dec 11 1968
White, Elmer E.                   Sep 11 1878    Jne 16 1939
Wicker, Fanny Spaulding           May 30 1853    Jan 20 1915
    d/o A.W. & Melvina Wicker
Wilcher, Charlie E.                      1899           1968
Williams, Eva P.                  Jul  4 1902    Dec  9 1968
Williams, Fred E.                 Mar 25 1901    Apr 19 1951
Wimberly, Mattie Lou w/o W.L.     Dec 21 1882    May 22 1918
Winters, Charles R.               Mar 10 1874    May 14 1921
Winters, Jessie Stephens          Apr 13 1878    Nov 17 1923
    w/o C.R.
Wynne, Janie Rackley              Jul 18 1898    Dec 29 1960
    w/o J.H.   d/o Willie C. & John F.
Wynne, Judson Holmes              Mar 10 1895    Apr 14 1963
    s/o Mamie Holmes & Wm. H.
Zeigler, C. Guy                          1902    Aug 21 1972
Zeigler, Lorena L.                       1882           1962
    w/o Wm. B.
Zeigler, Madge L.                        1903              L
    w/o C. Guy
Zeigler, William B.                      1875           1938
```

127.   SCHMIDT

```
Schmidt, Berry H.  MD           May  4 1882  Sep 27 1936
    Note:  interred in a large brick-rock mausoleum on
    edge of Keysville  (ed).
```

128.   <u>SMITH</u>

Smith, Wiley   Aug 18 1825   Jan 30 1914
  h/o Sallie <u>Note</u>: No children mentioned in his will.
  After wife's death property goes to two nieces of his
  wife, Clara J. Vinson & Maude Cox, daughters of Mrs.
  Mattie R. Wimberly, <u>Will Bk B, 189</u>.

129.   <u>SMITH</u>

Hines, Mary   age 18 y   Oct   1819
  w/o Churchill
Hines, Smithy   age 1 y   Sep 22 1819
  d/o C.M.
Smith, Noah   age 65 y   Dec 12 1836
Smith, Noah s/o N.& E.   age 18 m   Aug   1821
Tarver, Nancy   age 2y 6m   Jan   1829
  d/o Robert & Ava

130.   <u>SPEARS</u>

Spears, William   CSA   nd   nd
  Williams Volunteers, Co C 32nd Ga Regt

<u>Note</u>: At least two others are buried in unmarked
graves: Sue, w/o William and Sue ------, their granddaughter. No dates available (ed).

131.   <u>ST. MARKS METHODIST</u>
                            Sardis, Ga.

Bailey, Frank WW-I   Oct 2 1894 Mar 29 1957
  Ga PFC 31 Co Trans Corps
Bailey, Joseph C.   age 53 y   Jne 27 1956
Bailey, R. Louie   1891   1963
Bailey, Sallie Joe   Sep 3 1905 Oct 9 1923
Broxton, Benjamin G.   Jne 10 1852 May 4 1908
Broxton, Dock I.   Sep 30 1881 May 22 1957
Broxton, Gilbert D. WW-II   Dec 20 1918 Nov 21 1944
  Ga Staff Sgt 333 Inf 84 Inf Div
Broxton, James   1919   1919
Broxton, Martha   Jul 12 1860 Nov 3 1938
Broxton, Minnie   Nov 10 1891 Jul 24 1913
  w/o D.B.
Buxton, Hubert R.   Dec 21 1897 Feb 13 1965
  s/o Florence Haeseler & Wm. Robt.
Buxton, Lucille Vance   Jul 26 1904 Feb 23 1969
  w/o Hubert R.   d/o Mary Jones & William
Chance, Doretha   Apr 11 1937 Aug 18 1939
Chance, Mary E.   Apr 1 1909   nd
  w/o Remor B.
Chance, Remor B.   Mar 2 1908 Aug 13 1956
Chance, Samuel W. WW-II   Dec 12 1927 Mar 12 1960
  Ga SGT HV Tank Co 15 Inf Regt Korea

```
Chandler, Lovic P.                              1892            1945
Chandler, Mamie S.                              1895            19--
   w/o Lovic P.
Deason, Paul P.                      Jan 22 1920                   L
Deason, Sylvia Belle                 May  5 1923                   L
   w/o Paul P.
Dickey, Robert A.                    Jul 15 1917   Jul 19 1917
   s/o M.A. & A.S.
Dixon, Thomas Charles                Oct 15 1918   May 13 1952
Duncan, Della M. Lively              May  6 1871   Mar  7 1940
Duncan, William Wesley               Jne 17 1869   Aug 19 1944
Elliott, Bronnie DeLaigle            Sep 23 1890   Dec 24 1970
   w/o Charlie    d/o Annie & N.L.
Elliott, Carol L. Kor W              Nov 30 1931   Aug 31 1960
   s/o Bronnie & Charlie
Elliott, Nelle M.                    Jan 25 1900   Nov 22 1957
Ellison, Annah Scott                 Jan 12 1882   Nov 25 1960
   w/o Samuel J.
Ellison, Clarence Irving             May 24 1882   Jul 19 1960
Ellison, Emma Mock                   Oct 25 1889   Oct  7 1968
   w/o Clarence
Ellison, Gladys                      Sep 23 1917   Oct  7 1917
   d/o S.J. & A.S.
Ellison, Samuel Joseph               Nov 10 1885   Sep 21 1968
Ellison, Scott                       Jne  9 1913   same   date
   s/o S.J. & A.S.
Fisher, James W. WW-I                Apr 15 1897   Jan 21 1968
   No Car. Pvt US Marine Corps  Military marker gives
   April 5 as birth date (ed).
   h/o Eleanor Marshall    s/o Susan & James
Fitzgerald, James Garnet                        1882            1945
Frazier, Charlie Mack                Sep  9 1943   Sep  5 1960
Frazier, Frances Elliott             May 10 1917                  nd
Frazier, Major Mack, Jr. WW-II Feb 24 1919  Jne 26 1944
   T/5 HQ Co 34th Inf Div Purple Heart
Godbee, Almond                       Mar  3 1895   Jne 13 1909
   s/o G.W. & L.T.
Godbee, George W. F&AM               Oct 27 1860   Apr  2 1919
Godbee, J.M. CSA                                1832            nd
   Alexander Greys, Co K 32 Reg Ga Vol Inf Army of Tenn
Godbee, Lula Cochran                 Apr 28 1870   Aug 24 1965
   w/o G.W.
Godbee, Sarah E.                     Jul  6 1832   Mar  9 1916
   w/o J.M.
Graham, Infant                       May 10 1904   May 16 1904
   s/o G.W. & L.M.
Griffin, Mattie Belle                Apr 26 1882   Jul  8 1955
Haeseler, Edna Buxton                Jne 27 1877   Nov 23 1966
   w/o Julian Gray    d/o Josephine & Samuel Buxton
Haeseler, Julian Gray                Oct 24 1874   Jan 11 1954
   s/o Frances Chance & Samuel Burchardt
Hannah, Robert Lewis WW-II           Sep 14 1917   Dec 12 1964
   Ga CPL Army Air Forces
```

```
Herndon, Clyde  WW-I              Nov  7 1896   Jne  9 1965
  PHM3 USNR
Herndon, Nettie Godbold           May  9 1898   Dec 29 1969
  w/o Clyde
Herrington, Caroline L.           Jul 17 1842   Feb 20 1908
Jenkins, Annie L. Godbee          Nov 28 1900   May 22 1945
  w/o Ernest W.
Jenkins, Ernest W.                Oct 12 1897   Jul 30 1970
Jenkins, Florence Haeseler        Dec 11 1907             L
  w/o Frank L.   d/o Edna B. & Julian G.
Jenkins, Frank Leslie             Feb 13 1896   Jul 10 1965
Jenkins, George Wilson            May 15 1917   Apr 24 1961
Jenkins, Helen Murray             Oct  8 1917   Apr 20 1956
  w/o Geo. W.   d/o Irene D. & Robt. L.
Johnson, William E.               age 87 y      Jan  9 1966
Jordan, William Lovett            Aug 21 1909   Apr  5 1944
Littlefield, Infant               only   date   Jne  3 1910
  of Sam. H. & Mattie
Littlefield, Samuel H.            Mar 25 1857   Feb 14 1914
Long, Marie C.                    Aug 30 1921             L
  w/o 1st Perry M. Long;  2nd Furman Mun
Long, Perry M., Sr.               Jan 12 1918   Aug 20 1968
  h/o Marie C.
Lovett, Arrabella                 Jne  1 1875   Aug  6 1902
  w/o W.L.
Lovett, Edith Bargeron            Jul 21 1879   Jul  4 1966
Lovett, Mary A.                        1851          1903
  w/o Thos. Y.
Lovett, Thomas Y.  CSA                 1848          1901
  Co D 27 Ga Inf
Lovett, W. Lanier                 Jne 12 1870   Jan  9 1936
Lovett, William J.  WW-I          Aug 23 1897   Feb 18 1952
  Ga Cpl 177 Adm Labor Co ASC
Mallard, H. Grady                 Oct  4 1925   Aug 13 1946
  d/o Henrietta & Walker
Mallard, Joseph G.                Aug 31 1922   Jne 16 1944
  s/o Henrietta & Walker
Mallard, Joseph Rowland           May 20 1901   Oct 22 1958
  s/o Bertha Rowland & Jos. L.
Mallard, Joseph Rowland, Jr.      Jne 29 1925   Jan 18 1936
  s/o Maude Murray & Jos. R.
Marshall, John Markham            Jne 15 1893   Dec 15 1967
  b Linden, Va.   s/o Eleanor Trumbo & H.M.
McMillan, Marian R.                    1965          1965
Mills, Ashley Ruedolph            Feb 12 1912   Sep  4 1916
  s/o Mr. & Mrs. J.A., Jr.
Mills, Bessie Chance              Dec 19 1888   Jul 19 1959
  w/o Jno. A.
Mills, Infant                     May    1908   same   date
  s/o Mr. & Mrs. J.A., Jr.
Mills, John Ashley                May 10 1886   Apr  7 1935
Mulkey, Carrie Bell Griffin       Mar 27 1888   Oct 20 1972
  w/o Euley L.
Mulkey, Euley L.                  Dec  2 1887   Feb 11 1972
  s/o Luvincia & Jas. W.
```

```
Mulkey, James William            Mar  4 1852   Dec  8 1929
Mulkey, Luvincia Mallard         Dec 20 1859   Oct 24 1957
  w/o James W.
Murray, George Laurie (Buck)     Feb 26 1897   Feb  4 1966
  s/o Turlie H. & S.W.L. (Fate)
Murray, Ira L.                   Jul  9 1907   Nov 21 1970
  s/o Turlie H. & S.W.L. (Fate)
Murray, Irene DeLaigle           Aug  9 1889   Nov 15 1954
  w/o Robt. L.  d/o Annie & N.L.
Murray, Lovick L.                Apr 20 1893   Apr 11 1970
  s/o Turlie H. & S.W.L. (Fate)
Murray, Mertie Daughtry          May 16 1895             L
  w/o L.L.
Murray, Robert Lloyd             Jan 27 1895   Feb 20 1962
  s/o Turlie H. & S.W.L. (Fate)
Murray, S.W.L.                   Jan 14 1858   Oct 31 1938
  s/o Mary A. & Dempsey
Murray, Turlie F. Herrington     Jan  6 1870   Sep  2 1943
  w/o S.W.L. (Fate)   d/o Mary Hurst & Bill
Murray, William                  Feb  9 1905   Oct 10 1906
  s/o S.W.L. & T.F.
Parkerson, Essie Mallard         Jne 17 1903             L
  w/o Furman J.
Parkerson, Furman James          Sep 22 1889   Jul 21 1972
Parkman, Benjamin Gordon         only    date   Aug 15 1961
Roberts, Annie L. Murray         Aug 22 1891             L
  w/o Carl   d/o Turlie H. & S.W.L.
Roberts, Attys                   Mar 26 1921   Dec  4 1923
  s/o Annie L. Murray & Carl
Roberts, Carl A.                 Jul  5 1885   Apr 24 1968
Roberts, Lloyd Rayford           May  3 1913   Feb 18 1971
  s/o Annie L. Murray & Carl A.
Roberts, Mary Mead               Sep 21 1920             L
  w/o Lloyd
Roberts, Ruth                    May 29 1924   Oct  5 1924
  d/o Annie L. Murray & Carl A.
Robey, Charles Wesley, Sr.       Jne 17 1894   Jne 23 1972
  WW-I  Ala PFC USA
Robey, Florence G.                       1897            nd
  w/o Charles W.
Robinson, Bertha Gnann                   1903            L
  w/o J. Wesley   d/o Hortensia Shearouse & Walter A.
Robinson, Irene Smith            Jan 10 1896   May 30 1973
  w/o Ivens L.
Robinson, Ivens L.  WW-I         Apr 18 1892   Oct 23 1966
  Ga Pvt USA
Robinson, J. Wesley                      1897          1968
  s/o Hattie Kemp & George W.
Smith, Dorothy D.                Sep 17 1924   Mar 26 1960
Smith, Hinton H.                 Apr  6 1887   Sep  9 1962
Smith, Lucy Joyner               Sep  4 1895   Dec 10 1966
Smith, Richard, III (Bubba)      Mar 28 1956   May  2 1972
West, Lillian Lowrie             Apr 16 1899   Jan  8 1948
  w/o J.S.
```

132.   SYMS

Syms, Gilbert L. CSA   Mar 24 1832 Nov 27 1861
  b Silverton, S. C.   d Richmond, Va.
Syms, Henry Britt   1859   1952
Syms, Infant   Oct 29 1888 Nov 18 1888
  s/o McD. & S.J.
Syms, Julia B.   Oct 21 1851 Apr 1 1860
  d/o Thomas & Mary Ann
Syms, Mary Ann   Dec 21 1825 Apr 30 1911
  w/o Thos. H.
Syms, McDuffie   Oct 14 1863 Mar 6 1923
Syms, McDuffie, Jr.   Dec 31 1892 Mar 20 1898
  s/o McD. & S.J.
Syms, Sallie J.   Dec 31 1860 Nov 5 1942
  w/o McDuffie
Syms, Thos. Henry   Jul 25 1828 Oct 21 1883

Note: Four Syms children: Thomas, Dora, Jack, and
Johnnie are buried in this cemetery but their graves
have no markers (ed).

133.   TARVER
                    Richmond Co.

Tarver, F.A.   Jul 21 1798 Mar 24 1867
Tarver, Sallie Green   Mar 16 1850 Aug 27 1850
  d/o L.A. & M.E.
  Note: Four other infant graves have slabs but are
  without inscriptions (ed).
Tarver, Samuel   Sep 30 1795 Jne 29 1855

134.   TARVER
                    Richmond Co.

Tarver, Elizabeth S.   Jan 11 1805 Sep 27 1880
  w/o John R.
Tarver, John R.   age 41 y   Jan 4 1842
Tarver, Margaret Ann   Feb 21 1825 Jan 21 1897
  eldest d/o John R. & Elizabeth S.
Tarver, Robert   Mar 24 1826 Nov 1 1849
  only s/o J. Robinson & Elizabeth
Wall, Eleanor Martha   Apr 6 1832 May 6 1854
  w/o Robert T.   d/o Elizabeth S. & John R. Tarver
  b Richmond Co   d LaGrange, Ga.

135.   TAYLOR

Taylor, Mrs. Emma Matthews   age c. 55y   Mar 10 1914
Taylor, G. C.   Oct 19 1884 Jan 15 1899

136.   TINLEY
                    Richmond Co.

Cadle, Cyrus Andrew   age 73 y   Sep 13 1927

223

Cadle, James W.	Nov 10 1877	Nov 3 1904
s/o Cyrus A. & Mary R.		
Cadle, Mrs. M. R.	Jul 12 1851	Oct 27 1906
w/o Cyrus		
Moseley, Infant	nd	nd
s/o J.H. & Mattie		
Moseley, James Richard	Oct 22 1854	Dec 6 1925
Moseley, John	Sep 19 1912	Dec 7 1914
Moseley, Nancy Virginia	Aug 12 1862	Jne 5 1936
w/o James R.		
Neely, Benjamin J.	1873	1922
Neely, Elizabeth R.	1883	1950
w/o Benj. J.		
Neely, Infant	1935	1935
d/o Mr. & Mrs. Horace B.		
Seals, Mattie Ruth	Aug 23 1901	Oct 4 1910
Seals, Mattie V.	1881	1911
w/o Rev. R. B.		
Seals, Rev. Robert B.	1871	1944
Tinley, David	nd	nd
s/o Frank C.		
Tinley, Frank Capers	1893	1963
Tinley, George D., Sr.	Oct 15 1887	Dec 18 1958
Tinley, Infant	only date	Apr 28 1890
of J.J. & C.E.		
Tinley, Infants (two)	nd	nd
of Frank C.		
Tinley, J. J.	Jan 15 1866	Sep 10 1893
Tinley, John	Mar 8 1826	May 5 1897
md Martha A. Smith, Feb 15, 1844. Ordained to the		
deaconship of Piney Grove Church, Nov. 1867		
Tinley, John P.	Aug 6 1881	Apr 29 1934
Tinley, W. M.	Aug 9 1848	Oct 16 1875
s/o J. & M.		

137.   TOMLIN

Tomlin, Charlotte	Dec 7 1793	May 1 1838
Tomlin, Mary	age 59 y	Nov 20 1847
Tomlin, Zilphia A.	age 61 y	Mar 2 1854

Note: No marker exists today on Zilphia Tomlin's grave. The dates are from the earlier research of Mrs. Anne MacKenzie Humphrey. Zilphia's will established the one-half acre cemetery on her plantation. Edward A. & Robert G. Tomlin, mentioned in the Ordinary Court action, may have been her brothers (ed). Will Book A, 102-05.

138.   TOMLIN

Tomlin, Caroline	Dec 7 1793	May 1 1838
Tomlin, Elizabeth	age 50 y	Nov 20 1847

139.   TORBIT

Torbit, H.D., MD   age 50 y   Aug 1 1879
   b Chester Co, S. Car.
Torbit, M.H.   Mar 3 1860 Dec 25 1882
   b Burke Co
Torbit, Sallie A.   Aug 12 1842 Dec 3 1909
Note: Cemetery enclosed by brick wall; in good
condition (ed).

140.   USHER-MIXON

Deal, Amelia Mixon   May 8 1835 Jan 31 1897
   w/o W.M.
Hawes, Mary A.   Jan 21 1856 Nov 11 1861
   d/o Savannah & Edward V.
Mixon, Floyd   age 1 y   1853
   s/o Michael & Sarah
Mixon, Johnny   age 10 d   Feb 3 1869
   s/o John J. & Josephine
Mixon, Michael   Oct 27 1790 Sep 17 1870
Mixon, Michael, Jr.   age 38 y   Aug 12 1864
   s/o Michael & Sarah
Mixon, Sarah   age 74 y   Jan 1 1869
   w/o Michael
Usher, Henry O.   May 27 1895 May 20 1910
Usher, Hugh T.   1924   1929
Usher, Little Mike   Nov 12 1905 Jul 6 1906
   s/o W.E. & A.B.
Usher, Savannah Mixon   age 73 y   Nov 30 1905
   w/o O.E.
Usher, Sterling J.   Mar 4 1873 Jan 21 1907
Usher, Wm. E.   Feb 4 1870 Feb 9 1906
Weathersbee, Jane   age 34 y   Nov 19 1857
   w/o Johnson d/o Michael & Sarah Mixon

141.   VALLOTTON

Vallotton, Rosabellar Hall   Jan 15 1833 Mar 22 1852
   1st w/o John R. md 1850   m/o Rosabella (Rozzie),
   b Mar 9 1852   md Jack Cooper.
   Note: The Hall parents are believed to have emigrated
   to Lowndes Co., Ga. Rosabella Cooper is buried in
   Blythe Methodist cemetery (ed).

142.   VALLOTTON

Vallotton, Amanda E.   Mar 17 1855 Jne 19 1855
Vallotton, Andrew E.   Aug 20 1870 Jan 7 1874
Vallotton, Francis Stephen   Apr 6 1796 Jul 15 1859
   s/o Rachel Nowland (niece of Governor David Emanuel)
   & Francis. b Richmond Co.
   Note: Children mentioned in his will: Savannah

Boulineau, Rachel T. (Arnold), Sarah Mariah
(Trowbridge), Elizabeth Ann (Trowbridge), Amanda
I., Winnefred C., Robert E. & John R. Will Bk A,
157-158.

Vallotton, Infant	nd	nd
Vallotton, Infant	Jan 6 1861	only date
Vallotton, John R., Jr.	Dec 20 1867	Sep 29 1969
Vallotton, John Robinson	Sep 15 1826	May 31 1885

  s/o Sarah Tarver & Francis Stephen; md 1st Rosabellar
  Hall (1850), 2nd Nancy Frederick Wise (1854)

Vallotton, Nancy Frederick   Dec 19 1836 Dec 30 1903
  2nd w/o John R.   /Wise   md May 18 1854
  d/o Nancy Daniel & Frederick Wise
Vallotton, Robert T.   Mar 7 1862 Sep 26 1865
Vallotton, Sarah Tarver   Mar 16 1798 Aug   1879
  w/o Francis Stephen
  d/o Nancy Robinson & Etheldred Tarver, Sr.
Whitman, Amanda Isabella   Sep 10 1830 Feb   1885
  w/o Robert G.   /Vallotton
  d/o Sarah Tarver & Francis Stephen
Whitman, Robert Goldshaw   nd Mar   1885
  b Spartanburg Co., S. Car.

Note: This old cemetery is being restored by Hugh L.
Vallotton, Valdosta, Ga., according to a plat made about
1900 showing the location of each grave. Through his
courtesy, we have the names and dates for several
unmarked graves, together with additional data on the
Vallotton family (ed).

143.   WALKER

Walker, Robert T.   nd Oct   1832
Walker, Wm. E.   Apr 26 1829 Jan 18 1854

Notes: 1) Three children's graves are without inscriptions. Cemetery enclosed by a brick wall almost
completely in ruins.
        2) Two additional Walker cemeteries are in
Richmond Co. The Old Walker Plantation cemetery
contains nine marked graves. The oldest is of the
original Thomas Walker (age 90 y d 1809). A much
larger and more important one is in Augusta, adjoining the northwest corner of the former U. S.
Arsenal grounds (now the Augusta College campus).
See Reese, op. cit., Vol. III, 74-76 for the plantation cemetery, and Vol. III, 153-188 for the large
cemetery (ed).

144.   WALLACE
                     Jenkins Co.

Carter, Alexander G.   May 1 1856 Aug   1890
Perkins, David   Oct 20 1773 Nov 20 1857
Perkins, David   Feb 25 bkn   bkn
  s/o D.S. & F.A.

Perkins, Ella	age 12y 12d	Aug 17 1867
d/o D.S. & F.A.		
Perkins, Enoch	May 28 1839	Jne 14 1861
s/o Nancy & Newton		
Perkins, Frances A.	age 38y 11m	Jan 4 1864
w/o D.S. Perkins, MD	3d	
Perkins, Mamie Lee	age 8m 5d	Feb 9 1872
d/o S.M. & T.M.		
Perkins, Newton	Nov 20 1778	Sep 10 1867
Perkins, Newton, Jr.	Feb 2 1804	Feb 19 1870
Perkins, Rebecca	Jan 31 1794	Sep 5 1859
Scarborough, Miss Amelia	Jan 7 1829	Jan 7 1858
Wallace, Alice	1869	1895
Wallace, Andrew W.	Feb 27 1893	Nov 6 1894
s/o Freeman & Judy		
Wallace, Bertha	1877	Mar 1894
Wallace, Idalee	1896	1896
d/o Clarence & Rozzie		
Wallace, Louderick	1875	1904
Wallace, Lucy Ann	Nov 29 1864	May 1945
Wallace, Mary Drucilla	Feb 12 1847	May 5 1911
w/o Stirling C. / Perkins	md Nov 1 1860	
Wallace, Mary Sue	1903	1903
d/o Clarence & Rozzie		
Wallace, Matthew	Mar 29 1820	Mar 5 1856
Wallace, Raymond	1887	nd
Wallace, Stiring C.	May 27 1838	1903

145.   **WARD**

Ward, Betsy	Apr 6 1889	Sep 17 1893
Ward, Charles E. MD CSA	Sep 2 1847	Aug 3 1912
Pvt Co F 2nd Ga Regt State Troops		
Ward, Charles E., Jr.	Oct 6 1891	Dec 18 1901
Ward, Rosa P., Jr.	May 26 1886	Sep 15 1893

146.   WAYNESBORO CONFEDERATE MEMORIAL

Soon after the close of Civil War hostilities, some
dedicated ladies organized the Ladies Memorial Association of Burke County and began the work of gathering
from scattered graves the remains of Confederate soldiers,who,in late 1864, died during the fighting in Burke
with Sherman's army. They were strangers from other
parts of the Confederacy but were being brought to rest
side by side with Burke's own comrades who had given
their lives for the common cause. In 1877 the Memorial
Association erected a massive, 25-foot monument to
honor all Confederate soldiers interred in Burke. This
handsome memorial faces west, and before it, in a small
green-sodded parade ground are two rows of markers, the
front and rear ranks, symbolizing all those who had
marched bravely to their death. The "unknown soldiers"

number twelve. Seven were unidentifiable. Only five
bear names: Captain Bedell (unit unknown), Captain
Bess (5th Ga. Cav.), Cotting (unit unknown),W. A.
Curry (2nd Ga. Cav.), and Peyton D. Kennedy (7th
Texas. Cav.). All are without birth and death dates,
but they rest at the center of Burke's official
Confederate Memorial Cemetery and within sight of
three plaques, high on the monument, which bear
mightier testimony:

In A Country's	They Who Die	To The
Memory	For Their	Confederate Dead
Her Heroes	Country	Who Fell In The
Are	Fill Honored	Struggle For The
Immortal	Graves	"Lost Cause"
		1861-1865

Elsewhere in the cemetery, nine iron crosses
mark CSA graves whose names are no longer available
from tombstones. Other known CSA soldiers bring the
total Confederate graves in this cemetery to forty-
nine (ed).

Addison, Sarah Lawson   age 48 y   1878
   w/o Thomas   d/o Barbara Tuttle & Alexander J. Lawson
   m/o Willie Leora Addison (who md R.C. Neely).
Ashton, R. William   CSA   nd   nd
   s/o Col. John D. Ashton   Pvt Co D 2nd Ga. Regt (Burke
   Sharpshooters). Col John D. was a leading W-Boro
   atty before and after the Civil War; later practiced
   elsewhere. He may be buried in this section. His
   daughter, Julia, married James White of Athens, Ga.
   A son, John D., Jr., lived in Dublin, Ga. See
   The Herald & Expositor, Mar 19 & 26, 1884.
Attaway, Frances Cates   Apr 12 1853 Nov 4 1924
   w/o James   d/o Susan Douglas Addison & Hosea B. Cates
   m/o Heman Perry, Hope MacKenzie, James, Jr. & Douglas
   Attaway (Shreveport, La).
Attaway, James   CSA   Nov 26 1833   Jul 17 1910
   s/o Eliza Taylor & David (1784-1853); md 1st Cath-
   erine Parish, issue David (Houston, Tex.); 2nd
   Frances Cates, issue four sons. Enlisted Burke Guards
   under Capt. Musgrove. Obit. T.C. Jul 23 1910
Baduly, Pamela   age 32 y   Nov 17 1834
   Probably a daughter, or granddaughter, of William
   Baduly, Clerk of Court of Ordinary, Burke Co., who
   died W-borough Feb 14, 1806. *See Warren op. cit., 4.
Banks, Dora Gresham   May 19 1855   Jul 31 1883
   w/o Gilbert T.   d/o Sarah M. Anderson & Edmund B.
   Gresham. See Clark, op. cit., 163; Will Bk A,
   350-51.
Banks, Infant   Mar 21 1883   Sep 11 1883
   of Dora Gresham & Gilbert T.

Berrien, Elizabeth Palmer   Feb 22 1854   Jul 21 1883
    w/o Thomas M. d/o Judge Edward Palmer m/o Noble,
    Laura Maria, Margaret & John (ed).
Berrien, John   1881   1901
    s/o Eliz. Palmer & Thos. M. Never married.
Berrien, Laura Maria   Nov 1 1877 Aug 14 1962
    d/o Eliz. Palmer & Thos. M. Never married. First
    woman admitted to Georgia Bar, Atty-at-Law, Washing-
    ton, D.C., President of the National Association of
    Woman Lawyers. Aunt of Elizabeth Berrien Harnsberger
    of Markham, Va. Obit. T.C. Aug 15, 1962
Berrien, Judge Thomas Moore   age 72 y   Jne   1860
    h/o Caroline Virginia Left a stepson, James Mabry,
    Will Bk A, 170. One of early attys in Burke; at
    first a junior partner with A.M. Allen about 1821.
    An uncle of later atty with same name who married
    Elizabeth Palmer. A memorial to him in Minutes of
    The Superior Court of Burke Co., 1857-1866, 409.
    Grave no longer marked (ed).
Berrien, Thomas Moore CSA   Jan 7 1844 Dec 20 1901
    md 1st Elizabeth Palmer (four children); 2nd Eliza
    Godbee (widow of Homer W.), who is buried at Old
    Church; s/o Weems Berrien b near Rome, Ga. Left
    Annapolis to join the Confed. Navy. Lawyer. Obit.
    T.C. Dec 21, 1901
Blount, Abbey E.   age 12y 3m   Sep 16 1858
    d/o Martha Attaway & Edward H.
Blount, Abigail (Abbie)   Jne 25 1821 Jan 9 1902
    w/o Thomas H. md Jul 14, 1838 d/o Martha & Elijah
    Attaway m/o Martha Virginia (md A.M. Rodgers), Albert
    Hamilton, David Chesley, Miss Annie R., Mrs. Callie
    Perry, Mrs. Lewis R. Ford, Herbert, & Charles Edward.
    Obit. T.C. Jan 11, 1902.
Blount, Amarintha Jane   age 11y 8m   Nov 20 1854
    d/o Martha Attaway & Edward H.
Blount, Mrs. Ella Bass   age 85 y   May   1931
    3rd w/o Robert Broadnax md Jan 22, 1893 m/o Mrs. C.C.
    Clarke, Chicago, Ill. Obit T.C. May 15, 1931.
Blount, Ella Humphrey   1861   1892
    2nd w/o Robert Broadnax. md Jan 10, 1883 m/o
    Charlie, Warnoch & Bartow. Ten grandchildren.
Blount, Cecil O.   Jne 25 1880 Sep 9 1881
    s/o Georgia Mims & John Sturges
Blount, Edward Howard   1811   1893
    h/o Martha Attaway s/o Eliza E. Winn & Stephen W.
Blount, Georgia Mims   Nov 21 1861 Apr 22 1945
    w/o John Sturges d/o Lavinia Byrd & Leonidas Mims
    m/o Reginald & Marion Obit. T.C. Apr 30 1945
Blount, John Sturges   Apr 20 1855 Oct 17 1915
    h/o Georgia Mims br/o Edward Carter Blount Obit.
    T.C. Oct 23, 1915 and Mrs. J.S. Cates (her Obit T.C.
    Dec 21, 1895).

229

Blount, Martha Attaway   Mar 13 1823   1880
w/o Edward Howard md Mar 27, 1848 d/o Martha &
Elijah Attaway m/o William Augustus, Amarintha Jane,
Abbey Elizabeth, Thomas, Robert Lee, Mary L., Eliza
Searson.
Blount, Mary L.   age 1y 4m   Aug 3 1857
d/o Martha Attaway & Edward H.
Blount, Robert Broadnax   Apr 15 1841 May 25 1894
h/o 1st Louise Dillard md Dec 22, 1859; 2nd Ella
Humphrey md Jan 10, 1883; 3rd Ella Bass md Jan 22,
1893. Father of eight. Known as "Tige". s/o Axalina
Clark & Stephen W. Obit T.C. May 26, 1894.
Blount, Robert Lee   age 25 y   nd
s/o Martha Attaway & Edward H.
Blount, Ruby L.   Aug 9 1883 Sep 1 1884
d/o Georgia Mims & John Sturges
Blount, Thomas Hamilton   Dec 8 1806 Jne 3 1876
h/o Abigail Attaway s/o Eliza E. Winn & Stephen W.
Blount, Warnoch H. WW-I   Dec 25 1888 Jan 15 1962.
Ga Cpl US Army s/o Ella H. & Robert Broadnax.
Never married.
Bostick, Mrs. Eva   Feb 15 1862 May 4 1880
Unidentified; possibly the wife of Dr. C.A.W. Bostick
whose name appears several times in The True Citizen
in 1884, or a relative of Nat Bostick, a merchant in
Waynesboro, two decades later (ed).
Burdell, Emma F.   age 33y   Oct 6 1880
w/o Dr. Thomas d/o Joanna Shewmake & Isaiah Carter,
II. m/o two sons: Carter and Thomas Ferdinand (ed).
Burdell, Thomas, MD CSA   Feb   1832 Jul 15 1881
s/o Matilda Melville Moss of Athens, Ga. &
Ferdinand Victor Burdell b Augusta d Waynesboro
md Emma F. Carter of Waynesboro, Nov. 1870. See
Calhoun, op. cit., 58-59.
Burdell, Thomas Ferdinand   Jul   1871 Sep   1903
s/o Emma F. Carter & Dr. Thomas br/o Carter Burdell
Both were orphaned at an early age and reared by their
father's sister, Sarah Burdell Thompson (Mrs. Wm.
Vance T.) (ed).
Burton, Harriet Gresham   1851   1935
w/o Robert H. Burton CSA. No children. d/o Sarah
M. Anderson & Edmund B. Gresham See Fothergill,
op. cit., 150; Clark, op. cit., 162.
Byne, Charlotte Augusta   age 78 y   Jul 12 1906
w/o Edmund b Screven Co. d/o Major Willis Young
(veteran of Mexican War). For 45 yrs a member of
Pres. Church. m/o Mrs. Florence Byne Whitehead
sis/o Mrs. Bird of Halcyondale. Obit T.C. Jul 14, 1906
Byne, Edmund   age 67 y   Nov 16 1894
h/o Charlotte Augusta; for years a leading Elder in
the First Pres. Church of Waynesboro. Obit T.C.
Nov 17 1894
Byne, Edmund G.   Jul 11 1872 Oct 3 1900
s/o Margaret Jones Murphree & John S.

Byne, John Gordon   Nov 20 1857   Jan 31 1899
   s/o Margaret Jones Murphree & John S.
Byne, John S.   Apr 19 1829 Nov 20 1888
   h/o Margaret J. Murphree s/o Nancy Gordon & John;
   step-son of Benjamin E. Gilstrap. See latter's will,
   Will Bk. A, 83-85.
Byne, Margaret J.   Sep 5 1839 Oct 2 1902
   w/o John S. d/o Jane Jones (b 1802, daughter of
   Thomas Jones) & Wright Murphree m/o three sons: J.
   Gordon, Edmund G., Dr. J. Miller, Sr. and three
   daughters: Mrs. W. Tennent Houston, Mrs. Lula Wilson
   & Mrs. Maggie M. Walker. Fothergill op. cit. 149.
   Obit. T.C. Oct 4, 1902.
Byrd, V. A.   nd   nd
   Buried in Ashton section; possibly a CSA comrade of
   one of the sons of Col. John D. Ashton (ed).
Carpenter, Grace C.   Mar 25 1814 Feb 19 1833
   d/o A. & L. Buried in same section with Angelina M.
   Carter (ed).
Carter, Alexander, Esq.   age 70 y   Jne 24 1823
   Family tradition is that he had three wives, but
   their names are not now known. Hetty Carter, a
   daughter, md Major George Poythress. Their son, John
   Carter Poythress, was Alexander's only grandchild.
   Alexander built the historic Carter House (later the
   Carter-Poythress House and ultimately the Munnerlyn
   House), and there entertained President George Wash-
   ington during his one night visit to Waynesborough,
   a planned stop between Savannah and Augusta, on his
   Southern Tour. Alexander was a large landowner in,
   south, and west of what became the Town of Waynesborough. He was one of the Board of Incorporators
   of the new town in 1813, and was elected one of the
   first five commissioners (ed).
Carter, Angelina M.   Dec 16 1816 Jan 2 1897
   w/o Dr. Edward J. d/o Elizabeth & John Carpenter
   For the Carpenter family, see his will, Will Bk A,
   260-65. m/o Brig. Gen. John C. Carter, CSA, Mrs.
   Charlotte Carter Perry & Mrs. Julia Carter Miller.
   Obit. T.C. Jan 9, 1897. Note: John Carpenter was
   born Oct 26, 1789; Elizabeth, his wife, on Apr 7,
   1782. They were married June 26, 1808 (from family
   Bible) (ed).
Carter, Ann   age 21 y   Jan 21 1800
   Believed to be the unmarried daughter of Alexander
   Carter, Esq. She is buried in section with him and
   his grandson, John Carter Poythress. Note: This
   is the oldest marker in this cemetery (ed).
Carter, Edward Alexander, II   1874   1878
   s/o Sarah Augusta Lawson & Edward Alexander Carter,
   (who was a son of Isaiah, II & Joanna Shewmake) (ed).

Carter, Edward J. MD   Oct 4 1814 Jul 9 1869
    h/o Angelina Carpenter s/o Sarah Redd (or Reid)
    (the widow Tuttle) & Isaiah Carter, I. Edw. J. &
    Isaiah Carter, II were brothers and nephews of
    Alexander Carter, Esq. Dr. Carter was an intellect-
    ual and a fine physician. Studied at the Jefferson
    Med. College, Phila. See his will in Will Bk A,
    297-98.
Carter, Ella L.   1873   1874
    d/o Sarah Augusta Lawson & Edward Alexander Carter, I
Carter, Isaiah, I   age 53 y   Jan 8 1817
    md 1st Esther Walker (see Walker cem) 2nd Sarah Redd
    or Reid (the widow Tuttle) br/o Alexander Carter,
    Esq. & Mary Carter Lawson s/o Thomas Carter of St.
    John's Parish. Early merchant in Waynesborough and
    substantial land owner (ed).
Carter, Isaiah, II   Aug 11 1811 Sep 15 1861
    md 1st Emily Carpenter 2nd Johanna Shewmake (a sis/o
    John Troup Shewmake) & 3rd Electra Varner. s/o Sarah
    Redd or Reid (the widow Tuttle) & Isaiah Carter, I.
    br/o Dr. Edward J. Carter. Will Bk A, 186-187.
Carter, Jefferson (infant)   dates ileg
    s/o Isaiah Carter, II
Carter, Mary Isaiah   Dec 7 1861 Dec 13 1862
    d/o Electra Varner & Isaiah, II
Cary, Mamie P.   age 62 y   Nov 23 1944
    d/o Ella L. Buxton & J.E. Prescott. d Macon, Ga.
    buried next to her mother (ed).
Cates, Bartow   age 9 m   nd
    s/o Emily MacKenzie & Frank Forth
Cates, Frank   age 2y 7m   nd
    s/o Emily MacKenzie & Frank Forth
Cates, Frank Forth   age 32 y   nd
    h/o Emily MacKenzie s/o Susan Douglas Addison &
    Hosea B. See his wife's Obit. T.C. May 5, 1894.
Cates, MacKenzie   age 4 d   nd
    s/o Emily MacKenzie & Frank Forth
Chandler, Johannah Hurst   Aug 2 1843 Aug 25 1927
    w/o George M. d/o Margaret Coutteau & Geo. W. Hurst
    Member of Bethlehem Baptist before coming to Waynes-
    boro. Left a niece, Mrs. Frank S. Burney and nephews:
    Charlie & T.J. Hurst, Colquitt Parnell, Edgar Barg-
    eron, Robert Bargeron and Grady Bargeron. Obit. T.C.
    Aug 27, 1927.
Collins, Jack P. WW-I   nd Oct 10 1926
    Ga Pvt Co H 11th Cav b Dublin, Ga.
Cooley, Mrs. Adeline E.   Apr 18 1855 Sep 25 1895
    Unidentified. It is possible that she was the wife,
    or mother, of a Dr. J. W. Cooley, dentist, of
    Eatonton, Ga. who, in the 1880's, periodically
    advertised in The True Citizen that he would be in
    Waynesboro on certain dates for practice. He and
    his family may have subsequently moved to, or retired
    in, Waynesboro (ed).

Corker, Stephen A. CSA   May 7 1830   Oct 18 1879
   md Margaret M. Palmer   d/o Jane Allen & Edmund Palmer
   (and a sis/o Prof. James E. Palmer of Emory College).
   f/o Palmer L. (founder of 1st Nat'l Bank of Waynesboro), Frank G. (a banker in Dublin), and Stephen
   (broker in New Orleans). Capt. Co A 3rd Ga Regt ANV
   Captured at Gettysburg. Atty-at-law. Member of
   Forty-first U.S. Congress. Will Bk A, 428. See
   memorial to him in Minutes of the Burke Superior
   Court, Bk H, 1877-1880, 433-34. After his death, his
   wife md Judge Weaver, Madison, Ga. She is buried
   at Madison.
Cornwall, George   age 5 m   nd
   s/o Annabel & George
Davis, Kate MacKenzie   marker removed
   w/o ------ Davis, d/o Elizabeth Attaway & Alexander
   MacKenzie m/o Marion Davis, MD Note: After the
   Civil War Mrs. Kate Davis for some years conducted
   a fine preparatory school for girls (ed).
Evans, Joshua K.   1854   Oct   1897
   h/o Sarah H. s/o Elizabeth & Esham Evans (who are
   buried in Louisville City cem.) Obit. T.C. Oct 9,
   1897. Will Bk B, 23-25.
Evans, Sarah H.   1860   1893
   w/o Joshua K. d/o T.H. Holleyman m/o Arthur, Charles
   William, Mary & Ruth
Garlick, Amarintha E.   age 78 y   May 12 1896
   w/o Edward
Garlick, Edward   age 55 y   Apr 20 1858
   h/o Amarintha E. s/o Samuel Garlick. Samuel was one
   of five incorporators of Town of Waynesborough, and
   elected one of first five commissioners; also a
   leading courthouse official. Three families: Seaborn
   H. Jones, Samuel Garlick & Rogers- constituted
   practically the full membership of the First Methodist
   Church of W-borough in its infancy. From 1830-1851
   two sons, John J. Jones & Edward Garlick, succeeded
   to their father's roles in the church. Edward was
   Judge of Ordinary Court for years (ed).
Garlick, Julia Blount   nd   nd
   w/o Edgar Simmons d/o Celia Thomas & Henry Jackson
   Blount m/o Rosa, Lucy, Mrs. Henry Vaughn, Carroll
   (md Mary Boyd), Mrs. Marvin Cox, Sr., of Washington,
   D.C. & McClesky Garlych. Now an unmarked grave (ed).
Garlick, Lucy   Sep 23 1869   Apr 20 1958
   d/o Julia Blount & Judge Edgar Simmons Garlick
   Obit. T. C., Apr 24, 1958
Garlych, McClesky WW-I   May 10 1891   Nov 2 1963
   s/o Julia Blount & Judge Edgar Simmons Garlick.
   Newspaper man and author. Never married. Ga Pvt
   US Army d Aiken, S.C. Obit. T.C. Nov 6, 1963
Gray, C. Blunt   Jan 28 1868   Apr 16 1870
   s/o Elizabeth & Simeon A.

Gray, Charlie   Apr 3 1891   Oct 8 1891
  s/o Tommie McElmurray & Charles A.
Gray, Elizabeth E.   Oct 7 1835   May 9 1897
  w/o Simeon A. d/o Stephen W. Blount m/o Alice (md
  Thos. Quinney), Clifford (md W.L. McElmurray), Emma
  (md W.H. Walters), Charles A. & Frank A. Charter
  member of the Margaret Jones Chapter of the UDC
  Obit. T. C., May 15 1897.
Gray, Sarah   Nov 9 1837 date   ileg
  d/o Jane & Robert H. Note: Robert H. Gray was at
  one time postmaster at W-Boro (ed).
Gray, Simeon Alexander CSA   Nov 3 1829 Jul 9 1899
  h/o Elizabeth s/o Minchi and his first wife. b near
  W-Boro br/o James Gray. Served in 1864-65 as 1st Lt.
  3rd Co 17th Ga. Mil. in protection of Waynesboro
  against Kilpatrick's Cavalry. For 52 years was a
  progressive and leading merchant and a planter.
  Owner of an early newspaper. A civic-minded citizen;
  served as Mayor of City of W-Boro Obit. T.C.,
  Jul 15, 1899.
Gray, S. Wheeler   Aug 29 1864 Apr 1 1871
  s/o Elizabeth & Simeon A.
Gray, Steven William   Jne 19 1862 Sep 16 1863
  s/o Elizabeth & Simeon A.
Gray, Thomas   Jan 6 1886 Aug 10 1886
  s/o Tommie McElmurray & Charles A.
Gresham, Edmund B.   age 63 y   Sep 18 1872
  s/o Mary Jones & Job (parents buried in Gresham cem.)
  Planter and a Burke delegate to Georgia's Secession
  Convention (ed). See Clark, op. cit., 161-163;
  Will Bk A. 350-51.
Gresham, Floyd   age 7½ y   Jne 14 1895
  d/o Leora (Lola) Scales & Oscar R. Gresham
Gresham, Margaret H.   age 18 y   Oct 7 1877
  d/o Sarah M. Anderson & Edmund B.
Gresham, Sarah Adeline   1841   1927
  d/o Sarah M. Anderson & Edmund B. Will Bk B. 332-34.
  Note: "Miss Addie" was a beloved school teacher;
  taught in the Hephzibah High School and the Waynesboro
  Academy. Obit. T. C. Apr 2, 1927. See also Clark,
  op. cit., 163.
Gresham, Mrs. Sarah M.   Nov 18 1817 Aug 23 1888
  w/o Edmund B. md May 15 1838 d/o Jane H. McCullers
  & Elisha Anderson, Jr. Will Bk A. 532-33. For the
  eight children of Sarah M. & Edmund B., see Clark,
  op. cit., 162-163.
Haeseler, Frances Marion   Aug 13 1839 Jan 29 1884
  w/o Samuel Burchardt (md Apr 4, 1867; widow of Robt.
  R. Lewis) d/o Sally Carpenter Mills & Henry Chance.
  Children by both husbands (ed).
Haeseler, Otto Augustus   Sep 18 1872 Jan 12 1893
  s/o Frances M. Chance & Samuel Burchardt. Never
  married.

234

Haeseler, Samuel Burchardt CSA Nov 10 1837 Jul 19 1895
    b Brunswick, Germany md Chance sisters: 1st Frances
    Marion (Lewis), 2nd Sarah (widow of Joel Reese) Co F
    Cobb's Legion Cav (Grubb's Hussars)
Hardwick, Grattan   nd   nd
    s/o Allie Chance & Andrew. Never married.
    Note: One son of Allie & Andrew, Redding C., md
    Mamie Carroll; lived in S. Car. and is not buried in
    this cemetery. Andrew was one of four children of
    Mrs. Hannah Hardwick: J. William, Andrew, Selena (md
    Goodwin), and Harriet (md Lightfoot) (ed).
Hardwick, Ruth   nd   nd
    d/o Allie Chance & Andrew. Never married.
Hardwick, Walter   nd   nd
    s/o Allie Chance & Andrew. Never married.
Hardwick, Whitehead (child)*   nd   nd
    s/o Alice Hardwick & David M.
Harlow, Betsey Bethiah   Nov 4 1814 Nov 20 1817
    d/o Rebecca Walker & Dr. Southworth
Harlow, George Thacher   Sep 1 1825 Jne 23 1826
    s/o Rebecca Walker & Dr. Southworth
Harlow, John A. MD   1823 Jul 2 1863
    s/o Rebecca Walker & Dr. Southworth. CSA Capt Co D
    48th Regt Ga Vol Inf ANV Killed at Gettysburg battle.
    Never married.
Harlow, Laura Green   Sep 26 1830 Oct 30 1832
    d/o Rebecca Walker & Dr. Southworth
Harlow, Mary Eliza   May 2 1820 Jne 7 1821
    d/o Rebecca Walker & Dr. Southworth
Harlow, Mary Whitehead   Aug 26 1812 Sep 26 1815
    d/o Rebecca Walker & Dr. Southworth. b Augusta
Harlow, Rebecca Walker   1790   1865
    w/o Dr. Southworth d/o Bethiah Whitehead & Isaac
    Walker m/o ten children; seven died in infancy;
    three reached maturity: John A., Ruth & Sarah (*md
    Dr. Benj. Green). See Rebecca's sketch in Myers,
    op. cit., 1542. Unmarked grave. See *Warren &
    White op. cit., 51.
Harlow, Ruth   1830 Mar 14 1877
    d/o Rebecca Walker & Dr. Southworth. Never married.
Harlow, Dr. Southworth MD   Jan 26 1781 Feb 23 1832
    Skillful & distinguished physician. Active in
    medical circles, and one of incorporators of Town
    of Waynesborough in 1813.
Harlow, Susan Ann   Feb 14 1817 Jne 2 1821
    d/o Rebecca Walker & Dr. Southworth
Harlow, William James   Sep 20 1818 Jul 8 1827
    s/o Rebecca Walker & Dr. Southworth
Holmes, Jane B. Blount   Dec 14 1799 Jne 8 1879
    d/o Charlotte Prioleau & Stephen Blount of Savannah.
    Buried in the Whitehead section. sis/o Elizabeth A.
    Jones m/o Lt-Col Wm. R. Holmes, MD, CSA. Will Bk A,
    417-18. Note: The "B" in her name is probably for
    Broadbelt (ed).
*Hardwick should be Humphrey.
235

Holmes, William R. MD   c. 1821 Sep 17 1862
  s/o Jane B. Blount & Joseph B. Holmes of Charleston,
  S.C. (parents md May 10, 1820). Nephew of Elizabeth
  A. Blount Jones. Never married. Will Bk A, 226.
  Capt. of the Burke Sharpshooters. Promoted to Lt.
  Col., Apr 28, 1862. Killed at Sharpsburg, Md.
  defending a bridge against tremendous Union odds.
  One of Burke's most distinguished Confed. officers.
  Probably buried in Neyland section (ed).
Humphrey, Alice Hardwick   Apr 28 1856 Aug 18 1921
  d/o Allie Chance & Andrew w/o David Martin
  m/o Moselle (md Judson Clements Gray), John Franklin
  (md Annie R. MacKenzie), Alice (md Pickens Hall
  Videtto), Floyd (md Louise Cox), and Hugh Walter
  (md Alice McClure). sis/o Redding C. & Mrs. Zorn.
  (ed). Obit. T.C. Aug 20, 1921.
Humphrey, David Martin   Oct 31 1849 Oct 27 1930
  h/o Alice Hardwick s/o Margaret Stoutmeyer & Robert
  Burgess A Waynesboro merchant. Obit. T.C. Oct 31,
  1930
Humphrey, Margaret Stoutmeyer   nd   nd
  w/o Robt. Burgess m/o David Martin
Humphrey, Minnie (child)   nd   nd
  d/o Alice Hardwick & David M.
Humphrey, Nora (child)   nd   nd
  d/o Alice Hardwick & David M.
Humphrey, Robert Burgess   nd   nd
Hurst, Charles William   Apr 12 1851 Apr 11 1914
  h/o Martha Chandler s/o Margaret Coutteau & George W.
  Baptist. Sheriff of Burke Co for a number of years.
  Sketch in Memoirs of Georgia, Vol II, 367, Southern
  Hist. Assoc., 1895. Obit. T. C. Apr 18, 1914
Hurst, Grover Cleveland   Aug 23 1884 Sep 16 1884
  (triplet) s/o Martha C. & Charles W.
  Obit. T.C. Sep 19, 1884
Hurst, Martha Chandler   Mar 31 1853 Apr 28 1911
  w/o Chas. William d/o Jane Darlington & Wm. Chandler
  m/o Mrs. Frank S. Burney, Mrs. Hamp Hickson, Roger C.
  Hurst and Mrs. W.R. Calloway of Clarksville, Ga. (ed).
Hurst, Mary Hendricks   Aug 23 1884 Apr 5 1886
  d/o M.C. & C.W. (triplet)
Hurst, Thomas Hendricks   Aug 23 1884 Sep 16 1884
  (triplet) s/o Martha C. & Charles W.
Jones, Eliza Temperance   Nov 13 1846 Dec 17 1905
  d/o P.E.H. Jones sis/o Harvey and Mrs. Sarah Frances
  Thornton of Alabama. Baptist. "Miss Tempie" lived
  near Waynesboro for nearly 40 years. Obit. T.C.
  Dec 23, 1905.
Jones, Elizabeth Ann Blount   c. 1801 Dec 29 1863
  w/o James W. No issue. d/o Charlotte Prioleau &
  Stephen Blount of Savannah. Will Bk. A, 234. Buried
  in the Whitehead section (ed). Her husband was the
  s/o Sarah Jones & James Jones. In Fothergill,
  op. cit., 108 James W. is listed as the husband of
  Elizabeth H. Blount. For his will, see Will Bk. A,
  121-22.

Jones, Harvey   Jne 10 1844   Jan 10 1911
   eldest s/o P.E.H. Jones   b Crawfordsville, Ga.   Moved
   to Jefferson Co. 1858 and to Burke 1865.   Lived first
   near Herndon, and for 40 years on the Ivanhoe Plantation.   d at his store about one mile south of Waynesboro.   Obit. T.C.   Jan 14, 1911.

Jones, Mat   Aug 29 1855   Jan   6 1894
   d at his home near Waynesboro.   Had a family.
   Obit. T.C. Jan 13, 1894.   Probably a son of P.E.H.
   (ed).

Jones, P.C.   Mar   2 1868   Mar 29 1885
   Probably a son of P.E.H.   (ed).

Jones, P.E.H.   Mar 29 1815   May 16 1887
   b Jefferson Co.; lived there most of his life, but for
   a time in Taliaferro Co.   Moved to Burke after the
   Civil War.   Obit. T.C., May 20, 1887.   Mentions two
   daughters, Eliza Temperance and Sarah Frances Jones,
   in his will, Will Bk. A, 520-21.

Jones, Philip Sapp   Dec   9 1854   Oct 16 1892
   h/o Ida Elizabeth Jones (1855-1912) who was the d/o
   Maria Law of Conn. & Seaborn Augustus Jones (she is
   buried at Fairhaven cem.) s/o Sidney Ann Eliz. Sapp
   & Dr. Wm. Beaman Jones (both buried at Birdsville).

Jones, Seaborn A.   Jne   6 1856   Nov 20 1881
   Never married.   s/o Martha Maria Law of New Haven,
   Conn. & Seaborn Augustus   Lived mainly in Hephzibah.
   Mentions in his will his mother, brother Thomas L.,
   two sisters, Mary Augusta Chew and Ida Elizabeth,
   and a cousin, Kate C. Wakelee.   Will Bk. A, 459-60.
   See also Fothergill, op. cit., 152 and Clark, op.
   cit., 168-169.

Jones, W.B.   Apr 20 1862   Jul 29 1883
   Probably a son of P.E.H. Jones.   Eliza Temperance,
   Harvey, Mat, P.C., P.E.H., and W.B. Jones are all
   buried in the same section   (ed).

Lambeth, Caroline Roberts   Dec   1836   Oct   1898
   w/o Capt. Amos P. (who was an F&AM)

Lambeth, Eugene P.   May   1 1860   Aug 19 1901
   s/o Capt. Amos P.   Obit. T.C., Aug 24, 1901.

Lawson, Alexander James, Sr.   Oct 17 1796   Mar   1863
   h/o Barbara Tuttle, who was the d/o Sarah Reid (or
   Redd) & Edward T.   s/o Mary Carter & John Lawson, Sr.
   & grand s/o Thomas Carter of St. John's Parish.
   Large planter.   Active in politics: Judge of
   Inferior Court, State Senator for years, defeated by
   Robert Toombs in a Congressional race;   opposed to
   secession in 1861   (ed).

Lawson, Alexander James, II   May 21 1848   Dec 16 1905
   s/o Ella L.V. Brown & Robert R.R.   Never married.

Lawson, Judge Edward Floyd CSA   Jan 22 1835   Oct 13 1906
   h/o Leora A. Martin   No issue.   s/o Barbara Tuttle &
   Alexander J., Sr.   Commissioned 2nd Lt in Jones
   Hussars.   Promoted to Major.   Judge of Ordinary Court.
   Successful atty-at-law.   Sketch in Memoirs of Georgia,
   Vol II, 370-71. Southern Hist. Assoc. 1895. Obit.
   T.C. Oct 13, 1906.

Lawson, Ella Louise   Apr 15 1829   Dec 11 1909
  /Virginia Brown w/o Robert R.R.   d/o Sarah Perry
& Wade Brown
Lawson, Florence R.   Feb 5 1863   Oct 5 1868
  d/o Ella L.V. Brown & Robt. R.R.
Lawson, George Troup   Mar 25 1859   Jne 24 1912
  s/o Ella L.V. Brown & Robert R.R. Never married.
Lawson, George Foster Pierce   Sep 19 1838   1862
  s/o Barbara Tuttle & Alexander J., Sr.
  CSA Co C 5th Ga Cav; d in army hospital
Lawson, Leora Aziline   Jne 6 1842 Sep 11 1921
  w/o Judge Edward F, d/o Eliza Walker & John Martin
  b Macon, Ga. An aunt of Leora Scales (Gresham)
  (Davis). Obit T.C. Sep 17 1921
Lawson, Robt. Raymond Reid   Sep 24 1823 Oct 25 1863
  CSA s/o Barbara Tuttle & Alexander J., Sr. A Burke
  Co-born Savannah journalist. Commissioned by Governor
  in August 1863 as Brig-General of troops for state
  defense; died two months later in army camp; no
  active combat service (ed). h/o Ella L.V. Brown
  Lawson.
Lewis, Robert Henry   Nov 24 1860 Jul 22 1882
  s/o Frances Marion Chance & Robert R. Lewis.
  Never married.
Lewis, Robert R. CSA   1828   1863
  1st h/o Frances Marion Chance f/o Robert Henry &
  Willie Walton (md Greene O'Neal Buxton). d in Confed.
  service, Atlanta (ed).
MacKenzie, Alexander   1823 Jne 7 1860
  h/o Elizabeth Attaway s/o Mary Ann Campbell &
  Alexander MacKenzie of Redcastle, Scotland.
  Atty-at-law. See memorial to him in Minutes of the
  Superior Court of Burke Co., 1857-1866, 409.
  His parents are buried in Augusta (ed).
MacKenzie, Angelina May   May 29 1853 Feb 18 1931
  w/o James Hope   /Lawson md Apr 3, 1877 Grave
  marker no longer in section (ed).
MacKenzie, Campbell   Jul 4 1881 Jne 7 1888
  s/o May Lawson & James Hope
MacKenzie, Charlie   Aug 15 1883 Jul 25 1884
  inf s/o May Lawson & J. Hope
MacKenzie Colin   nd   nd
  s/o Mary Ann Campbell & Alexander. His parents are
  buried in Augusta (ed).
MacKenzie, Elizabeth Attaway   Aug 7 1829 Aug 4 1891
  w/o Alexander md Feb 6 1848 d/o Martha (d Jan 30,
  1836) and Elijah (1795-1848)   m/o Margaret, Emily,
  Charles, Kate & James Hope. Grave no longer marked
  (ed).
MacKenzie, James Hope   Dec 10 1850 Aug 20 1922
  h/o Angelina May Lawson s/o Elizabeth Attaway &
  Alexander MacKenzie f/o Campbell, little Charlie,
  Lewis F., Tracy, & Annie MacKenzie Humphrey (Mrs.
  John Franklin)

MacKenzie, Lewis F.   Oct 4 1886 Feb 19 1917
   s/o May Lawson & James Hope   Never married.
MacKenzie, Tracy   Dec 3 1879 May 2 1954
   s/o May Lawson & James Hope
Manau, Henry   Oct 13 1893 Nov 30 1894
   s/o M.L.B. & H.H. b in Germany Obit. T.C. Dec 1,
   1894
Mandell, John Poythress   Sep 18 1846 Aug 30 1853
   s/o Mary E. & George A.
Mandell, Mary E.   Dec 14 1828 Sep 11 1912
   w/o George Addison (a nephew of John Carter Poythress
   by his half-sister). She was born Turner; niece of
   James Henry Royal. See his will, Will Bk. A, 431-32.
   m/o John Poythress Mandell and Annie R. (md Munnerlyn). Donor with Mrs. Mary Bennett of the City Park
   adjoining St. Michael's Episcopal Ch. Obit. T.C.
   Sep 14, 1912. See Poythress will, Will Bk. A, 207-9.
Marmelstein, Maud L.   Oct 3 1872 Sep 25 1896
   w/o C. Marmelstein d/o Louise Dillard & Robert
   Broadnax Blount. No issue.
McCathern, Henry Lamar   Feb 8 1885 Jan 24 1886
   s/o Sarah J. & Walker
McCathern, Meta Jane   Mar 12 1889 Aug 7 1889
   only d/o Sarah J. & Walker
McCathern, Otis A.   Mar 17 1877 Jul 13 1922
   s/o Sarah J. & Walker h/o Sallie Kate Tinley
   f/o Walker
McCathern, Sarah J.   Jan 7 1849 Feb 23 1924
   w/o Walker eldest d/o Leslie Darlington & William
   Chandler m/o Wm. Walker, Porter F., J. Jenks, Otis A.
   G. Metz and Sidney. Obit. T.C. Mar 1, 1924.
McCathern, Walker CSA   Feb 10 1840 Oct 14 1915
   h/o Sarah J. s/o William b Richmond Co. Baptist.
   Mayor of Waynesboro. Burke Guards Co. Made a
   spectacular escape from Fort Delaware, a Union prison.
   Obit. T.C. Oct 16, 1915.
McCleskey, Georgia Bird   Nov 25 1882 Aug 27 1886
   d/o E.S. & Rev. J.R., minister of First Methodist
   Church, Waynesboro, 1886-1888
McCleskey, Lee Lamar   Jul 1 1884 Aug 27 1886
   s/o E.S. & Rev. J.R., minister of First Methodist
   Church, Waynesboro, 1886-1888
McCullough, John Edward   1858   1895
McCullough, Malvine Elizabeth   1855   1933
   An aunt of Robert Allen Templeton. One large marker
   lists both families as follows:

   McCullough   Templeton
John Edward 1858-1895   Robert Allen 1870-1927
Malvine Elizabeth 1855-1933 Josephine Wade 1864-1934

McElmurray, Corlotta   Jne 30 1898 Nov 8 1898
   d/o H.E. & J.S.
Milledge, Sadie   Mar 20 1876 Sep 21 1877
   d/o Rosa Gresham & Richard (Dick) Milledge.
   See Clark, op. cit., 163.

Miller, Hugh   Jan 29 1878   Jul 1 1878
   s/o Julia Carter & Joseph Baldwin
Miller, John Polhill   Jul 29 1857   Aug 2 1877
   1st h/o Emma Gray (see Walters, Emma Gray _infra_).
   s/o Cornelia Polhill & Dr. B.B.
Miller, Joseph Baldwin   Jan 26 1855   Aug 25 1879
   h/o Julia Carter   s/o Cornelia Polhill & Dr. Baldwin
   Buckner. Atty-at-law.
Miller, Julia Carter   Jul 28 1855   Nov 19 1932
   w/o Joseph Baldwin   d/o Angelina M. Carpenter & Dr.
   Edward J. Carter. Graduated from Mrs. Kate Davis'
   School; studied at Mary Baldwin Seminary. Long a
   member of First Pres. Church of W-Boro. Obit. _T.C._
   Nov 25, 1932.
Mitchell, Mary Lavinia   Jne 9 1835   Dec 16 1895
   w/o 1st Leonidas Mims   2nd L.M. Mitchell   b in S. Car.
   m/o W.L. Mims, Georgia Mims Blount, Mrs. Wells and
   Walter Mitchell   Obit. _T.C._   Dec 21, 1895.
Mobley, Leila Blount   nd   Jan 16 1883
   w/o R.F.   md Dec 15, 1881. No issue.
Moore, Prioleau Clanton   Jul 3 1854   Oct 10 1903
   s/o Martha & William Moore   See will of latter,
   Will Bk. A, 132-34.
Moseley, J.W.   Sep 9 1847   Sep 12 1895
   Leaves a wife and two children. Died at home of his
   son-in-law, D.E. Hunter. Obit. _T.C._ Sep 7 & 12, 1895.
Munnerlyn, Annie R.   Nov 25 1848   May 13 1918
   w/o John D., Sr.   d/o Mary E. & George A. Mandell
   m/o four children but only John D., Jr. survived
   infancy. Inherited the historic Carter-Poythress
   house, later known as the Munnerlyn house (ed).
Munnerlyn, Infant   Aug 8 1872   Sep 13 1872
   of Annie R. & John D.
Munnerlyn, John D., Jr.   May 13 1868   Dec 23 1910
   s/o Annie R. & John D., Sr.
Munnerlyn, John Daniel, Sr.   Jul 27 1842   Mar 22 1895
   h/o Mrs. Annie R.   WOW   CSA   Came to Waynesboro from
   Savannah. Munnerlyn Station on Central of Georgia
   named for him.
Munnerlyn, Mary Emma   Feb 17 1870   Oct 10 1870
   d/o Annie R. & John D.
Munnerlyn, Poythress   Feb 6 1867   Dec 24 1867
   s/o Annie R. & John D.
Neely, Thomas William   Mar 10 1881   May 1 1883
   s/o Willie Leora & Robert C.
Neely, Willie Leora   Nov 27 1860   Jan 25 1885
   1st w/o Robert C.   d/o Sarah Lawson & Thomas Addison
Neyland, Charlotte S. Prioleau Apr 19 1778   1823
   d/o John & Jane Broadbelt Prioleau of Charleston,
   S.C. md 1st Stephen Blount of S. Car. & Savannah;
   two daughters, Jane B. & Elizabeth Ann; 2nd John
   Barton Gibbons, no issue; 3rd, Rev. Gilbert Ney-
   land, issue: John Prioleau Neyland & Mary Rebecca
   B. Neyland. Buried in Neyland section   (ed).

Neyland, Rev. Gilbert   1777   Mar 11 1818
  md Charlotte S. Prioleau Jan 27, 1810 f/o John
  Prioleau Neyland (May 4 1817-Jne 7 1855) who is buried
  in Savannah, and the grand f/o Tallulah G. Neyland
  Whitehead. Buried in Neyland section (ed).
Oliver, James H. MD   Sep 3 1830 May 31 1889
  h/o Mary J. s/o Martha & W.W. Oliver. A leading
  physician in county. CSA f/o two daughters and three
  sons: one attorney and two physicians (ed).
Oliver, Mary J.   Oct 12 1829 Feb 1 1913
  w/o Dr. James H. m/o Taney D., Dr. Shelly Oliver,
  Dr. Sam Oliver, Mrs. Chas. C. Brown, Macon, Ga. and
  Mrs. Wm. H. Pace. Obit. T.C. Feb 8, 1913.
Oliver, Taney D.   Dec 23 1857 Dec 26 1897
  s/o Mary J. & Dr. James H. Never married. An atty-
  at-law; elected to General Assembly. d in Atlanta,
  an honored representative. Obit. T.C. Jan 1, 1898.
Owen, Carroll   nd   nd
  Note: A child's grave next to John Blackstone Owen.
  Last name missing; believed to be an Owen (ed).
Owen, John Blackstone   Oct 22 1830 Feb 6 1860
Palmer, Martha Jane   Mar 10 1843 Jan 29 1896
  w/o 1st Robert Allen Rowland 2nd Jasper Palmer (not
  connected with Burke Palmers). Buried beside her
  first husband. Born Martha Jane Wooding of Columbia
  Co., Ga. m/o Rosa Allen (md Geo. Dwelle), Roberta
  Pearl & Mary Victoria (both are buried in W-Boro
  Magnolia cem. next to Enon E. Chance) (ed).
  Obit. T.C., Feb 1, 1896
Parnell, Colquitt H.   Jul 2 1880 Feb 25 1931
  s/o Margaret Hurst & Leonidas. h/o Mrs. Susie Ivey
  Parnell Merchant in Waynesboro, later merchant and
  farmer, Davisboro, Ga. Survived by wife, a step-son,
  Dr. Mallard Page of Davisboro and four nephews in
  Girard. Obit. T.C. Feb 25, 1931.
Parnell, Leonidus   Dec 31 1846 Jan 19 1889
  h/o Margaret Hurst
Parnell, Margaret Hurst   Mar 12 1846 Feb 11 1924
  w/o Leonidas d/o Margaret Coutteau & George W. Hurst
  Survived by two children: Mrs. Horace Odom & Col-
  quitt Parnell Obit. T.C. Feb 16, 1924.
Perry, Charlotte Elizabeth   Nov 15 1844 May 15 1886
  w/o Judge Heman H. /Carter d/o Angelina M. Carpen-
  ter & Dr. Edward J. Carter m/o Angie, Percy, &
  John Carter
Perry, Judge Heman H. CSA   Apr 13 1835 Feb 14 1908
  h/o Charlotte Carter s/o Mary Fryer & Hardy Perry
  (b Va.) br/o Hettie Perry (Mrs. John Richard
  Scruggs). T.C.Sep 18, 1931. Capt. & Adj-Gen Wright's
  Brig under Gen. G. M. Sorrel.   Lawyer, judge, &
  newspaper editor. Member constitutional convention
  1877, State senator. Obit. T.C. Feb 15, 1908.
Perry, John Carter   Jan 12 1871 Mar 22 1892
  s/o Charlotte Carter & Judge Heman H. Never married.
  Obit. T.C. Mar 26, 1892.

Perry, Percy   nd   nd
    inf s/o Charlotte Carter & Judge Heman H.
Phelps, Frank W.   May 9 1887   Oct 5 1935
    s/o Emma Gray & Robert L. Never married. br/o Simeon
    A. of Waynesboro & R.L., Jr. of Brooklet, Ga.
    Obit. T.C. Oct 1J, 1935.
Phelps, R.L.   Jul 3 1858   Oct 18 1889
    h/o Emma Gray f/o Simeon A., Frank W., & Robert L.
    Obit. T.C. Oct 19, 1889.
Phelps, Simeon A. WW-I   Feb 18 1882   Jne 2 1948
    h/o Agnes Sherwood of Eastern Maryland   md Nov 14,
    1909. s/o Emma Gray & Robert L. f/o Virginia (md 1st
    Dr. Everett A. Bargeron 2nd Carlton Fulford), Edith
    (md W.V. Brown), & Sherwood A. Pvt Inf Ga N.G. Mex.
    Border duty Obit. T.C. June 10, 1948
Polhill, Cora Gertrude   Dec 24 1857   Feb 18 1928
    w/o Joseph A. (pharmacist), md Jan 1, 1880 d/o Ella
    W.V. Brown & Robert R.R. Lawson. Obit T.C.
    Feb 25, 1928.
Polhill, Infant   only date   1880
    s/o Cora Gertrude & Joseph A.
Poythress, John Carter   Sep 14 1796   Sep 12 1862
    s/o Hetty Carter (the d/o Alexander Carter, Esq.) &
    Major George Poythress of Virginia. Major Poythress
    md a second time, so that John C. had a half-sister,
    Mary Elizabeth Poythress. She married Addison
    Mandell. Their son was George A. Mandell, h/o Mrs.
    Mary E. Mandell. John C. md a Miss Morris, a sis/o
    Wm. S.C. Morris. In his will, Will Bk A, 207-09,
    John C. excluded his nephew, George A., and left his
    property to his wife's niece, Maria B.M. McIntosh
    (the d/o Wm. S.C. Morris), and to his nephew's wife,
    Mrs. Mary E. Mandell and her daughter, Annie R.
    Mandell (Munnerlyn). In the settlement of John C.'s
    large estate, the historic Carter-Poythress House,
    with all its fine silver and furniture, passed into
    the hands of Mrs. Mandell and ultimately to Mrs.
    Munnerlyn. Thus the house for decades became known
    as the Munnerlyn House (ed).
Prescott, Ella L. Buxton   Aug 15 1855   Mar 29 1905
    w/o J.E. m/o Mrs. Mamie P. Cary of Macon, Ga.
    Obit. T.C. Apr 1, 1905.
Ramsdale, Mary M.   nd   Dec 23 1887
    buried near the Gray section. She was brought to
    Waynesboro from New York City to manage the dress and
    millinery department of Gray's Emporium (department
    store) (ed).
Reynolds, Angie Perry   Dec 10 1868   Nov 4 1926
    w/o Joseph Jones Reynolds d/o Charlotte Carter &
    Judge Heman H. Perry m/o Charlotte, Barbara, Joseph
    J., Jr., Heman & Oliver Obit. T.C. Nov 6, 1926
Reynolds, Elizabeth M.A.   Jul 9 1836   Apr 1 1912
    2nd w/o J. Jones Reynolds, CSA d/o James S. Anderson
    (1793-1854), One sister survived, Mrs. J.O. Clark of
    Macon, Ga. Presbyterian. Obit. T.C. Apr 6, 1912

Reynolds, J. Jones CSA   Jan 25 1838 Mar 16 1900
   md 1st Rosina V. Anderson 2nd Eliz. M.A. Anderson
   s/o Mary Ann Jones (b Nov 1, 1814) & James Madison
   Reynolds (1809-1878). Obit. T.C. Mar 24, 1900 Co F
   Cav Cobb's Legion (Grubb's Hussars). For Mary Ann
   Jones, James Madison Reynolds and their children, see
   Fothergill, op. cit., 150-151.
Reynolds, Joseph J., Sr.   1866   1939
   h/o Angie Perry s/o Rosina V. Anderson & J. Jones
   Reynolds, CSA
Reynolds, Rosina V. Anderson   Aug 31 1838 Dec 21 1872
   1st w/o J. Jones Reynolds, CSA d/o James S. Anderson
Reynolds, Rozina   Feb 20 1900 Mar 6 1900
   d/o Angie F. & Joseph Jones
Roberts, D.B. CSA   nd   nd
   Pvt Co D 2nd Ga Regt (Burke Sharpshooters). Buried in
   the Ashton section, along with R.W. Ashton, V.A. Byrd,
   & possibly Col. John D. Ashton, able atty-at-law
   (ed).
Rodgers, Alpheus M. CSA   nd May 18 1887
   h/o Virginia Blount Rodgers An atty-at-law.
   Obit. T.C., May 20, 1887
Rodgers, Frank Preston   age 2 y   nd
   s/o Virginia Blount & Alpheus M. Rodgers
Rodgers, Thomas Blount (inf)   nd   nd
   s/o Virginia Blount & Alpheus M. Rodgers
Rodgers, Virginia Blount   nd Nov 22 1893
   w/o A.M. Rodgers, atty-at-law d/o Abbie Attaway &
   Thomas Hamilton Blount d at home of her son, Julien
   S. Rodgers, Macon, Ga. Leader in organizing the
   Ladies Memorial Assoc. of Burke Co. Obit. T.C.
   Nov 25, 1893
Routzahn, Louis H.   age 50 y   Aug 1 1885
   1st h/o Florence Byne A merchant; came to Waynesboro
   from North Carolina f/o three daughters: Bertha,
   Haidee & Madeline (ed).
Rowland, Marian Wallace   Apr 5 1874 Jul 17 1899
   1st w/o Clarence L. / Whitehead d/o Tallulah Neyland
   & Dr. Amos G. Whitehead m/o Grattan Whitehead
   Rowland. Obit. T.C. Jul 22, 1899
Rowland, Robert Allen   May 17 1819 Apr 25 1877
   s/o Benjamin b Richmond Co. d Waynesboro
   md Martha Jane Wooding of Columbia Co., Ga. (see
   Palmer, Martha Jane, who is buried in the same
   section).
Smith, Elizabeth Blount   Dec 22 1862 Jul 18 1886
   w/o J.
Stewart, H.D.   Dec 21 1861 Aug 5 1895
   F&AM Obit. T.C. Aug 10, 1895
Sturges, Georgia Anna Ward   1826 Feb 18 1905
   w/o William U. md Aug 10, 1847 d/o Thomas A. Ward
   m/o John R. (infant), Sarah Clifford (age 1 year in
   1850 census, not in 1860 census), Philoclia Whitehead
   and William Ward. sis/o Elizabeth Ward Anthony of
   Augusta and Thomas A. Ward, MD (buried in this

cemetery) Obit. T.C. Feb 25, 1905 The two first-mentioned children are probably buried in the Sturges section (ed).

Sturges, Jane Robinson   Nov 30 1809   Aug 17 1817
d/o Rachel Lowrey & Samuel

Sturges, John R.   CSA   1827   Jul 1 1862
s/o Rachel Lowrey & Samuel   b in Georgia   An atty-at-law.   Went to front with Burke Guards in 1861 as a 1st Lt.; promoted to Major and to Lt Col, 3rd Ga. Regt in 1862. Killed at Malvern Hill, Va. Jul 1, 1862. Never married. In his will, Will Bk A, 203-05, he mentions his "beloved brother", Wm. Urquhart and "my niece Mrs Abby S. Jones, wife of Henry H. Jones." Note: According to an article by Henry H. Jones The Southern World, May 1, 1884, "the body of the gallant Sturges was interred in a gentleman's garden at Gen. Longstreet's Hdqs., three miles from Richmond. There it slumbered until about six years ago, when loving hands removed the last relics of the dauntless soldier to their final resting place in Waynesboro, the home of his ancestors". (ed).

Sturges, Philoclia Whitehead   1853   Jan 31 1931
d/o Georgia Anna Ward & William U.   Never married. Music teacher in Waynesboro Academy; later on staff of Lucy Cobb Institute, Athens, Ga. and Agnes Scott College, Decatur, Ga.   b Waynesboro   d Decatur Lived in Decatur nearly 20 years. Widely known as "Miss Philo". Obit. T.C. Feb 6, 1931.

Sturges, Rachel Lowrey   Oct 18 1786   1837
w/o Samuel   md May 3, 1804   b in Georgia   m/o Abigail Eliza, Jane Robinson, Nathaniel Lewis, Sarah Ann, William Urquhart, Samuel, Julia & John R.   Grave no longer marked (ed).
Notes: 1) Children with unmarked graves in this section probably include Nathaniel Lewis (no dates), Samuel (1818-32), and Julia (1824-no date).
      2) Abigail Eliza Sturges (1807-28) md Samuel Dowse (see Bath cem) and Sarah Ann Sturges (b Mar 11, 1812 d 1833) md John W. Reynolds (ed).

Sturges, Samuel   Nov 5 1774   Oct 6 1831
h/o Rachel Lowrey   s/o Abigail Lewis & Samuel Sturges b Fairfield, Conn.   br/o Nathaniel Lewis Sturges who settled in Augusta. Samuel arrived in Georgia, possibly in 1795 but certainly by 1801. Living in Waynesborough by 1804. One of 5 members Board of Town Incorporators; elected 1813 as one of first five commissioners to govern new Town. For many years, Ordinary of Burke Co. Grave no longer marked (ed).

Sturges, William Urquhart   1816   May 1 1884
s/o Rachel Lowrey & Samuel   b in Georgia. Was a resident of Waynesboro all his life. Obit. The Herald & Expositor. May 7, 1884

Sturges, William Ward   1855   nd
  s/o Georgia Anna Ward & William U. age 14 in 1870
  census; probably died between 1870 and 1880 census
  dates. One marker for both William and Philoclia
  reads: "Sister and brother" (ed).
Sullivan, Annie Gresham   nd   nd
  w/o Wm. Decatur b Greene Co., Ga.
Sullivan, Miss Hattie   nd   ·nd
  d/o Annie Gresham & Wm. Decatur
Sullivan, Mathilda Becker   nd   nd
  w/o Sterling L. from Hamburg, Germany
Sullivan, Sterling Lawrence   nd   nd
  s/o Annie Gresham & William Decatur
Sullivan, William Decatur CSA   nd   nd
  Founder, publisher & first editor of The True Citizen,
  April, 1882. He was an experienced newspaper man.
  Confed. iron cross marks his grave (ed).
Tant, Anna Lee   nd   nd
  inf d/o Thomas & Martha
Tant, Lela   age 3 y   Oct 10 1870
  d/o Thomas & Martha Note: Thomas Tant, merchant,
  returned to Waynesboro in 1884 to open a store. The
  Herald & Expositor, Mar 26, 1884
Taylor, Mary Street   Nov 30 1831 Apr 4 1887
  d/o Hon. Patrick Connelly of Jefferson Co. m/o Mrs.
  James Heyward and Mrs. Dr. Roland Steiner.
  b Louisville, Ga. d at her home near Holcombe
  Obit. T.C. Apr 8, 1887
Templeton, Josephine Wade   1864   1934
  w/o Robert Allen m/o Louise (Mrs. Robert Harrison)
  Slaughter of Washington, D.C. grand m/o Robert,
  Blair B., & Ellen Slaughter (ed).
Templeton, Robert Allen   1870 Sep   1927
  F&AM & Shriner. For a number of years was Tax
  Collector of Burke Co. Nephew of Mrs. M.E.
  McCullough Obit. T.C. Sep 10, 1927
Thomas, Charles H.   Oct 13 1854 Jan 16 1913
  h/o Ruth Miller s/o Nancy Cates & Jethro
  Obit. T.C. Jan 18, 1913
Thomas, Jethro CSA   Mar 4 1823 Sep 3 1885
  s/o Axalina Clark & Ethelred md 1st Jane Blount (one
  son, Judge George Thomas of Athens, Ga.) 2nd Nancy
  Cates (Davenport). Co D 5th Ga Cav Prisoner for 6
  mos at Point Lookout, Union Prison. Charter member
  First Bapt. Ch. of W-Boro, Judge of Inferior Court,
  Mayor of Town, County Commissioner. Obit. T.C.
  Sep 11, 1885
Thomas, Jethro   Nov 29 1880 Apr 25 1885
  s/o Ruth Miller & Charles H. Obit. T.C. May 1, 1885
Thomas, Nancy   Sep 13 1831 Oct 2 1911
  w/o 1st ------ Davenport; 2nd Jethro Thomas.
  d/o Araminta Hodges & Joseph Cates m/o Charles H.,
  Jethro B. & Kate (md 1st George A. Green, 2nd Dr.
  C.T. Milner) Obit. T.C. Oct 7, 1911

Thomas, Ruth Miller   Dec 2 1859 Jan 2 1940
w/o Chas. H. d/o Cornelia Polhill & Dr. Baldwin
Buckner Miller m/o Nell, Kate and Jethro (d young)
(ed).
Underwood, Mrs. E.J.   Dec 1 1833 Mar 25 1889
A business woman who opened in June 1884 a millinery
and fancy goods store in Waynesboro. T.C. June 2,
1884. Her brother, G.H. Montgomery, administered her
estate. T.C. May 11, 1889.
Walker, Julia   nd Oct 11 1880
Walters, Emma Gray   Apr 5 1857 Jne 19 1940
w/o 1st John P. Miller 2nd Robert L. Phelps
3rd William H. Walters d/o Elizabeth & Simeon Gray
m/o five sons: S.A. Phelps, Frank W. Phelps, R.L.
Phelps, Jas. H. Walters and Wm. H. Walters.
Obit. T.C. June 20, 1940
Ward, Thomas A. MD   Mar 28 1825 Mar 31 1895
s/o Thomas A. br/o Georgia Anna Ward Sturges.
Whitehead, Amos Grattan MD   Feb 14 1841 Mar 23 1904
md 1st Tallulah G. Neyland 2nd Florence Byne
(Routzahn) s/o Mary Ann Wallace Dent & John P.C.
Leading Burke physician. President of the State Med.
Ass'n. For his CSA record, see sketch in Biograph-
ical Souvenir of the States of Georgia and Florida
(1889), 838-39.
Whitehead, Florence Byne   Dec 19 1847 Feb 9 1925
w/o 1st L.H. Routzahn 2nd Dr. A.G. Whitehead;
d/o Charlotte Young & Edmund Byne m/o Bertha R.
(md George M. Gordon), Haidee R. (md Judson S.
McElmurray) and Madeline R. (md Jas. H. Whitehead)
Obit. T.C. Feb 14, 1925
Whitehead, Hattie Cope   Aug 16 1876 Oct 1 1879
d/o Tallulah Neyland & Dr. A.G.
Whitehead, Tallulah   Sep 15 1846 Jne 8 1886
/ Gilbertine Neyland 1st w/o Dr. Amos Grattan, MD
md Jan 31, 1871 d/o Agnes C. Cline & John Prioleau
Neyland b Savannah m/o Marian Wallace Whitehead
(md Clarence L. Rowland) (ed).
Williams, W.B.   age c. 58y Jne 1901
Native of Chester, Ga. A painter at Sanders' Wagon
Works. Left a daughter and son-in-law at Chester.
Obit. T.C. June 15, 1901
Wilson, Alice Perry   Oct 14 1871 Oct 24 1895
w/o O.V. Left a husband and two young children, one
an infant a few weeks old. Obit. T. C. Oct 26, 1895
Wilson, Infant   age 1m 12d Nov 27 1895
s/o A.P. & O.V. A few weeks before the father had
moved his family from Munnerlyn to Waynesboro to
accept a position with Central of Ga. R.R.
T.C. Sep 14, 1895
Wimberly, Callie Chandler   Jne 22 1857 Jan 13 1948
w/o W.M. d/o Jane Darlington & William Chandler
m/o Miss Willie and Chandler W. Baptist. Obit. T.C.
Jan 22, 1948

Wimberly, William Mathis   Jul 26 1857 Mar 28 1887
   h/o Callie Chandler s/o Julia A. Mathis & Wilson
   Joseph Obit. T.C. Apr 1, 1887
Wimberly, Willie Inez   Mar 22 1886 Aug 9 1973
   d/o Callie Chandler & William Mathis Wimberly.
   Never married.
Zorn, Nora Hardwick   Feb 25 1859 Mar 6 1926
   w/o Wm. Elijah d/o Allie Chance & Andrew b Burke Co
   sis/o Alice Hardwick Humphrey & Redd C. Hardwick,
   atty-at-law, S.Car. T.C. Jan 6, 1894. m/o W.E. Zorn,
   Jr., Jacksonville, Fla; Mrs Marion Hope, Denmark,
   S.C.; Miss Julia Zorn, Los Angeles, Cal., and Mrs.
   Inez LeMaster, Americus, Ga. Obit. T.C. Mar 13, 1926
Zorn, William Elijah   Mar 16 1855 Dec 25 1889
   h/o Nora Hardwick Obit. T. C. Dec 28, 1889
   Note: "Baby Strojer" appears on combined husband
   and wife marker (ed).
---bkn--, Oswell   May 15 1860 Jne 12 1879
   "Oswell was a good and industrious boy laboring for
   his own support when 8 years old. A regular SS
   scholar, he spent his last hours singing their hymns.
   Let his rest be peaceful".

Notes: 1) For assistance with annotations to some of
the above markers, we are especially indebted to Miss
Catherine Stewart Jones, Macon (Sturges section),
Grattan Whitehead Rowland, Atlanta (Neyland, Sturges,
& Whitehead sections), Mrs. Charlotte Reynolds Gavin,
Lakeland, Fla. (Carter, Perry & Reynolds sections),
Mrs. Frank Cates, Jr., Waynesboro (MacKenzie-Cates
section) and W.H. Walters, Waynesboro (Gray & Blount
sections) (ed).
        2) "Obit. T.C." indicates an obituary in
Waynesboro's weekly newspaper, The True Citizen
(ed).

147.   WAYNESBORO MAGNOLIA

Agerton, Zillah Bostick   1871   1961
   w/o 1st Jno. A. Redd 2nd E.T. Agerton d/o Mary
   Alma Marshall & John E. See sketch of her in T.C.
   Jul 19, 1961.
Alford, William Little   Aug 28 1919 Mar 1 1966
   md Eula E. Lewis Jul 20 1940 s/o Louise Little &
   Roy Stephens
Allen, Cecil Lamar WW-II   Aug 2 1911 May 15 1970
   h/o Myrtle Lee Stroud s/o Martha Caroline Ballard
   & Tarver Singleton Ga Cpl USA
Anderson, Annie Green   Apr 20 1901 Dec 26 1923
   w/o Grover C. d/o Annie L. Cox & Walter G.
Anderson, Charles Lawson   Aug 12 1934 May 5 1959
   s/o Marian Poston & Lawson W.
Anderson, Comfort Floy Cullen   Mar 6 1892 Jne 14 1958
   w/o Harvey Lee

247

Anderson, Gracie B.   Jan 17 1881   Oct 27 1959
Anderson, Grover Cleveland   Oct 21 1888   Apr 18 1963
  WW-I s/o Ellen McNair & C. Q. 2nd Lt 167 Inf 42 Div
  b Wrens, Ga Began practice of law in W-Boro about
  1918. Judge of the Superior Court, Augusta Circuit,
  1946-1963.
Anderson, Harvey Lee   May 4 1889   Nov 9 1968
  s/o Augusta Anne Ray & Thomas Francis
Anderson, Lawson W. WW-II   Apr 17 1912   Mar 27 1972
  s/o Mary Wilburn & Harvey L. Cpl US Marine Corps
Anderson, Lena Houston   1888   L
  w/o 1st H.C. Daniel 2nd G.C. Anderson d/o Savannah
  Heath & Jos. W.
Anderson, Marion Wilburn   Aug 19 1942   Oct 26 1944
  s/o Marian Poston & Lawson W.
Anderson, Mary Wilburn Cramer   Dec 22 1888   Sep 24 1917
  1st w/o Harvey Lee
Anderson, Rev. W.M.   Aug 17 1867   Aug 23 1923
  b Rock Castle Co Ky Pastor 1st Baptist Church
  (W-Boro) 1922-1923
Andrews, Alda Ouzts   Mar 11 1894   Apr 8 1959
  w/o J.C. d/o Milbria & Albert P.
Andrews, Joseph C.   May 14 1879   Nov 11 1962
Applewhite, Emmie Cates   Mar 4 1879   Dec 19 1951
  w/o John O. d/o Margaret McKenzie & Wm. Jos.
Applewhite, John O.   Feb 16 1866   Apr 7 1926
  s/o Sarah Owen & John N.
Applewhite, William Owen   Mar 7 1908   Apr 30 1930
  s/o Emmie C. & John O.
Armstrong, Patsy Quinney   Apr 3 1887   Nov 26 1964
  w/o Dr. Klatte d/o Alice Gray & Thomas
Arnette, James Arthur, Jr.   only   date   Sep 13 1972
  (infant)
Arnold, Cyril S.   1880   1939
  s/o Sarah Bobo & Benjamin
Arnold, Margaret Boyle   1882   _ 1964
  w/o Cyril S. d/o Mary Mulligan & Wm.
Bailey, Otis M. WW-I   Dec 12 1891   Jul 10 1955
  h/o Thelma Rhodes s/o Georgia C. & Jack
  Cpl 572 Casual Co
Bailey, Virginia (infant)   only   date   Jan 9 1945
  d/o Thelma Rhodes & Otis M.
Baldwin, Nell Hillhouse   Jne 23 1906   Apr 20 1966
  w/o John Charles d/o Nell Thomas & Wm. C.
Banks, Billy West WW-II   Jul 9 1928   Apr 5 1956
  h/o Dean Martin s/o Anabell & Lansdell B.
  Sgt US Army Korea
Banks, Gilbert T.   1855   1925
  h/o Dora Gresham See Cem #146
Banks, Henry W.   age 73 y   nd
Banks, James Louie Viet W   Nov 15 1944   Aug 5 1972
  h/o Sylvia McFeely s/o Anabell & L.B. Ga Adj3 USN
Banks, Lansdell B.   Apr 7 1900   Jan 3 1965
  h/o Anabell West

Bargeron, Edgar   May 20 1876 Feb 12 1947
  h/o Ada Newsome s/o Martha Hurst & John T.
Bargeron, Dr. Everett A. MD   Jan 2 1906 Aug 27 1961
  1st h/o Virginia Phelps s/o Ada Newsome & Edgar
Bargeron, Fairbelle Houston   Dec 29 1883 Jan 5 1968
  w/o Robert H. d/o Savannah Heath & Jos. W.
Bargeron, Henry Grady   Jne 12 1891 Nov 14 1956
  s/o Martha Hurst & John T.
Bargeron, Leila   1879   19__
  w/o W. Bass
Bargeron, Pearl Odom   Oct 8 1894   L
  w/o Henry Grady d/o Lillie J. Heath & J.F.
Bargeron, Robert Herbert   Jan 27 1870 Aug 13 1951
  s/o Mary Ellison & Ezekiel
Bargeron, W. Bass   1875   1944
Bargeron, W. Bass, Jr.   1910   1914
  s/o Leila & W.B.
Barnes, Bessie Houston   Jne 30 1892   L
  w/o Horace D. d/o Savannah Heath & Jos. W.
Barnes, Horace Bruce   Aug 4 1912 Dec 25 1960
  s/o Bessie Houston & Horace D.
Barnes, Horace D.   Apr 15 1885 Nov 4 1953
  h/o Bessie Houston s/o Dona Clayton & Buren B.
Bartlett, Wardner P.   Aug 19 1888 Jul 3 1957
  b Croden, N.H. s/o Mary Powers & Geo. Wardner
Bateman, Albert P. Sp-Am W   nd   nd
  Co B 2 Ga Inf
Bateman, Maggie Stoy   Feb 25 1876 Oct 30 1936
  w/o R.F.
Bateman, R.F.   Aug 15 1863 Mar 17 1914
Bates, Annie Bell   Dec 6 1882 Sep 10 1966
  w/o Sidney B. d/o Emma Chandler & Simeon
Bates, Sidney Berry   Jan 16 1875 May 20 1952
  s/o Martha Herrington & John F.
Baxley, Hughie Eugene   Sep 14 1935 Mar 15 1944
  s/o Lillie Bell O. & James Jasper
Baxley, James Jasper   1900   L
Baxley, Lillie Bell O.   1903   L
  w/o James Jasper
Bell, Ada Blount   Jul 9 1870 Dec 16 1939
  w/o Ransom A. d/o Georgia Cates & Wm. Augustus
Bell, Emma Chandler   Sep 17 1860 Jan 14 1947
  w/o Simeon, Sr. d/o Jane L. Darlington & Wm.
Bell, Georgia Cates   Aug 5 1900 Sep 29 1951
  d/o Ada Blount & Ransom A.
Bell, Joseph W.H.   1832   1908
Bell, Mamie Corker   Jan 23 1886 May 26 1963
  w/o Simeon, Jr. d/o Melrose Attaway & Palmer L.
Bell, Pearl Claxton   nd   L
  w/o Rufus E. d/o Georgia Bailey & Robert
Bell, Ransom Archibald   Oct 22 1866 Oct 22 1922
  s/o Sarah Lewis & R.A.
Bell, Rufus Ernest   Jne 4 1892 Jul 25 1930
  s/o Lula Agnes Edenfield & Bernie Ernest

Bell, Simeon   May 29 1853 May 9 1916
    s/o Eliz. Herrington & Simeon Sketch in Cyc of
    Georgia, I, 161-162 (ed).
Bell, Simeon, Jr.   Jne 17 1885 May 11 1946
    s/o Emma Chandler & Simeon
Belt, Susan Whitehead   Sep 21 1862 Mar 30 1944
    w/o Dr. Lloyd Jones d/o Margaret Harper & John P.C.
Bentley, Patterson M.   CSA   nd   nd
    Ga Co D Inf 27 EN
Black, Cecil Carter   Oct 8 1901 Nov 15 1901
    s/o L.A. & S.M.
Black, Mrs. Sarah May   Feb 26 1876 Oct 9 1901
    w/o L.A. Black d/o Edw. A. & Sarah A. Carter
    Obit. T.C. Oct 12, 1901
Blackman, Trottie WW-II   only   date Mar 3 1939
    Ga Pvt 148 Inf 37 Div Note: Names of the others in
    the section are spelled "mon". Two other adult-sized
    slabs unmarked (ed).
Blackmon, Earnest   1900   1949
Blackmon, Miss Georgia   Jul 8 1896 Mar 1 1967
Blackmon, Simmie   age 64 y   Dec 8 1967
Blackwell, W.T.   Sep 11 1865 Apr 2 1901
Blount, Annie Lorine Smith   Nov 26 1870 Dec 23 1953
    w/o Wm. Thos.
Blount, Asa Holt   Oct 5 1860 Dec 25 1935
    s/o Louise Dillard & Robert Broadnax
Blount, Asa Holt, Jr.   Aug 7 1896 Mar 20 1939
    s/o Harriet Wood & Asa H. md 1st Daisy Netherland
    2nd Lucile Meyers
Blount, Avra Martin   Nov 25 1890 Mar 28 1973
    2nd w/o Robt. B., Jr. d/o Mary Tomlin & Alex.
Blount, Bertha Odom   nd   nd
    w/o F. Hamilton (Hamp) d/o Nancy V. & Sylvester
Blount, Bessie Redd   Nov 18 1870   nd
    w/o Frank A. d/o Caroline Missouri Elliott &
    Wm. Mack
Blount, Carl A.   Jne 19 1898 May 13 1968
    h/o Ethel McMurrain s/o Bessie Redd & Frank A.
Blount, Chesley Alpheus   Sep 28 1901 Jne 22 1902
    s/o Maude C. Youngblood & David Alpheus
Blount, Edward Carter   Sep 7 1852 Aug 15 1922
    h/o Lucy Jordan. See Blount, John Sturges in W-Boro
    Confed. Mem. cem. (ed).
Blount, Edward Hosea   Nov 1 1874 Sep 10 1931
    h/o Nina Thompson s/o Georgia Cates & Wm. Augustus
Blount, Edwin Fitzgerald CSA   Jan 7 1838 Oct 4 1932
    h/o Margaret Allen s/o Axalina Clark & Stephen W.
Blount, Eleanor Palmer   Nov 9 1888 Feb 18 1958
    w/o Henry W. d/o Anna Rheney & J. Price
Blount, Ethel Johnston   Nov   1877 Oct   1911
    1st w/o Robt. B., Jr. d/o Sallie A. & Geo. W.
Blount, F. Hamilton (Hamp)   Dec 11 1877 Jan 27 1934
    s/o Georgia C. & Wm. Augustus
Blount, Frank A.   Dec 22 1868 Jan 8 1925
    s/o Louisa Dillard & Robert Broadnax

Blount, Frank Lamar   Apr 3 1897   Jul 16 1897
  s/o Bessie Redd & Frank A.
Blount, George Alpheus   1901   1935
  s/o Ethel Johnston & Robt. B., Jr. Pvt Ga 82 Aero 20
Blount, Georgia Cates   Apr 24 1847   Apr 2 1910
  w/o Wm. Augustus d/o Susan Douglas Addison & Hosea B.
Blount, Harriet Wood   Jan 25 1861   Dec 22 1939
  w/o A.H. d/o Harriet Crawford & Jno. Henry
Blount, Henry Wood   Nov 18 1887   Oct 27 1959
  s/o Harriet W. & Asa H.
Blount, Hugh M.   Jan 16 1881   Feb 9 1946
  h/o Emma Smith s/o Georgia C. & Wm. Augustus
  no children
Blount, Infant   only   date   Jan 27 1889
  of Maude C. Youngblood & David Alpheus
Blount, Infant   nd   nd
  s/o Bertha Odom & F.H. (Hamp)
Blount, Infant   only   date   Feb 4 1914
  d/o Frances Stallings & John Allen
Blount, Infant   only   date   Jan 23 1916
  d/o Frances Stallings & John Allen
Blount, James Herbert   Aug 9 1857   Dec 6 1918
  s/o Abigail (Abbie) Attaway & Thos. H.
Blount, Jennie Blount   Dec 17 1869   Mar 10 1905
  w/o John Allen d/o David Chesley
Blount, John Allen   Nov 20 1866   Apr 1 1942
  s/o Margaret Allen & Edwin Fitzgerald
Blount, Josephine Bell   Oct 19 1859   May 30 1943
  w/o James Herbert d/o Sarah Lewis & Joe
Blount, Leonidas D.   Jul 24 1878   Jne 17 1933
Blount, Lewis Donald   Jan 27 1900   Apr 22 1972
  s/o Josephine Bell & Jas. H.
Blount, Lucile Meyers   age 69 y   Dec 13 1973
  w/o Asa H., Jr.
Blount, Lucy Jordan   Feb 5 1855   Jan 25 1948
  w/o Edward Carter d/o Mr. & Mrs. F.D.
Blount, Lucy Tarver   Jan 29 1885   Jul 23 1956
  w/o Reginald
Blount, Mary Lou Williams   Jul 6 1896   Jne 19 1973
  w/o Perry, Sr. d/o Rev. & Mrs. Wm. J.
Blount, Mildred Grace   Oct 1 1915   Oct 18 1915
  d/o Nina Thompson & E. Hosea
Blount, Palmer Smith (infant)   only   date   Nov 23 1918
  s/o Eleanor Palmer & Henry W.
Blount, Perry, Sr.   Jul 2 1887   Dec 24 1957
  s/o Mr. & Mrs. Joe Note: There is no known
  connection between this family and other Blounts
  in Burke Co (ed).
Blount, Reginald M. WW-I   Dec 27 1881   Feb 16 1956
  s/o Georgia Mims & John Sturges Capt Co A 34 Inf
Blount, Robert Ashton   1904   1938
  s/o Ethel J. & Robert Broadnax, Jr.
Blount, Robert Broadnax, Jr.   Apr 15 1878   Aug 26 1946
  s/o Louisa Dillard & Robert Broadnax

Blount, Simeon G. Sp-Am W   nd   nd
  Co B 2 Ga Inf s/o Margaret Allen & Edwin Fitzgerald
  Never married   (ed).
Blount, Stephen W.   Feb 14 1873 Sep 25 1957
  s/o Margaret Allen & Edwin Fitzgerald. Never
  married   (ed).
Blount, William Augustus CSA   Oct 25 1841 Apr 29 1904
  s/o Martha Attaway & Edw. Howard
  Co D 2nd Ga Vol Inf ANV Pvt
Blount, William J.   Nov 21 1916 Apr 6 1952
  M/Sgt 59 AF Air Base GE
Blount, William Thomas   Jne 2 1865 Apr 10 1910
  s/o Louisa Dillard & Robert Broadnax
Bonnell, Mary O.   Sep 25 1871 Mar 16 1950
Boyd, John Lee   Oct 27 1866 Feb 13 1934
  s/o Anna Owens & Abe Boyd
Boyd, Martha Virginia Scott   Oct 4 1846 Jan 3 1933
  w/o John
Boyd, Ollie Pace   Dec 5 1870 Jan 22 1962
  w/o John L. d/o Mr. & Mrs. Geo. M.
Boyd, Percy C.   1876   1938
  s/o Mary Gould & J.J. Note: See Botsford Cemetery
  (ed).
Boynton, Larry E.   1945   1945
Bragg, Crawford WW-II   nd   nd
  PFC HQ Co 6 Armored Regt
Braswell, Annie Watts   May 28 1882 May 15 1941
  w/o James R. d/o Mary Frances Joiner
Braswell, Edwin Fulcher   Jul 28 1922 Nov 2 1923
  s/o Lillian Fulcher & Albert Monroe (who was b
  Elberton, Ga. s/o Emma Hyslop and Barton Braswell)
  (ed).
Braswell, James R.   Feb 14 1886 Feb 11 1968
  s/o Anna Jane McNeely & James Lee
Braswell, Johnnie B.   Oct 13 1906 Jan 21 1974
  s/o Annie Watts & James R. Never married.
Braswell, Lucille Sikes   Dec 14 1914   L
  w/o Robt. Harold d/o Mary Ellen Dismake & John
  Thomas Sikes
Braswell, Robert Harold   Jan 22 1912   L
  s/o Annie Watts & James R.
Brinson, Annabelle Sibley   Sep 17 1881 Jan 27 1948
  w/o James H. d/o Geo. R. & Emma T.
Brinson, Annie Hearne   Jan 14 1850 May 9 1926
  w/o Edward L. No issue.
Brinson, Edward Loraine   Apr 10 1854 Jul 17 1922
  With Atty R.O. Lovett, published The Herald &
  Expositor in Waynesboro. Last issue was Vol. 7,
  No. 39, June 18, 1884. Judge of the Superior Court,
  Augusta Circuit, 1899-1903 (ed).
Brinson, Frank L., Sr.   Mar 28 1853 Dec 31 1904
  s/o Mary Ann Wallace & James F&AM
Brinson, Frank Lafayette, Jr.   Oct 1 1887   L
  s/o Martha E. & F.L., Sr.

252

Brinson, Franklin L., III   Nov 10 1911 Nov 29 1953
  s/o Sarah McElmurray & Frank L., Jr.
Brinson, Harry Wingfield   Sep 1 1889 Dec 21 1889
  s/o M.E. & F.I..
Brinson, Hattie Perkins   Feb 14 1889 Jul 9 1963
  w/o John Wright d/o Lula Cross & Wm. Penn
Brinson, James H.   Nov 16 1882 Nov 16 1956
  s/o M.E. & F.L., Sr.
Brinson, John Wright   Sep 19 1888 Jan 28 1958
Brinson, Martha E.   Oct 10 1855 Dec 8 1932
  w/o Frank L., Sr. d/o Nancy Pollock & Robert
  Herrington
Brinson, Robert   Jne 8 1893 Sep 19 1895
  s/o M.E. & F.L.
Brinson, Sarah McElmurray   Dec 19 1887 May 17 1971
  w/o Frank L., Jr. d/o Mary Chandler & Thos. J.
Brown, Lois Sibley Brinson   Jne 24 1911 Dec 11 1939
  w/o James P. d/o Annabelle S. & Jas. H.
Brown, Neva Cox   Feb 17 1906 Sep 21 1932
  w/o Malcolm d/o Beulah Burch & J. Floyd
Broxton, Jasper A.   Oct 28 1889 May 25 1951
Broxton, Mary Julia Johnson   Sep 1 1892   L
  w/o Jasper A. d/o Alice Freeman & Jesse Eugene
Broxton, Maude D.   1879   1945
  w/o T.R.
Broxton, T. Regile   1879   1938
Bull, Thomas WW-I   Sep 20 1891 Jan 22 1960
  Pvt USA
Burch, Kim Louise   Jne 30 1956 Nov 4 1961
  d/o Louise Pittard & Frank
Burley, Henry H. WW-I   1893   1973
  s/o Susie Perry & J.B. Pvt 19 Co 5th Regt
  157 Depot Brigade
Burley, Mae Miller   1886   1969
  w/o 1st P.C. Boyd 2nd H.H. Burley
Burney, Frank S.   Mar 9 1877 May 1 1958
  s/o Rev. & Mrs. Samuel A.
Burney, Sarah Joe Hurst   May 11 1882 Aug 21 1963
  w/o Frank S. d/o Martha C. & C.W.
Burton, Annie E.   Sep 25 1873 Jul 1 1957
  d/o Sarah J. Shewmake & Thos. J.
Burton, Clarence C.   May 10 1902 Feb 15 1963
Burton, Fannie Herrington   1873   1949
  w/o J. Virgil d/o Frances L. & Berry
Burton, Infant   only date Jan 23 1904
Burton, J. Virgil WOW   1863   1947
  s/o Sarah J. Shewmake & Thos. J.
Burton, Sarah J. Shewmake   Apr 15 1839 Jne 19 1918
  w/o Thos. J. d/o Caroline Hankinson of S. Car. &
  Joseph Allen
Burton, Thomas J. CSA   Apr 18 1833 Dec 5 1883
  s/o Susan Jones & Charles A. See Fothergill, op.
  cit., 149. Co A 3rd Regt Ga Vol Inf ANV F&AM

Busbee, James M.   Jul 20 1869   Dec 5 1925
  s/o Martha Ann Williams & Pleasant
Butler, Simeon Bell WW-II   Oct 2 1925   Apr 2 1972
  S 2 USN
Butler, Vera L. Anderson   Aug 20 1901   Nov 10 1952
  w/o Chas. W.
Buxton, Elizabeth Rouse   Jan 18 1881   Oct 31 1928
  w/o Thos. F. d/o Emmie & John B.
Buxton, Thomas Fowell   Sep 16 1879   Feb 26 1961
  s/o Josephine Dixon & Samuel
Buxton, Thomas Fowell, Jr.   Mar 24 1908   Apr 29 1910
  s/o Elizabeth R. & T.F.
Byne, Infant   only   date   Jne 15 1913
  s/o J.M. & M.W.
Byne, James Miller, Sr. MD   Mar 17 1879   May 3 1961
  s/o Margaret Murphree & John Steptoe
Byne, John Heggie   Jne 15 1913   Sep 10 1915
  s/o Mary W.H. & J.M., Sr.
Byne, Mary W. Heggie   Sep 22 1882   Jne 16 1959
  w/o J.M., Sr. d/o Mary Tibiatha Smith & Wm.
Callaway, Lessie Hurst   Sep 24 1877   Oct 6 1949
  w/o W.R. md Nov 12 1901 d/o Martha Chandler &
  Chas. W.
Callaway, William Robert   Sep 14 1870   Dec 26 1915
  s/o Lucy Howard & Rev. Brantley M. of Wilkes Co.,
  Ga. Atty-at-law.
Carrington, Francis Gresham   Jul 28 1881   Sep 26 1941
  w/o 1st Louis Powell 2nd Randolph C.
  d/o Leora Scales & Oscar Gresham
Carswell, Arabella Walker   Mar 3 1868   Nov 8 1931
  w/o Porter W. md Apr 3, 1895 d/o Lucy Pearson &
  Clarence V. b Augusta, Ga. Obit. T.C. Nov 13, 1931
Carswell, Clarence Valentine   Jul 3 1897   May 14 1899
  s/o Arabella & P.W.
Carswell, James Kilpatrick   Feb 3 1861   Aug 10 1942
  s/o Harriet K. & Matthew J.
Carswell, Lillian Cates   Feb 15 1863   Aug 2 1942
  w/o Jas. K. d/o Susan Douglas Addison & Hosea B.
Carswell, Mary L.   1896   1896
  d/o Arabella W. & P.W.
Carswell, Porter Wilkins   Jan 7 1867   Sep 5 1905
  s/o Linda Royal & John Devine
Carswell, Wallis Cates   Dec 19 1891   Feb 25 1972
  h/o Mary Lee Davis s/o Lillian C. & J.K.
Carter, Alice Skinner   age 72 y   Dec 6 1973
  w/o Ben
Carter, Celestine Irving   1898   1964
  w/o R.L.
Carter, Edward Alexander CSA   1841   1906
  Co D 2nd Ga Vol Inf ARV s/o Joanna Shewmake &
  Isaiah, II. md Sarah Augusta Lawson (ed).
Carter, Jacob Lee   May 16 1888   Nov 23 1971
  s/o Agnes McMillan & Jacob Franklin
Carter, Mose J.   Sep 11 1923   Sep 15 1937
  s/o Sarah Johnson & Jacob Lee

Carter, Ocie Leen Cullen   Nov 3 1886 Nov 11 1960
  w/o R. Mc.
Carter, Richard McMillan   Sep 30 1883 Feb 15 1937
  s/o Agnes McMillan & Jacob Franklin
Carter, Robert Lawson Sp-Am W   1878   1940
  Co C 2nd Ga Inf s/o Sarah Augusta Lawson & Edward
  Alexander Carter. I   md Celeste Irwin.
Carter, Sarah Augusta Lawson   Aug 20 1846 Feb 17 1905
  w/o Edw. Alexander, I d/o Ella L.V. Brown & Robt.
  R.R. Lawson
Carter, Sarah Johnson   May 13 1894   L
  w/o J.L.
Cates, Augustus B.   Dec 31 1860 Sep 13 1899
  s/o Susan Douglas Addison & Hosea B.   F&AM
Cates, Eva Blount   1869   1942
  w/o J.D. d/o Rosa C. White & Stephen Wm., II
Cates, Francis   Jul 14 1913 Jul 21 1913
  s/o Susan Douglas & F.M., Jr.
Cates, Francis Marion, Sr.   Mar 25 1854 Jan 21 1931
  s/o Mary Ann Rebecca Knight & Robt. H.
Cates, Francis Marion, Jr.   Sep 10 1890 Jul 27 1959
  s/o Julia Boyd & F.M., Sr.
Cates, John D., Jr.   Feb 17 1905 Jan 12 1966
Cates, John Douglas   1864   1944
  s/o Susan D.A. & Hosea B.
Cates, John Douglas, Jr.   1899   1900
Cates, Juanita Moore   Mar 27 1924 Mar 31 1968
  w/o James d/o Susie Whitaker & Milton M.
Cates, Julia Boyd   May 29 1867 Nov 22 1929
  w/o Francis M., Sr. d/o Martha Virginia Scott & John
Cates, Lena Agerton   1891   L
  w/o Thomas Eddie   d/o Sarah M. Sikes & E.T.
Cates, Margaret MacKenzie   Jne 10 1853 Oct 6 1930
  w/o Wm. Joseph d/o Eliz. Attaway & Alexander
Cates, Mary Ann Rebecca   Dec 31 1830 Feb 27 1911
  w/o Robert H. /Knight Note: Mrs. Cates was buried
  beside her husband in the Rocky Creek Bap. cem (#122).
  When part of the cem. was used for a hwy, her marker
  was removed to the family section in Magnolia. Her
  name is listed in both cemeteries (ed).
Cates, Mary Rogers   Oct 8 1894 Mar 14 1896
  d/o Julia B. & F.M., Sr.
Cates, Paul Davis   Jan 3 1897 Oct 15 1938
  h/o Frances McElmurray s/o Julia B. & F.M., Sr.
Cates, Paul Davis, Jr.   Jne 2 1920 Jul 22 1925
  s/o Frances McE. & Paul
Cates, Robert Boyd WW-I   Sep 17 1887 Jne 22 1937
  s/o Julia B. & F.M., Sr. 2nd Lt Adj Gen 82 Div
  Never married.
Cates, Susan Burton   Apr 18 1870 Jul 19 1955
  w/o Augustus B. d/o Sarah J. Shewmake & Thos. J.
  See Fothergill, op. cit., 149.
Cates, Thomas Eddie   1887   1963
  s/o Mattie Blount & Jas. S.

Cates, William Joseph   Feb 12 1850   Jne 26 1903
    s/o Susan D.A. & Hosea Berrien
Chance, Bobby   Jul 23 1932   Jan 31 1938
    s/o R.W. & T.I.
Chance, Enon Elton   Jul 10 1867   Feb 10 1946
    s/o Mary Ann Lovett & Reuben C. Shriner Sketch in
    Cyc of Georgia, I, 340-341.
Chance, Franklin W. Kor W   Jne 29 1929   Mar 16 1972
    AB3 US Navy
Chance, H. Rackley   1890   1956
Chance, Lessie H.   1892   1971
Chance, Mamie Rowland   Jan 21 1865   Sep 30 1938
    w/o 1st W.T. Rogers 2nd E. E. Chance
    d/o Martha Jane Wooding & Robt. Allen
Chance, Marion Moore   Jul 13 1881   Apr 30 1901
Chance, Mary Lovett   Dec 26 1843   Sep 27 1908
    w/o Reuben C. d/o Ann Herrington & Anthony Buck
Chance, Pearl Rowland   Dec 23 1873   Apr 14 1896
    1st w/o E.E. d/o Martha Jane Wooding & Robt. Allen
    See Palmer, Martha Jane in W-Boro Confed. Mem. Cem.
    (ed).
Chance, Reuben Carpenter CSA   Sep 2 1835   Apr 16 1920
    s/o Sallie Carpenter & Henry
Chance, Reuben Carpenter, II   Aug 27 1907   Oct 14 1965
    s/o May Hopper & Henry Carpenter
Chance, Thomas L.   Nov 19 1875   Sep 28 1901
    s/o Mary L. & R.C.
Chance, Thompson Kennedy, Jr.   Jan 25 1931   Aug 7 1951
    s/o Helen Rowland & Thompson
Chance, Tilda T.   1907   1953
Chance, Walter O. WW-I   May 20 1892   Dec 13 1954
    Cpl USA
Chance, Warren T.   1875   1949
Chance, Winnie V.   1889   1968
    w/o Warren T.
Chandler, Elizabeth Cates   Apr 15 1875   Mar 6 1931
    w/o Walter Chandler
Chandler, Frank C.   Dec 19 1900   May 26 1926
    s/o Elizabeth Cates & Walter
Chandler, Infant   only date   Jan 1 1937
    of Mary M. & Louie L.
Chattman, Bert C., Jr.   1927   1928
Claxton, Charles W. WW-I   nd   Oct 21 1934
    Pvt ICL Gen Hosp 39
Claxton, Georgia Bailey   1874   1944
    w/o Robert
Claxton, John A. WW-I   Jul 5 1895   May 11 1953
    Pvt Evacuation Hosp 24
Cochran, Hubert H. WW-II   Jan 19 1919   May 16 1960
    Cpl Btry A 133 AAA Bn CAC s/o Lillie Taylor & Jesse
Cochran, Jesse L.   1887   1956
    s/o Ella Ellison & Charlie B.
Cochran, Lillie Taylor   1893   1962
    w/o Jesse L. d/o Georgia Lowe & Jos. L.

Cochran, Thomas Mosley   age 55 y   Sep   1970
  s/o Lillie Taylor & Jesse L.
Coleman, Charles H. WW-II   Nov 9 1911 Sep 4 1956
h/o Sadie Fulcher s/o Nancy McMillan & F. Woodrow
  Lt USN
Colson, John Hammond   May 19 1856 Aug 26 1903
Colson, Kate Roberts Hall   Dec 27 1871 Apr 2 1944
  w/o J.H. d/o Margaret E. & P.B.
Colson, Warren Hammond   Sep 23 1896 Oct 26 1905
  s/o Kate H. & J.H.
Cooley, Dr. Joseph Dillard   Nov 30 1887 Jan 12 1974
  h/o Alice Fulcher s/o Martha Dean & Jos. D.
Cooper, G. Harold   Jul 23 1893 Sep 12 1973
Cooper, Infant   only   date   1943
  d/o Thomas & Marie
Cooper, John C.   Oct 25 1860 Jan 20 1930
Cooper, Marie B.   1916   1943
  1st w/o Thomas
Cooper, Mary Wicker   Dec 21 1870 Jan 2 1953
  w/o John C.
Copeland, Maude D.   Oct 29 1900   L
  w/o Newton
Copeland, Newton WW-I   Mar 21 1890 Mar 25 1962
  Pvt USA
Corker, Melrose Attaway   Sep 15 1862 Dec 29 1935
  w/o Palmer L., Sr. md 1880 d/o Mary V. Parrish &
  John Attaway
Corker, P.L., Jr. WW-I   Aug 11 1888 Apr 30 1944
  s/o Melrose A. & P.L., Sr. Co B 118 FA 31 Div
Corker, Palmer L., Sr.   Aug 7 1860 Feb 11 1920
  s/o Margaret M. Palmer & Stephen A.
  Sketch in Cyc of Georgia, I, 500-01.
Corker, Stephen A.   Apr 11 1884 Feb 16 1940
  s/o Melrose A. & P.I., Sr.
Cowart, Levi   age 5 y   Jul 19 1919
Cox, Annie Garlick   Jan 16 1885 Dec 9 1942
  w/o Marvin H. d/o Julia Blount & Edgar S.
Cox, Beulah Burch   1872   1940
  w/o J. Floyd d/o Alfred E. CSA
Cox, Carol   Feb 18 1913 Dec 27 1970
  d/o Annie Garlick & Marvin H. Atty-at-law
Cox, George Fulcher   1869   1941
  s/o Alona F. & P. Duncan
Cox, Infant   only   date Oct 8 1907
  of Beulah & Floyd
Cox, J. Floyd   1870   1949
  s/o Louisa Wimberly & H.H.
Cox, Jackson Elliott Viet W   Sep 15 1941 Mar 25 1967
  s/o Emily E. & Sidney C. 2nd Lt US Marine Corps
  killed in action Vietnam Bronze Star with combat
  medal "V" Navy commendation Purple Heart
Cox, Louisa Wimberly   1849   1928
  w/o Harmon H. d/o Rachel McNorrill & Zack
Cox, Marion Dent   Jan 5 1872 Jul 22 1952
  w/o Sidney C. d/o Maria Harper & Dr. John M.

Cox, Marvin Hill   May 26 1882   Jul 28 1918
  s/o Alona Fulcher & P. Duncan
Cox, Mary Toombs Jones   1886   1948
  w/o Geo. F. d/o Evalina Toombs & John J.
Cox, Ruby Mobley   Apr 29 1886   Dec 18 1952
  w/o Dr. Cicero
Cox, Sidney Clarence   Oct 20 1875   Oct 9 1946
  s/o Louisa W. & Harmon H.
Cox, William Turner WW-I   Aug 26 1891   Mar 26 1922
  s/o Beulah B. & J. Floyd
  Reg Sgt Maj Batt C 1st Reg 118th Field Arty
Crangle, George Martin   Apr 7 1891   Dec 16 1965
Crangle, Nina Horton   May 23 1894   Aug 13 1969
  w/o Geo. Martin
Crapnell, Mattie Stewart   1908   1964
Cullen, David H.   Mar 26 1866   Mar 18 1941
Cullen, Fred B.   Dec 22 1903   Feb 5 1959
  s/o Mary Merritt & David
Cullen, James Asa   Mar 1 1885   Mar 4 1951
  s/o Comfort Merritt & Wyatt
Cullen, Mary M.   Feb 28 1867   Sep 16 1942
  w/o D.H.
Cullen, Miller Byne   Dec 20 1905   Sep 25 1968
Cullen, Rosa Lee Quick   Oct 3 1914   L
  w/o M.B. d/o Essie May Bell & Willie Fulton
Cunningham, John   age 45 y   Mar 2 1917
Currington, Charles Cleveland   1896   1943
Daniel, Carrie McNorrill   Nov 28 1879   Jan 21 1972
Daniel, Charles Roswell, Jr.   Apr 21 1907   Jan 31 1908
  s/o Hattie L.B. & C.R.
Daniel, Floyd E.   Sep 9 1879   Nov 6 1928
  s/o Carrie McNorrill & Warren
Daniel, Henry C.   1875   1929
  s/o Annie Blanton & Charles P.
Daniel, J.C. (Moody)   1914   1968
  s/o Lucile Carter & James C.
Daniel, James Carswell, Sr.   Jul 1 1891   Sep 4 1940
Daniel, Myra C.   1878   1949
  w/o W.M.
Daniel, "Our Baby,"   only   date Jne 30 1908
  s/o Hattie L. Blount & C.R.
Daniel, W.M.   1874   1936
Davis, Barbara Ann   Jan 30 1939   Dec 12 1940
  d/o J.C. & Margaret
Davis, Gertrude H.   1902   19__
  w/o Robt. E.
Davis, Henry Jefferson   Jne 2 1861   Sep 26 1941
  s/o Eliza J. Gaddy & Henry H.
Davis, Ibrey Smith   Jan 29 1918   Oct 21 1945
  w/o L.F. d/o Belle Hyatt & Thos. Walter
Davis, John H.   1882   1941
Davis, Katie Hayes   May 29 1892   Feb 22 1970
  w/o L. Frank d/o Lydia Ansley & Elias Grady Hayes
Davis, L. Frank, Sr.   Mar 31 1896   Jan 19 1969
  s/o Eliza Jane Hester & Rev. Lee Carswell

258

Davis, Leora Scales Gresham   Dec 10 1856   Dec 23 1934
  w/o 1st Oscar Gresham   2nd H. J. Davis
  d/o Francis Rebecca Martin & Robert Watt Scales
Davis, Malverda A.   1881   1961
  w/o J.H.
Davis, Marie Wilkins   Jne 10 1878   Nov 1 1900
  w/o Wm. H. d/o Fannie Warren & Joseph H.
Davis, Robert E.   1878   1945
Davis, Robert Henry   Dec 16 1899   May 7 1900
  s/o H. Jeff & Leora S.
Davis, Thomas E. WW-I   Sep 11 1891   Mar 28 1951
  Pvt 157 Depot Brigade
Davis, Judge Wm. Hudson   Feb 2 1865   Feb 4 1928
  s/o Sarah A. Kilpatrick & Rev. Wm. Hudson Atty-at-
  law; Judge of City Court; President Board of Trustees
  Mercer Univ.; trustee of Georgia State College for
  Women; President of the First National Bank of W-Boro.
  Obit. T.C. Feb 11, 1928; editorial Feb 25, 1928.
Davis, Little Will   Oct 25 1900   nd
  s/o Marie Wilkins & Wm. H.
Day, Evelyn Jackson   Jul 21 1884   Nov 18 1969
Day, Lee V. WW-II   Feb 1 1909   Jan 31 1965
  Ga CM 3 USNR
Deason, Neal E.   Mar 17 1887   Feb 5 1928
  h/o Sallie K. Tinley (McCathern)
  s/o Laura Brauda & Wm. Hiram
Deck, William L., Jr. WW-II   Jan 31 1920   Mar 31 1953
  s/o Kathleen & W.L.   DFC 2OLC AM 2OLC-PH
Deck, William L., Sr.   Dec 24 1876   Dec 3 1942
  h/o Kathleen Merk
DeLaigle, Felix   Dec 28 1949   Jan 1 1950
  s/o Herman & Sally Clark
DeLaigle, Herman WW-II   Feb 9 1921   Apr 7 1957
  S/Sgt USA s/o Jennie Quick & Nick L.
DeLaigle, Nick L. WW-I   Sep 19 1896   Jul 6 1973
  h/o Jennie Quick s/o Nicklous L. & Annie Godbee
  Pvt USA
DeLaigle, Roy WW-II   May 31 1926   Jan 26 1969
  Cpl USA s/o Jennie Quick & Nick L.
DeLaigle, Wyatt Cullen   Aug 14 1951   Aug 17 1951
  s/o Roy & Frances Cullen
DeLoach, Louise Porter   Apr 26 1907   Mar 12 1970
  w/o Clarence W. d/o Annie & L.J.
Dent, Caroline Elizabeth   Aug 6 1882   Jul 27 1947
  d/o Maria Harper & Dr. John M.
Dent, Charles Andrew   Dec 31 1872   Oct 16 1949
  s/o Maria Harper & Dr. John M.
Dent, Daisy Dickinson   Dec 16 1881   Sep 3 1922
  w/o Wm. H. d/o Anna Walker & Capt. Wm.H.
Dent, Edwin G.   Dec 28 1861   Mar 19 1935
  s/o Maria Harper & Dr. John M.
Dent, Fanny Dickinson (Boyd)   Sep 23 1869   Dec 14 1949
  w/c Wm. H. d/o Anna Walker & Capt. Wm. H.
Dent, John Marshall   Jne 5 1911   Dec 21 1969
  h/o Novine Holcomb s/o Daisy Dickinson & Wm. Harper

Dent, John Marshall MD CSA   Jul 16 1834 Nov 20 1922
  s/o Sarah McIntosh & Dr. John Co A 12th Ga Bn
  Note: His father, an Augusta physician. was a member
  of the first State Board (1825) to license physicians;
  a trustee of the Medical Academy of Georgia (1828)
  which ultimately became the Medical College of the
  University of Georgia. One year, 1832-33, he filled
  the Professorship of Theory & Practice of Medicine
  (ed).
Dent, Mamie Holleyman   Mar 5 1863 Mar 20 1942
  w/o Edwin G. d/o Mollie & Thomas
Dent, Maria   Dec 4 1867 Sep 10 1905
  d/o Maria Harper & Dr. John M.
Dent, Maria Harper   Jul 22 1836 Feb 17 1908
  w/o Dr. John M. d/o Mary Ann Cashin & Wm.
Dent, William Harper   Nov 8 1869 Jul 20 1954
  s/o Maria Harper & Dr. John M.
Dickey, Mitchell   nd   nd
Dietrich, Lily Mae Blount   Nov 5 1886 Jne 18 1960.
  w/o Wm. S. d/o Josephine Bell & James H.
Dietrich, William S.   Feb 19 1886   nd
Dinkins, Alva Grady WW-I   Feb 17 1889 Jne 12 1935
  s/o Cornelia Tinley & C.N. USNR
Dinkins, Ellen Rackley   Dec 5 1890 Jne 7 1971
  w/o A. Grady d/o Willie C. & Jno. F.
Dinkins, John Rackley WW-II   Nov 6 1919 Dec 30 1956
  h/o Elizabeth Stowers s/o ElJen & A.G. JV6 Mo MM 1
  USN Shriner
Dufft, August Frederick   Dec 18 1863 Mar 3 1955
Dufft, Sara Rumble   Oct 10 1870 May 31 1945
  w/o A.F.
Durden, Dade   Sep 22 1888 Nov 8 1937
  h/o Emma J. Davis s/o Mary Rountree & George Walter
Durham, Clarence   1883   1951
Durham, Maggie Little   1884   1949
  w/o Clarence
Dye, Paul Byron   Apr 14 1905 Apr 19 1969
  h/o Alden Rowland s/o Allie May Henderson & James Lee
Edenfield, Floyd D.   Jne 27 1910 May 17 1967
  h/o Billie Sapp s/o Iona Hayes & Rufus L.
Edenfield, Iona Hayes   Dec 23 1882 Nov 29 1950
  w/o Rufus L.
Edenfield, Rufus L.   Apr 14 1889 Feb 16 1948
  s/o Susan M. Morgan & Linton H.
Elliott, Ben F.   Nov 4 1880 Mar 5 1954
Elliott, William C. Kor W   Oct 30 1930 May 31 1957
  Sgt Med Corps
Ellis, Frank W. WW-I   May 27 1894 Nov 12 1930
  s/o Mattie Duke & J.H. Cpl Postal Ex Serv
Ellis, James H.   Nov 13 1863 Nov 30 1903
Ellison, Edward   Aug 7 1875 Oct 26 1938
  s/o Josephine & Robt. J.
Ellison, George E.   May 1 1884 Sep 10 1884
  s/o Josephine & Robt. J.

Ellison, Josephine Herrington   Sep 20 1852   Sep 15 1923
  w/o Robt. J.   d/o Frances L. & Berry
Ellison, Julian WW-I   nd   Dec 6 1936
  s/o Josephine & Robt. J.   Pvt 364 Inf 91 Div
Ellison, Linwood H.   Jan 1 1874   May 30 1883
  s/o Josephine & Robt. J.
Ellison, Otis   Dec 2 1880   Oct 27 1920
  s/o Josephine & Robt. J.
Ellison, Robert J., Sr.   Nov 11 1847   Jul 28 1900
Ellison, Robert Jasper   Nov 8 1885   Nov 7 1960
  h/o Jessie Hillis s/o Josephine & Robt. J.
Ellison, Warren   May 3 1887   Jne 10 1887
  s/o Josephine & Robt. J.
Evans, Annie Wright Clark   Dec 5 1889   Jan 19 1968
  w/o Chas. A. d/o Adella Rheney & Wm. E.
Evans, Arthur Forte   Sep 13 1881   Nov 1 1968
  s/o Sarah Holleyman & Joshua K.
Evans, Elizabeth Macaulay   Oct 4 1890   Mar 4 1953
  w/o Arthur F. d/o Sallie McMaster & David J.
Evans, Infant   Mar 11 1916   same   date
  s/o Elizabeth Macaulay & Arthur F.
Evans, Margaret Kirkman   Sep 14 1895   Nov 26 1964
  w/o Wm. F. /(Miss Maggie) d/o Laura Ann Dickens
  & Marmaduke M.
Evans, William F.   Jan 4 1890   Jne 30 1949
  s/o Sarah Holleyman & Joshua K.
Farrar, Doris Aliene   1920   1922
  d/o Virgil & Ettie B.
Farrar, Ettie Barnes   nd   L
  w/o Virgil P. d/o Mary Dona Clayton & Buren B.
Farrar, Janie Ponder   1869   1934
  w/o Jeff E.
Farrar, Virgil Payne   1888   1921
  s/o Janie Ponder & Jeff E.
Flakes, Arnold   1942   1956
  s/o John & Josie
Flakes, Maria Quick   1905   1973
Flakes, Ray   1941   1942
  s/o James L. & Maria
Ford, Fannie Blount   Mar 30 1854   Nov 29 1925
  w/o Dr. Lewis R. d/o Abbie Attaway & Thos. H.
Ford, Frank G.   Nov 23 1874   May 30 1927
  s/o Fannie Blount & Dr. Lewis R. Never married.
  Shriner
Ford, Dr. Lewis R. CSA   Nov 22 1843   Jne 26 1903
  s/o Dr. Lewis D. Ford of Augusta, Ga., one of early
  professors in the Medical Academy (Institute) which
  developed into the Medical College of the University
  of Georgia (ed).
Foreman, Annie Lee   May 19 1871   Aug 11 1962
  sis/o Maude Stembridge d/o Jane Rountree & Isaac
  Foreman
Foster, Agnes Phillips   Jne 10 1903   Jan 11 1967
  w/o B.L. d/o Nancy & Wiley B. of Tarrytown, Ga.

261

Foster, Herbert J.   May 12 1903   Jul 24 1944
  s/o Jerry Lee Prescott & Samuel E.
Foster, Infant   only   date   1928
  s/o Agnes Phillips & Bertie Lee
Foster, Leo Daniel   1877   1938
  w/o Bill
Foster, Murray Irving   Feb 25 1886   Apr 24 1958
  s/o Jerry Lee Prescott & Samuel E.
Foster, Samuel E.   Jan 17 1850   Apr 12 1923
  h/o Jerry Lee Prescott   s/o Mary Ward & Henry
Foster, Seaborn L., Sr.   age 62 y   Nov 10 1973
  s/o Katie Tomlin & Jim
Foster, Thelma Martin   Jul 22 1913   Sep 8 1944
  1st w/o Seaborn   d/o Annie L. & Norman
Foster, Thomas D.   Nov 24 1900   Jan 6 1959
  s/o Leo Daniel & Bill
Franklin, Frances Reese   May 15 1919   Apr 17 1972
  w/o David Francis   d/o Josie Hatcher & J.H.
Freeman, Beulah J. Robinson   Mar 22 1879   nd
  w/o J.M., Sr.
Freeman, John M., Jr.   Mar 15 1910   Jul 21 1911
  s/o Beulah J. & J.M., Sr.
Freeman, John M., Sr.   WOW   Apr 18 1886   Feb 14 1936
Frey, Augusta   1860   1939
Fryhofer, George William   May 4 1874   Oct 1 1932
  h/o Ruth Green   s/o Louisa DeWyke & Geo. W.
Fulcher, Almeda Pauline   Sep 11 1847   Sep 8 1905
  2nd w/o Valentine
Fulcher, Edwin   Sep 30 1856   Sep 8 1924
  s/o Melvina & Valentine   md 1st Osee Herrington
  2nd Margaret Bell Herrington   Note: See Fulcher
  cemetery #45   (ed).
Fulcher, Elizabeth McElmurray   nd   L
  w/o Heywood E.   d/o Clifford Gray & Wm. Leslie
Fulcher, George Glenn   May 17 1892   Dec 17 1921
  s/o Osee Herrington & Edwin
Fulcher, George Pierce   CSA   1847   1878
  s/o Louisa Wimberly & Vincent W.
Fulcher, Heywood E.   WW-I   Oct 11 1896   Feb 18 1952
  s/o Osee Herrington & Edwin   Calif. Cpl 78 Field
  Arty 6 Div
Fulcher, John Lafayette   Sep 29 1883   Nov 28 1955
  s/o Mozelle Melton & John Bryant
Fulcher, Julian LeRoy   1851   1911
  s/o Louisa Wimberly & Vincent W.
Fulcher, Lamar L.   WW-I   Dec 22 1887   Mar 22 1966
  s/o Osee Herrington & Edwin   Ga Pvt 161 Inf Co
Fulcher, Lou May   1856   1879
  d/o Louisa Wimberly & Vincent W.
Fulcher, Louisa Wimberly   1825   1915
  w/o Vincent Warren   d/o Mary Cox & Wiley
  Note: Louisa & Vincent were the parents of six sons
  and six daughters, all of whom grew to adulthood:
  Simpson R., George P., Vincent M., Julian L.,

William M., M. Ousley, Mary Virginia (McNorrill)
Lou May, T. Alona (Cox), Carrie (Green), Lillian
(Lewis), and Rosa (Simmons) (ed).
Fulcher, Mae Fuller   May 17 1890 Nov 20 1966
  w/o John L. d/o Mattie Parkman & Jacob M.
Fulcher, Margaret   Mar 1 1920 Oct 19 1920
  d/o Margaret B. Herrington & Edwin
Fulcher, Marion Ousley MD   May 20 1870 Jan 16 1935
  Sp-Am W h/o Winifred Winston s/o Louisa Wimberly
  & Vincent W. Medical Corps Cuba & P.I.
Fulcher, Mary S. Moffett   Dec 30 1889   L
  w/o Roger E. d/o Annie Brown & Morton Clement
Fulcher, Osee Herrington   Jul 4 1863 Dec 2 1904
  w/o Edwin d/o Frances L. & Berry
Fulcher, Roger Edwin   Aug 19 1885 Mar 2 1944
  s/o Osee Herrington & Edwin
Fulcher, Sarah Crawford   May 27 1876 Jan 27 1934
  w/o William Marcus /Dent (Sadie) d/o Maria Harper
  & Dr. John M.
Fulcher, Vincent Melville   Sep 12 1853 Nov 3 1925
  s/o Louisa Wimberly & Vincent W.
Fulcher, Vincent Warren   1814   1889
  s/o Mary Colson & John Note: See Fulcher
  cemetery #45 (ed).
Fulcher, William Marcus   Dec 3 1858 Nov 30 1935
  s/o Louisa Wimberly & Vincent W. Clerk of Superior
  Court, 1902-1917. Founder of the People's Savings
  Bank of Waynesboro. Shriner
Gage, Herbert S.   1872   1929
Gage, Nelle Doty   1881   nd
  w/o Herbert S.
Game, Clifford Bunyan   Aug 1 1877 Jul 18 1954
  h/o Lizzie Lou Gray
Garlick, Carroll B.   Jul 10 1882 Jul 13 1925
  h/o Mary Boyd s/o Julia Blount & Edgar S.
Gilman, Anita Story   Nov 4 1899 Oct 15 1965
  w/o Preston N. d/o Ida Gresham & S.G., II
Gilman, Preston Nathaniel   Dec 13 1880 Jul 16 1943
Glisson, Freddie Lee Glisson   1907   1967
  w/o Morris V. d/o Sallie Royal & Jas. Willie
Glisson, James Lester   Apr 9 1911 May 4 1951
  s/o Mary Alice Laricy & George Hinton
Glisson, Mary Alice Laricy   Feb 7 1880 Jne 2 1953
  w/o Geo. H. d/o Mary Ellen Toole & Henry
Glisson, Morris Victor   1903   L
  s/o Mary Alice Laricy & George Henley
Glover, Evelyn Wingard   1908   1959
  w/o John L. d/o Mr. & Mrs. C.W.
Glover, John L.   1903   1957
  s/o Sarah Rowell & Wm. Morgan
Godbee, Brigham R.   Oct 30 1907 Dec 14 1924
  s/o Vannie Brigham & F.W.
Godbee, Florence B.   Jul 27 1888 Aug 19 1913
  w/o W.S.

Godbee, Frank W., Sr.   Jan 9 1883 Mar 24 1959
   h/o Vannie Brigham s/o Bertha & Russell J. For the
   family of Russell J., see Will Bk B, 237
Godbee, Margaret Gresham   Nov 26 1882 May 12 1958
   w/o Simeon A. d/o Annie Lassiter & Job A.
Godbee, Ralph J. WW-II   Jul 2 1916 Aug 26 1954
   s/o Vannie Brigham & F.W. Tec3 531 Ord H V Maint Co
Godbee, Simeon A.   Sep 24 1882 Jne 13 1921
Godbee, Walter S.   Feb 28 1857 Aug 18 1913
Gordon, Bertha F. Routzahn   Oct 22 1875 Oct 24 1899
   w/o Geo. M. d/o Florence B. & L.H.
Gordon, George M.   Dec 29 1875 Aug 25 1935
   s/o Elizabeth Winter & George M.
Gordon, Ronald Byne   Mar 24 1899 Feb 13 1918
   s/o Bertha R. & Geo. M.
Gordon, Wm. Morgan, Jr.   Oct 24 1911 Jne 10 1912
Gray, Charlie A.   1859   1944
   s/o Elizabeth & Simeon A.
Gray, Frank A. WOW   Aug 2 1874 Jne 19 1941
   s/o Elizabeth & Simeon A.
Gray, Hugh H.   1902   L
   s/o Tommie McElmurray & Chas. A.
Gray, Judson Clements   Jne 22 1887 Jne 7 1951
   s/o Tommie McElmurray & Chas. A.
Gray, Julia Williams   Mar 16 1878 Apr 16 1939
   w/o Frank A.
Gray, Moselle Humphrey   Nov 11 1890 Jan 20 1971
   w/o Judson C. d/o Alice Hardwick & David M.
Gray, Tommie McElmurray   1863   1941
   w/o C.A. d/o Louisa Barron & Thos. J.
Green, Annie Lou Cox   Jan 19 1868 May 2 1956
   w/o Walter Gresham d/o T. Alona Fulcher & P. Duncan
Green, Arvelle McPhail   Nov 28 1902 Mar 30 1958
   w/o Millard M.
Green, Carrie Fulcher   Apr 8 1861 Mar 5 1952
   w/o Moses Edwin d/o Louisa W. & V.W.
Green, George Edwin   Aug 31 1887 Dec 24 1888
   s/o Carrie F. & M.F.
Green, Hugh WW-I   Jan 7 1889 Apr 20 1963
   s/o A.L. Cox & W.G., Sr. PFC 5th Ord Repair Detach-
   ment
Green, Jesse Patterson, III   Nov 15 1859 Jne 15 1931
   h/o Sallie Meyer s/o Mary J. Gresham & Jesse P., II
   See Green cemetery #56 (ed).
Green, Jesse P., IV   Nov 18 1886 Sep 24 1961
   s/o Sallie M. & J.P., III h/o Eva Mae Stokes
Green, Julian Cox   Sep 3 1898 Jan 20 1970
   s/o A.L. Cox & W.G., Sr.
Green, Martha Hugh   Oct 28 1918 Nov 22 1954
   d/o Sallie Bailey & Hugh
Green, Millard Meyer   Mar 1 1885 Jne 6 1950
   s/o Sallie M. & J.P., III
Green, Millard Meyer, Jr.   Jul 22 1928 Apr 5 1974
   s/o Arvelle McPhail & Millard M.

Green, Moses Edwin   Dec 21 1850 Feb 2 1893
  s/o Martha Thompson Anderson & Moses P. See Green
  cemetery #56. (ed).
Green, Moses P.   Jan 10 1876 Feb 8 1909
  s/o Kate L.T. & George Augustus. Never married.
Green, Sallie Bailey   Oct 4 1890 Nov 22 1967
  w/o Hugh d/o Georgia C. & A.B. (Jack)
Green, Sallie Meyer   Dec 6 1864 May 6 1950
  w/o Jesse P., III
Green, Walter Gresham, Sr.   Jan 23 1862 Jul 26 1933
  s/o Mary J. Gresham & Jesse P., II
Greene, James Rufus   1852   1941
Greiner, Alline V.   Feb 17 1882 Apr 1 1912
  d/o Ella Hatsfield & John D.
Greiner, Charles Clinton   Jul 9 1878 Jul 15 1972
  h/o Nan Rackley s/o Ella & John David
Greiner, Daniel Evans   Dec 26 1894 Sep 19 1969
  s/o Peter
Greiner, Ella Venona Hatfield   May 3 1860 Jan 16 1954
  w/o John David
Greiner, Joe Hightower   May 26 1883 Jan 7 1959
  s/o George
Greiner, John David   Dec 21 1856 Feb 9 1926
Greiner, Josephine Cosnahan   Apr 11 1902 Jul 26 1968
  w/o Daniel
Greiner, Laurie Battle   age 74 y   Jan 11 1974
  s/o Laura Nesbit & Robert Henry
Greiner, Lillie Mae Lyons   Sep 8 1891 Mar 31 1964
  w/o Joe H.
Greiner, Nan Rackley   Apr 28 1874 May 16 1974
  w/o C.C. d/o Mary V. & S.T.
Gresham, Annie Lassiter   1856   1939
  w/o Job A. d/o Mary Burke & Orrin
Gresham, Arthur   Aug 15 1888 Oct 10 1953
  h/o Ruth E. Jones md Jne 23, 1915 s/o Ella
  Lassiter & John Jones
Gresham, DeForrest McElmurray   nd   L
  w/o Wylie O. d/o Sallie Godbee & Minis H.
Gresham, Ella Lassiter   Oct 17 1851 Oct 3 1936
  w/o John Jones d/o Mary Burke & Orrin
Gresham, Emmet B., Jr. WW-II   Mar 25 1923 Feb 25 1954
  h/o Rebecca Spaatz d/o Gen. Carl A. Spaatz   USAF
  s/o Nona Johnston & Emmett 1st Lt. HQ3 Fighter Comd
  Am & 4 OLC PH & OLC Note: spelling of Emmet, Jr's
  name with one t (ed).
Gresham, Emmett Burdell   Mar 7 1875 May 17 1936
  s/o Annie Lassiter & Job A.
Gresham, Job Anderson CSA   1843   Nov 14 1940
  s/o Sarah M. Anderson & Edmund B. Co D 48 Regt Ga Vol
Gresham, Job Anderson   Nov 25 1911 Jan 4 1944
  s/o Nona Johnston & Emmett B.
Gresham, John Jones CSA   Mar 25 1845 Jne 6 1910
  s/o Sarah M. Anderson & Edmund B. Co C 5th Ga Regt
  Anderson's Brig. Wheeler's Cav

Gresham, Jones   Mar 6 1918 May 6 1919
  s/o Arthur & Ruth Jones
Gresham, Mary Dorothy Tomlin   Apr 10 1916 Dec 27 1969
  w/o Phil J. d/o Hattie Barnes & Ben Jones
Gresham, Mary Dye   1875   1946
  w/o Orrin L. d/o Jas. M. CSA
Gresham, Natalie Thomas   Jne 24 1886 Oct 21 1918
  1st w/o Wylie O. d/o Emma M. & Nathaniel Pinckney
Gresham, Nona Johnston   Mar 15 1886 Apr 28 1964
  w/o Emmett B. d/o Lena Shewmake & Philip P.
Gresham, Orrin Lassiter   Feb 25 1877 May 24 1958
  s/o Ella L. & J.J.
Gresham, Oscar Milledge WW-I   1889   1964
  s/o Annie L. & Job A.
Gresham, Wylie Oscar   1880   1937
  s/o Leora Scales & Oscar
Gresham, Wylie Oscar, Jr.   1924   1960
  s/o DeForrest McE & W.O.
Griffin, Shelley A.   Mar 17 1908 Jan 31 1967
  h/o Mary Cates s/o Martha E. & Ellison
Griner, Bradfert   1921   1944
Griner, Joe Noah   May 13 1898 Mar 17 1966
Griner, Rosa Lucile   1927   1947
Guess, James E.   Jul 31 1882 Mar 23 1928
Guess, Mattie Duke   1875   1942
  w/o J.E. md 1st J.H. Ellis d/o B.F.
Hall, Frank Butler   May 25 1870 Jul 9 1950
  s/o Margaret & P.B.
Hall, John P.   Dec 5 1866 Apr 12 1905
  s/o Margaret & Pickens B.
Hall, Margaret E.   Mar 12 1842 Aug 23 1910
  w/o P.B.
Hall, Pickens B. CSA   Oct 26 1842 Oct 26 1920
  Co H 9th Ga Regt
Hall, William Ashton   Aug 5 1911 Mar 15 1969
  h/o Margaret Manau
Hallman, Arthur C.   Jul 25 1898 Jne 12 1961
  h/o Flora Mae Turner s/o Alice Wayne & Joe B.
Hankinson, John C. WW-I   Feb 25 1895 Mar 12 1964
  Ga Cpl USA
Hankinson, Sara W. Blount   Feb 23 1905 Nov 3 1964
  w/o John C. d/o Edith Whitner & L.D.
Hargrove, Annie Katherine   Feb 24 1931 Jne 21 1947
  d/o Pearl & Roy Belmont
Hargrove, Henry W.   Dec 5 1921 Nov 29 1968
  s/o Mary Blount & Wm. C.
Hargrove, Katherine Lee   Oct 2 1870 May 12 1940
  w/o Wm. W. /Herrington d/o Abigail Reeves &
  Crawford T.
Hargrove, Pearl Folsom   Mar 18 1898 Jul 26 1973
  w/o Roy B. md Feb 23 1924 d/o Mr. & Mrs. J.J.
  Folsom of Boston, Ga.
Hargrove, Roy Belmont WW-I   Aug 18 1889 Aug 14 1950
  s/o K.L. Herrington & Wm. W. 2nd Lt Inf

Hargrove, William Clifford   Mar 28 1891   Jul 7 1936
  h/o Mary Blount   s/o Kitty L. Herrington & Crawford T.
Hargrove, William W.   Aug 10 1863   Jan 17 1935
  s/o Sarah Perkins & John Green
Harner, Joseph Edward   Jul 29 1934   Feb 16 1959
  h/o Cynthia Ann Hattaway s/o Ida Belle Hendry &
  Jos. W.   2nd Lt 3550 AF Hospital
Harner, Joseph Winfred   Jul 31 1880   Dec 28 1954
  h/o Ida Belle Hendry s/o Eliza Cook & John
Harner, S/Sgt Wm. C. WW-II   Oct 30 1924   1943
  s/o Ida Belle Hendry & Jos. W. Lost his life at sea
  aboard British troopship Rohna
Harrell, Miriam Green   Apr 25 1888   Jan 3 1971
  w/o Wm. Green d/o Sallie Meyer & Jesse P., III
Harrell, Wm. Green   Jul 28 1889   Jne 24 1960
Hatcher, Benjamin J.   Feb 10 1873   Dec 1 1942
  s/o Arrah N. & J. Newton
Hatcher, Benjamin J., Jr.   Oct 5 1913   Sep 16 1956
  WW-II h/o Frances Scott   s/o Denie Miller & Benj. J.
  As USNR
Hatcher, Charlie Hughes   Aug 18 1893   Feb 1 1947
Hatcher, Denie Miller   Nov 18 1874   Jul 18 1929
  w/o 1st Thos. B. Cox 2nd B.J. Hatcher d/o Georgia
  Godbee & Marcellus F.
Hatcher, Ella Mary Greiner   1884   1960
  2nd w/o R.N. d/o Ella H. & John David
Hatcher, Infant   Feb 7 1909   Sep 30 1909
  d/o Mamie Cox & Lindsey E.
Hatcher, Lindsey E.   May 16 1881   Mar 21 1948
  s/o Geraldine Thomas & Wm. J.
Hatcher, Mamie Cox   Oct 22 1884   Mar 25 1946
  w/o Lindsey E. d/o Laura Rogers & Thos. B.
Hatcher, Mattie Mae James   Jul 27 1901   nd
  w/o C.H.
Hatcher, Minnie L.   1886   1970
  w/o W.A.
Hatcher, Robert Newton   1877   1937
  h/o 1st Bertha Wimberly 2nd Ella Mary Greiner
  s/o Geraldine Thomas & Wm. J.
Hatcher, Walter A.   1868   1940
Hatcher, Mrs. Willie Green   May 20 1860   Jul 8 1923
Hayes, Harold B., Jr.   Aug 7 1902   Aug 25 1957
  s/o Bertha & Harold B.
Hayes, Nona Lowe   Aug 9 1896   Jan 7 1973
  w/o Wm. Grady d/o Serena Atkins & John W.
Hayes, William Grady   Jan 11 1890   Jan 12 1958
  s/o Lydia Ansley & Elias
Heath, Evans V.   Feb 9 1889   Aug 8 1926
  h/o Florence Fulcher s/o Mary Rouse & Justin B.
  Able atty and State Senator. He and Rufus E. Lester
  (1873-79) are the only Burke Senators to preside over
  the Georgia Senate since the Civil War. Heath was
  elected President Pro Tem in 1918 (ed).
Heath, Infant   only date Sep 13 1917
  s/o Florence Fulcher & Evans V.

267

Henry, Fay Dufft   Oct 20 1893   Jan 9 1934
   d/o Sara Rumble & August F.
Herrington, Abbie A. Reeves   Aug 27 1849   Oct 23 1914
   w/o Crawford T.
Herrington, Andrew Jinks   Oct 30 1886   Oct 2 1963
   h/o Bertice Bargeron s/o Adelaide Hargrove & John
   Fletcher
Herrington, Annie Laurie Davis Oct 6 1868   Oct 28 1940
   w/o Dr. Lovick Pierce
Herrington, Crawford T. CSA   Sep 1 1847   Dec 5 1921
   Co D 27 Ga Regt s/o Frances L. & Berry
Herrington, Capers L.   Feb 11 1874   Jul 17 1927
   s/o Abigail Reeves & Crawford T.
Herrington, Edwin F., II   Oct 22 1946   Nov 26 1946
   s/o Anne Johnston & Edwin F.
Herrington, Effie Tinsley   Jne 16 1886   Mar 31 1927
   w/o Capers L. b Columbia, Tex. md Apr 15, 1903
   One son, Clayton Obit. T.C.Apr 9, 1927
   d/o Mr. & Mrs. S.P.
Herrington, Eula R.   1890   1971
   w/o John G.
Herrington, Henry C.   May 25 1902   Aug 30 1958
   h/o Clyde s/o Adelaide Hargrove & John Fletcher
Herrington, Ivy Perry, Sr.   1893   ·1952
   s/o Adelaide Hargrove & John Fletcher
Herrington, John G.   1889   1944
   s/o Adelaide Hargrove & John Fletcher
Herrington, John Linwood   Mar 19 1883   Dec 22 1944
   h/o Kathleen Cates s/o Nannie Cates & Seaborn R.
Herrington, Lovick Pierce MD   May 27 1858   Nov 8 1920
   s/o Frances L. & Berry
Herrington, Lucy Smith   1892   1971
   w/o I. Perry d/o Sarah Bell & E.A.
Herrington, Mims L.   1882   1966
   s/o Leila Thorn & Andrew
Herrington, Willie Mae Mallard   1901   L
   w/o Mims L.
Hersey, Warren C.   Oct 8 1901   Sep 25 1948
   s/o Alice Leon & Warren W.
Hewitt, John S.   Apr 11 1892   Dec 21 1964
Hewitt, Louise Blount   May 23 1896   L
   w/o John S. d/o Jennie Blount & John A.
Hickman, Annie M.   1882   1951
   w/o Joseph W.
Hickman, Joseph W.   1878   1951
Hickson, Margaret Hurst   Nov 13 1886   Nov 22 1934
   w/o Wade H. d/o Martha Chandler & Chas. W.
Hickson, Wade Hampton   Aug 30 1876   Jne 12 1944
Hiers, Benjamin J.   Oct 9 1905   Aug 22 1968
Hiers, Elizabeth Gray   Aug 4 1908   Jan 15 1972
   w/o Ben J. d/o Julia & Frank A.
Hill, Benjamin U.   Apr 13 1879   Nov 5 1930
Hill, Bessie Rowland   May 17 1894   Jan 6 1968
   w/o Jas. W. d/o Janie Renfroe & Elmo

Hill, Eva Downs   Jan 9 1889   Sep 4 1968
   w/o Benj. U.
Hill, James Whitehead   Sep 17 1892   Feb 7 1961
   s/o Mary Whitehead & Leonard Dozier
Hill, John James   Dec 16 1860   Jne 26 1905
Hill, L. Dozier   Sep 13 1894   Feb 26 1907
   s/o Mr. & Mrs. Leonard Dozier
Hill, Leonard Dozier   Feb 2 1867   Sep 25 1927
Hill, Mary Amin   Sep 3 1913   Jne 4 1914
Hill, Mary Ann Whitehead   Jan 10 1864   Jne 16 1942
   w/o Leonard Dozier d/o Margaret Ireland Harper &
   John P.C. md Nov 17 1891
Hill, Robert D.   Sep 4 1891   Apr 1 1952
Hillhouse, Nell Thomas   Jan 10 1879   Mar 29 1967
   w/o Wm. C. d/o Ruth Miller & Charles H.
Hillhouse, Wm. Chambus   Dec 12 1868   Oct 7 1944
   s/o Martha Ann Steele & Capt. Wm. C. CSA
   Note: Chambus should read "Chambers." The latter
   is a family name dating from pre-Rev. days on the
   western Penn. frontier (ed).
Hirleman, Sara Applewhite   Apr 14 1903   Jne 29 1972
   w/o Dr. Ward B. d/o Emmie C. & John O.
Hirleman, Dr. Ward B.   May 2 1888   Aug 4 1958
Hogan, Emily Ola   Nov 13 1890   Nov 27 1937
Holland, Annie R.   May 12 1916   Apr 23 1956
Holland, Infant   nd   Jul 14 1970
Holton, Albert P.   Sep 13 1905   Dec 7 1969
   s/o Mary A. & Geo. T.
Holton, George T.   Dec 16 1874   Jul 28 1959
   s/o Josephine Cobb & Henry Clark
Holton, Mary A.   Jul 24 1878   Aug 12 1958
   w/o Geo. T. d/o Amanda Cato & Clark Amerson
Holton, Sally F.   Sep 2 1908   Feb 25 1972
   w/o Albert P.
Hopkins, Enon Chance MD   Aug 7 1921   Jne 13 1966
   h/o Catherine Cooper s/o Mary Pearl Chance & Henry C.
Hopkins, Henry Cormac   Aug 2 1888   Jne 24 1953
   h/o Mary Pearl Chance s/o Martha B. Key & Matthew H.
Hopkins, Mary Catherine   Feb 13 1946   Jne 17 1951
   d/o E.C. & C.C.
Hopper, Roger W.   1896   1952
   s/o Mattie Rogers & Claude W.
Hopper, Taney Oliver   1902   L
   w/o Roger W. d/o Eleanor & Dr. Shelley
Horton, Clifford O.   May 31 1887   Feb 7 1950
Horton, Dora Attwell   Apr 12 1887   Jan 22 1949
   w/o Clifford O.
Hudson, Lota B.   1880   1943
Hughes, Clyde L.   Oct 4 1899   May 6 1949
Hughes, Effie Mabel   May 7 1877   Aug 27 1903
   w/o W.P.
Hughes, Gladys B.   Feb 12 1911   Jul 23 1933
Hughes, Leon   1908   1969
Hughes, William Patrick   1877   1939

Humphrey, Annie MacKenzie   Feb 20 1878   Apr 30 1974
   w/o John F.   d/o Angelina May Lawson & James Hope
Humphrey, Floyd Lawson   May 26 1893   Sep 27 1970
   s/o Alice Hardwick & David M.
Humphrey, Infant   Aug 28 1920   Aug 29 1920
   d/o Louise Cox & Floyd L.
Humphrey, Floyd Lawson, III   Apr 17 1946   Apr 18 1946
   s/o Betty Ferree & Floyd L., Jr.
Humphrey, John Franklin WOW   Dec 8 1875   Dec 7 1935
   s/o Alice Hardwick & David M.
Humphrey, Louise Cox   Nov 6 1898   L
   w/o Floyd d/o Denie M. & Thos. B.
Hunter, David Edward F&AM   Aug 1 1868   Jne 25 1903
Hunter, Mary Mosely Morris   Aug 23 1874   Dec 8 1957
   w/o David E.   md 1st W.C. Morris d/o Rebecca Gray &
   J.W. Mosely
Hurst, Charlie W.   Dec 15 1892   Sep 14 1969
   s/o Sarah V. Smith & Thomas Jefferson
Hurst, Francis Marion Sp-Am W May 24 1876   Nov 10 1933
   h/o Irene Trowbridge s/o Sarah V. Smith & Thos. J.
   USA 1898-1900 WOW
Hurst, John Gorden   Jne 10 1880   May 23 1901
   s/o Sarah V. Smith & Thomas Jefferson
Hurst, Roger Coutteau   Jan 10 1880   Jan 11 1925
   h/o Jennie Brigham s/o Martha Chandler & Charles W.
Hurst, Ruby Kelly   Aug 27 1891   Oct 7 1960
   w/o Thos. J., Jr.
Hurst, Sarah V. (Sallie) Smith Jul 5 1855   Mar 3 1926
   w/o Thomas Jefferson
Hurst, Stella Ward   Oct 9 1895   L
   w/o Charlie W. d/o Mattie Tomlin & Charlie
Hurst, Thomas Jefferson   Nov 15 1848   Jan 22 1910
   s/o George W.
Hurst, Thomas J., Jr.   May 29 1882   Feb 2 1953
   s/o Sarah V. Smith & Thomas Jefferson
Ison, Mrs. Sallie J. Redd   Oct 15 1867   Mar 1 1913
   d/o Caroline Missouri Elliott & Wm. Mack
James, Frank Cheatham   May 20 1888   Jul 21 1942
James, Mamie Herrington   Aug 12 1889   Apr 19 1946
   w/o Frank C. d/o Abbie Reeves & C.T.
Jenkins, Dianne   Mar 6 1961   Mar 6 1961
Jenkins, Earl F. Kor W   Dec 11 1905   Jne 22 1957
   Sgt Med Corps Korea
Jenkins, Eddie   age 31 y   Jan 16 1915
Jenkins, Louis   nd   Mar 10 1915
Jenkins, Melody   Jul 21 1962   Nov 24 1962
Jenkins, Robert Fulton, Sr.   May 22 1884   May 12 1966
   s/o Agnes Crozier & Berry
Jernigan, L.M. WW-II   only date   Apr 19 1943
   Gunner's Mate 3CI USN
Jernigan, Lena Gainey   1886   1944
Jernigan, Lyde Miller   1881   1944
Jester, Guy L. WW-II   Nov 14 1915   Aug 30 1947
   S/Sgt Field Arty

Johnson, Annie B.H.   Oct   9 1896   nd
  w/o W.C.
Johnson, Edgar A.   Aug   7 1896   Nov   6 1967
  h/o 1st Reba McGrady 2nd Florrie Daniel
  s/o Alice Freeman & Jesse Eugene
Johnson, Reba Irene McGrady   Aug 29 1898   Mar 12 1937
  1st w/o Edgar A. d/o Mollie E. Main & Thos. B.
Johnson, Roy Wayne (infant)   only   date   1938
Johnson, W.C. (Buck)   Jul 25 1904   Aug 15 1973
Johnston, George W. CSA   Nov 27 1846   Aug 22 1918
  Pvt Co K 16th Ga Regt Wafford's Brig Longstreet's
  Corps Lee's Army
Johnston, James Jesse   Sep 11 1875   Nov 17 1960
  h/o Annie May Tyler s/o Susan Elizabeth Senn &
  Lemuel Casper
Johnston, John S. WW-I   nd Jne 26 1925
  Pvt ICL Qm Corps USA s/o Lena Hewmake & Philip P.
Johnston, Lena Shewmake   1858   1934
  w/o Philip P. d/o Elizabeth Penelope Jones & John
  Troup Shewmake
Johnston, Louise Green   Jan 23 1891   Dec 24 1973
  w/o Wm. Giles d/o A.L. Cox & W.G.
Johnston, Philip Pelatiah   Sep 19 1854   Jne 29 1910
  b in Fla s/o Mariah Whitehurst & George
Johnston, Sallie A.   Dec 13 1849   Jul   7 1919
  w/o Geo. W.
Johnston, Samuel T.   Nov 15 1886   May   7 1901
  s/o G.W. & S.A.
Johnston, William Giles   Mar 30 1890   Jne 15 1930
  s/o Mary Rearden & Edward Taylor
Joiner, Lester J. WW-II   Oct 27 1911   Jne 23 1970
  PFC USA
Joiner, Martha L.   Mar   8 1917   Jne 23 1968
  w/o Lester J.
Jones, Boss H.   1873   1944
Jones, Evalina Toombs   Jan 31 1830   Nov 17 1900
  w/o John James d/o Mary Flournoy & Lawrence C.,
  who was a br/o Robert Toombs
Jones, Helen Gresham   Dec 15 1873   Dec   8 1943
  w/o Seaborn H. d/o Ella E. Lassiter & John Jones
Jones, Henry Rice WW-II   Mar 23 1906   Feb   1 1949
  1st h/o Pearl Smyly PFC Ga 39 Inf
Jones, Inez Florida Wilkins   Aug   4 1862   Dec 27 1931
  w/o Wm. E. d/o Moselle Carswell & Major Wm. A.
Jones, John James CSA   Sep 13 1824   Oct 19 1898
  s/o Margaret A. Jones & Seaborn H. Note: Lawyer and
  U.S. Congressman. Colonel on Governor Brown's staff
  See Jones cemetery #82 (ed).
Jones, Kathleen Mitchelson   nd Dec   6 1958
  w/o Sidney C.
Jones, Maude Wells   1874   1934
  w/o B.H. d/o Mr. & Mrs. Thos. B.
Jones, Moselle (infant)   nd   nd
  d/o Inez W. & W.E.

```
Jones, Nina Treutlen                    Oct  3 1884   Mar  5 1959
    d/o Inez Wilkins & Wm. E.
Jones, Seaborn Henry                    Dec 20 1861   Dec 17 1921
    s/o Evalina Toombs & John James
Jones, Sydney Carswell                  Jul  2 1883   Oct  3 1947
    s/o Inez Wilkins & Wm. E.
Jones, Wm. Everett                      Oct 12 1856   Jul 27 1904
    s/o Sidney Ann Sapp & Dr. Wm. Beaman
    Note:  See Jones cemetery #81  (ed).
Jones, Wm. Wilkins                      Jne 23 1881   Oct  3 1908
    s/o Inez Wilkins & Wm. E.
Jordan, Bethiah Douglass                May 12 1833   Jne 26 1902
    w/o Francis D.
Jordan, Effie S.                        Feb  9 1898   Feb  2 1970
Jordan, Joseph P.                       Oct  1 1893   May 11 1944
Joyner, Howell Caloway                  Mar  3 1896   Oct 29 1953
    s/o Cora T. & Thomas
Joyner, Marie Stephens                  Aug  6 1899   Mar  7 1974
    w/o Howell C.  d/o Nora Dugan & Arthur Hampton
Kelley, Janet Norvell                   Apr 11 1892   Feb 20 1962
    w/o U.H.
Kelley, Lee Cates                       Feb 29 1864   Sep 22 1940
Kelley, Upton Hollifield   MD           Mar 19 1881   Jul 10 1935
Kelly, Andrew Jackson                   May 15 1868   Nov 10 1935
Kelly,  Earlie McDaniel                      1892            1934
    w/o Oliver J.
Kelly, Guy Baxley                       May 10 1900   Jan 21 1973
    s/o Rebecca Inglett & Andrew J.
Kelly, Guy Baxley, Jr. Kor W    Jul 21 1932   Apr 15 1953
    s/o Zannie McC. & Guy B.  Ser/FC Inf USA   killed in
    action
Kelly,  Oliver Jackson                       1892            1968
    s/o Rebecca Inglett & Andrew J.
Kelly, Rebecca Inglett                  Aug 12 1875   May 21 1932
    w/o A.J.
Kelly, Willie Mims                      age 39 y      Dec 29 1970
Kelly, Zannie McClelland                Feb 17 1909            L
    w/o Guy B.  d/o Minnie Clark & John F.
Kendrick, Annie Mae Boyd                Nov 25 1889   Apr 28 1957
    w/o Nisbit Stovall  d/o Ollie Pace & John L.
Kendrick, John Boyd  WW-II              Oct 31 1915   Nov 28 1945
    s/o Annie M. Boyd & N.S.  USA Army
Kendrick, Nisbit Stovall                May  5 1882   Oct 25 1966
Kilpatrick, Celia Avret                 Feb 28 1878   Jne 16 1950
    w/o Louis Jones
Kilpatrick, George Pulaski              Jne  5 1868   Aug  7 1924
    s/o Sarah E. Schick & Rev. Washington L.
Kilpatrick, Irene Baxley                Nov 10 1871   Feb 22 1943
    w/o Geo. P.  d/o Rebecca Ward & Dr. Wm. H., Sr.
Kilpatrick, John N.                     Feb  2 1913   Oct  9 1918
    s/o Celia Avret & L. Jones
Kilpatrick, Jones Avret                 Jne  1 1899   May 16 1944
    s/o Celia Avret & L. Jones
Kilpatrick, Louis Jones                 Apr 12 1864   Jan 26 1918
    s/o Elmira Chance & John
```

Kilpatrick, Marie   1900   1973
  d/o Celia Avret & L. Jones
King, Mary Hatcher Willis   Nov 5 1904 Dec 19 1968
  w/o 1st Paul H. Willis 2nd John King
  d/o Mamie Cox & L.E.
Kirkman, Genie   Aug 13 1922 Dec 7 1923
  d/o Mr. & Mrs. Arthur
Kirkman, M.D. F&AM   Sep 15 1859 Aug 31 1911
Kitchens, Henry J.   1884   1945
Kitchens, Iola K.   1886   1970
  w/o Henry J.
Lamb, Alice W.   age 58 y   Oct 3 1973
Lance, Jack Junior   Feb 24 1915 Nov 9 1928
  s/o Alice Rose Erwin & Thos. J. Note: His father
  was then Supt. of the Waynesboro City Schools; later
  President of Young Harris College (ed).
Lassiter, Agnes Walsh   1874   1944
  w/o Wm. P.
Lassiter, Mary Burke   Nov 27 1831 Jan 19 1914
  w/o Orrin
Lassiter, Michael Edward   Jul 7 1898 Feb 19 1953
  s/o Agnes Walsh & Wm. P. 1st h/o Lena Holland; one
  daughter Teresa L. (Phillips)
Lassiter, William P.   1859   1943
Law, Carolyn Palmer   Jul 24 1915 Mar 19 1969
  1st w/o Wilkes A., Jr. d/o Bessie Thomas & Jesse
  C., Sr.
Law, Carrie Lane   Sep 22 1888 Mar 24 1971
  w/o Joseph d/o Emma Rylander & Davis T.
Law, Joseph   Aug 4 1886 Nov 22 1940
  s/o Clara E. Jones & Robert Judge of the Ordinary
  Court, Burke Co.
Law, Madelle Benson   Aug 9 1891 Apr 26 1970
  w/o Wilkes Aiken, Sr. d/o Annie Brinson & Henry
Law, Wilkes Aiken, Sr.   Jne 5 1888 Dec 14 1940
  s/o Clara E. Jones & Robert
Law, Wilkes Aiken, III   Aug 9 1935 May 23 1949
  s/o Carolyn Palmer & W.A., Jr.
Law, William A.   age 79 y   Mar 7 1960
Lester, Lillian Ellison   Jan 6 1877 Jan 27 1959
  w/o Pharos R. d/o Josephine & Robert J.
Lester, Paul E. WW-II   Jne 27 1900 Apr 1 1961
  h/o Pearl Smyly s/o Lillian Ellison & Pharos R.
  Florida Sk2 USN
Lester, Pharos Rufus   Dec 3 1868 Nov 28 1908
Lewis, Alma King   Apr 14 1903   L
  2nd w/o G. Alvin d/o Cora B. & John T.
Lewis, Clifford McElmurray   Aug 11 1900 Jan 27 1946
  w/o Preston B., Jr. d/o Clifford Gray & Wm. Leslie
Lewis, Emma Bell   Sep 23 1918 Jan 16 1919
  d/o Winnie Bell & Dr. Jas. B.
Lewis, George Alvin WW-I   Jne 20 1891 Mar 23 1971
  s/o Lena Chance & G.W. Pvt USA Shriner
Lewis, James Barnette MD   Jan 7 1888 Oct 24 1942
  s/o Lena Taylor & Jas. T.

Lewis, Jettie Thomas   May 7 1898 Oct 30 1945
   1st w/o G. Alvin d/o Eula Redd & Jethro B.
Lewis, Julian Fulcher WW-II   Oct 30 1902 Jul 15 1970
   s/o Lillian Fulcher & Preston Brooks Lt Col (ret)
   US Army Shriner
Lewis, Lillian Fulcher   May 19 1863 Jul 26 1928
   w/o Preston Brooks, Sr. d/o Louisa Wimberly &
   Vincent Warren
Lewis, Mattie Julia Fields   Feb 7 1908 Apr 23 1967
   w/o Ralph Elliott d/o Urney West & Seth Spencer Hill
Lewis, Preston Brooks, Sr.   Nov 16 1857 Nov 24 1927
   b Edgefield Co., S.C. s/o Mary Ann May & Goody F&AM
Lewis, Preston Brooks, Jr.   Mar 20 1891 Aug 19 1965
   WW-I h/o 1st Clifford McElmurray 2nd Janie Coleman
   (Edmond) s/o Lillian Fulcher & Preston Brooks, Sr.
   1st Lt Co A 151 Mach Gun Bn Rainbow Div AEF   F&AM
   Attorney-at-law.
Lewis, Ralph Elliott WW-I & II Sep 6 1892 Dec 19 1962
   WW-I & II   s/o Lillian Fulcher & Preston Brooks, Sr.
   WW-I 2nd Lt F Batt FA 3rd Div WW-II J A Dept Lt-Col
   (ret) US Army F&AM Atty-at-law.
Lewis, Virginia Dare Lansdell   Oct 18 1919   L
   w/o Julian F. d/o Jennie Godbee & Dare S.
Lewis, William Cecil WW-I   Sep 29 1889 Apr 14 1953
   h/o Ruth Lester s/o Lena Chance & G.W.
   Pvt Depot Brigade
Lewis, Winnie Bell   Oct 20 1887 Jul 20 1962
   w/o Dr. James B. d/o Emma Chandler & Simeon
Lively, Charles B.   Feb 11 1874 Feb 26 1937
Lively, Jennie B.   Nov 29 1882 Jan 27 1973
   w/o Chas. B.
Lively, Josie B.   Aug 6 1901 Sep 27 1963
Lovett, Ida Dixon   Jne 18 1880 Apr 16 1954
   w/o J. Marvin d/o Eliz. Pollock & T. Jas.
Lovett, Infant   Nov 30 1942 Dec 3 1942
   s/o Ruby Ratliff & John McFerrin
Lovett, J. Marvin   May 24 1876 Oct 3 1956
   s/o Virginia Burton & Jas. R.
Lovett, James Cuyler   1906   1969
   s/o J. Marvin & Ida Dixon
Lovett, Julia Ward   1906   L
   w/o James Cuyler
Lovett, Marjorie James   Jne 7 1916 Jan 7 1939
   w/o R.C., Jr. d/o Mamie Herrington & Frank
Lovett, Mary Elizabeth   Feb 7 1935 May 2 1937
   d/o Myrtis Lowrey & Paul Lively
Lovett, Mary Valinda Lively   1882   1962
   w/o Robt. C. d/o Sarah Cates & Matthew
Lovett, Myrtis Lowrey   Jul 29 1914   L
   w/o Paul L. d/o Laura Hersey & Carl D.
Lovett, Paul Lively   Sep 28 1912 Aug 19 1961
   s/o Mary V. Lively & Robert C.
Lovett, Robert C., Jr. WW-II Aug 14 1911 Jul 28 1969
   h/o Ruth Powell s/o Mary V. Lively & Robt. C.

Lovett, Robert Cleveland   1885   1955
   s/o Virginia Burton & Jas. R.
Lovett, Ronald   Jne 24 1925   Jne 28 1969
   h/o Eugenia s/o Mary V. Lively & Robt. C.
Lovett, Ronald E.   1943   1972
Lowrey, Carl Dethridge WOW   Jne 12 1882   Dec 13 1937
   s/o Elvina Abney & Melvin
Lowrey, Dorothy Walker   Jul 24 1911   same   date
   d/o Laura H. & Carl D.
Lowrey, John Pettigo   Feb 28 1888   Jne 25 1936
   s/o Elvina Abney & Melvin
Lumpkin, W.O.   Nov 3 1855   Mar 20 1917
Macaulay, Hugh Angus MD   Sep 4 1885   Feb 4 1931
   1st h/o Elizabeth McMaster md Sep 21 1916
   s/o Sallie McMaster & David J.
Maddox, John Lindsey   Feb 16 1936   Feb 19 1936
   s/o Lucile Hatcher & M.A.
Malabar, Benjamin Franklin   Aug 10 1870   Jan 15 1925
   s/o Martha Godbee & John
Malabar, Kate Fulcher   Feb 24 1875   Jne 16 1940
   w/o B.F. d/o Almeda Heath & Valentine
Manau, Edwin S.   Dec 30 1908   Nov 8 1913
   s/o Marie Louisa Becker & H.H.
Manau, Hans   Feb 9 1892   Nov 16 1961
   s/o Marie Louisa Becker & H.H.
Manau, Hans Henry   May 3 1859   Jan 4 1917
   b Hamburg, Germany
Manau, Henry WW-I   May 12 1896   Jan 10 1968
   s/o Marie Louisa Becker & H.H. Ga Cox USN
Manau, Louisa B.   Dec 30 1908   Aug 20 1973
   d/o Marie Louisa Becker & H.H.
Manau, Marie Louisa A. Becker   Mar 24 1866   Apr 4 1910
   w/o H.H.   b Hamburg, Germany
Manau, Mathilda (Tillie)   Jan 24 1895   Aug 8 1973
   d/o Marie Louisa Becker & H.H.
Manau, Ruth Kelly   Jan 21 1900   May 23 1957
   w/o Henry d/o Rebecca Inglett & Andrew J.
Manau, Willy   Mar 5 1903   Jul 31 1904
   s/o Marie Louisa Becker & H.H.
Marsh, Mulford W.   Nov 26 1957   Dec 4 1905
Martin, Annie Lambert   Nov 3 1895   Apr 15 1955
   w/o Norman L.
Martin, Leona   Sep 20 1915   Mar 15 1954
   d/o Annie Lambert & Norman L.
Martin, Norman L.   Dec 26 1892   Jul 18 1961
Mays, Annie R.   Jul 11 1868   Jan 18 1951
   w/o J.R.
Mays, Jabus R.   Feb 1 1867   Jne 13 1962
Maxwell, Hugh McCullough   May 15 1834   Nov 16 1912
Maxwell, Sophie Luckenbach   Apr 1 1844   Jul 4 1915
   w/o H.M.
McCampbell, Robert P. WW-II   Aug 19 1919   Jan 14 1969
   h/o Catherine Jones s/o Barbara Preble & Henry
   Butler   Nebraska   Lt Col USA

McCathern, Charlotte Reynolds 1890 L
w/o Sidney J.; two children, Sidney J., Jr. &
Marcia (Stille); md 2nd David Gavin d/o Angie Perry
& J. J.
McCathern, Hugh Walker 1901 1959
s/o Kathryn Woodward & Wm. W.
McCathern, Kathryn Woodward 1877 1951
w/o Wm. Walker d/o Catherine Stallings & James
Monroe
McCathern, Sidney J. WW-I 1888 1928
s/o Sarah J. Chandler & Walker. Parents buried in
W-Boro Confed. Cem. Inf TOTC
McCathern, Sidney J., Jr. 1925 1932
s/o Charlotte Reynolds & S.J.
McCathern, William Walker 1872 1930
s/o Sarah J. Chandler & Walker. Parents buried
in W-Boro Confed. Cem. (ed).
McClellan, Agnes Martin Jul 18 1913 Mar 27 1949
w/o Torbit M. d/o Annie Mae & John Hamilton
McClellan, Deanie Bargeron 1883 1967
w/o Wm., Sr. d/o Mellie Ward & Richard
McClellan, James E. Aug 4 1937 Jul 4 1938
s/o Evelyn Walden & Rufus
McClellan, John E. Aug 7 1901 Jne 6 1970
s/o Minnie & John E.
McClellan, John E. Oct 28 1875 Sep 19 1941
s/o Susan O'Kelly & Doss
McClellan, Minnie Jne 27 1882 Sep 4 1960
w/o J.E.
McClellan, Richard A. Apr 13 1909 Dec 14 1957
s/o Deanie B. & Wm., Sr.
McClellan, Rufus W., Sr. May 5 1911 Sep 1 1953
s/o Deanie B. & Wm., Sr.
McClellan, Torbit M. Mar 3 1905 Jne 12 1972
s/o Deanie B. & Wm., Sr.
McClellan, William, Jr. Jan 28 1917 May 22 1972
s/o Deanie B. & Wm., Sr.
McClellan, William, Sr. 1878 1938
s/o Susan O'Kelly & Doss
McClellan, Willie M. WW-II Oct 21 1912 Aug 7 1965
Pvt HQ Btry 177 Fld Arty
McClure, Alva Herrington 1868 1930
w/o H.E. d/o Abbie Reeves & Crawford T.
McClure, Hiram Edward 1853 1919
McCray, Dorothy Anne Sep 19 1921 Jne 29 1972
McCray, Jasper Roscoe WW-I Aug 2 1893 May 23 1955
Ga PFC USA
McCray, Mollie Hanks Dec 24 1892 May 3 1965
w/o Jasper Roscoe
McCullough, Jessie B. Dec 31 1908 Mar 24 1971
s/o Minnie R. & Leonard L.
McDaniel, Nancy Jul 3 1862 Jan 13 1942
McDonald, Verona Calvert May 10 1904 Jne 3 1906
d/o Mr. & Mrs. A.L.
McDowell, John Pleasant Apr 4 1896 May 23 1971

McDowell, Mamie Durham   Feb 1 1905   Sep 6 1971
  w/o John Pleasant
McElhenny, Albert J.   Dec 10 1896   Sep 22 1953
McElhenny, Mabel Robinson   Aug 20 1903   Jan 6 1967
  w/o A.J. md 2nd Henry Manau
McElmurray, Clifford Gray   Jan 31 1872   Jne 29 1964
  w/o Wm. L. d/o Eliz. & Simeon A. Parents buried in
  W-Boro Confed. Cem.
McElmurray, Evan Howell WW-I   Jan 30 1890   Oct 1 1932
  s/o Mary Chandler & Thomas J. Capt. Battery A 118
  F A 31st Div AEF
McElmurray, Haidee Routzahn   Oct 10 1871   Sep 17 1960
  w/o Judson S. d/o Florence Byne & L.H.
McElmurray, Henry Grady   Jan 30 1890   Dec 16 1944
  h/o Grace Ouzts s/o Mary Chandler & Thos. J.
McElmurray, John Thomas   Dec 9 1918   May 30 1919
  s/o Grace Ouzts & H. Grady
McElmurray, Joseph H. WW-I   Dec 6 1891   Sep 17 1933
  s/o Mary Chandler & Thos. J. Ga Wagoner 118 F Arty
  21st Div AEF
McElmurray, Judson S.   Aug 17 1866   Nov 25 1930
  s/o Louisa Barron & Thos. J. See Will Bk B, 36-39
McElmurray, Louise   Sep 13 1894   Dec 9 1901
  d/o Clifford Gray & Wm. L.
McElmurray, Minis H.   Apr 30 1868   Jul 22 1914
  s/o Louisa Barron & Thos. J.
McElmurray, Mary Chandler   Feb 22 1855   Sep 28 1915
  w/o Thomas J. d/o Jane L. Darlington & Wm.
McElmurray, Sallie Godbee   Dec 15 1871   Mar 21 1946
  w/o M.H. d/o Bertha & Russell J. For family of
  Russell J., see Will Bk B, 237.
McElmurray, Thomas J.   Aug 15 1898   Oct 20 1938
  s/o Sallie Godbee & M.H.
McElmurray, Thomas J. CSA   Mar 1 1841   Apr 9 1898
  s/o Emily J. & Minis H. F&AM Note: See cemeteries
  #1 & #126 (ed).
McElmurray, Wm. Leslie   Feb 22 1862   Jan 26 1943
  s/o Louisa Barron & Thos. J. See Will Bk B, 36-39.
  Mother buried at Old Church cem. (ed).
McFerrin, Dr. John Porter CSA   1843   1926
  Beloved pastor of the First Methodist Church of
  W-Boro, 1915-1920 (ed).
McFerrin, Julia Patten   1847   1926
  w/o Dr. John P.
McFerrin, Mary   1870   1955
  d/o Julia Patten & Dr. John P.
McJunkin, W.D.   Oct 5 1860   Mar 28 1916
McKenzie, Annie E.   Jan 21 1875   Apr 6 1959
McKie, James Baker   Apr 21 1851   Jan 20 1934
  s/o Elizabeth Fuqua Griffin & Thos. Ross
McKie, Julia Kingman   Apr 6 1852   Nov 7 1924
  w/o James B. d/o Margaret E. Hammond & Samuel
McMaster, Hugh Buchanan MD   Feb 13 1856   Aug 21 1908
  s/o Eliz. Fleming & Hugh B. b Winnsboro, S. Car.

McMaster, Rosa Moore   Jne 30 1875   Jne 14 1964
  w/o Dr. H.B.   d/o Eliz. Sandeford & J.W. Shultz
McNair, James William   1900   1964
  s/o Lula Wright & Robt. Harris
McNair, Mary Jones   Sep 17 1882   Mar 4 1958
  d/o Mattie & Gabriel
McNair, Jane Blount   age 73 y   1926
  w/o Wm. md Mar 1 1877 d/o Celia Thomas & Henry
  Jackson
McNair, Lula Wright   1867   1935
  w/o Robert H.
McNair, Neva Johnson   1903   L
  w/o Jas. Wm. d/o Alice Freeman & Jesse Eugene
McNair, Thomas Gray   Apr 18 1890   Apr 4 1967
  h/o Lois Fox s/o Jane Blount & Wm.
McNair, William CSA   1847   1909
Messex, Harold David   Jul 8 1939   Nov 20 1958
  s/o Stanley
Messex, James Austin   1907   19
Messex, M. Stanley   Oct 28 1911   Oct 10 1973
Messex, Margaret Goodwin   1915   19__
  w/o James Austin
Messex, Rosa Lee Sikes   Feb 6 1901   Nov 17 1969
  w/o M. Stanley
Milledge, Mary Gresham   Dec 8 1869   Aug 16 1944
  w/o John md June 30, 1896 d/o Ella Lassiter &
  John Jones
Miller, Dean Joyner   Jne 21 1875   L
  w/o Robert Lee No issue. Leader of the WCTU's
  d/o Mary J. Graybill & Virgil S. See sketch &
  editorial T.C. Oct 7, 1964 & June 17, 1970
Miller, Robert L. MD   Sep 26 1870   Mar 31 1936
  s/o Cornelia Polhill & Dr. B.B.
Mills, Marie Green   Jan 21 1890   Sep 5 1961
  w/o W.L. d/o Sallie Meyer & Jesse P.
Mills, Wm. Littlefield   Aug 17 1883   Jan 22 1964
  s/o Susan Littlefield & John A.
Milner, Charles T. 'MD   Dec 31 1867   Jul 14 1916
Milner, Kate Thomas   Apr 12 1856   Dec 6 1928
  w/o 1st George A. Green 2nd C.T. Milner MD
  d/o Nancy Cates & Jethro
Mims, Mrs. Clifford W.   nd Sep 25 1897
  w/o W.L. d/o Henry White six children survive.
  Obit. T.C. Oct 2, 1897.
Mims, Dr. Willie   nd Dec 29 1970
Mobley, Alice Banks   Aug 28 1923   Jne 7 1949
  w/o Malcolm d/o Martha & Torbit
Mobley, Beulah Bailey   Mar 12 1883   May 31 1973
  w/o James d/o Georgia Chandler & A.B. (Jack)
Mobley, Floyd M. WW-I   Feb 15 1896   Sep 24 1964
  Pvt USA
Mobley, James   May 8 1882   Oct 5 1938
  s/o Louisiana Dixon & Malcolm M.
Mobley, Mary Odom   1893   1971
  w/o Floyd

```
Mobley, Owen                        Sep  1 1905  Mar 17 1938
Moffett, Annie Brown                Apr 12 1868  May 27 1954
  w/o M.C.
Moffett, Morton Clement             Jul 28 1860  Jul 16 1941
  s/o Sara A. Nisbet & Alexander
Moody, Walter R.  WOW               Jne 17 1876  Nov 13 1926
  1st h/o Minnie Carter  s/o Julia Dixon & Walter Reuben
Moore, Infant                       Feb 23 1897  Aug 22 1899
Moore, Maggie J.                    Jan 22 1841  Mar 20 1915
Moore, Marian Louise (infant)           nd           nd
  d/o E.B. & L.S. Parents moved from W'boro in the
  early 1900's (ed).
Morris, Lennie R.                   Sep 14 1875  Apr 16 1945
  w/o W.N.
Morris, Willard N.                  Oct 20 1876  Apr 15 1933
Mosley, Carl E.                          1886         1944
Mulder, Arminda Anne                Dec 16 1879  Dec 13 1951
  w/o Edgar Stephen
Mulder, Edgar Stephen               May 28 1883  Jan  9 1963
Mundy, John Ernest                  Apr  4 1881  Feb  3 1969
  s/o Martha Thompson & John Madison
Mundy, Louise Moate                 Jul 20 1882  Jul 15 1964
  w/o John Ernest  d/o Carolyn G. Bass & John Wesley
Murphy, Ruth Evans                  Sep 25 1892  Sep 11 1920
  w/o A.(Leck) T.  d/o Sarah Holleyman & Joshua K.
  Parents buried in W-Boro Confed. Mem. Cem. (ed).
Murrow, George W.                        1891         1957
  s/o Mary R. Wallace & Gershom
Murrow, Irene M.                         1893         1967
  w/o Geo. W.  d/o Fannie L. Harrell & Wm. Lowry
Neely, Alvin Wilkins  WW-I          Apr 12 1887  Apr 15 1971
  h/o Julia Abbott  s/o Lillian Wilkins & Robt. C.
  1st Lt Co B Mach Gun Bn AEF France
Neely, Grace                        Jan  5 1901  May 10 1902
  d/o Grace Maxwell & John F.
Neely, Grace Maxwell                     1879         1948
  w/o John F.
Neely, John Flewellyn                    1865         1925
  s/o Philoclea Whitehead & Thos. Wm.
Neely, Lillian Wilkins                   1863         1930
  w/o Robert C., Sr.  d/o Moselle Carswell & Major W.A.
Neely, Louise Calhoun Phinizy   Sep  1 1889  Jan  5 1965
  w/o R.C., Jr.  d/o Marion Pickens Coles & Stewart
Neely, Robert Caldwell                   1856         1923
  s/o Philoclea Whitehead & Thos. Wm.  Leading planter,
  merchant, banker, and civic-minded citizen.  Founder
  of Citizens' Bank of Waynesboro;  Mayor of City;
  member of State Highway Board  (ed).
Neely, Robert Caldwell, Jr.     Jne 27 1888  May 30 1964
  s/o Lillian W. & Robert C.  Mayor of City  (ed)
Nelson, Leighton E.                 Dec  4 1897  Dec 29 1953
Netherland, Erma Davis              Nov 17 1904
  w/o Olin C.
Netherland, Olin C.  WW-I           Jan 10 1897  Apr 26 1953
  S 2 USNRF  s/o Nora & J.E.
```

Newton, Adrian Lester   Apr 13 1904 Mar 18 1951
  s/o Georgia Lane & Russell D.
Newton, Georgia Ophelia Lane   Mar 6 1883 May 22 1957
  w/o Russell D. md Dec 21 1902 d/o Isabella Lewis
  & Thomas
Newton, Russell DeCalb   Oct 1 1879 Oct 27 1965
  s/o Dicey Oglesby & John C.C.
O'Connell, Frances   Feb 20 1870 Aug 27 1954
  d/o Elizabeth Chapple & Daniel sis/o Mary O'Connell
  (Mrs. Clarence L.) Rowland (ed).
Odom, Hattie   1875   1932
  w/o Morgan
Odom, Morgan   1866   1934
Oglesby, Annie P.   1911   1945
  w/o Paul M.
Oglesby, Infant   only   date   1945
  of Paul M. & Annie R.
Oglesby, Richard James   Jne 1 1956 Apr 25 1963
Oglesby, William Dawson   only   date   1944
  s/o Paul M. & Annie R.
Oliver, Amye Lou Gay   May 11 1898   L
  w/o Mims R. d/o Alice Thomson & John Henry
Oliver, Emma Walters   1868   1922
Oliver, Lena Helmly   Sep 23 1876 Jul 18 1969
  w/o R.L. d/o Martha Hillis & John W.
Oliver, Mims R.   Oct 2 1899 Sep 4 1972
  s/o Lena Helmly & Richard L.
Oliver, Richard L.   Aug 20 1867 Jan 30 1940
  s/o Mary E. Lovett & Richard Wm.
Oliver, Dr. Samuel J.   Oct 28 1860 Jan 17 1915
  s/o Virginia & Dr. Jas. H.
Oliver, Virgil Baxley   1884   1943
Outland, Billie, Jr.   Nov 22 1936 Nov 24 1936
  s/o Naomi Ellis & Wm. A.
Ouzts, Chester K.   Jan 19 1900 Oct 14 1943
  s/o Milbria & Albert P.
Ouzts, Milbria Lee Williams   Apr 12 1866 Oct 24 1915
  w/o Albert Preston d/o Pamela T. & Dr. Goode
Owens, Mamie Clark   Jan 23 1884   nd
  w/o Wm. H.
Owens, Wm. Henry   Nov 1 1882 Jan 1 1962
Pace, Albert Twiggs   1867   1924
  br/o Wm. H.
Pace, Anna Greiner   1874   1958
  w/o Albert T.
Pace, Irene Kilpatrick   Apr 12 1910 Jne 2 1910
  d/o Anna G. & Albert T.
Pace, Mattie Oliver   nd Jul 10 1916
  w/o Wm. H. d/o Mary V. Kellum & Dr. J.H.
Pace, Ollie Mae   Jan 27 1903 Aug 29 1909
  d/o A.T. & A.L.
Pace, Robert Lewis   May 31 1914 May 18 1918
  s/o Anna G. & Albert T.
Pace, Taney James   Jan 23 1882 Jul 20 1899
  s/o Mr. & Mrs. Wm. H.

```
Pace, William H.                                      nd   Dec 13 1913
Pace-Anderson, Mary Ann McE.              1830              1904
Palmer, Bessie Quinney          Nov 16 1880   Mar 12 1920
  w/o Frank S.  d/o Alice Gray & Thomas
Palmer, Bessie Thomas           Feb 22 1893   Jne 28 1956
  w/o Jesse C.  d/o Eula Redd & J.B.
Palmer, Clifford Quinney                  1892              1963
  w/o Samuel  d/o Alice Gray & Thomas
Palmer, Frank                   Jan  5 1917   May 11 1918
  s/o Bessie Q. & Frank S.
Palmer, Frank Sidney            Aug 19 1879   May 19 1945
  md 1st Bessie Quinney  2nd Stella Farriba  s/o L.B.
  Palmer (agent of Methodist Publishing Co., Nashville,
  Tenn.)
Palmer, Infant                            nd               nd
  of Maud L. & John T.
Palmer, John Rheney                       1885             1949
  s/o Mary E. Rheney & W.C.
Palmer, John T.  WW-I           Apr  7 1892   May 23 1956
  h/o 1st Maud Long  2nd Irene T.  s/o Iola Boyd &
  John T.  Sgt Btry B 118 Field Arty 31 DIV AEF
Palmer, Lewis B.                          1900             1949
Palmer, Louise H.                         1897             1947
  w/o L.B.
Palmer, Maud Long               Dec  6 1887   Mar  2 1936
  w/o John T.  d/o Martha Burns & Thos. Wilson
Palmer, Moselle Neely                     1890             1967
  w/o John R.  d/o Lillian W. & R.C., Sr.
Palmer, Ruth McElmurray         Apr  3 1894   Oct 23 1971
  /Cothran  w/o 1st James Robeson Cothran, issue:
  J.R., Jr. & John McE.  md 2nd Jesse Campbell Palmer, I
Palmer, Samuel                            1892             1941
Palmer, Stella Farriba          Jan 30 1898   Mar 30 1949
  2nd w/o Frank Sidney
Parker, Ida Moore               Apr  7 1885   Jan 18 1958
  w/o William Silas
Parker, William Silas           Jan 31 1892   Nov  6 1969
Perkins, Lonnie Eton            Feb  1 1913   Oct 20 1957
Perkins, Lula Cross             Jan 24 1862   Jan  1 1936
  w/o W.P.
Perkins, William Penn           Aug 17 1859   May  4 1934
Perry, Amos P.  CSA             Sep  4 1847   Jne  2 1900
  Co D 27th Ga Bn
Perry, Martha                   Aug 15 1834   Nov 28 1912
Phelps, Gell W.                           1884             1943
Ponder, Ada Greiner                       1876             1965
  w/o Chas. A.  d/o Ella H. & John D.
Ponder, Charles Allen                     1876             1955
Porter, Annie G. Laramore       Mar 25 1883   Nov 12 1956
  w/o Lawrence J.
Porter, Lawrence Jefferson      Jan 27 1878   Jne  1 1963
Posey, Corrie Louise                      1922             1922
  d/o Corrie Ann Holley & Wm. Edward
Posey, Lena Mae                           1916             1918
  d/o Corrie Ann Holley & Wm. Edward
```

Posey, William Edward   Dec 9 1891 May 16 1951
   h/o Corrie Ann Holley s/o Elizabeth Maria Turner &
   Jas. Malachi
Powell, Francis Wylie WW-II   Mar 24 1908 Jne 30 1950
   s/o Francis G. & Dr. Louis E. Va Cpl Air Corps
Powell, Lillian Lewis   Jne 20 1895   L
   w/o Wm. Henry d/o Lillian Fulcher & Preston
   Brooks, Sr.
Powell, Louis Edmond MD   Jul 14 1876 Sep 26 1909
   F&AM s/o Mary J. Cresham & Green B.
Powell, Louis Edmond, Jr.   Aug 29 1904 Aug 30 1906
   s/o Francis G. & Dr. Louis E.
Powell, Mary J. Gresham   May 18 1839 Nov 24 1905
   w/o 1st Jesse P. Green 2nd Green B. Powell MD
   d/o Sarah M. Anderson & Edmund B.(Byne) See Clark,
   op. cit., 162.
Powell, Ralph Lewis, Jr.   Sep 4 1958 May 5 1961
   s/o Pauline Cooper & Ralph L.
Powell, William Henry   Feb 10 1895 Mar 4 1971
   s/o Moselle Griffin & Henry Cater F&AM
Powell, William Henry, Jr.   Jul 23 1927 Feb 8 1965
   WW-II (h/o Frances McNair s/o Lillian Lewis &
   Wm. H.) and
Powell, William Henry, III   Jan 7 1951 Feb 8 1965
   (s/o Frances McNair & Wm. H., Jr.) lost their lives
   in the crash of an Eastern Airlines flight in the
   Atlantic Ocean approximately 6 miles off shore from
   Jamaica, N. Y., on the evening of February 8, 1965.
Quick, B.B.   Sep 16 1900 Oct 24 1949
   s/o Mina Godbee & Henry
Quick, Charlotte Eileen   May 5 1943 Jul 26 1944
   d/o Mr. & Mrs. Sidney
Quick, David Wayman   May 15 1947 May 16 1947
Quick, Jeanette Ward   Mar 18 1905 Mar 31 1972
   w/o B.B. d/o Mr. & Mrs. Charlie
Quick, Needom WW-II   Jan 4 1925 Jne 25 1958
   s/o Virginia Frazier & Robert Fla MOM M3 USNR
Quick, Sidney Herbert   Feb 17 1923 Dec 15 1964
   s/o Jeanette W. & B.B.
Quinney, Alice Gray   Dec 8 1854 Oct 28 1938
   w/o Thomas d/o Eliz. & Simeon A. Parents buried in
   W-Boro Confed. cem. (ed).
Quinney, Alice May   Jan 4 1883 Jan 27 1953
   d/o Alice Gray & Thomas
Quinney, Callie Nowell   Oct 3 1878 Aug 30 1923
   1st w/o Gray
Quinney, Gray   Apr 7 1878 Dec 9 1965
   s/o Alice Gray & Thomas
Quinney, Madge Saunders   May 25 1899 Oct 27 1966
   2nd w/o Gray
Quinney, Thomas   Aug 11 1849 Mar 19 1923
Rackley, Barbara Reynolds   Nov 14 1892 May 22 1956
   w/o J. Frank, Sr. d/o Angie Perry & Jos. J.
Rackley, George W.   Nov 23 1876 Nov 19 1908
   s/o Mary V. Cates & Steve T.

Rackley, Hattie Allen   Jne 11 1863   Oct 26 1912
  w/o J.V.
Rackley, Infant   nd   nd
  s/o Mr. & Mrs. G.W.
Rackley, J. Frank, Jr.   Nov 8 1930   Sep 22 1965
  s/o Barbara Reynolds & J. Frank
Rackley, J. Frank, Sr.   Apr 18 1897   Apr 27 1949
  s/o Hattie Allen & Jos. V.
Rackley, John Franklin   Jul 9 1856   Dec 2 1953
  s/o Mary V. Cates & S.T.
Rackley, John Hugh   Mar 18 1891   Jul 8 1905
  s/o Willie Cates & John F.
Rackley, Joseph Virgil   Oct 1 1860   Dec 7 1906
  s/o Mary V. Cates & S.T.
Rackley, Lila   Sep 20 1902   Jne 16 1921
  d/o Willie Cates & John F.
Rackley, Mary V. Cates   Oct 10 1836   Oct 16 1921
  w/o S.T.
Rackley, Stephen T. CSA   Jne 10 1834   Sep 3 1904
  Pvt 7th Regt 2nd Brigade 1st Div Ga Mil
Rackley, Willie Cates   Jne 7 1861   Jan 28 1930
  w/o John Franklin
Radcliff, Drannon W.   Nov 11 1922   Dec 16 1937
Radcliffe, Atha Russell   1887   1952
Radcliffe, Woodrow W.   Apr 9 1914   Jul 20 1953
Rafferty, Thomas Edward   Apr 29 1865   Dec 10 1907
  1st h/o Lula Hurst (Summerfield)
Raley, Mollie C.   1846   1933
  sis/o Nannie Raley Vinson
Ratcliff, Clara D.   Sep 10 1917   nd
Ratcliff, Mary Pauline   Mar 4 1923   Jul 23 1923
Ratcliff, Robert R.   Nov 10 1898   Jul 14 1957
Ratliff, James P.   Oct 6 1884   Jan 26 1956
  s/o Rebecca Gulledge & Gaston
Ratliff, Sallie Jones   Oct 23 1888   Mar 29 1973
  w/o James P. d/o Sarah Morgan & Nathaniel
Redd, Annie M.   Jne 30 1862   Jan 5 1916
  d/o Caroline Missouri Elliott & Wm. Mack
Redd, John Allen   1860   1922
  1st h/o Zillah Bostick s/o Caroline Missouri Elliott
  & Wm. Mack
Redd, W.M.   Sep 25 1872   Apr 26 1908
  s/o Caroline Missouri Elliott & Wm. Mack
Reese, John Harvey   Jan 15 1885   Jan 17 1956
Reese, Josie Hatcher   Feb 11 1883   May 1 1960
  w/o J.H. d/o Geraldine Thomas & Wm. J.
Reeves, Ann Taylor   Apr 1 1920   Feb 12 1971
  w/o L.R. d/o Emma Usher & John Carey
Reeves, Eleanor Hill Bartlett   Aug 21 1900   Mar 11 1969
  w/o 1st E.W. Bartlett: one son, Ernest Jr.
  md 2nd S.A. Reeves, no issue; d/o Eleanor Doneghue
  & Ernest Eugene Hill b Cornish, N.H.
Reeves, Ida Lee Carpenter   Sep 12 1895   Sep 7 1966
  w/o Mallory T. d/o ------ Rogers & John Nelson

Reeves, Leslie R.   WW-II   Apr 26 1914   Apr 28 1960
    s/o Lola Lewis & Riley W.   PFC H&S Co 207 Engr C Bn
Reeves, Mallory Thomas   Jne 9 1891   Mar 27 1967
    s/o Cora Davenport & David Brooks
Reeves, Nancy Lynn (infant)   only   date   1955
    d/o Thomas & Edna Jester
Reynolds, Oliver H.   Apr 2 1904   Nov 23 1968
    h/o Mary Osee Gordon   s/o Angie Perry & J.J., Sr.
Rhodes, Fannie G.   Apr 6 1886   May 2 1960
    w/o Wesley P.
Rhodes, Wesley P.   Nov 15 1879   Jne 28 1959
Ridgedill, Ada Perkins   Jul 1 1898   L
    w/o Elton W.
Ridgedill, Elton W.   Oct 5 1897   Oct 30 1963
Roberson, Anna Burton   Dec 26 1866   Mar 3 1939
Roberson, Homer Clem   Aug 16 1861   Mar 21 1940
Roberson, Roscoe Burton   Sep 23 1887   Jul 18 1918
Robinson, Allen   CSA   age 79 y   Mar 2 1928
    Co G 2 SC Arty   Obit. T.C., Mar 3, 1928.
Robinson, Mrs. Allen F.   age 82 y   Feb 23 1928
    w/o Allen, CSA Survived by two daughters, Mrs. W.G.
    Sapp, Mrs. J.M. Freeman and a brother, J.M. Foster.
    Obit. T.C., Feb 25, 1928.
Robinson, Bessie Oxyner   Apr 23 1903   Nov 16 1973
    w/o John R.
Robinson, Helen L.   Sep 20 1915   Apr 13 1916
Robinson, Jas. Edw.   age 78 y   Dec 31 1967
Robinson, Jethro T. WOW   Nov 5 1881   Nov 16 1924
Robinson, John R., Sr.   May 1 1896   Nov 23 1965
Robinson, Josef Emil   Sep 30 1908   Mar 18 1973
Robinson, Joseph A.   Jne 5 1875   Jan 23 1924
Robinson, Mabel Burke   Aug 20 1882   Mar 16 1957
Rogers, Fred   WW-II   Dec 25 1907   Nov 22 1961
    Ga MM3   USNR
Rogers, Fred Olin, Jr.   Jan 5 1958   Jan 7 1958
Rogers, Marie Kimball   nd   nd
    w/o Sam Alvin
Rogers, Sam Alvin   nd   nd
Rogers, Warren T.   Nov 21 1861   Aug 11 1894
    1st h/o Mamie Rowland
Rollins, Daisy Coursey   Apr 27 1908   Jan 14 1964
    w/o Rufus Elester d/o Lota Woodard & Wm. Perry
Rollins, Rufus Elester, Sr.   Dec 11 1900   L
    s/o Eliza Cain & John R.
Roof, Ada Jean Vickery   Aug 28 1918   Dec 12 1959
    w/o Daniel J., Jr. d/o Lizzie Holland & Stafford
    Stanley
Roof, Daniel Joseph   1886   1973
Roof, Daniel Joseph   Dec 8 1913   Aug 25 1964
    s/o Hattie & Daniel
Roof, Hattie B.   1885   1956
    1st w/o Daniel J.
Roof, Myrtie Moak   Oct 26 1900   Jul 15 1962
    2nd w/o Daniel J., Sr.

```
Ross, Eugene H.                              1914          1973
  s/o Mattie Elizabeth Best & Wm. Henry
Ross, Maggie M.                              1923           nd
  w/o Eugene H.  d/o Cora Kilpatrick & Will
Rowell, Annie L.                   May  5 1862  Nov 23 1924
Rowell, R.T.                       Jan 15 1855  Jan  7 1923
Rowland, Clarence Leonard          May 21 1872  Aug  6 1938
  s/o Catherine Barnes Whitehead & Charles Alden
Rowland, Francis Jefferson         May  7 1903  Feb  8 1914
  s/o Mary O'Connell & Clarence L.
Rowland, Freddie Haeseler          Mar 12 1868  Jan  4 1952
  w/o R.B.  d/o Frances Chance & Samuel Burchardt
Rowland, Mary O'Connell            Jan  8 1872  Dec 24 1948
  w/o Clarence L.  d/o Elizabeth Chapple & Daniel
Rowland, Robert Buxton             Sep 30 1863  Mar 17 1898
Rowland, Robbie                    Apr 14 1898  Jul 13 1901
  d/o Robt. & Freddie
Royal, Herbert Ludine              Jan 31 1937  Feb 21 1965
Royal, Oregon B.                   Nov  6 1872  Jne 11 1958
  w/o W.W.
Royal, Walter W.                   Jan 25 1869  Sep 24 1956
Russell, Bertie Magnolia           Sep 21 1913  Jul 21 1963
  w/o Theodore R.
Russell, Theodore Roosvelt         Oct 13 1910  Oct 13 1969
Russell, Willis D.                 Mar 14 1936  Sep 23 1954
  Ga PFC HQ Co 1 Bn  188 ABN Inf Bn USA
Sandeford, Gratt W.                Nov 20 1894  Mar 25 1897
  s/o M.J. & Wm. C.
Sandeford, Minnie Jarrett          Nov 15 1853  Feb 12 1932
  w/o Wm. C.
Sandeford, Wm. C.  WW-I                    nd  Jul 18 1940
  s/o Minnie J. & Wm. C.  Pvt 157 Depot Brig
Sandeford, William Capers          Feb 18 1849  Nov  4 1911
  s/o Mary & Hill  See will of his father, Will Bk A,
  446-47.  Parents buried in Old Church Cem.  (ed).
Sanders, John David                Dec 31 1857  Feb  1 1941
Sanders, Sallie Burton             Dec 13 1868           nd
  w/o J.D.
Sapp, Addie Robinson               Jul 16 1886  Jul 13 1963
  w/o Wm. Gratten, Jr.
Sapp, Beulah Katie                 Oct  7 1915  Jne 18 1917
  d/o Addie Robinson & Wm. G., Jr.
Sapp, Fred Gene  Kor W             Dec  3 1928  Jne  7 1953
  s/o May Brown & Harvey L.  M/Sgt 101 AAA Gun Bn
Sapp, Harvey L.                    Aug 13 1886  Dec 25 1930
  s/o Willie Brookins & Wm. Gratten
Sapp, Hayward Daniel                        1906          1965
  s/o Lavonia Bunn & Hayward D.
Sapp, Henry Jasper                 Dec 13 1917  Dec 26 1919
  s/o May Brown & Harvey L.
Sapp, Infant                       Nov 23 1916  Dec  6 1916
  s/o Myrtie Youngblood & Oscar L.
Sapp, James                        age 47 y    Oct 17 1965
  s/o Addie Robinson & Wm. Gratten, Jr.
```

Sapp, Louise Cochran   1911   L
  w/o Hayward D. d/o Lillie Taylor & Jesse A.
Sapp, Myrtle Youngblood   nd   L
  w/o Oscar L. d/o Mary Baugh & Wesley Jackson
Sapp, Oscar Lee   Apr 17 1879 Dec 9 1937
  s/o Willie Brookins & Wm. Gratten
Sapp, William Gratten, Jr.   Sep 13 1876 Feb 1 1928
  h/o Addie Robinson s/o Willie Brookins & Wm. G.
  f/o four sons and one daughter: Floyd, Joseph, James
  & Paul & Mrs. Forrest Place. Obit. T.C.. Feb 4, 1928
Sasser, Gregory Lee   Mar 12 1953 Mar 16 1958
Saxon, Wm. E.   1879   1936
Scales, Floyd Lawson   Jul 15 1870 Apr 26 1909
  s/o Francis Rebecca Martin & Robt. Watt Atty-at-law
  md Mary Scales Pillow of Greenwood, Miss br/o Leora
  Scales (Gresham) (Davis) (ed).
Scott, Edward L.   Jul 4 1861 Jul 6 1925
Scott, John Stephens   1894   1941
  s/o Martha Rackley & Edw. L.
Scott, Martha Rackley   Apr 9 1863 Apr 2 1946
  w/o Edw. L.
Scott, Naomi Odom   1895   nd
  w/o John S. d/o Nora Jane Houston & Jas. Richard
Scott, Robert E. WW-I   Nov 12 1896 Feb 3 1963
  s/o Martha & Edward L. Ga Pvt USN
Seeger, Samuel Todd   Feb 21 1891 Apr 11 1956
Seeger, Shelly Pace   nd   L
  w/o S. Todd d/o Mattie Oliver & Wm. H.
Sentell, Cynthia Louise   nd   nd
  inf d/o Thelma H. & Ben
Sheppard, Arthur Lee   Jne 26 1900 Mar 1 1974
  h/o Florine Turk s/o Bessie Horton (Thigpen) &
  Enoch. For many years owner & operator of the
  movie theater (ed).
Shuman, John Jarvin   Feb 25 1950 Feb 28 1950
  s/o Carolyn Mundy & R. Dan
Sikes, James A., Jr.   Jan 19 1930 Mar 4 1963
Sikes, Mack Frank   Dec 31 1894 Feb 11 1945
Simmons, James A., Jr.   May 16 1912 May 23 1963
  h/o Evelyn Godbee s/o James & Willie B.
Simmons, James Alfred   1882   1967
  s/o Mary Ola Simmons & Rev. John Wesley
Simmons, Roy N. WW-II   1916   1945
  s/o Willie B. & J.A. USNR d in Manila, P.I.
Simmons, Willie Brunson   1888   L
  w/o James A. d/o Emma Martha Yates & Harvey H.
Simons, Mattie Clarke   1888   nd
  w/o Wm. A.
Simons, Wm. Andrew   1880   1945
Sims, Ellen   1907   1934
Skinner, Charles W., Jr.   Apr 21 1901 Mar 26 1955
  s/o Minnie Caraker & Chas. W., Sr. President of the
  Bank of Waynesboro (ed).

Skinner, Charles Wesley, Sr.   May 23 1863   Jan 16 1931
  s/o Sarah Tabb & John J. President of the Bank of
  Waynesboro and leading merchant. Obit. T.C., Jan 23,
  1931.
Skinner, Franklin M.   Nov 20 1907 Nov 5 1953
  h/o Mary Brinson s/o Minnie Caraker & Chas. W., Sr.
Skinner, Henrietta Boyer   Feb 22 1907 May 8 1972
  w/o Chas. W., Jr. d/o Lena McKenzie Lovejoy &
  Mirabeau H.
Skinner, John Jones   Nov 5 1895 Nov 20 1959
  h/o Sara s/o Elizabeth Cates & Jones J.
Skinner, Julia R.   Sep 7 1843 Jul 25 1914
  d/o Sarah Tabb & John J.
Skinner, Minnie Caraker   May 25 1874 Apr 29 1940
  w/o Chas. Wesley Sr. md Mar 8, 1900
  d/o Elizabeth Bayne & Jacob Monroe
Skinner, Napoleon B.   May 15 1882 Jne 18 1953
Skinner, Rallie Trader   Sep 21 1886   nd
  w/o Napoleon B.
Smith, Belle Hyatt   1896   L
  w/o Thos. Walter d/o Jessie Stevens & Elisha Leonard
Smith, Catherine Bateman   1871   1941
Smith, D. Oliver WW-I   Dec 21 1892 Jan 11 1950
  Pvt USA
Smith, Edwin A.   Mar 25 1859 Mar 27 1920
Smith, Edwin A. Smith, Jr.   Aug 10 1895 Oct 6 1918
  WW-I Lost on the Otranto s/o Sarah E. & E.A.
Smith, Hilda Mozelle   Jan 16 1928 Jul 30 1946
  d/o Maude Register & Rufus Wm.
Smith, Joseph Walden   Jul 12 1861 Oct 13 1900
  h/o Ida Lewis
Smith, Lillie C.   1894   1965
  w/o D.O.
Smith, Rufus William   Sep 26 1902 Feb 12 1958
  s/o Josie Hartley & William
Smith, Sarah E.   Oct 20 1858 Aug 29 1948
  w/o Edwin A.
Smith, Thos. Walter   1892   1941
  s/o Josie Hartley & Wm.
Smith, Wm. Henry   1861   1943
Smith, Willie Mae   Sep 22 1895 Apr 19 1973
Smith, Zera Alice   Mar 3 1904 Feb 13 1958
  d/o Josie Hartley & Wm.
Smoot, George W.   1900   1963
Smoot, Ruth R.   1914   19__
  w/o George W.
Smyly, Euclid J.   1870   1943
Smyly, Euclid J., Jr.   1903   1958
  s/o Florence F. & Euclid J.
Smyly, Florence F.   1880   1930
  w/o E.J.
Smyly, Margaret Gordon   1914   19__
  w/o Euclid J., Jr. d/o Mamie Lou Fulcher & Wm. H.
Spears, Homer M.   1873   1912

Spears, Linnie Belle   1870   1955
  w/o H.M.
Spencer, Carlton   only   date   Feb 16 1933
  California Sgt ICL USA
Steadman, George Alfred   Jne 30 1883   Jul 6 1932
  s/o Rachel Mary Hane & Jonathan Elbert
Steadman, Georgia Thomas   Jne 20 1889   Sep 22 1954
  w/o Geo. A. d/o Emma Marsh & Nathaniel P.
Stembridge, Henry Hansel, Sr.   Aug 1 1875   Jan 10 1937
  s/o Elizabeth Hawkins & Henry. Pharmacist; one son,
  Hansel, a Baptist minister (ed).
Stembridge, Maude Foreman   Oct 6 1876   Oct 16 1958
  w/o H.H., Sr. w/o Jane Rountree & Isaac
Stephens, Corbett E.   1898   1958
Stephens, Jake K.   Sep 20 1890   May 5 1904
Stephens, Jennie B.   1900   1951
  w/o Corbett E.
Stewart, George Alvin   1905   1946
Stewart, Mary Busbee   May 27 1881   May 25 1970
  w/o Samuel d/o Martha Ann Williams & Pleasant
Stewart, Samuel   Aug 15 1871   Apr 19 1950
  s/o Lydia Williams & ------Stewart
Story, Ida   Oct 30 1902   Jne 10 1958
  d/o Ida Gresham & Samuel Gaines, II
Story, Ida Gresham   May 21 1876   Apr 9 1942
  w/o Samuel G., II d/o Annie Lassiter & Job A.
  See Clark, op. cit., 162.
Story, Infant   only   date   Jul 12 1921
  of Willie Mae Malabar & S.G. Story, III
Story, Samuel Gaines, II   Oct 29 1870   Jul 25 1923
  s/o Burmah Steed & Samuel G., I
  See Hephzibah cem. (ed).
Story, Samuel Gaines, III   Jan 23 1897   Jne 4 1949
  WW-I S2 USNRF md 1st Willie Mae Malabar 2nd Lois
  Ward s/o Ida G. & S.G., II
Story, Samuel Gaines, IV   Nov 20 1922   Nov 18 1943
  WW-II s/o Willie M.M. & S.G., III AAF
Story, Willie Mae Malabar   May 31 1897   Jan 21 1931
  w/o S.G. Story, III d/o Kate Fulcher & Ben F.
Strange, Betty Ruth   Dec 9 1925   Jul 26 1932
Strange, W.T.   1875   1954
Strother, Albert   1854   1914
Strother, Albert Amos WW-I   Sep 14 1898   May 31 1968
  h/o Mary Riddle Ga S2 USN For Mrs. Strother's Obit.
  see T.C., Jan 29, 1932.
Stroud, Daniel Lee   Dec 18 1883   Dec 31 1966
  s/o Lula Truett & Perry
Stroud, Irene Robinson   Sep 15 1894   L
  w/o Daniel L. d/o Susie Virginia Jones & John
  Randolph
Stroud, Kathryn Tomlin   Dec 18 1921   May 19 1961
  w/o W.R. d/o Hattie Barnes & Bill J.
Sullivan, William Gresham   Apr 17 1857   Oct 21 1913
  s/o Annie Gresham & William Decatur

Sullivan, William Lester WW-I Mar 13 1881 Jne 23 1929
  s/o Winnie Lester & Wm. G. Sgt Field Arty
Summers, Ethel Greiner   Jul 2 1886 Dec 27 1966
  w/o A.D. d/o Ella Hatfield & John D.
Tanham, Frank   Apr 6 1892   nd
  The Tanhams lived in Plainfield, New Jersey (ed).
Tanham, Irene Kilpatrick   Sep 7 1895 Oct 14 1957
  w/o Frank d/o Irene Baxley & Geo. P.
Taylor, Dorothy   May 20 1912 Jne 19 1913
  d/o W.E. & R.M.
Taylor, Henry I.   1890   1973
Taylor, Mary H.   1890   1968
  w/o Henry I.
Taylor, Rosa Mims   1881   1950
  w/o Wm. E. d/o Clifford White & W.L. m/o two
  daughters: Clifford & Grace and a son, Wm., Jr.
  (ed). See T.C., June 12, 1931.
Taylor, William E.   1880   1940
Thigpen, Hal Battle   1886   1945
Thigpen, Infant   only date   1931
  d/o H.B. & O.B.
Thomas, Emma Marsh   Sep 15 1862 Jne 3 1934
  w/o Nathaniel P. d/o Georgia S. Walton & Isaac
Thomas, Emmett C.   Mar 9 1882 Jul 14 1945
Thomas, Eula Redd   Sep 25 1864 Apr 22 1934
  w/o Jethro B. d/o Caroline Missouri Elliott & Wm.
  Mack
Thomas, Jethro Beauregard   Oct 4 1861 Sep 18 1941
  s/o Nancy Cates & Jethro
Thomas, John H.   1902   Dec 2 1972
Thomas, Louise S.   1912   1968
Thomas, Nathaniel Pinckney   Apr 15 1863 Sep 23 1917
  See Will Bk. B, 208. A J. Pinckney Thomas (b Burke
  Co Apr 29, 1839; md Feb 1860 Mary L. Clanton,
  d/o Col. Turner Clanton of Augusta) was found in
  Samuel A. Echols, Biographical Sketches, Georgia's
  General Assembly of 1878, 94-95. This might be the
  father of the above Nathaniel (ed).
Thomas, Stella H.   Oct 16 1890 Jne 25 1954
  w/o Emmett C.
Thomas, William Roy   May 20 1891 Jne 21 1897
  s/o Eula R. & J.B.
Thompson, Dr. Cleveland, Sr.   Nov 7 1884 Aug 5 1958
  s/o Mary J. Wilkes & Thomas b Vidalia
Thompson, Eileen L.   Nov 27 1890 Feb 24 1958
  w/o Dr. Cleveland d/o Walter V. & Minnie Ogilvie
  Lanier b Allendale, S.C. For the Lanier family, see
  John Wright Boyd, op. cit., in "Source Books for
  Additional Data".
Thompson, Emmie McKie   Jul 1 1890 Aug 27 1969
  w/o Dr. Paul Francis d/o Julia Kingman & James Baker
  sis/o Ellen McK. Wimberly
Thompson, Florence McElmurray   Jul 4 1893 Sep 6 1963
  w/o F.W. d/o Haidee Routzahn & Judson S.

Thompson, Peyton Wade   WW-I   Aug 8 1892   Aug 2 1961
  s/o Josephine Wade & Wall Tattnall   Capt. AEF
Thompson, Peyton Wade, Jr.   Jul 16 1922   Aug 7 1944
  WW-II s/o Florence McE. & P.W.   2nd Lt Co C 120 Inf
  30 Inf Div killed in action near Mortain, France:
  buried in American cemetery there   (ed).
Thorne, Elma Johnson   Jul 23 1911   Jul 9 1944
  w/o Ernest Louis
Thorne, Ernest Louis   Aug 13 1906   Jul 9 1944
  s/o Anna Godbee & Edward L.
Tidwell, Hugh   Apr 18 1903   Mar 29 1951
Tinley, Annie Wilson   Jan 17 1892   Jul 8 1965
  w/o Lawton E.
Tinley, Frank E.   1914   1938
  1st h/o Florrie Daniel s/o Annie Wilson & Lawton E.
Tinley, Infant twins   only   date   1944,
  sons/o Billie Burnsed & Lewis
Tinley, John Henry   Jan 23 1854   Sep 28 1938
  s/o Martha Smith & John Henry
Tinley, Katie L. Tinley   Jne 14 1858   Apr 1 1941
  w/o John H.
Tinley, Lawton E.   Jan 11 1886   Feb 4 1953
  s/o Katie L. Tinley & John Henry
Tinley, Lewis S.   Jan 1 1890   May 23 1910
  s/o Katie L. Tinley & John Henry
Tinley, Sallie J. Mosely   Jne 26 1878   Apr 30 1904
  1st w/o W. Morris
Tompkins, Byrd B. WW-I   Jne 16 1890   Feb 21 1953
  2nd h/o Minnie Carter s/o Monte Hilldey & Benj. Hill
  Hospital Corps
Tomlin, Bill Jones   Jul 18 1889   Dec 30 1937
Tomlin, Hattie Barnes   Feb 6 1891   Feb 8 1959
  w/o B.J.
Tomlin, Infant   Apr 5 1920   Apr 7 1920
  d/o B.J. & H.B.
Trowbridge, Robert P.   age 50 y   Oct 13 1973
  h/o Tommie Gray
Tucker, Cecil Carroll   Jne 30 1907   Sep 19 1955
Tucker, Mamie Hill   Feb 23 1918   May 7 1919
  d/o M.H. & M. King
Tucker, Winston   May 19 1952   Mar 30 1953
Tufts, Eva Brinson   Feb 14 1875   Mar 6 1957
  d/o Martha E. Herrington & Frank L., Sr.
Turner, William H.   Feb 22 1892   Sep 10 1957
Tyler, John B.   Nov 9 1856   Jul 20 1919
  s/o Anne Caroline Kittrell & Capt. Thos. W.
Tyler, Statham McLendon   Jne 29 1863   Dec 12 1947
  w/o John B. d/o Mary Ann Stribling & Isaac A.
  McLendon
Tyler, Vivienne   Aug 25 1893   Jne 16 1918
  d/o Statham McL. & John B.
Vaughn, Daisy Garlick   Sep 3 1872   Jne 14 1924
  w/o James Henry d/o Julia Blount & Edgar S.
Vaughn, James Henry   Oct 18 1867   Jan 27 1926

Vaughan, James Henry, Jr.   Aug 2 1897 Aug 17 1897
    s/o Daisy Garlick & J. Henry
Vaughn, Pearl S.   1883   19___
    w/o R.D.
Vaughn, Richard D.   1882   1944
Vernon, James Edward   1894   1944
    Lt USN
Vickery, Alan Wayne   Mar 2 1951 May 27 1951
    s/o Dorothy Elizabeth Burnsed (of Eden, Ga.) &
    Julius Walter
Vinson, Gary   Oct 30 1873 Mar 30 1961
    s/o Nannie Raley & N.W. Hardware merchant. Bachelor
    Philanthropist to Baptist institutions (ed).
Vinson, Nannie Raley   1844   1927
    w/o N.W.
Walden, Pauline Hill Barnes   Nov 9 1914 Nov 23 1969
    d/o Bessie Rowland & Jas. W. Hill
Wallace, A. B.   Aug 3 1891 Mar 15 1938
    s/o Julia Stephens & Adam B.
Wallace, Adam Brinson   CSA   Sep 11 1847 Apr 22 1928
Wallace, Bessie Mays   Apr 26 1896 Aug 26 1962
    w/o A.B.
Wallace, David Garnett   Mar 14 1915 Dec 1 1921
    s/o Minnie L. & David J.
Wallace, David J.   Oct 15 1878 Nov 19 1943
    s/o Julia S. & Adam B.
Wallace, Florence L.   Nov 29 1913 Jul 12 1914
Wallace, Infant   only   date Apr 11 1906
    s/o M.L. & D.J.
Wallace, Julia Stephens   Sep 5 1847 Mar 14 1927
    w/o Adam Brinson
Wallace, Lovick Herrington   May 15 1889 Jul 16 1963
    s/o Julia S. & Adam B.
Wallace, Mamie P.   Feb 4 1907 Aug 15 1907
Wallace, Minnie Lane   Sep 13 1880 Feb 16 1957
    w/o D.J. d/o Emma Etta Cail & Milton J.
Wallace, Sallie Mae T.   Feb 13 1893   nd
    w/o Lovick H. d/o Anna Godbee & Edward L. Thorne
Walters, James Henry WW-I & II Jne 28 1897 Dec 12 1961
    h/o Laura Morgan s/o Emma Gray & Wm. H. WW-I Sea-
    man, USNRF 7th & 12th Co 1st Trng Reg WW-II Lt-Col
    Finance Dept
Ward, Charles E. WW-II   Jul 19 1909 Aug 14 1955
    Cpl 140 Base Unit AAF
Ward, Charlie Louis   Jan 21 1869 Feb 22 1945
    s/o Al Jarona Prescott & Calvin
Ward, Gilbert A.   Oct 7 1878 May 31 1956
Ward, Hugh L.   Feb 17 1885 Jan 15 1948
    s/o Minnie Spotswood & Seaborn Harris
Ward, James M. WW-I   Apr 10 1894 Jne 1 1966
    Ga Pvt USA
Ward, John Walter   Sep 4 1912 Dec 23 1950
    h/o Catherine Mobley s/o Adele McNorrill & G.A.
Ward, Julia Bell   May 22 1856 Dec 28 1941
Ward, Mattie Tomlin   Nov 10 1877 May 26 1957
    w/o Charlie Louis d/o Maria Godbee & Med

291

Ward, Paul L.   Feb 22 1923 Nov 22 1939
  s/o Mr. & Mrs. Hugh L.
Ward, Thomas E.   Oct 27 1900 Dec 10 1951
  s/o Mattie Tomlin & Charlie Louis
Ware, Sidney A.   Oct 25 1885 Sep 20 1904
Warnock, Ellie A.   Nov 20 1879 Jne 29 1880
  s/o Wm. & M.T.
Warnock, George O. CSA   Jan 29 1842 Dec 20 1924
  Co B 7th Ga Cav Prior to that he was with Co B 17th
  Ga Regt Ga Vol and the 21st Ga Cav. Wounded at
  Trevillian Station. Prisoner at Fort Delaware.
  Clerk of the Superior Court (ed).
Warnock, Margaret T.   Feb 5 1845 Mar 12 1901
  w/o William
Warnock, Nancy E.   1811 Apr 27 1888
Warnock, William CSA   Jne 17 1840 Oct 29 1886
  Co A 3rd Ga Regt, Wright's Brigade. Wounded at
  Sharpsburg.
Waters, Sadie Roberta   Jan 25 1917 Sep 19 1962
Watkins, Julien H.   Jan 31 1874 Feb 7 1946
Watkins, Temperance   Aug 8 1940 Oct 6 1903
Watson, Ollie G.   1903   1965
Watson, Verdie M.   1900   L
  w/o Ollie G.
Wetherhorn, Infants   nd   nd
  of Mr. & Mrs. J.
Wheat, George Grafton   1895   1950
Wheat, Minnie Holston   1900   1943
  w/o G.G.
Wheeler, Nellye G.   Aug 22 1885 Dec 17 1962
Wheeler, Samuel P.   Nov 9 1884 May 16 1938
White, Herschel H.   Apr 20 1898 Jul 2 1965
  h/o Marion Simmons s/o Theodosia Durrence & Rufus
  King
White, Marion Simmons   Sep 11 1907   L
  w/o Herschel H. d/o Willie Brunson & James Alfred
Whitehead, Carolyn McElmurray   Mar   1873 Jne   1898
  1st w/o James H. md Nov 27, 1895 d/o Annie E.
  Shewmake & John F.
Whitehead, James H.   Nov 19 1866 Jul 23 1928
  s/o Margaret Ireland Harper & John P.C. President
  of the Waynesboro Savings Bank and of the Citizens
  Bank of Waynesboro (ed).
Whitehead, Madeline Routzahn   Oct 17 1883 Mar 17 1910
  2nd w/o James H. md Mar 17, 1903 d/o Florence
  Byne & L.H.
Whitehead, Nora L. Edmondston   Sep 26 1886 Aug 31 1920
  3rd w/o James H. md Dec 2, 1919
Whitehead, Lula Cathrine   Jne 7 1915 Nov 17 1915
  d/o Wm. & Connie
Wilkins, Archibald   Jne 14 1885 Aug 28 1888
  s/o Fannie W. & Joseph H.

Wilkins, Fannie Warren   Oct 21 1849 Oct 18 1913
 w/o Jos. H. d/o Julia Battey & L.P.
Wilkins, Joseph Hamilton   Dec 13 1837 Sep 10 1891
Wilkins, Joseph Hamilton   Feb 27 1881 Jul 2 1881
 s/o F.W. & J.H.
Wilkins, Julia Battey   Feb 7 1871 Mar 29 1873
 d/o F.W. & J.H.
Wilkins, Lindsay Warren   May 27 1883 Aug 13 1883
 s/o F.W. & J.H.
Wilkins, Moselle Carswell Jul 27 1839 Jne 16 1892
 w/o Major William A. d/o Sarah Devine & Judge John
 Wright
Wilkins, Wm. A., Jr.   1873   1937
 s/o Moselle C. & W.A.
Wilkins, Wm. Archibald   Oct 9 1835 Feb 14 1907
 s/o Amanda Porter & Archibald md 1st Moselle Carswell
 2nd Kate Thomas b Liberty Co. Founder of Bank of
 Waynesboro; leading merchant; first Mayor when
 Waynesboro became a city; civic-minded, serving many
 years on the city council (ed).
Williams, Betsy Hobbs   Jul 16 1888 Feb 11 1953
Williams, Children (2)   nd   nd
 of Adris and Harvey Ford
Williams, James Carlos   Jne 10 1885 Aug 21 1964
 s/o Sarah Walden & James
Williams, Mattie Ford   Oct 6 1895 Jne 20 1958
 w/o James C. d/o Sarah Smallwood & James W.
Williams, Ollie Lee   1888   1940
 s/o Bertha Lee & Boggus Andrew
Williams, Othella Tinsley   1897   1954
 w/o Ollie L. d/o Georgia Carey & Thomas Warren
Williams, Thomas P.   1858   1916
Williams, Wanette Hayes   Aug 23 1917 Jul 14 1956
 w/o Leonard d/o Nona Lowe & Wm. Grady
Willis, John B.   1890   1945
Willis, Mary K.   1893   nd
Willis, Paul Harris   Dec 31 1896 Nov 1 1931
 h/o Mary Hatcher
Wimberly, Chandler Wilson May 20 1882 Jne 4 1952
 h/o Ellen McKie s/o Callie Chandler & Wm. Mathis
Wingard, C.W.   Sep 23 1885 Nov 19 1928
Wood, Benjamin T.   May 23 1890 Apr 16 1947
 s/o Betty & George
Wood, Bessie Johnson   Dec 23 1894   L
 w/o Benj. T. d/o Alice Freeman & Jesse Eugene
Wood, Infant   Mar 21 1920 Mar 25 1920
 s/o Bessie J. & Benj. T.
Wood, Roger L.   Apr 5 1919 Jne 29 1919
 s/o Bessie J. & Benj. T.
Woschke, Erich   Feb 9 1905 Jul 8 1973
 b in Germany d Waynesboro, Ga. Came from Savannah;
 lived in W-Boro only a few months (ed).
Wright, Esther K.   1907   1966

Wright, Inez Wilkins Jones   Nov 15 1890   Jan 25 1969
    w/o Geo. Livingston   d/o Inez Wilkins & Wm. E.
Wright, Mintie Barrow   May 15 1875   Jne 6 1971
Wright, T. Henry   1904   19
Youngblood, John A.   Nov 10 1883   Aug 22 1954
    s/o Mary Baugh & Wesley J.
Youngblood, Mary Baugh   Aug 12 1862   Aug 1 1925
    w/o Wesley J. d/o Martha Elizabeth & Andrew Jackson
Youngblood, Wesley Jackson   Jne 25 1856   Jne 9 1927
    s/o Martha Wesley & ------. Employee of Central
    of Ga. R.R. Survived by brother Thomas in Dallas,
    Tex. and four children. Obit. T.C., June 11, 1927.

148.   WAYS BAPTIST
                        Jefferson Co.

Adkins, Alexander H.S.   Dec 16 1855   Aug 14 1912
Adkins, Beulah Ethel   Jan 21 1906   Feb 13 1910
Adkins, Willie C. Jones   Jne 13 1869   Dec 16 1948
    w/o A.H.S.
Alexander, Dr. R.E.   age 55 y   Sep 25 1888
Allen, Heyward E.   1906   1961
Allen, Iris Estelle   Nov 11 1900   May 2 1910
    d/o Mae & Thomas
Allen, Mae G.   Mar 25 1878   Apr 1 1969
    w/o Thomas W.
Allen, Thomas W.   Mar 31 1872   May 18 1947
Anderson, Claudia S.   Oct 7 1891   Jne 14 1892
    s/o W.F. & Fannie
Anderson, James F.   Oct 6 1886   May 19 1911
Anderson, Morrison Eugene   Sep 17 1901   May 2 1904
    s/o W.F. & Fannie W.
Attaway, Edward G.   Oct 3 1855   Oct 29 1928
Attaway, Mattie Ann   age 80 y   nd
Atwell, Augusta Hill   Jne 9 1858   Jne 22 1894
Atwell, E.P.   nd   -   nd
Atwell, Fannie E.   Feb 18 1847   Oct 22 1915
    w/o James
Atwell, James   Jul 16 1848   Jul 11 1919
Atwell, John   Jul 28 1850   Apr 29 1892
Atwell, R. Allen   Feb 3 1871   Aug 7 1927
Avrett, Edward M.   CSA   age 48 y   Jan 10 1897
    Co D 12 Ga Mil
Avrett, Edward M., Jr.   Apr 14 1897   Mar 11 1905
Avrett, Florence   nd   May 3 1894
Avrett, George Stratton   Feb 6 1892   Jne 13 1966
Avrett, Mamie Pilcher   Sep 13 1877   Mar 13 1951
Avrett, Marion   nd   Apr 27 1898
Avrett, Robert Lee   Feb 18 1902   May 27 1953
Avrett, Ruth Brown   Oct 21 1892   nd
    w/o Geo. Stratton
Avrett, Walter Lee   Jne 6 1875   Sep 30 1944
Avrett-Beall, Sallie Tarver   Nov 17 1853   Feb 16 1943
Barrow, Anna Swan   Dec 26 1875   Nov 25 1932

                        294

```
Barrow, Cleone M.                              1895              1962
Barrow, G.P.                                   1889              1941
Barrow, Henry B.                               1885              1968
Barrow, Infant                      only    date                1962
  d/o Catherine & Eliott
Barrow, James A.                    Sep 14 1856    May   8 1929
Barrow, James E.                               1899              1962
Barrow, Lillian E.                             1884              1950
  w/o Henry B.
Barrow, Robert Lee WW-II            Jan  2 1903    Dec   5 1963
  Ga SF2 USNR
Barrow, Sallie C.                   Nov  1 1862    Feb 17 1940
  w/o James A.
Barrow, Thomas C.                   Jan 28 1901    Feb 18 1908
Baston, Adella Denny                Jne  7 1852    Aug 21 1924
  w/o Wm. E.
Baston, Annie Mae                   Oct 13 1884    Mar   9 1907
Baston, William Edward              Feb 10 1847    Jan 27 1925
Boulineau, Alex                                1907              1972
Boulineau, Betty G.                 Jan 26 1924                    nd
  w/o James E.
Boulineau, Catherine Anneta         May  7 1922    Apr   6 1926
Boulineau, Clayborn S.                         1876              1937
Boulineau, Ethel Avera                         1883              1962
  w/o Joe
Boulineau, Fannie J.                           1883              1969
  w/o Clayborn S.
Boulineau, J.P.                     Apr  8 1932    Oct   1 1933
Boulineau, James E.                 Jan 10 1913                    nd
Boulineau, Joe                                 1877              1954
Boulineau, Joseph Curry             Jul 22 1913    Oct 20 1913
Boulineau, Lorine                              1916                nd
  w/o Alex
Boulineau, Mary Bell Johnson        Jne 30 1879    Apr 30 1916
Brinson, Agnes                      Dec 25 1758    Jan 26 1828
  w/o Moses, Sr.
Brinson, Eben B.                    Mar 17 1850    May 17 1899
Brinson, Fred O.                    Jne  9 1873    Oct 18 1898
Brinson, Capt. John W.   CSA        Nov 26 1832    Apr 24 1896
  Co G 38 Ga Inf
Brinson, Moses, Sr.                 Feb  3 1765    Jan   7 1850
Brinson, Sarah E.                   May  3 1841    Dec   9 1888
  w/o John W.
Brown, B. Frank                     Oct 13 1835    Mar 30 1903
Brown, Infants (twins)              Sep  6 1927    Nov   5 1936
  sons/o O.B. & Mary
Brown, Louise                                  1885              1966
Brown, Mollie Williams                         1863              1941
Brown, Olin B., Sr.                            1857              1943
Brown, Olin Bryan                   May 25 1897    Oct   5 1957
Burkett, Anna H. Roberts            May 29 1867    Dec 20 1940
Carpenter, Claudia R.                          1916                nd
  w/o Hubert
Carpenter, Hubert P.                           1907              1964
Carswell, George M.                            1881              1955
```

```
Carswell, Julia Brown                      1848              1925
Carswell, Matthew A.            Aug  6 1848   Feb 21 1923
Carswell, Matthew A.                   1884              1906
Carswell, Wade H.               Mar 11 1876   Oct 26 1896
   s/o M.A. & J.J.
Chance, Belle                   Mar 17 1869   Dec 10 1898
   w/o H.F.
Chance, Ernest Eugene           Oct 30 1898   May  8 1899
   s/o H.F. & Belle
Chappelear, Georgia O.          Sep    1879   Aug    1901
Clark, Celia Parker             Jan 28 1895   Jne  4 1968
   w/o David E.
Clark, David E.                 Jne 22 1893   Mar 11 1945
Clements, Alma A.               Apr 19 1914              nd
   w/o John R.
Clements, Fannie Newsome        May  1 1884   Mar 18 1927
Clements, John R.               Jul  6 1912   Feb 17 1973
Comer, Mary Elizabeth           Oct 30 1838   Sep  9 1905
   w/o Daniel M.
Connell, Matilda P.                      nd                nd
   m/o Nathan, Nancy & Lawson
Corish, Corrie L.                      1900              1970
Coursen, Malcolm                Jne 30 1900   Nov  9 1900
Courson, Elizabeth Gay          Apr 27 1890   Apr  4 1948
   w/o John J.
Courson, John J.                Mar  4 1873   May 15 1929
Davis, Anna Ganus               Aug  2 1882   Mar 29 1947
   w/o Isaac Braswell
Davis, Arrenvy                  age 29 y      Feb 14 1836
   w/o Isaac B.
Davis, Arrenvy Virginia         age 2y 6m     Oct 24 1846
   d/o W.P. & E.M.
Davis, Ike B.                   Oct 22 1895   Nov 16 1897
   s/o E.J. & J.P.
Davis, Isaac B.                 age 59y 21d   Mar 21 1856
Davis, Isaac Braswell           Aug 23 1872   Aug  5 1940
Deaderick, Frances B.                  1928   -          1964
Delph, Annie Pilcher            Dec 27 1883   Jne 21 1931
Delph, John Waring              Sep 11 1907   May 16 1908
   s/o J.G. & A.P.
Delph, Preston Ioor             Feb 29 1916   Jul 30 1963
Delph, Sarah Elizabeth          Dec 13 1909   Oct 13 1911
   d/o J.G. & A.P.
Denny, George O.                Nov 20 1889   Nov 20 1917
Denny, James Edward                    1845              1905
Denny, John Andrew              Jul 23 1879   Jan 10 1882
   s/o James E. & Sarah J.
Denny, Marvin P.                Oct 12 1877   Mar 10 1915
Denny, Sallie Rogers                   1850              1923
   w/o James E.
Dorman, Alice Taylor            Jan  5 1892   Mar 11 1971
Duke, Cleo                             1888              1929
Duke, Gertrude                         1854              1928
Duke, James H.                  Nov 16 1875   Jul 22 1936
```

Name	Birth	Death
Duke, James Roy	Jne 11 1907	Feb 4 1913
s/o J.H. & N.B.		
Duke, Nonie Gay	Oct 8 1883	Feb 2 1947
w/o James H.		
Duke, Turner	1851	1928
Dukes, Alma W.	1900	nd
w/o Dorsey A. md Aug 26 1917		
Dukes, Dorsey A.	1894	1972
Dye, Benjamin A.	Apr 12 1889	Nov 7 1918
Dye, Homer E.	Jan 8 1882	Oct 3 1965
Dye, John E. CSA	nd	nd
Co D 2 Ga Inf		
Dye, Mae Milton	1895	1972
Dye, Mattie L.	Jan 9 1860	Jan 12 1921
Dye, Sarah Ela	Mar 24 1886	Nov 18 1944
w/o Homer E.		
Eaton, James Edward	Sep 20 1852	Mar 6 1936
Eaton, Ora Anna	May 31 1867	Jan 30 1919
w/o Jas. E.		
Farmer, Amelia	Mar 23 1783	Jan 20 1852
Farmer, Clara Denny	1882	1973
Farmer, George Denny, Sr.	Jul 26 1913	Apr 12 1969
Farmer, George S.	Jul 20 1858	Apr 6 1928
Farmer, George Samuel	Oct 11 1897	Jan 31 1954
Farmer, Gordon Ashton	Feb 5 1876	Oct 30 1920
Farmer, Henry R.	1878	1938
Farmer, Irma Sturkey	Feb 20 1892	Oct 6 1971
Farmer, J.J.	Dec 26 1816	Dec 21 1888
Farmer, John W., Sr.	1893	1959
Farmer, Josie G.	Jul 10 1863	Feb 22 1899
Farmer, Lena A.	Jul 16 1873	Dec 27 1910
Farmer, Leon Jackson	Mar 2 1890	Apr 30 1956
Farmer, Lucius Pierce WW-I	Jne 11 1881	May 1 1951
Ga 1st Lt Medical Corps		
Farmer, Martha I.	1847	1926
Farmer, Mary E.	Mar 1902	May 1902
Farmer, Rhesa E.	Oct 25 1845	May 6 1924
Farmer, Ruth	Oct 31 1822	Jul 13 1892
w/o J.J.		
Farmer, Ruth E.	Mar 2 1877	Apr 19 1898
Farrell, Kathryn Tabb	Sep 10 1899	Sep 10 1967
w/o Van Buren		
Farrell, Van Buren	Nov 25 1899	Apr 25 1972
Farrer, Asa M.	Oct 12 1897	Feb 7 1963
Farrer, Nellie E.J.	Jan 25 1904	Oct 16 1938
w/o Asa M.		
Fitzgerald, Arthur R. WW-I	Dec 21 1894	Sep 2 1966
Ga Pfc USA		
Gailes, Eva Irene	Aug 26 1877	Mar 18 1898
Gailes, Harvey Eugene	Feb 21 1901	Jan 6 1919
Gailes, John A., Sr.	Sep 15 1859	Jul 18 1949
Gailes, Minnie L.	Sep 10 1878	Sep 1 1941
w/o John A.		
Gailes, Nettie Inez	1896	Jul 18 1898
Ganus, Ely M.	Mar 30 1875	Jul 26 1945

Ganus, Julia V.	Oct 15 1850	Sep 15 1923
Ganus, Katherine J.	May 12 1892	Oct 5 1970
w/o Ely M.		
Gay, Alice D.	Jne 22 1882	Oct 14 1968
w/o James J.		
Gay, Andrew Jackson	Jul 27 1357	Feb 3 1929
Gay, Annie Way	1888	1953
Gay, Bessie Anna	nd	nd
Gay, E.L.O.	Aug 1873	Dec 24 1902
Gay, Edward	1914	1969
Gay, Mrs. Ellen E.	May 9 1849	Sep 11 1914
w/o Isaac Jackson		
Gay, Emma Lee	age 39 y	Sep 3 1900
Gay, Gussie E.	Apr 24 1891	Jne 4 1917
w/o James		
Gay, Ida Scott	1877	1944
w/o Reuben J.		
Gay, Isaac D. WW-II	Jan 25 1898	Jne 7 1970
Ark TEC5 USA		
Gay, Isaac Jackson	Jul 8 1852	Mar 20 1922
Gay, James J.	Dec 1 1853	Nov 16 1933
Gay, James M.	Dec 5 1886	Jul 26 1922
Gay, Mary Ponder	Jan 20 1854	Dec 11 1934
Gay, Mrs. R.S.	nd	nd
Gay, Reuben J.	1880	1948
Gay, Sam Ponder	Mar 22 1887	Nov 4 1956
Godowns, Alma M. Johnson	1903	1968
w/o Willis		
Godowns, Clinton Jackson	Dec 26 1897	Oct 28 1953
Godowns, Eugenia Joiner	1876	1955
w/o James J.		
Godowns, James J.	1873	1937
Godowns, Lois	Jan 5 1907	Jan 14 1917
d/o W.H. & Mozelle		
Godowns, Sarah Mozelle	1885	1955
w/o Wm. H.		
Godowns, Tarver Hill	1911	1936
Godowns, William H.	1876	1941
Gordy, Ebbie Ganus	Apr 19 1889	Aug 23 1952
w/o Robt. Lee		
Gordy, Robert Lee	Feb 6 1881	Feb 28 1956
Griswold, Elizabeth P.	Oct 12 1910	Apr 27 1972
in Ponder section		
Holmes, Mrs. L.	Sep 6 1826	Apr 25 1888
Holmes, Martha I.	Jne 6 1844	Jan 25 1876
w/o D.S.		
Holmes, Percy Lee	1877	1878
Holmes, R.W.	Nov 4 1819	May 3 1904
Hopper, George F., Jr.	nd	1956
s/o Geo. & June		
Hopper, Harden P.	1893	1958
Hopper, Mary Jo	1926	1931
d/o Harden & Hattie Ruth		
Hudson, Julia	Aug 29 1866	Mar 28 1886
w/o N.J.		

Hudson, N.J.	age 30 y 2m 28d	Feb 11 1887
Inglett, James Edward	Apr 8 1897	Jan 6 1919
Jackson, Cortez A.	1889	1970
Jackson, Edith Jones w/o Cortez A.	1898	1966
Jackson, Infant s/o C.A. & E.J.	only date	1927
Jackson, Infant s/o C.A. & E.J.	only date	1929
Johnson, Ann W.	1889	1947
Johnson, Beatrice w/o Sam W.	Jul 1 1893	Jne 14 1970
Johnson, Catherine d/o N.E. & D.S.	Nov 28 1918	Aug 15 1919
Johnson, Cora Swann w/o Wilson H.	1884	1972
Johnson, David B. WOW	Jne 29 1900	May 23 1922
Johnson, Eliza Matilda	Oct 7 1842	Jul 11 1926
Johnson, Hugh M.	Nov 13 1905	Mar 15 1973
Johnson, Macy P. w/o Thomas J.	Jan 30 1882	Oct 27 1973
Johnson, Mae Swan w/o Oswell B.	Oct 11 1878	Nov 8 1962
Johnson, Margaret Adella Swan w/o Nathan Edgar	Sep 3 1881	Oct 22 1969
Johnson, Mary Elizabeth w/o Moses J.	Aug 30 1859	Nov 4 1933
Johnson, Mary Elizabeth	Jan 20 1923	Jne 18 1925
Johnson, Moses J.	Apr 1 1860	Feb 6 1950
Johnson, Nathan Edgar	Jne 14 1878	Jan 6 1949
Johnson, Oswell B. WOW	May 5 1870	Jul 16 1936
Johnson, Sam W.	1881	1966
Johnson, Sarah F. w/o S.W.	Oct 16 1853	Apr 9 1896
Johnson, Sarah Ina Duke w/o Walter E.	Aug 3 1878	May 15 1952
Johnson, Thomas E.	Mar 6 1903	Mar 21 1916
Johnson, Thomas J. h/o Macy P.	Nov 23 1881	Jne 29 1912
Johnson, Walter E.	Oct 16 1875	Dec 5 1961
Johnson, William H.	1909	1936
Johnson, Wilson Hawes	1883	1965
Jones, Arthur A.	Apr 17 1875	Oct 28 1933
Jones, Arthur Ernest	Jne 10 1901	Dec 5 1924
Jones, Bessie d/o Julia E. Palmer & W.H.	Aug 14 1880	Aug 30 1883
Jones, Della H.	Jne 3 1860	Jul 24 1886
Jones, Ela R.	Aug 21 1862	Dec 9 1883
Jones, Fannie A. w/o Robert J.	Mar 2 1840	Nov 4 1914
Jones, Hubert C.	Nov 6 1903	Dec 7 1970
Jones, John Eben Brinson	1882	1953
Jones, John N.T.	Jan 17 1831	Mar 12 1886
Jones, Mamie Weeks w/o John Eben	1888	nd

Jones, Margaret M.	Sep 27 1839	Jne 1 1896
w/o John N.T.		
Jones, Mary Virginia	May 30 1895	Aug 10 1901
d/o Julia E. Palmer & W.H.		
Jones, Mattie Ina	Dec 7 1880	Jne 22 1942
w/o Arthur A.		
Jones, Ralph E.	1908	1941
Jones, Robert J.	Mar 10 1835	Oct 7 1910
Jones, Robert J.	Mar 7 1912	Apr 22 1972
Jones, Walter Palmer	Nov 28 1877	Aug 31 1883
s/o Julia E. Palmer & W.H.		
Jones, William Henry, Jr.	Dec 26 1876	Sep - 1877
s/o Julia E. Palmer & W.H.		
King, Carrie Davidson	Mar 24 1903	Mar 10 1927
King, Clyde Lanier	Mar 24 1903	Apr 17 1903
King, Emma Swan	Nov 24 1871	Mar 23 1957
w/o James		
King, Gussie Tabb	Aug 31 1893	Jan 20 1954
King, Hattie	Aug 4 1895	Jan 4 1973
King, Herbert A.	May 17 1900	Sep 15 1972
King, James	age 56 y	Oct 30 1890
King, James	Feb 11 1869	Oct 12 1928
King, Lois Fuller	Oct 22 1908	nd
King, Nancy	Sep 20 1829	Jne 2 1884
w/o James		
Lowe, Wylantie	age 47 y	Jul 16 1894
Luckey, Eddie Eugene WOW	Feb 22 1890	Apr 3 1920
Manning, Erskine M.	Apr 8 1877	Aug 21 1951
Matthews, Ann Elizabeth	age 1y 11m	Apr 20 1846
only d/o L.C. & E.A.	15d	
Matthews, Atwell	Jul 23 1881	Aug 27 1882
Matthews, Charles A.	1855	1931
Matthews, Elizabeth A.	Oct 28 1822	Jne 13 1857
w/o Levin C.		
Matthews, Levin C.	Jan 28 1815	Jne 26 1866
Matthews, Mary A.	1858	1937
w/o Charles A.		
Matthews, Sara Louise	Oct 6 1885	Jul 25 1903
Matthews, Thomas L.	Nov 11 1891	Nov 22 1913
Matthews, Worthington	Aug 13 1879	Sep 5 1883
Mauldin, Kenneth	1948	1971
Mays, Alex H.	Apr 20 1895	Mar 17 1897
s/o R.S. & J.V.		
McDearmon, Frances Jane Murray	May 20 1951	Aug 18 1972
McNair, Carl	Jul 12 1907	Aug 27 1908
s/o T.J. & S.L.		
McNair, Carter	May 25 1904	May 30 1905
s/o T.J. & S.L.		
McNair, Clara Dye	May 9 1900	Jne 11 1973
w/o James E.		
McNair, J.P.	1876	1941
McNair, James Elisha	Jul 19 1898	Dec 14 1952
McNair, John D.	Dec 9 1910	Oct 28 1911
s/o T.J. & S.L.		

Miles, Alice Swan	Nov 1 1897	Feb 5 1944
w/o Eulian Malone		
Miles, Eulian Malone	1892	1973
Milton, Clifford Ellmore	May 1883	Dec 12 1942
Milton, Fallie Ponder	Sep 1881	Jne 1929
Milton, Fannie R.	age 30 y	Apr 12 1893
w/o James J.	11m 26d	
Milton, Gertie May	Dec 24 1881	Mar 18 1899
Milton, James J.	1849	1940
Milton, James T.	Jan 9 1892	Dec 16 1898
s/o J.J. & Fannie		
Milton, Sarah W.	Dec 2 1814	Feb 13 1896
Minus, Bessie E. Dye	Aug 8 1895	nd
w/o Lloyd B.		
Minus, Clyde	May 12 1901	Sep 5 1903
Minus, Hugh F.	Jan 30 1891	Jan 8 1945
Minus, Hula Z.	1864	1926
Minus, Lloyd Bryant	Jan 8 1893	Jul 25 1957
Minus, Wm. Fulton	1886	1925
Minus, William S.	1858	1945
Murphy, Ellen Eulala	Mar 16 1884	Feb 8 1944
Murray, Carrie Lou Short	1874	1967
w/o Elliott		
Murray, Elliott	1871	1938
Murray, Elliott A.	Dec 10 1902	Mar 30 1971
Newsome, Addie N.	Mar 25 1907	nd
w/o J. Maurice		
Newsome, Annie Laura	Oct 16 1885	Nov 2 1934
w/o John N.		
Newsome, J.J.	Mar 12 1876	Sep 25 1900
Newsome, James Thomas	Feb 6 1853	Jan 6 1940
Newsome, John Maurice	Jne 27 1904	nd
Newsome, John N.	Jul 24 1880	Feb 19 1938
Newsome, Lawson	Feb 2 1899	Nov 20 1905
s/o Mr. & Mrs. J.T.		
Mewsome, Newman Price	Jul 8 1922	Oct 25 1931
Newsome, Rebecca Jane	Oct 13 1855	Aug 31 1933
Oliphant, Beulah V.	Aug 2 1872	Oct 24 1898
Oliphant, Conelia P.	1910	nd
w/o Judson W. Note: Name spelled Cornelia in a son's		
inscription (ed).		
Oliphant, Edgar Gene	1944	1971
Oliphant, Emily	Dec 8 1841	Sep 25 1910
w/o Noah		
Oliphant, Dr. J.N.	Jan 20 1834	Dec 27 1899
Oliphant, Rev. James H.	Jan 22 1824	Dec 12 1898
Oliphant, Jim H.	Apr 26 1872	Dec 30 1955
Oliphant, Juanita	Jan 14 1878	Jul 16 1967
Oliphant, Judson W.	1895	nd
Oliphant, Marcus Newton	Jan 8 1887	Dec 25 1958
s/o Judson & Cornelia		
Oliphant, Mattie Perdue	1887	1957
w/o Thomas A.		

```
Oliphant, Noah                          Dec  7 1832   Jan  2 1912
Oliphant, Thomas A.                          1883           1943
Oliphant, Truitt C.                     Oct  2 1910   Apr 12 1911
Oliphant, Wilanty A.                    age 30 y      Sep  4 1874
  w/o Dr. J.N.
Oliphant, Wilbur  WW-II                 Apr  6 1918   Apr  4 1950
  Ga Pfc 148 Inf 37 Inf Div BSM-PH
Oliphant, Wm. Chester                   Jne 19 1915   Jne 27 1925
  s/o Newt. & Mattie B.
Oliphant, Willie Y.                     Mar  4 1887   Aug  2 1924
Parish, Mary L.                         Oct 18 1886   Feb 22 1894
Parker, William S.                      Nov 26 1880   Nov 20 1899
Parrish, Kate M.                        Jne  6 1856   Dec  2 1911
  w/o J.D. Parish
Patterson, John J.                      age 51y 7m    Oct 23 1903
Patterson, Martha Elizabeth             Dec 28 1904   Jne 11 1906
Patterson, Mattie Allen                 Jne 10 1880   Aug  3 1925
Patterson, Mollie Smith                 Sep 17 1846   Nov 23 1908
Patterson, Robin H.                     Sep  7 1874   Aug 11 1911
Patterson, Sallie M. Pilcher            Jul 10 1874   Feb 18 1895
Pendrey, James J.                       Jul  1 1875   Jne 18 1909
Pendrey, P.L.                           Mar 23 1845   Jne  1 1915
  w/o F.A.
Pendrey, Robert I.                      Jan 27 1882   Aug 19 1901
Perdue, Annie Eliza                     Mar 26 1857   Aug 13 1895
Perdue, L.R.                                 1858     Sep 19 1913
Perkins, James Edward                   Sep 15 1859   Apr 20 1918
Pilcher, Elizabeth Stapleton            Aug 10 1858   Jul 29 1933
  w/o Dr. J.W.
Pilcher, James Wright  MD               Jan 30 1853   Nov 22 1920
Pilcher, Jimmie                         Sep 17 1879   Dec 27 1882
Ponder, Ina                                  1872           1909
Ponder, James H.                             1852           1927
Ponder, Lillie M.                       Jan  5 1890   Nov  1 1960
Ponder, Mary P.                              1850           1927
  w/o James H.
Ponder, Thomas W., Jr.                  only  date    Jul 18 1932
Ponder, Thomas W., Sr.                  Oct 24 1888   Oct 14 1962
Poole, Eva Irene                             1889           1900
Poole, Frances Comer                    Jne 29 1860   Jne  5 1920
  w/o Michael T.
Poole, Michael Thomas                        1856           1900
Poole, S.E.                             Sep 7 1837    Feb 11 1920
  w/o William P.S.
Poole, William P.S.   CSA               Jul  6 1840   Nov 10 1893
  Co I 1 Ga Inf
Powell, Leona Martin                    Aug 16 1903   Feb 27 1973
Prior, Hezekiah                         Oct 14 1812   Feb 12 1829
  s/o Robt. & Nancy
Pruett, Addie Wren Way                  Dec 18 1903   Dec 28 1960
Roberts, Alice M. Bowling               Aug 20 1876   Jul 30 1939
  w/o John Silas
Roberts, Floyd A.   F&AM                Apr  7 1849   Jan 21 1903
Roberts, John Silas                     Sep 29 1873   Dec  7 1937
```

Roberts, Matilda		1855		1878
Rogers, Alice Fell		1845		1922
Rogers, John S.	Mar 12 1834		Sep 5 1894
Rogers, Martha M.	Apr 17 1836		Mar 31 1900
w/o John S.			
Rogers, Rev. W.J.	Nov 18 1832		Dec 23 1899
Rogers, Willie A.	Jan 10 1858		Aug 22 1878
Rowland, Benjamin F.	Sep 7 1873		Jne 4 1942
Rowland, Ella L.		1927		1928
Rowland, Harriet E.	Oct 18 1843		May 13 1923
w/o B.F.			
Rowland, James Marion	Nov 17 1867		Apr 28 1929
Rowland, John Berry	Oct 7 1871		Nov 22 1936
Rowland, Phoebe Lorene		1958		1958
Rowland, Phoebe Salters	Mar 24 1883		nd
w/o Sam R.			
Rowland, Sam R.	Sep 15 1880		Apr 24 1954
Rowland, Thomas Jefferson	Feb 14 1870		Dec 31 1901
St. Marie, Mary Barrow		1905		1971
Salter, Martha Temples		1854		1928
Salter, Zed		1861		1942
Scruggs, Clemmie E.		1892		1965
w/o James P.			
Scruggs, James P.		1885		1955
Scruggs, Lois Geneva	Feb 4 1933		Jan 2 1934
d/o J.P. & C.G.			
Sellars, Ellie	Jan 27 1906		Feb 2 1906
d/o W.J.			
Sellars, Infant	Jan 27 1906		Feb 2 1906
s/o Mr. & Mrs. W.J.			
Simpson, Daisy Wasden	Aug 20 1876		Jne 15 1906
w/o J.H.			
Sinquefield, Mrs. E.J.	age 18 y		Oct 18 1829
Smith, Belle Joiner		1872		1952
w/o G. Absalom			
Smith, Ben J.		1896		1900
s/o Belle J. & G.A.			
Smith, Edgar Joseph	Jan 1 1904		Mar 9 1958
Smith, Eliza A.	Jul 28 1858		Aug 28 1910
Smith, Fannie R.		1890		1969
Smith, G. Absalom		1869		1927
Smith, George M.		1901		1904
s/o Belle J. & G.A.			
Smith, Helen Boulineau	Jul 2 1905		nd
w/o Edgar Joseph			
Smith, J.J.		1878		1935
Smith, Joan Elizabeth Tanner	Sep 28 1847		May 22 1881
w/o Herschel E. d/o Rebecca Adams & Wm. Tanner			
Smith, Joshua A.	Nov 7 1847		Apr 13 1909
Smith, Josie	Jan 26 1896		Feb 5 1897
d/o W.D. & Eliza			
Smith, Lillie J.	Aug 3 1857		Sep 5 1914
w/o Joshua A.			
Smith, Marie	Nov 7 1883		Apr 24 1887
d/o W.D. & Eliza A.			

Smith, Mary A.	age 20 m		1876
Smith, Mrs. Mary C.		1875	1959
Smith, Nancy Abigail	age 8 m	Feb 12	1834
d/o Noah & Narcissa			
Smith, Narcissa	age 31 y	Aug 27	1847
w/o Noah			
Smith, Noah	age 66y 2m	Feb 8	1891
Smith, Noah	Oct 9 1891	Feb 28	1914
Smith, Rachael Roland	Jan 2 1878	Jan 1	1900
w/o P.H.			
Smith, Robert Etheldred	Aug 26 1835	Mar 1	1836
s/o Noah & Narcissa			
Smith, Sarah	Nov 4 1821	Jne 27	1900
w/o E.A.			
Smith, W.T.		1885	1920
Smith, William D.	Feb 24 1853	Oct 25	1895
Snider, Almira Elizabeth	Sep 29 1885	Jan 31	1920
Stewart, Marie A.	Jan 24 1887	Mar 4	1947
Stewart, Thomas J. (Hamp)	Jul 9 1888	Feb 9	1953
Story, Frank J.	Dec 14 1873	May 19	1931
Swan, Alice B.	Apr 26 1842	Apr 8	1916
Swan, Andrew L.		1874	1945
Swan, Bryant S.	Dec 22 1853	Aug 1	1917
Swan, D. Perry		1911	1912
s/o Daniel & Pearl			
Swan, Daniel H.		1869	1946
Swan, J.B.	Apr 20 1895	Oct 4	1923
Swan, J. Paul	Nov 25 1900	Aug 27	1910
Swan, Captain John C. CSA		nd	nd
Co F Cobb's Ga Legion			
Swan, Mary		nd	nd
w/o John C.			
Swan, Pearl Reese		1880	1941
w/o Daniel H.			
Swan, Robert L.		1899	1973
Swan, Sallie Wren	Mar 1 1878	Feb 18	1954
w/o Andrew L.			
Swan, Thomas E.	Sep 4 1834	Oct 4	1899
Swann, Bertha Whittle	Jul 29 1893	Oct 9	1968
w/o Clayton L.			
Swann, Brightee B.	Aug 4 1891	Mar 22	1968
Swann, Mrs. Carrie Way	Mar 13 1861	Mar 13	1939
Swann, Clayton L.	Jan 6 1881	Feb 10	1953
Swann, Ellen M.	Nov 8 1889	Mar 27	1916
w/o Clayton			
Swann, Frances Wright	Apr 17 1916	Apr 21	1916
d/o W. E. & E.M.			
Swann, James Leonard		1915	1969
Swann, John W.	Sep 16 1886	Nov 8	1965
Swann, Lonnie B.		1892	1955
Swann, Mary A.	Mar 15 1858	Jan 17	1923
w/o T.J.			
Swann, Pearl		1891	1929
w/o Lonnie B.			

Name	Birth	Death
Swann, T.J.	Oct 26 1856	Feb 21 1916
Swann, W.G. WW-II	Aug 4 1920	Aug 19 1943
Lost at sea USN		
Swint, Julia Carswell	age 73y 5m 19d	Jul 27 1961
Tabb, Edward James	Feb 23 1859	Sep 15 1917
Tabb, Millie Way	Oct 4 1858	Aug 12 1943
w/o Edward J.		
Tabb, Sallie M.	Mar 27 1888	Apr 5 1958
w/o Wm. R.		
Tabb, Sara E.	1914	1914
Tabb, William R.	Nov 4 1885	Mar 27 1952
Taylor, A.G.	Aug 8 1855	May 11 1911
Taylor, Adella	Oct 23 1851	Oct 10 1915
Taylor, B.F.	Dec 21 1855	May 10 1928
Taylor, B. Frank	Mar 15 1830	Sep 3 1964
Taylor, Elbert Leroy	Sep 16 1860	Mar 25 1866
Taylor, Etta R.	Jul 28 1889	Oct 1 1970
Taylor, J.L.	Mar 21 1879	Dec 4 1959
Taylor, Julia	Feb 14 1882	Aug 18 1896
Taylor, Martha S.	1854	1928
w/o A.G.		
Taylor, Sallie Luella	Apr 29 1859	May 20 1871
Thompson, Mrs. Ammie L.	1918	1953
Thompson, Evelyn S.	1889	1972
w/o James L.		
Thompson, Idella Zeigler	Jne 12 1875	Feb 29 1960
Thompson, James L.	1885	1958
Thompson, Mary	1917	1935
Thompson, Sam	1910	1955
Tinley, Adeline Swann	1868	1955
Tompkins, Celestia A. Matthews	Jne 1846	Dec 19 1905
w/o John		
Vaughn, William B.	Aug 19 1904	Jul 13 1948
Waddell, C.T.	1883	1950
Waddell, H.W. F&AM	Oct 17 1852	Jan 9 1924
Walker, Amanda	Jul 1 1856	Oct 9 1900
w/o H.N.		
Walker, H.N.	Mar 25 1857	Jan 28 1916
Walton, Estelle Johnson Lic. N	May 14 1900	Apr 7 1970
w/o Robert G.		
Walton, Robert Gordon F&AM	Aug 26 1875	May 1 1932
Way, Allen E.	1899	1959
Way, Elbert W.	1858	1815
Way, Elizabeth Ann	age 41y 10m 18d	Mar 19 1825
w/o John		
Way, Emma	nd	Feb 4 1927
Way, Grady	1908	1940
Way, Hardy	Apr 28 1900	Feb 5 1949
Way, John	Jul 7 1779	Jne 28 1855
Way, Noah S.	1856	1939
Way, Sallie A.	1871	1946
w/o Elbert W.		
Way, Samuel Augustus	age 23y 8d	Nov 17 1847
s/o John & Elizabeth Ann		

Weeks, B.A.	Jul 24 1873	Oct 20 1899
Weeks, Charles E.	May 23 1859	Jan 26 1934
Weeks, Charlie E.	Sep 27 1909	Jne 10 1910
s/o C.E. & E.E.		
Weeks, Emily Miller	Dec 13 1867	Jan 26 1925
w/o Charles E.		
Weeks, Frank T.	Dec 6 1900	Jne 13 1924
Weeks, Gussie Emily	Dec 3 1904	Jne 8 1905
Weeks, Hattie B.	Aug 14 1895	May 15 1900
Weeks, Infant	same date	Jul 10 1906
s/o C.E. & E.E.		
Wheeler, Joe E., Sr.	1895	1969
Whitaker, Thomas W.	Nov 12 1880	Sep 2 1897
s/o J.W. & E.C.		
Williams, Bessie Swann	Nov 22 1886	Feb 30 1944
Williams, Helen Avrett	Aug 10 1900	Sep 4 1971
Williams, Lester L.	May 19 1890	Aug 2 1951
Woodall, Betty Godowns	Nov 2 1902	Jul 14 1945
Wren, Alice	Oct 22 1856	Jan 14 1911
w/o R.P.		
Wren, James Broadus	Feb 3 1880	Mar 15 1899
s/o R.P. & Alice		
Wren, R.P.	Mar 12 1855	May 3 1900
Wren, Robert LaFayette	Sep 1 1901	Jne 12 1902
s/o P.K. & A.L.		
Wright, Albert J.	Sep 6 1886	Apr 7 1935
Wright, E.M.	Apr 19 1857	Mar 15 1933
Wright, Mattie Y.	Sep 7 1868	Jul 14 1949
Wright, Nancy	age 56 y	Jne 17 1842
Wright, Porter H.	only date	Oct 13 1937
Ga Pvt USA		
Young, Clara Swan	Dec 26 1883	Jne 28 1971
w/o Frank		
Young, Frank	Mar 9 1878	Mar 21 1927
Young, William U.	Jne 22 1801	Jan 29 1852
Zeigler, Annie Mae G.	Sep 20 1903	Oct 28 1959
Zeigler, David Leland	Sep 17 1898	Apr 5 1969
Zeigler, Manley	May 31 1877	Sep 19 1920

149.   WETHERS

| Wethers, Evaline | Nov 21 1866 | Mar 15 1869 |
| d/o John & M.E. | | |

150.   WHITEHEAD

Floyd, Mrs. Jane B.   age 22 y   Oct 23 1808
    w/o Rev. Loami Floyd d/o John Logan, Esq. of St.
    Bartholomew's Parish, S. Car.
Whitehead, John, Sr. Rev War   age 72 y   Nov 18 1821
    s/o Alice & Thomas of Orange Co., N. Car. In Burke
    1764. During war moved to Liberty Co. A Captain.
    md Amarinthia Elliott (the widow Roberts). No child-
    ren. She was d/o Capt. John & Elizabeth Elliott.
    Later returned to Burke. See Rowland, op. cit. (ed).

151. WHITEHEAD

Dowse, Mary   May 3 1794   Jan 9 1822
  w/o Samuel md 1812 d/o Mary Wynne & Amos Whitehead
Whitehead, Dr. James MD   Apr 7 1786   Oct 11 1847
  s/o Mary Wynne & Amos
Whitehead, Mrs. Ruth Lowndes   Jne 9 1798   May 12 1839
  w/o Dr. James md Jne 30 1816   d/o Williamina Sarah
  Eliza Moore & Major John Berrien. Note: Annotations
  on both Whitehead cemeteries are from Rowland, op.
  cit., by permission (ed).

152.   WIGGINS

Wigins, Amos   d. in 54th y May 21 1837

153.   WILLIAMS

Williams, Ezekiel   age 61 y   Jan 1 1867
  Note: He mentions in his will a half sister, Mary
  Prescott and her two daughters; a sister, Sarah
  Williams, w/o William Allen of Houston Co., Ga. and
  her four daughters. One niece, Sarah Ophelia Allen,
  md William Cox. Ezekiel remained a bachelor.
  Will Bk A, 256-257.

154.   WIMBERLY

Cox, Maude Wimberly   Mar 7 1880   Mar 1 1917
  w/o Jinks   d/o Mattie Lawson & Jas. M.
Harlow, Frederick Nicholos   May 1 1871   May 27 1958
Harlow, Gertrude Wimberly   Apr 9 1878   Jul 10 1959
  name spelled Wimberley (ed). w/o Frederick N.
  d/o Mattie Lawson & Jas. M.
Hatcher, Bertha Wimberly   Mar 19 1874   Nov 27 1916
  w/o Robt. N. d/o Mattie Lawson & Jas. M.
Vinson, Clara Wimberly   1871   1950
  w/o Peach d/o Mattie Lawson & Jas. M. granddaughter
  of Zack Wimberly (ed).
Wimberly, James Marion   Mar 6 1849   Nov 1 1884
  s/o Rachel McNorrill & Zack
Wimberly, Mattie Lawson   Dec 10 1852   Jan 14 1924
  w/o James M.
Wimberly, Nina Ophelia   Mar 21 1884   Jne 26 1884
  d/o Mattie Lawson & Jas. M.
Wimberly, Mrs. Rachel   Jul 11 1813   May 30 1865
  w/o Zack   /McNorrill
Wimberly, Zack   Feb 10 1808   Feb 4 1872
  md 1st Rachel McNorrill 2nd Parmelia E. Gough Dawson,
  widow/o William Cullen Dawson, July, 1867; no children by second marriage (ed).
Wimberly, Zack Lawson   Apr 4 1876   Oct 1 1877
  s/o Mattie Lawson & Jas. M.

Ellis, Bryant   CSA   nd   nd
  Co G 3 S Car Lt Arty
Powell, Annie E.   May 27 1861   Oct 8 1941
  w/o Elbert d/o Ally & Simeon Wimberly
Powell, Elbert E. (Buck) CSA   Dec 24 1846   Dec 30 1939
  Co D Ga Bn
Powell, Infant   Jne 4 1888   Jul 21 1889
  of Annie E. & Elbert
Powell, Martha   Mar 7 1816   Dec 6 1894
  w/o Berry
Powell, William Z.T.   Jan 8 1849   Sep 9 1867
  half-br/o Elbert
Wimberly, Allen   CSA   nd   nd
  Co A 2 Ga Inf
Wimberly, Ally   Apr 15 1830   Jul 18 1889
  w/o Simeon
Wimberly, Edna Lucile   Aug 28 1916   Feb 5 1917
  d/o Ruby & Sim A.   name spelled Wimberley on marker
  (ed).
Wimberly, G.W.   Apr 8 1865   Feb 15 1885
  Year of birth illeg; could be 1805 (ed)
Wimberly, Jefferson   CSA   nd   Oct 18 1862
  Co D 48th Reg Ga Inf ANV
Wimberly, John   CSA   nd   nd
  s/o Mary Prescott & Allen   Co C 32 Ga Inf
Wimberly, Mary Prescott   age 70 y   nd
  w/o Allen
Wimberly, Simeon   Sep 6 1820   Jne 26 1886

Note: One flat slab and one bricked grave could not be
      identified (ed).

29.   CARSWELL

Carswell, Alexander   Rev War   age 74 y   Feb 11 1808*
  3 D Co Ga Batt'n   b County Antrim, Ireland   *died at
  his plantation, Burke Co. Founder of the Carswell
  family in Burke and other counties (ed).
Carswell, Alexander   age 60 y   Mar 7 1848
  h/o *Mary Palmer *md Mar 11, 1813
  s/o Sarah Wright & John
Carswell, E.C.   nd   nd
  probably a child (ed).
Carswell, Infant   age 17 hrs   May 4 1846
  d/o N.J. & E.H.
Carswell, Infant   age 7 hrs   Jul 16 1847
  s/o N.J. & E.H.
Carswell, Isabella Browne   nd   nd
  w/o Alexander, I d/o Wm. & Elizabeth (Rock) Browne
  b in County Claire, Ireland
Carswell, John   Rev War   age 54 y   Mar   1817
  s/o Isabella Browne & Alexander, I. md Sarah Wright
  (d Nov 12, 1808*). Ga Line 4th Ga Regt under General
  Twiggs.

Carswell, Mary Adeline   age 6m 7d   Jne 13 1888
Carswell, Mary Palmer   age 59 y   Jne 22 1847
  w/o Alexander (the s/o John) md Mar 11, 1813*
  d/o Mary Cureton & George Palmer
Carswell, Matthew   age 54 y   Apr 7 1849
  s/o Sarah Wright & John md Adelaide M. Williams
  See J.V. Michael Motes, "What's Your Family Line?",
  Georgia Magazine, May 1971 (ed).
Stubblefield, Eliza A.   Jul 5 1845 Aug 12 1850
  d/o B. & C. Stubblefield

Notes: 1) For above data marked with an asterisk (*),
see Warren, op. cit., 18.
       2) The Carswell Family Association, early in
1974, placed a new marker in this cemetery dedicated to
the pioneer mother of their line: "Lady Isabella/
Browne Carswell/ wife of /Alexander Carswell/ of
Ancient/Scottish Lineage/ Came with Her /Husband and
Their /Six Children in 1772 /To Settle Here and /
Help Found A Nation" (ed).

156.   ALLEN
              Jefferson Co.

Allen, Beatrice   1814   1837
Love, Rebecca Helen   age 23y 10m Jne 3 1837

157.   BRACK

Brack, Benjamin Rev War   Mar 12 1763 Apr   1827
  b St George's Parish md Christeon Fields
Brack, Christeon Fields   nd   nd
  w/o Benj. Note: A 6½ ft shaft marks the grave not
  only of Benjamin, but memorializes by name his wife
  and three children: Elizabeth, Seth & Benjamin,Jr.
  (ed).
Brack, John Rev War   nd   nd
  a brother of Benjamin
Brack, Miles Fields   Nov 28 1825 Oct 22 1872
  md Jane Harriet McCullers. They were the parents of
  Ottis LeVert, Chappin McCullers & Benjamin Calvin
  McCullers Brack (ed). Note: His marker was not
  found (ed).
Brown, Jane Ella   nd Oct 13 1840
  d/o Cynthia E. & J.T. Brown

Note: Mrs. Pauline Brack Lane, Midville, Ga., supplied
some of the above data from Brack family records (ed).

158.   BROOME
              Richmond Co.

Broome, Bertice Effie Napier   May 16 1877 Dec 31 1972
  w/o John C. d/o Mary Elizabeth Dye & Absalom Napier

Broome, C. Earl	1904	1929
s/o Bertice Napier & John C.		
Broome, Florrie	Oct 25 1920	Jul 17 1925
d/o Bertice Napier & John C.		
Broome, John Christopher	Jan 20 1872	Sep 20 1945
s/o Elizabeth B. Ward & John Wiley		
Broome, Selma Blanche	1905	1911
d/o Bertice Napier & John C.		
Collins, Georgia A.	Jan 30 1833	May 20 1880
w/o Lewis R.		
Collins, Lewis R.	Jul 16 1827	Jan 17 1907
Kersey, Larry A.	1943	1973
McManus, Cecil Clark	Dec 12 1904	Sep 30 1906
s/o Mary Lou & Oliver		
McManus, Mary Lou	1883	1927
w/o Oliver		
McManus, Oliver Brantley	1867	1931
Rountree, George C.	Jne 3 1880	Oct 16 1884
Rountree, James M.	Oct 20 1881	Sep 30 1888
Rountree, Jobe Lewis	Jul 10 1884	Jan 27 1885
Rountree, Mary E.	Mar 24 1857	Feb 17 1906
w/o David Meyer		
Rountree, Miriam Russell	age 3 y	Dec 13 1881
d/o D.M. & M.E. burned to death		
Westbrook, Mrs. D.A.	Oct 14 1861	Jul 14 1889
Westbrook, D. Cuthbert	Oct 15 1886	Feb 3 1932

159.   BUNN

Bunn, Dixie	Dec 1892	Dec 5 1920
Bunn, Mrs. Elizabeth Gordy	Aug 14 1866	Mar 16 1938
Bunn, John Walton	Feb 8 1860	Feb 13 1952
Bunn, Margaret Walea	Dec 10 1831	Oct 15 1887
Bunn, Mary Leslie	Feb 22 1923	May 18 1923
Bunn, Matthew W.	Oct 11 1825	Mar 30 1882
Bunn, Moses Servin	Sep 1897	Mar 1898
Bunn, Nora Sapp	nd	Oct 12 1912
w/o Robert L.		
Bunn, Robert L.	nd	Mar 28 1929
Bunn, Susie Bunn Coleman	Sep 8 1881	Apr 20 1966
Bunn, Tom Watson	Aug 1892	Sep 1896
Goodwin, Shawn	1964	1967
Joiner, Emily B.	Jan 11 1855	Oct 31 1895
Joiner, William B.	Aug 27 1884	May 5 1887
Watson, Nellie B.	Feb 13 1907	Dec 18 1930

Note: Four concrete upright markers, five loose brick
coping graves, and one concrete slab are without names
(ed).

160.   COLEMAN

Coleman, Daniel S	Jan 26 1865	Dec 13 1902
Coleman, Mattie	Jan 8 1896	Sep 10 1898
d/o D.S. & L.E.		

161.   MALONE
                     Richmond Co.

Boykin, Mrs. Elizabeth   age 64 y   May 2 185_
    bkn marker   d Oakland, Richmond Co
Malone, Jimmie   age 18 m   Aug 18 1865
    s/o M.J. & W.T. Malone
Malone, Mrs. Nancy H.   age 60 y   Mar 20 1861
    w/o Robert   d Oakland, Richmond Co
Malone, Robert   age 45 y   Mar 3 1838
    d Savannah, Ga.
Pierce, Ann D.   Jan 13 1826   Feb 4 1860
    d/o Nancy H. & Robert Malone
Varner, Frances King   Nov 26 1829   Feb 18 1857
    d/o Nancy H. & Robert

Note: For the Malone family and some of the descendants, see Clark op. cit., 174-77 (ed).

162. ·   McCULLERS-ANDERSON

        This cemetery has been denuded of its tombstones.
According to unconfirmed information, it originally had
markers on McCullers, Andersons, and Greenwoods. With
this as a basis we have supplied below genealogical
data obtained from the Elisha Anderson, Jr., family
Bible. We cannot assert that this is a complete list
of those buried in this cemetery, or that all listed
below are interred there (ed).

Anderson, Elisha, Jr.   nd Dec 24 1825
    s/o Mary Holzendorf & Elisha, Sr. Clark, op. cit.,
    35-37.
Anderson, James   Jan 12 1816 d. young
    s/o Jane H.M. & Elisha, Jr. Clark op. cit., 36-37.
Anderson, Jane Harriet   Jne 15 1796 Aug 17 1849
    /McCullers w/o Elisha, Jr. md June 27 1811
    Note: One daughter, Sarah M, who married Edmund
    B. Gresham, is buried in the Waynesboro Confederate
    cem. (ed).
Anderson, Louisa Elisha   Apr 15 1821   nd
    Never married. Clark op. cit., 37.
Anderson, Mary H.   Jul 8 1814 Oct 6 1815
    d/o Jane H.M. & Elisha, Jr.
Greenwood, Harriet Elizabeth   Apr 2 1824 May 26 1876
    w/o Henry D. md Dec 6, 1843 d/o Jane H.M. & Elisha,
    Jr. Clark, op. cit., 37, 164-5.
Greenwood, Henry D.   Mar 20 1822 May 7 1876
    See Clark, op. cit., 164-5.
Greenwood, John A.   Sep 16 1844 Jne 20 1881
    only s/o Harriet & Henry D. Never married.
    Clark, op. cit., 165.
Harris, Rosa Anderson   Jul 18 1823 Oct 28 1854
    w/o Elijah M. md May 27, 1840. d/o Jane H.M. &
    Elisha, Jr. Clark, op. cit., 36-37.

                        311

Note: The family Bible is in possession of Jane Gresham McLeod, Summerville, S. Car. An extract of the genealogical data has been deposited in the Burke County Library (ed).

163.   PERRY

Bartley, Clifford Perry	age 40 y	nd
Perry, Jeff D.	Jul 4 1864	Aug 6 1905
Perry, Lucian A.	age 55 y	nd

164.   ROBINSON

Fergusson, Caroline w/o A. Fergusson	age 23 y	Aug 16 1845
Robinson, Ann Eliza w/o Lewis Emanuel	nd	Oct 3 1833
Robinson, Lewis Emanuel	nd	Oct 3 1833

both "departed this life within a few hours of each other"

ADDENDA

Note: By mistake the following inscriptions were omitted from the Brushy Creek Baptist cemetery on page 60:

Atwell, Carl	May 17 1866	Oct 9 1906
Bass, Marion	May 31 1918	same date
Hankinson, Bessie Lee	Jne 29 1905	Oct 4 1910
Martin, C.E.	Nov 10 1847	May 20 1916
Martin, Paul Templeton s/o C.E. & S.M.	1889	1901

SOURCE BOOKS FOR ADDITIONAL DATA

Boyd, John Wright, A Family History: Wright-Lewis-Moore and Connected Families, published by author, Atlanta, 1968. 730 pp. (in Burke Co. Library). See especially for Laniers and the Cleveland Thompsons, pp. 354-365.

Brigham Emma E., The History of the Brigham Family, Vol. II, The Lertle Company, Rutland, Vt., 1927. 300 pp. Copyrighted.

Brigham, W. I. Tyler (edited by Emma E. & William E. Brigham), The History of the Brigham Family, Vol. I, The Grafton Press, New York, 1907. 636 pp. Copyrighted.

Brinson, Miriam Jones & Susan Elizabeth Jones Franklin, The Birdsville Jones Family, published by authors, Herndon, Ga., n.d. 66 pp. typed (available only from a family member).

Calhoun, Ferdinand Phinizy, The Phinizy Family In America, published by author, Atlanta, Ga., n.d. 176 pp. See for Burdell, Dales and Neelys, pp. 58-61, 84-88, 102.

Clark, Walter A., A Lost Arcadia or the Story of My Old Community, published by author, Augusta, Ga., 1909. 200 pp. (in Burke Co. Library).

Dumont, Wm. H., "Burke County, Georgia", National Genealogical Society Quarterly, Vol 54, No. 1, Mar. 1966, pp. 3-54.

Fairbank, Eula Mae (Priscilla) Sturdivant, History of the Mallard Family, published by author, Richmond, Va., 1960. 37 pp. (in Burke Co. Library).

Fothergill, Augusta B., Peter Jones and Richard Jones Genealogies, Genealogical Publishing Co., Baltimore, 1967. 363 pp. Reprint of 1924 edition.

Hillhouse, A.M., The Miller, Polhill, and Other Families, Chicago, Ill., 1936. 101 pp. typed (in Georgia Historical Society Library).

Hillhouse, Helen T. and Laurens Petigru, The Hillhouse Family (S. Car. Branch), Waynesboro, Ga., 1959. 75 pp. mimeo (in Georgia Historical Society & Library of Congress).

Hooks, Clyde, The Farrer and Scruggs Families of Jefferson County, Ga., published by author, Augusta, Ga., 1971. 8 pp. mimeo (in Burke Co. Library).

Index to the U.S. Census of Georgia For 1820, Georgia Historical Society, Savannah, 1963. 167 pp.

Myers, Robert Manson, The Children of Pride, Yale University Press, New Haven, Conn., 1972. 1845 pp. Copyrighted. See especially "Who's Who," 1449-1738.

Perkins, David E. (ed), Whistle Stops (Perkins, Millen, Lawton), 1883-1900, published by the editor, Waynesboro, Ga., 1964. 21 pp. (in Burke Co. Library).

Pound, Jerome B., Memoirs of Jerome B. Pound, published
by author, Chattanooga, Tenn., 1949. 340 pp. See
"The Palmer Family," 313-323.
Powell, Lillian Lewis, An Informal History of the First
Methodist Church of Waynesboro, Georgia, 1812-1968,
published by author, Waynesboro, Ga., 1969. 213 pp.
(in Georgia State Dept. of Archives, [Atlanta], Burke
County and Wesleyan College [Macon, Ga.] libraries.)
See especially the Appendix on the descendants of
Louisa Wimberly and Vincent W. Fulcher.
Prince, Beiman Otis, The Clark Family of Georgia,
Clark Family Association, Columbia, S. C. 1973.
66 pp.
Reese, Morton Lamar, Cemetery Records, Mainly from
Richmond County, Georgia, Augusta, Ga., 1949.
Approx. 800 pp. typed. Vols. I-III incl. are bound
together (available only at Richmond Co. Library).
Rowland, Grattan Whitehead, Sr., The Whiteheads of
Burke County, Georgia (in an advanced manuscript
form), Atlanta, Ga., 1974. Approx. 300 pp. typed
(information available only from author).
Vallentine, Dr. John F., Livelys of America, 1690-1968,
National Association of Lively Families, Provo,
Utah, 1971. 892 pp. Copyrighted. See especially
Chap. 2, "Burke County, Georgia Lively Line, 1715",
pp. 151-175 (in Burke County Library).
Warren, Mary Bondurant, Marriages and Deaths - 1763
to 1820, Heritage Papers, Danielsville, Ga., 1968.
155 pp. Copyrighted.
Warren, Mary Boundurant and Sarah Fleming White,
Marriages and Deaths - 1820 to 1830. Heritage
Papers, Danielsville, Ga., 1972. 191 pp.
Copyrighted.
Wimberly, Ellen McKie (Mrs. Chandler W.), Family
Bible Records, Burke County Families, etc., St.
George's Parish Chapter, Daughters of the American
Colonists, Waynesboro, Ga., n. d. 11 pp. typed
(in Burke County Library).
Wimberly, Ellen McKie (Mrs. Chandler W.), Some Records
of the Bates, Bell, Chandler, Chappell, Darlington,
Harden, & Wimberly Families, published by author,
Waynesboro, Ga., 1971. 21 pp. typed (in Burke
Co. Library).
Woodson, Hortense (ed), Charles May and His Descend-
ants (Who Settled at Mays Cross Roads in Old
Edgefield County, S. C.), May Family Association,
Edgefield, S. C., 1956. 287 pp. See especially
Chap. 5, "Lewis May Line" for the Burke County
Lewis Family, pp. 104-114.

Beall continued
  Mary S. Bowls 63
  William Walter 17
Beasley, Eva Agnes G. 75
  Marvin D. 75
  Wm. T., Jr. 75
Bebee, Annie Willis
  Atkins 6
Beckum, Doyle J., Sr. 17
  Edward Oliver 18
  Jefferson 18
  Joe H. 18
  John Hyden 17
  Julia Eloise 17
  Martha E. 18
  Mary Jane 71
  Mary Lou Roberson 17
  Nettie V. 18
  S. B. 18
  Sarah Buck 18
  Thelma N. 18
  Willie Mae 17
Becton, E. E. 58
Beesley, Sarah 99
Belcher, Deborah 87
  Donnie D. 87
  Eddie 87
  G. W. 87
  Isaiah G. 87
  Minna W. 87
  Roxie E. 87
Bell, Abbie Jane 61
  Ada Blount 147
  Mrs. Addie Kirkland 126
  Alcimus Overn 61
  Almeade G. 61
  Amanda J. 61
  Amos W. 58
  Berdie Brinson 126
  Berry 61
  Berry A. 61
  Clarence L. 18
  Dora Allmond 61
  Durwin Rhett 58
  Edgar T. 61
  Edla C. 61
  Effie Dawson 94
  Elbert Berrien, Jr. 126
  Elbert Berrien, Sr. 126
  Elizabeth C. Langley 61
  Elizabeth S. 87
  Ella Fair 61
  Emma 61
  Emma Chandler 147
  Eugene 126
  Fannie Crozier 61
  Feddie Clark 61
  Frederick D. 61
  Georgia Cates 147
  Hallie Henry 61
  Hardie J. 126
  Henry Green 61
  Hoke S. 61
  Isaiah A. 61
  J. B. 61
  James Horace 61
  Joe, Sr. 61
  Joe B. 61
  John Wesley 61 (2)
  Joseph W. H. 147
  Lloyd 61
  Lucy Lovett 126
  Maggie Chance 61
  Mamie Corker 147
  Mary Ola Herrington 61
  Ozzie F. 61
  Pearl Claxton 147
  Preston Wade 126
  Ransom Archibald 147
  Robert Lee 113
  Rufus Ernest 147
  Sarah G. 113
  Sarah Lewis 113
  Seaborn J., Sr. 113

Bell continued
  Seaborn O. 61
  Simeon 147
  Simeon, Jr. 147
  Tom J. 58
  Virgil H. 113
  William Daniel, Sr. 126
  William K. 113
  Wm. Thomas 61
  Willie 61
  Willie A. 61
  Willie M. Chance 61
  Willie S. 126
Belt, Richard B. MD 10
  Susan Whitehead 147
Bennett, Edna Royal 35
Bent, Hyland Fairbanks,
  MD 103
Bentley, Patterson M. 147
Benton, Roby Hinton 103
Bernstein, Katie 103
  Louis 103
Berrien, Eliza Godbee 113
  Elizabeth Palmer 146
  John 146
  Laura Maria 146
  Thomas Moore 146
  Judge Thomas Moore 146
Berrong, Edna Layton 68
  Millard A. 68
Berry, Charlie 126
  Eliza 126
Bewan (?lilg), Emelia 21
Biggs, Joseph A. 75
Bittinger, Sarah L. 96
  Solomon S. 96
Black, Arthur 61
  Cecil Carter 147
  Elizabeth B. 68
  Mrs. Sarah May 147
  Thomas Lamar 42
  William Mack 68
Blackburn, Dorothy W. 25
  Georgia N. 75
  Inez Rushton 25
  J. M. 25
  James R. 75
  L. Dean 25
  Marietta W. 78
  Robert L. 78
Blackman, Trottie 147
Blackmon, Earnest 147
  Miss Georgia 147
  Simmie 147
Blackston, Mamie B. 83
  William B. 83
Blackstone, Annie Inglett
  71
  William McKinley 71
Blackwell, W. T. 147
Blanchard, Ada Frances
  Hillis 13
  Edith Glover 13
  G. P. 13
  Mrs. I. M. 1
  John Francis 13
  Julia S. 13
  Thomas S. 1
Bland, Bertha Beatrice 21
Blizzard, Christopher N.
  68
Blocker, Amanda E. 12
  Barkley M. 12
  Ella F. 12
  Hugh L. 12
  Julia Reed 12
  Pierce Butler 12
  Sarah M. Heath 12
Blount, Abbey E. 146
  Abigail 146
  Amarintha Jane 146
  Annie Lorine Smith 147
  Asa Holt 147
  Asa Holt, Jr. 147

Blount continued
  Avra Martin 147
  Axalina Clark 16
  Bertha Odom 147
  Bessie Redd 147
  Carl A. 147
  Daisy Netherland 9
  E. M. 126
  Edward Carter 147
  Edward Hosea 147
  Edward Howard 146
  Edwin Fitzgerald 147
  Eleanor Palmer 147
  Mrs. Ella Bass 146
  Ella Humphrey 146
  Ethel Johnston 147
  F. Hamilton 147
  Frank A. 147
  George Alpheus 147
  Georgia Cates 147
  Georgia Mims 146
  Harriet Wood 147
  Henry Wood 147
  Hugh M. 147
  James Herbert 147
  Jennie Blount 147
  John Allen 147
  John Sturges 146
  Josephine Bell 147
  Leonidas D. 147
  Lewis Donald 147
  Mrs. Lou Setta B. 126
  Louisa Dillard 16
  Lucile Meyers 147
  Lucy Jordan 147
  Lucy Tarver 147
  Martha Attaway 146
  Mary Lou Williams 147
  Perry, Sr. 147
  Reginald M. 147
  Robert Ashton 147
  Robert Broadnax 146
  Robert Broadnax, Jr. 147
  Robert Lee 146
  Simeon G. 147
  Stephen W. 147
  Stephen William 16
  Thomas Hamilton 146
  Warnoch H. 146
  Wiley Dillard 123
  William Augustus 147
  William J. 147
  William Thomas 147
Bolton, Anna 58
  Georgia M. 58
  Jas. 58
  Octavia M. 58
  Robert 58
  Rev. W. L. 25
  Washington 58
  William M. 58
Bonnell, Albert Judson 126
  Ann 126
  Chas. E. 8
  Charles Otis 126
  Mrs. Clara R. 75
  Clyda 126
  J. Crawford 75
  James Everett 126
  James P. 126
  Louisa 126
  Mamie Ellison 126
  Mamie Joe 126
  Mary O. 147
  Myrtie H. 126
  Robert S. 126
Boon, Augusta M. 6
Bostick, Mrs. Eva 146
Bostock, John L. 68
  Julia L. 68
Bostwick, Chesley 91
  Floyd C. 113
Boulineau, Alex 148
  Betty G. 148

324

Green continued
  George Augustus 56 :
  George Edwin 147
  Gershom 55
  Henry T. 10
  Hugh 147
  Jesse P., Jr. 56
  Jesse P., Sr. 56
  Jesse P., II 56
  Jesse P., IV 147
  Jesse Patterson, III 147
  Jim 103
  John Gaybard 10
  Julian Cox 147
  Martha Hugh 147
  Martha Thompson A. 56
  Millard Meyer 147
  Millard Meyer, Jr. 147
  Moses Edwin 147
  Moses P. 56,147
  Roger N. 103
  Rosa E. 10
  Sallie Bailey 147
  Sallie Meyer 147
  Sarah Harlow 57
  Virginia A. Thompson 10
  Walter, Sgt. 103
  Walter Gresham, Sr. 147
Greene, Andrew Judson 25
  James Elmer 103
  James Rufus 147
Greenway, Elizabeth Ann 83
  Henry H. 83
Greenwood, Harriet
    Elizabeth 162
  Henry D. 162
  John A. 162
Gregory, A. B. 87
  John Brinson 87
Greiner, Alline V. 147
  Charles Clinton 147
  Daniel Evans 147
  Dove V. 18
  Ella Venona Hatfield 147
  Frederick B. 6
  Joe Hightower 147
  John D. 25
  John David 147
  John P. 25
  Josephine Connahan 147
  Laurie Battle 147
  Leland S. 33
  Lillie Mae Lyons 147
  Mary Anna 6
  Mary S. 25
  Nan Rackley 147
  Robert H. 59
Gresham, Annie Lassiter
    147
  Arthur 147
  DeForrest McElmurray 147
  Edmund B. 146
  Ella Lassiter 147
  Emmet B., Jr. 147
  Emmett Burdell 147
  Floyd 146
  Job 60
  Job Anderson 147 (2)
  John Jones 147
  Jones 147
  Margaret H. 146
  Mary Dorothy Tomlin 147
  Mary Dye 147
  Mary Jones 60
  Natalie Thomas 147
  Nona Johnston 147
  Orrin Lassiter 147
  Oscar Milledge 147
  Sarah Adeline 146
  Mrs. Sarah M. 146
  Wylie Oscar 147
  Wylie Oscar, Jr. 147
Griffin, Cleveland E. 75
  Ethel Buxton 12

Griffin continued
  Eva L. 75
  Hemon T. 75
  Isabella I. 75
  James W. 12
  Jane E. 75
  Jane R. 75
  Joicy M. 12
  L. E. 12
  Lillian G. 75
  Marion Thomas 75
  Martha C. E. 12
  Mary Clark Blount 83
  Mary E. Brinson 87
  Mattie Belle 131
  Mattie J. 75
  Shelley A. 147
  Thomas E. 75
  Vance A. 75
  W. L. 75
  Washington 12
  Willie E. 75
Griner, Arrie Oglesbee 75
  Bradfert 147
  Joe Noah 147
  Orrie H. 25
  Rosa Lucile 147
  Seaborn L. 25
  Susie F. Chance 126
  William P. 25
Griswold, Elizabeth P. 148
Guess, James E. 147
  Mattie Duke 147
Gunn, James 91
  Lewis A. F. 83
  Seabie Reeves 61
  Terry 61

Hadden, Mrs. Mary 94
Haeseler, Edna Buxton 131
  Frances Marion 146
  Joe A. 126
  Julian Gray 131
  Otto Augustus 146
  Samuel Burchardt 146
  Sarah Reese 61
Hair, Laura Richardson 117
  Winton Andrew 117
Halford, Alford F. 17
Hall, Bessie B. 12
  Charlie Bolton, Sr. 58
  D. Emmett 68
  Frank Butler 147
  Ida Davis 68
  John, Esqr. 62
  John P. 147
  M. B. 12
  Margaret E. 147
  Martha W. 58
  Mary Kilpatrick 61
  Pickens B. 147
  Thomas D. 12
  William Ashton 147
Hallman, Arthur C. 147
Ham, Mrs. S. E. 103
Hamilton, Florrie Oliver
    126
  John L. 75,126
  Stella Bargeron 126
Hamm, Jesse Thomas 103
  Mollie S. 103
Hammett, Mrs. Martha M. 17
Hammond, C. D. 107
  Charles D. 107
  Elizabeth Winter 107
Hancock, James T. 17
  Mattie M. 17
  William Bruce 103
Hand, C. M., Jr. 103
  Claude Matthew 103
  Eddie C. 103
Hankinson, Bessie Lee 24
  John C. 147

Hankinson continued
  Marion 35
  Sara W. Blount 147
  Thyrza Y. 92
  Wm. Bernard 35
Hannah, Clelia R. 25
  James L. 25
  Janie Heath 12
  Robert Lee 12
  Robert Lewis 131
Hardin, Claude F. 68
  Doris W. 68
  Hazel M. 68
Hardwick, Grattan 146
  Ruth 146
  Walter 146
Hardy, Eliza James 18
  J. W. 17
  Jerry M. 18
  Ruby Loree 68
  Samuel B. 18
Hargrove, Alma O. 58
  Annie Katherine 147
  Carey H. 58
  Florrie B. 58
  G. H. 58
  George W. 58
  H. Melton 61
  Henry W. 147
  Katherine Lee Herrington
    147
  Pearl Folsom 147
  Pharabe Wallace 58
  Quinnie 58
  Roy Belmont 147
  Mrs. Sallie J(osey?) 58
  Sarah F. 87
  William Clifford 147
  William W. 147
Hargroves, Henry 126
  John G. 87
  Martha 126
  S. A. 58
  William B., Sr. 58
Harlow, Frederick Nicholas
    154
  Gertrude Wimberly 154
  John A. MD 146
  Rebecca Walker 146
  Ruth 146
  Dr. Southworth MD 146
  William James 146
Harman, William H. 10
Harner, Joseph Edward 147
  Joseph Winfred 147
  S/Sgt. Wm. C. 147
Harrell, Charles S. 96
  Mary E. 63
  Mary L. 63
  Miriam Green 147
  Porter T. 63
  Thomas A. 63
  Wm. Green 147
Harris, Edwin Adolphus MD
    103
  Franklin 22
  Rosa Anderson 162
Harrison, Floy Smith 125
  Linton Stiles 21
  Martha M. Lines 21
  William H. 125
  William Kollock 21
Harter, Alexander 68
  Carrie G. 68
Hatcher, Mrs. Alice 66
  Annie Powell 19
  Arrah N. 19
  Augusta Virginia 65
  Benjamin J. 147
  Benjamin J., Jr. 147
  Bertha Wimberly 154
  Charlie Hughes 147
  Mrs. Christian C. 64
  Denie Miller 147

326

McElmurray continued
Evan Howell 147
Francis Lorraine 1
George Leslie 1
Haidee Routzahn 147
Henry Grady 147
J. K. 107
John F., Sr. 1
John F., Jr. 1
Joseph H. 147
Judson S. 147
Kate W. 1
Lizzie 117
Louisa Barron 113
Louise 147
Louise Hopkins 1
Mary A. 45
Mary Chandler 147
Mattie J. Lively 19
Minis H. 147
Minis Hunter 126
Sallie Godbee 147
Sallie Joe 1
Thomas J. 1,147 (2)
William L. 126
Wm. Leslie 147
McFerrin, Dr. John Porter
147
Julia Patten 147
Mary 147
McGarr, Irene Toole 103
Margaret Bland 103
Walter J., Sr. 103
McGee, Thomas Ellis 68
McGlohorn, ------ 58
Atticus H. 58
Fannie B. 58
Groover 58
Grover 58
John 58
McGowan, John Hampton 35
McGregor, Charles E. 35
Georgia A. 35
Laura Goodson 35
Capt. M. T. 35
Mitt O. 35
McIver, James B. 94
McJunkin, W. D. 147
McKenzie, Annie E. 147
McKie, James Baker 147
Julia Kingman 147
McKinley, Robert L. 71
McLelland, Beulah Vernon
Johnson 68
Cornelia H. 68
Joseph E. 68
McLendon, Green Bell 87
Harry 20
Moselle E. 87
McManus, Mary Lou 158
Oliver Brantley 158
McMaster, Hugh Buchanan MD
147
Rosa Moore 147
McMellon, Ada B. 13
McMillan, Nancy 58
McMillian, Henry A. 13
Marion G. 13
William D. 126
McNair, Addie Jones 17
Cinnie Rheney 18
Clara Dye 148
J. K. 18
J. P. 148
James Daniel 83
James Elisha 148
James William 147
Jane Blount 147
John W., Sr. 17
Lula Wright 147
M. Jones 17
Mary 17
Mary Ellen 83
Mary Jones 147

McNair continued
Neva Johnson 147
Sara B. 22
Sarah 17
Thomas Gray 147
William 147
McNatt, Adam 10
Mary Anna 10
Wm. 100
McNeely, John Russell 103
Mary Heath 12
McNorrill, Alfred Burke 19
Beatrice C. 19
Beatrice M. 25
Charlie D. 19
Effie M.(?) 19
Eliza A. Godbee 19
Eula T. 19
Howell Henry 19
Ida Lou 19
James T. 19 (2)
Janey B. 19
John C. 19
Joseph W. 19
Laura 19
Lee H. 25
Margaret C. 19
Martha Ann 19
Norman L. 19
Norman W. 19
R. Joseph, Jr. 19
Rufus 19
Rufus C. 19
Russell J. 19
Sallie 19
Sarah E. 19
Thomas F. 19
Virginia Fulcher 107
Dr. W. H. 19
Walter L. 19
Willet Howell 19
Rev. Wm. H. LaFayette 19
McTyre, Mary 109
Mead, Lecie 102
Sharon Acacia 19
Thomas 102
Meads, Ada B. 21
Charlie A. 21
George L. 126
Gerthie T. 21
J. H. 126
Mattie B. 126
Moses 126
Pauline D. 126
Sadie Amanda 21
Wade 21
Mears, Alice 21
Annie M. 21
Barsheba Lewis 21
C. Raymond 21
Joab Wilson 21
John B. 21
John Wilson 21
Lucy Buford 21
William H. 21
William Melton 21
Meeker, Gilford F. 25
Lillian G. 25
Meigs, Eliza A. 68
James 68
Mary Bowman 68
Melton, Amy 33
Edmond Louisa Elizabeth
C. 33
Edmund 33
Robert Edmund 33
Messex, Augusta 1
Carey C. 25
Charles W. 61
Cora K. 1
Ethel Raygood 58
Harold David 147
James Andrew 58
James Austin 147

Messex continued
L. J. 61
M. Stanley 147
Margaret Goodwin 147
Martha 61
Rosa Lee Sikes 147
Willie 1
Meyer, Bertie Miller 117
Carl Crockett 38
Carrie H. 117
Florrie Crockett 38
Julian Lofton 117
Rebecca J. 99
William W. 117
William Wallace 117
Michaels, Wayne Bruce 68
Miles, Alice Swan 148
Eulian Malone 148
Milledge, Mary Gresham 147
Miller, Mrs. Anna 99
Annie Louise Fulcher 117
Annie S. Wood 99
Baldwin Buckner MD 104
Bates 99
Benjamin F. 104
Benjamin S., Jr. 117
Clyde S. 13
Cornelia E. Polhill 68
Dean Joyner 147
Elizabeth 19
Elizabeth C. 11
Evans Smith 68
Evelyn 11
James F., Sr. 19
John Polhill 146
Joseph Baldwin 146
Josie Brinson 87
Julia Carter 146
Marshall A. 117
Mrs. Nancy 99
Robert L. MD 147
Rosa Anderson Morrison
104
Sallie Bates 99
Sarah Hanson 99
Sidney Lucile Turner 68
Stephen 99
Sgt. W. Henry 99
Mills, Bessie Chance 131
Carlton Joy, Sr. 126
Elizabeth 126
Floyd L. 107
George L. 126
Ina Herrington 126
John Alexander 126
John Ashley 131
Marie Green 147
Sarah Kemp 126
Sarah M. 107
Seabie Bell 126
Stephen B. 126
Susan Littlefield 126
Wm. Herbert, Sr. 126
Wm. Littlefield 147
Milner, Charles T. MD 147
Kate Thomas 147
Milton, Clifford Ellmore
148
Fallie Ponder 148
Fannie R. 148
Gertie May 148
James J. 148
Sarah W. 148
Mims, Alice 21
Allen Lines 21
Bessie Hardeman 21
Brian R. 68
Britton 21
Dr. Britton Robert 21
Mrs. Clifford W. 147
Emma H. 21
Fred Henry 68
Guy Baxley, Sr. 68(?)
Harry A. 68

Mims continued
  Hattie 21
  Ida Dixon 68
  Jack V. 68
  Dr. James A. 21
  Judith Scott 21
  Louise Rhodes 68
  Lucile Malcolm 68
  Mary Kathleen 21
  Mary Lessie 21
  Nellie E. Ray 68
  R. Leslie 68
  Susie Baxley 68
  T. K. 68
  Thomas S. MD 21
  Thomas S., Jr. 21
  Dr. Willie 147
Mincey, Lillie S. 25
Minor, Allen E. 19
  Annie May Jones 68
  Burmah T. 19
  Dalton L. 25
  Gertrude B. 25
  James D. 25
  John E. 19
  Lucile R. 25
Minus, Bessie E. Dye 148
  Hugh F. 148
  Hula Z. 148
  Lloyd Bryant 148
  Wm. Fulton 148
  William S. 148
Mitchell, Mary Lavinia 146
Nixon, Annie Gertrude 77
  C. J. 117
  Charley J. 105
  Chester 117
  Clara P. 105
  Ella R. 117
  Essie Lundy 105
  George 105
  George Henry 105
  Ina James 78
  Mamie M. 105
  Mary M. 117
  Michael 140
  Michael, Jr. 140
  Narcisus B. 105
  Pat M. 117
  Sarah 140
  Theodore F. 117
Mobley, A. J. S. 19
  Agnes E. 92
  Alice Banks 147
  Alice Woods 35
  Alma Odom 12
  Benj. H. 12
  Beulah Bailey 147
  Carolyn Rose 12
  Clinton 19
  Elizabeth Barrow 19
  Ernest C. 12
  Ernest C., Jr. 25
  Floyd M. 147
  Frances L. 12
  George Washington 12
  Grady H. 12
  Henry Grady 92
  Hettie Scruggs 19
  Ira A. 12
  J. F. 14
  Jack 25
  James 147
  James M. 19
  Jeff Davis 19
  Jennie Bonnell 126
  John Thomas 92
  Julian H. 92 (2)
  Leila Blount 146
  Lewis 25
  Lola 12
  Mrs. Luna Chance 75
  Malcom M. 12
  Margaret 75

Mobley continued
  Mary Helen 92
  Mary Louneal 92
  Mary Odom 147
  Minus 75
  Nettie Reddick 92
  Nellie W. 12
  Owen 147
  Robert 35
  Robert Virgil 35
  Samuel L. 25
  Samuel Tilton 92
  Sarah 25
  Sidney L. 92
  Sue 19
  Susan E. 14
  Thomas Lovett 92
  Ulysses E. 126
  Mrs. V. R. 92
  William B. 19
  Wm. C. 12
  William L. 14
  William O. 126
  Winnie B. 75
Mock, Arthur Lee, Jr. 14
  Bessie Whitfield 87
  Eva L. 58
  Sol 58
Moffett, Annie Brown 147
  Morton Clement 147
Moody, Adalaid 106
  Gara Ernestine 106
  Sweet Julia 106
  Walter R. 147
  Walter T. 106
Mooneyham, Mary F. 25
Moore, Debra Gail 25
  Elizabeth Penelope 113
  John M. 75
  John William Shultz 113
  Julia L. 18
  Louise Adelia 83
  Maggie J. 147
  Mollie 58
  Prioleau Clanton 146
  Thomas 58
  Tomsie A. 75
  Wyatt L. 117
Morris, Adolphus, Sr. 75
  Caroline Hardy 17
  Cathrine 17
  Cora E. 17
  Daisy S. 75
  Rev. Edmond 17
  Eugenia Carswell 71
  Eugenia Virginia 14
  G. Walter 17
  James Lovick 75
  Jasper H. 71
  John H. 75
  Lennie R. 147
  Rosa J. 17
  Susan Walker 10
  Willard N. 147
  Capt. Wm. St. Clair 10
Moseley, J. W. 146
  James Richard 136
  Joseph H. 117
  Mattie A. 117
  Nancy Virginia 136
Mosley, Carl E. 147
  Charles Seaborn 123
  Clifford 123
  Ida Bussey 123
  S. H. 123
Moss, Rev. William B. 22
Mosteller, Luther 123
  Sarah J. 123
Mountain, Mrs. S. A. 20
Moxley, Benjamin Lee 103
  Cathrine Lowry 123
  George Jordan 103
  Gladys Lamb 103
  H. Eugene 103

Moxley continued
  Homer Leonard 103
  Mary B. 87
  Nathaniel J. 87
  Ralph William 103
  William Jasper 123
Muck, Robert C. 117
Mulder, Arminda Anne 147
  Edgar Stephen 147
Mulkey, Carrie Bell
    Griffin 131
  Euley L. 131
  James William 131
  Luvincia Mallard 131
  W. A. 113
Mulling, Annie McGolrick
    103
  Charles B. 103
  Claiborne Sneed 103
  Cora G. 103
  Deborah 9
  Mr. E. H. W. 9
  Mrs. F. P. 9
  Hattie Cooper 9
  Henrietta G. 103
  Isaac Jefferson 103
  James A. 9
  Johnnie Bell Lamb 103
  Mrs. Kate I. Shaw 103
  Mamie Lou 9
  Mattie Helen Jordan 103
  Pinkin H. 103
  Susie Carswell 9
  Susie Nasworthy 103
  W. A. 9
  W. J. 9
  W. Lawson 103
  William C. 103
Mundy, John Ernest 147
  Julia 17
  Louise Moate 147
  R. M. 17
  Roy 17
Munnerlyn, Annie R. 146
  John D., Jr. 146
  John Daniel, Sr. 146
Muns, Lucy 14
Murdock, Susie A. 103
  Thomas C. 103
Murphey, Alexander 108
  Caroline Eliza 108
  Edmund 109
  Harriet Carswell 68
  Henrietta Brey 33
  Henry Lee 68
  Ida A. 33
  John F. 33
  John M. C. 68
  Margaret 108
  N. Eugenia Lansdell 68
  Nancy 109
  Nancy Rhodes 109
  Robert A. 9
  Sarah Jones 68
Murphree, Abraham W. 110
  Augustus William 103
  Charles Musgrove 103
  Charles O. 103
  Dora A. Hurst Gordy 103
  Mrs. Elizabeth 9
  Elizabeth Brack 110
  Elizabeth T. Jordan 103
  Emily Virginia 110
  Hannah E. 110
  Jane M. Jones 110
  John Byne 103
  Jones Jordan 103 (2)
  Letitia Inman Hodges 103
  Lillian McBride 20
  Lou Dudley 103
  Malachi 110
  May Parker 103
  Mills 110
  Robert M. 103

Oliphant continued
Wm. Chester 148
Willie Y. 148
Oliver, Amye Lou Gay 147
Caroline C. 126
Caroline Bentley 14
Clarence J. 9
Donnie Lee 21
Eleanor Chance 126
Eliza Goodwyn 35
Elizabeth 126
Emily Ophelia 14
Emma Walters 147
James H. MD 146
John William 126
Lafayette 14
Lena Helmly 147
Lula Estelle 75
Mary A. 14
Mary J. 146
Mims R. 147
Nina T. 75
Richard L. 147
Dr. Samuel J. 147
Shelley V., Jr. 126
Shelley V., Sr. 126
Taney D. 146
Thomas Wm. 35
Virgil Baxley 147
Virgil Brooks 35
W. Douglas 35
William R. 75
O'Quinn, Norman Franklin
 25
Orander, James Boaz 17
Marie W. 17
Osbon, Wilma V. 11
Ouzts, Chester K. 147
Milbria Lee Williams 147
Owen, John Blackstone 146
Owens, Joseph Holmes 103
Leila Hickson 103
Mamie Clark 147
Wm. Henry 147
Oxyner, Bessie Watson 68
James Luther 68

Pace, Albert Twiggs 147
Anna Greiner 147
Mattie Oliver 147
Ollie Mae 147
Taney James 147
William H. 147
Pace-Anderson, Mary Ann
 McE. 147
Padgett, Beatrice Sherrer
 83
Boyd P. 83
Deedy Oglesbee 35
Elbert P. 83
Hubert Lester, Sr. 83
Jackson L., Sr. 18
Rev. John Albert 35
Louiza 83
Mary E. Williamson 83
Myrtle G. 83
Nannie Hassie 83
Richard Newton 35
Palmer, Anna G. 33
Anna Rheney 33
Benjamin S. 33
Bessie Quinney 147
Bessie Thomas 147
Clifford Quinney 147
E. N. 45
Earnest 19
Miss Elefare Josephine
 71
Estelle B. 58
Frank Sidney 147
George 114
Georgia V. 33
Isabella Tarver 71

Palmer continued
J. Paul 33
J. Price 33
J. T. 33
John Rheney 147
John T. 19, 147
Levin E. 18
Lewis B. 147
Lillie Smith 18
Louise H. 147
Lucie Mae Reese 18
Martha Jane 146
Mary Cureton 114
Mary E. Finley 18
Mary Ellen Rheney 33
Mary Matilda Brown 71
Miss Mary Sabine 71
Maud Long 147
Miss Michigan Adelaide
 71
Moselle Neely 147
Olin H., Jr. 18
Olin Hagood 18
Robert C. 71
Ruth McElmurray Cothran
 147
Samuel 147
Samuel Anthony 18
Samuel E. 18
Stella Farriba 147
Truman N. 18
William Cureton 33
Paradise, Lena Bussey 123
Paris, Martha L. 35
W. C. 35
Parish, Mary L. 148
Parker, Ida Moore 147
Jimmie 83
Thomas A. 83
William Silas 147
Wilton J. 83
Zebula W. 83
William S. 148
Parkerson, Daisy J. 79
Essie Mallard 131
Furman James 131
Henry I. 79
Parnell, Colquitt H. 146
Leonidus 146
Margaret Hurst 146
Parrish, Kate M. 148
Parsons, Henry Philip 81
Julia Virginia 81
Melvina Virginia 81
Sarah M. 115
Patterson, Augustine Little
 94
Caroline Strong 94
Mrs. Eleanor L. 94
Ellen Edgeworth 94
James E. 94
John 94
John J. 148
Mattie Allen 148
Mittie J. 94
Mollie Smith 148
Nancy J. 94
Robin H. 148
Rosa Carswell 68
Sallie M. Pilcher 148
William 94
Pearce, Dollie Turner 17
Henry Lester, Jr. 17
Pearre, Emma Cody 63
Peek, Ethel N. 106
John Marion 117
Marion John 99
Noah L. 105
Peel, Bennie F. 58
Bennie W. 58
Bettie A. 103
Dempsey Frank 58
Gussie 58
Harriett 58

Peel continued
Henry W. 87
John T. 87
Johnie Otis 58
Levi 58
Levi S. 58
Lucy L. Sikes 87
Lula M. Bragg 58
Luther L. 58
Mary 58
Mary Frances Wallace 58
Mary Julia Dawson 52
Mathew W. 58
Mongin LeRoy 87
Nina Their 87
Olive Dickey 58
Quinton 58
R. E. 58
Richard Lawson 94
Robert J. 123
Robert Lee 58
Rosa Lee 58
Sarah Whigham 123
Susan McCoy 58
Susannah Wallace 87
W. M. 58
Wade H. 58
Pemberton, Atton 116
Pendrey, James J. 148
P. L. 148
Robert I. 148
Penington, Thos., Jr. 94
Fred Cook 18
Julia Dean Heisler 18
Mary Pearre 18
Minnie A. 94
Penrow, Asa H. 16
C. E. 53
John Ralph 123
Martha A. 16
Martha R. 16
Perdue, Annie Eliza 148
L. R. 148
Perkins, A. J. 87
Ann Barnes 96
B. L. 87
Beatrice 96
Bessie S. 96
C. E. 87
Capers D. 96
Carlos A. 87
Clarence E. 83
Clemmie Cross 103
Crawford 96
David 144 (2)
David Mills 96
Dr. E. A. 96
Effie 68
Eliza 58
Ella 144
Enoch 144
Ethel 96
Ethelyn Murrow 87
Eudora C. 96
Eunice A. 87
Frances A. 144
Mrs. Frank 96
Fred W., Sr. 96
Fulton J. 96
G. J. 87
George C. 96
George Mills 96
Georgie Adele 96
Harman Hampton 96
Harvey E. 83
Henry C. 87
Hugh C. 96
Ira E. 96
Irene 96
Iris Irene 96
J. Byron, Sr. 96
James Edward 148
James G. 96
John H., II 96

Rhodes continued
  Mary Elizabeth Atkins 68
  Mrs. Mary J. 121
  Mary White 68
  Mollie 68
  Mrs. Nancy Ann 109
  Pauline Carolina 103 (2)
  Pauline E. Simon 68
  R. L. 68
  Rebecca Tripp 103
  Robert A. 121
  Susan C. White 68
  T. S. W. 68
  W. E., Jr. 68
  W. T. 68
  Walter E. 68
  Walter Warren 68
  Wesley P. 147
  William J. 121
  Wm. Peyton 68
  Willie T., Sr. 68
Richardson, Jessie Edith 6
Ricker, Elizabeth P. 17
  Ethel 17
  Forrest L. 17
  James L. 17
  James Luther 71
  Leacy Phillips 17
  Mada Griffin 17
  Mary L. 71
  Melvina Gaines 71
  Paul Hayne 17
  William James 17
Riddle, John A. 96
Rider, Elbert 21
Ridgedill, Ada Perkins 147
  Elton W. 147
Ridlehoover, Jack B. 68
Riggs, Bruce 103
  James L. 25
  Nannie Lou 103
Roberson, A. J. 61
  Anna Burton 147
  Homer Clem 147
  Roscoe Burton 147
  Turner 61
Roberts, Alexander H. 68
  Alice Bowling 148
  Annie L. Murray 131
  Bessie Hill 24
  Bessie W. 103
  Carl A. 131
  Clarence H. 75
  Cora Rowland 18
  D. B. 146
  Desse A. 68
  Flyd A. 148
  George D. 103,107
  Green W. 18
  James Henry 68
  James R. 18
  Jane E. 75
  Jessie M. 75
  John Eben 68
  John Henry 68
  John Silas 148
  L. P. 71
  Lloyd Rayford 131
  Louisa Amelia Simon 68
  M. H. 75
  Maizie E. 68
  Mary 119
  Mary Mead 131
  Mathilda 148
  Titus Alganon 68
  William Eugene 68
Robey, Charles Wesley, Sr.
    131
  Florence G. 131
Robinson, Allen 147
  Mrs. Allen F. 147
  Ann Eliza 164
  Bertha Gnann 131
  Bessie Oxyner 147

Robinson continued
  Donna Ferrell 126
  Dora Bell 126
  Elizabeth Ponder 53
  Ellaree Zeigler 126
  Emory W. 126
  Ezekiel W. 126
  G. B. 53
  George W. 126
  Grace B. 126
  Hattie J. 126
  Irene Smith 131
  Ivens L. 131
  J. Wesley 131
  James 9
  Mrs. James Alice 53
  Jas. Edw. 147
  Jerome 126
  Jethro T. 147
  Jimmy R. 126
  John R. 9,83
  John R., Sr. 147
  John T. 61
  Josef Emil 147
  Joseph A. 147
  Kate A. 9
  Katherine 9
  Lemuel 126
  Lewis Emanuel 164
  Mabel Burke 147
  Mary Baughman 126
  Mary E. 126
  Moree Mixon 25
  Ralph Mills 126
  Richard 103
  Richard M. 103
  Sarah Virginia Jones 9
  Sidney J. 126
  Susan E. 126
  Thomas Edward 53
  W. J. 9
  Walter H. J. 126
  Zula Mills 126
Robsky, Louise Bargeron 68
Rockwell, Reuben L. 25
Rodgers, Alpheus M. 146
  Nancy J. McCullar 96
  Virginia Blount 146
Rogers, Alice Fell 148
  Alliean Lucile 61
  Dudley 126
  Fred 147
  Harriet 113
  J. Rufus 61
  James H. 107
  Jerry Leo 25
  John M. 107
  John S. 148
  Josephine Rebecca Buxton
    12
  Marie Kimball 147
  Martha M. 148
  May Godbee 107
  Nancy B. 61
  Sallie W. 126
  Sam Alvin 147
  Sarah 107
  Sarah C. 107
  Sarah J. 107
  Thomas 107
  Thomas Britton 107
  Thomas W. 107
  Rev. W. J. 148
  Warren T. 147
  Willie A. 148
Rollins, Daisy Coursey 147
  Eliza C. 20
  Henry Ulysses 123
  John 20
  John R. 20
  Johnnie Belle Burke 123
  Mrs. Mary Ann 20
  Rufus Elester, Sr. 147
  Sarah H. 20

Rollins continued
  Thomas McBride 20
  William P. 20
Roof, Ada Jean Vickery 147
  Daniel Joseph 147
  Daniel Joseph, Jr. 147
  Hattie B. 147
  Myrtie Moak 147
Rooks, Asa H. 68
  Lillian Lansdell 68
Rosier, Jane Hellen 124
  John A. 124
  Mary Elizabeth 124
  Sarah J. Winter 124
Ross, Eugene H. 147
  Maggie M. 147
Rosser, Caroline Jones 42
  Clarence C., Sr. 42
  Clarence Cocke, Jr. 42
Rountree, Allen Lon 11
  Carrie Cross 103
  Grace W. 103
  Hugh J., Jr. 103
  James M. 158
  Lewis R. 11
  Mary E. 158
Rouse, Emmie B. 12
  John B. 12
Routzahn, Louis H. 146
Rowe, Albert W. 75
  Charles D. 75
  Ella Chance 75
  Roe Ann 75
  William M. 75
Rowell, Annie L. 147
  James B., Sr. 25
  Louise Daniel 25
  R. T. 147
Rowland, Ada 12
  Anna Renfroe 123
  Benjamin B. 12
  Benjamin F. 148
  Benjamin Franklin 12
  Clarence Leonard 147
  Dorothy Pearson 123
  Eva Powell 12
  Francis Jefferson 147
  Freddie Haeseler 147
  Harriet E. 148
  Henry B. 18
  J. Charley 18
  Jacob 123
  James Elmo 123
  James M. 12
  James Marion 148
  James Monroe 12
  James R. 18
  John Berry 148
  Mae Thompson 123
  Marian W. Whitehead 146
  Mary O'Connell 147
  Phoebe Salters 148
  Robert Allen 146
  Robert Buxton 147
  Rosa Lee 18
  Roy A. 12
  Sam R. 148
  Sarah B. 18
  Savannah 12
  Thomas Jefferson 148
  Thomas R. 123
  Victoria 12
Royal, Alice Tobias 35
  Mrs. Annie L. Williams
    35
  Atticus Roscoe 12
  Benjamin F. 61
  Claudine O'Banion 12
  Cleveland Wayne 25
  Doughty 35
  Emmie 12
  Eticus 35
  Frances G. 119
  Frank 35

339

Singley, Hudle L. 25
Sinquefield, Mrs. E. J.
  148
Skillman, Ervin F. 68
Skinner, Alice Carten 11
  Alice Maude Bentley 61
  Benjamin Franklin 61
  Caroline 13
  Carroll C. 13
  Cathorine W. 68
  Charles W., Jr. 147
  Charles Wesley, Sr. 147
  E. N. 13
  Eliza 75
  Etta Rosetta P. 35
  Ezra W. 13
  Mrs. F. E. 61
  Franklin M. 147
  G. Millard 68
  George W. 13 (2)
  Harvey T. 68
  Henrietta Boyer 147
  Irene 13
  J. H. 61
  John Jones 147
  Jonas Hardy 61
  Julia R. 147
  L. Milton 126
  Lany 83
  Lavonia 13
  Lottie Jenkins 79
  Lovett C. 75
  Mamie G. 13
  Mary Dell 126
  Mattie Lee 13
  Mattie Trueza Chance 61
  Minnie Caraker 147
  Napoleon B. 147
  Nellie K. 13
  Nillie 75
  Oscar T. 83
  Paul F. 11
  Rallie Trader 147
  Robert Lee 61
  Sallie E. 13
  Sim B. 13
  Sim Thomas 79
  Simeon W. 13
  Susan M. Joyner 75
  T. Baldwin 22
  Thomas W. 126
  W. E. 75
  William Jasper 11
  William T. 11
Skrine, Quintillian 10
Smith, A. Eugenia 45
  Alice Templeton 17
  Ann Eliza 45
  Annie Mae 83
  Belle Hyatt 147
  Belle Joiner 148
  Benjamin 28
  Berry H. MD 17
  Bunyan A. 126
  Cathrine Bateman 147
  Charles O. 68
  Charles Otto 68
  Clarence L. 75
  Cleo W. 126
  Curby Lee 83
  D. Oliver 147
  David J. 99
  Dorothy D. 131
  Edgar Joseph 148
  Edwin A. 147
  Edwin A., Jr. 147
  Eli Sidney 103
  Eliza A. 148
  Elizabeth Blount 146
  Emma 12,92
  Essie G. 113
  Eva Weeks 123
  Fannie R. 148
  Frances Bell 113

Smith continued
  Frances R. 12
  Frank A. 45
  G. Absalom 148
  Grady D. 75
  Hattie Ponder 103
  Hazel Parish 103
  Helen Boulineau 148
  Henry McPherson 94
  Hilda Mozelle 147
  Hinton H. 131
  Homer W. 103
  Isaac H. 75
  J. J. 148
  J. Wyatt 45
  James 58
  James B. 126
  James H., Sr. 75
  James Russell 123
  Jannette Carswell 17
  Joan Elizabeth Tanner
  148
  John Hervy 17
  Joseph Walden 147
  Joshua A. 148
  Kenneth Mac 25
  L. E. 103
  Laura Bell 126
  Lillie C. 147
  Lillie J. 148
  Lon 83
  Lucia Williamson 83
  Lucy Joyner 131
  Lyddie 126
  Lydia Frances 126
  Macy B. 17
  Marion D. 99
  Martha 75,79
  Martha E. 9
  Mary A. 148
  Mary Ann 103
  Mrs. Mary C. 148
  Mrs. Mary E. 103
  Mary Eliza Carswell 68
  Mary Murphree 103
  Mattie A. 123
  Mattie Alexander 94
  Mattie L. 75
  Nancy Hargrove 126
  Narcissa 148
  Nathaniel 96
  Noah 129,148 (2)
  Patrick Bartow 103
  Patrick H. 103
  Philip E. 126
  Rachael Roland 148
  Richard, III 131
  Robert F. 45
  Robert H. 123
  Robert Homer 103
  Rosa 22
  Rufus William 147
  Ruth Hillis 75
  Mrs. S. J. 75
  Sallie Robinson 126
  Sarah 148
  Sarah E. 147
  Sarah H. Carroll 68
  Sarah I. 45
  Susan Murphree 103
  Thomas E. 68
  Thomas J. 126
  Thos. Walter 147
  Verlinder 99
  W. T. 148
  Walter Mallard 25
  Walter S. 17
  Wiley 128
  William D. 148
  William Devotie 103
  Wm. E. 9
  Wm. Henry 147
  William Henry 17
  Willie Mae 147

Smith continued
  Zera Alice 147
Smoot, George W. 147
  Ruth R. 147
Smyly, Euclid J. 147
  Euclid J., Jr. 147
  Florence F. 147
  Margaret Gordon 147
Snider, Almira Elizabeth
  148
Sorrier, G. Josephine
  Brinson 87
Sowell, Georgia E. Freeman
  14
  J. Alex 58
  Spears, Homer M. 147
  Linnie Belle 147
  William 130
Spence, Dyte Olliff 58
  Henry Baxley 103
  Marjorie Coleman 103
Spencer, Alvin H. 61
  Carlton 147
  Mamie Samuel 33
Spires, Crystbell C. 13
  Henry U. 13
  Lee G., Jr. 13
Stalnaker, Mary L. 58
Stanucha (?illeg.) C. E.
  22
Stapleton, Annie Adams 17
  John T. 17
  Mary B. 25
  Pauline Tarver 17
  Robert L. 25
  Wm. A. 17
  William A., Jr. 17
Steadman, George Alfred
  147
  Georgia Thomas 147
Steed, Gertrude Hudson 68
Stembridge, Henry Hansel,
  Sr. 147
  Maude Foreman 147
Stephens, Corbett E. 147
  Elmer Eugene 12
  Eva Barefield 13
  Ida J. 9
  Jake K. 147
  Jane 13
  Jennie B. 147
  Joanna E. 126
  John F. 126
  Myra B. 58
  Ruby Palmer 18
  Tampa J. 83
  W. Jack 13
  William V. 12
Stevens, Andrew Tarver 33
  Carl A. 103
  Henrietta Mulling 103
  Mary Palmer 33
Stewart, George Alvin 147
  H. D. 146
  Julia Burch 68
  Marie A. 148
  Mary Busbee 147
  Samuel 147
  Thomas J. 148
  William A. 148
Stockton, Letitia Jones
  103
  Louise Frances 103
  William Joseph 103
  William Joseph, Jr. 103
Stone, David Leroy, Jr. 25
  David Leroy, Sr. 25
  Drucilla Joiner 103
  Myrtis Tinsley 25
  Paul Sinclair, Jr. 25
Story, Charles 68
  Chester E. 68
  Emily Burmah Steed 68
  Frank J. 148

345

ERRATA

Bostwick, Nathan 91
Brown, Isabella 23
  James B. 23
  John S. 23
  Martha P. 23
  Nancy E. 23
Coleman, Pearl Elizabeth
  103

Daniel, Louisa J. 71
Dawson, Belle Boyd 94
Drew, Laura Earnest 103
Jones, Sidney Ann Sapp 81
Lane, Florence Drew 103
McNeely, Laura Drew 103
Morris, Whitfield Lee 71

Parkman, Benjamin Gordon
  131
Pool, Sarah Jane 83
Poole, Eva Irene 148
Vallotton, Elizabeth A.
  Erwin 71

Johnson, Kathleen, Morris should be Johnston 99

www.ingramcontent.com/pod-product-compliance
Lightning Source LLC
Chambersburg PA
CBHW031116020426
42333CB00012B/104